VIRGINIA MILITIA

IN THE

WAR^{OF}■1812

From Rolls in the Auditor's Office at Richmond

Volume II

Originally published under the title
Muster Rolls of the Virginia Militia in the War of 1812,
Being a Supplement to the Pay Rolls Printed and Distributed in 1851.
Richmond, Virginia, 1852.
Reprinted as *Virginia Militia in the War of 1812,* Volume II, by
Genealogical Publishing Company
Baltimore, Maryland, 2001.
Library of Congress Catalogue Card Number 00-136461
International Standard Book Number, Volume II: 0-8063-1670-5
Set Number: 0-8063-1672-1
Made in the United States of America

MUSTER ROLLS

OF THE

VIRGINIA MILITIA IN THE WAR OF 1812,

BEING A

SUPPLEMENT TO THE PAY ROLLS

PRINTED AND DISTRIBUTED IN 1851.

COPIED FROM ROLLS IN THE AUDITOR'S OFFICE AT RICHMOND.

☞ This Supplement contains the Companies and parts of Companies which were omitted in the printed Pay Rolls.

RICHMOND, VA.
WILLIAM F. RITCHIE, PUBLIC PRINTER.
1852.

TABLE OF CONTENTS.

FIELD AND STAFF OFFICERS.

COMPANIES.

* This is part of, and is included in, Capt. Ed. Marks' company.

MUSTER ROLL

Of the Field and Staff Officers of the First Regiment and First Brigade, Virginia Militia, commanded by General William Chamberlayne, in the Service of the United States during the year 1814.

NAMES.	RANK.	TIME OF SERVICE.		REMARKS.
		Months.	Days.	
Wm. Chamberlayne, -	General,	3	3	
James Byrne, - -	Colonel,	3		
James Scott, - -	Lt. Colonel,	3		
Philemon Holcombe, -	"	–	10	
Harwood Jones, - -	Major,	3		
Joseph G. Wilder, - -	"	3		
Saml. T. Winston, - -	Brig. Major,	3	3	
Wm. Armistead, -	Aid de Camp,	3	3	
Timothy Thorp, - -	Adjutant,	3		
John Nicholas. - -	"	–	10	
Edmond C. Goodwin, -	"	–	27	
Henry Curtis, - -	Surgeon,	–	11	
David Walker, - -	"	3		
James Henderson, - -	"	–	10	
——— Morgan, - -	Surg. Mate,	–	7	
John Bragg, - -	"	3		
Nicholas Scherer, - -	"	–	11	
John H. Brown, - -	Qr. Master,	3		
Nicholas Mills, - -	B. Q. Master,	3	3	
John Holcombe, - -	Qr. Master,	–	9	
Spencer Wooldridge. -	For. Master,	3	3	
Andrew Moore, - -	B. W. Master,	2	22	
Peter F. Barrow. - -	"	3	3	
Archibald Baugh, - -	Pay Master,	3		
Thomas G. Tinsley, -	"	–	–	Under arrest.
James Whitelaw, - -	"			
Ralph Wingfield, - -	Serg. Major,	–	5	
Joseph Caldwell, - -	"	3		
Henry Ligon, - -	"	–	6	
Armistead T. Townes, -	Q. M. Serg't,	–	9	
Benjamin Walker, - -	"	3		

(For rest of this company, see publication of Pay Rolls.)

MUSTER ROLL

Of the Field and Staff Officers of the Second Regiment, Virginia Militia, in the Service of the United States, at different periods during the years 1813 and 1814.

NAMES.	RANK.	TIME OF SERVICE.		REMARKS.
		Months.	Days.	
William Sharp,	Lt. Colonel,	–	23	
Thomas M. Bayley,	"	3	3	
John Ambler,	"	2	20	
William Brown,	"	2	20	
Archbold Richie,	Major,	–	23	
James Maurice,	"	–	23	
William R. Custis,	"	1	4	
John Finney,	"	–	3	
Archer Ball,	"	2	20	
Peter Ferguson,	Adjutant,	–	10	
John G. Joynes,	"	1	12	
George W. Cole,	Lt. Adjutant,	2	20	Promoted to adj't Sept. 1, 1814, in the place of A. S. Wooldridge, promoted.
Lewis Hansford,	Surgeon,	–	4	
Henry S. Fisher,	"	1		
Thomas R. Fisher,	Surg. Mate,	–	9	
Wm. A. O. Brown,	"	2	20	
John Hodges,	"	–	4	
Robert P. Archer,	"	2	20	
William A. Armistead,	Pay Master,	–	4	
Samuel Downing,	"	3	23	
John R. Walker,	"	2	20	
Thomas Vaden,	Qr. Master,	2	20	
Wm. A. Parker,	"	–	13	
John A. Bundick,	"	4	8	
Charles Rudder,	Q. M. Sergt.	–	2	
Francis Boggs,	"			
Wm. Renell,	"	3	15	
James Echelberger,	"			
Baker Wells,	"	2	20	
William Shannon,	Sergt. Major,	–	14	
P. O. Twiford,	"			
Edward S. Snead,	"	–	16	
Levin Parker,	"			
Robert R. Miller,	"	2	20	
Thomas Stanley,	Drum Major,	2	20	
Nelson B. Burton,	Fife Major,	2	20	

(For rest of this company, see publication of Pay Rolls.)

MUSTER ROLL

Of the Field and Staff Officers of the Third Regiment from the State of Virginia, in the Service of the United States, commanded by Lieutenant Colonel Francis M. Boykin.

NAMES.	RANK.	TIME OF SERVICE.		REMARKS.
		Months.	Days.	
Francis M. Boykin, - -	Lt. Colonel,	–	–	No time given.
Wm. C. Veale, - -	Major,			
Wiley Parker, - -	"			
II. W. Wills, - -	Adjutant,			
John Barber, -	Qr. Master,			
Thomas Purdie, -	Pay Master,			
James B. Southall, - -	Surgeon,			
George Wilson, - -	Surg. Mate,			
Mills F. Wills, - -	Q. M. Serg.			

MUSTER ROLL

Of Field and Staff Officers of the Sixth Regiment, Virginia Militia, in the Service of the United States during the year 1814.

NAMES.	RANK.	TIME OF SERVICE.		REMARKS.
		Months.	Days.	
Arch. Ritchie, - -	Lieut. Col.	–	10	
John Dangerfield, - -	"	–	4	
George W. Banks, - -	Major,	–	14	
Sam'l Muse, - -	"	–	10	
Charles Woodson, - -	"	–	5	
John Bellfield, - -	Adjutant,	–	4	
Carter M. Braxton, . -	"	–	10	
A. Brockenbrough, - -	Surgeon,	–	10	
Jas. H. Noel, - -	Surg. Mate,	–	10	
John Jones, - -	Pay Master,	–	14	
John L. Cox, - -	Qr. Master,	–	10	
John H. Upshaw, - -	"	–	10	
Wm. T. Banks, - -	Q. S. Mate,	–	10	
John Bohannon, - -	St. Mate,	–	10	
Sam'l Johnson, - -	F. M.	–	10	
Phil. Clarke, - -	D. M.	–	10	

MUSTER ROLL

Of Field and Staff Officers of the Seventh Regiment.

NAMES.		RANK.	TIME OF SERVICE.		REMARKS.
			Months.	Days.	
Will. Saunders,	- -	Adjutant,	–	9	
John Crouch,	- -	Surg. Mate,	–	20	
Jos. Watkins.	- -	Q. M. Serg't,	–	14	

(For rest of this company. see publication of Pay Rolls.)

MUSTER ROLL

Of the Field and Staff Officers of the Eighth Regiment.

NAMES.	RANK.	TIME OF SERVICE.		REMARKS.
		Months.	Days.	
Charles F. Wall,	Colonel,	3	28	
Henry Timberlake,	Lt. Colonel,	3	28	
Charles Woodson,	Major,	3	28	
Isaac Pleasants,	"	2	18	
James Robertson,	"	–	21	
David Rodes,	Adjutant,	2	10	
R. S. Sandridge,	"	1	15	Appointed brigade in-
Geo. W. Trueheart,	Qr. Master,	3	26	spector 12th Dec'ber
George Harris,	Pay Master,	3	26	1814.
A. Kean,	Surgeon,	3	26	
Jas. Minor,	Surg. Mate,	2	21	
J. W. Royster,	"	4	19	
T. R. Morris,	"	–	22	
M. Fox,	"	–	15	
G. W. Vaughan,	Steward,	2	1	
Samuel Ragland,	Sergt. Major,	3	26	
Peter Morton,	Q. M. Sergt.	3	26	
Michael Markwood,	D. Major,	3	24	
P. Barret,	"	–	25	
William Brown,	F. Major,	3	28	

(For rest of this company, see publication of Pay Rolls.)

MUSTER ROLL

Of the Field and Staff of the Ninth Regiment of Virginia Militia, commanded by Lieutenant Colonel William Boyd, in Service from the 2nd day of December 1814, to the 10th day of December 1814, both days inclusive.

NAMES.	RANK.	TIME OF SERVICE.		REMARKS.
		Months.	Days.	
William Boyd, - -	Lt. Colonel,	–	9	
Wily Campbell, - -	Major,	–	9	
John Hoskins, - -	Surgeon.	–	9	
Moore G. Fauntleroy, -	Surg. Mate,	–	9	
Robert B. Hill, - -	Pay Master,	–	9	
Jas. B. Taliaferro, -	Qr. Master,	–	9	
John G. Garnett, - -	Adjutant,	–	9	
Harris Carlton, - -	Sergt. Major,	–	9	
Henry Bagby, - -	Q. M. Sergt.	–	9	
Archibald Carlton, -	Drum Major,	–	9	

MUSTER ROLL

Of the Field and Staff Officers of the Sixteenth Regiment.

NAMES.	RANK.	TIME OF SERVICE.		REMARKS.
		Months.	Days.	
William F. Gray,	Adjutant,	–	26	
William P. Goodwin,	"	–	28	
Meredith Yeatman,	Q. Master,	–	28	
John Wigglesworth,	"	–	26	
Richmond Lewis,	Surgeon.	–	26	
Ashton Johnston,	Serg. Major,	–	17	
Nathaniel Browne,	"	–	22	
Benj. Eatherton,	Drum Major,	1	24	
Robert L. Rawlings,	Fife Major,	–	28	
James Wigglesworth.	Q. M. Serg't.	–	26	Attached to Major S. Crutchfield's detachment.
Stapleton Crutchfield,	Major,	–	26	Commanding separate detachment.
William Dillard,	S. Major.	–	26	
Thomas Frazer,	Ass't Q. M.	–	26	
Richard Johnson,	Serg't Major,	–	17	
Moses,	Drummer,	–	26	

(For rest of this company, see publication of Pay Rolls.)

MUSTER ROLL

Of Field and Staff Officers of the Nineteenth Regiment, Virginia Militia, commanded by Lieutenant Colonel John Ambler, in the Service of the United States from 18th to 27th March 1813, from 28th June to 3d July 1813, and from 26th August to the 30th September 1814.

NAMES.	RANK.	TIME OF SERVICE.		REMARKS.
		Months.	Days.	
John Ambler,	Lieut. Col.	–	16	
Christopher Tompkins,	Major,	–	16	
Hugh Davis,	"	2	15	
John Adams,	Surgeon,	1	21	
Thomas Massie,	S. Mate,	1	11	
John Hayes,	"	1	2	
Sam'l G. Adams,	Adjutant,	–	16	
William Hay, jr.	Pay Master,	–	16	
William Burnes,	Qr. Master,	–	10	
J. West,	"	–		
David Hanna,	Serg. Major,	1	29	

MUSTER ROLL

Of the Field and Staff Officers of the Twentieth Regiment of Virginia Militia, commanded by Lieutenant Colonel James Robinson, from 6th to 18th February. from 8th to 15th March, and from 5th to 28th September, in the year 1813.

NAMES.			RANK.	TIME OF SERVICE.		REMARKS.
				Months.	Days.	
James Robinson,	-	-	Lt. Colonel,	1	15	
William Nimmo,	-	-	Major,	–	21	
James D. Moseley,	-	-	Surg. Mate,	1	15	
Jonathan Hopkins,	-	-	Qr. Master,	2	2	
Jacob Valentine.	-	-	Q. M. Sergt.	–	21	
Willam Davis.	-	-	"	–	18	

MUSTER ROLL

Of the Field and Staff Officers of the Twenty-first Regiment of Virginia Militia, commanded by Lieutenant Colonel William Camp, in the Service of the United States during the years 1813, 1814 and 1815.

NAMES.	RANK.	TIME OF SERVICE.		REMARKS.
		Months.	Days.	
William Camp, - -	Lieut. Col.	12	4	Died March 1814, and William Jones promoted.
William Jones, - -	Lieut. Col.	11	6	
Nathaniel Burwell, - -	Major,	11	13	Died Feb. 1814, and Capt. Robert Thurston promoted.
William Jones, - -	"	7	21	Promoted to Lt. Col. vice William Camp, dec'd.
Robert Thurston, - -	"	11	27	
Thomas Hall, - -	"	18	27	
Mann Page, - -	"	4	15	
Overton Seawell, - -	Adjutant,	18	27	
John Page, - -	"	–	28	
John R. Cary, - -	Pay Master,	23	3	
John Dixon, - -	Qr. Master,	13	15	Appointed Jan. 7, '14, vice William Robins resigned.
Jasper C. Rowe, - -	"	3	6	Resigned May 20, 1813, and Wm. Robins appointed in his place.
Wm. Robins, - -	"	7	14	Resigned Jan. 7, 1814.
James Dabney, - -	Surgeon,	9	21	
Wm. Wiatt, - -	Surg. Mate,	20	7	
Thomas Whiting, - -	"	11	6	
John Lucas, - -	Serg't Major,	18	27	
Arch'd W. Janson, - -	Q. M. Serg't,	9	14	
Vincent Hudson, - -	Fife Major.	11	6	
William Hudson, - -	Drum Major.	11	6	

MUSTER ROLL

Of the Field and Staff of a detachment of the Virginia Militia from the County of Chesterfield, composing the Twenty-third Regiment, commanded by Colonel William Brown, in the Service of the State from 13th March to the 2nd of July, in the year 1813.

NAMES.	RANK.	TIME OF SERVICE.		REMARKS.
		Months.	Days.	
William Brown, - -	Colonel,	–	14	
Archer Ball, - -	Major,	–	12	
Tom N. Traylor, - -	"	–	12	
Bev. C. Stanard, - -	Adjutant,	–	13	
Abner Crump, - -	Surgeon,	–	13	
Wm. A. O. Brown, - -	Sergt. Major,	–	13	
John R. Walk, - -	Pay Master,	–	9	
Thomas Vaden, - -	Qr. Master,	–	11	
Marley Walthall, - -	Q. M. Sergt.	–	12	
Samuel Flournoy, - -	Sergt. Major,	–	12	
Nath'l Childers, - -	Qr. Master,	–	12	

MUSTER ROLL

Of the Field and Staff of the Twenty-fifth Regiment of Virginia Militia in the County of King George, commanded by Lieutenant Colonel Austin Smith, in the Service of the United States during the years 1813 and 1814.

NAMES.	RANK.	TIME OF SERVICE.		REMARKS.
		Months.	Days.	
Austin Smith, - -	Lieut. Col.	3	2	
William Thornley, - -	Major,	2	27	
Robert L. Yates, - -	"	2	18	
Will. Nelson, - -	"	–	9	
George Chadwell, - -	"	–	9	
Thomas Martin, - -	Adjutant.	2	18	
John S. Massey, - -	"	–	13	
Enoch Arnold, - -	Pay Master,	3	1	
Butler Washington, -	Qr. Master,	2	18	
West Ashton, - -	Q. M. Serg.	2	18	
W. J. Quessenberry, - -	Surgeon,	2	18	
Manus Rowan, -	"	–	12	
Geo. Fitzhugh, -	Surg. Mate,	2	18	
Benjamin Sedwrick, -	"	–	8	
Thomas B. Thornley, -	Serg. Major,	2	26	
Robert Frank, - -	Fife Major,	2	18	
John Frank, - -	Drum Major,	2	18	

MUSTER ROLL

Of the Field and Staff Officers of the Twenty-ninth Regiment of Virginia Militia, commanded by Major Joseph W. Ballard, in the Service of the State from the 23d of June to the 27th of July 1813.

NAMES.	RANK.	TIME OF SERVICE.		REMARKS.
		Months.	Days.	
Joseph W. Ballard, - -	Major,	–	18	
Andrew Woodley, - -	"	–	18	
Arthur Smith, - -	Adjutant,	–	18	
James Chalmers, -	Q. M. Serg.	–	20	
Robert Hines, - -	Pay Master,	1	5	
James B. Southall, - -	Surgeon,	–	18	
Joseph Blunt, - -	Surg. Mate,	–	21	
John K. Todd, - -	Serg. Major,	–	18	
Fielding Goodson. - -	Q. M. Serg.	–	18	

MUSTER ROLL

Of the Field and Staff Officers of a detachment of Militia from the Thirtieth Regiment, commanded by Major Reuben Tankersley, in the Service of the State of Virginia from the 3d to 9th December 1814.

NAMES.	RANK.	TIME OF SERVICE.		REMARKS.
		Months.	Days.	
Reuben Tankersley, -	Major,	–	6	
Edmund Taylor, -	Act'g Adju't.	–	6	
Geo. W. Baylor, -	Surg. Mate.	–	6	

MUSTER ROLL

Of the Field and Staff Officers of the Thirty-sixth Regiment of Virginia Militia, commanded by Lieutenant Colonel Enoch Rennoe, in the Service of the State of Virginia during the years 1813 and 1814.

NAMES.	RANK.	TIME OF SERVICE.		REMARKS.
		Months.	Days.	
Enoch Rennoe,	Lt. Colonel,	–	7	
Thomas Chapman,	Major,	–	22	
Thomas Thornton,	Surgeon,	–	15	
John Spence,	"	–	6	
Thomas Thornton,	Surg. Mate,	–	6	
John Bronaugh,	"	–	7	
Peyton Narvell,	"	–	7	
David Davis,	"	–	8	
James Hays,	Adjutant,	–	21	
Thomas Tebbs,	Q. M. S.	–	2	
Robert Boughanan,	"	–	21	
William Barron,	"	–	6	
David Boyle,	P. M.	–	21	
Henry Fairfax.	Q. M.	–	15	
George Smith,	"	–	6	
William Purnel,	F. M.	–	15	
Peyton Narvell,	"	–	8	
Allan Duffey,	D. M.	–	15	
Thomas Montgomery,	Sergt. Major,	–	6	

Field and Staff of the Thirty-seventh Regiment.

NAMES.	RANK.	TIME OF SERVICE.		REMARKS.
		Months.	Days.	
Thomas D. Downing, -	Lieut. Col.	7		
Hiram Blackwell, - -	Major,	7		
Samuel Downing, - -	"	7		
Joseph Basye, - -	Surgeon,	7		
John McAdam, - -	Surg. Mate,	9	18	
Mottrom Ball, - -	Surgeon.			
Thomas Towles, - -	Pay Master,	7		
James Smith, - -	"	–	22	
Royster Betts, -	Qr. Master,	7		
Peter C. Rice, - -	Adjutant,	7		
Griffin Edwards, - -	Qr. Master.			
Thomas S. Sydnor, - -	Q. M. Serg't,	–	20	

(For rest of this company, see publication of Pay Rolls.)

MUSTER ROLL

Of the Field and Staff Officers of the Thirty-ninth Regiment of Virginia Militia, commanded by Lieutenant Colonel James Byrne, in Service from 30th June to 12th July 1813.

NAMES.	RANK.	TIME OF SERVICE.		REMARKS.
		Months.	Days.	
James Byrne, - -	Lieut. Col.	–	–	Absent.
Joseph G. Wilder, - -	Major,	–	13	
John Hamlin, - -	"	–	6	
William B. Branch, - -	Adjutant.			
Arch'd Baugh, - -	Pay Master,	–	6	
Charles Cowling, - -	Qr. Master,	–	6	
David Walker, - -	Surgeon,	–	6	
John Gilliam, - -	S. Mate.	–	6	
Joseph Caldwell, - -	Serg't Major,	–	13	

MUSTER ROLL

Of the Field and Staff Officers of the Forty-first Regiment of Virginia Militia, commanded by Lieutenant Colonel Vincent Branham, in the Service of the United States during the years 1813 and 1814.

NAMES.	RANK.	TIME OF SERVICE.		REMARKS.
		Months.	Days.	
Vincent Branham, - -	Lt. Colonel,	–	19	
Moore F. Brockenbrough, -	Major,	–	26	
John W. Belfield, - -	"	–	14	
Daniel Garland, - -	Adjutant,	–	19	
William Settle, - -	Qr. Master,	–	14	
Henry M. Dobyns, - -	Q. M. Sergt.	–	8	
William Stanley, - -	Sergt. Major,	–	14	
Thomas Spence, - -	"	–	7	
Horace Welford, - -	Surg. Mate,	–	14	
Austin Neale, - -	Pay Master,	–	14	

MUSTER ROLL

Of the Field and Staff Officers of the Forty-fifth Regiment.

NAMES.	RANK.	TIME OF SERVICE.		REMARKS.
		Months.	Days.	
Samuel H. Peyton, - -	Lt. Col.	–	10	
Benjamin Tolson, - -	Major,	–	10	
Robert Crutcher, - -	"	1	26	
Thomas Fristoe, - -	Adjutant,	–	9	
John Moncure, -	Pay Master,	–	17	
Coleman R. Brown, - -	Qr. Master,	–	11	
William P. Bailey, -	Commissary,	–	20	
John Fant, - -	Q. M. Serg.	–	10	
Elijah McIntire, - -	F. Master,	–	20	
Benj. H. Hall, -	Surgeon,	–	10	
Alexander Fitzhugh, -	Surg. Mate,	–	10	
Wm. Buchanan, - -	"	–	9	
Wm. Seddon, -	Serg. Major,	–	10	
Rowzee Peyton, -	Cl'k & Adj't,	–	18	
Joseph Reddish, -	Capt.	–	10	
Jeremiah B. Templeman, -	Lieut.	–	10	
James Browne, -	Serg't,	–	10	
Rich'd Gaines, -	Ensign,	–	10	

(For rest of this company, see publication of Pay Rolls.)

MUSTER ROLL

Of Field and Staff Officers of the Fifty-second Regiment of Virginia Militia, commanded by Lieutenant Colonel John H. Christian, in the Service of the United States at different periods in the years 1813 and 1814.

NAMES.	RANK.	TIME OF SERVICE.		REMARKS.
		Months.	Days.	
John D. Christian, -	Lt. Colonel,	1	15	
John D. Watkins, -	Major,	1	15	
Wm. H. Gregory, -	"	–	15	
John Minge, - -	Qr. Master,	1	15	
Thos. Gilliam, -	D. Q. Master,	1		
Robert Christian, jr. -	Pay Master,	1	15	
David Glass, -	Adjutant,	1		
William M. Massey, -	Surgeon,	1	15	
Jno. F. Christian, -	Surg. Mate,	1	15	
William F. Walker, -	D. Q. Master,	1		
Richard Graves, -	Adjutant,	–	15	
Patrick Hendren, -	Sec. to Col.	1		
Robert B. Clopton, -	S. Major,	–	15	
Robert W. Christian,	Clerk,	–	15	
Robert Perkins, -	Captain,	–	16	
Wm. Taylor, - -	"	–	16	
Arch'd Lacy, - -	"	–	16	
Wm. Slater, - -	"	–	16	
Seaton W. Crup, - -	"	–	16	
Parks Ball, - -	Lieutenant,	–	16	
John Minge, - -	"	–	15	
Robert Christian, jr.	"	–	15	
David Glass, - -	"	–	15	
John Rankas, -	"	–	15	
Robert Christian, -	"	–	15	
James H. Wilkinson, -	"	–	16	
Ch. Miller, - -	"	–	16	
Daniel Slater, -	"	–	16	
Thos. C. Tunstall, -	"	–	10	
Rich'd Crump, -	"	–	16	
Ancil Bailey, - -	Ensign,	–	16	
Ed. V. Graves, -	"	–	16	
Wm. Ratcliffe, -	"	–	16	
Richard Crump, -	"	–	16	
Norborne Crump, -	"	–	16	
Richard Hillard, -	"	–	16	
Cary Wilkinson, - -	"	–	14	Cavalry.

MUSTER ROLL

Of the Field and Staff Officers of the Fifty-ninth Regiment of Virginia Militia, commanded by Lieutenant Colonel Josiah Riddick, jr., called into the Service of the United States from the County of Nansemond, from the 18th day of March 1813, when last mustered, to the 17th day of April 1813.

NAMES.	RANK.	TIME OF SERVICE.		REMARKS.
		Months.	Days.	
Josiah Riddick,	Lieut. Col.	1		

MUSTER ROLL

Of the Field and Staff Officers of the Sixty-first Regiment Virginia Militia.

NAMES.			RANK.	TIME OF SERVICE.		REMARKS.
				Months.	Days.	
John P. James,	-	-	Qr. Master,	3		
William Bohannon,	-	-	Qr. M. Serg't,	3		
A. G. Cushman,	-	-	Qr. Master,	–	7	
Joseph C. Marigne,	-	-	Serg't Major,	–	13	
Bart. Gayle,	-	-	S. Mate.			
Wm. Taliaferro,	-	-	"	–	3	

(For rest of this company, see publication of Pay Rolls.)

MUSTER ROLL

Of the Field and Staff Officers of the Sixty-second Regiment, Virginia Militia, commanded by Colonel Miles Selden, in the Service of the State of Virginia from the 27th June 1813 to the 9th July 1813.

NAMES.			RANK.	TIME OF SERVICE.		REMARKS.
				Months.	Days.	
Miles Selden,	-	-	Lt. Colonel,	–	13	
William Mattox,	-	-	Major,	–	13	
Richard Williams,	-	-	"	–	13	
Samuel Rains,	-	-	Qr. Master,	–	13	
Thomas Cocke,	-	-	Pay Master,	–	13	
Ashley Davis,	-	-	Surgeon,	–	13	
Thomas Daniel,	-	-	Adjutant,	–	13	
Peyton Rives,	-	-	S. Major,	–	13	
Wm. Hobbs,	-	-	Drum Major,	–	13	
John Tucker,	-	-	Fife Major,	–	13	

MUSTER ROLL

Of the Field and Staff Officers of the Sixty-eighth Regiment, Virginia Militia, commanded by Lieutenant Colonel William Walker, in the Service of the United States at different periods in the years 1813 and 1814.

NAMES.	RANK.	TIME OF SERVICE.		REMARKS.
		Months.	Days.	
Wm. Walker, - -	Lt. Colonel,	–	17	
Robert McCandlish, - -	Adjutant,	–	16	
Robert Anderson, - -	"	1		
Philip Smith, - -	Surgeon,	–	17	
James C. Madison, - -	S. Mate,	–	17	
John Bush, - -	Qr. Master,	1		
Edmond S. Briggs, - -	Surg. Mate,	1		
John Walker. - -	P. M. pro tem.	–	12	

(For rest of this company, see publication of **Pay Rolls**.)

MUSTER ROLL

Of the Field and Staff Officers of the Seventy-first Regiment, Virginia Militia, commanded by Lieutenant Colonel Wm. Allen, in the Service of the United States at different periods during the years 1813 and 1814.

NAMES.			RANK.	TIME OF SERVICE.		REMARKS.
				Months.	Days.	
William Allen,	-	-	Lt. Colonel,	–	23	
William Blow,	-	-	Major,	–	12	
Langley C. Wills,	-	-	"	–	6	
Edwin Jones,	-	-	"	–	11	
John Peter,	-	-	"	–	5	
Edward S. Holt,	-	-	Capt. Com'g,	–	6	
James D. Edwards,	-	-	Adjutant,	–	23	
Francis Ruffin,	-	-	Qr. Master,	–	12	
Benjamin Cocke,	-	-	Pay Master,	–	23	
Charles H. Graves,	-	-	Surgeon,	–	22	
John Pretlow,	-	-	Surg. Mate,	–	14	
Fred. B. Power,	-	-	"	–	10	
Joseph Blunt,	-	-	"	–	14	
William E. Chambliss,		-	Q. M. Serg.	–	7	
William B. Moody,	-	-	Serg. Major,	–	15	
Joseph Warren,	-	-	Drum Major,	–	23	
William P. Ryland,	-	-	F. Major,	–	23	

MUSTER ROLL

Of the Field and Staff Officers of the Seventy-fourth Regiment of Virginia Militia, commanded by Colonel William Trueheart, in the Service of the United States from 20th March to 2nd July in the year 1813.

NAMES.	RANK.	TIME OF SERVICE.		REMARKS.
		Months.	Days.	
Wm. Trueheart, - -	Lt. Colonel,	3	12	
Thomas Starke. - -	Major,	3	12	
Parke Street. - -	"	3	12	
Edmond G. Goodwin, -	Adjutant,	3	12	
William Bowe, - -	P. Master,	3	12	
John W. Ellis. - -	Q. Master,	3	12	
Charles Morris, -	Surgeon,	3	12	
Joseph M. Sheppard, -	S. Mate,	3	12	

MUSTER ROLL

*Of the Field and Staff Officers of the Eighty-third Regiment, Virginia Militia,
in the County of Dinwiddie, commanded by Lieutenant Colonel James Scott,
in the Service of the United States from 1st to 6th July in the year 1813.*

NAMES.			RANK.	TIME OF SERVICE.		REMARKS.
				Months.	Days.	
James Scott,	-	-	Lieut. Col.	—	6	
Armstead Burwell,	-	-	Major,	—	6	
William Wynne,	-	-	"	— .	6	
Henry Young,	-	-	Adjutant,	—	6	
Tingnal Jones,	-	-	Surgeon,	—	6	
John Manlove,	-	-	"	—	6	
John C. Pegram,	-	-	Surg. Mate,	—	6	
John C. Boisseau,	-	-	Pay Master,	—	6	
Thomas Thweatt,	-	-	Qr. Master,	—	6	
Herbert Gregory,	-	-	Qr. Serg't,	—	6	
Joseph Sturdivant,	-	-	Serg't Major,	—	6	
Calvin Hine,	-	-	Fife Major,	—	6	

MUSTER ROLL

Of the Field and Staff Officers of the Ninety-second Regiment of Virginia Militia, commanded by Lieutenant Colonel John Chowning, in the Service of the United States at different periods during the years 1813 and 1814.

NAMES.	RANK.	TIME OF SERVICE.		REMARKS.
		Months.	Days.	
John Chowning,	Lt. Colonel,	–	25	
Spencer George,	Major,	–	25	
John Biscoe.	"	–	22	
William B. Mitchell,	Adjutant,	–	25	
Thomas James,	"	–	3	
Thomas K. Ball.	Surgeon,	–	25	
Charles Carter,	Surg. Mate,	–	19	
James Gibson,	"	–	6	
Wm. Lee Ball,	Pay Master,	–	25	
Ellison Currie.	Qr. Master,	–	19	
Leroy P. Leland,	"	–	13	
Raw. Dunnaway,	Q. M. Sergt.	–	25	
James Kesterson,	"	–	9	
Joseph Shearman,	"	–	6	
Wm. Pollard,	"	–	3	
Bidkah George,	Sergt. Majr.	–	6	
Wm. J. Payne,	"	–	19	

(For rest of this company, see publication of Pay Rolls.)

MUSTER ROLL

Of the Field and Staff Officers of the Ninty-ninth Regiment, Virginia Militia, commanded by Lt. Col. Charles Bagwell, in the Service of the United States at different periods during the years 1813 and 1814.

NAMES.	RANK.	TIME OF SERVICE.		REMARKS.
		Months.	Days.	
Charles Bagwell, - -	Lt. Colonel,	19	7	
James Gillet, - -	Major,	19	7	
William Conquest, - -	"	19	7	
John K. Evans, - -	Adjutant,	19	7	
George Scherer, - -	Surgeon,	19	7	
Peter Hack, - -	Surg. Mate,	19	7	
William W. Burton, - -	Qr. Master,	19	7	
Samuel Crippen, - -	Pay Master,	19	7	

MUSTER ROLL

Of the Field and Staff Officers of the One Hundred and Ninth Regiment of Virginia Militia, commanded by Lieutenant Colonel Elliott Muse, in Service at different periods during the years 1813 and 1814.

NAMES.	RANK.	TIME OF SERVICE.		REMARKS.
		Months.	Days.	
Elliott Muse, - -	Lt. Col.	–	5	
Seaton Humphreys, - -	Major,	1	5	
Rich'd M. Segar, - -	"	–	5	
George D. Nicholson. -	Surgeon,	–	5	
G. W. McIntire, - -	Surg. Mate,	–	5	
Peyton Grymes, - -	Pay Master,	–	5	
John Thruston, - -	Adjutant,	–	25	
Rich'd Claybrooke, - -	"	–	12	
Taliaferro Hunter, - -	Q. Master,	–	5	
James Healy, - -	Q. M. Serg.	1	26	
Absolam Griffin, - -	"	–	20	
Philip Montague, - -	Drum Major,	–	5	
John Saunders, -- -	Serg. Major,	–	9	
P. Woodward, - -	"	–	11	
Henly Woodward, - -	"	–	12	
Lewis Montague, - -	Fife Major,	–	23	

(For rest of this company, see publication of Pay Rolls.)

MUSTER ROLL

Of the Field and Staff Officers of the One Hundred and Eleventh Regiment, Virginia Militia, commanded by Colonel Richard E. Parker, in the Service of the United States at different periods during the years 1813 and 1814.

NAMES.			RANK.	TIME OF SERVICE.		REMARKS.
				Months.	Days.	
Richard E. Parker,	-	-	Colonel,	4	16	
William Nelson,	-	-	Major,	3	12	
John Turberville,	-	-	"	2		
George W. Banks,	-	-	"	1	21	
Daniel Carmichael,	-	-	Pay Master,	2	3	
Richard T. Brown,	-	-	"	1	3	
Richard T. Brown,	-	-	Qr. Master,	—	27	
Charles S. Collins,	-	-	Surgeon.	2	22	
Nathaniel W. Clopton,		.	Surg. Mate,	3	25	
Robert Murphy,	-	-	"	—	21	
George Payne,	-	-	Adjutant,	3	10	
Richard Croxton,	-	-	Qr. M. Serg't,	2	8	
J. W. Jones,	-	-	S. Major,	1		
John L. Mayo,	-	-	"	—	28	
Daniel Payne,	-	-	"	3	7	
Robert Bailey,	-	-	Qr. Master,	1	3	
Henry S. Yeatman,	-	-	"	1	19	
Samuel Johnson,	-	-	F. Major,	1	3	
John Johnson,	-	-	D. Major,	1	3	
William Middleton,	-	-	Captain,	—	19	
Mroth M. Marmaduke,	-	-	"	—	7	
Allen S. Dozier,	-	-	"	—	17	
Jno. B. Murphy,	-	-	Lieutenant,	—	5	
Wm. M. Walker,	-	-	"	—	7	
Stephen Bailey,	-	-	"	—	13	
Edward Spencer,	-	-	"	—	7	
Thomas Prickard,	-	-	Ensign,	—	15	
James English,	-	-	"	—	9	

MUSTER ROLL

Of the Field and Staff of the One Hundred and Fifteenth Regiment, Virginia Militia, commanded by Lt. Col. Henry Howard, in Service from 26th June to 7th July 1813.

NAMES.			RANK.	TIME OF SERVICE.		REMARKS.
				Months.	Days.	
Henry Howard,	-	-	Lt. Colonel,	—	12	
Henry Tabb,	-	-	Major,	—	12	
Augustine Moore,	-	-	"	—	1	
Samuel Colton,	-	-	Surgeon,	—	1	
Maurice Langhorne,	-	-	Q. Master,	—	1	
Everard Robinson,	-	-	Pay Master,	—	1	
George Winder,	-	-	Surg. Mate,	—	1	
Robert Anderson,	-	-	Adjutant,	—	13	

Field and Staff of the Second Elite Corps at Charles City Court-house.

NAMES.	RANK.	TIME OF SERVICE.		REMARKS.
		Months.	Days.	
P. B. Tindall, - -	Surgeon,	–	–	Time not given.

(For rest of this company, see publication of Pay Rolls.)

Field and Staff of the Fourth Brigade from 20th August to 31st October 1814.

NAMES.	RANK.	TIME OF SERVICE.		REMARKS.
		Months.	Days.	
Arch'd Perkins, - -	Brig. Insp'tor,	–	15	
Thomas Harding, - -	W. Master,	–	14	
William May, - -	F. Master,	–	9	
Benj. Harris, - -	As't F. Master,	–	13	

(For rest of this company, see publication of **Pay Rolls.**)

MUSTER ROLL

Of the Field and Staff Officers of a detachment of the Virginia Militia, commanded by Major Robert Crutchfield, attached to the Brigade of General Wm. Madison, in the Service of the United States from the 4th day of September 1814 to the 12th day of September 1814, inclusive.

NAMES.	RANK.	TIME OF SERVICE.		REMARKS.
		Months.	Days.	
Robert Crutchfield, - -	Major,	–	9	

MUSTER ROLL

Of the Field and Staff Officers of a detachment of Virginia Militia stationed at Fort Powhatan, from the 26th of July to the 17th of September 1813.

NAMES.	RANK.	TIME OF SERVICE.		REMARKS.
		Months.	Days.	
James Williams, - -	Major,	1	24	
Ashley Davis, - -	Surgeon,	1	24	
Charles Perrow, - -	Pay Master,	1	24	
James Garland, - -	Q. Master and Sec. to Com't.	2	6	

(For rest of this company, see publication of Pay Rolls.)

MUSTER ROLL

Of the First Brigade, Virginia Militia, commanded by Brigadier General William Chamberlayne, in Service during the year 1814.

NAMES.	RANK.	TIME OF SERVICE.		REMARKS.
		Months.	Days.	
William Chamberlayne, -	Brig. Gen'l,	4	9	
S. J. Winston, -	B. Major,	4	8	
Abraham S. Wooldridge, -	Aid de Camp,	3		
William Armstead, - -	"	3		
Andrew Stevenson, - -	"	1	5	
Joshua West, - -	B. Q. Master,	–	4	
Nicholas Mills, - -	"	1	29	
—— Smithers, - -	B. F. Master,	–	6	
Wm. Winston, - -	"	–	2	
Richard W. Michaux, -	B. T. Master,	–	4	
James Fowlks, - -	"	–	23	
Spencer Wooldridge, -	B. F. Master,	1	22	
Wm. Stark, - -	"	1	4	
Andrew Moore, - -	B. W. Master,	1	22	
Peter F. Farrow, - -	"	–	12	
Cincinnatus Stith, - -	"	1	5	
—— Booker, - -	Servant,	1	5	
Sam. Hall, - -	"			
Geo. Lindsay, - -	"			

MUSTER ROLL

Of the Staff Officers of the Battalion of Artillery of Virginia Militia, in the Service of the United States, from the 7th of October to the 16th November 1814, both days inclusive.

NAMES.			RANK.	TIME OF SERVICE.		REMARKS.
				Months.	Days.	
Jno. Armistead,	-	-	Capt. Com'dt.			
Robert P. Archer,	-	-	Surgeon,	1	11	On furlough.
James B. Southall,	-	-	Qr. Master,	1	11	
Lewis C. Tyler,	-	-	Adjutant,	1	10	

MUSTER ROLL

Of the Field and Staff of the detachment of Troops in Service at Smithfield, under the command of Major Joseph W. Ballard, from the 18th of March 1813, to the 8th of April 1813.

NAMES.	RANK.	TIME OF SERVICE.		REMARKS.
		Months.	Days.	
Joseph W. Ballard, - -	Major,	–	22	
Arthur Smith, - -	Adjutant,	–	22	
Nathaniel Young, - -	Qr. Master,	–	9	
James Chalmers, - -	"	–	22	
Robert Hines, - -	Pay Master,	–	22	
John H. Purdie, - -	Surgeon,	–	22	
John R. Todd, - -	Serg't Major,	–	22	
William Cole, - -	Q. M. Serg't,	–	22	

MUSTER ROLL

Of the Staff of the Eighth Brigade, Virginia Militia, in the Service of the State of Virginia, under the command of Lieutenant Colonel Francis M. Boykin, called into Service under General Orders of the 27th day of August 1814, and rendezvoused at Smithfield from the 29th day of August 1814, to the 13th day of September 1814, when last mustered, both days inclusive.

NAMES.	RANK.	TIME OF SERVICE.		REMARKS.
		Months.	Days.	
Francis M. Boykin,	Lt. Col. Comdt.	–	16	
Henry W. Wills,	Maj. & Brig. Insp'r,	–	16	
Fielding W. Loodson,	Brig. Qr. Master,	–	16	
John Faircloth,	Ass't Commissary,	–	16	

MUSTER ROLL

Of the Staff Officers of a detachment of Virginia Militia, under the command of his Excellency the Governor of Virginia, composing the Army for the defence of the State, in the Service of the United States from the 28th day of August 1814, to the 28th day of November 1814.

NAMES.	RANK.	TIME OF SERVICE.		REMARKS.
		Months.	Days.	
David Campbell,	Aid de Camp,	2	24	
Philip Nicholas,	"	3		
Benj. W. Leigh.	"	3		
Hugh Nelson,	"	3		
James Maurice,	Adj't General,	3		
C. W. Gooch,	Ass. Ad. Gen.	3		
Ch. F. Mercer,	Insp. General,	2	13	
Wm. Randolph,	Ass. Ins. Gen.	1	12	
Jno. Randolph of Roanoke,	Top. Engin'r.			
Nathaniel Cargill,	Q. M. Gen'l,	3		
George Blow,	As. Q. M. Gen.	3		
Robert Rochelle,	"	3		
James Jones,	Surg. Gen'l,	3		
Philip Thornton,	Hosp. Surg.	3		
Micajah Clark,	"	3		
Meredith Fox,	"	3		
Carter B. Page,	Prin. Forager,	3		
M. B. Poitiaux,	Ass't "	3		
Harrison Jones,	Hos. Steward,	3		
Jesse Burton.	P. W. Master.	3		
John T. Anderson.	Ward Master.	3		

MUSTER ROLL

Of the Quarter Master General and Hospital Departments, in the City of Richmond, in the Service of the United States from the 29th day of November 1814, when last mustered, to the 28th of February 1815.

NAMES.			RANK.	TIME OF SERVICE.		REMARKS.
				Months.	Days.	
James Maurice.	-	-	Adj't Gen'l,	2	25	
Nathaniel Cargill,	-	-	Q. M. Gen'l,	3		
George Blow.	-	-	A. D. Q. M. Gen'l,	–	15	
Robert Rochelle,	-	-	"	3		
Carter B. Page.	-	-	P. F. Master,	3		
M. B. Poitiaux.	-	-	Ass't F. Master	3		
Ptolemy L. Watkins.	-	-	Ass't T. Master	5	18	
John L. Duffel,	-	-	Ass't T. Master	2	22	
Jesse Burton,	-	-	P. W. Master,	1	8	
James Jones,	-	-	Surg. General,	–	17	
Philip Thornton,	-	-	Hosp'l Surg.	–	17	
M. Clark,	-	-	H. Surg. Mate,	–	18	
M. Fox,	-	-	H. L. Mate,	3		
H. Jones,	-	-	H. Steward,	–	10	
John T. Anderson,	-	-	Ward Master,	2	22	

MUSTER ROLL

Of the Field and Staff Officers of a detachment of the Virginia Militia compos-
ing the Flying Camp, now in the Service of the United States, composing the
Regiment commanded by Colonel James McDowell, from the 3d of July 1813,
when last mustered, to the 16th of August 1813.

NAMES.			RANK.	TIME OF SERVICE.		REMARKS.
				Months.	Days.	
James McDowell,	-	-	Col. Comd't,	1	15	
Chamberlin Jones,	-	-	Major,	1	15	
John Floyd,	-	-	Surgeon,	1	15	
Hardin Massie,	-	-	Surg. Mate,	1	15	
Samuel M. D. Reid,	-	-	Adjutant,	1	15	
John Irvine,	-	-	Insp'r Master,	1	15	
Benjamin Moseby,	-	-	Forage Mast'r,	1	15	
Joshua Yoe,	-	-	Ass't F. Mas'r,	1	15	
George Cayner,	-	-	Wag. Master,	1	15	
Peter Bowyer,	-	-	Q. M. Serg't,	1	15	
James R. Robinson.	-	-	Serg. Major,	1	15	

MUSTER ROLL

Of the Field and Staff Officers of a Division of the Virginia Militia in the Service of the United States, commanded by Major General John Pegram, from the 27th of August 1814, to the 1st December 1814.

NAMES.			RANK.	TIME OF SERVICE.		REMARKS.
				Months.	Days.	
John Pegram,	-	-	Major Gen'l,	3	4	
John Fitzgerald,	-	-	Aid de Camp,	3	4	
Daniel Eppes,	-	-	"	3	4	
Armistead Burwell,	-	-	Div. Inspector.	3	4	
Edward Pegram,	-	-	Div. Q. Mas'r,	3	4	
Beverley Tucker,	-	-	Ass't Adj. Gen.	3	4	
John B. Strachan,	-	-	Hosp. Sur. of Div.	3	4	
				3	4	
John Field,	-	-	Hosp'l Surg. Mate,	3	4	
John Pegram,	-	-	"			
John Roane,	-	-	"	3	4	
John L. Martin,	-	-	Issuing Com'y,	3	4	
Benj. W. Moss,	-	-	Ass't Q. Mas'r,	3	4	
Fendal Gregory,	-	-	Forage Mas'r,	3	4	
Cincinnatus Stith,	-	-	Wag. Mas'r,	3	4	
William Stark,	-	-	Ass't F. Mas'r,	3	4	
Edward Randolph,	-	-	"	3	4	
Rich'd Cunningham,		-	Ass't D. Insp.	3	4	

MUSTER ROLL

*Of Field and Staff Officers of the First Corps d'Elite of the Army of Virginia.
one month in Service, composed of frequently changed Companies of organized
Draughts and Volunteers for the particular occasions, united by Proclamation,
and established Volunteer Companies of Cavalry, Artillery, and Light Infantry,
commanded by Thomas M. Randolph.*

NAMES.	RANK.	TIME OF SERVICE.		REMARKS.
		Months.	Days.	
Thos. Mann Randolph,	Lieut. Col.	–	4	
Daniel Watson,	Major,	–	4	
John Grattan Gamble,	Lieutenant,	–	4	
George Watson,	Surgeon.	1		
Jas. Murray Morris,	Surg. Mate,	1		
John Young Stockdale.	"	–	8	Richmond Riflemen.
John Randolph,	"	–	8	Second sergeant in Archer's.
Wm. F. Braxton,	Qr. Master,	–	4	
Samuel Dyer,	"	–	9	
William Caulfield,	"	–	20	Richmond Light Infantry.
Charles Wonegardner,	Ass't Q. M.	1	–	Richmond Riflemen.
John Randolph,	For. Master,	–	24	Private of Archer's.
Edward Geddie,	Ass't Q. M.	–	29	
George Robertson,	"	–	28	Richmond Light Infantry.
James Ragland,	Adjutant,	1	9	Carr's Cavalry.

MUSTER ROLL

Of the Field and Staff of a Squadron of Dragoons, commanded by Major John T. Woodford, in the Service of the United States during the years 1814 and 1815.

NAMES.	RANK.	TIME OF SERVICE.		REMARKS.
		Months.	Days.	
John T. Woodford, - -	Major,	7	4	
Armistead Hoomes, - -	Adjutant,	4	18	
James Henderson, - -	Surgeon.	6	15	
William Leftwich, - -	P. Master,	5	25	
Fabius Lawson, -	Q. M. Serg.	2	4	
Joseph B. Anderson, - -	Serg. Major,	2	4	
Augustine Leftwich, - -	Serg. Major,	3	2	
Charles Whitley, - -	Q. M. Serg.	7	4	
William Woodford. - -	Serg. Major.	2	25	

PAY ROLL

Of a detachment of Infantry of the Eighty-seventh Regiment, 14th Brigade, of Virginia Militia, commanded by Major Thomas Hill, from the County of King William, called into the Service of the United States for the month of December 1814.

NAMES.	RANK.	TIME OF SERVICE.		REMARKS.
		Months.	Days.	
Thomas Hill,	Major,	—	17	
William L. Abraham.	Captain,	—	17	
Reuben Lipscomb.	Lieutenant,	—	17	
Richard King,	"	—	17	
Robert Hill,	"	—	17	
Robert Row,	Ensign,	—	17	
Cornelius Dabney,	"	—	17	
William S. Johnson,	Sergeant,	—	17	Sub. for Jas. Willroy.
Presley Ellett,	"	—	17	Sub. for P. Croxton.
Fendal S. Trimmer,	"	—	17	
George M. Powell,	"	—	17	
Samuel B. Edwards,	"	—	17	
Joseph Tompkins,	"	—	17	
John F. Tuck,	"	—	17	
William Terry,	Corporal,	—	17	
Henry Dabney,	"	—	15	Sub. for H. Dabney.
Josiah Pollard,	"	—	17	Sub. for Jas. Cock.
Thos. Patterson, jr.	"	—	17	
Stephen Hughes,	"	—	17	
Henry Sanders,	Drummer,	—	17	
William Blake,	Fifer,	—	17	
John Addams,	Private.	—	17	
Acquilla Alexander,	"	—	17	
Warren Addams,	"	—	17	
Churchill Alexander,	"	—	17	
Thomas Ancarrow,	"	—	17	
John Acree,	"	—	17	
Martin Ancarrow,	"	—	17	
Alexander Agnew,	"	—	17	Sub. for William E. Bowes.
Thomas T. Allen,	"	—	17	Sub. for J. Slaughter.
Reuben Baker,	"	—	17	
William Batchedor,	"	—	17	
Joel Beadles,	"	—	17	
William Baker,	"	—	17	
Edward Burke,	"	—	17	
Thomas Blakerby,	"	—	17	Sub. for John Bradberry.
Thomas Bradberry,	"	—	17	Sub. for R. D. Grundy.
William Chick,	"	—	17	
John Catlett,	"	—	17	
John S. Crump,	"	—	17	
Warner Cook,	"	—	17	Sub. for J. Glover.
Thos. B. Chamberlayne,	"	—	17	Sub. for Cs. C. Page.
Pleasant Davice,	"	—	17	
Mordecai B. Dabney,	"	—	17	
Pleasant D. Ellett,	"	—	17	Sub. for P. Robinson.
Thomas G. Edmondson,	"	—	17	Sub. for J. Glover.

NAMES.		RANK.	TIME OF SERVICE.		REMARKS.
			Months.	Days.	
Thos. K. Foster,	- -	Private,	–	17	Sub. for Js. Foster.
William T. Fleet,	- -	"	–	17	
Bailey Fox,	- -	"	–	17	Sub. for Thos. Rose.
John B. Foster,	- -	"	–	17	Sub. for Js. Smither.
Jos. Gwathmey, jr.	- -	"	–	17	Sub. for W. Mearix.
Thomas Garnett,	- -	"	–	17	
William Gunter.	- -	"	–	17	
Robert Garnett,	- -	"	–	17	
Jack Gravitt,	- -	"	–	17	
Philip Gatewood,	- -	"	–	17	
John Gary.	- -	"	–	17	
Ralph R. Horn,	- -	"	–	17	Sub. for J. C. Cox.
Gideon Hay,	- -	"	–	17	
Francis Horth,	- -	"	–	17	
John Houchings,	- -	"	–	17	
James R. Houchings,	- -	"	–	17	
John R. Horn,	- -	"	–	17	
Ellett Houchings,	- -	"	–	17	
Rich'd Hay.	- -	"	–	17	
George Heath,	- -	"	–	17	Sub. for C. Johnson.
Robert Johnson,	- -	"	–	17	
Addison Johnson,	- -	"	–	17	
Rich'd C. Lowers,	- -	"	–	17	Substitute for T. Satterwhite.
Caleb Longest,	- -	"	–	17	
Henry Lipscomb,	- -	"	–	17	
Thomas A. Lipscomb,	-	"	–	17	
Peter Lendrum,	-	"	–	17	
Thos. J. Madison,	- -	"	–	17	Sub. for F. Dujar.
John McCarty,	- -	"	–	17	Sub. for Thos. Glover.
Thomas Mason,	- -	"	–	17	
John Martin,	- -	"	–	17	
George Martin,	- -	"	–	17	
William Mahon,	- -	"	–	17	
James Maxwell,	- -	"	–	17	
Donald McNabb,	- -	"	–	17	
Stephen Monday,	- -	"	–	17	
Gregory Madison,	- -	"	–	17	Sub. for E. L. Powell.
James O. Neal,	- -	"	–	9	Deserted 14th Dec.
John M. Powers,	- -	"	–	17	Sub. for Jno. Alvey.
John Pemberton,	- -	"	–	17	Sub. for T. C. Nelson.
John Pitts.	- -	"	–	17	Sub. for W. D. Puller.
Charles Pigg.	- -	"	–	17	Sub. for Js. Croxton.
Benjamin Pendleton,	- -	"	–	17	
Thos. G. Pollard,	- -	"	–	17	
James Phillips,	- -	"	–	17	
Isaac Powers,	- -	"	–	17	
James Powell.	- -	"	–	17	
George Powell,	- -	"	–	17	
Robert F. Quarles,	- -	"	–	17	
Samuel Rice,	- -	"	–	17	
Nathaniel Row,	- -	"	–	17	
William Rice,	- -	"	–	17	
Charles Rogers,	- -	"	–	17	
Michael S. Rice,	- -	"	–	17	
Thomas Starke,	- -	"	–	17	Sub. for J. Bowles.
James Shadwick,	- -	"	–	17	Sub. for Js. Fox.
John R. Stewart,	- -	"	–	17	Sub. for Thos. Floyd.
William Sanders,	- -	"	–	17	Sub. for A. Leftwich.
James Sullins,	- -	"	–	17	Sub. for T. Leftwich.
John Smith,	- -	"	–	17	
John Sullins, jr.	- -	"	–	17	
Stephen Slaughter,	- -	"	–	17	
Rich'd Sullins,	- -	"	–	17	

NAMES.	RANK.	TIME OF SERVICE.		REMARKS.
		Months.	Days.	
Henry Smith, - -	Private,	–	17	
James Smith, jr. - -	"	–	17	
William Slaughter, - -	"	–	17	Sub. for G. Slaughter.
Thomas Smith, - -	"	–	17	
James Sanders, - -	"	–	17	
William G. Tuck, - -	"	–	17	
Obadiah Trimmer, - -	"	–	17	Sub. for William Trimmer.
Reuben Trimmer, - -	"	–	17	
James Taylor, - -	"	–	17	
George Tuck, - -	"	–	17	
James Turner, - -	"	–	17	Sub. for T. Turner.
Thomas Tuck, - -	"	–	17	
Robert Tuck, - -	"	–	17	
Josiah Tuck, - -	"	–	17	
Joseph Tuck, - -	"	–	17	
Henry Tuck, - -	"	–	17	
Wm. Taliaferro, - -	"	–	17	
George P. Terry, - -	"	–	17	
William Terry, - -	"	–	17	Sub. for Thomas Edwards.
Vincent S. Terry, - -	"	–	17	
David Valentine, jr. - -	"	–	17	
John W. Valentine, - -	"	–	17	
James P. Woody, - -	"	–	17	Sub. for J. Wooddy.
George Woollard, - -	"	–	17	
James Warters, jr. - -	"	–	17	
Wm. Woollard, - -	"	–	15	Died 19th Dec. 1814.
Richard Wadkins, - -	"	–	17	
John Wooddy, - -	"	–	17	Sub. for P. Longist.
Thomas Wheatley, - -	"	–	17	Sub. for R. W. King.
William Webb, - -	"	–	17	Sub. for J. S. Grant.
Jeremiah Walker, - -	"	–	17	Sub. for Jas. Buckner.

PAY ROLL

Of the Militia of the Ninety-second Regiment, from Lancaster County, commanded by Major John Chowning, jr., in Service from 3d April to the 9th of the same month in the year 1813.

NAMES.	RANK.	TIME OF SERVICE.		REMARKS.
		Months.	Days.	
John Chowning, jr.	Major,	—	7	
Samuel M. Shearman,	Captain,	—	7	
John Hunt.	"	—	5	
John Biscoe,	"	—	7	
William C. Carpenter,	"	—	7	
Thomas Armstrong,	"	—	7	
Thomas Yerby,	"	—	6	
John Gaines.	Lieutenant,	—	3	
Ralph Edwards,	"	—	5	
John Hathaway,	"	—	7	
John Rogers,	"	—	7	
William T. Yerby,	"	—	7	
William H. Rogers,	"	—	7	
William Blackstone,	Ensign,	—	7	
William B. Mitchell,	"	—	7	
Opie Beane,	"	—	7	
James Kirk.	"	—	5	
Timothy McNamara,	"	—	5	
Thomas Mason,	Sergeant,	—	7	
Bailey George,	"	—	7	
John Thrall,	"	—	7	
Nicho. P. Buchan,	"	—	7	
James Brent,	"	—	7	
John Kirk,	"	—	7	
Thomas Y. Hunton,	"	—	7	
Robert Percifull,	"	—	7	
James Kisterson,	"	—	7	
William T. Payne,	"	—	7	
William George,	"	—	7	
William Pitman.	"	—	7	
Hilkiah Ball,	"	—	7	
Burges K. Keen,	"	—	7	
John Edwards, jr.	"	—	7	
Leonard Stamper,	"	—	7	
William Dunnaway,	"	—	7	
Overton Carpenter,	"	—	7	
Armstead T. Palmer,	"	—	7	
John Kem,	"	—	7	
Robert Daniel,	"	—	7	
John Taff.	Corporal,	—	7	
James Sutton,	"	—	7	
Joseph Wirt,	"	—	7	
William Hill,	"	—	7	
Walter Arms,	"	—	7	
William Chitwood,	"	—	7	
William Hathaway,	"	—	7	
George Pullen,	Drummer,	—	7	
Ben. Doggett,	"	—	7	

NAMES.	RANK.	TIME OF SERVICE.		REMARKS.
		Months.	Days.	
John Stott, - -	Fifer,	–	7	
Radham Kent, - -	"	–	7	
Nathaniel Alford, - -	Private,	–	7	
Archbold Anderson, - -	"	–	7	
George Ashburne, - -	"	–	7	
James Ashburn, - -	"	–	7	
James Adkerson, - -	"	–	7	
Thomas Bush, - -	"	–	7	
Theo. Bland, - -	"	–	3	
Spencer Brown, - -	"	–	7	
William Boatman, - -	"	–	7	
Robert Biscoe, - -	"	–	7	
Charles Bailey, - -	"	–	7	
Thomas Biscoe, - -	"	–	7	
John Boatman, - -	"	–	7	
Middleton Brent, - -	"	–	7	
Newby Barrack, - -	"	–	7	
William Brown, - -	"	–	7	
Raleigh Brown, - -	"	–	7	
Thomas P. Ball, - -	"	–	7	
Addington Brent, - -	"	–	7	
Peter Beane, - -	"	–	7	
Robert Beane, - -	"	–	7	
John S. Chowning, - -	"	–	7	
Thomas Coats, -	"	–	7	
William H. Chowning, -	"	–	7	
John Cundiff, - -	"	–	7	
Hiram Chilton, - -	"	–	7	
Stephen Chilton, - -	"	–	7	
Richard Cundiff, - -	"	–	7	
Thomas Christopher, - -	"	–	7	
Richard Coats, - -	"	–	7	
Griffin Carpenter, - -	"	–	7	
Hiram Carpenter, - -	"	–	7	
Robert Chum, - -	"	–	7	
Richard Cockrell, - -	"	–	7	
Isaac Cundiff, - -	"	–	7	
John Currell, - -	"	–	7	
Isaac Currell, - -	"	–	7	
Thomas Cattrell, - -	"	–	7	
George Carter, - -	"	–	7	
Dennis Doggett, - -	"	–	7	
James Doggett, - -	"	–	4	
Joseph Dozier, - -	"	–	7	
William Drivon, - -	"	–	7	
Joseph Duvvenday, - -	"	–	7	
William Doggett, - -	"	–	7	
Landon Dudley, - -	"	–	7	
Daniel F. Davenport, -	"	–	7	
William Dawson, - -	"	–	7	
James Ewell, - -	"	–	7	
William Ford, - -	"	–	7	
John Flowers, - -	"	–	7	
William Fleming, - -	"	–	7	
James Fleming, - -	"	–	7	
Thomas N. Ford, - -	"	–	7	
Elias Fendley, - -	"	–	7	
Isaac George, - -	"	–	7	
Thos. D. George, - -	"	–	7	
William Garner, - -	"	–	7	
John Gresham, - -	"	–	7	
John Gundry, - -	"	–	7	
James Gaines, - -	"	–	7	
John George, - -	"	–	7	

NAMES.	RANK.	TIME OF SERVICE.		REMARKS.
		Months.	Days.	
Spencer George, - -	Private,	–	7	
Thomas Goodrick, - -	"	–	7	
Nicholas George, - -	"	–	7	
William George, - -	"	–	7	
Eppa George, - -	"	–	7	
Martin George, - -	"	–	7	
John W. Hunton, - -	"	–	7	
Archbold Henton, - -	"	–	7	
Armstead Hayden, - -	"	–	7	
Thomas Hayden, - -	"	–	7	
Griffin Hayden, - -	"	–	7	
Lewis Hayden, - -	"	–	7	
Osburn Hayden, - -	"	–	7	
Lewis Hammonds, - -	"	–	7	
B. Hughlett, - -	"	–	7	
John Hubbard, - -	"	–	7	
George Hathaway, - -	"	–	7	
Richard Hutchings, - -	"	–	7	
Roystin Hughlett, - -	"	–	7	
Martin Hughlett, - -	"	–	7	
Richard Hinton, - -	"	–	7	
Jesse Hammonds, - -	"	–	7	
James Hammonds, - -	"	–	7	
Thomas Hugh, - -	"	–	7	
Charles Ingram, - -	"	–	7	
Richard Ingram, - -	"	–	7	
William James, - -	"	–	7	
Charles James, - -	"	–	7	
John Kemp, - -	"	–	7	
James Kirk, - -	"	–	7	
Westley Kirk, - -	"	–	7	
James Kem, - -	"	–	7	
Lodovick Kent, - -	"	–	7	
Charles Kelley, - -	"	–	7	
William Keebig, - -	"	–	7	
Joel Kirk, - -	"	–	7	
Richard Keem, - -	"	–	7	
John Lowry, - -	"	–	7	
Henry Law, - -	"	–	7	
William Lockham, - -	"	–	7	
Hiram Locke, - -	"	–	7	
William Lawson, - -	"	–	7	
Joseph Morgan, - -	"	–	7	
Thomas Martin, - -	"	–	7	
Robert Miller, - -	"	–	7	
Thomas Miller, - -	"	–	7	
Wm. C. McTyre, - -	"	–	7	
John McNamara, - -	"	–	3	
John Mason, - -	"	–	7	
Thomas Mason, jr. - -	"	–	7	
William Mason, - -	"	–	7	
William Martin, - -	"	–	7	
Thomas Newgrant, - -	"	–	7	
Rawleigh Nover, - -	"	–	7	
Robert Nutt, - -	"	–	7	
Moseley Nutt, - -	"	–	7	
James L. Norris, - -	"	–	7	
James Nutt, - -	"	–	7	
Alexander Nawel, - -	"	–	7	
Joseph Nutt, - -	"	–	7	
William Pitman, - -	"	–	7	
William Pullen, - -	"	–	7	
John Y. Percifull, - -	"	–	7	
Edward Percifull, - -	"	–	7	

NAMES.	RANK.	TIME OF SERVICE.		REMARKS.
		Months.	Days.	
Henry Pullen, - -	Private,	–	7	
Edward Payne, - -	"	–	7	
Isaac Pitman, - -	"	–	7	
George Roberts, - -	"	–	7	
James Robinson, - -	"	–	7	
John Rice, - -	"	–	7	
Raleigh Rains, - -	"	–	7	
Richard Rant, - -	"	–	7	
Edward Richard, - -	"	–	7	
Andrew Robinson, - -	"	–	7	
Lemuel Robinson, - -	"	–	7	
John Richardson, - -	"	–	7	
Daniel Ruse, - -	"	–	7	
George Smith, - -	"	–	7	
William Sutton, - -	"	–	7	
Samuel Stanham, - -	"	–	7	
George Spermare, - -	"	–	7	
Thos. Schofield, - -	"	–	7	
Daniel Shelton, - -	"	–	7	
John Simmonds, - -	"	–	7	
John Sampson, - -	"	–	7	
William B. Snydor, - -	"	–	7	
William Simmonds, - -	"	–	7	
Henry Schofield, - -	"	–	7	
William Spilman, - -	"	–	7	
Dempsey Treckley, - -	"	–	7	
William Thrall, - -	"	–	7	
Richard Tawell, - -	"	–	7	
George Thomas, - -	"	–	7	
Thomas I. Talley, - -	"	–	2	
Thornley Tankersley, - -	"	–	7	
James Tankersley, - -	"	–	7	
John Talman, - -	"	–	7	
George Talley, - -	"	–	7	
Henry Tapscott, - -	"	–	7	
Thomas Thrall, - -	"	–	7	
Partuer Tawles, - -	"	–	7	
George Welsh, - -	"	–	7	
James Warwick, - -	"	–	7	
Griffin Welsh, - -	"	–	7	
John Walker, - -	"	–	7	
Thomas L. Warwick, - -	"	–	7	
John Wilder, - -	"	–	7	
John Yerby, - -	"	–	7	

MUSTER ROLL

Of the Sick Noncommissioned Officers and Privates belonging to a detachment of Militia, commanded by Colonel James McDowell and left at Camp Holly Spring Hospital on the 13th October 1813.

NAMES.	RANK.	TIME OF SERVICE.		REMARKS.
		Months.	Days.	
In Capt. Danl. Huffman's Company.				
John Grizsby, - -	Sergeant.			
George Hosshorth, - -	Private,	-	-	Died 22d October 1813.
In Capt. John Gilkerson's Co.				
Robert Stevenson, - -	Private.			
Joseph Guy, - -	"			
In Capt. Joseph Hanna's Co.				
Geo. Jourdan. - -	Private.			
Peter Franklin, - -	"			
John Johns, - -	"			
Daniel Core, - -	"			
Ferman Sievens, - -	"			
Anderson Manuel, - -	"			
Matthias Hover, - -	"			
John Newcomb, - -	"			
In Capt. James Cartmell's Co.				
James L. Turner, - -	Sergeant.			
Jacob Switzer, - -	Private.			
William Dunbar, - -	"			
Samuel Hamilton, - -	"			
John Holland, - -	"			
Jacob Bolton, - -	"			
Merit Martin, - -	"			
John Campbell, - -	"			
William Overhain, - -	"			
John M. Culley, - -	"			
Samuel Gross, - -	"			
Charles Weaver, - -	"			
John Cohon, - -	"			
Joseph Gladden, - -	"			
Geo. Fultz, - -	"			
Joshua Snyder, - -	"			
Moses Skelton, - -	"			
John Lawson, - -	"			
Joshua Tate, - -	"			
James Switzle, - -	"			

MUSTER ROLL

Of Artificers under the command of Philip B. Winston, Superintendent of Artificers in the Service of the United States, selected from the Fourth Brigade, Virginia Militia, commanded by Brigadier General John H. Cocke—Camp Carter.

NAMES.	RANK.	TIME OF SERVICE.		REMARKS.
		Months.	Days.	
Charles Anderson,	Carpenter,	4	21	Detailed from Capt. Gannaway's co.
Samuel Bridgwater,	—	2	14	
William Clibourne,	—	1	13	
William Cogbill,	—	1	03	
John Dowdy,	—	2	11	
Jacob Deals,	Blacksmith,	4	25	Detailed from Capt. Estis' Company.
James Davenport,	Gunsmith,	4	14	Detailed from Capt. Penick's company.
Thos. Epperson,	—	2	17	
Peyton Fuqua,	—	2	11	
John A. Flippen,	Blacksmith,	4	12	Detailed from Capt. Timberlake's co.
John Garrett,	Carpenter,	4	7	Detailed from Capt. Gannaway's co.
Thos. Holmes,	—	2	11	
Charles T. Howard,	Carpenter,	4	21	Detailed from Capt. Tinsley's co.
John Hopper,	"	1	14	Detailed from Capt. Ford's co.
John Ladd,	Gunsmith,	4	26	Detailed from Capt. Massy's co.
Wm. C. Martin,	Carpenter,	4	—	Detailed from Capt. Gannaway's co.
H. McMamers,	—	1	06	
Henry Niece.	Carpenter,	1	—	Detailed from Capt. Scott's co.
Turner Southall,	—	1	10	
Wm. Tyree,	—	1	10	
George Vaden,	—	2	10	
Edward Wills,	Blacksmith,	3	20	Detailed from Capt. Field's co.
William Waite,	"	4	25	Detailed from Capt. Estis' co.
William Walton,	—	2	14	
Thos. Wayard,	—	1	17	

MUSTER ROLL

Of Captain Ephraim G. Alburtis' Company, in the First Regiment of Virginia Volunteers commanded by Colonel John F. Hamtramck, called into the Service of the United States by the President, under the Act of Congress approved May 13, 1846, from the 21st January 1847, for during the War with Mexico.

NAMES.	RANK.	WHEN ENROLLED.	REMARKS.
Ephraim G. Alburtis,	Captain,	Nov. 21, 1846.	
Otker H. Harrison,	1st Lieutenant,	" "	
David W. Gray,	2d "	Nov. 27, "	
George W. Chambers,	2d "	Dec. 20, "	
Edward W. Maxwell,	1st Sergeant,	Nov. 21, "	
John C. Reed,	Sergeant,	" 27, "	
Robert Pollock,	"	Jan. 6, 1847.	
John Jamison,	"	Nov. 27, 1846.	
Daniel Poisal,	Corporal,	" 21, "	
Wm. H. Page,	"	Dec. 26, "	
Thornton Coontz,	"	Nov. 29, "	
Wm. Sherrard,	"	" 27, "	
John W. Keef,	Drummer,	" 21, "	
Benjamin W. Blondell,	Fifer,	Dec. 30, "	
Anderson Bennett,	Private,	Jan. 6, 1847.	
John A. Beales,	"	Nov. 21, 1846.	
John H. Blessing,	"	Dec. 27, "	
John Brown,	"	Jan. 6, 1847.	
Peter A. Brown,	"	" 11, "	
Wm. J. Brown,	"	" 6, "	
Geo. W. Blakney,	"	Nov. 21, 1846.	
Jacob Crowl,	"	Dec. 19, "	
Wm. C. Cain,	"	Jan. 1, 1847.	
John Q. Creamer,	"	Nov. 21, 1846.	
Wm. D. Done,	"	Jan. 6, 1847.	
Andrew Duffey,	"	Nov. 30, 1846.	
Carlisle Dobb,	"	Jan. 6, 1847.	
Wm. W. Dunn,	"	" 21, "	
James Evans,	"	Dec. 9, 1846.	
Charles Erwin,	"	Jan. 6, 1847.	
Henry S. Free,	"	" 21, "	
Aaron K. Gordon,	"	Nov. 21, 1846.	
Robert Gainor,	"	" 30, "	
Lewis H. Grove,	"	Dec. 26, "	
Andrew M. Griffin,	"	Jan. 4, 1847.	
John S. Gallaher,	"	" 4, "	
Arthur Hagan,	"	" 6, "	
Jacob H. Heilfeinstein,	"	Nov. 24, 1846.	
Josiah Heller,	"	Dec. 16, "	
David Heck,	"	" 19, "	
George Hodges,	"	Jan. 6, "	
John W. Hood,	"	Dec. 1, "	
John H. Hunter,	"	" 26, "	
James D. Harwood,	"	" 16, "	
William Hooven,	"	Jan. 6, 1847.	
Francis W. M. Hooser,	"	" 21, "	
John Jones,	"	" 6, "	

NAMES.	RANK.	WHEN ENROLLED.	REMARKS.
Joseph Johnston, - -	Private,	Jan. 6, 1847.	
Otho Kisinger, - -	"	Dec. 17, 1846.	
Charles H. Klein, - -	"	Jan. 6, 1847.	
William Kinley, - -	"	" 6, "	
Charles Loftin, - -	"	" 6, "	
James Lewis, - -	"	Nov. 22, 1846.	
Wm. McCommack, - -	"	Jan. 6, 1847.	
Robert Mansford, - -	"	Dec. 28, 1846.	
John M. Miller, - -	"	" 15, "	
Thompson Mason, - -	"	" 21, "	
Joseph McMinn, - -	"	" 15, "	
Richard G. Moore, - -	"	Jan. 6, 1847.	
John Mimey, - -	"	" 6, "	
Bernard D. Magee, - -	"	" 6, "	
Patrick Meguire, - -	"	" 6. "	
Alex. C. McCorkle, - -	"	" 21, "	
William Nopie, - -	"	" 6. "	
John H. Ott, - -	"	Nov. 21, 1846.	
Socrates Prather, - -	"	Dec. 4, "	
John Peare, - -	"	" 14, "	
James Pentony, - -	"	" 14, "	
James Peace, - -	"	" 12, "	
Jacob Rinor, - -	"	" 23, "	
George T. Robbins, -	"	Jan. 6, 1847.	
Jeremiah R. Reese, - -	"	Nov. 27, 1846.	
John T. Reamy, -	"	Jan. 1, 1847.	
Wm. L. Shoemaker, -	"	" 6, "	
John P. Stewart, - -	"	Nov. 23, 1846.	
Jacob Shank, - -	"	" 27, "	
Wm. Seigler, - -	"	Dec. 27, "	
Richard H. Stephens, -	"	" 29, "	
William Sorber, - -	"	Jan. 6, 1847.	
John C. Vauhorn, - -	"	" 6, "	
Abram G. Vanmetre, -	"	Nov. 26, 1846.	
Paskil Vaden, - -	"	Jan. 13, 1847.	
John Vanlier. - -	"	" 6, "	
George L. Weast, - -	"	Dec. 18, 1846.	
Henry Wilhelm, - -	"	" 26, "	
John R. Williams, - -	"	Jan. 6, 1847.	
Richard Winter, - -	"	" 6. "	
Charles Whiteman, - -	"	" 6, "	

MUSTER ROLL

Of Captain Fletcher H. Archer's Company, in the First Regiment of Virginia Volunteers, commanded by Colonel John F. Hamtramck, called into the Service of the United States by the Secretary of War, under the Act of Congress approved May 13th, 1846, from the 15th day of December 1846, (date of this Muster,) for during the War with Mexico, unless sooner discharged.

NAMES.	RANK.	WHEN ENROLLED.	DISTANCE TO PLACE OF RENDEZVOUS.
Fletcher H. Archer,	Captain,	Nov. 28, 1846,	22 miles.
Franklin Pegram,	Lieutenant,	" 30, "	22 "
David A. Weisiger,	2d "	" " "	22 "
Peter A. Peterson,	2d "	" 26, "	22 "
Peyton Pollard,	1 Sergeant,	" 28, "	22 "
Thomas Scott,	Sergeant,	" 30, "	22 "
Samuel G. Wilson,	"	" " "	22 "
Richard A. Bailey,	"	" " "	22 "
Andrew Jackson,	Corporal,	" 27, "	22 "
Charles B. Drinkard,	"	Dec. 1, "	22 "
James S. Foley, jr.	"	Nov. 30, "	22 "
Harrison C. Cock,	"	" " "	22 "
George W. Williams,	Drummer,	Dec. 5, "	22 "
Edward Watkins,	Fifer,	" 10, "	35 "
James H. Atkins,	Private,	Nov. 30, "	22 "
William E. Alley,	"	" 28, "	22 "
James H. Barnes,	"	Dec. 1, "	22 "
Alexander E. Brichett,	"	Nov. 28, "	22 "
George S. Bain,	"	" 30, "	22 "
James T. Ballow,	"	Dec. 1. "	22 "
Joseph P. Brevitt,	"	" " "	22 "
James C. N. Brown,	"	" 4, "	28 "
Jesse C. Choate,	"	Nov. 26, "	22 "
Joseph L. Carter,	"	Dec. 5, "	22 "
Nathaniel E. Cargill,	"	Nov. 30, "	52 "
Nathaniel D. Cain,	"	Dec. 8, "	47 "
Solomon B. Doudge,	"	Nov. 20, "	141 "
James A. Dunn,	"	" 30, "	22 "
James M. Donnan,	"	" 28, "	22 "
Robert N. Eagle,	"	Dec. 2, "	22 "
James C. Eanes,	"	" 4, "	22 "
Edward W. Fitzgerald,	"	Nov. 30, "	22 "
Thomas A. Farley,	"	" 29, "	22 "
Richard Fust,	"	" 30, "	22 "
Robert F. Fewqua,	"	" " "	22 "
Joseph Galloway,	"	" " "	22 "
Arthur M. Goodwin,	"	Dec. 1, "	31 "
Thos. B. Greenhow,	"	Nov. 30, "	22 "
Isaac T. Graham,	"	Dec. 4, "	22 "
Archibald B. Goodwin,	"	Nov. 28, "	37 "
Hezekiah Hughes,	"	Dec. 3, "	22 "
Francis Hoy,	"	" 2, "	22 "
John F. Henderson,	"	Nov. 30, "	22 "
Joseph N. Harrison,	"	Dec. 2, "	22 "
Hamlin E. Harris,	"	" 1, "	22 "
William H. J'Anson,	"	Nov. 30, "	22 "

NAMES.	RANK.	WHEN ENROLLED.	DISTANCE TO PLACE OF RENDEZVOUS.
William N. B. Judkins,	Private,	Dec. 1, 1846,	22 miles.
Samuel T. Knox,	"	" 4, "	22 "
William T. Lightfoot,	"	" 1, "	22 "
John H. Lahmeyer,	"	" 1, "	22 "
Charles F. Loomis,	"	" 8, "	22 "
Samuel Landes,	"	Nov. 28, "	22 "
George B. Lipscomb,	"	" 28, "	22 "
Napoleon B. Long,	"	Dec. 1, "	22 "
James Lunsford,	"	" 1, "	22 "
James Martin, jr.	"	" 4, "	22 "
William H. Moore,	"	" 1, "	22 "
Fleming C. McGee,	"	" 1, "	47 "
George B. P. Marye,	"	Nov. 30, "	22 "
Joseph McIntosh,	"	Dec. 1, "	22 "
Thomas J. McCaleb,	"	" 3, "	22 "
William T. Peterson,	"	Nov. 26, "	22 "
Edward T. Price,	"	" 26, "	22 "
Edward G. Partin,	"	Dec. 1, "	22 "
William L. Pritchett,	"	" 1, "	22 "
Samuel H. Prichard,	"	" 2, "	22 "
George B. Parr,	"	" 5, "	55 "
Benjamin Ricaud,	"	" 2, "	22 "
James A. Robinson,	"	" 1, "	22 "
James B. Robertson,	"	Nov. 28, "	22 "
Samuel Smith,	"	" 29, "	22 "
James Smith,	"	" 30, "	22 "
David F. Shields,	"	Dec. 5, "	22 "
Robert Simpson,	"	Nov. 30, "	22 "
Edward J. Spotswood,	"	" 30, "	22 "
Richard Seymore,	"	" 28, "	22 "
John E. Tenaa,	"	" 26, "	22 "
Richard B. Traylor,	"	Dec. 1, "	22 "
John W. Thompson,	"	" 1, "	22 "
William A. C. Vernon,	"	" 3, "	22 "
Mordica Vaiden,	"	" 3, "	22 "
Joseph L. White,	"	" 1, "	22 "
Richard H. Westmore,	"	" 3, "	22 "
Joseph Wilkinson,	"	" 1, "	22 "
William J. Wello,	"	Nov. 30, "	22 "
Edward Williams,	"	Dec. 8, "	60 "

[Company organized 11th January 1847—mustered into Service 25th February 1847.]

MUSTER ROLL

Of Captain Wm. B. Archer's Company, in the First Regiment of Virginia Volunteers commanded by Colonel John F. Hamtramck, called into the Service of the United States by the Secretary of War, under the Act of Congress approved May 13, 1846, from the 25th day of February 1847, (date of this Muster,) during the War with Mexico, unless sooner discharged.

NAMES.	RANK.	WHEN ENROLLED.	DISTANCE TO PLACE OF RENDEZVOUS.
Wm. B. Archer, - -	Captain,	Nov. 15, 1846.	
Lindsay M. Shumaker, -	1st Lieutenant,	Jan. 10, 1847,	185 miles.
Robert R. Keeling, - -	2d "	Nov. 15, 1846.	
Wm. A. Allen, - -	2d "	" 15, "	
Joseph E. Sandige, - -	1st Sergeant,	Feb. 25, 1847.	
Wm. L. Taylor, - -	Sergeant,	" 5, "	
James L. Clark, -	"	" 5, "	
Jacey P. Hodgden, - -	"	" 22, "	
Ellerson Russell, - -	Corporal,	" 5, "	
John G. Binford, - -	"	Dec. 1, 1846,	45 "
James S. Kellam, - -	"	" 1, "	200 "
John H. Willis, - -	Drummer,	Jan. 2, 1847.	
Bartlett P. Adams, - -	Private,	" 10, "	
Edward H. Acree, - -	"	" 15, "	
James Alexander, - -	"	Feb. 22, "	
Augustus L. Austin, -	"	Jan. 10, "	160 "
Jackson Baker, - -	"	Feb. 23, "	
Richard B. H. Bailey, -	"	Jan. 10, "	160 "
Anderson N. Barnett, -	"	" 10, "	200 "
Merrett W. Bootright, -	"	Feb. 15, "	40 "
Robert Bowles, - -	"	Jan. 10, "	160 "
William A. Burks, - -	"	" 10, "	160 "
Sydney S. Cantor, - -	"	" 25, "	160 "
John A. Clark, - -	"	Feb. 23, "	
Robert Clark, - -	"	Nov. 20, "	
Samuel Crawford, - -	"	Jan. 10, "	160 "
Henry Custer, - -	"	" 10, "	160 "
Henry Dixon, - -	"	Feb. 5, "	130 "
Jos. E. Ellett, - -	"	Jan. 10, "	160 "
Obadiah Ellis, - -	"	" 1, "	
John G. Evans, - -	"	" 20, "	45 "
William T. Francis, -	"	Feb. 5, "	
Wm. B. Garrison, - -	"	Jan. 1, "	200 "
Samuel Gennet, - -	"	" 15, "	
Wm. Gough, - -	"	" 10, "	146 "
Henry L. Goulden, - -	"	" 10, "	160 "
Henry S. Green, - -	"	" 1, "	140 "
Henry Hammons, - -	"	" 25, "	200 "
Musty Hannah, - -	"	Feb. 1, "	
Franklin G. Hayden, -	"	Jan. 10, "	147 "
James Harland, - -	"	" 30, "	
Burton Henderson, - -	"	Dec. 1, 1846,	200 "
Thomas D. Henderson, -	"	Feb. 1, 1847,	200 "
Joseph M. Hobson, - -	"	Jan. 25, "	

NAMES.	RANK.	WHEN ENROLLED.	DISTANCE TO PLACE OF RENDEZVOUS.
Nicholas R. Horne, - -	Private,	Jan. 1, 1847.	
Thomas A. Holland, -	"	Feb. 19, "	145 miles.
James Howle, - -	"	" 9, "	20 "
Rhoten Hurst, - -	"	Jan. 10, "	160 "
James Jennings, - -	"	Feb. 5, "	120 "
Charles R. Jones, - -	"	Jan. 10, "	160 "
Richard Jones, - -	"	" 10, "	160 "
James Kennon, - -	"	Feb. 5, "	
William Kidd, - -	"	" 5, "	
Valentine Logwood, -	"	Jan. 10, "	160 "
Andrew J. Marshall, -	"	" 1, "	30 "
Chas. H. Marshall, -	"	Feb. 4, "	40 "
Wm. A. Martin, - -	"	Jan. 10, "	160 "
Wm. J. Mills, - -	"	Feb. 4, "	250 "
James Neighbours, -	"	Jan. 10, "	160 "
Moses G. Noble, - -	"	" 10, "	160 "
John Richardson, - -	"	" 20, "	146 "
Chas. G. Salmon, - -	"	Dec. 1, 1846,	45 "
Jesse L. Snead, - -	"	Jan. 1, 1847.	
John S. Spencer, - -	"	" 10, "	160 "
Henderson Stanfield, -	"	" 10, "	160 "
Augustus Stone, - -	"	Dec. 10, 1846,	80 "
Wm. B. Sweeney, - -	"	Jan. 10, 1847,	160 "
Miles Talley, - -	"	" 30, "	
George Taylor, - -	"	" 25, "	
Benjamin J. Walker, -	"	" 10, "	160 "
Robert Wallace, - -	"	Feb. 6, "	
John Watson, - -	"	" 7, "	250 "
James L. Weisiger, -	"	Nov. 16, "	
Joseph J. Woodrah, -	"	Jan. 10, "	160 "
Wm. C. Wyatt, - -	"	Dec. 1, "	200 "

MUSTER ROLL

Of Captain Smith P. Bankhead's Company, in the First Regiment of Virginia Volunteers, commanded by Colonel John F. Hamtramck, called into the Service of the United States by the Secretary of War, under the Act of Congress approved May 13, 1846, from the thirty-first day of December 1846, (date of this Muster,) for the term of during the War with Mexico, unless sooner discharged.

NAMES.	RANK.	WHEN ENROLLED.	DISTANCE TO PLACE OF RENDEZVOUS.
Smith P. Bankhead, - -	Captain,	Dec. 1, 1846,	40 miles.
Thomas S. Garnett, - -	1st Lieutenant,	" 18, "	40 "
Robert F. Coleman, - -	2d "	" 1, "	60 "
Washington L. Mahan,	2d "	" 29, "	40 "
William W. Wallace, -	1st Sergeant,	" 29, "	40 "
Thomas S. Mason, - -	Sergeant,	" 29, "	40 "
Thomas B. Coghill, - -	"	" 13, "	50 "
Geo. F. Barrell,	"	" 30, "	40 "
Jonathan Good, - -	Corporal,	" 29, "	40 "
Isaac Keiter, - -	"	" 30, "	40 "
Henry Maygar, - -	"	" 29, "	40 "
Francis H. Clair, -	"	" 30, "	40 "
Frederick Waugh, - -	Drummer,	" 30, "	40 "
Wm. Jennings, -	Fifer,	" 18, "	60 "
John W. Andrews, -	Private,	" 30, "	40 "
Harvie Albertson, - -	"	" 30, "	40 "
James Bullard, - -	"	" 18, "	60 "
Lawrence Battaile, -	"	" 13, "	45 "
John S. Burruss. - -	"	" 13, "	60 "
Theodore Blendel, - -	"	" 8, "	40 "
Michael Bradley, - -	"	" 29, "	40 "
Thomas C. Black, - -	"	" 29, "	40 "
Wm. S. Briggs, -	"	" 12, "	64 "
Joseph Brown, - -	"	" 29, "	40 "
Charles B. Brown, - -	"	" 1, "	40 "
John W. Carter, - -	"	" 18, "	70 "
Albert G. Collins, - -	"	" 18, "	60 "
John Calhoun, - -	"	" 18, "	60 "
Jasper S. Clayton, -	"	" 18, "	40 "
Bery Cain, - -	"	" 29, "	40 "
Robert Chase, - -	"	" 29, "	40 "
Franklin Carroll, - -	"	" 18, "	60 "
Lewis Campbell, - -	"	" 30, "	40 "
Andrew Carmichael, -	"	" 29, "	40 "
Thomas Davis, - -	"	" 1, "	40 "
Richard Field, - -	"	" 30, "	40 "
William Finnall, - -	"	" 10, "	60 "
Lafayette Franklin, -	"	" 10, "	60 "
Jacob H. Fagunders, -	"	" 30, "	40 "
Thomas M. Graham, -	"	" 13, "	40 "
Joseph Haywood, - -	"	" 18, "	60 "
Benjamin Hood, - -	"	" 30, "	40 "
John L. Hart, - -	"	" 20, "	55 "
John Heays, - -	"	" 18, "	75 "
Theodore Hesser, - -	"	" 29, "	40 "
Joseph Hillard, - -	"	" 18, "	60 "

NAMES.	RANK.	WHEN ENROLLED.	DISTANCE TO PLACE OF RENDEZVOUS.
Thomas H. Hurston, - -	Private,	Dec. 30, 1846,	40 miles.
George Hall, - -	"	" 30, "	40 "
George Jones, - -	"	" 30, "	40 "
Nathaniel Jackson, - -	"	" 30, "	40 "
Elhanan Johns, - -	"	" 30, "	40 "
Charles Lewis, - -	"	" 27, "	40 "
Joseph Lewis, - -	"	" 29, "	40 "
John Leckie, - -	"	" 30' "	40 "
John Landrum, - -	"	" 25, "	60 "
Moses A. Little, - -	"	" 18, "	60 "
Lewis Lawson, - -	"	" 15, "	40 "
Thomas T. Mahan, - -	"	" 30, "	40 "
Peter McPhelin, - -	"	" 13, ..	60 "
Edwin P. Merritt, - -	"	" 10, "	40 "
John Milholland, - -	"	" 29, "	40 "
Levi McGathey, - -	"	" 29, "	40 "
Samuel McFarland, - -	"	" 30, "	40 "
David W. Morgan, - -	"	" 30, "	40 "
William Otter, - -	"	" 30, "	40 "
Joseph F. Piper, - -	"	" 24, "	60 "
John Roach, - -	"	" 30, "	40 "
Alexander Riddle, - -	"	" 30, "	40 "
John Shelton, - -	"	" 22, "	65 "
James F. Simmons, - -	"	" 30, "	40 "
Harrison Sarrell, - -	"	" 25, "	40 "
William Sampson, - -	"	" 31, "	60 "
Francis L. Turner, - -	"	" 30, "	40 "
John R. Taliaferro, - -	"	" 24, "	65 "
John Taylor, - -	"	" 29, "	40 "
Thomas Taylor, - -	"	" 29, "	40 "
Robert Wallace, - -	'.	" 29, "	40 "
James E. White, - -	"	" 30, "	40 "
Geo. W. Widdifield, - -	"	" 29, "	40 "

[Company organized 27th November 1846.]

MUSTER ROLL

Of Captain Edward C. Carrington, jr.'s Company, in the First Regiment of Virginia Volunteers, commanded by Colonel John F. Hamtramck, called into the Service of the United States by the Secretary of War, under the Act of Congress approved May 13, 1846, from the 16th day of December 1846, (date of this Muster,) during the War with Mexico, unless sooner discharged.

NAMES.	RANK.	WHEN ENROLLED.	DISTANCE TO PLACE OF RENDEZVOUS.
Edward C. Carrington, jr. -	Captain,	Nov. 18, 1846.	
George A. Porterfield, -	1st Lieutenant,	" 18, "	180 miles.
Carlton R. Munford, -	2d "	" 18, "	
Henry W. Williamson, -	2d "	" 24, "	140 "
Abram N. Womack, -	1st Sergeant,	Dec. 10, "	75 "
Lafayette W. Gray, -	Sergeant,	Nov. 28, "	146 "
John Kurt. -	"	" 28, "	
Wm. W. Murphy, -	"	" 18, "	
Van R. Otz. -	Corporal,	Dec. 1, "	146 "
Sam'l S. Pleasants, -	"	" 5, "	
Andrew J. Didlake. -	"	Nov. 28, "	146 "
Benjamin T. Wharton, -	"	" 18, "	
Henry Starke, -	Drummer,	" 28, "	
Benj. Montgomery. -	Fifer,	Dec. 16, "	
Geo. W. Alexander, -	Private,	Nov. 18, "	
Richard Armstrong, -	"	Dec. 2, "	36 "
Edward Aken, -	"	" 7, "	25 "
William Barker, -	"	Nov. 18, "	
Philip A. Bradley, -	"	" 23, "	
Robert Barry, -	"	" 25, "	
Lewis J. Beadles, -	"	" 28, "	
Albert A. Banks, -	"	" 28, "	146 "
Richard C. Burnett, -	"	" 28, "	
John G. Brown, -	"	" 28, "	
Farmer Converse, -	"	Dec. 5, "	
Zacariah Carter, -	"	Nov. 18, "	
John H. Coleman, -	"	Dec. 2, "	
John A. Driscoll, -	"	Nov. 18, "	
Archibal W. Diddep, -	"	" 18, "	
Thomas H. Dunn, -	"	" 28, "	146 "
Joseph Ellis, -	"	" 25, "	22 "
John English, -	"	Dec. 1, "	
Lafayette H. Fitzhugh, -	"	" 7, "	80 "
John H. Fitzhugh, -	"	" 7, "	80 "
Martin D. Fielder, -	"	Nov. 28, "	
William Grant, -	"	Dec. 15, "	
John R. Graves, -	"	Nov. 18, "	
Benj. A. Grimes, -	"	" 28, "	
Geo. N. Giles, -	"	" 25, "	
Thomas Goosley, -	"	" 28, "	
Henry Goodwin, -	"	Dec. 3, "	20 "
Geo. W. Hubbard, -	"	Nov. 28, "	
Wm. Hudnall, -	"	Dec. 1, "	
Joseph Haskins, -	"	Nov. 28, "	15 "

NAMES.	RANK.	WHEN ENROLLED.	DISTANCE TO PLACE OF RENDEZVOUS.
Wm. A. Haskins, - -	Private,	Nov. 28, "	15 miles.
Thomas F. King, ' - -	"	Dec. 11, "	
Henry Kolp, - -	"	" 3, "	
Wm. E. Kidd, - -	"	" 5, "	
John R. Lewellen, - -	"	Nov. 18, "	
Joseph N. Lynch, - -	"	" 18, "	
John Lennox, - -	"	" 18, "	
William Langford, - -	"	Dec. 14, "	
John Moore, - -	"	Nov. 18, "	
Arthur McNutty, - -	"	" 28, "	
William T. McAllister, -	"	" 28, "	
Philip B. Minor, - -	"	Dec. 8, "	
Chas. H. Montgomery, -	"	" 14, "	
John M. Nees, - -	"	Nov. 26, "	
Charles G. Newhall, - -	"	Dec. 14, "	55 "
Felix O'Neil, - -	"	" 14, "	
Williamson Price, - -	"	Nov. 28, "	
Romulus T. Pullen, - -	"	" 18, "	
Robert H. Philips, - -	"	" 18, "	
Edward Powell, - -	"	" 26, "	
John Poor, - -	"	" 28, "	
Robert Powell, - -	"	Dec. 8, "	
Wm. Rilen, - -	"	" 1, "	
John H. Shell, - -	"	Nov. 28, "	
Wesley C. Simmons, -	"	Dec. 8, "	
Richard Starke, - -	"	Nov. 29, "	
Stephen Schwitzer, - -	"	" 28, "	150 "
Joseph P. Scott, - -	"	" 28, "	
Samuel M. Snead, - -	"	" 28, "	146 "
Thomas Winfree, - -	"	" 18, "	
John W. Williams, - -	"	" 18, "	
John Wade, - -	"	" 28, "	
Thomas B. Waller, - -	"	" 30, "	10 "
Nicholas Ward, - -	"	Dec. 16, "	146 "
Hiram Woodroof, - -	"	" 16, "	146 "

MUSTER ROLL

Of Captain Montgomery D. Corse's Company, in the First Regiment of Virginia Volunteers, commanded by Colonel John F. Hamtramck, called into the Service of the United States by the Secretary of War, under the Act of Congress approved May 13, 1846, from the 13th day of December 1846, (date of this Muster,) for the term of during the War with Mexico, unless sooner discharged.

NAMES.	RANK.	WHEN ENROLLED.	DISTANCE TO PLACE OF RENDEZVOUS.
Montgomery D. Corse, - -	Captain,	Nov. 20, 1846,	114 miles.
Turner W. Ashby, - -	1st Lieutenant,	" 20, "	114 "
Benj. G. Waters. - -	2d "	" 20, "	114 "
James S. Douglass, - -	2d "	" 20, "	114 "
John H. Hisden, - -	1st Sergeant,	" 20, "	111 "
William G. Minor, - -	Sergeant,	" 30, "	114 "
John T. Gong, - -	"	" 30, "	114 "
Wm. Jenkins, - -	"	" 30, "	114 "
Charles F. Force, - -	Corporal,	" 30, "	114 "
Silas Moore. - -	"	" 30, "	114 "
Benedict J. Fenwick. - -	"	" 30, "	114 "
Washington Marman, - -	"	" 27, "	114 "
Wm. Doyle, - -	Drummer,	Dec. 12, "	114 "
John J. Jones, - -	Fifer,	" 21, "	
Gurden C. Ashton, - -	Private,	" 12, "	114 "
John Acton, - -	"	Nov. 20, "	114 "
John W. Baugs, - -	"	" 20, "	114 "
Charles A. Baker, - -	"	Dec. 10, "	114 "
John C. Belt, - -	"	" 26, "	140 "
John Brooks, - -	"	Nov. 30, "	114 "
John Brown, - -	"	Dec. 12, "	114 "
Wm. P. Bloxham, - -	"	" 5, "	114 "
McHenry Bramblett, - -	"	" 19, "	180 "
James W. Brown, - -	"	" 21, "	114 "
Thompson M. Chichester, - -	"	" 1, "	114 "
Henry Caddis, - -	"	Nov. 20, "	114 "
John E. Carter, - -	"	Dec. 22, "	20 "
Noah Carmey, - -	"	" 5, "	114 "
Hampton Carr, - -	"	" 6, "	130 "
Chas. H. Cawwood, - -	"	" 12, "	114 "
Thomas L. Coppedge, - -	"	" 19, "	146 "
James Compton, - -	"	" 10, "	114 "
Fayette D. Carpenter, - -	"	" 26, "	114 "
John S. Delany, - -	"	" 12, "	114 "
Benjamin Dossey, - -	"	" 19, "	114 "
Robert Ferguson, - -	"	Nov. 20, "	114 "
Amos T. Fisher, - -	"	Dec. 5, "	114 "
Joseph S. Farrow, - -	"	" 6, "	114 "
Joseph W. Ford, - -	"	" 12, "	114 "
John Felts, - -	"	" 27, "	115 "
James H. Fowler, - -	"	" 14, "	
Thomas Fegan, - -	"	" 21, "	
Isaiah Fisher, - -	"	" 22, "	114 "
John F. Goodrich, - -	"	" 5, "	114 "
Jesse C. Green, - -	"	" 3, "	114 "

NAMES.	RANK.	WHEN ENROLLED.	DISTANCE TO PLACE OF RENDEZVOUS.
Henry Gordon, - -	Private,	Dec. 19, 1846,	114 miles.
Jacob Howard, - -	"	" 10, "	114 "
William Hall, -	"	" 1, "	114 "
Zachariah P. Hunter, -	"	" 1, "	114 "
John H. Heninger, - -	"	" 5, "	114 "
Frederick Hoffmaer, -	"	" 22, "	
Richard Jones, - -	"	" 1, "	114 "
—— Keilhotts, - -	"	" 19, "	114 "
John Lotts, - - -	"	" 1, "	114 "
Wm. Maxwell, -	"	" 13, "	114 "
Robert Mullen, -	"	" 5, "	114 "
Charles Mullen, - -	"	" 5, "	114 "
Albert G. Minor, -	"	Nov. 20, "	114 "
Michael Morlick, -	"	Dec. 1, "	114 "
George A. Moody, -	"	" 1, "	114 "
Robert Mitchell, -	"	" 19, "	114 "
Peter Morton, -	"	" 13, "	114 "
Daniel Murphy, -	"	" 18, "	114 "
Robert Mathews, -	"	" 18, "	114 "
Dougald McPhail, -	"	" 18, "	140 "
Wm. H. Nugle, -	"	" 13, "	114 "
Wm. W. Owens, -	"	" 1, "	114 "
Albert W. Orison, -	"	" 16, "	114 "
John F. Preston, -	"	Nov. 20, "	114 "
Michael Reinheut, -	"	Dec. 1, "	114 "
Daniel Ressinger, -	"	" 18, "	114 "
Thomas Self, -	"	" 1, "	114 "
Andrew Sullivan, -	"	Nov. 20, "	114 "
G. R. Snyder, -	"	" 20, "	114 "
Benjamin Swan, -	"	" 20, "	114 "
James E. Stephenson, -	"	Dec. 14, "	114 "
Elias Shaw, - -	"	" 14, "	114 "
John Tridle, - -	"	" 1, "	114 "
William Thompson, -	"	" 10, "	114 "
James R. Vanzant, -	"	" 10, "	114 "
Philip White, -	"	Nov. 20, "	114 "
John Weeks. -	"	Dec. 22, "	
Covington West, -	"	" 13, "	114 "

MUSTER ROLL

Of Kenton Harper's Company of Volunteers, commanded by Colonel John F. Ham-
tramck, called into the Service of the United States by the Secretary of War,
under the Act of Congress approved May 13th, 1846, from the 6th January 1847,
(date of original Muster,) for the term of during the War with Mexico, unless
sooner discharged.

NAMES.	RANK.	WHEN ENROLLED.	REMARKS.
Kenton Harper, - -	Captain,	Dec. 7, 1846,	
Robert Henry Kinney, -	1st Lieutenant,	Nov. 27, "	
Vincent Epley Geiger, -	2d "	" 27, "	
Wm. Henry Harmon, -	2d "	" 27, "	
George W. Allen, - -	1st Sergeant,	Dec. 7, "	
Charles H. Ball, -	Sergeant,	Nov. 27, "	
William Dunlap, - -	"	Dec. 7, "	
Wm. Blackburn, - -	"	" 7, "	
Wm. O. Bickle, - -	Corporal,	" 7, "	
Lewis H. Clarke, - -	"	" 19, "	
Lewis C. Lavall, - -	"	" 27, "	
Benj. F. Imboden, -	"	" 7, "	
Archibald A. Gordon, -	Drummer,	" 27, "	
Morgan Hasson, - -	Fifer,	" 24, "	
George Alexander, -	Private,	" 12, "	
Jos. M. Bishop, jr. - -	"	Jan. 5, 1847,	
John Bowles, - -	"	Nov. 27, 1846,	
James B. Brown, - -	"	" 27, "	
George W. Britt, - -	"	" 27, "	
Preston Brown, - -	"	Dec. 28, "	
Abel D. Chase, - -	"	Nov. 27, "	
Wm. Carroll, - -	"	Dec. 7, "	
Richard Cole, - -	"	" 12, "	
Andrew Crist, - -	"	Nov. 30. "	
John Dubecq, - -	"	Dec. 7, "	
James W. Eyrse, - -	"	" 7, "	
Wm. G. Eyrse, - -	"	" 7, "	
John Emerson, - -	"	" 7, "	
Addison Fisher, - -	"	Nov. 27, "	
Wm. Ferguson, - -	"	Dec. 19, "	
Alexander Grove, -	"	Nov. 27, "	
John B. Grove, - -	"	Jan. 6, 1847,	
Valentine Gladwell, -	"	Dec. 7, 1846,	
Augustus A. Gregory, -	"	" 5, "	
James S. Graham, -	"	" 7, "	
Wm. Goens, - -	"	" 3, "	
James Goens, - -	"	" 3, "	
Samuel Helms, - -	"	" 7, "	
George Harlan, - -	"	" 7, "	
Arington Hoffman, -	"	" 7, "	
Grey H. Halvey, - -	"	" 10, "	
Wm. H. Hull, - -	"	" 15, "	
Samuel Johnson, - -	"	" 7, "	
Richard Johnson, - -	"	" 7, "	
Isaac W. Johnson, -	"	" 7, "	
Jacob Illick, - -	"	" 5, "	

NAMES.	RANK.	WHEN ENROLLED.	REMARKS.
Isaac Kurts, - -	Private,	Dec. 7, 1846,	
John Knowles, - -	"	" 15, "	
Jacob Long, - -	"	" 7, "	
Henry Lambert, - -	"	" 7, "	
John J. Logan, - -	"	" 7, "	
William Long, - -	"	" 22, "	
Christian G. Merritt, -	"	Nov. 27, "	
William Miller, - -	"	Dec. 7, "	
Alexander C. Milon, -	"	" 7, "	
Hugh D. Noon, - -	"	" 20, "	
John Peer, - - -	"	Nov. 27, "	
John S. Parent, - -	"	" 27, "	
James Powers, - -	"	Dec. 7, "	
Alpheus W. Poage, -	"	Nov. 27, "	
Israel Peck, - -	"	Dec. 26, "	
James T. Petter, -	"	Jan. 6, 1847,	
Wm. C. Robertson, -	"	Dec. 7, 1846,	
Wm. E. Skeen, - -	"	" 7, "	
Andrew J. Shackelford, -	"	" 7, "	
Miles Simes, - -	"	Jan. 6, 1847,	
Robert L. Smead, -	"	Dec. 7, 1846,	
Samuel Searl, - -	"	Jan. 6, 1847,	
Daniel A. Stofer, -	"	Nov. 30, 1846,	
Jonathan Smith, - -	"	Dec. 22, "	
Wm. M. Sly, - -	"	" 22, "	Deserted at Richmond,
John H. Steel, - -	"	Nov. 27, "	Jan. 1, 1847.
Wm. G. Taylor, - -	"	Dec. 10, "	
Abram Tar, - -	"	" 7, "	
Lewis K. Terrell, -	"	" 20, "	
Greenbury B. Terrell, -	"	Jan. 6, 1847,	
Samuel W. Wilson, - -	"	Dec. 7, 1846,	
Cyrus C. White, - -	"	" 7, "	
Samuel P. Wade, - -	"	" 22, "	

MUSTER ROLL

Of Captain Wm. Murray Robinson's Company, in the First Regiment of Virginia Volunteers, commanded by Colonel John F. Hamtramck, organized in Petersburg 5th January 1847, and mustered into the Service of the United States 15th January 1847 at Richmond, Va.

NAMES.	RANK.	WHEN ENROLLED.	REMARKS.
Wm. Murray Robinson,	Captain,	Dec. 10, 1846,	
James L. Bryan,	1st Lieutenant,	" 22, "	
Aurelius R. Shands,	2d "	" 26, "	
Wm. G. McGowan,	2d "	" 24, "	
Benj'n W. Collier,	1st Sergeant,	Jan. 4, 1847,	
Benj'n F. Wingfield,	Sergeant,	Dec. 10, 1846,	
Jas. B. Baldwin,	"	" 11, "	
Jas. W. Rivers,	"	" 22, "	
Nathaniel Pebworth,	Corporal,	" 19, "	
Wm. F. Rives,	"	" 31, "	
Harman T. Burns,	"	" 29, "	
Jno. W. Fisher,	"	Jan. 4, 1847,	
Jos. D. Procise,	Drummer,	Dec. 26, 1846,	
Drury B. Stith,	Fifer,	Jan. 5, 1847,	
Edwin C. Archer,	Private,	" 14, "	
Jos. C. Adams,	"	" 4, "	
St. Lawrence Adams,	"	Dec. 20, 1846,	
Isaac A. Anderton,	"	Jan. 4, 1847,	
H. Bentley,	"	" 22, "	
Wm. H. Britt,	"	Dec. 29, 1846,	
Wm'son S. Clanton,	"	" 21, "	
Jos. D. Cheatzom,	"	" 21, "	
Francis D. Clements,	"	" 28, "	
Fitzwm. J. Comann,	"	Jan. 5, 1847,	
Wm. S. Crocket,	"	" 25, "	
Jas. B. Crowder,	"	" 5, "	
Jas H. Davis,	"	" 4, "	
George Duncan,	"	" 8, "	
Jas. Franklin,	"	Dec. 23, 1846,	
Lewis H. Foster,	"	Jan. 12, 1847,	
Jas. F. Gibbs,	"	" 17, "	
Benj. H. Gray,	"	Dec. 31, 1846,	
Robert A. Goodwin,	"	Jan. 5, 1847,	
Wesley B. Garrett,	"	" 6, "	
William Heath,	"	" 17, "	
Alexander Henderson,	"	Dec. 23, 1846,	
Rodolphus Hammond,	"	Jan. 22, 1847,	
George W. Harrison,	"	" 3, "	
Richard Hamlin,	"	" 8, "	
Jno. R. Hobgood,	"	" 28, "	
Edw'd Hobgood,	"	" 5, "	
Cornelius Holloway,	"	" 12, "	
Wm. T. Howle,	"	" 29, "	
Jno. W. Hudgins,	"	" 6, "	
Alexander Jordan,	"	Dec. 30, 1846,	
Wm. H. James,	"	Jan. 4, 1847,	
Jas. H. Johnstone,	"	" 6, "	

NAMES.	RANK.	WHEN ENROLLED.	REMARKS.
John T. Lanier, - -	Private,	Dec. 22, 1846,	
Mendoza Maynard, - -	"	" 11, "	
Dennis McCarthy, - -	"	" 11, "	
Daniel McCollum, - -	"	Jan. 8, 1847,	
James M. Moore, - -	"	" 4, "	
Jno. Moyler, - -	"	" 5, "	
Jno. J. Moss, - -	"	" 6, "	
Wm. D. Martin, - -	"	" 6, "	
J. W. Murdaugh, - -	"	" 9, "	
Benj. C. Newell, - -	"	Dec. 21, 1846,	
David W. Nicholson, -	"	Jan. 6, 1847,	
Landon Noel, - -	"	" 3, "	
Wm. T. Payne, - -	"	Dec. 28, 1846,	
Edw'd F. Payne, - -	"	" 29, "	
Robert F. Payne, - -	"	" 30, "	
Geo. W. Perkinson, -	"	Jan. 11, 1847,	
J. W. Poynts, - -	"	" 3, "	
Robt. H. Phipps, - -	"	Dec. 30, 1846,	
Thos. Paocise, - -	"	Jan. 3, 1847,	
Alfred Rittenburg, - -	"	" 5, "	
Theodore B. Smiley, -	"	" 1, "	
Chas. C. Spooner, - -	"	" 8, "	
Jas. J. Spalding, - -	"	" 1, "	
William N. Shepherdson, -	"	" 2, "	
Wm. W. Stuart, - -	"	" 4, "	
Albert A. Smith, - -	"	" 5, "	
Wm. B. Smith, - -	"	" 7, "	
Calvin N. Smith, - -	"	" 7, "	
Richard Tudor, - -	"	Dec. 28, 1846.	
Jno. Totty, - -	"	" 31, "	
Thomas H. Towner, -	"	Jan. 8, 1847,	
Robt. H. Vaden, - -	"	" 9, "	
Alfred J. Vaughan, -	"	Dec. 21, 1846,	
Thos. Wigden, - -	"	" 31, "	
Jno. Wyatt, - -	"	Jan. 1, 1846,	
Jas. Womack, - -	"	" 1, "	
Armistead B. Wills, -	"	" 12, "	
Jno. H. Wells, - -	"	" 12, "	
Benj'n Wilkins, - -	"	" 19, "	

[Date organization of Company, 23d December 1846.]

MUSTER ROLL

Of Captain John William Rowan's Company, in the First Regiment of Virginia Volunteers, commanded by Colonel John F. Hamtramck, called into the Service of the United States by the Secretary of War, under the Act of Congress approved May 13, 1846, from the 27th day of January 1847, (date of this Muster,) for the term of during the War with Mexico, unless sooner discharged.

NAMES.	RANK.	WHEN ENROLLED.	DISTANCE TO PLACE OF RENDEZVOUS.
J. W. Rowan,	Captain,	Dec. 1, 1846,	180 miles.
John Avis,	1st Lieutenant,	" 1, "	180 "
Lawrence B. Washington,	2d "	" 6, "	180 "
Wm. McCormick,	2d "	" 12, "	180 "
George Wm. Fairfax,	1st Sergeant,	" 10, "	180 "
John W. Gallaher,	2d "	" 1, "	180 "
Lewis D. Ball,	3d "	" 9, "	180 "
John M. English,	4th "	" 20, "	180 "
James W. Duke,	Corporal,	" 1, "	180 "
James R. Copeland,	"	" 1, "	180 "
Joseph Jones,	"	" 12, "	180 "
Wm. C. McClure,	"	Jan. 4, 1847,	180 "
Thomas H. Douglass,	Drummer,	" 2, "	145 "
John Cunningham,	Fifer,	" 1, "	180 "
Wm. A. Baker,	Private,	Dec. 24, 1846,	180 "
Wm. F. Bragg,	"	" 29, "	180 "
Benjamin H. Bradford,	"	Jan. 5, 1847,	180 "
John P. Brock,	"	" 26, "	125 "
Wm. Bryant,	"	" 5, "	100 "
James H. Boxer,	"	Dec. 9, 1846,	200 "
James B. Ball,	"	" 9, "	200 "
Peter Boughn,	"	" 24, "	200 "
Wm. Birkit,	"	" 24, "	180 "
Vance W. Bush,	"	Jan. 20, 1847,	200 "
Emanuel Beam,	"	" 1, "	203 "
Cornelius P. Barr,	"	Dec. 20, 1846,	200 "
James W. Bateman,	"	Jan. 20, 1847,	172 "
Cornelius Carlin,	"	Dec. 17, 1846,	200 "
Fayette Cole,	"	Jan. 26, 1847,	125 "
Andrew J. Copenhafer,	"	Dec. 9, 1846,	200 "
Henry L. Cabell,	"	" 9, "	200 "
Henry Davy,	"	" 27, "	180 "
Joseph L. Everett,	"	" 11, "	180 "
Joseph Evans,	"	" 11, "	180 "
Samuel Ellis,	"	" 20, "	200 "
Charles French,	"	Jan. 20, 1847,	180 "
Wm. C. Gover,	"	" 1, "	180 "
Carter Gibson,	"	" 24, "	150 "
John Grandberry,	"	Dec. 26, 1846,	145 "
David B. Glasscock,	"	Jan. 21, 1847,	150 "
Henry Gallenar,	"	" 21, "	
Joseph L. Hampton,	"	Dec. 29, 1846,	180 "
John A. B. Harding,	"	" 4, "	180 "

NAMES.	RANK.	WHEN ENROLLED.	DISTANCE TO PLACE OF RENDEZVOUS.
Dennis Herrington, - -	Private,	Dec. 17, 1846,	180 miles.
Joseph Henning, - -	"	" 29, "	200 "
Stephen D. Hurst, - -	"	" 7, "	180 "
John M. Heflin, - -	"	Jan. 20, 1847,	200 "
Morriss B. Howell, - -	"	Dec. 17, 1846,	180 "
John F. Hogan, - -	"	" 20, "	180 "
Richard W. Heafer, - -	"	" 13, "	180 "
James M. Harry, - -	"	" 20, "	180 "
John V. Howell, - -	"	" 14, "	180 "
Wm. Hillard, - -	"	" 29, "	180 "
William Kirk, - -	"	" 11, "	180 "
William Kendall, - -	"	" 20, "	110 "
George W. Kile, - -	"	Jan. 2, 1847,	180 "
Beverley W. Lancaster, -	"	Dec. 6, 1846,	180 "
James W. McKinney, -	"	" 25, "	180 "
Pilate McKay, - -	"	" 11, "	180 "
Thomas McCroig, - -	"	Jan. 20, 1847,	200 "
Peter Miller, - -	"	Dec. 24, 1846,	200 "
Joseph Meyer, - -	"	Jan. 20, 1847.	200 "
Elijah L. Mindenall, -	"	Dec. 20, 1846,	200 "
George W. Mack, - -	"	" 26, "	
John F. Poland, - -	"	Jan. 20, 1847,	200 "
Thomas R. Satterfield, -	"	Dec. 20, 1846,	180 "
James F. Shryock, - -	"	" 20, "	200 "
Wm. P. Shipman, - -	"	" 28, "	180 "
James C. Seabright, - -	"	" 28, "	200 "
John Wm. Sheets, - -	"	" 1, "	180 "
Barnardt Shelling, - -	"	" 25, "	
James Thompson, - -	"	" 26, "	180 "
Charles M. Thompson, -	"	" 20, "	200 "
Henry G. Vonreason, -	"	Jan. 20, 1847,	200 "
John B. Whiting, - -	"	Dec. 9, 1846,	180 "
Charles Waddell, - -	"	" 23, "	200 "
Treadwell S. Wall, - -	"	" 23, "	200 "
David H. Watson, - -	"	Jan. 20, 1847,	200 "
Andrew J. Wood, - -	"	Dec. 29, 1846,	180 "

MUSTER ROLL

Of Captain William A. Talbott's Company, of Virginia Volunteers commanded by Colonel John F. Hamtramck, called into the Service of the United States by the Secretary of War, under the Act of Congress approved May 13, 1846, for the term of during the War with Mexico, unless sooner discharged.

NAMES.	RANK.	WHEN ENROLLED.	REMARKS.
Wm. A. Talbott, - -	Captain,	June 21, 1846.	
Wm. A. Scott, - -	1st Lieutenant.	Aug. 27, "	Joined by transfer at Fort Monroe.
Wm. H. Pleasants, - -	2d "	May 15, "	" " "
Robert F. Astrop, -	2d "	Sept. 8, "	" " "
John F. Stagg, -	1st Sergeant,	May 15, "	" " "
Robert W. Folks, -	Sergeant,	Aug. 29, "	" " "
Joseph A. Johnson, -	"	July 15, "	" " "
Richard D. Wills, -	"	Aug. 29, "	" " "
Thos. G. Flagg, -	Corporal,	June 6, "	" " "
Wm. C. Brown, -	"	July 15, "	" " "
Sterling L. Wallace, -	"	Sept. 13, "	" " "
Upton A. Edmundson, -	"	" 2, "	" " "
Francis Valiett, -	Musician,	July 25, "	" " "
Reuben B. Wilkes, -	"	" 3, "	" " "
Wm. C. Boswell, -	Private,	Sept. 6, "	" " "
Wm. T. Booker, -	"	June 20, "	
Bartlett Breeden, -	"	Aug. 1, "	
Wm. H. Burke, -	"	July 1, "	
Jacob Beck, -	"	Sept. 2, "	
Jesse P. Bradley, -	"	Oct. 7, "	" " "
Samuel Bowers, -	"	Sept. 10, "	" " "
Jesse P. Brown, -	"	" 10, "	" " "
George W. Chick, -	"	Aug. 1, "	
Alexander J. Cropp, -	"	" 7, "	
John Clark, -	"	Nov. 10, "	
A. M. Crowder, -	"	Sept. 7, "	" " "
John Comerford, -	"	Nov. 4, "	" " "
John Cotton, -	"	" 23, "	" " "
John Q. A. Dillard, -	"	Aug. 10, "	
Wm. E. Donevant, -	"	" 1, "	
John Diamond, -	"	July 7, "	
Charles C. Dixon, -	"	Aug. 9, "	
Nelson C. Etheridge, -	"	Nov. 25, "	
D. M. Eustace, -	"	" 30, "	
Jas. H. Eaves, -	"	" 9, "	" " "
John D. Frazier, -	"	Aug. 28, "	
Algernon R. Folks, -	"	" 16, "	
Elijah Foster, -	"	" 1, "	
John R. Featherston, -	"	July 1, "	
Edward Garther, -	"	June 30, "	
John L. Goodwin, -	"	Oct. 4, "	
George W. Golden, -	"	July 5, "	
Washington Goodwyn, -	"	Sept. 2, "	" " "
Lewis Hammock, -	"	" 2, "	" " "
Daniel Hudson, -	"	" 15, "	" " "
George W. Halsey, -	"	Nov. 17, "	" " "

NAMES.	RANK.	WHEN ENROLLED.	REMARKS.
John R. Humphreys, -	Private,	Sept. 20, 1846,	Joined by transfer at Fort Monroe.
Thomas R. Jones, - -	"	Aug. 1, "	
Francis A. Johnson, -	"	July 5, "	
John A. Johnson, - -	"	May 26, . "	
John Jenkins, -	"	July 5, "	
Edward W. Jones, - -	"	Aug. 29, "	" " "
William H. Johnson, -	"	Nov. 17, "	" " "
Robert W. Lee, - -	"	July 13, "	
Edwin T. Lucado, -	"	June 22, "	
Jacob G. Miller, - -	"	" 16, "	
John Miller, - -	"	Nov. 17, "	
Thomas F. Marable, -	"	June 1, "	
Francis P. Muloy, - -	"	Oct. 7, "	
Josiah Manson, -	"	Sept. 2, "	" " "
Albert Meador, - -	"	Aug. 29, "	" " "
James O. Moss, -	"	" 29, "	" " "
John W. Nicholson, -	"	Nov. 11, "	" " "
John T. Organ, -	"	July 7, "	
Richard W. Outland, -	"	Sept. 4, "	
Henry B. Olcott, - -	"	Nov. 26, "	
Joseph J. W. Pinnell, -	"	Aug. 10, "	
Wm. N. Parrish, -	"	Sept. 5, "	" " "
Robert H. Phillips, -	"	Aug. 29, "	" " "
Anthony Pevenlly, -	"	Nov. 17, "	" " "
Walter Powers, -	"	" 4, "	" " "
D. S. Robertson, -	"	" 18, "	
Wm. H. Stafford, -	"	" 18, "	
Paul L. Savage, -	"	July 5, "	
William H. Scott, -	"	Nov. 10, "	
James Smith, -	"	" 4, "	
Joseph Tiffin, - -	"	Aug. 1, "	
Henry Thorpe, -	"	" 1, "	
John Taylor, -	"	Nov. 13, "	
Albert G. Wingfield, -	"	Aug. 1, "	
Peter H. Wilson, -	"	Sept. 2, "	
James Warden, -	"	July 1, "	
Robert A. Whitlock, -	"	Aug. 26, "	
William Wills, -	"	Sept. 10, "	" " "
Benjamin W. Wilks, -	"	" 2, "	" " "
Thomas R. Williams, -	"	Aug. 8, "	" " "
David M. White, -	"	Oct. 20, "	" " "
Ira Willis, -	"	Nov. 23, "	" " "
Wm. M. Yates, -	"	Aug. 27, "	" " "

MUSTER ROLL

*Of Captain John P. Young's Company, in the First Regiment of Virginia Volun-
teers, commanded by Colonel John F. Hamtramck, called into the Service of the
United States by the Secretary of War, under the Act of Congress approved
May 13, 1846, from the Twenty-eighth day of January 1847, (date of this
Muster,) for the term of during the War with Mexico, unless sooner discharged.*

NAMES.	RANK.	WHEN ENROLLED.	DISTANCE TO PLACE OF RENDEZVOUS.
John P. Young,	Captain,	Nov. 23, 1846,	145 miles.
John K. Cooke,	1st Lieutenant.	" 23, "	145 "
Edward J. Blamire,	2d "	" 23, "	145 "
William M. Levy,	2d "	" 23, "	145 "
James W. Butt,	1st Sergeant,	" 23, "	145 "
John Loppin,	Sergeant,	" 23, "	146 "
Augustus G. Tabb,	"	" 23, "	145 "
Nathaniel G. Rodgers,	"	" 24, "	145 "
Richard T. Montague,	Corporal,	" 23, "	145 "
Henry K. Edwards,	"	Dec. 18, "	145 "
Eugene D. Councill,	"	Nov. 28, "	145 "
Francis W. Parker,	"	" 24, "	145 "
Christopher Lawrence,	Drummer,	" 24, "	145 "
John P. Forbes,	Fifer,	" 24, "	145 "
James S. A. Brigham,	Private,	" 23, "	145 "
Joseph Boykin,	"	Dec. 29, "	190 "
Jesse Benton,	"	" 20, "	145 "
John Burdine,	"	" 24, "	
Zerah Boothe,	"	Jan. 22, 1847.	
John Bames,	"	Nov. 23, 1846.	
Francis L. Benson,	"	Jan. 15, 1847.	
Samuel J. Beatty,	"	" 22, "	
Thomas Callaghan,	"	" 10, "	
Lewis Cohen,	"	" 25, "	
William Cherry,	"	Dec. 28, 1846.	
Charles J. Creekmur,	"	Jan. 11, 1847.	
David Cherry,	"	" 18, 1847.	
Elijah Corden,	"	" 22, 1847.	
John Conner,	"	" 22, "	
James Caterson,	"	" 22, "	
Frederick A. Cunningham,	"	" 26, "	
Bailey Callis,	"	" 28, "	
Alexander Dyes,	"	Dec. 28, 1846.	
Nathaniel Dyes,	"	" 28, "	
John S. Donnell,	"	" 28, "	
Joshua Grimes,	"	" 24, "	145 "
James Grimes,	"	" 24, "	145 "
Benjamin Gayle,	"	" 18, "	145 "
Charles Gilmore,	"	Jan. 18, 1847,	145 "
Nathaniel B. Hawkins,	"	" 26, "	
John W. Haslay,	"	" 6, "	145 "
Richard S. Howell,	"	Dec. 23, 1846.	145 "
John E. Hinchman,	"	" 23, "	145 "
Sparrell Jones,	"	" 13, "	145 "
William D. James,	"	Nov. 23, "	145 "
Joseph H. James,	"	" 23, "	145 "

NAMES.	RANK.	WHEN ENROLLED.	DISTANCE TO PLACE OF RENDEZVOUS.
William M. Joiner, - -	Private,	Dec. 24, 1846,	145 miles.
Richard E. Johnson, - -	"	Jan. 12, 1847,	145 "
Samuel Lamb, - -	"	" 20, "	145 "
John Misley, - -	"	Dec. 22, 1846,	145 "
James E. Moore, - -	"	" 21, "	145 "
James Moss, - -	"	" 6, "	145 "
Jeremiah McCrady, - -	"	Jan. 29, 1847,	145 "
William W. Manning, -	"	Nov. 23, 1846,	145 "
John Majer, - -	"	Jan. 20, 1847,	145 "
Samuel W. Miller, - -	"	" 20, "	145 "
Daniel Morse, - -	"	" 20, "	145 "
William T. Nottingham, -	"	Dec. 22, 1846,	145 "
Christopher Norfleet, -	"	Jan. 22, 1847,	160 "
George W. Orton, - -	"	Dec. 24, 1846,	145 "
Virginius L. Pitts, - -	"	Jan. 3, 1847,	145 "
James W. Peed, - -	"	Dec. 22, 1846,	145 "
James D. Pollard, - -	"	Jan. 20, 1847,	145 "
Richard Peel, - -	"	Dec. 18, 1846,	165 "
William Reed, - -	"	" 11, "	145 "
Samuel Reynolds, - -	"	Jan. 5, 1847,	145 "
John Shelling, - -	"	Nov. 26, 1846,	145 "
John T. Spratt, - -	"	" 23, "	145 "
James W. Spratt, - -	"	Dec. 21, "	145 "
Edward G. Stewart, -	"	Jan. 9, 1847,	145 "
John Spencer, - -	"	Nov. 23, 1846,	145 "
Thomas Shinn, - -	"	Jan. 20, 1847,	145 "
Henry Turner, - -	"	Nov. 23, 1846,	145 "
Samuel Totten, - -	"	Jan. 18, 1847,	145 "
James Whitson, - -	"	Dec. 16, 1846,	145 "
Andrew Williamson, -	"	" 28, "	145 "
Francis S. Wilson, - -	"	" 15, "	145 "
Isaac Waples, - -	"	Jan. 15, 1847,	145 "
Henry Webster, - -	"	" 20, "	145 "
William White, - -	"	" 20, "	145 "

MUSTER ROLL

Of Captain Samuel G. Adams' Company of Militia of the Nineteenth Regiment, commanded by Lt. Colonel John Ambler, in the Service of the United States from the 18th to the 27th March, and from the 27th day of June to the 3d day of July 1813.

NAMES.	RANK.	TIME OF SERVICE.		REMARKS.
		Months.	Days.	
Samuel G. Adams, - -	Captain,	—	16	
John S. Stubbs, - -	Lieutenant,	—	16	
Jacob Weisiger, - -	Ensign,	—	16	
Thomas Anslow, - -	Sergeant,	—	16	
Charles Kelley, - -	"	—	10	
John Yore, - -	"	—	10	
Francis J. Lewis, - -	"	—	16	
Geo. Watt, - -	"	—	6	
John Oram, - -	"	—	6	
William B. Lupton, - -	Corporal,	—	16	
Richard Finch, - -	"	—	10	
Charles Word, - -	"	—	10	
Thomas Turner, - -	"	—	6	
Crosher Graves, - -	"	—	6	
Samuel Quay, - -	"	—	6	
James S. Smithers, - -	"	—	6	
Nathan Abbott, - -	Private,	—	16	
Francis Austin, - -	"	--	16	
James Adams, - -	"	—	16	
Ignatius H. Allen, - -	"	—	16	
James Aspey, - -	"	—	10	
Bently Anderson, - -	"	—	10	
Thos. H. Alley, - -	"	—	10	
Edward Brown, - -	"	—	16	
William Brown, - -	"	—	16	
William W. Brown, - -	"	—	4	
Thos. Briggs, - -	"	—	16	
Alex. Barker, - -	"	—	6	
Joshua Brotherhood, - -	"	—	16	
Jason J. Brightwell, - -	"	—	16	
Joseph Bertrand, - -	"	—	4	
Geo. Brock, - -	"	—	4	
John Baptist, - -	"	—	4	
Amos Bemis, - -	"	—	10	
Ely Bennet, - -	"	—	10	
Samuel Bowers, - -	"	—	10	
John Clarke, - -	"	—	16	
William Coggin, - -	"	—	16	
John Cramey, - -	"	—	6	
Andrew Dunn, - -	"	—	16	
Joshua Doing, - -	"	—	16	
Benj. Darby, - -	"	—	16	
Berkett Doudall, - -	"	—	16	
John Drinkard, - -	"	—	6	
Charles Daniel, - -	"	—	4	
James Enders, - -	"	—	6	
James Earle, - -	"	—	16	

NAMES.	RANK.	TIME OF SERVICE.		REMARKS.
		Months.	Days.	
Thomas M. Everson, -	Private,	–	16	
Charles Elliott, - -	"	–	6	
Pleasant Franklin, - -	"	–	16	
Ralph Fenn, - -	"	–	16	
William Fleming, - -	"	–	16	
Sam'l Gathwright, - -	"	–	16	
John Gathwright, - -	"	–	4	
Chas. F. Gretter, - -	"	–	16	
Major T. Garnett, - -	"	–	16	
Thomas Green, - -	"	–	6	
William Garraw, - -	"	–	4	
Sam'l D. Hart, - -	"	–	16	
Geo. B. Haines, - -	"	–	4	
Sam'l Houston, - -	"	–	6	
Noah Jones, - -	"	–	16	
John Johnston, - -	"	–	13	
William S. Johnston, -	"	–	6	
Thomas Jones, - -	"	–	4	
Thomas Kesey, - -	"	–	6	
Joseph Key, - -	"	–	16	
Daniel Lucas, - -	"	–	16	
John Lancaster, - -	"	–	6	
Nath'l Long, - -	"	–	16	
William Miller, - -	"	–	16	
John McElligott, - -	"	–	4	
Geo. Myers, - -	"	–	4	
Thomas Oliver, - -	"	–	16	
Reuben Pleasants, - -	"	–	16	
Robert Pleasants, - -	"	–	16	
Geo. W. Payne, - -	"	–	16	
Philip Peach, - -	"	–	16	
Laurance Ryan, - -	"	–	16	
Jonathan Rogers, - -	"	–	6	
William Sheran, - -	"	–	16	
Charles Smith, - -	"	–	16	
Geo. Smith, - -	"	–	16	
Stephen Smith, - -	"	–	16	
John Sexsmith, - -	"	–	16	
Reuben M. Sizer, - -	"	–	16	
Jonas P. Slade, - -	"	–	16	
John Starr, - -	"	–	5	
Francis Sharp, - -	"	–	4	
Baylor Stubbs, - -	"	–	4	
Abner W. Turner, - -	"	–	16	
Richard Turner, - -	"	–	16	
Roddy Towers, - -	"	–	16	
Ambrose Turner, - -	"	–	16	
Joseph Thompson, - -	"	–	5	
John West, - -	"	–	16	
Cornelius West, - -	"	–	4	
Robert White, - -	"	–	4	
Beverly T. Wells, - -	"	–	16	
John Worrock, - -	"	–	16	
Thomas Whitlow, - -	"	–	16	
John Willock, - -	"	–	6	
John Wright, - -	"	–	16	
Edm'd Wright, - -	"	–	16	
Alex'r Parker, - -	"	–	10	
Henry Wright, - -	"	–	10	
Charles Hughes, - -	"	–	10	
James Snell, - -	"	–	10	
Joseph Palmer, - -	"	–	10	
Wyatt Hines, - -	"	–	10	
Hugh Warder, - -	"	–	10	

NAMES.	RANK.	TIME OF SERVICE.		REMARKS.
		Months.	Days.	
Francis Childress, - -	Private,	–	10	
Levy Pickrell, - -	"	–	10	
Purley Hughes, - -	"	–	10	
Ephraim Leonard, - -	"	–	10	
William J. Williams,	"	–	10	
Nath'l Miller, - -	"	–	10	
Joseph Now, - -	"	–	10	
Geo. N. Haynes, - -	"	–	10	
William Massie, - -	"	–	10	
John Nettles, - -	"	–	10	
John Grantland, - -	"	–	10	
Philip Holtz, - -	"	–	10	
John Oram, - -	"	–	10	
Joseph Murdock, - -	"	–	10	
William Kesee, - -	"	–	10	
Jabez Parker, - -	"	–	10	
William Tate, - -	"	–	10	
James Gibbs, - -	"	–	10	
Geo. Watt, - -	"	–	10	
Nicholas Scherer, - -	"	–	10	
Samuel Sherer, - -	"	–	10	
Geo. Reed, - -	"	–	10	
James Whitefield, - -	"	–	10	
William Mitchell, - -	"	–	10	
Christ. Drummond, - -	"	–	10	
Crosher Graves, - -	"	–	10	
Benj. Hubbard, - -	"	–	10	
Martin Turner, - -	"	–	10	
Geo. Merry, - -	"	–	10	

MUSTER ROLL

Of Captain Lewis Alexander's Company of Infantry, in the Forty-fifth Regiment of Virginia Militia, commanded by Lieutenant Colonel Samuel H. Peyton, in the Service of the United States from 22d day of July 1814, to the 18th August 1814.

NAMES.			RANK.	TIME OF SERVICE.		REMARKS.
				Months.	Days.	
Lewis Alexander,	-	-	Captain,	–	28	
Samuel Wilcocks,	-	-	Lieutenant,	–	28	
John S. Knose,	-	-	Ensign,	–	28	
Burdett Cliffton,	-	-	"	–	28	
Boswell Alsop,	-	-	Sergeant,	–	28	
Thomas Tutt,	-	-	"	–	28	
Daniel B. Doggett,	-	-	"	–	28	
William Langfit,	-	-	"	–	28	
Richard Gaines,	-	-	Corporal,	–	28	
William Latham,	-	-	"	–	28	
William S. Dunington,	-	-	"	–	28	
William Alexander,	-	-	Private,	–	–	Transferred July 22d, 1814.
Thornton Alexander,	-		"	–	28	Thos. D. Harrison his substitute.
William Brooke,	-	-	"	–	–	Transferred July 22d, 1814.
William C. Beale,	-	-	"	–	28	
David Briggs,	-	-	"	–	28	In the staff.
William Burton,	-	-	"	–	28	
William Buchanan,	-	-	"	–	28	In the staff as assistant S. Mate.
Thomas Butler,	-	-	"	–	28	
John Bell, jr.	-	-	"	–	28	
Ire Burton,	-	-	"	–	28	
Whitfield Brooke,	-	-	"	–	15	
Thomas W. Cowne,	-	-	"	–	–	Transferred July 22d, 1814.
Frederick Cline,	-	-	"	–	28	
John Chiles,	-	-	"	–	28	
James Curtis,	-	-	"	–	28	
James S. Carter,	-	-	"	–	28	
Sanford Carter,	-	-	"	–	28	
John Dosier,	-	-	"	–	28	
John England,	-	-	"	–	28	
Murray Forbes,	-	-	"	–	28	In the staff—assistant Q. Master.
David Grinnan,	-	-	"	–	28	
James R. Hewett,	-	-	"	–	28	Benjamin Gilbert substitute.
Benj. H. Hall,	-	-	"	–	28	In the staff—2d Surgeon's Mate.
George Kiger,	-	-	"	–	28	R. Manabez substitute, and transferred.
Henry Lewis,	-	-	"	–	28	Geo. Lewis substitute.
George Leach,	-	-	"	–	28	James Edwards "
John Lewis,	-	-	"	–	28	

NAMES.	RANK.	TIME OF SERVICE.		REMARKS.
		Months.	Days.	
William W. McNeale,	Private,	–	28	Secretary to Maj. Folson.
Ebenezer Marray,	"	–	–	Transferred July 22d. 1814.
Rodham Myers,	"	–	28	
James Miles,	"	–	28	
Benjamin Maccoy,	"	–	28	
George Payne,	"	–	28	
Dearson Payne,	"	–	28	
Theodosius Payne.	"	–	28	
John Payne,	"	–	28	
John Rogers,	"	–	28	
William Stringfellow,	"	–	28	Made Suttler.
Thomas C. Scott,	"	–	28	Marmian Sullivan substitute.
William Skidmore,	"	–	28	
William Thompson,	"	–	28	
George F. Vowles,	"	–	28	Secretary to Colonel Peyton.
John W. Wallace.	"	–	28	Thos. Wallace sub.
William Wallace,	"	–	28	

Captain Thomas C. Alexander's Company—Forty-fifth Regiment.

NAMES.	RANK.	TIME OF SERVICE.		REMARKS.
		Months.	Days.	
Thomas C. Alexander,	Captain,	–	9	
Jesse Custis,	Lieutenant,	–	9	
Aaron H. Ball,	Ensign,	–	9	
Thomas McGuire,	Sergeant,	–	9	
Francis Hewit,	"	–	9	
William Walker,	"	–	9	
John Rouse,	"	–	28	
Robert Fennell,	Corporal,	–	17	
Thomas Curtis,	"	–	17	
James Rowe,	"	–	9	
George Davis,	"	–	17	
Ellis Gravatt,	"	–	28	
Rasal Rollow,	"	–	28	
James Armstrong,	"	–	28	
Peter Cox,	Fifer,	1	15	
John Cox,	"	–	28	
William Bates,	Private,	–	17	
William Bryant,	"	–	17	
William Butler,	"	–	28	
John Ball,	"	–	28	
Francis Brown,	"	–	9	
Samuel Brown,	"	–	9	
Thomas Burton,	"	–	9	
John Burton,	"	–	9	
Reubin Berry,	"	–	9	
Samuel Cox,	"	–	9	
John Curtis,	"	–	28	
James A. Curtis,	"	–	28	
Charnock Cox,	"	–	28	
Thomas Chilton,	"	–	8	
Thornton Chilton,	"	1	7	
William Chilton,	"	–	17	
James Cox,	"	–	8	
Rolley Chin,	"	–	17	
James Curtis,	"	–	9	
Joseph A. Carter,	"	–	9	
Joseph Curry,	"	–	17	
Newton Cox,	"	–	17	
George Cox,	"	–	17	
Joseph Carter,	"	–	8	
Benjamin Cox,	"	–	9	
Thomas Davis,	"	–	17	
Henry Dillon,	"	–	17	
Thomas Edwards,	"	–	17	
David Fines,	"	–	28	
Charles Fox,	"	–	28	
Samuel Geter,	"	–	17	
William Hewitt,	"	–	9	
Gilson Jett,	"	–	9	
William T. Jones,	"	–	28	
Peter Jett,	"	–	17	
Vincent Limbrick,	"	–	17	
John Limbrick,	"	–	9	
James Limbrick,	"	–	17	

NAMES.			RANK.	TIME OF SERVICE.		REMARKS.
				Months.	Days.	
James Long,	-	-	Private,	–	17	
Elijah Leach,	-	-	"	–	28	
Abner Leach,	-	-	"	–	17	
John Leach,	-	-	"	–	17	
Elijah Leach,	-	-	"	–	17	
James Leach,	-	-	"	–	9	
Samuel Montieth,	-	-	"	–	17	
John McGune,	-	-	"	–	28	
Isaac Newton,	-	-	"	–	17	
Berry Newton,	-	-	"	–	9	
Stephen Pratt,	-	-	"	–	9	
William Payne,	-	-	"	–	9	
Burkitt Pratt,	-	-	"	–	28	
Aaron Pates,	-	-	"	–	28	
Thomas Robertson,	-	-	"	–	28	
Francis Rolly,	-	-	"	–	9	
Jesse Rowe,	-	-	"	–	28	
Benj. Sullivant,	-	-	"	1	7	
Thomas Sullivant,	-	-	"	–	17	
James Sullivant,	-	-	"	–	28	
Casson Sullivant,	-	-	"	–	28	
Dawson Sullivant,	-	-	"	–	9	
James Spilman,	-	-	"	–	17	
Alex. Sorrel,	-	-	"	–	28	
Robert Toombs,	-	-	"	–	28	
James Welch,	-	-	"	–	28	
George White,	-	-	"	1	7	
James White,	-	-	"	–	17	
Daniel White,	-	-	"	–	9	
James Williams,	-	-	"	–	9	

(For rest of this company, see publication of Pay Rolls.)

MUSTER ROLL

Of a detachment of Cavalry commanded by Lieutenant James Allen, jr. and attached to the Sixth Regiment of Virginia Militia, called into actual Service by Lieut. Col. John Daingerfield at Tappahannock in Essex County, on the 5th day of April 1813.

NAMES.	RANK.	TIME OF SERVICE.		REMARKS.
		Months.	Days.	
James Allen, jr. - -	Lieutenant,	–	4	
William Newbill, - -	2d "	–	1	
Thomas Dix, -	Sergeant,	–	5	
William Crittendon, -	"	–	3	
Samuel Croxton, -	Private,	–	4	
James W. Upshaw, - -	"	–	3	
John Boughan, - -	"	–	3	
Major J. Boughan, - -	"	–	3	
Washington Purkins, -	"	–	5	
Isaac Tigner, - -	"	–	3	
Adderson Allen, - -	"	–	5	
Thomas Allen, jr. - -	"	–	3	
James Andrews, - -	"	–	3	
John Andrews, - -	"	–	3	
John Beazley, - -	"	–	5	
Lewis Rouse, - -	"	–	3	
Carter M. Braxton, - -	"	–	4	
William F. Micou, - -	"	–	4	
William Croxton, - -	"	–	4	
John B. Burke, - -	"	–	6	
Thomas Parker, - -	"	–	3	
Thomas S. Latane, - -	"	–	4	

MUSTER ROLL

Of Lieutenant Robert Allen's Company of Artillery of Virginia Militia, from the Twenty-third Regiment, in the Service from the 18th day of March 1813, to the 30th of March 1813.

NAMES.			RANK.	TIME OF SERVICE.		REMARKS.
				Months.	Days.	
Robert Allen,	-	-	Lieutenant,	–	12	
W. A. Martin,	-	-	Sergeant,	–	12	
Jas. Cunningham,	-	-	"	–	12	
Jas. Adkins,	-	-	Private,	–	12	
Woodford Alvis,	-	-	"	–	12	
W. E. Gales,	-	-	"	–	12	
W. Shell,	-	-	"	–	12	
John Whillock,	-	-	"	–	12	
Jas. Branch,	-	-	"	–	12	
Jesse Russell,	-	-	"	–	12	
John Rancock,	-	-	"	–	12	
Dav. Brodel,	-	-	"	–	12	
W. Cary,	-	-	"	–	12	

Captain Samuel V. Allen's Company—First Regiment.

NAMES.	RANK.	TIME OF SERVICE.		REMARKS.
		Months.	Days.	
Samuel V. Allen. - -	Captain,	–	13	
William L. Venable, -	Lieutenant,	–	13	
Henry E. Watkins, - -	"	–	13	
Samuel L. Lockett, - -	Cornet,	–	13	
Archer Fuqua, - -	Sergeant,	–	13	
Peyton Randolph, - -	"	–	13	
Pugh W. Price, - -	"	–	13	
Booker Foster, - -	"	–	13	
James J. Foster, - -	Corporal,	–	13	
Henry N. Watkins, - -	"	–	13	
Obadiah Marton, - -	"	–	13	
James D. Wood, - -	Musician,	–	13	
Leonard Anderson, - -	Private.			
James R. Allen, - -	"	–	13	Appointed Sword Master Sept. 7, 1814.
Merit B. Allen, - -	"	–	13	
Cary C. Allen, - -	"	–	13	
Samuel Anderson, - -	"	–	13	
William B. Booker, - -	"	–	13	
Richard Booker, - -	"	3	18	
Archer Brown, - -	"	3	18	
Patrick Boothe, - -	"	–	13	
Thomas Ellington, - -	"	–	13	
Paschal Foulkes, - -	"	–	13	
Peter Foster, - -	"	–	13	
Jennings Foulkes, - -	"	–	13	
William Foulkes, - -	"			
William Fleming, - -	"	–	13	
Francis Flippin, - -	"	–	13	
Thos. Goode, - -	"	–	13	
Joseph Goode, - -	"	–	13	
John Holcombe, - -	"	–	13	
Simon Hughs, - -	"	–	13	
Theodorick C. Haskins, -	"	–	13	
Henry W. Holland, - -	"	–	13	
Thomas Jackson, - -	"	–	13	
Nathan G. McGehee, -	"	–	13	
Nath. Morris, - -	"	–	13	
Charles Morris, - -	"	3	5	
Samuel Morris, - -	"	–	13	
William Martin, - -	"	–	13	
John F. Nash, - -	"	–	13	
Edwin Price, - -	"	–	13	
Daney Purman, - -	"	–	13	
Hastin Poe, - -	"	–	13	
James Price, - -	"	–	13	
Benjamin H. Price, - -	"	–	13	
William Price, - -	"	–	13	
William G. Price, - -	"	–	13	
Charles W. Price, - -	"	–	13	
William Phillips, - -	"	–	13	
John Redford, - -	"	–	13	
Josiah M. Rice, - -	"	–	13	
Stephen C. Richardson, -	"	–	13	

NAMES.			RANK.	TIME OF SERVICE.		REMARKS.
				Months.	Days.	
John Rice,	-	-	Private,	–	13	
James S. Smith,	-	-	"	–	13	
Lion F. Spencer,	-	-	"	–	13	
Jos. H. Thurston,	-	-	"	–	13	
Henry H. Vaughan,	-	-	"	–	13	
John H. Venable,	-	-	"	–	13	
Nath. Venable,	-	-	"	–	13	
William Venable,	-	-	"	–	13	
Thomas Wilbourne,	-	-	"	–	13	
Wm. H. Walthall,	-	-	"	–	13	
Francis Walthall,	-	-	Saddler,	–	13	
Samuel Worsham,	-	-	Private,	–	13	
Richard Woodson,	-	-	"	–	13	
Augustus Watkins,	-	-	"	–	13	
John Williams,	-	-	"	–	13	
John A. Watson,	-	-	"	–	13	

(For rest of this company, see publication of Pay Rolls.)

MONTHLY PAY ROLL

Of Captain William Allen's Company of Infantry, from Thirty-third Regiment of Virginia Militia, in the Service from the 19th to the 29th March, 1813.

NAMES.		RANK.	TIME OF SERVICE.		REMARKS.
			Months.	Days.	
William Allen,	- -	Captain,	–	5	
John Pemberton,	- -	Lieutenant,	–	4	
John Carter,	- -	Ensign,	–	5	
Christian Allen,	- -	Sergeant,	–	5	
Claiborne Bethell,	- -	"	–	5	
William Baker,	- -	"	–	5	
John Morris,	- -	"	–	5	
William Eacho,	- -	Private,	–	5	
Hazlewood Bottom,	- -	"	–	5	
James Smith,	- -	"	–	5	
Terry Hill, -	- -	"	–	5	
Geo. Leach, -	- -	"	–	5	
Daniel Tucker,	- -	"	–	5	
Ishmael Lawrence,	- -	"	–	5	
Therwood Binford,	- -	"	–	5	
John Eacho,	- -	"	–	5	
John Warriner,	- -	"	–	5	
Thomas Wade,	- -	"	–	5	
Ansel Gathright,	- -	"	–	5	
Reuben Matthews,	- -	"	–	5	
William Austin,	- -	"	–	5	
Thomas Johnson,	- -	"	–	4	
Jonathan Brackett,	- -	"	–	5	
John Turner,	- -	"	–	5	
Littlebery Allen,	- -	"	–	5	
William Gathright,	- -	"	–	5	
John Valentine,	- -	"	–	5	
John Childreys,	- -	"	–	5	
Thomas Bethel,	- -	"	–	5	
Carter Bethel,	- -	"	–	5	
James Matthews,	- -	"	–	5	
Moses Woodfin,	- -	"	–	5	
Thomas Goodman,	- -	"	–	5	
John Dunn,	- -	"	–	5	
Robt. Bethell,	- -	"	–	5	
Samuel Barker,	- -	"	–	5	
William Carter,	- -	"	–	5	
Samuel Gathright,	- -	"	–	5	
William Barker,	- -	"	–	5	
Samuel Lawrance,	- -	"	–	5	
George Savage,	- -	"	–	5	
Joseph Wade,	- -	"	–	5	
Carter Gathright,	- -	"	–	5	
Richard Allen,	- -	"	–	5	
Fleming Pollard,	- -	"	–	5	
Thomas Holmes,	- -	"	–	5	
John Hailes,	- -	"	–	5	
Winston Harwood,	- -	"	–	5	
Moses Carter,	- -	"	–	5	

NAMES.			RANK.	TIME OF SERVICE.		REMARKS.
				Months.	Days.	
William Matthews,	-	-	Private,	–	5	
John Clark,	-	-	"	–	5	
Pleasant Smith,	-	-	"	–	5	
Thomas Gathright,	-	-	"	–	5	
William Ferress.	-	-	"	–	5	
Edward Gathright,	-	-	"	–	5	
John Francis,	-	-	"	–	5	
Edward Morriss,	-	-	"	–	5	
John W. Royster,	-	-	"	–	3	
Hobson Warriner,	-	-	"	–	5	
Jacob Truman,	-	-	"	–	5	
Dandridge Carter,	-	-	"	–	5	
Stephen Warriner,	-	-	"	–	2	
James Austin,	-	-	"	–	5	
Thomas Hamblett,	-	-	"	–	5	
Matthews Carter,	-	-	"	–	5	
John W. Lawrence,	-	-	"	–	5	
Joseph Goodman,	-	-	"	–	5	

MUSTER ROLL

Of Lieutenant William Allen's Guard of Infantry of Virginia Militia, Sixty-eighth Regiment, in the Service of the United States from the 3d day of December, 1814 to the 3d of January, 1815.

NAMES.	RANK.	TIME OF SERVICE.		REMARKS.
		Months.	Days.	
William Allen, - -.	Lieutenant,	1		
William Combs, - -	Ensign,	1		
Archibald B. Cambell, -	Sergeant,	1		
William Jones, - -	"	–	28	
William Thomas, - -	"	–	9	
Whitaker Lee, - -	Corporal,	–	28	
William M. Patrick, - -	"	1		
Joseph Volentine, - -	"	–	12	
—— Bacon, - -	Private,	–	6	
Dandridge Claiborne, -	"	1		
James Christain, - -	"	–	8	
—— Crowdus, - -	"	–	6	
William Durfey, - -	"	–	28	
—— Dunkin, - -	"	–	26	
Thomas Gayle, - -	"	–	26	
Leven Gordon, - -	"			
Howard Shield, - -	"	1		
James Scemple, - -	"	1		
Bayley Smith, - -	"			
Eddingborough, - -	Wagoner,			
Joseph Waid, - -	Private,	–	2	

Captain Joseph Ames' Company—2d Regiment.

NAMES.	RANK.	TIME OF SERVICE.		REMARKS.
		Months.	Days.	
Joseph Ames, - -	Captain,	–	7	
Charles Smith, - -	Lieutenant.	–	7	
Abel W. Kellum, - -	Ensign,	–	7	
James Kellum, - -	Q. M. Serg't.	–	7	
William Collonna, - -	1st Sergeant,	–	13	
William Collorind, - -	"	–	6	
Richard Ames, - -	2d "	–	7	
Thomas H. Ames, - -	3d "	–	19	
John F. Mears, - -	4th "	–	13	
John Benson, - -	Drummer,	–	7	
Samuel Ames, - -	Fifer,	–	13	
Thomas C. Mears, - -	Private,	–	13	
Samuel Tradon, - -	"	–	7	
Stringer Kellum, - -	"	–	13	
Babel Sturgis, - -	"	1	7	
John M. Ames, - -	"	–	9	
William Addison, - -	"	–	19	
Selby Copes, - -	"	–	13	
William Slaths, - -	"	–	7	
William McHolloms, - -	"	–	7	
Jonathan Killim, - -	"	–	19	
William Martin, - -	"	–	7	
Ezekiel Mason, - -	"	–	7	
George Mason, - -	"	–	7	
Churchil Ames, - -	"	–	7	
William Person, - -	"	–	7	
John A. Ames, - -	"	–	7	
Henry Window, - -	"	–	7	
Luther Mears, - -	"	–	13	
Edward Martin, - -	"	–	13	
Richard Turner, - -	"	–	7	
Edmund Hutchinson, - -	"	–	7	
William Turner, - -	"	–	13	
John Hornsby, - -	"	–	13	
James Stewart, - -	"	–	24	
Calvin Kellum, - -	"	–	19	
Augustine Waterfield, - -	"	–	13	
John Smith, (R. S.) - -	"	–	7	
William Waterfield, - -	"	–	21	
Luther Kellum, - -	"	–	7	
Evans Kellum, - -	"	–	13	
Shepherd Kellum, - -	"	1	19	
John Mason, - -	"	–	3	
John Copes, - -	"	–	7	
James Hornsby, - -	"	–	7	
Southa Satchell, - -	"	–	13	
William Satchell, - -	"	–	7	
David Watson, - -	"	–	7	
Michell S. West, - -	"	–	16	
Jessee Ames, - -	"	–	7	
Rich'd Cutler, - -	"	–	6	
Jehu Davis, - -	"	–	6	
Thos. V. Hack, - -	"	–	18	
James Ritchinson, - -	"	–	14	

NAMES.	RANK.	TIME OF SERVICE.		REMARKS.
		Months.	Days.	
Ezekiel Ashby, - -	Private,	–	16	
George Babe, - -	"	–	24	
Nehemiah Copes, - -	"	–	8	
Henry Hornsby, - -	"	–	8	
William P. Johnson, -	"	1	8	Or Fowler.
Henry Fowles, - -	"	–	4	
Henry Howley, - -	"	–	24	
Henry Stewart, - -	"	–	8	
James Ames, - -	"	–	26	
Pary Belote, - -	"	–	21	
Benjamin Ames, - -	"	–	17	
James Daily, - -	"	–	17	
Henry Fowler, - -	"	–	8	
John Wise, - -	"	–	16	
Severn Young, - -	"	–	18	
James Bunting, - -	"	–	9	
James Colonna, - -	"	–	9	
Thomas Pusey, - -	"	–	9	
Churchill Ames, - -	"	–	6	

(For rest of this company, see publication of Pay Rolls.)

Captain Walter Anderson's Company—Thirty-seventh Regiment.

NAMES.	RANK.	TIME OF SERVICE.		REMARKS.
		Months.	Days.	
Thos. Keeve, - -	1st Sergeant,	–	4	
Richard Morrison, - -	3d "	–	7	
Thos. Cambell, - -	Fifer,	–	6	
Samuel Berry. - -	Private,	–	27	
Spencer M. Bluford, - -	"	–	16	
James Beattey, - -	"	–	16	
Thomas Conaway, - -	"	–	24	
Hiram Corbell, - -	"	–	9	
Samuel Cackarill, - -	"	–	1	
George Coles. - -	"	–	17	
Joseph L. Edwards, - -	"	–	19	
John George, - -	"	–	16	
John W. Hayes, - -	"	–	17	
James Harrison, - -	"	–	8	
George Hays, - -	"	–	1	
John Hunt, jr. - -	"	–	11	
John Hunt, sr. - -	"	–	20	
William Jones, - -	"	–	18	
Samuel Jones, - -	"	–	14	
John Kenedy, - -	"	–	7	
Charles S. Kent, - -	"	–	2	
John Moore, - -	"	–	9	
John Nelms, - -	"	–	19	
William Sebred, - -	"	–	4	
Henry Waren, (or Warren,)	"	–	15	
Joseph Walker, - -	"	–	15	
Martin Williams, - -	"	–	3	
William Wilkins, - -	"	–	3	

(For rest of this company, see publication of **Pay Rolls.**)

MUSTER ROLL

Of Captain Patrick Anderson's Company of the Seventy-fourth Regiment, Virginia Militia, commanded by Lieutenant Colonel William Trueheart, in the Service of the United States from 20th to 29th March, from 27th to 29th June, and from 1st to 2d July, in the year 1813.

NAMES.	RANK.	TIME OF SERVICE.		REMARKS.
		Months.	Days.	
Patrick Anderson, - -	Captain,	–	14	
James Gentry, - -	Lieutenant,	–	11	
Thomas G. Tinsley, - -	Ensign,	–	14	
Henry Langford, - -	Sergeant,	–	14	
Obadiah Archer, - -	"	–	14	
Dimack Hay, - -	"	–	14	
James Kirby, - -	"	–	14	
Bartlett Anderson, - -	Private,	–	14	
John Anderson, - -	"	–	14	
James Andrews, - -	"	–	13	
Obadiah Atkinson, - -	"	–	14	
Benjamin Brand, - -	"	–	13	
Overton Butler, - -	"	–	1	
John Brooks, - -	"	–	14	
Nathan Bumpass, - -	"	–	14	
David Clarke, - -	"	–	12	
Henry Curtis, - -	"	–	14	
James B. Clarke, - -	"	–	14	
David R. Clarke, - -	"	–	14	
Christopher Corthan, - -	"	–	2	
Joseph Clarke, jr. - -	"	–	4	
Pitman Dobson, - -	"	–	14	
Wm. C. Eggleston, - -	"	–	14	
Joseph N. Edmundson, - -	"	–	3	
Richard Epperson, - -	"	–	4	
William Gardner, - -	"	–	14	
Henry D. Gentry, - -	"	–	14	
Fleming Green, - -	"	–	14	
Edward B. Geddy, - -	"	–	14	
Jeremiah Hooper, - -	"	–	14	
Rice Hughes, - -	"	–	14	
Fleming Hughes, - -	"	–	1	
John Haw (or Hane,) - -	"	–	14	
Isaac Hay, - - -	"	–	14	
Richard H. Johnson, - -	"	–	14	
John Jenkins, - -	"	–	14	
John Jones, - - -	"	–	14	
Elisha Kirby, - -	"	–	14	
Matthew Kersey, - -	"	–	14	
Francis E. Kindrick, - -	"	–	4	
Thomas Lumpkin, - -	"	–	14	
Robert Lumpkin, - -	"	–	14	
James Littlepage, - -	"	–	14	
William Lyle, - -	"	–	14	
John K. Miller, - -	"	–	14	
Robert Martin, - -	"	–	14	
Hezekiah Muntillo, - -	"	–	14	

NAMES.	RANK.	TIME OF SERVICE.		REMARKS.
		Months.	Days.	
Henry W. Nicholes, -	Private,	—	14	
William R. Nelson, - -	"	—	14	
Isaac Oliver, - -	"	—	14	
John Oliver, - -	"	—	13	
Thomas B. Puller, - -	"	—	14	
Robert Page, - -	"	—	14	
John Puller, - -	"	—	14	
John Patterson, -	"	—	14	
Cobbett Richardson, -	"	—	14	
Patrick Roane, - -	"	—	4	
George W. Rabinan, -	"	—	10	
William Sizer, -	"	—	14	
William Sansom, - -	"	—	14	
William Smith, -	"	—	14	
Robert Sherlock, jr. - -	"	—	13	
Thomas Tyler, - -	"	—	14	
Benjamin Tyler, - -	"	—	12	
Thruston Thomas, - -	"	—	14	
Nicholas Talley. -	"	—	12	
James Thomas, - -	"	—	14	
William Thomas, - -	"	—	14	
William Tombs, - -	"	—	14	
Lewis Trueheart, - -	"	—	14	
James V. Tyler, - -	"	—	14	
John P. Tyler, - -	"	—	14	
Skelton Tyler, - -	"	—	12	
John Talley, - -	"	—	14	
James Tyler, - -	"	—	12	
Elkanah Talley. -	"	—	14	
John Talley, (son of Billey,) -	"	—	14	
Billey Talley, - -	"	—	14	
Benjamin B. Tyler, -	"	—	14	
Nathaniel Talley, - -	"	—	14	
Zachariah Tyler, - -	"	—	4	
William Via, - -	"	—	14	
Claiborne Wicker, - -	"	—	4	
Robert White, - -	"	—	14	
Charles Whitlock, - -	"	—	14	
James Whitlock, - -	"	—	7	
Benjamin West, - -	"	—	13	
Nathaniel Whitlock, -	"	—	9	
David Wade, - -	"	—	12	
William White, - -	"	—	14	
Elliott Wicker, - -	"	—	11	

[Muster Roll missing—Pay Roll copied.]

PAY ROLL

Of Captain Branch Archer's Company of Mounted Infantry, commanded by Col.
T. M. Randolph, in the service of the United States, attached to the Corps d'Elite.

NAMES.			RANK.	TIME OF SERVICE.		REMARKS.
				Months.	Days.	
Branch Archer,	-	-	Captain,	–	21	
John Matthews,	-	-	1st Lieutenant,	–	21	
William A. Shelton,	-	-	2d "	–	16	
Anthony M. Dupey,	-	-	Ensign,	–	21	
Samuel Flournoy,	-	-	1st Sergeant,	–	21	
John Randolph,	-	-	2d "	–	4	Promoted Sept. 3d.
John Bentley,	-	-	3d "	–	21	
Charles Clark,	-	-	4th "	–	21	
Charles Littlepage,	-	-	1st Corporal,	–	21	
Rich'd Randolph,	-	-	2d "	–	21	
William Wash,	-	-	3d "	–	21	
James R. Vaughan,	-	-	4th "	–	21	
Samuel Booker,	-	-	Private,	–	21	
Hugh Orven,	-	-	"	–	21	
Katita Townly,	-	-	"	–	21	
Geo. B. Poindexter,	-	-	"	–	21	
Samuel Hunter,	-	-	"	–	21	
William Cosby,	-	-	"	–	21	
Geo. Hunt,	-	-	"	–	21	
John Briggs,	-	-	"	–	21	
Walker Bowler,	-	-	"	–	21	
William H. Barker,	-	-	"	–	21	
John Butler,	-	-	"	–	21	
Edward Cox,	-	-	"	–	21	
Peter Archer,	-	-	"	–	21	
John Goode,	-	-	"	–	21	
Edw'd Morgan,	-	-	"	–	21	
Rich'd Wilkinson,	-	-	"	–	21	
Benj'n Watkins,	-	-	"	–	21	
George Harris,	-	-	"	–	21	
Thomas Woodfin,	-	-	"	–	21	
Wm. G. Povall,	-	-	"	–	21	
Stokes Tinstall,	-	-	"	–	21	
William A. Cocke,	-	-	"	–	21	
Henry Watkins,	-	-	"	–	21	
Elam Ross,	-	-	"	–	21	
Elijah Caruthers,	-	-	"	–	21	
Elbert Mosby,	-	-	"	–	21	
William Taylor,	-	-	"	–	21	
Jos. Mosby,	-	-	"	–	21	
John Netherland,	-	-	"	–	21	
Thurston Netherland,	-	-	"	–	21	
Samuel Flanagan,	-	-	"	–	21	

NAMES.			RANK.	TIME OF SERVICE.		REMARKS.
				Months.	Days.	
Samuel Flanagan,	-	-	Private,	–	21	
Uriah Owen,	-	-	"	–	21	
Charles A. Scott,	-	-	"	–	21	
John Dyer,	-	-	"	–	21	
Reuben Lewis,	-	-	"	–	21	
Charles L. Banket.	-	-	"	–	21	
Geo. Wood,	-	-		–	21	
Peter Garland,	-	-	"	–	21	
Chs. M. Brand,	-	-	"	–	21	
Nelson Shelton.	-	-	"	–	21	

MUSTER ROLL

Of Captain Edward Archer's Company of Virginia Militia, from Twenty-third Regiment, commanded by Colonel William Brown, in the Service from 17th to the 29th of March, from 27th to 28th of June, and from 30th day of June to the 20th day of July, 1813.

NAMES.	RANK.	TIME OF SERVICE.		REMARKS
		Months.	Days.	
Edward Archer, - -	Captain,	—	18	
Thomas Stratton, - -	Lieutenant,	—	18	
Samuel Clay, - -	Ensign,	—	18	
Henry Cox, - -	1st Sergeant.	—	18	
Charles E. Featherton, -	2d "	—	18	
John Walthall, - -	3d "	—	13	
Frank Walthall, - -	4th "	—	13	
Thomas Lambert, - -	Private,	—	15	
Joseph Dillon, - -	"	—	18	
William Stewart, - -	"	—	18	
James Hall, - -	"	—	18	
George Cox, - -	"	—	18	
Thomas Cousin. - -	"	—	18	
Armstead Hill, - -	"	—	15	
Thomas Hare, - -	"	—	18	
Thomas Wilson, - -	"	—	18	
David Johnston, - -	"	—	18	
John Stewart, - -	"	—	18	
John Varner, - -	"	—	18	
Benjamin Walthall, -	"	—	18	
Thomas Howlett, - -	"	—	18	
John Covington, - -	"	—	18	
Robert Royall, - -	"	—	18	
Rich'd Warwick, - -	"	—	18	
Peter F. Edwards, -	"	—	18	
Jacob Breutt, - -	"	—	18	
Henry Varner, - -	"	—	18	
Peter Varner, - -	"	—	18	
Thomas Hatchet. - -	"	—	18	
William Munk. - -	"	—	18	
Erby Fuqua, - -	"	—	18	
William Moody, - -	"	—	18	
Anthony K. Erby, -	"	—	18	
Theo. F. Strachen, -	"	—	18	
William Covington, -	"	—	18	
Joseph Whiteford, -	"	—	15	
Alexander Biggleston, -	"	—	18	
Solomon Baugh, - -	"	—	15	
Thomas Butte, - -	"	—	18	
Edw'd A. May, - -	"	—	18	
Bur. O. Descar, - -	"	—	13	
Simon Fraserx, - -	"	—	13	
James Stuart, - -	"	—	13	
John Jackson, - -	"	—	13	
John Nobes, - -	"	—	13	
Samuel Goode, - -	"	—	13	

NAMES.	RANK.	TIME OF SERVICE.		REMARKS.
		Months.	Days.	
Joseph Dudley, - -	Private,	–	13	
Peyton Fuqua, - -	"	–	13	
Thomas Marsh, - -	"	–	13	
Emanuel Blankenship, -	"	–	13	
John Childers, - -	"	–	13	

Captain Thomas Archer's Company—68th Regiment.

NAMES.	RANK.	TIME OF SERVICE.		REMARKS.
		Months.	Days.	
Thomas Austin, - -	Corporal,	—	22	
Quarles Bohannon. - -	Private,	—	11	
Williams Inge, senr. - -	"	—	7	
Joseph Wade, -	"	—	13	
William H. Wynn, - -	"	—	22	
William Williams, - -	"	—	22	
Matthew Wood, - -	"	—	22	
Richard Preston, - -	Drummer,	—	19	
Edingborough, - -	Wagoner,	—	26	
William Hubberd, - -	"	—	14	
Simeon Block, - -	"	—	22	
William Charles, senr. -	"	—	12	
Henry Charles, - -	"	—	—	
William Ernest, - -	"	..	—	Time not given.
Elliott Kemp, - -	"	—	—	
John Garrett, - -	"	—	22	
Thomas Harwood, - -	"	—	22	
Robert Lee, - -	"	—	22	
John Hague, - -	"	—	13	
John Moss, - -	"	—	2	
William Patrick, - -	"	—	22	
William Proby, - -	"			
Zac. Shackeford. - -	"	—	4	
Nathaniel Young, - -	"	—	22	
Otway Shields, - -	"	—	20	
John Crawley, - -	"	—	24	
Hugh Freeman, - -	"	—	18	
John Jones, - -	"	—	25	
Daniel Jones, - -	"			
Francis Moody, - -	"	—	5	
John Pearman, - -	"			
John D. Smith, - -	"	—	26	
Robert B. Travis. - -	"			
Bowling Vaughan. - -	"	—	23	

(For rest of this company, see publication of Pay Rolls.)

MUSTER ROLL

Of Captain David Armistead's Company of Infantry, from the Fifty-second Regiment, Virginia Militia, in the Service from 28th June to the 13th July, 1813.

NAMES.	RANK.	TIME OF SERVICE.		REMARKS.
		Months.	Days.	
David Armistead, - -	Captain,	–	17	
Alex. Walker, - -	Lieutenant,	–	17	
Benjamin Marrable, -	Ensign,	–	17	
John Lambe, -	Sergeant,	–	17	
William R. Colgin, - -	"	–	17	
Robert Holdcraft, - -	"	–	17	
Jno. Willison, - -	"	–	17	
Charles Barrow, - -	Corporal,	–	17	
Joseph Jerdone, - -	"	–	17	
Robert West, - -	"	–	17	
Edw'd Young, - -	"	–	17	
William Ammons, - -	Private,	–	17	
John F. Brown, - -	"	–	17	
John Dean, - -	"	–	17	
William Haynes, - -	"	–	17	
John Hughes, - -	"	–	17	
William Snips, - -	"	–	17	
Geo. B. Taylor, - -	"	–	17	
Benj. Worberton, - -	"	–	17	
Thos. Worberton, - -	"	–	17	
Isaac Woodcock, - -	"	–	17	
John Young, - -	"	–	17	
Major Taylor, - -	"	–	17	
William Apperson, - -	"	–	17	
John Barrow, - -	"	–	17	
John Hall, - -	"	–	17	

Captain John Armistead's Company—52d Regiment.

NAMES.	RANK.	TIME OF SERVICE.		REMARKS.
		Months.	Days.	
John Armistead,	Captain,	–	16	
Henry Armistead,	1st Lieutenant,	–	16	
William Edloe,	2d Lieutenant,	–	16	
James Harrison,	Sergeant,	–	16	
James B. Southall,	"	–	16	
Henry Walker,	"	–	16	
Joseph Gresham,	Corporal,	–	16	
Anthony H. Lamb,	"	–	16	
Richmond Finch,	"	–	16	
Nat. Eshon,	Drum Major,	–	16	
John Binns,	Private,	–	16	
M. S. Bradley,	"	–	16	
John Bullifant,	"	–	16	
David Blanks,	"	–	16	
John Blayton,	"	–	16	
James J. Bullifant,	"	–	16	
John L. Bacon,	"	–	16	
George Chandler,	"	–	16	
James Charles,	"	..	16	
Jno. C. Chandler,	"	–	16	
Rivers Collier,	"	–	16	
Nick Dillard,	"	–	16	
John Dolly,	"	–	16	
William Davidson,	"	–	16	
Henry Davidson,	"	–	16	
Christopher P. Deane,	"	–	16	
James M. Hopkins,	"	–	16	
Robert A. Hill,	"	–	16	
Robert Meauley,	"	–	16	
Thomas Orange,	"	–	16	
Patrick Pond,	"	–	16	
John Presson,	"	–	16	
Edward Mocock,	"	–	16	
John Ricketts,	"	–	16	
John Spraggins,	"	–	16	
John W. Shearman,	"	–	16	
William L. Shell,	"	–	16	
Stephen Southall,	"	–	16	
Manton D. Shell,	"	–	16	
Peyton Via,	"	–	16	
John Wright,	"	–	16	
William B. Wilcox,	"	–	16	
Com. Young,	"	–	16	
Henry H. Southall,	4	–	16	Appointed door-keeper to the Virginia legislature.
Benj. Vaughan,	2	–	16	Ditto.

(For rest of this company, see publication of Pay Rolls.)

MUSTER ROLL

Of Captain John P. Armistead's Company of Infantry of the One Hundred and Fifteenth Regiment, commanded by Lieutenant Colonel Henry Howard, in Service from the 24th October to 7th November, 1814.

NAMES.		RANK.	TIME OF SERVICE.		REMARKS.
			Months.	Days.	
John P. Armistead,	- -	Captain,	1		
Thomas W. Cary,	- -	1st Lieutenant,	–	15	
John W. Jones,	- -	Lieutenant,	–	15	
G. M. Armistead,	- -	Ensign,	–	15	
William Langhoone,	- -	Sergeant,	–	15	
Henry Robinson,	- -	"	–	15	
Robert Seymour,	- -	"	–	15	
Geo. Hope,	- -	"	–	15	James Wood substitute.
William R. Guy,	- -	"	–	15	
Robert Noel,	- -	Corporal,	–	15	
Robert Toppin,	- -	"	–	15	
Thomas Marrow,	- -	"	–	15	
William Hope,	- -	"	–	15	
John Routon,	- -	"	–	15	
Merit Parson,	- -	Drummer,	–	15	
William Armistead,	- -	Private,	–	15	
William Bean,	- -	"	–	15	
Smith Burton,	- -	"	–	15	
William Bushel,	- -	"	–	15	
Edward Bains,	- -	"	–	13	
John C. Brown,	- -	"	–	13	
John Bushell,	- -	"	–	13	
William Calvert,	- -	"	–	13	
Type L. Charles,	- -	"	–	15	
Henry B. Cooper,	- -	"	–	15	
William Davis,	- -	"	–	24	
Thomas Dewbrey,	- -	"	–	15	Robt. Seldon sub.
Ezekiel Drummond,	- -	"	–	15	Will'm Parkinton sub.
John Daws,	- -	"	–	13	Jno. Stansworth sub.
George Fisher,	- -	"	–	15	
Devorax Gordon,	- -	"	–	13	
Samuel Guy,	- -	"	–	15	
Nathaniel Haughten,	- -	"	–	15	
Jesse Hopkins,	- -	"	–	10	
William C. Hicks,	- -	"	–	15	
William Hope,	- -	"	–	15	Edward Bennet sub.
William Hickman,	- -	"	–	12	Robert Turlington sub.
William Hawkins,	- -	"	–	15	Rich'd Barrow sub.
Will'm S. Ironmonger,	- -	"	–	15	
Joseph S. Latimer,	- -	"	–	15	William Clark sub.
Moses Lawrence,	- -	"	–	15	
Bagwell Lawrence,	- -	"	–	15	
John Lewis,	- -	"	–	15	
George Latimer,	- -	"	–	14	
Thomas Latimer,	- -	"	–	14	
Rich'd McIntosh,	- -	"	–	14	
William Means,	- -	"	–	14	
George Melson,	- -	"	–	14	

NAMES.	RANK.	TIME OF SERVICE.		REMARKS.
		Months.	Days.	
Thomas Minson, - -	Private,	–	10	
Thomas Melson, - -	"	–	15	
Thomas Moning, - -	"	–	15	William Russel sub.
William S. Mallory, - -	"	–	15	John Crandal sub.
Allen McHolland, - -	"	–	14	
William V. Netles, - -	"	–	15	
George Randolph, - -	"	–	14	
Zerobabel Roberts, - -	"	–	1	
John Pool, jr. - -	"	–	10	
James Smaw, - -	"	–	15	
William Smaw, - -	"	–	11	
John Sherrington. - .	"	–	15	
Levin Smith, - -	"	–	15	
Richard Tennis, - -	"	–	15	Rob't Wilson sub.
Branson Turner, - -	"	–	14	
Will'm Whitaker, - -	"	–	14	
James Wilson, - -	"	–	14	
Edward Whitaker, - -	"	–	15	
George Wills, - -	"	–	14	Will'm Budd sub.
John Waymouth, - -	"	–	14	
Severn Watson, - -	"	–	13	
John Wilson, - -	"	–	14	
Richard Wilson, - -	"	–	13	
Thomas Young, - -	"	–	14	

Captain Thomas Armstrong's Company—Fourth Regiment.

NAMES.	RANK.	TIME OF SERVICE.		REMARKS.
		Months.	Days.	
Leonard Stamper, - -	1st Sergeant,	–	5	
John Lunsford, - -	"	–	5	
William Dunaway, - -	"	–	15	
Henry Pullin. - -	Corporal,	–	5	
William C. McTyre - -	"	–	5	
William Doggett, - -	Private,	5		
Thos. Garner, - -	"	–	5	
John Dunaway, - -	"	–	3	
William Berrick, - -	"	1	28	
Thomas Sullivant, - -	"	–	2	
Frederick Walker, - -	"	–	5	
John Langsford, - -	"			

(For rest of this company, see publication of Pay Rolls.)

MUSTER ROLL

Of Lieutenant John Arnold's Company of Virginia Militia, from the Twenty-fifth Regiment, commanded by Lieutenant Colonel Austin Smith, in the Service of the United States from the 20th of July to 5th August and from the 23d day of August to 3d September, 1814.

NAMES.	RANK.	TIME OF SERVICE.		REMARKS.
		Months.	Days.	
John Arnold, - -	Lieutenant,	–	27	
Joel T. Doniphan, - -	Ensign,	–	12	
Joseph Suttle, ..	"	–	14	
George H. Bullard, - -	Sergeant,	–	12	
John Payne, - -	"	–	28	
William D. Green, - -	"	–	12	
William Kelly, - -	"	–	12	
Massey Thomas, - -	"	–	14	
Austin Suttle, - -	"	–	14	
James Dishman, - -	Corporal,	–	23	
Watts Jones, - -	"	–	12	
John Spilman, - -	"	–	27	
James Went, - -	"	–	12	
Stephen Wilkerson, - -	"	–	14	
Philip Jones, - -	–	–	14	
Geo. Armstrong, - -	Private,	–	27	
Thornton Atwell, - -	"	–	26	
John N. Ashton, - -	"	–	12	
James E. Buller, - -	"	–	26	
Leftridge Bruce, - -	"	–	12	
James Bruce, - -	"	–	12	
Standly Baissa, - -	"	–	12	
Bennett Chrismond, - -	"	–	26	
Lewis Carter, - -	"	–	10	
John Davis, - -	"	–	12	
William Davis, - -	"	–	12	
William Dodd, - -	"	–	14	
John Fisher, - -	"	–	25	
Jeremiah Elkins, - -	"	–	12	
John Elkins, - -	"	–	12	
John Goldsmith, -	"	–	24	
John L. Gubernaton, -	"	–	24	
Daniel Garner, - -	"	–	12	
Burdett Heflin, - -	"	–	27	
James Holliday, - -	"	–	12	
Benjamin Hailes, - -	"	–	12	
Edward Inscoe, - -	"	–	8	Deserted 30th August 1814.
Elijah Inscoe, - -	"	–	8	" " "
William Johnson, - -	"	–	12	
James Jackson, - -	"	–	12	
Sidney Jones, - -	"	–	12	
Joseph Jones, - -	"	–	26	
George Jones, - -	"	–	14	
William Jett, - -	"	–	12	
James Lee, - -	"	–	12	
John Limbrick, - -	"	–	12	

NAMES.	RANK.	TIME OF SERVICE.		REMARKS.
		Months.	Days.	
Enus Monteeth. - -	Private,	–	12	
Gilbret Morgan, - -	"	–	21	Deserted 28th August 1814.
John McCarty. - -	"	–	12	
Thomas Morgan, - -	"	–	21	Deserted 28th August 1814.
John H. Micou, - -	"	–	26	
William Marders, - -	"	–	26	
William R. Massey, - -	"	–	14	
Geo. Pollard, - -	"	–	12	
James Prim, - -	"	–	26	
William Rollins, - -	"	–	26	
Samuel Rollins, - -	"	–	26	
William Rose, - -	"	–	12	
Gustavius G. Rogers. - -	"	–	12	
James Stephens. - -	"	–	27	
William Scott, - -	"	–	12	Sub. Henry Wallace.
James Staples. - -	"	–	15	
Thomas Stephens, - -	"	–	15	
William Thompson. - -	"	–	27	
John White, - -	"	–	12	
John Worrell, - -	"	–	27	
Augustin Weedon, - -	"	–	27	
Isaac Wood, - -	"	–	12	
John Wine, - -	"	–	12	
Stephen White. - -	"	–	12	
Geo. White, - -	"	–	12	
William White, - -	"	–	12	

Captain David Ashby's Company—Second Regiment.

NAMES.		RANK.	TIME OF SERVICE.		REMARKS.
			Months.	Days.	
Rich'd Tatham,	- -	4th Corporal.	–	8	
Abel Burfoot, sr.	- -	Private,	1	3	
William Bell,	- -	"	–	17	
Savage Davis,	- -	"	1	7	
John Garrison,	- -	"	–	6	
James Glen,	- -	"	–	6	
Benj. Harrison,	- -	"	–	17	
Custis Kellam,	- . -	"	–	23	
Jesse Lewis,	- -	"	–	25	
John Mears, (of Levin,)	-	"	–	23	
Geo. Mapp,	- -	"	–	29	
William Richardson,	- -	"	–	27	
Jeremiah Stockley,	- -	"	–	24	
William F. Savage,	- -	"	–	11	
Rickets Tatham,	- -	"	–	15	
James Mears, (of E.)	-	"	–	6	
Lewis Mears,	- -	"			
James Walker,	- -	"	–	6	
John Ames,	- -	"	–	6	

(For rest of this company, see publication of Pay Rolls.)

MUSTER ROLL

Of Captain John N. Ashton's Company of Infantry of Virginia Militia, from Twenty-fifth Regiment, in the County of King George, in the Service from July 15 to July 1813.

NAMES.	RANK.	Months.	Days.	REMARKS.
John N. Ashton,	Captain,	–	12	
David T. Chevis,	Lieutenant,	–	8	
James Edwards,	Ensign,	–	12	
Geo. T. Riding,	1st Sergeant,	–	8	
Enoch Edwards,	2d "	–	12	
William Piper,	3d "	–	12	
John Payne,	4th "	–	12	
Charles Jones,	Private,	–	8	
Edward Inscoe,	"	–	8	
Gilbert Morgan,	"	–	12	
Geo. Pritchett,	"	–	12	
Stephen Marders,	"	–	11	
John Worrell, jr.	"	–	12	
James Pursley,	"	–	8	
James Marders,	"	–	8	
John Berry,	"	–	12	
Peter Jones,	"	–	12	
William Marders,	"	–	12	
Thomas Morgan,	"	–	8	
Thomas Pursley,	"	–	8	
William Greenlaw,	"	–	3	Sub. J. Marders.
Thomas Inscoe,	"	–	8	
William Potts,	"	–	7	
William Berry,	"	–	12	
John Dickerson,	"	–	12	
Thomas Eskridge,	"	–	12	
Elijah Inscoe,	"	–	12	
Samuel Atwell,	"	–	12	
James Lunsford,	"	–	8	
Benjamin Johnson,	"	–	12	
William Rollins,	"	–	12	
Reuben Cookley,	"	–	8	
Littleton Pursley,	"	–	8	
George Armstrong,	"	–	12	
James Bailey,	"	–	8	
Thomas Rose,	"	–	8	
John Prin,	"	–	12	
John Marders,	"	–	12	
Benjamin Prichett,	"	–	8	
Felding Owens,	"	–	8	
John Boutwell,	"	–	12	
Monga R. Micou,	"	–	11	Or George
Samuel O. Wilkinson,	"	–	11	
John Woodell, sr.	"	–	12	
Ritchie Alsop,	"	–	11	
William Marders,	"	–	11	
Richard Potts,	"	–	12	
Benjamin Rogers,	"	–	8	
David Jones,	"	–	8	
John Marders, sr.	"	–	9	

MUSTER ROLL

Of Ensign Archibald Atkinson's Company of Riflemen, Virginia Militia, detached from 29th Regiment, commanded by Lieut. Col. Francis M. Boykin, in the Service of the State of Virginia, from 28th day of August to the 13th day of September, 1813.

NAMES.	RANK.	TIME OF SERVICE.		REMARKS.
		Months.	Days.	
Archibald Atkinson,	Ensign,	–	17	
Mills Stephenson,	1st Sergeant,	–	17	
David Tynes,	2d "	–	17	
Benjn. L. Edwards,	3d "	–	17	
William Dixon,	4th "	–	17	
James Jones,	1st Corporal,	–	17	
George Gray,	2d "	–	17	
Robert Montgomery,	3d "	–	17	
Hardy Jones,	4th "	–	17	
Josiah Jones,	Musician,	–	17	
Thomas Bullock,	Private,	–	17	
Thomas S. Cofer,	"	–	17	
John Dixon,	"	–	17	
Richard Gray,	"	–	17	
Harrison Glover,	"	–	17	
Joseph Hall,	"	–	17	
George Hall,	"	–	17	
Jonathan Holleman,	"	–	17	
Samuel Harriss,	"	–	17	
John Harriss,	"	–	17	
Peter Holcome,	"	–	17	
Benjamin Hutchins,	"	–	17	
Thomas Jones,	"	–	17	
James Murray,	"	–	17	
Ridick Montgomery,	"	–	17	
Alexander McDougall,	"	–	17	
Travis Philips,	"	–	17	
Cartwright Price,	"	–	17	
Elisha Sutland,	"	–	17	
Joseph Stroud.	"	–	17	
James Stallings,	"	–	17	
James Shivers,	"	–	17	
Henry Tynes,	"	–	17	
David Tynes,	"	–	17	
Charles Wailo,	"	–	17	

[Pay Roll copied—Muster Roll missing.]

PAY ROLL

Of Captain Joseph Atkinson's Troop of Cavalry of the Twenty-ninth Regiment, Virginia Militia, commanded by Lieutenant Colonel Francis M. Boykin, in the Service from 29th August to 8th September, and from 27th September to 21st October, in the year 1814.

NAMES.	RANK.	TIME OF SERVICE.		REMARKS.
		Months.	Days.	
Joseph Atkinson,	Captain,	1	7	
Robert West,	1st Lieutenant.	1	7	
Geo. Wilson,	2d "	1	7	
Thomas Day,	1st Sergeant,	1	7	
Nathaniel Cocke,	2d "	1	7	
James Johnson,	3d "	1	7	
William Davis,	4th "	—	11	
James Wilson,	1st Corporal,	—	11	
William Gibbs,	2d "	—	11	
Edmund Pedin,	3d "	—	11	
Merit Jordon,	4th "	—	11	
Levy Addison,	Trumpeter,	1	7	
George Aplewhaite,	Private,	1	7	
John Buckhurst,	"	1	7	
Benjamin Bailow,	"	—	11	
Jessee Brett,	"	1	7	
John Bowden,	"	—	26	
David Clark,	"	—	11	
Samuel Carrol,	"	—	11	
Bailey Davis,	"	1	7	
John Dannel,	"	1	7	
Robert Deford,	"	—	26	
Thomas Dews,	"	—	11	
Edward Gray,	"	1	7	
Ludwell Gualtney,	"	—	11	
William Gills,	"	—	26	
Morriss Hatchel,	"	1	7	
William Holleman,	"	—	26	
Lewis Johnson,	"	1	7	
Joseph Joyner,	"	1	7	
Joseph Jordan,	"	—	11	
Robert Lawrence,	"	—	26	
John Levy,	"	1	7	
Josiah Mercer,	"	1	7	
Thomas McWilliams,	"	1	7	
Benjamin Nelson,	"	—	11	
Edmund Pedin,	"	—	26	
Samuel Thomas,	"	—	11	
Josiah Thomas,	"	—	11	
Mills Whitfield,	"	1	7	
James White,	"	—	11	
James Wheadon,	"	1	7	

Captain Thomas T. Attwell's Company—37th Regiment.

NAMES.	RANK.	TIME OF SERVICE.		REMARKS.
		Months.	Days.	
Hamor Webb,	Ensign,	–	15	
Washington Haynie,	Sergeant,	–	9	
Charles Betts,	"	–	6	
John L. Chinn,	"	–	10	
Holland H. Spriggs,	Drummer,	–	11	
John George,	Fifer,			
Joseph Humphries.	Private,	–	16	
Bridgar Haynie,	"	1	9	
Elias Haynie,	"	–	20	
Jordan Haynie,	"	–	10	
Isaac Haynie,	"	–	3	
Peter Hall,	"	–	3	
Austin Haynie,	"	–	10	
Willis W. Hudnall,	"	–	2	
Hiram Haynie,	"	–	10	
Elias Hughlett,	"	–	11	
Chichester Haynie,	"	–	6	
Stephen Hall,	"	–	3	
Lally Haynie,	"	–	10	
Henry Haynie,	"	–	7	
Gideon Haynie,	"	–	2	
Winder Haynie,	"	–	8	
Catesby Jones,	"	–	24	
Creton Jones,	"	–	17	
Morris Jones,	"	1	3	
John S. Kesterson,	"	–	28	
William Morrison,	"	–	10	
John Morrison,	"	–	10	
Thornton Marsh,	"	–	11	
John McCane (or McCaul,)	"	–	3	
Thomas Miller,	"	–	3	
Thomas Marsh,	"	–	7	
Holland Marsh,	"	–	2	
James Nightengill,	"	–	18	
Elismond Pitman,	"	–	3	
Gabriel Pritchett,	"	–	10	
Sam'l Robinson,	"	–	8	
Richard Swann,	"	1	3	
William Sullivant,	"	–	19	
Thomas T. Sydnor,	"	–	3	
William Swann,	"	–	10	
Aaron Spicer,	"	–	3	
Job M. Simms,	"	–	3	
Vincent Thomas,	"	–	7	
Lewis Ticer,	"	–	8	
William Ticer,	"	–	8	
Benjamin Walker,	"	–	7	
Jessee Burriss,	"	–	10	
Isaac Bailey,	"	–	17	
Joseph Burriss,	"	–	7	
Royston Botts, sen.	"	–	28	
William Betts,	"	–	8	
Isaac Bailiss,	"	–	15	

NAMES.	RANK.	TIME OF SERVICE.		REMARKS.
		Months.	Days.	
Richard Coles. - -	Private,	—	10	
Robert Crowther, - -	"	—	10	
William Crowther, - -	"	—	10	
Randall Crowther, - -	"	—	10	
Thomas Crowther, -	"	—	7	
Robert Christopher, -	"	—	8	
Samuel Y. Davis, - -	"	—	3	
John Dawson, - -	"	—	3	
William Dougherty, - -	"	—	10	
Robt. Davis, - -	"	—	10	
Richard Denny, - -	"	—	12	
Isaac Edwards, - -	"	—	10	
Richard Edwards, - -	"	—	3	
Griffin H. Foushee, - -	"	—	2	
James Farbush. - -	"	—	10	
Thos. French. - -	"	—	3	
Shap. P. Gill. - -	"	—	3	
Elisha Fallin. - -	"	—	12	

(For rest of this company, see publication of Pay Rolls.)

MUSTER ROLL

Of Captain John Bagby's Company of Virginia Militia, from the Fourth Regiment, commanded by Lieutenant Colonel Elliott Muse, in Service from the 4th to 14th April, 1813, and from the 2d to the 10th December, 1814.

NAMES.	RANK.	TIME OF SERVICE.		REMARKS.
		Months.	Days.	
John Bagby, - -	Captain,	–	19	
John Gill, - -	1st Lieutenant,	–	9	
Geo. Hill, - -	2d "	–	19	
Whit. Campbell, -	"	–	9	
Churchil Anderson, -	Cornet,	–	19	
Robt. S. Jones, -	"	–	10	
Baylor Temple, -	1st Sergeant,	–	19	
William Watts, -	2d "	–	19	Promoted
Reuben Garrett, -	3d "	–	9	
John Richards, -	4th "	–	9	
Zachariah Lewis, -	1st Sergeant.	–	10	
Thomas Walker, -	3d "	–	10	
Benony Gresham, -	1st Corporal,	–	19	"
Rich'd U. Buckner, -	2d "	–	19	"
Samuel Orrill, -	3d "	–	19	"
Thomas Atkins, -	Private,	–	10	
Henry A. Brown, -	"	–	9	
Richard Brown, -	"	–	9	
William Brown, -	"	–	19	
William Broaddus, -	"	–	19	
Lewis Brooks, -	"	–	9	
Ira Carlton, -	"	–	19	
William Carlton, -	"	–	9	
Thomas Carlton, -	"	–	9	
Thomas Covington. -	"	–	10	
Philip Clavely, -	"	–	10	
Nathan Carlton, -	"	–	10	
John Didlic, -	"	–	9	
Edward Fox, -	"	–	9	
Leroy Farenholtz, -	"	–	9	
Rich'd C. Faulkner, -	"	–	10	
Robt. Garrett, -	"	–	9	
Thomas Garrett, jr. -	"	–	19	
Thomas Garrett, sen. -	"	–	19	
Joseph Gatewood, -	"	–	19	
Asa Gresham, -	"	–	9	
James Guthrie, -	"	–	9	
John Gibson, -	"	–	9	
Henry Gleason, -	"	–	9	
Banks Garrett, -	"	–	10	
Thomas Golder, -	"	–	9	
Thomas W. Hart, -	"	–	9	
William B. Haskins, -	"	–	10	
Spencer Hoskins, -	"	–	10	
John Lumpkin, -	"	–	9	
Iverson Lewis, -	"	–	10	
Martin Lipscomb, -	"	–	10	
William Mann, -	"	–	9	

NAMES.	RANK.	TIME OF SERVICE.		REMARKS.
		Months.	Days.	
Richard Miller. - -	Private,	–	9	
John G. Meridith, - -	"	–	10	
Thomas Mecarty, - -	"	–	9	
Thomas Motley. - -	"	–	9	
John C. Montague, - -	"	–	9	
John G. Meredith, - -	"	–	9	
Henry Nunn, - -	"	–	9	
Thomas Nunn. - -	"	–	19	
William Newbill, - -	"	–	9	
Samuel Orrell, - -	"	–	10	
Robert Orrill, - -	"	–	10	
James Owen. - -	"	–	10	
John Pemberton. - -	"	–	19	
Robt. Pollard, - -	"	–	9	
John Radford. - -	"	–	10	
James Shackleford. - -	"	–	19	
Leonard Shackleford. -	"	–	10	
James Smith. - -	"	–	10	
Thomas Sebولis. - -	"	–	10	
Isaac Tignor. - -	"	–	9	
Rich'd Wyatt. - -	"	–	9	
Geo. Wyatt, - -	"	–	19	
Thomas Wyatt. - -	"	–	19	
William Wright. - -	"	–	19	
Henry Walker, - -	"	–	9	
John Watkins, - -	"	–	10	

MUSTER ROLL

Of Sergeant John Bagwell's detachment of Cavalry, from the Second Regiment, commanded by Lieutenant Colonel Thomas M. Bayley, in the Service of the United States, from the 4th to the 11th July, 1814.

NAMES.	RANK.	TIME OF SERVICE.		REMARKS.
		Months.	Days.	
John Bagwell,	1st Sergeant.	–	8	
Edward Boismard.	2d "	–	8	
Chas. Mason,	4th "	–	8	
William C. White.	Corporal.	–	8	
John C. Copes.	Private.	–	8	
William Grinalds,	"	–	8	
Thomas James.	"	–	8	
Nehemiah Stockley.	"	–	8	
John Poulson.	"	–	8	
Wiley J. Twiford.	"	–	8	

MUSTER ROLL

Of Lieutenant Ephraim Baird's Company of Militia, detached from Sixty-second Regiment, commanded by Colonel Miles Selden, in the Service of the State of Virginia, from the 30th June to 10th July, 1813.

NAMES.			RANK.	TIME OF SERVICE.		REMARKS.
				Months.	Days	
Ephraim Baird,	-	-	Lieutenant,	–	11	
Francis E. Rives,	-	-	Ensign,	–	11	
James L. Gee,	-	-	Sergeant,	–	11	
Thos. Gee,	-	-	"	–	11	
William Moore,	-	-	"	–	11	
William Simmons,	-	-	"	–	11	
Coleman Simmons,	-	-	Corporal,	–	11	
Peter Minger,	-	-	"	–	11	
John P. Hunnicut,	-	-	"	–	11	
Peter Tatum,	-	-	"	–	11	
James Baxter	-	-	Private,	–	11	
James T. Devenpart,	-	-	"	–	10	
Joseph Daniel,	-	-	"	–	11	
Dudley Fewqua,	-	-	"	–	10	
John Grammer,	-	-	"	–	10	
Henry Lee,	-	-	"	–	10	
Fredrick Grantham,	-	-	"	–	10	
Nicholas Hatch,	-	-	"	–	10	
William Heath,	-	-	"	–	10	
Joseph Heath,	-	-	"	–	10	
Rodrick Heath,	-	-	"	–	7	
Peter Ivy,	-	-	"	–	11	
John Livesay,	-	-	"	–	10	
Joel Livesay,	-	-	"	–	10	
Joel Lee,	-	-	"	–	11	
Alex. Lee,	-	-	"	–	11	
Francis Livesay,	-	-	"	–	10	
Wyatt Livesay,	-	-	"	–	10	
Larkin Smith,	-	-	"	–	7	
John Moore,	-	-	"	–	10	
Wilkins Smith,	-	-	"	–	10	
Joel Simmons,	-	-	"	–	9	
James G. Tatum,	-	-	"	–	10	
Hubbard Womack,	-	-	"	–	10	

PAY ROLL

Of Captain Briscoe G. Baldwin's Company—Thirty-second Regiment.

NAMES.		RANK.	TIME OF SERVICE.		REMARKS.
			Months.	Days.	
Peter G. Bower,	- -	Sergeant,	–	15	
Patrick Mellon,	- -	Musician,	1	13	
Hugh Hillis,	- -	"	1	13	

(For rest of this company, see publication of Pay Rolls.)

PAY ROLL

Of Captain John C. Baskins' Company—Thirty-second Regiment.

NAMES.			RANK.	TIME OF SERVICE.		REMARKS.
				Months.	Days.	
Tride Golady,	-	-	Ensign,	–	12	
Thomas Nowland,	-	-	Private,	1	10	
Daniel Nowles,	-	-	"	–	21	

(For rest of this company, see publication of Pay Rolls.)

PAY ROLL

Of Captain Samuel Blake's Company—One Hundred and Ninth Regiment.

NAMES.	RANK.	TIME OF SERVICE.		REMARKS.
		Months.	Days.	
James Baker, - -	Private,	–	11	
David Barrick. - -	"	–	11	

(For rest of this company, see publication of Pay Rolls.)

PAY ROLL

Of Sergeant Willis Barham's Guard of Militia, ordered out by Lieutenant Colonel William Allen, Commandant of the Seventy-first Regiment, in Service 5 days.

NAMES.	RANK.	TIME OF SERVICE.		REMARKS.
		Months.	Days.	
Willis Barham, - -	1st Sergeant,	–	5	
Thomas Jones, - -	"	–	5	
Robert Pyland, - -	"	–	5	
James Barham, - -	"	–	5	
Randolph H. Price. - -	"	–	5	

MUSTER ROLL

Of Captain Samuel Baugh's Company of Virginia Militia, from the Sixty-second Regiment, in the Service from the 28th to 30th June, and from the 1st to the 10th July, 1813.

NAMES.			RANK.	TIME OF SERVICE.		REMARKS.
				Months.	Days.	
Samuel Baugh,	-		Captain,	—	13	
William E. Rives,	-	-	Lieutenant,	—	3	
James Baugh,	-	-	"	—	9	
James Sturdivant,	-	-	Ensign,	—	13	
Rich'd Twiny,	-	-	1st Sergeant,	—	13	
Henry Lee,	-	-	2d "	—	3	
James Brownley,	-	-	2d "	—	10	
Richard H. Moore,	-	-	3d "	—	3	
Daniel B. Fenn,	-	-	3d "	—	10	
William Moore,	-	-	4th "	—	3	
Richard Hamlin,	-	-	4th "	—	10	
William H. Bassere,	-	-	1st Corporal,	—	3	
Jere. Aldridge,	-	-	1st "	—	9	
David Todd,	-	-	2d "	—	3	Promoted since the 30th June 1813
William Smith,	-	-	2d "	—	10	
Lahen Leadbetter,	-	-	3d "	—	3	
Benjamin Newell,	-	-	3d "	—	10	
Peter Ivey,	-	-	4th "	—	3	
Abraham Tucker,	-	-	4th "	—	8	
William Simmons,	-	-	Private,	—	3	
Peter Tatum,	-	-	"	—	3	
Peter Minga,	-	-	"	—	3	
John Swisdy,	-	-	"	—	3	
Joel Swisdy,	-	-	"	—	3	
John Moore,	-	-	"	—	3	
Joel Lee,	-	-	"	—	3	
Nicholas Hatch,	-	-	"	—	3	
Roderick Heath,	-	-	"	—	3	
James T. Davenport,	-	-	"	—	3	
Joseph Heath,	-	-	"	—	3	
William Smith, jr.	-	-	"	—	3	
Frederick Grantham,	-	-	"	—	3	
James Baxter,	-	-	"	—	3	
Nathaniel Raines,	-	-	"	—	3	
Littleburry Lee,	-	-	"	—	3	
Jesse Mustlewhite,	-	-	"	—	3	
Wood Burge,	-	-	"	—	3	
Armistead Harrill,	-	-	"	—	3	
Seth Harrell,	-	-	"	—	3	
William Alley,	-	-	"	—	3	
Elijah Harrill,	-	-	"	—	3	
Reubin Wright,	-	-	"	—	3	
Reubin Tucker,	-	-	"	—	3	
Reaps Ambrose,	-	-	"	—	3	
William Bishop,	-	-	"	—	3	
Edmond Bishop,	-	-	"	—	3	
Wm'son Cotton,	-	-	"	—	3	
Daniel S. Chieves,	-	-	"	—	3	

NAMES.	RANK.	TIME OF SERVICE.		REMARKS.
		Months.	Days.	
Daniel B. Fenn, - -	Private,	–	3	
Benjamin Newell, - -	"	–	3	
Thomas Tucker, - -	"	–	3	
Peter Tucker, - -	"	–	3	
Thomas Newell, - -	"	–	13	
Epes Tatum, - -	"	–	13	
Henry Williamson, - -	"	–	3	
Richard Gary, - -	"	–	13	
Samuel Smith, - -	"	–	3	
William Berchett, - -	"	–	3	
Jesse Minge, - -	"	–	13	
William Smith, - -	"	–	3	
William Rosser, - -	"	–	13	
Thomas Tucker, - -	"	–	10	
Peter Tucker, - -	"	–	10	
Thomas Temple, - -	"	–	10	
Aaron Alley, - -	"	–	10	
Benjamin Tamonds, - -	"	–	10	
Nath'l B. Sturdevant, - -	"	–	10	
Daniel Hunnicutt, - -	"	–	10	
Herbert Pittway, - -	"	–	10	
Edward Hobbs, - -	"	–	10	
Ro. Smith, - -	"	–	10	
Samuel Smith, - -	"	–	10	
William Burkett, - -	"	–	10	
Robt. Minge, - -	"	–	9	
Coleman Burge, - -	"	–	9	
Liston Temple, - -	"	–	10	
Howell Barhom, - -	"	–	10	
John Sturdevant, - -	"	–	10	
William H. Baugh, - -	"	–	10	
Henry Wilkins, - -	"	–	10	
John Chappell, - -	"	–	10	
Mark Hunnicutt, - -	"	–	10	
Robt. Hunnicutt, - -	"	–	10	
William Potts, - -	"	–	10	
Persons Magee, - -	"	–	10	
William Moody, - -	"	–	10	

MUSTER ROLL

Of Captain Thomas Beacham's Company of Virginia Militia, from the Thirty-seventh Regiment, commanded by Lieutenant Colonel T. D. Downing, in the Service from the 7th to the 21st April, from 15th to 30th July, and from 7th to 11th of November, 1813.

NAMES.	RANK.	TIME OF SERVICE.		REMARKS.
		Months.	Days.	
Thomas Beacham,	Captain,	1		
Thomas Bell,	Lieutenant,	1	5	
Samuel Cralle,	Ensign,	1		
Charles L. Fulks,	Sergeant.	–	21	
Alexander Rock,	"	–	16	
John C. Hudson,	"	–	21	
Wm. L. Self,	"	–	4	
Lewis Lumpkin,	"	–	5	
Bushrod M. F. Beacham,	Corporal.	–	20	Promoted since 30th June.
Peter G. McClanahan,	"	–	20	Promoted since 30th June.
Steward R. Pursell,	"	–	5	
John Weymouth,	"	–	5	
Geo. Burton,	Drummer.	1		
Presley Hudson,	Fifer,	–	28	
Haynie Ashburn,	Private.	–	13	
Jesse Bryant,	"	–	20	
Thomas Brann,	"	–	4	
Stephen Bryant,	"	–	4	
Geo. L. Beacham,	"	–	4	
Saml. Clarke,	"	–	22	
John S. Cralle,	"	–	4	
Pemberton Claughton, jr.	"	–	4	
Saml. Clarke, jr.	"	–	4	
William Fulks,	"	–	4	
Robert Forrest,	"	–	3	
James C. Gill,	"	–	22	
Mathew Harrison,	"	–	20	
Richd. Holliday,	"	–	24	
Geo. H. Headley,	"	–	24	
Thomas T. Hudson,	"	–	19	
Randall Headley,	"	–	24	
Lumsford Hall,	"	–	4	
Robert Holmes,	"	–	4	
John Hughes, jr.	"	–	4	
Moses Hale,	"	–	4	
James S. Hale,	"	–	4	
John C. Hudson,	"	–	4	
John Hughs,	"	–	4	
Benjamin H. Hale,	"	–	3	
Willis Jones,	"	–	24	
William B. Lewis,	"	–	20	
Peter G. McClanahan,	"	–	3	
Stewart R. Pursell,	"	–	18	
Bazil Pritchett,	"	–	23	
John Peck,	"	–	5	

NAMES.	RANK.	TIME OF SERVICE.		REMARKS.
		Months.	Days.	
John Kock, - -	Private,	–	4	
Saml. A. Self, - -	"	–	24	
James B. Self, - -	"	–	4	
Mottrom B. Self, - -	"	–	3	
John Weymouth, - -	"	–	20	
Wilson L. Williams, - -	"	–	20	
Richard Walker, - -	"	–	4	
William G. Walker, - -	"	–	4	
Thomas Whittington, - -	"	–	3	
Henry Dawson, - -	"	–	21	
Christopher Dawson, - -	"	–	20	
John C. Dameron, - -	"	–	20	
Luke Dameron, jr. - -	"	–	20	
William Dameron, jr. - -	"	–	16	
Benjamin Dawson, - -	"	–	4	
John C. Dawson, - -	"	–	4	

MUSTER ROLL

Of Captain Edwin Beasley's Company from Thirty-ninth Regiment, Virginia Militia, commanded by Major Jo. G. Wilder, in the Service from the 30th day of June, 1813, to the 12th of July, 1813.

NAMES.	RANK.	TIME OF SERVICE.		REMARKS.
		Months.	Days.	
Edwin Beasley,	Captain,	–	13	
John Hanserd,	Lieutenant,	–	13	
Rob't Ritchie,	1st Sergeant,	–	13	
Henry Marks,	2d "	–	13	
William Robertson,	3d "	–	13	
John L. Merten,	4th "	–	13	
James Boisseau,	1st Corporal,	–	13	
William Hawthorn,	2d "	–	13	
John Batley,	3d "	–	13	
Clement Hawks,	4th "	–	13	
Benj'n B. Anderson,	Private,	–	13	
Hezekiah B. Anderson,	"	–	13	
Daniel Baugh,	"	–	13	
John Baird,	"	–	13	
Herbert Baird,	"	–	13	
Peter Baird,	"	–	13	
Thos. C. Batte,	"	–	13	
William Berry,	"	–	13	
Eli Bennett,	"	–	13	
Lewellen R. Cain,	"	–	13	
James Cole,	"	–	13	
William Couch,	"	–	13	
William Cathbert,	"	–	13	
John R. Daniel,	"	–	13	
William P. Daniel,	"	–	13	
Marvil Dunivant,	"	–	13	
Ira A. Ester,	"	–	13	
Belfield Fauntleroy,	"	–	13	
Bailey Gee,	"	–	13	
Nath'l Harris,	"	–	13	
Moses Jeffres,	"	–	13	
Robert K. Jones,	"	–	13	
William H. Jones,	"	–	13	
Thomas E. Lacy,	"	–	13	
Samuel Leech,	"	–	13	
Eaton Lamb,	"	–	13	
Charles Mann,	"	–	13	
Hector McMillen,	"	–	13	
William Mottley,	"	–	13	
William Meikle,	"	–	13	
James Merrow,	"	–	13	
William Old,	"	–	13	
James Orr,	"	–	13	
Peter Peterson,	"	–	13	
Sylvester Plumb,	"	–	13	
Samuel Peniston,	"	–	13	
William Russell,	"	–	13	
William B. Ritchie,	"	–	13	

NAMES.	RANK.	TIME OF SERVICE.		REMARKS.
		Months.	Days.	
Beverly H. Randolph, -	Private,	–	13	
Richard Richards, - -	"	–	13	
John Roper, - -	"	–	13	
Jabez Smith, - -	"	–	13	
John Somerville, - -	"	–	13	
James Selby, - -	"	–	13	
Lewis G. Simmons, - -	"	–	13	
William Stevenson, - -	"	–	13	
Sceva Thayer, - -	"	–	13	
Henry Tharp, - -	"	–	13	
Carter Wells, - -	"	–	13	
Ebenezer Watts, - -	"	–	13	
Wyllie Wells, - -	"	–	13	
Henry Wright, - -	"	–	13	
Baker Woodward, - -	"	–	13	
John Zimmerman, - -	"	–	13	
Jonathan Zimmerman, -	"	–	13	

MUSTER ROLL

Of Captain Joseph Belfield's Company, from Forty-first Regiment, Virginia Militia, under command of Lieut. Col. Vincent Branham, in the Service of the United States, from 5th to 8th October, and from 1st to 8th December, in the year 1814.

NAMES.	RANK.	TIME OF SERVICE.		REMARKS.
		Months.	Days.	
Joseph Belfield,	Captain,	—	12	
William K. Bragg,	Lieutenant,	—	12	
Richard N. Marriner,	Ensign,	—	12	
David Saunders,	1st Sergeant,	—	12	
James Saunders,	2d "	—	12	
Hudson Morriss,	3d "	—	12	
Allen W. Mothershead,	4th "	—	12	
James Brown,	1st Corporal,	—	12	
James Hudson,	2d "	—	12	
Robert Jinkins,	3d "	—	12	
Allen Saunders,	4th "	—	12	
John Balderson,	Private,	—	12	
Berriman Balderson,	"	—	12	
James P. Balderson,	"	—	12	
Gibbs H. Balderson,	"	—	12	
William Balderson,	"	—	12	
Daniel Carter,	"	—	12	
Robert Conniller,	"	—	12	
Samuel Coats,	"	—	12	
James Coats, jr.	"	—	12	
William C. Crash,	"	—	12	
William R. Carpenter,	"	—	12	
Jeremiah Carpenter,	"	—	12	
Charles Fones,	"	—	12	
Thomas Fones.	"	—	12	
James Gutnage,	"	—	12	Or Gutrage.
Reuben Hart,	"	—	12	
George Hinson,	"	—	12	
Meredith Hammons,	"	—	12	
William H. Hall,	"	—	12	
John Jenkins, jr.	"	—	12	
Thomas Jenkins,	"	—	12	
James Mothershead,	"	—	12	
William Mothershead,	"	—	12	
Henry J. Mothershead,	"	—	12	
Daniel Morriss,	"	—	12	
Reubin Marks,	"	—	3	
James Nash,	"	—	12	
Henry Nash,	"	—	12	
John Nash,	"	—	12	
William Oliff,	"	—	12	
James Oliff, jr.	"	—	12	
James Pratt,	"	—	12	
John Ryalds,	"	—	12	
Jacob A. Rayne,	"	—	12	
Thomas Saunders, jr.	"	—	12	
Thomas Saunders, sen.	"	—	12	
James Saunders, jr.	"	—	12	

MUSTER ROLL

Of Lieutenant John Bell's Company, from Seventy-first Regiment, Virginia Militia, commanded by Lieutenant Colonel William Allen, in the Service from the 23d March to the 5th of April, 1813.

NAMES.	RANK.	TIME OF SERVICE.		REMARKS.
		Months.	Days.	
John Bell,	1st Lieutenant,	–	14	
Philip Smith,	Sergeant,	–	14	
Robert Crittenden,	"	–	12	
Willis Thompson,	"	–	12	
Anthony D. White,	"	–	12	
Samuel Bell,	Corporal,	–	12	
Joseph Warren,	"	–	14	
Joseph Raimey,	"	–	14	
Miles Cary,	Private,	–	14	
Peter T. Spratley,	"	–	14	
Patrick H. Hill,	"	–	14	
Lewis M. Spratley,	"	–	14	
William Bailey,	"	–	14	
David Long,	"	–	12	
Nathaniel Smith,	"	–	12	
John Adkinson,	"	–	12	
Elijah Holloway,	"	–	8	
Thomas C. Edwards,	"	–	12	
John M. St. George,	"	–	12	

Ensign Thomas Benn's Company—Fifty-ninth Regiment.

NAMES.	RANK.	TIME OF SERVICE.		REMARKS.
		Months.	Days.	
William Woodward. -	Sergeant,	–	18	
John Taylor, - -	Corporal,	–	18	
William Benn, - -	Private,	–	1ꞩ	
Jesseo Fulgam, - -	"	–	18	
William Jordon, - -	"	–	18	
Will Pitt, - - -	"	–	18	
William Wainright, - -	. "	–	18	
Willis Wright, - -	"	–	18	

(For rest of this company, see publication of Pay Rolls.)

Captain Carter B. Berkeley's Company—One Hundred and Ninth Regiment.

NAMES.	RANK.	TIME OF SERVICE.		REMARKS.
		Months.	Days.	
Carter B. Berkeley, - -	Captain,	1	12	
James Chewning, - -	Lieutenant,	1	13	
Carter Perkins, - -	"	–	8	
Charles G. Layton, - -	"	1	3	
Benj. H. Holder, - -	Sergeant,	1	13	
Carter Perkins, - -	"	1	13	
George W. Layton, - -	"	1	13	
James Stiff, - -	"	–	10	
Thomas Clear, - -	"	–	8	
John Robinson, - -	"	1	3	
John B. Clayton, - -	"	–	3	
Thomas Clear, - -	Corporal,	1	13	
John B. Garland, - -	"	1	13	
John Layton, - -	"	1	13	
George Wortham, - -	"	1	9	
William Cundiff, - -	"	–	2	
Bailey Barnet, (or Banick,) -	"	–	8	
Braxton Dunlany, - -	Fifer,	1	13	
Robert Clear, - -	Drummer,	1	13	
John Anderson, - -	Private,	1	27	
Thomas D. Blake, - -	"	1	27	
Jacob S. Blake, - -	"	2	2	
Warner C. Blake, - -	"	1	19	
George Blake, - -	"	1	13	
Bailey Banick, - -	"	1	21	
George Burnes, - -	"	1	15	
John B. Banick, - -	"	1	21	
David Banick, - -	"	1	21	
Wm. R. Baker, - -	"	1	9	
Wm. R. Brooks, - -	"	–	10	
John Chewning, - -	"	1	21	
William Cundiff, - -	"	1	23	
Stapleton H. Davis, - -	"	1	13	
William Deagle, - -	"	1	13	
John Daniel, - -	"	2	2	
James W. Dunlavy, - -	"	1	25	
Selby Howard, - -	"	1	29	
John Hanks, - -	"	1	24	
John B. Hall, - -	"	2	6	
Richard Jackson, - -	"	2	3	
John Jefferson, - -	"	1	13	
Thomas Layton, - -	"	–	7	
John Mercer, - -	"	1	21	
Thomas Pearce, - -	"	1	13	
Thomas Palmer, - -	"	1	13	
James Pierce, - -	"	–	4	
Peter Reveer, - -	"	1	16	
John Robinson, - -	"	–	4	
William Robinson, - -	"	1	6	
Charles Robinson, - -	"	1	12	
Thomas Saunders, - -	"	2	6	

NAMES.	RANK.	TIME OF SERVICE.		REMARKS.
		Months.	Days.	
Davis H. Stapleton, - -	Private,	–	8	
James Stiff, - -	"	1	3	
George Trader, - -	"	1	11	
John Woodley, - -	"	2	17	
Thomas Woodley, - -	"	1	25	
William Williams, - -	"	1	13	
John Williams, - -	"	1	29	
William Wilkins, - -	"	1	13	
James Wilkins, - -	"	1	·9	
John Wilkins, - -	"	1	19	
John G. Wade, - -	"	1	9	
Daniel S. Ward, - -	"	–	14	

(For rest of this company, see publication of Pay Rolls.)

MUSTER ROLL

*Of Ensign Newton Berryman's Company of Virginia Militia, Westmoreland
County, from the One Hundred and Eleventh Regiment, under the command
of Major William Nelson, in the Service from the 15th to the 20th July, 1813.*

NAMES.		RANK.	TIME OF SERVIC .		REMARKS.
			Months.	Days.	
Newton Berryman,	-	Ensign,	—	5	
Waters Berryman,	- -	"	—	5	Acting as Lieutenant.
Weeks Berryman,	-	"	—	5	Acting as Ensign.
Robert P. Marshall,	-	Sergeant,	—	5	
Abner James,	- -	"	—	5	
Taliaferro Jete,	- -	"	—	5	
William Frank,	- -	"	—	5	
Spencer B. Worth,	- -	Private,	—	5	
David Curley,	- -	"	—	5	
Robert G. Robb,	- -	"	—	5	
Benjamin Weaver,	- -	"	—	5	
Henry D. Stoke,	- -	"	—	5	
George Short,	- -	"	—	2	
William Berkley,	- -	"	—	5	
Weedon Jete,	- -	"	—	5	
Lewis Bell,	- -	"	—	3	
William T. Sanders,	- -	"	—	5	
Charles White,	- -	"	—	5	
Rich'd Wilkins,	- -	"	—	4	
J. H. Mothershead,	- -	"	—	2	
Thomas Bran,	- -	"	—	5	
Samuel Lampkin,	- -	"	—	5	
Henry Deatley,	- -	"	—	5	
Robt. Ralph,	- -	"	—	5	
James Coats,	- -	"	—	3	
George Crask,	- -	"	—	2	
Benjamin P. Smith,	- -	"	—	5	
George McKenney,	- -	"	—	3	
Alpha H. Shaw,	- -	"	—	5	
George Picket,	- -	"	—	5	
Thomas Bulger,	- -	"	—	2	
Sylus Short,	- -	"	—	5	
Warner Hudson,	- -	"	—	5	
Walter Gimbo,	- -	"	—	4	
Robert S. Hipkins,	- -	"	—	5	
Henry Penn,	- -	"	—	2	
William McKenny,	- -	"	—	4	
John B. Deatley,	- -	"	—	5	
George Johnston,	- -	"	—	5	
Charles Butler,	- -	"	—	4	
James Miller,	- -	"	—	4	
Octavious A. Harvey,	- -	"	—	4	
Thomas W. Landrum,	- -	"	—	5	
Henry W. Weaver,	- -	"	—	4	
Frederick Campell,	- -	"	—	4	
Daniel Sanford,	- -	"	—	4	

MUSTER ROLL

Of Captain Charles Betts' Troop of Cavalry, from the First Regiment, in the Service of the United States, under the orders of the Deputy Adjutant General of the State of Virginia, from the 31st August to the 12th September, 1814.

NAMES.	RANK.	TIME OF SERVICE.		REMARKS.
		Months.	Days.	
Charles Betts,	Captain,	–	13	
John Bigger,	1st Lieutenant,	–	13	
Edmund Hardy,	2d "	–	13	
John W. Scott,	Cornet,	–	13	
John Buford,	1st Sergeant,	–	13	
Joseph A. Watson,	2d "	–	13	
Gillie M. Bacon,	3d "	–	13	
Benjamin Oliver,	4th "	–	13	
John L. Williams,	1st Corporal.	–	13	
Joseph Williamson,	2d "	–	13	
John Riggins,	3d "	–	13	
John Norvell,	4th "	–	13	
Edward M. Jones,	R. Master,	–	13	
George Hatchell,	Qr. Master,	–	13	
Thomas Chambers,	D. Q. Master.	–	13	
William Brown,	Sw'd Master.	–	13	
Henry S. Ellis,	Farrier,	–	13	
John W. Rogers,	B. Smith.	–	13	
James Anderson,	Private,	–	13	
Benj'n Alexander,	"	–	13	
David Allmonds,	"	–	13	
Boston Betts,	"	–	13	
Richard Boran,	"	–	13	
Richard C. Bacon.	"	–	13	
John Billups,	"	–	13	
John Boswell,	"	–	13	
Thomas Butte,	"	–	13	
John Brown,	"	–	13	
James Brown,	"	–	13	
Anderson Bagley,	"	–	13	
Richard Bragg.	"	–	13	
Hamblin Cole,	"	–	13	
William Clarke.	"	–	13	
Field Clarke,	"	–	13	
Samuel Cary,	"	–	13	
Howell Crowder,	"	–	13	
Edw'd R. Chambers.	"	–	13	
Henry P. Crenshaw.	"	–	13	
Theophilus Denten,	"	–	13	
Bowler Dobbyns.	"	–	13	
Joseph Dupree,	"	–	13	
Rich'd C. Ellis,	"	–	13	
Benj. Edmondson,	"	–	13	
Hezekiah Freeman,	"	–	13	
William C. Fowlkes,	"	–	13	
William J. Fowlkes,	"	–	13	
Thomas Fowlkes,	"	–	13	

NAMES.	RANK.	TIME OF SERVICE.		REMARKS.
		Months.	Days.	
Robert Garland. - -	Private,	—	13	
William R. Geers, - -	"	—	13	
Leonard Goodwin, - -	"	—	13	
Benj'n Gwatney, - -	"	—	13	
Isaiah Hawkins, - -	"	—	13	
Haynie Hatchell, - -	"	—	13	
John Hazlewood, - -	"	—	13	
Eaton Hudson. - -	"	—	13	
Valentine Hudson, - -	"	—	13	
Irby Hudson, - -	"	—	13	
Munford Hunt, - -	"	—	13	
Edmund Irby, - -	"	—	13	
Thomas Jorden, - -	"	—	13	
Edward Jorden, - -	"	—	13	
James Jorden, - -	"	—	13	
Branch Jorden, - -	"	—	13	
John Jorden, - -	"	—	13	
Benj'n W. Johnston, - -	"	—	13	
James Jennings, - -	"	—	13	
Thomas Knight, - -	"	—	13	
John Lipford, - -	"	—	13	
Burnett Lester, - -	"	—	13	
Jeremiah Morgan, - -	"	—	13	
Samuel B. Morgan, - -	"	—	13	
Reuben Morgan, - -	"	—	13	
Jesse Moon, - -	"	—	13	
Martin Peters, - -	"	—	13	
Jesse Pilkinton, - -	"	—	13	
John Ogburne, - -	"	—	13	
Richard L. Smithson, - -	"	—	13	
Jas. A. Smithson, - -	"	—	13	
Ralph Stegall, - -	"	—	13	
Wiltshire Tucker, - -	"	—	13	
George Tucker, - -	"	—	13	
Robt. Thompson, - -	"	—	13	
Bassfield Winn, - -	"	—	13	
Jonathan P. Winn, - -	"	—	13	
Josiah Wilson, - -	"	—	13	
Benjamin Wyatt, - -	"	—	13	
William Williams, - -	"	—	13	
Rich'd Williams, - -	"	—	13	
John J. Wells, - -	"	—	13	
Rowland Whitworth, -	"	—	13	

MUSTER ROLL

Of Captain Thomas Bevill's Company of Virginia Militia, in the Eighty-third Regiment, Dinwiddie County, under the command of Lieutenant Colonel James Scott, in the Service from the 1st to the 6th July, 1813.

NAMES.	RANK.	TIME OF SERVICE.		REMARKS.
		Months.	Days.	
Thomas Bevill,	Captain,	–	6	
John Smith,	Lieutenant.	–	6	
Arch'd J. Bevill,	Ensign,	–	6	
William Malone,	Sergeant.	–	6	
John Malone,	"	–	6	
Williamson Knight,	"	–	6	
David Harrison,	"	–	6	
John Goodwin,	Corporal,	–	6	
George R. Watts,	"	–	6	
John C. Harman,	"	–	6	
Daniel Harman,	"	–	6	
Lewis Brown,	Drummer,	–	6	
Mason Harwell,	Fifer,	–	6	
Green Jackson,	Private,	–	6	
Thomas Pilkington,	"	–	6	
Edward Perkins,	"	–	6	
James Dugger,	"	–	6	
Christopher Daniel,	"	–	6	
Francis Daniel,	"	–	6	
Joshua Perkins,	"	–	6	
William Noble,	"	–	6	
Harper Malone,	"	–	6	
Johnson Suit,	"	–	6	
Berryman Chappell,	"	–	6	
Briggs Chappell,	"	–	6	
John Abernathy.	"	–	6	
Thomas Goodrich.	"	–	6	
Henry Heath,	"	–	6	
Benjamin Malone,	"	–	6	
Henry Tucker,	"	–	6	
William Sturdivant,	"	–	6	
Robert Malone,	"	–	6	
Benjamin H. Copeland,	"	–	6	
John Stanton.	"	–	6	
Staunton Butler,	"	–	6	
James Binford,	"	–	6	
Micajah Peebles,	"	–	6	
Howell Hines,	"	–	6	
Bernard M. Perkins,	"	–	6	
David Smith,	"	–	6	
Robert Davis,	"	–	6	
Burwell Brown,	"	–	6	
Ethiel Crowder,	"	–	6	
Augustin Suit,	"	–	6	
John H. Hall,	"	–	6	
Noah Brown,	"	–	6	Sub. for Jesse Spiers.
Charles B. Rives,	"	–	6	
Foster Tucker,	"	–	6	
James Wilbourne,	"	–	6	

NAMES.			RANK.	TIME OF SERVICE.		REMARKS.
				Months.	Days.	
William P. Smith,	-	-	Private,	–	6	
William Kerkland,	-	-	"	–	6	
Roger Daniel,	-	-	"	–	6	
Charles Mingge,	-	-	"	–	6	
John Mingge,	-	-	"	–	6	
David Chappell,	-	-	"	–	6	
James Hawkes,	-	-	"	–	6	
William C. Tucker,	-	-	"	–	6	
Elijah Scoggin,	-	-	"	–	6	
Benjamin Heath,	-	-	"	–	6	

Captain Richard Bidgood's Company—Twenty-ninth Regiment.

NAMES.	RANK.	TIME OF SERVICE.		REMARKS.
		Months.	Days.	
Joseph Johnson, - -	Lieutenant.	—	21	
Joseph Godwin, - -	"	—	18	
Robert Adams. - -	Private.	—	18	
Geo. Bowen. - -	"	—	21	
William Cowper. - -	"	—	21	
Joseph Chapman, - -	"	—	18	
Jordan Goodwin. - -	"	1	9	
Ralph Gibbs, - -	"	—	18	
Samuel Hunt, - -	"	—	18	
Thomas Harris, - -	"	—	21	
Pitt Hall. - -	"	—	21	
James Moody, - -	"	—	18	
Samuel McCoy, - -	"	—	16	
Joseph Pitt, - -	"	—	18	
Stephen Smith, - -	"	—	21	
Elias Williamson, -	"	—	21	
Wilkinson Whitefield, -	"	—	20	
William Wilbern. - -	"	—	21	

(For rest of this company, see publication of Pay Rolls.)

PAY ROLL

Of Captain John Billups' Company.

NAMES.			RANK.	TIME OF SERVICE.		REMARKS.
				Months.	Days.	
Gabriel Miller,	-	-	Sergeant,	–	1	On detachment from
Isaac Ayres,	-	-	Private,	1	9	Capt. B. Digges.
John Anderson.	-	-	''	–	5	
Job Digges,	-	-	''	–	1	'' '' ''
Joel Digges,	-	-	''	–	1	'' '' ''
Joseph Foster,	-	-	''	–	8	
Albert Foster,	-	-	''	–	1	'' '' ''
John Hudgin,	-	-	''	1	14	'' '' ''
Hugh Hudgin,	-	-	''	–	1	'' '' ''
Anthony Hudgin.	-	-	''	–	1	'' '' ''
James Hudgin,	-	-	''	–	1	'' '' ''
Patrick Horan,	-	-	''	–	1	'' '' ''
Richard James,	-	-	''	–	17	
Robert Williams,	-	-	''	–	13	
Thomas Willis,	-	-	''	–	6	
Christ. Weston,	-	-	''	–	1	

(For rest of this company, see publication of Pay Rolls.)

MUSTER ROLL

Of Captain Driny Birchett's Company of Virginia Militia, from Sixty-second Regiment, commanded by Lieutenant Colonel Miles Selden, in the Service from 27th June to 9th July, 1813.

NAMES.	RANK.	TIME OF SERVICE.		REMARKS.
		Months.	Days.	
Driny Birchett,	Captain,	–	13	
John Birchett,	Lieutenant,	–	13	
Thomas Vaughan,	Ensign,	–	13	
Joel Titmash,	Sergeant,	–	13	
Williamson Williams,	"	–	13	
Alexander Hobbs,	"	–	13	
Geo. Vaughan,	"	–	13	
Pleasant Hobbs,	"	–	13	
Wills Floyd,	"	–	13	
Joseph Womack,	"	–	13	
Samuel Fenqua,	"	–	13	
Allen C. Hobbs,	Drummer,	–	13	
Geo. Adams,	Private,	–	13	
David Hobbs,	"	–	13	
John Finch,	"	–	13	
Collen Hobbs,	"	–	13	
Hartwell Hackney,	"	–	13	
James Williams,	"	–	13	
Jackariah Williams,	"	–	13	
Grieff Williams,	"	–	13	
James McCann,	"	–	13	
Daniel Jamison, jr.	"	–	13	
John H. Jamison,	"	–	13	
Anthony Allen,	"	–	13	
William Allen,	"	–	13	
Wilson Hobbs,	"	–	13	
Robt. Day,	"	–	13	
Thomas Allen,	"	–	13	
Robert Commings,	"	–	13	
Saml. Wammack,	"	–	13	
Josiah Fenqua,	"	–	13	
Josiah Adams,	"	–	13	
Henry Gill,	"	–	13	
Joshua W. Roberts,	"	–	13	
Robt. Brockwell,	"	–	13	
William L. Waugh,	"	–	13	
Thos. Owney,	"	–	13	
Peter W. Bookwell,	"	–	13	
Littleberry Murry,	"	–	13	
Hartwell Heath,	"	–	13	
William Brockwell,	"	–	13	
William C. Hobbs,	"	–	13	
Samuel Bridgewater,	"	–	13	
Nath'l Wammack,	"	–	13	
William Hackney,	"	–	13	
John Hatch,	"	–	13	
Geo. Bonner,	"	–	7	
John Pointer,	"	–	3	

MUSTER ROLL

Of Captain William Birchett's Company of Virginia Militia, from the Twenty-second Regiment, Mecklenburg County, in the Service from the 30th August to the 13th September, 1814.

NAMES.	RANK.	TIME OF SERVICE.		REMARKS.
		Months.	Days.	
William Birchett, - -	Captain,	–	16	
John G. Baptist, - -	1st Lieutenant,	–	16	
Mathew L. Baptist, -	2d Lieutenant,	–	16	
Hume R. Field, - -	Cornet,	–	16	
Thomas Blackborne, -	1st Sergeant,	–	16	Transferred to Capt. Pryor's company.
William C. Wall, - -	2d "	–	16	
David Crenshaw, - -	3d "	–	16	
James A. M. P. Stewart, -	4th "	–	16	Transferred to Capt. Pryor's company.
Richard P. Montgomery, -	Q. M. Serg.	–	16	
Giles R. Norment, - -	Corporal,	–	16	
Osborn Crooke, - -	"	–	16	
John Nelson, - -	"	–	16	Transferred to Capt. Pryor's company.
Richard S. Jeffres, - -	"	–	16	
Thomas Atkins, - -	Private,	–	16	
Edward B. Brown, - -	"	–	16	
Pleasant Brommall, -	"	–	16	
William Baptist, - -	"	–	16	
Francis Blackborne, -	"	–	16	
John Bigger, - -	"	–	16	
Grey Blackborne, - -	"	–	16	
Francis B. Bailey, - -	"	–	16	
Alexander Boyden, - -	"	–	16	
Josiah Crews, - -	"	–	16	
Miles T. Crowder, - -	"	–	16	
Thomas Crow, - -	"	–	16	
Little B. Carter, - -	"	–	16	
John P. Carter, - -	"	–	16	
Geo. Doggett, - -	"	–	16	
John Farrar, - -	"	–	16	
John S. Field, - -	"	–	16	
Richard Field, - -	"	–	16	
Thomas Gregory, - -	"	–	16	
Barnett Gregory, - -	"	–	16	
Daniel Hudson, - -	"	–	16	
Stephen Hudson, - -	"	–	16	
William C. Hudson, -	"	–	16	
Sam'l G. Hunt, - -	"	–	16	
Edward Jones, - -	"	–	16	
Paul C. Jeffers, - -	"	–	16	
William Keen, - -	"	–	16	
John Loafman, - -	"	–	16	
Nath'l McCann, - -	"	–	16	
Thomas Marshall, - -	"	–	16	
Champion C. Marrable, -	"	–	16	
Green Moss, - -	"	–	16	
Abner Moody, - -	"	–	16	
Stephen Mayes, - -	"	–	16	

NAMES.	RANK.	TIME OF SERVICE.		REMARKS.
		Months.	Days.	
William Neal, - -	Private,	−	16	
John J. Norment, - -	"	−	16	
Achilles Norment, - -	"	−	16	
Thos. J. Norment, - -	"	−	16	
Thomas Norment, - -	"	−	16	
Lewis Nunn, - -	"	−	16	
Joseph Ogborne, - -	"	−	16	
Philip Poindexter. - -	"	−	16	
John Puryear, - -	"	−	16	
Thomas Puryear. - -	"	−	16	
Rich'd C. Puryear. - -	"	−	16	
Lewis Roffe, - -	"	−	16	
Robt. Richardson, - -	"	−	16	
John Tabb, - -	"	−	16	
Richard H. Walker. - -	"	−	16	
William Williamson. - -	"	−	16	
Charles Yancey, - -	"	−	16	
John Young, - -	"	−	16	
James L. Summervill. -	"	−	16	
Philip Lackett, - -	"	−	16	
Shearwood Colley. - -	"	−	16	
William Nelson, - -	"	−	16	Transferred to Capt.
William Towns, - -	"	−	16	Pryor's company.
Erasmus Kennon, - -	"	−	16	
Alexander Clausel. - -	"	−	16	
Farley Wade, - -	"	−	16	

Captain Robert Blakey's Company—One Hundred and Ninth Regiment.

NAMES.	RANK.	TIME OF SERVICE.		REMARKS.
		Months.	Days.	
Robert Blakey,	Captain,	1	4	
William Jesse,	Lieutenant,	1	4	
Thomas L. L. Steptoe,	"	–	16	
John C. Warwick,	Cornet,	1	4	
James B. Bristow,	Sergeant,	1	4	
Chs. Harwood,	"	–	18	
Christopher Howard,	"	1	4	
Warner Roane,	"	–	12	
William Crittenden,	"	–	7	
Zach. N. Crittenden,	"	–	7	
Anthony New,	"	–	13	
Thomas Kidd,	Corporal,	6	27	
William M. Burk,	"	–	16	
Mathew Major,	"	–	9	
Lewis Seward,	"	6	16	
Cary R. Dudey,	"	–	13	
Henry Muse,	"	6	–	
Philip Lee,	"	6	17	
Edwd. Micklebaugh,	"	6	13	
Joseph Lipscomb,	"	6	–	
James Trice,	"	1	11	
Wm. L. Burke,	Private,	–	3	
Leonard Bristow,	"	1	2	
Austin Ball,	"	7	5	
Lewis Brooke,	"	–	26	
William Blake,	"	–	17	
John Ball,	"	1	5	
John Brown,	"	1	12	
Parmenias Bird,	"	–	8	
Wm. M. Burke,	"	–	2	
Samuel Brooks,	"	–	7	
James Burk,	"	–	3	
William Blackey,	"	–	27	
Henry Cloudas,	"	6	16	
Richard Claybrooke,	"	–	7	
Thomas Dyke,	"	–	17	
Henry Dunn,	"	–	6	
John Dudley,	"	–	17	
Thomas Edward,	"	7	24	
Vincent W. Fawcett,	"	–	21	
James Frazer,	"	1	9	
Edward L. Ferrell,	"	–	18	
John Gibson,	"	–	12	
Payton Grymes,	"	–	13	
William Goughney,	"	–	2	
William George,	"	–	14	
Thomas Groom,	"	–	16	
Edmund Healy,	"	–	2	
Walter Healy,	"	–	16	
Mathew Hibble,	"	–	15	
John Jesse,	"	–	13	
James Johnson,	"	–	16	
Thomas Jones,	"	–	16	
Richard Jackson,	"	6	7	

NAMES.	RANK.	TIME OF SERVICE.		REMARKS.
		Months.	Days.	
Thomas Kidd, - -	Private,	–	7	
Burgess Kidd, - -	"	1	3	
Elliott Kidd, - -	"	12	6	
James Kidd, - -	"	–	11	
Allen Kidd, - -	"	6	–	
Tartius Kuningham, -	"	–	4	
Philip Lee, -	"	–	15	
Jas. H. T. Lorimer, -	"	–	25	
Robert T. Lee, - -	"	6	6	
Ralph Lomax, -	"	–	6	
Saml. W. Layre, - -	"	–	11	
Matthew Lewis, -	"	–	27	
George Murray, - -	"	1	3	
Matthew Major, - -	"	–	28	
Henry Muse, -	"	–	18	
Edward Micklebrough, -	"	–	8	
Francis Newcomb, -	"	6	22	
Henry Perkins, -	"	1	5	
Phillip Patterson, -	"	–	28	
Warner Roane, -	"	–	13	
William Robinson, -	"	6	14	
Henry Robinson, -	"	–	6	
John B. Roane, -	"	–	11	
William R. Robinson, -	"	–	9	
Benj. F. Robinson, -	"	–	7	
Geo. Revene, -	"	–	7	
Nelson Stamper, -	"	–	15	
Saml. Stamper, - -	"	1	1	
James Stamper, -	"	6	2	
Edmund Simcoe, -	"	–	11	
George Steptoe, -	"	–	11	
Lewis Seward, -	"	–	7	
Rowland Sutton, -	"	–	16	
Walter J. Steptoe, -	"	–	7	
James R. Steptoe, -	"	–	7	
Thomas H. Stiff, -	"	–	17	
James Trice, - -	"	1	2	
Edward Trice, -	"	–	7	
Henry Thruston. -	"	–	13	
Thomas Trice, -	"	–	7	
Valentine Vowell, -	"	–	28	
Robert Woody, -	"	–	2	
James Williams, -	"	–	16	
John Wood, - -	"	1		

(For rest of this company, see publication of Pay Rolls.)

MUSTER ROLL

Of Lieut. Robert Bland's Company of Virginia Militia, from 9th Regiment, commanded by Lieut. Col. William Boyd, in the Service from 2d to 10th day of December, 1814.

NAMES.	RANK.	TIME OF SERVICE.		REMARKS.
		Months.	Days.	
Robert Bland, - -	Lieutenant,	–	9	
John Harper, - -	Ensign,	–	9	
William A. Smith, - -	Sergeant,	–	8	
William Bland, - -	"	–	8	
Thomas Watts, - -	"	–	8	
John G. Ribe, - -	Corporal,	–	4	
William Brown, - -	Drummer,	–	9	
Charles Colly, - -	Fifer,	–	9	
Thomas Adams, - -	Private,	–	9	
John Y. Burton, - -	"	–	9	
James Bland, - -	"	–	9	
Richard Bland, - -	"	–	9	
William Bowden, - -	"	–	9	
Edmond Corr, - -	"	–	8	
Isaiah Clegg, - -	"	–	9	
Thomas Corr, - -	"	–	3	
Laban Clegg, - -	"	–	9	
Zachariah Collins, - -	"	–	9	
Baylor Dudley, - -	"	–	9	
George B. Dudley, - -	"	–	6	
Jedediah Darning, - -	"	–	9	
William Dillard, - -	"	–	9	
John Faulkner, - -	"	–	9	
Vinsen Hart, - -	"	–	9	
John Lambath, - -	"	–	9	
Henry Milby, - -	"	–	9	
William Newcomb, - -	"	–	9	
James Seward, - -	"	–	4	
William Southern, - -	"	–	9	
William Seward, - -	"	–	9	
William Thurston, - -	"	–	9	
Henry Tankersley, - -	"	–	5	
Armstead Thurston, - -	"	–	9	
Samuel Thurston, - -	"	–	9	
Samuel Thurston, - -	"	–	9	
Thomas Williams, - -	"	–	6	
Lewis Williams, - -	"	–	9	

MUSTER ROLL

Of Captain John Blunt's Company of Virginia Militia, from Twenty-ninth Regiment, commanded by Lieut. Col. Francis M. Boykin, in the Service of the State of Virginia, from 23d June to the 10th July, 1813, and from 28th August to 13th September, in the year 1814.

NAMES.			RANK.	TIME OF SERVICE.		REMARKS.
				Months.	Days.	
John Blunt,	-	-	Captain,	—	26	
Jordan Parr,	-	-	1st Lieutenant.	—	26	
Exum Eley,	-	-	1st "	—	17	
William Crocker,	-	-	Ensign,	—	9	
Miles W. Gray,	-	-	Ensign,	—	17	
Samuel Jefferson,	-	-	1st Sergeant,	—	9	
John Crocker,	-	-	2d "	—	9	
David Clarke,	-	-	3d "	—	9	
Samuel P. Jordan,	-	-	1st Sergeant,	—	17	
Edmund Godwin,	-	-	2d "	—	17	
Thomas Applewhite,	-	-	3d "	—	17	
William Sikes,	-	-	4th "	—	17	
Henry Crocker,	-	-	1st Corporal,	—	9	
Robert Gibbs,	-	-	2d "	—	9	
Edmond Humphreys,	-	-	3d "	—	9	
Burwell Edwards,	-	-	4th "	—	9	
Davis Chapman,	-	-	1st Corporal,	—	17	
Exum Chapman,	-	-	2d "	—	17	
Hezekiah Vellines,	-	-	3d "	—	17	
Richard Stringfield,	-	-	4th "	—	17	
Hardy Reade,	-	-	Fife Major,	—	17	
Moses Atkins,	-	-	Private,	—	26	
Samuel Addison,	-	-	"	—	17	
Francis Branch,	-	-	"	—	9	
Jesse Bounds,	-	-	"	—	9	
Lee Busby,	-	-	"	—	9	
James Braswell,	-	-	"	—	9	Substituted by David Ponsonby.
William Brewer,	-	-	"	—	26	
Thomas Bridger,	-	-	"	—	9	
Robert Brown,	-	-	"	—	17	
James Brantley,	-	-	"	—	17	
Thomas Bell,	-	-	"	—	17	
Silas Beal,	-	-	"	—	17	
Mills Butler,	-	-	"	—	17	
Elias Beal,	-	-	"	—	17	
Allen Bradshaw,	-	-	"	—	17	
Samuel Batten,	-	-	"	—	17	
Exum Britt,	-	-	"	—	17	
Samuel Bridger,	-	-	"	—	17	
Thomas Bowden,	-	-	"	—	17	Substituted by John Sikes.
Robert Butler,	-	-	"	—	17	
James Bowden,	-	-	"	—	17	
Charles D. Broadfield,	-	-	"	—	17	
William Busby,	-	-	"	—	17	
William Bradshaw,	-	-	"	—	17	
William Batten,	-	-	"	—	17	

NAMES.	RANK.	TIME OF SERVICE.		REMARKS.
		Months.	Days.	
Clements Batten, - -	Private,	—	17	
Exum Chapman, - -	"	—	9	
Davis Chapman, - -	"	—	9	
John Cousin, - -	"	—	9	
John Clayton, - -	"	—	9	
John Cofer, - -	"	—	17	
Joseph J. Crocker, - -	"	—	17	
Henry Colicote, - -	"	—	17	
Thomas Cocks. - -	"	—	17	
Littleton A. Coanes, - -	"	—	17	
Lewis Coggin, - -	"	—	17	
Samuel Cutchen, - -	"	—	17	
Hardy Council, - -	"	—	17	
Robert Carson, - -	"	—	17	
Joseph Cutchen. - -	"	—	17	
Hardy Davis, - -	"	—	7	
Lemuel Davis, - -	"	—	9	
Joshua Duggin, - -	"	—	17	
Joshua Daughtry, - -	"	—	17	
Samuel Davis, - -	"	—	17	
Hardy Darden, - -	"	—	17	
Jesse Duck, - -	"	—	17	Deserted.
Everitt Daughtry, - -	"	—	17	
John Ellis. - -	"	—	9	
Joseph Ellis, - -	"	—	26	
Burwell Edwards, - -	"	—	17	
Nathan English, - -	"	—	17	
John W. English, - -	"	—	17	
Cary Ellis. - -	"	—	17	
Benjamin Eley, - -	"	—	19	
John Forrest, - -	"	—	14	
Thomas Flake, - -	"	—	17	
Allen Fulgham, - -	"	—	17	
Abraham Fowler, - -	"	—	17	
Silas Fowler, - -	"	—	17	
Edmund Fowler, - -	"	—	17	
Job C. Fowler, - -	"	—	17	
Harrison Glover, - -	"	—	9	
Jordan Goodson, - -	"	—	26	
Henry Goodson, - -	"	—	26	
Samuel Garrison, - -	"	—	17	
Joseph Goodson, - -	"	—	17	
Benjamin Glover, - -	"	—	17	
John B. Gale, - -	"	—	17	
John Goodson, - -	"	—	17	
Robert Gibbs, - -	"	—	17	
Thomas Harris, - -	"	—	17	
Thomas Hargrave, - -	"	—	14	
Major Heath, - -	"	—	17	
Edward Humphries, - -	"	—	17	
Job Holland. - -	"	—	17	
Edward Howell, - -	"	—	17	
Edmond Joyner, - -	"	—	17	
John James, - -	"	—	17	
Benjamin J. Jones, - -	"	—	17	
Thomas Judkins, - -	"	—	17	
Jordan Johnson, - -	"	—	17	
Stephen Johnson, - -	"	—	17	
Aaron Johnson, - -	"	—	17	
William Latimer, - -	"	—	17	
William Lester, - -	"	—	17	
William Mintz, - -	"	—	17	
Richard Madrey, - -	"	—	17	
Joseph McCallester, - -	"	—	17	Sub'd by Fr's Taylor.

NAMES.	RANK.	TIME OF SERVICE.		REMARKS.
		Months.	Days.	
Edmond Murry, - -	Private,	–	17	
Cary Morris, - -	"	–	17	
William Montford, - -	"	–	17	
William Milby. - -	"	–	17	
Zack. Matthews, - -	"	–	17	
Thomas Nosworth, - -	"	–	17	
Mathew Pope, - -	"	–	17	
Daniel Pope, - -	"	–	17	
James Powell. - -	"	–	17	
William Powell, - -	"	–	17	
Andrew Redd, - -	"	–	17	
Willis Robertston, - -	"	–	17	
Joseph Sikes, - -	"	–	17	
Richard Stringfield, - -	"	–	17	
John Sikes, - -	"	–	17	
James Sikes, - -	"	–	17	
Allen Spivey, - -	"	–	17	
Mills Spivey, - -	"	–	17	
Zuckariah Turner. - -	"	–	17	
James Tallough, - -	"	–	17	
Henry Turner, - -	"	–	17	
Jacob Turner, - -	"	–	17	
Jordan Taylor, - -	"	–	17	Deserted.
Isham Underhill, - -	"	–	17	
Nath'l Vellines, - -	"	–	17	
Hezekiah Vellines, - -	"	–	17	
Samuel Vaughn, - -	"	–	17	
Josiah Whitley, - -	"	–	17	
Jack Whitehead, - -	"	–	17	
George Williamson, - -	"	–	17	
Thomas West, - -	"	–	17	

MUSTER ROLL

Of Captain William Bolling's Troop of Cavalry, Thirty-eighth Regiment, Virginia Militia, in the Service of the State of Virginia, from September 4th to September 13th, 1814.

NAMES.	RANK.	TIME OF SERVICE.		REMARKS.
		Months.	Days.	
William Bolling.	Captain,	—	10	
James B. Furguson,	1st Lieutenant.	—	10	
Charles J. Eins,	"	—	10	
John Royster,	"	—	10	
Warner Lewis,	Cornet,	—	10	
John Philpots,	1st Sergeant,	—	10	
Granvill Smith,	"	—	10	
William George,	"	—	10	
Thomas H. Crouch.	"	—	10	
Joseph S. Clarke,	"	—	10	
Alexander S. Dandridge,	Corporal,	—	10	
William Humber,	"	—	10	
Francis W. Royster,	"	—	10	
Neil B. Gay,	"	—	10	
Richard Garrett,	"	—	10	
Anthony Cabiness,	"	—	10	
Moses Overton,	"	—	10	
Edward Bruce,	"	—	10	
Jessee Bother,	"	—	10	
Anderson Jackson,	"	—	10	
John R. Bell,	"	—	10	
Robert Oliver,	"	—	10	
Paulin Anderson,	Private,	—	10	
Dandridge Bradshaw,	"	—	10	
Peyton Bailey,	"	—	10	
Russel B. Belcher,	"	—	10	
Ambos Brooks,	"	—	10	
Peyton Baughan,	"	—	10	
James Burton,	"	—	10	
Henry D. Carver,	"	—	10	
Alex'r A. Cambell,	"	—	10	
James L. Cocke,	"	—	10	
Kenner Cralle,	"	—	10	
Moses Collier,	"	—	10	
Francis Carter,	"	—	10	
Asa Cabiness,	"	—	10	
Pleasant Clark,	"	—	10	
William Crittenten,	"	—	10	
Thomas Dunevant,	"	—	10	
John Dunevant,	"	—	10	
James W. Druprey,	"	—	10	
Joshua Davis,	"	—	10	
John Dickerson,	"	—	10	
Jessee Ellis,	"	—	10	
John Foster,	"	—	10	
Pascal Foster,	"	—	10	
Gideon Foster,	"	—	10	
Gabriel Fowlkes,	"	—	10	
Cradock Fowlkes	"	—	10	

NAMES.			RANK.	TIME OF SERVICE.		REMARKS.
				Months.	Days.	
Tarlton Fleming,	-	-	Private,	–	10	
Wyatt Fleming,	-	-	"	–	10	
Edward Gay,	-	-	"	–	10	
Edmund George,	-	-	"	–	10	
Reuben George,	-	-	"	–	10	
William Gill,	-	-	"	–	10	
Anderson Gill,	-	-	"	–	10	
James Goodwin,	-	-	"	–	10	
Edward Humber,	-	-	"	–	10	
Daniel Hardaway,	-	-	"	–	10	
Younger Hardaway,		-	"	–	10	
Thomas L. Holiday,		-	"	–	10	
William Hardaway,		-	"	–	10	
John Holoway,	-	-	"	–	10	
John B. Humbers,	-	-	"	..	10	
Isaiah Humphries,	-	-	"	–	10	
Spicer Humphries,	-	-	"	–	10	
William Hicks,	-	-	"	–	10	
David Jarret,	-	-	"	–	10	
Freeman Jordan,	-	-	"	–	10	
Thomas P. Jackson,	-	-	"	–	10	
Asa Jeffries,	-	-	"	–	10	
John W. Jennings,	-	-	"	–	10	
Leweling Jones,	-	-	"	–	10	
Benj'n Jackson,	-	-	"	–	10	
Simon C. Jackson,	-	-	"	–	10	
Robert Key,	-	-	"	–	10	
Tiscamer Knight,	-	-	"	–	10	
William Leeds,	-	-	"	–	10	
Arch'd B. Lewis,	-	-	"	–	10	
Charles May,	-	-	"	–	10	
Kenneth McRae,	-	-	"	–	10	
Thomas Miller,	-	-	"	–	10	
David Mines,	-	-	"	–	10	
John Morrison,	-	-	"	–	10	
John Mullins,	-	-	"	–	10	
Sygnal Moore,	-	-	"	–	10	
Edward Morriss,	-	-	"	–	10	
Pauncey Nuckols,	-	-	"	–	10	
Thomas Nelson,	-	-	"	–	10	
Daniel Nelson,	-	-	"	–	10	
Rice Newman,	-	-	"	–	10	
John B. Oliver,	-	-	"	–	10	
Alex'r P. Payne,	-	-	"	–	10	
Thomas Payne,	-	-	"	–	10	
Sam'l H. Pankey,	-	-	"	–	10	
Thompson Penick,	-	-	"	–	10	
James Reynolds,	-	-	"	–	10	
Thomas Richardson,	-	-	"	–	10	
Samuel D. Rawlins,	-	-	"	–	10	
John Stanley,	-	-	"	–	10	
Shederick Saidsbury,		-	"	–	10	
William Smith, (son of Hall,)			"	–	10	
Thomas Salmous,	-	-	"	–	10	
William Smith,	-	-	"	–	10	
Ezekiel Saidsbury,	-	-	"	–	10	
John P. Samson,	-	-	"	–	10	
William Tourman,	-	-	"	–	10	
Samuel Thomas,	-	-	"	–	10	
Thos. C. Vaughan,	-	-	"	–	10	
John P. Woodson,	-	-	"	–	10	
George W. Watkins,		-	"	–	10	
Ambrose Wade,	-	-	"	–	10	
Daniel Wade,	-	-	"	–	11	
Bassett Watson,	-	-	"	–	10	
William Wright,		-	"	–	10	

Captain James Bonner's Company—Sixty-second Regiment.

NAMES.	RANK.	TIME OF SERVICE.		REMARKS.
		Months.	Days.	
James Bonner, - -	Captain,	4		
William H. Harrison, -	Lieutenant,	4		
Richard Heath, - -	Ensign,	4		
Williamson B. Heath, -	1st Sergeant,	4		
Baker Andrews, - -	2d "	4		
Edwin Hobbs, - -	3d "	4		
Charles Cain, - -	4th "	4		
James Fenn, - -	4th "	3		
Robert Sturdivant, - -	1st Corporal,	4		
Braxton Harrison, - -	2d "	4		
Nicholas R. Cain, - -	3d "	4	–	Promoted since 13th February.
Samuel Bennet, - -	4th "	4	–	Promoted since 13th February.
John Lee, - - -	1st "	4	–	Promoted 13th June.
James Sturdivant, - -	Drummer,	4		
Stephen Andrews, - -	Fifer,	4		
Robert Andrews, - -	Private,	4		
William Bonner, - -	"	1		
William Braxton, - -	"	4		
John Bacon, - -	"	1		
James Bradley, - -	"	4		
William Dowain, - -	"	4		
Stephen Dilister, - -	"	3		
Edward Finney, - -	"	3		
James Goulder, - -	"	4		
Edmund Goulder, - -	"	4		
James Harrison, - -	"	1		
William Hamlin, - -	"	4		
Frederick T. Hall, - -	"	4		
Samuel Harwell, - -	"	4		
Theodrick P. Harrison, -	"	4		
Carter Harrison, - -	"	4		
Daniel Hunnicutt, - -	"	1		
William Hall, - -	"	4		
John Hamlin, - -	"	4		
Peter Hamlin, - -	"	–	7	
James Hardiman, - -	"	4		
Peter Johnston, - -	"	4	–	Enlisted in the service of United States 19th April 1813.
Miles Johnston, - -	"	4	–	Enlisted in the service of United States 19th April 1813.
John Johnson, - -	"	3	–	Enlisted in the United States service 19th April 1813.
Augustine Johnson, -	"	3	–	Enlisted in the United States service 19th April 1813.
John Kirby, - -	"	2	25	Enlisted in the United States service 9th June.
Willy Livesay, - -	"	1		

NAMES.	RANK.	TIME OF SERVICE.		REMARKS.
		Months.	Days.	
John Livesay, jr. - -	Private,	4		
David Lee, - - -	"	1	–	Substitute D. Lee, jr.
Jessee Lanthrope, - -	"	4		
Amos Livesay, - -	"	3		
Alex'r Lee, - - -	"	3		
Henry S. Mouring, - -	"	4		
Marchy McKan, - -	"	4	–	Or McHan.
Thomas Musslewhite, -	"	4		
Henry C. Machen, - -	"	4		
Edmond Miles, - -	"	4		
Thomas Murry, - -	"	4		
Daniel Newell, - -	"	1		
Mathew Noland, - -	"	1	12	
Peter Pepples, - -	"	1		
William Philips, - -	"	4		
Willy Poythriss, - -	"	4		
Mack Roberts, - -	"	4		
John Newill, - -	"	1		
William Stainback, -	"	4		
Larkin Smith, - -	"	3		
Eppes Tatum, - -	"	4		
David Temple, - -	"	4		
William Wells, - -	"	4		
Wyatt Williams, - -	"	4		
Ambrose Wilkins, - -	"	3		
Robert Watkins, - -	"	1		

(For rest of this company, see publication of Pay Rolls.)

Captain George Bookers' Company—Nineteenth Regiment.

NAMES.	RANK.	TIME OF SERVICE.		REMARKS.
		Months.	Days.	
George Booker.	Captain,	–	10	
John Drewry,	Lieutenant,	–	10	
William Taylor,	Ensign,	–	10	
Joseph S. James,	"	–	24	
John Kenedy,	"	–	22	Promoted.
M. B. Portiaux,	Lieutenant,	–	9	
Francis Wood.	"	–	24	
Thomas Clarke,	Sergeant,	–	10	
William Boler.	"	–	10	
John Goddin.	"	–	10	
Lewis Atkinson,	"	–	22	
Christopher Irvine,	"	–	12	
Thomas Jude,	"	–	12	Transferred to comp'y as assistant.
Joshua Lomax,	"	–	24	
John Wood,	"	–	16	
Ebenezer Jones,	"	–	24	
John Parkhill,	"	–	24	
Robert B. Fife,	"	–	24	
Adolph Dill,	Corporal,	–	10	
Anderson Barrett,	"	–	10	
Abner Robinson,	"	–	10	
Francis Mills,	"	–	10	
John Powell.	"	–	12	
George W. Holmes,	"	–	12	Transferred to comp'y as assistant.
William Dickerson,	"	–	12	
Henry Pollard,	"	1	6	
John Southall,	"	–	24	
Henry Cower,	"	–	24	
John Rynax,	"	–	24	
Moses H. Judah,	"	–	24	
Samuel Andrews,	Private,	–	24	
James C. Anthony,	"	–	24	
Leary Andrews,	"	–	1	
David Allen,	"	–	10	
Gilliam Anderson,	"	–	10	
Lewis Atkinson,	"	–	10	
John G. Beck,	"	–	24	
Robert Bullington,	"	–	12	
Edward Bradley,	"	–	12	
William Baker,	"	–	10	
William Bosher,	"	–	2	Joined Capt. Stevenson's company.
Samuel Bingham,	"	–	10	
Thomas Baker,	"	–	10	
John Bosher,	"	–	10	
C. Baker,	"	–	10	
Benjamin Baker,	"	–	10	
Joshua Beale,	"	–	10	
J. Blair.	"	–	10	
James Bexhall,	"	–	10	
John Benson,	"	–	10	
William Badger,	"	–	2	Left the company.

NAMES.	RANK.	TIME OF SERVICE.		REMARKS.
		Months.	Days.	
William Bush, - -	Private,	–	2	
Charles Christian, - -	"	–	24	
Thomas Conclain, - -	"	–	25	Deserted.
Charles A. Cox, - -	"	–	–	Joined Capt. Wirt's F. artillery.
Milton Clarke, - -	"	–	24	
Elisha Copland, - -	"	–	24	
J. B. Cotton, - -	"	–	14	
William Crane, - -	"	–	24	
Henry Clarke, - -	"	–	24	
Frederick Clarke, - -	"	–	24	
Thomas Clark, - -	"	–	11	
Richardson Curle, - -	"	–	2	Joined some other company.
Reuben Crealy, - -	"	–	10	
James Cannon, - -	"	–	10	
Andrew Carleton. - -	"	–	4	
William W. Dickerson, - -	"	–	24	
William Dabney, - -	"	1	4	
Samuel Dunn, - -	"	–	10	
Charles Dunbar, - -	"	–	10	
Samuel Dayle, - -	"	–	10	
William Ellis, - -	"	–	10	
James Epperson. - -	"	–	10	
Ambrose Edwards, - -	"	–	4	Joined some other company.
James Edwards, - -	"	–	4	Joined some other company.
Daniel Ellis, - -	"	–	22	
William Elliott, - -	"	–	2	Joined another company.
Macon Ford, - -	"	–	24	
William Finch, - -	"	–	24	
Philip Fister, - -	"	–	24	
Elijah Folks, - -	"	–	24	
Nelson Farrar, - -	"	–	12	
William Foster, - -	"	–	14	Joined Capt. Wrist's (or Wirt's) artillery.
William Ford, - -	"	–	10	
Robert Fuller, - -	"	–	10	
R. B. Gwathney, - -	"	–	17	
James Gray, - -	"	–	24	
R. H. Goldthwait, - -	"	–	24	
John Garth, - -	"	–	24	
Mathew Gentry. - -	"	–	6	
Samuel Greenhow, - -	"	–	10	
William Guy, - -	"	–	10	
John A. Glass, - -	"	–	4	
John S. Hughes, - -	"	–	24	
Wyatt Hynes, - -	"	–	24	
John F. Hendley, - -	"	–	12	
John Hanley. - -	"	–	22	
William L. Hedenburgh, - -	"	–	–	Deserted.
George Hamilton, - -	"	–	10	
James Holcroft, - -	"	–	10	
Leopold Jones, - -	"	–	21	
Edwin James, - -	"	–	24	
Dexter Jones, - -	"	–	10	
Christ. Irvine, - -	"	–	10	
Henry King, - -	"	–	24	
Daniel Lipscomb, - -	"	–	24	
Oliver Lipscomb, - -	"	–	21	Deserted.
William Lawrence, - -	"	–	24	
James Lowns, jr. - -	"	–	24	
Roger Lipscomb, - -	"	–	10	

NAMES.	RANK.	TIME OF SERVICE.		REMARKS.
		Months.	Days.	
John Miller, - -	"	–	16	
Thomas Massie, - -	"	–	24	
Sublett McGruder, - -	"	–	24	
W. G. Meriwether, - -	"	–	18	
William McEury, - -	"	–	24	
Thomas Michall, - -	"	–	10	
Joseph Mays, - -	"	–	10	Appointed Serg. Maj.
Otis Mason, - -	"	–	10	
Peter Mayse, - -	"	–	1	
John Noel, - -	"	–	24	
Hector Organ, - -	"	–	24	
James Oldham, - -	"	–	10	
Asa Otis. - -	"	–	11	
Henry Owen, - -	"	–	22	
Thomas Ponsenbuy, - -	"	–	5	
Lawson Puckett, - -	"	–	24	
Charles Paine, - -	"	–	18	
George Parker, - -	"	–	4	Deserted.
John Puryear, - -	"	–	12	Transferred to company as assistant.
David Perry, - -	"	–	12	
Thomas Prosser, - -	"	–	10	
William Powell, - -	"	–	10	
Lindley Quesy, - -	"	–	10	
Richard Roddy, - -	"	–	9	Deserted.
Lodovicus Reed, - -	"	–	11	
William Richards, - -	"	–	24	
Elias Reed, - -	"	–	21	
Tho. Richardson, - -	"	–	3	Joined some other company.
Paschal Robertson, - -	"	–	10	
Samuel Stillman, - -	"	–	24	
John Slade, - -	"	–	24	
William Sheppard. - -	"	–	24	
Nathaniel Sheppard, - -	"	1	4	
William Saunderson. - -	"	–	21	
Samuel Swan, - -	"	–	24	
John Scott, - -	"	–	12	
Philip Sturdivant, - -	"	–	4	Joined Capt. Wrist's (or Wirt's) artillery.
Nath'l Shapard, - -	"	–	12	
George Spooner, - -	"	–	10	
John Sims, - -	"	–	10	
Yancy Thompson, - -	"	–	12	
William Tyree, - -	"	–	10	Deserted.
Caleb Tyree, - -	"	–	10	
W. P. Thatcher, - -	"	–	18	
Thos. Tinsley, - -	"	–	10	
Edward Valentine, - -	"	–	10	
R. C. Wortham. - -	"	–	24	
Harvie Williams, - -	"	–	24	
Edward Walford, - -	"	–	24	
Orin Williams, - -	"	–	24	
Isaac White, - -	"	–	24	
John Wright, - -	"	–	24	
Charles William, - -	"	–	24	
William Wild. - -	"	–	19	
Christopher Whiting, - -	"	–	12	
David Wood, - -	"	–	–	Deserted.
Josiah Williams, - -	"	–	10	
Henry Williams, - -	"	–	1	Joined some other company.
Thomas Winston, - -	"	–	10	
Thomas Ware, - -	"	–	10	

(For rest of this company, see publication of Pay Rolls.)

MUSTER ROLL

Of Captain Thomas S. Booth's Company of Virginia Militia, from the 39th Regiment, under the command of Major John G. Wilden, from the 1st to 6th July, 1813.

NAMES.	RANK.	TIME OF SERVICE.		
		Months.	Days.	
Thomas S. Booth,	Captain,	–	7	
Edward Watkins.	Lieutenant.	–	7	
Peter Vaden,	Ensign,	–	7	
Vivant Quimchet,	Sergeant,	–	7	
John Lee,	''	–	7	
Nathaniel Gray,	''	–	7	
David Thacker,	''	–	7	
Frederick B. Overby,	Corporal,	–	7	
Nelson Crowder,	''	–	7	
Peter Bedlock,	''	–	7	
Westley Crowder,	''	–	7	
Atkinson, Robert	Private,	–	7	Sub. by Geo. Day.
Atkinson, Thomas	''	–	7	Do Ananias Crowder.
Aldridge, Littleberry	''	–	7	
Andrews, Robert	''	–	7	
Andrews, Joseph	''	–	7	
Brown, Archer	''	–	7	
Branton, William	''	–	7	
Butler, Jonathan	''	–	7	
Butler, Micajah	''	–	7	
Butler, Joseph	''	–	7	
Butler, Samuel	''	–	7	
Butler, Robt. H.	''	–	7	
Binford, Robert	''	–	7	
Crowder, Wiley	''	–	7	
Crowder, Joseph	''	–	7	
Clements, Nicholas	''	–	7	
Dabney, Nathaniel	''	–	7	
Fiby, Henry	''	–	7	
Gresham, Henry	''	–	7	
Gray, Frederick	''	–	7	
Harwell, Batte	''	–	7	
Jolley, Daniel	''	–	7	
Jones, Henry	''	–	7	
Jones, Edmond	''	–	7	
King, Wiley	''	–	7	
Lewis, Thompson	''	–	7	
Lewis, William	''	–	7	
Moody, Kerby	''	–	7	
Moody, David	''	–	7	
McCulloch, Cad.	''	–	7	
Pillion, Thomas	''	–	7	
Pillsborough, Moses B.	''	–	7	
Stowe, Wiley	''	–	7	
Sandifer, Joshua	''	–	7	
Stonton, John	''	–	7	
Tudor, Richard	''	–	7	
Thomas, Ebenezer	''	–	7	

NAMES.	RANK.	TIME OF SERVICE.		REMARKS
	Private,	Months.	Days.	
	"			
Vaughan, Berayman -	"	–	7	
Williams, Thomas - -	"	–	7	
Wells, Jessee - -	"	–	7	
Whitehead, Jeremiah -	"	–	7	
Wells, Adam - -	"	–	7	
Yates, Benjamin P. -	"	–	7	

Captain Nathaniel Bowe's Company—Seventy-fourth Regiment.

NAMES.	RANK.	TIME OF SERVICE.		REMARKS.
		Months.	Days.	
Nath'l Bowe, - -	Captain.	–	25	
James Christian. - -	Private.	1		
Jacob Christian, - -	"	1		
Francis Taylor, - -	"	–	9	Furnished a substitute.
Attached to Captain Jones' Co.				
Ch. D. Alvis, - -	"	–	10	
Henry Arnall, - -	"	–	10	
Davis Arnall, - -	"	–	10	
Rich'd Arnall, - -	"	–	10	
Thomas Bowles. - -	"	–	10	
Peter Bowles, - -	"	–	10	
Joseph Bowles, - -	"	–	10	
Ambrose Brooks, - -	"	–	10	
John Bell, - -	"			
Daniel Caker, - -	"	–	10	
Chas. Childress. - -	"	–	10	
Alex'r Chisholm, - -	"	–	24	Joined Capt. Wingfield on the 20th June.
Chris. Cawthon. - -	"	–	10	
Geo. Davis, - -	"	–	10	
John Donnolly, - -	"	–	10	
Pleasant Ford, - -	"	1		
Thomas F. Green, - -	"	–	10	
James Higgason, - -	"	–	10	
Norman Harvey, - -	"	–	10	
Ben. Harris, - -	"	–	10	
Ben. Jenkins, - -	"	–	10	
Ben. Jenkins, - -	"	–	10	
John Jude, - -	"	–	2	
Ed. Maynard, - -	"	–	10	
Joseph Patterson, - -	"	–	10	
William Pearson, - -	"	–	10	
James B. Parker. - -	"	–	10	
Neal D. McCook, - -	"	–	10	
Thomas Richardson, - -	"	–	10	
Tindall Ragland. - -	"	–	10	
Thomas Turner. - -	"	–	10	
Joseph Shelton, - -	"	–	10	

(For rest of this company, see publication of Pay Rolls.)

MUSTER ROLL

Of Captain Joseph Bragg's Company of Virginia Militia, (Infantry,) from Thirty-ninth Regiment, commanded by Major Jo. G. Wilder, in the Service from 30th June to the 12th July, 1813.

NAMES.	RANK.	TIME OF SERVICE.		REMARKS.
		Months.	Days.	
Joseph Bragg,	Captain,	–	13	
Richard F. Hannon.	Lieutenant,	–	13	
Thomas Wilcox,	Ensign,	–	13	
Solomon High.	Sergeant,	–	13	
James B. Coggbill.	"	–	13	
Steven Aldridge,	"	–	13	
David A. Rawlings.	Corporal,	–	13	
Thomas Rosser,	"	–	13	
Joseph Bacon,	"	–	13	
Joel Aldridge,	Private,	–	13	
James D. M. Anderson,	"	–	13	
William Branch,	"	–	13	
Armistead O. Butler.	"	–	13	
William Clarke, jr.	"	–	13	
William Cain,	"	–	13	
William Clarke,	"	–	13	
Richard Cotton,	"	–	13	
Silas Canterbury,	"	–	13	
Andrew Cross,	"	–	13	
James Cain,	"	–	13	
George J. Cain,	"	–	13	
Nathan Dumphe,	"	–	13	
Herbert Elder,	"	–	13	
Pleasant Elam.	"	–	13	
Francis R. Farlamb,	"	–	13	
William H. Gent,	"	–	13	
Dinwiddie Goodwyn,	"	–	13	
James Harriss.	"	–	7	
Cary Hobbs,	"	–	13	
Hartwell P. Heath,	"	–	13	
Robert Harris,	"	–	13	
George King,	"	–	13	
Peter Kendall,	"	–	13	
Peyton Lynch,	"	–	13	
William Leavy,	"	–	13	
James Lea,	"	–	13	
John McKetrich,	"	–	13	
Allen Mitchell,	"	–	13	
Elijah Mitchell,	"	–	13	
John McLean,	"	–	13	
Robert McLean,	"	–	13	
Edward Powell,	"	–	13	
John Powell,	"	–	13	
Ezra Pride,	"	–	13	
Robert P. Potts,	"	–	13	
George Patterson,	"	–	13	
Elgin Russell,	"	–	13	

NAMES.	RANK.	TIME OF SERVICE.		REMARKS.
		Months.	Days.	
Joseph Rowlett, - -	Private,	–	8	
William Robertson, - -	"	–	13	
Daniel Stringer, - -	"	–	13	
Isaac Sharp, - -	"	–	13	
John B. Smith, - -	"	–	13	
Alba Sexton, - -	"	–	13	
Theodore Trezvant, - -	"	–	13	
William E. Turner, - -	"	–	13	
Hartwell Webb, - -	"	–	13	
John H. Warwich, - -	"	–	13	
Edward Williams, - -	"	–	13	
Duncan Watts, - -	"	–	13	

MUSTER ROLL

Of Carter M. Braxton's Company of Infantry of the Line, of the 111th Regiment, commanded by Lieutenant Colonel Richard E. Parker, in the service of the United States, from the 5th day of August to the 25th day of September, 1814.

NAMES.	RANK.	TIME OF SERVICE.		REMARKS.
		Months.	Days.	
Carter M. Braxton, - -	Captain,	1	20	
George Wright, -	Lieutenant,	–	27	
Thomas C. Braxton, - -	Ensign,	1	20	
William R. Jeffries, - -	Sergeant,	1	20	
James Carter, - -	"	1	20	
John H. John, - -	"	1	20	
Vincent Ramsey, - -	"	1	20	
James Trible, - -	Corporal,	1	20	
Griffin Harper, - -	"	1	20	
Richard H. John, - -	"	1	20	
Joseph Hester, - -	"	1	20	
Lawson Johnson, -	Fifer,	1	20	
Lawrence Andrews, - -	Private,	1	20	
Abraham Brizendine, -	"	1	20	
Vincent Brizendine, - -	"	1	20	
Lewis Beaman, - -	"	1	20	
Henry Brown, - -	"	1	20	
William Beazley, - -	"	1	20	
Benjamin Boughton, - -	"	1	20	
Reuben Cox, - -	"	1	20	
George Campbell, - -	"	1	20	
James Cooper, - -	"	1	20	
Richard N. Calliss, - -	"	1	20	
Lewis Coleman, - -	"	1	20	
Robbin Crow, - -	"	1	20	
Evan Davis, - -	"	1	20	
Thomas Durham, - -	"	1	20	
Lewis Davis, - -	"	1	20	
Drura Dobbins, - -	"	1	20	
Robinson Davis, - -	"	–	25	
William L. Day, - -	"	–	4	
Jackson H. Dunn, - -	"	–	25	
Robert Elliott, - -	"	–	25	
Alexander Elliott, - -	"	–	25	
Churchill Fidler, - -	"	–	25	
Greenwood Fisher, - -	"	1	20	
John Giss, - -	"	1	20	
Jessee Griggs, - -	"	1	20	
John Greenwood, - -	"	1	20	
Isaac Greenwood, - -	"	1	20	
Thomas Gatewood, - -	"	1	20	
Garnett Greenstreet, - -	"	–	25	
Spencer Graves, - -	"	–	25	
Lewis Gatewood, - -	"	–	25	
Philip P. Gatewood, - -	"	–	25	
Thomas Hogges, - -	"	1	20	
Major Hogges, - -	"	1	20	

NAMES.			RANK.	TIME OF SERVICE.		REMARKS.
				Months.	Days.	
John T. Hill,	-	-	Private,	–	25	
Morning Johnson,	-	-	"	1	20	
Philip E. Jones,	-	-	"	–	25	
Benjamin Jones,	-	-	"	–	25	
John Long,	-	-	"	–	25	
Roderick Lumpkin,	-	-	"	–	25	
Elijah McKan,	-	-	"	1	20	
James McKendry,	-	-	"	1	20	
Elijah Moody,	-	-	"	1	1	
Hunley Moody,	-	-	"	1	20	
Jameson Moody,	-	-	"	–	25	
Lewis Munday, jr.	-	-	"	–	25	
John Mahon,	-	-	"	–	25	
Charles Minter,	-	-	"	–	25	
Larkin Moody,	-	-	"	–	25	
Muscoe Munday,	-	-	"	–	25	
Lewis Munday, jr.	-	-	"	–	25	
George Purkins,	-	-	"	1	20	
Mordecai Rouse,	-	-	"	1	20	
Anderson Rowe,	-	-	"	–	25	
Allen D. Smith,	-	-	"	1	20	
Reubin Sale,	-	-	"	–	25	
George Treble,	-	-	"	1	20	
Richard Thomas,	-	-	"	–	25	
Ludy Taylor,	-	-	"	1	20	
John Tucker,	-	-	"	1	20	
Upton Williams,	-	-	"	1	20	

MUSTER ROLL

Of Captain Charles H. Braxton's Company of Cavalry, attached to the First Regiment, commanded by Lieutenant Colonel Phil. Holcomb, in the Service of the State of Virginia, from 3rd to 13th September, 1814.

NAMES.	RANK.	TIME OF SERVICE.		REMARKS.
		Months.	Days.	
Charles H. Braxton,	Captain,	–	11	
William H. Spiller,	1st Lieutenant,	–	11	
Lodwick Slaughter,	2d "	–	11	
John Skyim,	Cornet,	–	11	
Herbert A. Clairborne,	Sergeant,	–	11	
John Crafton,	"	–	11	
Richard S. Taylor,	"	–	11	
Collin C. Spiller,	"	–	11	
William Newman,	Corporal,	–	11	
Warner L. Womley,	"	–	11	
Reubin Crouch,	"	–	11	
Edward Pollard,	"	–	11	
Dudly Armstrong,	Private,	–	7	
Thos. Anchews,	"	–	11	
Samuel Banass,	"	–	11	
John W. Baylor,	"	–	3	
Isaac Cock,	"	–	11	
John Castlen,	"	–	11	
Drewby Dugen,	"	–	11	
John B. Foster,	"	–	11	
Larkin Garrett,	"	–	11	
Robert Johnson,	"	–	11	
Warren Lipscomb,	"	–	11	
Christopher Lipscomb,	"	–	4	
John C. Pollard,	"	–	7	
William Powell,	"	–	6	
Thomas J. Powell,	"	–	6	
John B. Richardson,	"	–	11	
Joseph Row,	"	–	11	
Geo. Simpkins,	"	–	11	
Benjamin C. Spiller,	"	–	11	
Robert Simpkins,	"	–	11	
Warner Shackelford,	"	–	11	
John B. Stuart,	"	–	11	
John H. Taliafero,	"	–	11	
Robert Taliafero,	"	–	11	
W. W. F. Tompkins,	"	–	11	
William W. Timberlake,	"	–	11	
Nathaniel Trunner,	"	–	4	Appointed wagon master on 6th.
John Woody,	"	–	11	
John H. Walker,	"	–	11	

Captain Hugh Brent's Company—Fourth Regiment.

NAMES.	RANK.	TIME OF SERVICE		REMARKS.
		Months.	Days.	
Hugh Brent,	Captain,	–	13	Dead.
Williamson P. Jones,	"	2	3	
Williamson P. Jones,	Lieutenant,	–	9	Promoted to captaincy on death of Captain Brent.
Rich'd Berryman,	"	–	7	
Joseph B. Downman,	"	2	13	
Cyrus Ball,	"	2	3	
Leroy P. Leland,	Cornet,	–	13	
Geo. W. Downman,	"	1	28	
Joseph B. Downman.	Sergeant,	–	6	
William Pitman,	"	–	6	
Lawson Huthaway,	"	2	14	
William Payne,	"	2	10	
Bartley James,	"	2	14	
Thomas Biscoe,	"	–	13	
Jesse Hubbert,	Corporal,	2	8	
William Lawson,	"	2	4	
William Gibson,	"	2	7	
James Brent,	"	2	4	
John Gibson,	Qr. Master,	2	20	
Wm. L. Ball,	"	–	7	
Edward Blackmore,	Commissary,	–	7	
Armstead Cerrill,	"	–	4	
Joseph Shedrenom,	"	–	7	
George Brent,	Ass't "	–	2	
James Gibson,	Surgeon,	–	3	
James K. Ball,	Surg. Mate,	–	7	
Spencer George,	Major,			
Nicholas P. Buchan,	Private,	–	16	
James Brent, jr.	"	–	7	
James Brent,	"	–	6	
William Barrack.	"	–	7	
George Brent,	"	–	7	
Charles Brent,	"	–	7	
Cyrus Ball,	"	–	8	
Peter Beane,	"	4	19	
Thomas Biscoe,	"	4	23	
Thomas Carter,	"	–	9	
Lancelott B. Corbin,	"	2	24	
Humphrey F. Carter,	"	6	17	
Rawleigh Carter,	"	3	29	
James Carrell,	"	2	3	
Robert Clark,	"	1	14	
Willis Dameron,	"	2	21	
George W. Downman,	"	–	22	
Richard Dodson,	"	–	7	
William Davnoson,	"	–	6	Or Davidson.
John Edmonds,	"	5	17	
William Eustace,	"	3	13	
James Ewell,	"	2	13	
George England,	"	2	6	
John Gibson,	"	–	7	
William Gibson,	"		26	

NAMES.	RANK.	TIME OF SERVICE.		REMARKS.
		Months.	Days.	
Robert Gilman, - -	Private,	–	6	
Thomas Garner, - -	"	–	7	
Martin George, - -	"	–	3	
Lawson George, - -	"	–	7	
Robert G. Gilmour, - -	"	2	13	
John W. Hunton, - -	"	4	5	
Richard T. Hinton, - -	"	5	28	
Jesse Hubbard, - -	"	–	27	
John Hunt, - -	"	1	28	
Richard Hutchings, - -	"	–	19	
Lawson Hathaway, - -	"	1	18	
Bartley James, - -	"	–	7	
David H. James, - -	"	1	23	
John Kirk, - -	"	2	16	
Moses Lunsford, - -	"	2	23	
William Lunsford, - -	"	–	6	
Arthur Lee, - -	"	3	4	
William Lawson, - -	"	–	13	
Richard Mitchell, - -	"	2	10	
Thad's Mitchell, - -	"	2	4	
John McNamara, - -	"	–	10	
James Mitchell, - -	"	–	12	
John Newby, - -	"	6	18	
Robert Nutt, - -	"	2	27	
Collin Nutt, - -	"	2	3	
Matthew H. Oliver, - -	"	4		
William Oldham, - -	"	5	26	
Presley Peal, - -	"	–	7	
Edward C. Pitman, - -	"	3	8	
William Payne, - -	"	–	6	
Richard Payne, - -	"	2	10	
Thomas G. Robinson, - -	"	–	7	
Thomas Sharman, - -	"	–	7	
Cornelius Sullivan, - -	"	3	4	
Joseph Sherman, - -	"	1	25	
Thomas Towell, - -	"	–	22	
Portuse Towls, - -	"	1	11	
Warner Tapscott, - -	"	–	6	
Wm. L. Watt, - -	"	3	21	
George Webb, - -	"	1	29	
George Wall, - -	"	4	5	
Griffin Webb, - -	"	2	2	
Charles Yerby, - -	"	2	2	

(For rest of this company, see publication of Pay Rolls.)

MUSTER ROLL

Of Ensign James Brent's Company of the Ninety-second Regiment, Virginia Militia, in Service from 30th November to 10th December, 1814.

NAMES.	RANK.	TIME OF SERVICE.		REMARKS.
		Months.	Days.	
James Brent, - -	Ensign.	–	11	
Thomas Y. Hunton, - -	Sergeant.	–	11	
Elias Fendley, - -	"	–	11	
William Keeling, - -	"	–	11	
Thomas Schofield, - -	"	–	11	
John Flowers, - -	Corporal.	–	11	
James Atkerson, - -	"	–	11	
Thomas Miller, - -	"	–	11	
Robert Miller, - -	"	–	11	
Augustin Hughlett, - -	Private.	–	11	
Royston Hughlett, - -	"	–	11	
Anderson Hull, - -	"	–	11	
Roody Miller, - -	"	–	11	
Eppa Lunceford, - -	"	–	11	
Thomas Oliver, - -	"	–	11	
Daniel Rew, - -	"	–	11	
John Richson, - -	"	–	11	
Thornley Tankersley, -	"	–	11	

MUSTER ROLL

Of Captain Richard Brother's Company of Virginia Militia, in the Fifty-ninth Regiment, commanded by Lieut. Col. Josiah Riddick, jr., in the Service from March 19th to April 1st, 1813.

NAMES.	RANK.	TIME OF SERVICE.		REMARKS.
		Months.	Days.	
Richard Brothers,	Captain,	—	13	
James McLenney,	Lieutenant,	—	13	
Benjamin Riddick,	Ensign,	—	13	
Miles Griffin,	Sergeant,	—	10	
Riddick Brother,	"	—	13	
Nath'l Lassiter,	"	—	13	
Peter Brinkley,	"	—	13	
Isam Butler,	Corporal,	—	13	
Nath'n Brinkley,	"	—	13	
Dan'l Franklin,	"	—	13	
Jacob Brinkley, sen.	Private,	—	13	
Robert Booth,	"	—	13	
Willis Brinkley, sen.	"	—	13	
Wiley Brinkley,	"	—	13	
Ivajah Butler,	"	—	13	
Eli Branton,	"	—	13	
Jacob Brothers,	"	—	13	
Elisha Brinkley,	"	—	13	
William B. Bailey,	"	—	10	
Eli Carr,	"	—	13	
William Ellis,	"	—	13	
Lemuel Eley,	"	—	11	
Joseph Ellis,	"	—	8	
Richard Goodwin.	"	—	11	
Jethro Harrell,	"	—	13	
Wright Holland,	"	—	12	
James Harrell,	"	—	11	
David Holland, jr.	"	—	6	
James Jones,	"	—	13	
Rob. Johnson,	"	—	13	
Arthur Jones,	"	—	12	
John King,	"	—	10	
Abraham Lassiter.	"	—	13	
Jason Lassiter,	"	—	13	
Kedar Lassiter,	"	—	4	
Seth Morrison,	"	—	11	
John Murfre,	"	—	10	
Elisha Norfleet,	"	—	13	
Mills Nichols,	"	—	13	
John Poulson,	"	—	13	
Kedar Raby,	"	—	13	
Edw'd Riddick,	"	—	13	
William Raby,	"	—	13	
Robert Stallings,	"	—	13	
Geo. Skinner,	"	—	13	
William Sumner,	"	—	13	
Shadrack Wilkins,	"	—	13	
Samuel Wilkins,	"	—	13	

MUSTER ROLL

Of Captain Bentley Brown's Company of the Seventy-fourth Regiment, Virginia Militia, commanded by Colonel William Truehcart, in the Service of the United States at different periods in the year 1813.

NAMES.			RANK.	TIME OF SERVICE.		REMARKS.
				Months.	Days.	
Bentley Brown,	-	-	Captain,	–	23½	
William Smith,	-	-	Lieutenant.	–	23½	
William Woolfolk,	-	-	Ensign,	–	23½	
Thomas Taylor,	-	-	Sergeant.	–	23½	
James Sharp,	-	-	"	–	23½	
Benjamin Spicer,	-	-	"	–	23½	
Dabney Dickinson,	-	-	"	–	23½	
William Arnall,	-	-	Private.	–	23½	
Genet Anderson,	-	-	"	–	13	
John Butler,	-	-	"	–	23½	
John Byars,	-	-	"	–	23½	
Miller Brown,	-	-	"	–	21½	
Nelson Brooks,	-	-	"	–	14	
George Bumpass.	-	-	"	–	14	
Thomas W. Claybrook,	-	-	"		23½	
Richard Chase,	-	-	"	–	23½	
John Dickinson,	-	-	"	–	19½	
Lewis Day,	-	-	"	–	23½	
Nathaniel Dickinson,	-	-	"	–	23½	
William D. Goodwin,	.	-	"	–	19	
John Gunnel,	-	-	"	–	12	
James Hall,	-	-	"	–	23½	
James Harris,	-	-	"	–	23½	
Terry Hewlett,	-	-	"	–	23½	
William Hargrave,	-	-	"	–	19	
Francis V. Howlet,	-	-	"	..	23½	
John Hancock,	-	-	"	–	19½	
Joseph Hancock,	-	-	"	–	23½	
Henry J. Hall,	-	-	"	–	23½	
Aaron Hall,	-	-	"	–	23½	
Zephaniah Hall,	-	-	"	–	23½	
Jacob Holloway,	-	-	"	–	23½	
Simeon Hall,	-	-	"	–	23½	
James Hall,	-	-	"	–	19½	
Tarlton Hancock,	-	-	"	–	23½	
David Hanes,	-	-	"	–	23½	
Garland Hall,	-	-	"	–	23½	
Pleasant Hinchey,	-	-	"	–	23½	
John Hall,	-	-	"	–	21	
William Harper,	-	-	"	–	23½	
Benjamin Hancock.	-	-	"	–	23½	
William Hall,	-	-	"	–	23½	
William Johnson,	-	-	"	–	15	
Richard F. Jones,	-	-	"	–	23½	
John Lester,	-	-	"	–	23½	
Garrett Lowry,	-	-	"	–	23½	
William Luck,	-	-	"	–	23½	
William Lawrence,	-	-	"	–	19	

NAMES.	RANK.	TIME OF SERVICE.		REMARKS.
		Months.	Days.	
Robert Mallory, - -	Private,	–	23½	
Warner W. Minor, - -	"	–	23½	
John Martin, - -	"	–	19½	
John Moody, - -	"	–	19½	
Nicholas Mills, - -	"	–	23½	
Charles Mills, - -	"	–	15	
Thomas Nelson, - -	"	–	19½	
William Noel, - -	"	–	23½	
Thos. Nelson, (son of Wm.)	"	–	21	
Samuel Oldham, - -	"	–	23½	
William Philips, - -	"	–	23½	
Lewis Philips, - -	"	–	23½	
Austin Pate, - -	"	–	21	
Edward Patterson, - -	"	–	14	
James Quarles, - -	"	–	23½	
William Seay, - -	"	–	23½	
Luke A. Seay, - -	"	–	23½	
James Smith, - -	"	–	23½	
Solomon Stanley, - -	"	–	21	
John Stanley, - -	"	–	23½	
Benjamin Stanley, - -	"	–	23½	
Charles Swift, - -	"	–	23½	
Robert Sharp, - -	"	–	21	
William Swift, - -	"	–	23½	
Strangeman Stanley, -	"	–	23½	
William Stanley, (son of O.)	"	–	23½	
William Stanley, (son of J.)	"	–	21½	
Thomas Stanley, - -	"	–	23½	
William B. Syms, - -	"	–	23½	
Lewis Smith, - -	"	–	21½	
Zachariah Smith, - -	"	–	21½	
Maddox Stanley, - -	"	–	23½	
John T. Smith, - -	"	–	21½	
Edward Thacker, - -	"	–	23½	
Chesley Thacker, - -	"	–	23½	
Thomas Price, - -	"	–	23½	
James Taylor, - -	"	–	23½	
Charles Terrell, - -	"	–	23½	
Edmund Terrell, - -	"	–	21½	
John Terrell, - -	"	–	23½	
Garland Thompson, - -	"	–	19	
David Terrell, - -	"	–	21	
Francis Thompson, - -	"	–	23½	
Roger Thompson, - -	"	–	19½	
Overton Watkins, - -	"	–	23½	
Thomas Watkins, - -	"	–	19½	
Horatio G. Winston, -	"	–	23½	
William Wash, - -	"	–	13	
Richard White, - -	"	–	23½	
Joel Walton, - -	"	–	21½	
Pleasant Yeamans, - -	"	–	21½	
Austin Yeamans, - -	"	–	21½	
Charles Yeamans, - -	"	–	23½	
Preston Yeamans, - -	"	–	2	

MUSTER ROLL

Of Captain Irby Brown's Company of Virginia Militia, from the Eighty-third Regiment, commanded by Lieutenant Colonel James Scott, in the Service from the 1st to the 6th of July, 1813.

NAMES.	RANK.	TIME OF SERVICE.		REMARKS.
		Months.	Days.	
Irby Brown,	Captain,	–	6	
Burwell Goodwyn,	Lieutenant,	–	6	
Balaam Wells,	Ensign,	–	6	
Joseph Sturdevant,	Sergeant,	–	6	
Edward Young,	"	–	6	
Jessee Goodwin,	"	–	6	
Green Rivers,	"	–	6	
William J. Aldridge,	Corporal,	–	6	
Barney Hawkins,	"	–	6	
Claiborne Wells,	"	–	6	
Thomas Rose,	"	–	6	
Philip Hawkins,	Private,	–	6	
John Hawks,	"	–	6	
Lewis Hawkins,	"	–	6	
Francis Gent,	"	–	6	
Peter Lewis,	"	–	6	
Joshua Young,	"	–	6	
Josiah Pebles,	"	–	6	
Abner T. Meanley,	"	–	6	
Grief Hardaway,	"	–	6	
Daniel Hawkins,	"	–	6	
Berry Hawkins,	"	–	6	
Arms'd Hawkins,	"	–	6	
Markham Hardaway,	"	–	6	
Mason Wells,	"	–	6	
Henry Jackson,	"	–	6	
William Davis,	"	–	6	
David Meanley,	"	–	6	
William Hawkins,	"	–	6	
William Waller,	"	–	6	
John Vaughan,	"	–	6	
Thomas G. Hardaway,	"	–	6	
Norman Crawford,	"	–	6	
James Kidd,	"	–	6	
Robert Hunnicutt,	"	–	6	
William Thrift,	"	–	6	
Fras. Walthall,	"	–	6	
Green Hawkins,	"	–	6	
James Hunnicutt,	"	–	6	
Thomas Scott,	"	–	6	
William Moody,	"	–	6	
Thomas Coleman,	"	–	6	
Robert Hawkins,	"	–	6	
Francis Lewis,	"	–	6	
Lemuel Stanton,	"	–	6	
Thomas Firth,	"	–	6	
Robert Sturdivant,	"	–	6	

MUSTER ROLL

Of Captain John Brown's Company of Infantry, Virginia Militia, from the One Hundred and Eleventh Regiment, under the orders of Major John Turberville, in the Service from the 15th of July to the 5th August, 1813.

NAMES.	RANK.	TIME OF SERVICE.		REMARKS.
		Months.	Days.	
John Brown, - -	Captain,	–	22	
Armstrong McKenney, -	Lieutenant,	–	11	
Allen S. Dosier, -	"	–	12	
Westley Porter, - -	Ensign,	–	22	
Austin Dozier, -	Sergeant,	–	22	
John Pursley, -	"	–	22	
James Greggorey, - -	"	–	11	
Jessee A. Muse, - -	"	–	11	
William Johnson, - -	"	–	12	
Peter P. C. Straugn, - -	"	–	12	
James Davis, - -	Drummer,	–	22	
Samuel Davis, -	Fifer,	–	22	
Rich'd B. Hutt, -	Private,	–	22	
William McGuiere, - -	"	–	11	
James Davis, jr. - -	"	–	11	
Newman McKenny, - -	"	–	11	
Zechariah Scott, - -	"	–	11	
Gerard McKinney, - -	"	–	8	
Beckhram Thomas, - -	"	–	11	
James Donahan, - -	"	–	11	
Barnett Sisson, - -	"	–	11	
Thomas Sisson, - -	"	–	22	
John Sanford, - -	"	–	22	
John Davis, - -	"	–	11	
Travis McGuire, - -	"	–	11	
Alexander McGuire, - -	"	–	11	
Youell F. Howsin, - -	"	–	11	
George Davis, - -	"	–	11	
John Anthony, - -	"	–	22	
William Sutton, - -	"	–	11	
William Thomas, - -	"	–	11	
William Stone, - -	"	–	15	
Job Davis, - -	"	–	10	
Peyton Sisson, - -	"	–	21	
Henry Pritchett, - -	"	–	8	
Lewis Ponter, - -	"	–	3	
William Reynolds, - -	"	–	8	
Joseph Brown, - -	"	–	17	
Berret M. Crabb, - -	"	–	8	
Corbin Brown, - -	"	–	8	
John Allen, - -	"	–	8	
Thos. Edwards, - -	"	–	17	
James T. Scott, - -	"	–	17	
Vincent Brann, - -	"	–	11	
Dan'l Hardwick, - -	"	–	11	
James Harrison, - -	"	–	11	
William Porter, - -	"	–	11	
Daniel Harrisson, - -	"	–	11	

NAMES.	RANK.	TIME OF SERVICE.		REMARKS.
		Months.	Days.	
Sam'l Gilbert, - -	Private,	–	11	
Allen McKinney, - -	"	–	11	
Joseph Elmore, - -	"	–	11	
William Gawn, - -	"	–	11	
George M. Cluskey, - -	"	–	11	
Corbin Strawn, - -	"	–	11	
John Pope, - -	"	–	11	
Nathaniel Lefavour, - -	"	–	11	
James Kirk, - -	"	–	11	
Thomas King, - -	"	–	11	
Jeremiah Clusky, - -	"	–	11	
John Kirk, - -	"	–	11	
Henry Greggory, - -	"	–	11	
Solomon S. Hutt, - -	"	–	11	
Thomas Parmer, - -	"	–	11	

Captain John E. Brown's Company—Sixty-eighth Regiment.

NAMES.	RANK.	TIME OF SERVICE.		REMARKS.
		Months.	Days.	
John Arnold,	Lieutenant,	–	18	
Thomas Jenkins,	"	–	8	
Thompson Doniphan,	Ensign,	–	8	
Geo. H. Ballard,	Sergeant,	–	28	
Geo. Thomas,	"	–	11	
Kendal Moss,	"	–	8	
Benjamin Elkins,	Corporal,	–	8	
John McCarty,	"	–	8	
Mahone Willis,	..	–	24	
Jos. Valentine,	"	–	13	
Spraggins Francis,	"	–	27	
William Anderson,	Drummer,	–	8	
Geo. Armstrong,	Private,	–	18	
Thornton Atwell,	"	–	18	
James Allen, sen.	"	–	8	
William Acred,	"	–	8	
William Allen,	"	–	8	
Thomas Bruce,	"	–	8	
Geo. Burton, (or Benton,)	"	–	6	
Roger Betty,	"	–	8	
James E. Butler,	"	–	18	
—— Bacon,	"	–	8	
Bennet Chrismond,	"	–	18	
Pearson Clift,	"	–	8	
—— Crowdus,	"	–	8	
Edmund Clift,	"	–	9	
Washington Clift,	"	–	4	
Thomas Chandler,	"			
Jas. Christian,	"	–	8	
William Dodd,	"	–	18	
—— Dunkin,	"	–	28	
Alexander Donaphan,	"	–	8	
John Fisher,	"	–	18	
John Goldsmith,	"	–	18	
Horatio Griffin,	"	–	3	
Burdet Hefferlin,	"	–	18	
John Hunsbrough,	"	–	8	
Alexander S. Hooe,	"	–	8	
William James,	"	–	8	
Edward Inscoe,	"	–	18	
Elijah Inscoe,	"	–	18	
Geo. Jones,	"	–	18	
Joseph Jones, jr.	"	–	18	
Gilbert Morgan,	"	–	18	
Thomas Morgan,	"	–	18	
John H. Micou,	"	–	18	
William Mardes,	"	–	18	
William Massey,	"	–	18	
Robert B. Massey,	"	–	7	
John Martin,	"	–	25	
Gordon Oliver,	"			
James Prim,	"	–	18	
John Payne,	"	–	6	

NAMES.	RANK.	TIME OF SERVICE.		REMARKS.
		Months.	Days.	
Gabriel Piggott, - -	Private,			
Pearson Piggott, - -	"			
Francis Pierce, - -	"	—	14	
James Owens, - -	"	—	13	
John Rollings, - -	"	—	8	
William Rollings, - -	"	—	18	
Samuel Rollings, - -	"	—	18	
Gustavus Rodgers. - -	"	—	18	
John Spilman, - -	"	—	18	
James Staples, - -	"	—	18	
James Stephens. - -	"	—	8	
Thomas Stephens, - -	"	—	18	
Austin Settlers, - -	"	—	6	
James Self, - -	"	—	2	
Bayly Smith, - -	"			
Edmund Southard. - -	"	—	12	
Thomas Sacra, - -	"	—	6	
Thomas Spraggins. - -	"			
William Thompson, - -	"	—	18	
William C. Thompson. - -	"	—	5	
Gayle Thomas, - -	"	—	22	
William B. Taylor, - -	"			
John Taylor, - -	"	—	9	
John Warrell, - -	"	—	18	
Augustine Weadon. - -	"	—	6	
Geo. Willis, - -	"	—	22	
Joseph Wase, - -	"	—	2	

(For rest of this company, see publication of Pay Rolls.)

[Muster and Pay Rolls missing—Receipt Rolls copied.]

RECEIPT ROLL

Of Captain Samuel Brown's Company of Virginia Militia, from the Thirty-third Regiment, in the Service from the 19th to 29th March, 1814.

NAMES.			RANK.	TIME OF SERVICE.		REMARKS.
				Months.	Days.	
Samuel Brown,	-	-	Captain,	–	5	On duty every other day.
Josiah Peck,	-	-	Lieutenant.	–	5	
William B. Ellis,	-	-	Ensign,	–	5	
William Ellis,	-	-	Sergeant.	–	5	
Cabil David,	-	-	"	–	5	
Martin Pait,	-	-	"	–	5	
Machichi Feriley,	-	-	"	–	5	Or Tinsley.
Richard Clarke,	-	-	Corporal.	–	5	
Reubin Allen,	-	-	"	–	5	
Daniel Brown,	-	-	"	–	5	
William Cottrell,	-	-	"	–	5	
William Hutcherson,		-	Private.	–	5	
Richard Sampson,	-	-	"	–	5	
William Brown,	-	-	"	–	5	
Anderson Taylor.	-	-	"	–	5	
John Miller,	-	-	"	–	5	
John Ellis,	-	-	"	–	5	
Stephen Duval.	-	-	"	–	5	
Wilson Price,	-	-	"	–	5	
Charles Woodward,	-	-	"	–	5	
Joseph Blackbourn,	-	-	"	–	5	
William Baughan.	-	-	"	–	5	
Henry Willis,	-	-	"	–	5	
John Baughan,	-	-	"	–	5	
Samuel Cottrell,	-	-	"	–	5	
David Powers,	-	-	"	–	5	
Ellis Brown,	-	-	"	–	5	
Samuel Conway,	-	-	"	–	5	
William Blackborne.	-	-	"	–	5	
Reaves Tinsley,	-	-	"	–	5	
John Thomas,	-	-	"	–	8	
Alexander Gordan,	-	-	"	–	5	
Nathaniel Tinsley,	-	-	"	–	5	
John Blackborne,	-	-	"	–	5	
Geo. Montgurmery.	-	-	"	–	5	
John Montgomery.	-	-	"	–	5	
James Ellis,	-	-	"	–	5	
Wilson Coats,	-	-	"	–	5	
Overton B. Pettit,	-	-	"	–	5	
Joseph W. Campbell,	-	-	"	–	5	
Stephen Stone,	-	-	"	–	5	
John R. Whome,	-	-	"	–	5	

NAMES.			RANK.	TIME OF SERVICE.		REMARKS.
				Months.	Days.	
John Fanant,	-	-	Private,	–	5	
James Jones,	-	-	"	–	5	
Joseph Ellis,	-	-	"	–	5	
Thomas Duke,	-	-	"	–	5	

Captain John F. Bryan's Company—Sixty-eighth Regiment.

NAMES.	RANK.	TIME OF SERVICE.		REMARKS.
		Months.	Days.	
John F. Bryan, - -	Captain,	–	19	
William Waller, - -	Lieutenant,	–	19	
William Walter, - -	"	–	3	
Auther King, - -	Ensign,	1	4	
Rich'd Powers, - -	Ord'ly Serg.	–	18	
John Wright, - -	Sergeant,	–	19	
Otway B. Shields, -	"	–	16	
William Tinny, - -	"	–	19	
James L. Lawson, - -	"	–	19	
James Lebby, - -	Corporal,	–	14	
Reuben Washn. - -	"	–	11	
Thomas Orrell, - -	"	–	11	
John Moore, - -	"	–	22	
Nath'l Cox, - -	"	2	10	
William Broadrib, - -	Private,	–	28	
Geo. Ball, - -	"	–	25	
Joseph Barber, - -	"	–	22	
Elisha Bates, - -	"	–	19	
Theo. Blassingham, -	"	–	19	
Kemp Charles, - -	"	–	19	
John Dewberry, - -	"	3	3	
William Duncan, - -	"	–	24	
William L. Ellis, - -	"	–	19	
Burwell Graves, - -	"	–	18	
William Hankin, - -	"	–	26	
Pryor Hankin, - -	"	–	21	
Jorden Harrison, - -	"	–	19	
Benja. Hazelwood, - -	"			
Henry Hazelwood, - -	"	–	19	
Daniel Jones, jr. - -	"	–	26	
Robert Jackson, - -	"	1	9	
Lively James, - -	"	–	28	
Benjamin Jolley, - -	"	–	4	
Abener Piggot, - -	"	–	11	
Robert Lee, - -	"	–	19	
William Lusely, - -	"	–	11	
Medes Lewis, - -	"	–	27	
Richard Randolph, - -	"	–	9	
Geo. Rigg, - -	"			
Edward Shags, - -	"	–	18	
Nath'l Tinney, - -	"	–	3	
Thos. Willsford, - -	"	–	6	
Samuel Wright, - -	"			
Joseph Wade, - -	"	–	2	
Erasmus Welch, - -	"	–	19	
Norris Williams, - -	"			

(For rest of this company, see publication of **Pay Rolls**.)

Captain Wilson Bryan's Company—Nineteenth Regiment.

NAMES.	RANK.	TIME OF SERVICE.		REMARKS.
		Months.	Days.	
Wilson Bryan, - . -	Captain,	–	10	
John Lipscomb, - -	Lieutenant,	–	10	
John Perry, - -	"	1	5	
Daniel Hutchinson, - -	Ensign,	–	11	
Jacob Weisiger, - "		–	23	
Thomas Ritchie, - -	Sergeant.	–	6	
Chauncey Carter, - -	"	–	11	
Charles Christian, - -	"	–	5	
Warner Thomas. - -	"	–	6	
John H. Jude, - -	"	–	9	
Robert Snuden, - -	"	–	24	
Thomas Hatcher. - -	"	–	23	
William Butler, - -	"	–	23	
John Quarles, - -	"	–	23	
Wilman Gilman, - -	"	–	10	
John L. Turner, - -	"	–	10	
Richard Scott, - -	"	–	10	
Samuel Evans, - -	Corporal,	–	16	
Peter Letellier, - -	"	–	6	
Alex'r Grant, - -	"	–	6	
Thomas Atkinson, - -	"	–	10	
William Tyree, - -	"	–	3	
Richard Edwards, - -	"	–	10	
George Boasher, - -	"	–	23	
William Granberry, - -	"	–	24	
Ellis Carlton, - -	"	–	5	
Nelson G. Phillips. - -	"	–	23	
Madison McLauren, - -	"	–	23	
Reuben Nash, - -	"	–	12	
James H. Royster, - -	"	–	12	
Samuel Queay, - -	"	–	8	
J. New, - -	Drummer,	–	17	
Robert Andrews, - -	Private,	–	23	
Thomas M. Ambler, - -	"	–	23	
Charles Anderson, - -	"	–	5	
Thomas Atkerson, - -	"	–	2	
George Atkerson, - -	"	–	3	
Charles J. Bingham, - -	"	–	5	
George Boswell, - -	"	–	12	
Royall Brown, - -	"	1		
James Bailess, - -	"	–	7	
William Barnes, - -	"	–	23	
John Benson, - -	"	–	2	
John Bransford, - -	"	–	6	
Samuel J. Bagby, - -	"	–	12	
Thomas Butler, - -	"	–	5	
G. H. Bacchus, - -	"	–	23	
Thomas Baish, - -	"	–	23	
Daniel Baugh, - -	"	–	23	
Wilson Bracket, - -	"	–	23	
James Brock, - -	"	–	23	
Samuel Brame, - -	"	–	23	
William Burke, - -	"	–	23	
Charles Bennet, - -	"	–	22	
Joshua Brotherhood, - -	"	–	23	
William Bressie, - -	" .	–	23	
Samuel Bull, - -	"	–	1	

NAMES.	RANK.	TIME OF SERVICE.		REMARKS.
		Months.	Days.	
John Bath, - -	Private,	–	3	
James Booker, - -	"	–	1	
John Barnes, - -	"	–	1	
Joseph Butler, - -	"	–	1	
James Burchell, -	"	–	4	
Jonathan Collingworth, -	"	–	16	
Robert Cracker, - -	"	–	6	
Ralph Crutchfield, -	"	–	14	
Henry Calloway, -	"	–	7	
James Connelly, -	"	–	2	
John Craw, -	"	–	3	
Geo. R. Cocks, -	"	–	23	
Samuel Churchill, -	"	–	23	
Samuel N. Cardozo, -	"	–	23	
B. W. Coleman, -	"	–	23	
George Carter, -	"	–	23	
Charles Carter, -	"	–	13	
Edward Cunningham, -	"	–	7	
Walter Cameron, -	"	–	24	
John Carter, -	"	–	10	
Joseph Carter, -	"	··	10	
Charles Christian, -	"	–	10	
Anthony Croussell, -	"	–	3	
Thomas Cook, -	"	–	3	
William Cousins, -	"	–	1	
John J. Dickenson, -	"	–	10	
John Dean, -	"	–	9	
Abraham Delape, -	"	–	12	
Alex'r S. Dean, -	"	–	6	
John Durham, -	"	–	6	
Richard Davis, -	"	–	23	
John Drinkard, -	"	1	3	
Andrew Dunn, -	"	–	23	
Benjamin Daiby, -	"	–	12	Or Dailey.
William Darning, -	"	–	4	
Obediah Duvall, -	"	–	10	
Hilary Driver, -	"	–	13	
John Enders, -	"	–	23	
Charles Ellis, -	"	–	14	
Theodorick Fergason, -	"	–	23	
Alexander Fulcher, -	"	–	23	
James Grassett, -	"	–	9	
Michael H. Gilliam, -	"	–	12	
John Goode, -	"	–	23	
William Garrow, -	"	–	23	
John Grantland, -	"	–	23	
Francis Gilmer, -	"	–	4	
John G. Gamble, -	"	–	2	
Alexander Grant, -	"	–	10	
Mich'l W. Hancock, -	"	–	16	
Garland Haynes, -	"	–	16	
William Harding, -	"	–	14	
Major Horner, -	"	–	16	
William Haynes, -	"	–	2	
Samuel Hawkins, -	"	–	5	
Thomas Hedrick, -	"	–	18	
James Herron, -	"	–	23	
John Hove, -	"	–	3	
John Hollins, -	"	–	10	
William Holloway, -	"	–	12	
Martin Holloway, -	"	–	3	
Henry Huxford, -	"	–	23	
Isaac Harnard, -	"	–	23	
Daniel Jones, -	"	1	3	

NAMES.	RANK.	TIME OF SERVICE.		REMARKS.
		Months.	Days.	
John Jamerson, -	Private,	–	2	
John Jude, - - -	"	–	2	
Richard Jeffries, - -	"	–	4	
Charles A. Jacob, - -	"	–	23	
John Jones, - -	"	–	3	
John Johnson, - -	"	–	23	
Harrison Jones, - -	"	–	12	
Benjamin Johnston. - -	"	–	1	
Fred. Jude, - -	"	–	10	
John M. Key, - -	"	–	23	
Bashforth Irvin, - -	"	–	1	
Yancy Lipcomb. - -	"	–	4	
William Loyall, - -	"	1	19	
Thomas Letellier, - -	"	–	6	
Charles Langmead, - -	"	–	2	
Nathaniel Long, - -	"	–	23	
Thomas Lee, - -	"	–	23	
Isaac Leonard, - -	"	–	23	
Francis Lewis, - -	"	–	2	
David Lemmon. - -	"	–	10	
Austin Lipscomb, - -	"	–	10	
Beverly B. Lipscomb, -	"	–	10	
Peter Letellier, - -	"	–	10	
John Murphy, jr. - -	"	–	16	
Alex'r McKim, - -	"	1	16	
John Marcus, - -	"	–	14	
Patrick McDonough, -	"	–	16	
John Moore, - -	"	–	16	
Archelaus Mays, - -	"	–	16	
Samuel Meridith, - -	"	–	6	
James M. Morris, - -	"	–	2	
John McBride, - -	"	–	4	
Charles J. McMurdo, -	"	–	23	
James McAllister, - -	"	–	23	
Alexander Morris, - -	"	–	23	
William Massenburg, -	"	–	23	
Archelaus Mays, - -	"	–	18	
William Morrissett, - -	"	–	10	
Reuben Merideth, - -	"	–	10	
Samuel Mallory, - -	"	–	10	
John McCurne, - -	"	–	1	
Hugh Moore, - -	"	–	10	
Edmond S. Norvell, - -	"	–	23	
Reubin Nash, - -	"	–	11	
Robert McCracken, - -	"	–	10	
Joseph Neale, - -	"	–	11	
George Olphin, - -	"	–	10	
Richard Olphin, - -	"	–	10	
James Oliver, - -	"	–	2	
John Ormond, - -	"	–	6	
Daniel G. Pleasants, - -	"	–	12	
Joseph Perryman, - -	"	–	4	
Anthony Perryman, - -	"	–	6	
Edward Peticolo, - -	"	–	23	
Jabez Parker, - -	"	–	23	
Thomas Peckrill, - -	"	–	23	
Daniel G. Pleasant, - -	"	–	12	
Noblin Puryear, - -	"	–	10	
Thomas Puryear, - -	"	–	2	
Samuel Quay, - -	"	–	15	
Nathan H. Rice, - -	"	–	16	
John Rutherfoord, - -	"	–	6	
Samuel Roberts, - -	"	–	2	
Richard Redford, - -	"	–	23	

NAMES.	RANK.	TIME OF SERVICE.		REMARKS.
		Months.	Days.	
John Roberts, - -	Private,	–	23	
James H. Royster, - -	"	–	11	
Thomas Ritchie, - -	"	–	10	
John Robertson, - -	"	–	10	
James Rudd, - -	"	–	10	
Thomas E. Sanford, - -	"	–	16	
William Shapard, - -	"	–	2	
James Seal, - -	"	–	10	
Briton Sharpe, - -	"	–	1	
Thomas Skidmore, - -	"	–	5	
William C. Shield, - -	"	–	23	
Samuel Smith, - -	"	–	23	
George Smith, - -	"	–	23	
William Sharan, - -	"	–	23	
James Snell, - -	"	–	23	
Solomon Simon, - -	"	–	23	
Charles Smith, - -	"	–	23	
Jacob Smith, - -	"	–	23	
Reuben M. Sizer, - -	"	–	13	
Joseph Trent, - -	"	1	3	
John L. Turner, - -	"	–	2	
Zachariah Tyler, - -	"	–	1	
Caleb Tyre, - -	"	–	2	
Thomas Warner, - -	"	–	2	
Chiles Terrell, - -	"	–	23	
Thomas Wilson, - -	"	–	23	
William Talley, - -	"	–	9	
James Taylor, - -	"	–	23	
Thomas Benaja, - -	"	–	23	
Michael Tucker, - -	"	–	23	
Watson Tyler, - -	"	–	23	
Amos Vibert, - -	"	–	3	
Jacob Valentine, - -	"	–	10	
William Wright, - -	"	–	6	
Jesse Willis, - -	"	–	16	
David Wallace, - -	"	–	13	
John Watkins, - -	"	–	16	
William Wirt, - -	"	–	10	
Erasmus Welsh, - -	"	–	10	
Lewis Wingfield, - -	"	–	10	
Samuel Winston, - -	"	–	23	
John Warrick, - -	"	–	23	
Benjamin Waller, - -	"	–	23	
Hugh Warden, - -	"	–	23	
Edmond Warner, - -	"	–	23	
Ambrose Watkins, - -	"	–	21	
Charles Word, - -	"	–	2	

(For rest of this company, see publication of Pay Rolls.)

PAY ROLL

Of Sergeant Tapley Bryant's Guard of Virginia Militia, under the orders of Major William Nelson of the One Hundred and Eleventh Regiment, in Service from the 21st August to the 17th September, and from 1st to 17th November, in the year 1813.

NAMES.			RANK.	TIME OF SERVICE.		REMARKS.
				Months.	Days.	
Tapley Bryant.	-	-	Sergeant.	1	14	
John Barrott,	-	-	Private.	–	17	
Thomas W. Clarke.	-	-	"	–	17	
Job Crask,	-	-	"	–	17	
William Dodd,	-	-	"	–	27	
Spencer Mullin,	-	-	"	–	17	
Thomas Jenkins,	-	-	"	–	27	
John Reed,	-	-	"	–	27	
Henry Ryley,	-	-	"	–	27	
William Sceats,	-	-	"	–	17	

Captain Abram Buford's Company—Eighth Regiment.

NAMES.	RANK.	TIME OF SERVICE.		REMARKS.
		Months.	Days.	
Winston Askew, - -	Private.	–	14	
William A. Bibb, - -	"	1	19	
John Cawthorn, - -	"	–	4	
Asa Crenshaw, - -	"	–	–	Transferred to Captain Tinsley.
Ephraim Eckles. - -	"	–	–	" " "
Samuel Flannagan, - -	"	1	27	
David H. Gray, - -	"			
William R. Head. - -	"			
Eli Hudson, - -	"	–	11	Substitute for George Sheffield.
Walter Key, - -	"	–	20	
Thomas Sprouse. - -	"	1	20	Sub. for Ro. Gillaspie, 29th December.
John Smith, - -	"	1	20	Sub. for James Smith, 29th December.
Geo. Smith, - -	"	–	28	Sub. for L. F. Waller, 29th November.
James Smith, - -	"	1	20	Sub. for Jos. Smith, 29th December.
Thomas Wright. - -	"	–	13	Sub. for P. Gentry, 14th December.

(For rest of this company, see publication of Pay Rolls.)

MUSTER ROLL

Of Captain David Bunow's Company of Virginia Militia, from Sixty-second Regiment, commanded by Colonel Miles Selden, in the Service of the State of Virginia, from the 27th of June to 9th July, 1813.

NAMES.	RANK.	TIME OF SERVICE.		REMARKS.
		Months.	Days.	
David Bunow,	Captain,	–	13	
Thomas Boisseau,	Lieutenant,	–	13	
William Keese,	Ensign,	–	12	
William Newell,	Sergeant,	–	13	
Joseph Boisseau,	"	–	13	
Joshua Hobbs,	"	–	13	
John Harrison,	"	–	13	
Randolph Whitmore,	Corporal,	–	13	
Jos. Warthen,	"	–	13	
Alfred Butts,	"	–	13	
Jas. Searhough,	"	–	13	
Evans Andrews,	Drummer,	–	10	
Geo. Bishop,	Fifer,	–	13	
Joshua Garden,	Private,	–	13	
Littlebery Brockwell,	"	–	13	
Nathan Williamson,	"	–	13	
William Hollingneroth,	"	–	13	
Rich'd Richardson,	"	–	13	
Jacob Bishop,	"	–	13	
Edm'd Whitman,	"	–	13	
John T. Brown,	"	–	12	
William Willey,	"	–	13	
Benj'n R. Glover,	"	–	10	
Thos. Waithen,	"	–	13	
John Seamwell,	"	–	12	
Austin Jones,	"	–	12	
William Brockwell,	"	–	13	
Rich'd J. Bishop,	"	–	13	
James Bishop,	"	–	13	
Jones Stephen,	"	–	13	
Benjamin Stephen,	"	–	13	
Geo. Grapwith,	"	–	13	
James Richardson,	"	–	7	
Thomas Grapwith,	"	–	13	
Hubbard Livesay,	"	–	13	
Samuel Harrison,	"	–	13	
Hamlin Stephen,	"	–	13	
Lewis Baugh,	"	–	13	
Beverly Drinkard,	"	–	13	
Joseph Taylor,	"	–	13	
Collin Harrison,	"	–	13	
William H. Tollman,	"	–	13	
Henry Cox,	"	–	12	
James Whitmore,	"	–	13	
Uriah Williamson,	"	–	13	
Benj'n Roe,	"	–	10	
William Robertson,	"	–	12	
William Stephens,	"	–	11	

NAMES.			RANK.	TIME OF SERVICE.		REMARKS.
				Months.	Days.	
Walter Waithen,	-	-	Private,	—	13	
William J. Bishop,	-	-	"	—	12	
James Brockwell,	-	-	"	—	13	
Hamlin Bishop,	-	-	"	—	5	
Sam'l Larrby,	-	-	"	—	6	
Benj'n Williams,	-	-	"	—	8	
Jessee Brockwell,	-	-	"	—	1	
Edm'd Mayrard,	-	-	"	—	5	Or Maynard.

MUSTER ROLL

Of Captain Lawson Burfoot's Company of Virginia Militia, from the Twenty-third Regiment, Chesterfield County, under the command of Lieutenant Colonel William Brown, in Service from the 18th to 30th March, from 26th to 28th June, and from the 30th June to the 2d July, 1813.

NAMES.	RANK.	TIME OF SERVICE.		REMARKS.
		Months.	Days.	
Lawson Burfoot,	Captain,	–	18	
William G. Elam,	Lieutenant,	–	18	
James Elam,	Ensign,	–	18	
Thomas H. Bass,	Sergeant,	–	15	In the requisition one of these tours.
Richard Cheatham,	"	–	15	With Capt. Graves one of these tours.
Pleasant Cheatham,	"	–	18	
William Blankenship,	Fifer,	–	18	
Thomas Godsay,	Private,	–	18	
Mackness Blankinship,	"	–	6	
Obediah Bailey,	"	–	18	
Ezekiel Blankenship,	"	–	18	
William Bailey,	"	–	18	
Geo. Blankenship,	"	–	18	
Henry Bailey,	"	–	18	
William Brown,	"	–	18	
Richard Bass,	"	–	18	
King Bailey,	"	–	18	
Benjamin Bowles,	"	–	18	
Elisha Bailey,	"	–	18	
James Baker,	"	–	12	
Mark Blankenship,	"	–	12	
Abijah Cheatham,	"	–	18	
James Clairbone,	"	–	18	
Young Condrey,	"	–	18	
Geo. Crump,	"	–	18	
Francis Dunnevant,	"	–	18	
Noah Elam,	"	–	18	
William B. Elam,	"	–	18	
Ammon Elam,	"	–	18	
Joshua Elam,	"	–	18	
Robert Elam,	"	–	18	
Peter Elam,	"	–	18	
Benja. Farmer,	"	–	15	
John Farrell,	"	–	3	
Thomas Flournoy,	"	–	18	
Mark Flournoy,	"	–	18	
John Farell,	"	–	15	
Joseph Goode,	"	–	18	
John Gates,	"	–	18	
Robert Haskins,	"	–	15	
James Hubbard,	"	–	12	
Benjamin James,	"	–	3	
William Lockett,	"	–	6	
King Lockett,	"	–	18	
Joshua Lacy,	"	–	18	

NAMES.	RANK.	TIME OF SERVICE.		REMARKS.
		Months.	Days.	
Joshua Lacy, - -	Private,	–	18	
Alexander Moore, - -	"	–	18	
William Martin, - -	"	–	18	
Barnett Moore, - -	"	–	18	
William Moody, - -	"	–	18	
James Purker, - -	"	–	6	
John Purdie, - -	"	–	18	
Isaac D. Parker, - -	"	–	6	
Jeremiah Parker, - -	"	–	6	
Frederick Rudd, - -	"	–	18	
Henry Robertson, - -	"	–	6	
Henry Roberts, - -	"	–	18	
John Sims, - -	"	–	15	
Thomas Turpin, - -	"	–	18	
William Turpin, - -	"	–	18	
William Trent, - -	"	–	18	
Henry Turpin, - -	"	–	18	
John Winfree, - -	"	–	18	

MUSTER ROLL

Of Captain Thomas Burfoot's Company of Virginia Militia, from the 23d Regiment, commanded by Col. William Brown, in Service from 18th to 30th March, from 27th to 28th June, and from 30th June to 2d day of July, 1813.

NAMES.	RANK.	TIME OF SERVICE.		REMARKS.
		Months.	Days.	
Thomas Burfoot, - -	Captain,	—	19	
Francis Lockett, - -	1st Lieutenant,	—	16	
Henry Winfree, - -	2d "	—	19	
John Harley, - -	Cornet,	—	19	
William Gates, - -	Sergeant,	—	19	
Robert Aiken, - -	"	—	19	
Robert Wood, - -	"	—	19	
Robert Haskins, - -	"	—	19	
Peter Morisett, - -	Private,	—	19	
Henry Branch, - -	"	—	19	
William Walthall, - -	"	—	19	
Pleas't Taylor, - -	"	—	19	
Richard C. Hudson, -	"	—	19	
Joseph Stewart, - -	"	—	19	
John Jennings, - -	"	—	19	
Newby Hancock, - -	"	—	19	
Mark Turner, - -	"	—	19	
Pleas't Aikin, - -	"	—	19	
John Andrews, - -	"	—	16	
William Bragg, - -	"	—	16	
James Alvis, - -	"	—	16	
William Jackson, - -	"	—	19	
Marvell Winfree, - -	"	—	19	
Thomas Vaden, - -	"	—	16	
Spencer B. Andrews, -	"	—	16	
Joseph T. Hudson, -	"	—	16	
Claiborne Conway, -	"	—	3	
William Hancock, - -	"	—	16	

MUSTER ROLL

Of a detached Guard of Infantry, commanded by Sergeant James Burke, of the One Hundred and Ninth Regiment, under the command of Major Richard M. Segar, in the Service of the United States from 21st to 23d April, 1814.

NAMES.			RANK.	TIME OF SERVICE.		REMARKS.
				Months.	Days.	
James Burke,	-	-	Sergeant,	–	3	
John Jackson,	-	-	Corporal,	–	3	
James Falkner,	-	-	Private,	–	3	
James Harrow,	-	-	"	–	3	
John Long,	-	-	"	–	3	
Thomas Montague.	-	-	"	–	3	
Daniel G. Reade,	-	-	"	–	3	
Robert Reade,	-	-	"	–	3	
Bailey Reade,	-	-	"	–	3	
John Woods,	-	-	"	–	3	

PAY ROLL

Of Captain Robert C. Burwell's Company of the Fifty-first Regiment.

NAMES.				RANK.	TIME OF SERVICE.		REMARKS.
					Months.	Days.	
Joshua Yoe,	-	-	-	Sergeant.	–	20	
Abram Shue,		-	-	Private,	1	14	
Moses Smith,		-	-	"	1	14	

(For rest of this company, see publication of Pay Rolls.)

[Receipt Roll copied—Muster and Pay Rolls missing.]

We, the Subscribers, belonging to the P. George Troop of Cavalry, called into service, do acknowledge to have received of Thomas Cocke, Pay Master to Sixty-second Regiment, Virginia Militia, the sum annexed to our names respectively, being in full of our pay for the period herein expressed.

NAMES.	RANK.	TIME OF SERVICE.		REMARKS.
		Months.	Days.	
Will. Baugh, - -	Sergeant,	–	9	
E. Newcomb, - -	"	–	15	
P. A. Wamack, - -	"	–	15	
G. Grammer, - -	"	–	15	
R. Bland, - -	Corporal,	–	15	
R. Wilkins, - -	"	–	15	
G. Grantham, - -	"	–	15	
E. T. Harrison, - -	"	–	15	
S. G. Aires, - -	Private,	–	20	
P. Andrews, - -	"	–	15	
Lewis Batte, - -	"	–	15	
W. Brown, - -	"	–	15	
W. Baxter, - -	"	1		
T. Comer, - -	"	–	20	
C. Cocke, - -	"	–	15	
Dry Dunn, - -	"	–	15	
Wm. Eppes, jr. - -	"	–	15	
Peter Fenn, - -	"	–	15	
O. Green, - -	"	–	24	
T. W. Harrison, - -	"	–	24	
H. Harrison, - -	"	–	24	
Is. Hite, - -	"	–	24	
H. Heath, - -	"	–	24	
Is. Harrison, - -	"	–	15	
H. G. Heath, - -	"	–	20	
B. Harrison, - -	"	–	20	
C. Harrison, - -	"	–	20	
H. Marks, - -	"	–	15	
John Moody, - -	"	–	24	
Wm. Marks, - -	"	–	24	
Benj. Marks, - -	"	–	15	
E. H. Niblett, - -	"	–	15	
S. Perkins, - -	"	–	24	
Wm. Peebles, - -	"	–	24	
T. Perkinson, - -	"	–	15	
Josias Sibbert, - -	"	–	15	
L. Traylor, - -	"	–	20	
Peter Tatum, - -	"	–	20	
P. B. Thweat, - -	"	–	15	
A. Wilkins, - -	"	–	20	

(There is nothing to shew who is the Captain of this company.)

Captain Thomas Carey's Company—Twenty-first Regiment.

NAMES.	RANK.	TIME OF SERVICE.		REMARKS.
		Months.	Days.	
George B. Field, - -	Ensign,	–	23	
William Blackburn, - -	Private,	–	3	
James Berry, - -	"	–	29	
James Bully, - -	"	–	28	
Thomas Baytop, - -	"	–	9	
Gibson Cleverius, -	"	–	15	
John Crew, - -	"	–	24	
Charles Dobson, - -	"	–	6	
John Field, - -	"	–	14	
Charles Grymes, - -	"	–	15	
Charles Hobday, - -	"	–	21	
James Hall, - -	"	–	15	
Horatio G. Harwood, -	"	–	21	
Robert Haywood, - -	"	–	16	
Henry Lewis, - -	"	–	29	
Henry Mourning, - -	"	–	25	
Paul Watlington, - -	"	–	9	
Edw'd Williams, - -	"	–	7	
Washington Watlington, -	"	–	9	
Francis West, - -	"	–	1	

(For rest of this company, see publication of Pay Rolls.)

Captain William C. Carpenter's Company—Ninety-second Regiment.

NAMES.	RANK.	TIME OF SERVICE.		REMARKS.
		Months.	Days.	
William C. Mitchell, -	Ensign,	–	5	
Armstead J. Palmer, -	Sergeant,	–	5	
John Gresham, - -	"	–	11	
John Hubbard, - -	"	–	11	
John Edwards, - -	Corporal.	–	11	
John Rice, -	"	–	5	
Robert Chinn, - -	"	–	5	
Robert Forester, - -	"	–	3	
Walter Arms, - -	Private.	–	14	
John Alford, - -	"	–	29	
Rawleigh Brown, - -	"	–	18	
William Brown, - -	"	–	8	
Thomas Bean, jr. - -	"	–	5	
John Baysay, - -	"	–	11	
John Boatman, - -	"	–	11	
Middleton Brent, - -	"	–	20	
Richard Cockrell, - -	"	–	8	
Richard Edwards, - -	"	–	29	
John Flowers, - -	"	–	29	
William Ford, - -	"	–	29	
William Garner. - -	"	–	29	
Isaac George, - -	"	–	29	
Thomas D. George, - -	"	–	10	
Thaddeus Goodridge, -	"	–	28	
John Hutchings, - -	"	–	3	
Elias Hazard, - -	"	–	8	
Hugh Hutchings. - -	"	–	11	
John Knights, - -	"	–	8	
George Myers, - -	"	–	29	
George Mason, - -	"	–	14	
Edward Pinchard, - -	"	–	8	
Cyrus Pitman, - -	"	–	29	
William Pitman, - -	"	–	14	
John Richardson, - -	"	–	29	
Alfred Rains, - -	"	–	10	
Nicholas Sebre, - -	"	–	18	
Michael Samuel, - -	"	1	1	
Charles Simmons, - -	"	–	8	
George Smith, - -	"	–	29	
John M. Smith, - -	"	–	14	
George Thomas, - -	"	–	5	
James W. Tapscott, - -	"	–	8	
Champn. Talley, - -	"	–	10	
Thomly B. Tankersley, -	"	–	29	
Joseph West, - -	"	–	29	

(For rest of this company, see publication of **Pay Rolls**.)

MUSTER ROLL

Of Captain Samuel Carr's Troop of Cavalry, of the Eighty-eighth Regiment, Virginia Militia, from the County of Albemarle, called into the Service of the United States by the Proclamation of the Governor of Virginia, of the 26th August, 1814, commencing the 29th day of August and ending the 20th day of September, in the year 1814.

NAMES.	RANK.	TIME OF SERVICE.		REMARKS.
		Months.	Days.	
Samuel Carr,	Captain,	—	22	
John H. Craven,	Lieutenant,	—	22	
James Ragland.	"	—	22	
Peter Minor,	Cornet,	—	22	
Pleasant Sandidge,	Q. M. Serg't,	—	22	
John Neilson,	Sergeant,	—	22	
Archbold Buckner,	"	—	22	
Achilles Broadhead,	"	—	22	
Daniel F. Carr,	"	—	22	
John Walker,	Corporal,	—	22	
James Minor,	"	—	22	
John F. Carr,	"	—	22	
William H. Coleman,	"	—	22	
Eli Alexander.	Private,	—	22	
Obadiah Austin,	"	—	22	
John Barksdale,	"	—	22	
Daniel M. Bailey,	"	—	22	
Briscoe G. Baldwin.	"	—	22	
Peter Carr,	"	—	22	
Francis Catterton,	"	—	22	
James Crawford.	"	—	22	
James O. Carr,	"	—	22	
Thompson Crutchfield,	"	—	22	
Davis Dunett,	"	—	22	
Robert Dunett,	"	—	22	
Charles M. Dickerson,	"	—	22	
William Donahue,	"	—	22	
Robert Doulhert,	"	—	22	
William Davis,	"	—	22	
William Digges,	"	—	22	
Richard Duke,	"	—	22	
William F. Garden,	"	—	22	
Francis W. Gilmer,	"	—	22	
Benjamin Gillaspy,	"	—	22	
Pleasant C. German,	"	—	22	
George Gilmer,	"	—	22	
Valentine Head,	"	—	22	
Alsatone Johnson,	"	—	22	
Larkin Kirby,	"	—	22	
William Lindsay,	"	—	22	
John Minor,	"	—	22	
James M. Macon,	"	—	22	
Conway Macon,	"	—	22	
Thomas Miller,	"	—	22	
Thomas W. Nash,	"	—	22	
Charles Penn.	"	—	22	
Harden Quinn,	"	—	22	

NAMES.	RANK.	TIME OF SERVICE.		REMARKS.
		Months.	Days.	
William Robertson, - -	Private,	–	22	
William Smithson, - -	"	–	22	
Daniel Shackleford, - -	"	–	22	
Hazlewood Ship, - -	"	–	22	
John Shiplet, - -	"	–	22	
Mathew Turner, - -	"	–	22	
Dubray Terrell, - -	"	–	22	
Arthur Whitehurst, - -	"	–	22	
William White, - -	"	–	22	

MUSTER ROLL

Of Ensign G. M. Carrington's Company, in the Nineteenth Regiment of Virginia Militia, commanded by Lieutenant Col. John Ambler, called into the Service of the United States, from the 27th day of August to the 7th day of September, in the year 1814.

NAMES.	RANK.	TIME OF SERVICE.		REMARKS.
		Months.	Days.	
G. M. Carrington.	Ens'n Comd't,	–	13	Transferred to Captain Turner.
Joseph Mayo,	Lieut. by brev.,	–	13	
N. K. Thomas,	Ens'n by "	–	13	
F. G. Crenshaw,	Sergeant,	–	13	" " "
Chas. T. Toomer,	"	–	13	" " "
Reuben Ragland,	"	–	13	" " "
Dan'l P. Organ,	"	–	13	" " "
Richard Anderson,	Private.	–	5	" " "
John Armistead,	"	–	13	" " "
William Barksdall,	"	–	2	
Simon Block,	"	–	13	" " "
Alexander Brown,	"	–	13	" " "
John Cline,	"	–	13	" " "
William M. Chick,	"	–	13	" " "
William H. Carroll,	"	–	11	
Nathaniel Dunlop,	"	–	10	
William Dunn,	"	–	13	" " "
Russel Dutton,	"	–	13	" " "
Geo. W. Hill,	"	–	13	" " "
Daniel Higginbotham,	"	–	6	" " "
John Henderson,	"	–	3	" " "
Edward Hallam,	"	–	13	" " "
John James,	"	–	13	" " "
Nathaniel M. Johnson,	"	–	13	" " "
Bennett Kirby,	"	–	13	" " "
William F. Micou,	"	–	8	Deserted.
John McMarra,	"	–	13	Transferred to Captain Turner.
Lewis Minor,	"	–	13	" " "
Elisha May,	"	–	9	" " "
John Marques,	"	–	13	" " "
Chas. M. Mitchell,	"	–	13	" " "
Daniel Mitchell,	"	–	13	" " "
Philip McGathy,	"	–	13	" " "
John Perkins,	"	–	13	" " "
John B. Ogg,	"	–	7	" " "
John Rowland,	"	–	13	" " "
Edward W. Roots,	"	–	13	" " "
Geo. Read,	"	–	13	" " "
Alexander Reid,	"	–	7	" " "
David Roper,	"	–	13	" " "
Mathew H. Rice,	"	–	8	" " "
Seamore Scott,	"	–	6	" " "
Larkin Smith,	"	–	13	" " "

NAMES.	RANK.	TIME OF SERVICE.		REMARKS.		
		Months.	Days.			
Samuel Sublett, - -	Private,	–	10			
Samuel Shepheard, - -	"	–	13	Transferred to Captain		
Alexander Sharp, - -	"	–	13	Turner,		
Edward W. Trent, - -	"	–	13	"	"	"
Hez'h Veach, - -	"	–	13	"	"	"
Jos. W. Vaughan, - -	"	–	7	"	"	"
Conquest Wyott, - -	"	–	13	"	"	"
Sylvester Walkley, - -	"	–	13	"	"	"
James Watson, - -	"	–	8	"	"	"

MUSTER ROLL

Of Captain Edward Carter's Troop of Cavalry, attached to a Regiment of Cavalry of the United States, commanded by Colonel P. Holcombe, in the Service of the United States, from the 3rd day of September to the 12th day of the same month, in the year 1814.

NAMES.	RANK.	TIME OF SERVICE.		REMARKS.
		Months.	Days.	
Edward Carter, - -	Captain,	–	10	
James Gurland, - -	1st Lieutenant,	–	10	
James Henton, -	2d "	–	10	
Horatio Thompson,	Cornet,	–	10	
Rawley W. Carter, - -	Sergeant,	–	10	
Christopher L. Carter, -	"	–	10	
Josiah Ferguson, -	"	–	10	
John Muse, - -	"	–	10	
Nathan Hutcherson, -	Corporal,	–	10	
John Thompson, -	"	–	10	
William A. Townes, -	"	–	10	
Archibald Hatcher, - -	"	–	10	
James R. Allen, - -	Private,	–	10	
Nathaniel Adams, - -	"	–	10	
Thomas B. Amos, - -	"	–	10	
John Adams, - -	"	–	10	
Thomas Allen, -	"	–	10	
James K. Buckley, - -	"	–	10	
Ozias Bowe, -	"	–	10	
George Boyd, - -	"	–	10	
Davis Barden, - -	"	–	10	
Bartlett Bennett, -	"	–	10	
Charles W. Bobbett, -	"	–	10	
Samuel Blair, - -	"	–	10	
James Bolling, -	"	–	10	
John Bolling, -	"	–	10	
Abner Bennett, -	"	–	10	
John Crider, -	"	–	10	
John F. Craddock, - -	"	–	10	
John Clark, -	"	–	10	
Jessee Carter, -	"	–	10	
Thomas Davis, -	"	–	10	
Samuel Dawson, -	"	–	10	
Joseph Davis, -	"	–	10	
Jordan Davis, -	"	–	10	
Thomas Easley, -	"	–	10	
George Edwards, - ' -	"	–	10	
Lovell Ferguson, -	"	–	10	
William Faris, -	"	–	10	
John Ferguson, -	"	–	10	
Edmond Fitzgerald, -	"	–	10	
John Giles, -	"	–	10	
Robert Haymes, -	"	–	10	
Walter Hailey, -	"	–	10	
Joshua Harrison, -	"	–	10	
Stephen Hamlett, -	"	–	10	
David Haymes, -	"	–	10	

NAMES.	RANK.	TIME OF SERVICE.		REMARKS.
		Months.	Days.	
William Haynes, - -	Private,	–	10	
James Harmon, - -	"	–	10	
Hezekiah Hubbard, - -	"	–	10	
Moses Hubbard, - -	"	–	10	
Thornton Hulson, - -	"	–	10	
John Hundley, - -	"	–	10	
John James, - -	"	–	10	
Gregory Jarratt, - -	"	–	10	
John M. Johns, - -	"	–	10	
Daniel Johns, - -	"	–	10	
James Jones, - -	"	–	10	
Sanford Jones, - -	"	–	10	
Richard G. Keatts, - -	"	–	10	
James Lovelass, - -	"	–	10	
James A. Luck, - -	"	–	10	
John McClanahan, - -	"	–	10	
Thomas O. Meaux, - -	"	–	10	
James H. Mitchell, - -	"	–	10	
Elisha Mitchell, - -	"	–	10	
John Mitchell, - -	"	–	10	
Henry L. Muse, - -	"	–	10	
Thomas Muse, - -	"	–	10	
James Myers, - -	"	–	10	
Jesse Oakes, - -	"	–	10	
John Oakes, - -	"	–	10	
Elisha Parkes, - -	"	–	10	
Allen Parrish, - -	"	–	10	
Thomas Parrish, - -	"	–	10	
Martin Pearson, - -	"	–	10	
John W. Pegram, - -	"	–	10	
Philip B. Price, - -	"	–	10	
Fountain Price, - -	"	–	10	
Joseph Reynolds, - -	"	–	10	
William Riddle, - -	"	–	10	
Abraham Rorrer, - -	"	–	10	
John Rorrer, - -	"	–	10	
George K. Smith, - -	"	–	10	
Vincent H. Shelton, - -	"	–	10	
Wesley Shelton, - -	"	–	10	
Reubin Smith, - -	"	–	10	
Samuel Settle, - -	"	–	10	
William Thompson, - -	"	–	10	
Elijah Toler, - -	"	–	10	
John Turner, - -	"	–	10	
Cornelius Turner, - -	"	–	10	
William M. Waller, - -	"	–	10	
Thomas Waller, - -	"	–	10	
William H. Watson, - -	"	–	10	
Thomas Watson, - -	"	–	10	
William Wammack, - -	"	–	10	
John Wells, - -	"	–	10	
Ephraim Witcher, - -	"	–	10	
James Witcher, - -	"	–	10	

MUSTER ROLL

Of R. W. Carter's Troop of Cavalry of Virginia Militia, attached to the Forty-first Regiment, in the Service of the United States, from 1st to 9th December, in the year 1814.

NAMES.	RANK.	TIME OF SERVICE.		REMARKS.
		Months.	Days.	
Robert W. Carter, - -	Captain,			
David L. M. Carter, - -	Lieutenant,			
Isaac Smith, - -	"	–	8	
Thomas Yerby, - -	Cornet,	–	8	
John Peck, - -	Sergeant,	–	4	
Jeremiah Northen, - -	"	–	8	
Christopher L. Dobyns, -	"			
Peter Morgan, - -	"			
Thomas M. Belfield, - -	Private,	–	8	
Charles Beale, - -	"			
Samuel Bailey, - -	"	–	8	
Thomas P. Ball, - -	"	–	6	
John R. F. Corbin, -	"	–	8	
William Crisonbury, - -	"	–	5	
Griffin Dudley, - -	"			
Thomas Dobyns, - -	"			
William Dobyns, - -	"			
Richard Efford, - -	"	–	8	
Israel Ferris, - -	"			
John Haywood, - -	"	–	8	
John Haurmack, - -	"	–	8	
Hudson Lyell, - -	"	–	8	
James Lewis, - -	"	–	8	
Carter Mitchell, - -	"			
William D. McCarty, -	"	–	8	
Robert W. McCarty, -	"	–	8	
George G. McCarty, -	"	–	8	
George Northen, - -	"	–	8	
Edward Northen, - -	"	–	8	
Eppa L. Neasom, - -	"			
Em'l Peck, - -	"			
William Palmer, - -	"	–	7	
Charles Palmer, - -	"	–	7	
John N. Roots, - -	"			
John Sandy, - -	"			
Thomas J. Scrimger, -	"			
Lewis Tune, - -	"	–	4	
Moore F. Tomlin, -	"			
Williamson B. Tomlin, -	"	–	8	
William Y. Weathers, -	"	–	9	
Richard Wall, -	"			
John G. White, - -	"	–	9	
William G. Yerby, - -	"	–	8	

MUSTER ROLL

Of Captain John R. Cary's Company of Light Infantry, of the Twenty-first Regiment, commanded by Lieutenant Colonel William Jones, in the Service of the United States from 22d to 24th and 28th to 30th October, from 22d to 24th November, and from 16th December in the year 1813 to 15th February, from 28th February to 9th March, and from 23d March to 6th April in the year 1814.

NAMES.	RANK.	TIME OF SERVICE.		REMARKS.
		Months.	Days.	
John R. Cary,	Captain,	2	21	
John Page,	Lieutenant.	3	5	
Richard M. Janson,	Ensign,	2	21	
William S. Thornton,	"	–	12	
Thomas Stoakes,	Sergeant,	3	5	
William Harvey,	"	3	5	
William Freeman,	"	3	5	
Reavel Sturgis,	"	–	–	Elected 7th Jan. 1814, served 25 days as private, and 46 days as sergeant, in place of Pippin, broke.
James Smith,	Corporal,	3	5	
Levi Diggs,	"	3	5	
Christ'n Stoakes.	"	3	5	
William Powell,	"	–	–	Elected 7th Jan. 1814, served 20 days as private, and 51 days as corporal, in place of Bland, discharged.
Vincent Hudson,	Fifer,	3	5	
William Hudson,	Drummer,	3	5	
Richard Allard,	Private,	3	5	
Samuel Bland,	"	–	29	Discharged 6th Jan'y 1814, and Powell elected to fill vacancy.
Churchill Boswell,	"	3	5	
William Cooke,	"	3	5	
Major Coloney,	"	3	5	
George Cake,	"	3	5	
Stephen Cake,	"	–	11	
Miles Camp,	"	–	12	
William Dunford,	"	3	5	
Isaiah Diggs,	"	3	5	
William Dews,	"	3	5	
William Dudley,	"	3	5	
John Dobson,	"	3	5	
Banks Dudley,	"	3	5	
Thomas Evans,	"	3	5	
William Eury,	"	3	5	
Thomas Freeman,	"	3	5	
Charles Grymes,	"	–	8	
Enos Hunt,	"	1	23	
John Hobday,	"	–	12	
Robert Harris,	"	3	5	
Thomas Hall,	"	3	5	
Edward Heywood.	"	3	5	

NAMES.	RANK.	TIME OF SERVICE.		REMARKS.
		Months.	Days.	
James Hogg, - -	Private,	3	5	
Richard Hogg, - -	"	3	5	
William Hogg, - -	"	3	5	
Solomon Jenkins, - -	"	3	5	
Arch'd W. Janson, - -	"	3	20	
Randall Jenkins, - -	"	3	5	
William James, - -	"	3	5	
Fielding Jenkins, - -	"	3	5	
Harwood Jenkins, - -	"	3	5	
Isaac King, - - -	"	3	5	
William Moore, - -	"	3	5	
Samuel Moore, - -	"	3	5	
John Newton, - -	"	3	5	
Oliver Gravly, - -	"	3	5	
Richard Pippin, - -	"	3	5	Broke Dec. 24, 1813, and Sturgis elected to fill vacancy.
Richard Powell, - -	"	—	29	
Edmund Powers, - -	"	3	5	
Joseph Powell, - -	"	1	12	
Charles Pleacy, - -	"	3	5	
James Powell, - -	"	3	5	
William Pippin, - -	"	3	5	
William Potts, - -	"	3	5	
Seymour Powell, - -	"	3	5	
Joseph Pippin, - -	"	3	5	
John Rider, - -	"	—	28	
Joseph Rider, - -	"	—	27	
James H. Ransone, - -	"	3	5	
James Rowe, - -	"	3	5	
Hansford Rowe, - -	"	3	5	
John Rowe, - -	"	3	5	
James Robins, - -	"	3	5	
George Rowe, - -	"	3	5	
David Spencer, - -	"	6	15	
Chrs. Smith, - -	"	—	23	
Warner Shackelford, - -	"	3	5	
William Shackelford, - -	"	3	5	
Benjamin Shackelford, - -	"	3	5	
James Shackelford, - -	"	—	16	
Richard Spann, - -	"	3	5	
Francis Spencer, - -	"	3	5	
Robert Stonkes, - -	"	3	5	
Thomas Tilledge, - -	"	3	5	
Wm. Tilledge, - -	"	—	10	
Hugh Thompson, - -	"	3	5	
John Vaughan, - -	"	3	5	
Wm. Walker, - -	"	3	5	
Edward Walker, - -	"	—	8	
Francis West, - -	"	3	5	
Nathaniel Walden, - -	"	3	5	
William Williams, - -	"	3	5	

(For rest of this company, see publication of Pay Rolls.)

MUSTER ROLL

Of Captain Miles Cary's Company of Infantry of the First Battalion, One Hundred and Fifteenth Regiment, Virginia Militia, called into Service under the orders of Lieutenant Colonel Henry Howard, from the 13th day of March to the 3d day of April, and from the 22d day of June to the 8th day of July, 1813.

NAMES.	RANK.	TIME OF SERVICE.		REMARKS.
		Months.	Days.	
Miles Cary,	Captain,	1	7	
Gill A. Cary,	Lieutenant,	1	7	
Gill Armistead,	Ensign,	1	7	
George Hope,	Sergeant,	1	7	
John Needham,	"	1	7	
John Dewbre,	"	1	7	
Benjamin West,	"	1	7	
Charles Philips,	Corporal,	1	7	
Robert Toping,	"	–	20	
Elijah Phillips,	"	1	7	
Wm. Kirby,	"	–	20	
George Phillips,	"	–	17	
Thomas Jennings,	"	–	17	
John Guy,	Drummer,	1	7	
Charles Paul,	Fifer,	1	7	
James Almond,	Private,	1	7	
Wm. Armistead,	"	–	17	
Smith Ames,	"	1	7	
George Armistead,	"	1	7	
Joseph Bushell,	"	–	17	
William Burge,	"	1	7	
Richard Brown,	"	–	17	
Richard Barron,	"	1	7	
Nathaniel Benthall,	"	–	17	
Ayel Benthall,	"	–	20	
Stokely Croswell,	"	1	7	
Lawson Croswell,	"	–	17	
John Cooper,	"	1	7	
Smith Drummond,	"	–	17	
Ezekiel Daws,	"	1	7	
George Drummond,	"	1	7	
James Dewbre,	"	1	7	
Thomas Dewbre,	"	1	7	
George Dunn,	"	–	15	
Henry Elliott,	"	1	7	
Jacob Elliott,	"	–	3	
Richard Fornsis,	"	–	17	
James Featham,	"	–	17	
Wm. Featherly,	"	1	7	
Jonathan Frayser,	"	1	7	
Hugh Freeman,	"	–	20	
Devorax Godwin,	"	–	17	
John Gayle,	"	1	7	
Samuel Guy,	"	–	17	
Joseph Godwin,	"	–	20	
Wm. Hickman,	"	1	7	
Charles Hopkins,	"	1	7	

NAMES.	RANK.	TIME OF SERVICE.		REMARKS.
		Months.	Days.	
Jessee Hopkins, - -	Private.	1	7	
Edward Ironmonger. -	"	–	17	
William Lewis, - -	"	–	17	
Wm. Lewis, jr. - -	"	–	17	
John Lewis, - -	"	1	7	
William Mears, - -	"	–	17	
Robert Melson, - -	"	1	7	
Littleton Mears, - -	"	1	7	
Joseph Outten, - -	"	1	7	
James Phillips, - -	"	1	7	
Dawson Provo. - -	"	1	5	
George Phillips, - -	"	–	20	
Richard Pool, - -	"	–	17	
Corbin Sprigg, - -	"	1	7	
William Stores, - -	"	1	7	
William Shelton, - -	"	–	25	
James Shelton, - -	"	–	17	
William Stake. - -	"	1	7	
Wilson Stores, - -	"	–	17	
George Topping. - -	"	1	7	
James Topping. - -	"	1	7	
Joseph Thomas, - -	"	–	17	
Robert Topping. - -	"	–	17	
John P. Topping. - -	"	–	17	
James Tatum, - -	"	–	20	
Richard Tennis, - -	"	–	20	
James Taylor, - -	"	–	20	
Joseph Thomas, - -	"	–	20	
John Tyler, - -	"	–	19	
Matthew Watts, - -	"	–	17	
John Wroughton, - -	"	1	7	
George Watkins, - -	"	1	7	
Matthew Wallace, - -	"	–	17	
Parker Wallace, - -	"	–	17	
Samuel Watts, - -	"	–	13	

Captain William Byrd Chamberlayne's Company—First Brigade.

NAMES.	RANK.	TIME OF SERVICE.		REMARKS.
		Months.	Days.	
William W. Christian, -	Private,	3	24	
John Turner, - -	"	1	5	
Jesse Willis, - -	"	–	8	Transferred to U. S. Army.

(For rest of this company, see publication of Pay Rolls.)

Captain Thomas W. Cary's Company—One Hundred and Fifteenth Regiment.

NAMES.	RANK.	TIME OF SERVICE.		REMARKS.
		Months.	Days.	
William Whitaker, - -	Private,	1		
James Wallace, - -	"	1		

(For rest of this company, see publication of Pay Rolls.)

Captain Mitchell Chandler's Company—Second Regiment.

NAMES.	RANK.	TIME OF SERVICE.		REMARKS.
		Months.	Days.	
James A. Twiford,	Ensign,	–	22	
Thomas B. Custis,	"	–	12	
John Bagwell,	Sergeant,	–	14	
George Bull, (of Caty,)	Corporal,	–	24	
Edward Ayres,	Private,	–	22	
Litt. Ayres,	"			
Edward Bell,	"	–	21	
George Bull,	"	–	6	
Ebern Bird,	"	–	14	
Parker Copes,	"	–	8	
Thomas Chandler,	"	–	22	
George Chandler,	"	–	3	
Elisha Chandler,	"			
Jno. Crowsand,	"	–	23	
Thos. Custis, (of Only.)	"	–	14	
Thos. B. Custis,	"			
Peter Duberly,	"	–	14	
John B. Edwards,	"			
John Fox,	"	–	20	
Spencer D. Fletcher,	"	–	27	
Charles Fitzgerald,	"	–	16	
Jno. Flaherty,	"	–	8	
Gilbert Hall,	"	–	24	
Robert Hall,	"			
Thomas Husk,	"	–	2	
Luther Jaquish,	"			
Jno. Kelley,	"			
Rich'd Kelley,	"	1	1	
Sam'l Lumber,	"	–	22	
Nath'l Lang,	"	–	13	
Josiah Melson,	"	–	8	
John McMouth,	"	–	16	
Jas. Melson, (of R.)	"	–	8	
Zadoc Poulson,	"	–	8	
Raymond Rolly,	"	–	8	
Samuel Singleton,	"	–	14	
William Scott,	"	–	8	
Nat. Trader,	"	1	14	
George Tignor,	"	–	8	
Litt. Watson,	"	–	8	

(For rest of this company, see publication of Pay Rolls.)

MUSTER ROLL

Of Captain Thomas Chappell's Company of the Eighty-third Regiment, Virginia Militia, in the County of Dinwiddie, called into actual Service under the General Orders of the 30th June, 1813, from the 1st day of July to the 6th day of the same month in the year 1813.

NAMES.	RANK.	TIME OF SERVICE.		REMARKS.
		Months.	Days.	
Thomas Chappell,	Captain,	–	6	
Henry Young,	Lieutenant,	–	6	
Patrick Roney,	Ensign,	–	6	
Wm. P. Pool,	Sergeant,	–	6	
Wood Jackson,	"	–	6	
William Chappell,	"	–	6	
Jon. M. Jackson,	"	–	6	
Williamson Moore,	Corporal,	–	6	
Nathan Withers,	"	–	6	
Reuben Williams,	"	–	6	
Silas Hine,	"	–	6	
William Jackson,	Musician,	–	6	
Jacob Barnes.	"	–	6	
Francis Aldridge,	Private,	–	6	
Joseph Darby,	"	–	6	
Freeman Gibbs,	"	–	6	
Joel Hitchcock,	"	–	6	
Thomas Hill,	"	–	6	
Charles S. Harrison,	"	–	–	On duty at Norfolk.
David Jackson,	"	–	6	
Coleman Jackson,	"	–	6	
Daniel Jackson,	"	–	6	
James Jackson,	"	–	6	
Samuel Johnson,	"	–	6	
Jesse Jackson,	"	–	–	In the service of the U. States.
Julius King,	"	–	6	
John W. King,	"	–	–	On duty at Norfolk,
William King,	"	–	6	In the service of the U. States.
John Lantroop,	"	–	6	
Jesse Lewis,	"	–	6	
Francis Lewis,	"	–	–	On duty at Norfolk.
Peterson Moore,	"	–	6	
John K. Perkins,	"	–	–	" " "
Richard Rose,	"	–	6	
Thomas Robinson,	"	–	6	
William N. Slater,	"	–	6	
James Slate,	"	–	6	In the service of the U. States.
Luther Tucker,	"	–	6	
Berryman T. Tucker,	"	–	6	
Robert Wynne, jr	"	–	6	
Thomas Warren,	"	–	6	
Tilman Wells,	"	–	6	
William Warren,	"	–	6	
Geo. M. Warren,	"	–	–	On duty at Norfolk.
Drury Wells,	"	–	–	In the service of the U. States.

MUSTER ROLL

Of Captain Thomas Cheatham's Company of Infantry of the Twenty-third Regiment, Virginia Militia, in the County of Chesterfield, called into actual Service from 18th to 29th March, from 27th to 28th June, and from 1st to 2d day of July, in the year 1813.

NAMES.	RANK.	TIME OF SERVICE.		REMARKS.
		Months.	Days.	
Thomas Cheatham,	Captain,	—	15	
Robertson Beasley,	Lieutenant,	—	15	
Daniel Chalkley,	Ensign,	—	15	
Obed Hatcher,	Sergeant,	—	15	
Wm. Hatcher, sen.	"	—	15	
Wm. Hatcher,	"	—	13	
Nelson Farmon,	"	—	2	
Hobson Chalkley,	"	—	13	
William Gady,	"	—	2	
Joel Belcher,	Private,	—	15	
Thomas Branch,	"	—	13	
Thomas N. Brooking,	"	—	15	
William Beasley,	"	—	11	
Dudley Brown,	"	—	11	
William Blankinship,	"	—	11	
Isham Belcher,	"	—	15	
Branch Chalkley,	"	—	15	
Josiah Chalkley,	"	—	11	
Jno. Chalkley,	"	—	11	
M. Chalkley,	"	—	15	
David Chalkley,	"	—	15	
Archer Chalkley,	"	—	15	
Bartlett Chalkley,	"	—	15	
Obed Chalkley,	"	—	15	
Hobson Chalkley,	"	—	2	
Oratio Chalkley,	"	—	2	
Nathaniel Davidson,	"	—	11	
Peter Farmer,	"	—	15	
Archer Farmer,	"	—	15	
William Fisher,	"	—	15	
Samuel Fuqua,	"	—	11	
William Fuqua,	"	—	11	
Nelson Farmer,	"	—	13	
Oratio Farmer,	"	—	13	
Peyton Fuqua,	"	—	4	
Peter Gary,	"	—	15	
James Gary,	"	—	15	
Wm. Gary,	"	—	11	
Edmund Gary,	"	—	15	
William Gregory,	"	—	13	
William Harner,	"	—	13	
Jno. Hancock,	"	—	15	
Jno. Hobbs,	"	—	15	
Stephen Hobbs,	"	..	15	
Josiah W. Hatcher,	"	—	11	
Jno. Hamblin,	"	—	11	
Branch Hatcher,	"	—	15	

NAMES.			RANK.	TIME OF SERVICE.		REMARKS.
				Months.	Days.	
Chs. R. Hatcher,	-	-	Private,	–	13	
Jno. Kelley,	-	-	"	–	11	
Jno. Moody,	-		"	–	15	
Michael K. Muney,	-	-	"	–	11	
Jas. McGee,	-	-	"	–	15	
Randolph Martin,	-	-	"	–	15	
Robert McClelland,	-	-	"	–	15	
Danl. Nunnally,	-	-	"	–	11	
Bernard Nunnally,	-	-	"	–	15	
Daniel Nobbs,	-	-	"	–	11	
James Nunnally,	-	-	"	–	15	
Arthur Nunnally,	-	-	"	–	15	
Jas. Oup,	-	-	"	–	11	
Cole Powell,	-	-	"	–	15	
Temple Reed,	-	-	"	–	13	
Archer Short,	-	-	"	–	11	
William Sadler,	-	-	"	–	11	
John Sims,	-	-	"	–	15	
Onot Short,	-	-	"	–	13	
William F. Smith,	-	-	"	–	2	
Richard Taylor,	-	-	"	–	15	
Robert Temple,	-	-	"	–	15	
Jno. Turpin.	-	-	"	–	15	
Jno. Turpin,	-	-	"	–	11	
Richard Tomson,	-	-	"	–	13	
James Vest,	-	-	"	–	2	
John Woodson,	-	-	"	–	15	
Daniel Wilson,	-	-	"	–	15	
Wm. Winfree,	-	-	"	–	2	

Captain Reuben Chewning's Company—Seventh Regiment.

NAMES.	RANK.	TIME OF SERVICE.		REMARKS.
		Months.	Days.	
Henry Beach, - -	Private,	2	25	Deserted.
William L. Harris, - -	"	–	10	
William W. Johnson, -	"	–	10	
Lewis Thomason, - -	"	–	28	

(For rest of this company, see publication of Pay Rolls.)

Captain Alexander Campbell's Company—Second Elite Corps.

NAMES.	RANK.	TIME OF SERVICE.		REMARKS.
		Months.	Days.	
Jacob Bever, - -	Private.			
Carter C. Elie, - -	"	–	10	
Christian Mountcastle, - -	"	–	5	
John Riley, - -	"		–	Deserted.

(For rest of this company, see publication of Pay Rolls.)

PAY ROLL

Of Captain William Childrey's Company of Infantry, Virginia Militia, from the Second Battalion, Thirty-third Regiment, called into Service the 19th and discharged the 29th of March, 1813.

NAMES.	RANK.	Months.	Days.	REMARKS.
William Childrey,	Captain,	–	5	
John Lindsay,	Lieutenant,	–	5	
John Hobson,	Ensign,	–	4	
Thomas Goode,	Sergeant,	–	5	
Samuel Norment,	"	–	5	
Jno. R. Pierce,	"	–	5	
Lewis Throgmorton.	"	–	5	
Billard Ammens,	Private,	–	5	
Joseph Bailey,	"	–	5	
Stanhope Bradley,	"	–	5	
Enes Bottoms,	"	–	1	
William Crittenden,	"	–	5	
Samuel Crenshaw,	"	–	5	
Edward Coghill,	"	–	5	
William Dandridge,	"	–	5	
Ahay Duke,	"	–	5	
Edward Eppes, jr.	"	–	5	
Edward Eppes, sr.	"	–	5	
Benj. A. Foster,	"	–	5	
Edward Goode,	"	–	1	
Benjamin Goode,	"	–	5	
Isaac Goode,	"	–	5	
Arch'd Goode,	"	–	5	
Hobson Goode,	"	–	5	
Jno. Goode,	"	–	5	
Robert Goode,	"	–	5	
Turner Hutchings,	"	–	5	
Henry G. Heath,	"	–	4	
James E. Hardyman,	"	–	5	
Robert Jolley,	"	–	5	
William Keepell,	"	–	5	
Francis Lewis,	"	–	5	
Moses Lindsay,	"	–	5	
Elijah Lindsay,	"	–	5	
Jonathan M. Laine,	"	–	5	
Benjamin Mosby,	"	–	3	
Jno. G. Mosby,	"	–	5	
William H. Minson,	"	–	5	
Hartwell M. Manners,	"	–	2	
William Profer,	"	–	5	
William Pierce,	"	–	5	
Samuel Robinson,	"	–	3	
Nathaniel S. Robinson,	"	–	5	
Peter Robinson,	"	–	5	
John Roper,	"	–	5	
Milner Redford,	"	–	5	

NAMES.	RANK.	TIME OF SERVICE.		REMARKS.
		Months.	Days.	
James Robertson, - -	Private,	–	5	
—— Sharps, -	"	–	5	
John Sanrenic, -	"	–	5	
Jesse Throgmorton, - -	"	–	5	
Robert Throgmorton, -	"	–	5	
Arch'd Taylor, - -	"	–	2	
Jno. Vaughan, . - -	"	–	5	
Thomas J. West, - -	"	–	5	
James Whitlock, - -	"	–	5	
Peter West, -	"	–	5	

Captain Jones R. Christian's Company—Fifty-Second Regiment.

NAMES.			RANK.	TIME OF SERVICE.		REMARKS.
				Months.	Days.	
John Redwood,	-	-	Lieutenant,	–	20	
William Douglass,	-	-	"	–	20	
Edward Roper,	-	-	Cornet,	–	20	
Edmund Morecock,	-	-	Sergeant,	1	10	
Thomas Tende,	-	-	"	–	7	
Wm. B. Graves,	-	-	"	–	15	
Holt Richardson,	-	-	"	–	20	
John Vaiden,	-	-	"	–	20	
Porterfield Bradley,	-	-	Corporal,	1	10	
Charles Christian,	-	-	"	–	20	
Thomas Morecock,	-	-	"	–	14	
Jordan Christian,	-	-	"	–	11	
Richard Allen,	-	-	Private,	1	7	
Edmund Apperson,	-	-	"	–	14	
John Ammons,	-	-	"	–	15	
Edmund J. Bacon,	-	-	"	1	10	
John Benns,	-	-	"	–	20	
Thomas Browdy,	-	-	"	–	20	
Henry Bowry,	-	•	"	–	20	
Fellany Barrow,	-	-	"	–	20	
Marston Bradley,	-	-	"	–	20	
Jesse Barnes,	-	-	"	1	4	
Richard Burns,	-	-	"	–	14	
Littleberry H. Bradley,	-	-	"	–	15	
Edwin Boyd,	-	-	"	–	15	
Gideon Christian,	-	-	"	–	20	
Nathaniel Cowles,	-	-	"	1	10	
Edmund Crump,	-	-	"	–	20	
Bartlett Crump,	-	.	"	–	20	
George W. Clayton,	-	-	"	–	20	
Josiah Crump,	-	-	"	1	6	
Bathurst Claiborne,	-	-	"	1	4	
James Christian.	-	-	"	–	14	
John Colgin,	-	-	"	1	2	
Richard Crump.	-	-	"	–	20	
Edward Carter,	-	-	"	–	15	
John B. Christian,	-	-	"	–	15	
John Creighton,	-	-	"	–	15	
Sheldone Crump,	-	-	"	–	15	
Peter Demoville,	-	-	"	–	14	
Reuben Francis,	-	-	"	–	14	
Thomas Gannaway,	-	-	"	–	20	
William B. Graves,	-	-	"	–	5	
Alexander Harrison,	-	-	"	1	10	
William E. Hill,	-	-	"	–	15	
Samuel Harwood,	-	-	"	–	20	
John Ireland,	-	-	"	–	20	
Ambrose Jenkins,	-	-	"	–	15	
John Jones,	•	-	"	–	15	

NAMES.	RANK.	TIME OF SERVICE.		REMARKS.
		Months.	Days.	
Burnet Lewis, - -	Private,	— •	15	
Abner Mitchell, - -	"	1	10	
Thomas Meux, - -	"	—	20	
Joseph Marshall, - -	"	—	17	
Gannaway Morgan, - -	"	—	14	
Nelson Mason, - -	"	—	6	
Miles Macon, - -	"	—	21	
Francis Marshall, - -	"	—	15	
William Mason, - -	"	—	15	
Meary Davy, - -	"	—	15	
Herman R. Otter, - -	"	1	10	
Nelson Parrish, - -	"	1	10	
Edward Poindexter, - -	"	—	15	
Elisha Pollard, - -	"	—	20	
John P. Poindexter, - -	"	—	20	
Charles Pearson, - -	"	—	11	
Wm. B. Price, - -	"	—	12	
Harry Poindexter, - -	"	—	15	
William C. Smith, - -	"	—	15	
Thomas B. Shearman, - -	"	—	15	
Francis Tyree, - -	"	1	10	
James Timberlake, - -	"	1	19	
Henry Timberlake, - -	"	—	14	
George B. Taylor. - -	"	—	15	
John Timberlake, - -	"	—	14	
William Taylor, - -	"	—	14	
Lewis Vaughan, - -	"	—	20	
John Vaiden, - -	"	—	5	
John Warren, - -	"	—	20	
Curry Wilkinson, - -	"	—	8	
Cary Wilkinson, - -	"	—	6	
Cary Wilkinson, - -	Surgeon,	—	14	
Wm. B. Westmore, - -	Private,	—	15	
Edward Wilcox, - -	"	—	15	
Josiah Wilson, - -	"	—	4	

(For rest of this company, see publication of Pay Rolls.)

Captain William A. Christian's Company—Twenty-seventh Regiment.

NAMES.	RANK.	TIME OF SERVICE.		REMARKS.
		Months.	Days.	
William A. Christian, -	Captain,	–	9	
William White, - -	Lieutenant,	–	9	
Thomas Johnson, - -	"	–	9	
William S. Drummond, -	Sergeant,	–	9	
George Wescot, - -	"	–	9	
Isaac Andrews, - -	"	–	9	
Major Wescot, - -	"	–	9	
Jesse Ross, - - -	Corporal,	–	9	
Custis Turhurn, - -	"	–	9	
Abel West, - - -	"	–	9	
William Clark, - -	"	–	9	
Solomon S. Burting, -	Drummer,	–	9	
Thomas Wyatt, - -	Fifer,	–	9	
Edmund Brustone, - -	Private,	–	9	
Sam'l C. Barnes, - -	"	1	15	
Laborn Belcoat, - -	"	–	9	
William B. Clarke, - -	"	1	15	
Josiah Dowty, - -	"	–	9	
Samuel Dennis, - -	"	–	9	
Major Dennis, - -	"	–	9	
Victor Ewing, - -	"	–	9	
John T. Elliott, - -	"	–	9	
Bagwell Garretson, - -	"	–	9	
Litt'y Godwin, - -	"	–	9	
John Hallett, - -	"	–	9	
Laborn Johnson, - -	"	–	9	
James Johnson, - -	"	–	9	
Zadock Lewis, - -	"	–	9	
Wm. Mears, - -	"	–	9	
Harrison Nottingham, -	"	–	9	
William Parkersburg, -	"	–	9	
Jacob Petit, - -	"	–	9	
John Richardson, - -	"	–	9	
Eli Richardson, - -	"	–	9	
James Roberts, - -	"	–	9	
Thos. Smith, jr. - -	"	–	9	
Jonathan Smith, - -	"	–	9	
James Turner, - -	"	–	9	
George Taylor, - -	"	–	9	
Teagle S. White, - -	"	–	9	
Thomas White, - -	"	–	9	

(For rest of this company, see publication of Pay Rolls.)

MUSTER ROLL

Of Captain Thomas Claiborne's Company of Infantry of the Thirty-ninth Regiment, Virginia Militia, in the County of Dinwiddie, called into actual Service under the general orders of the 30th of June 1813, from the 30th June to the 12th July, inclusive, in the year 1813.

NAMES.	RANK.	TIME OF SERVICE.		REMARKS.
		Months.	Days.	
Thomas Claiborne,	Captain,	–	8	
Drewry Burge.	Lieutenant,	–	11	
Allen Archer,	Ensign,	–	11	
Arthur Leath,	Sergeant,	–	11	
Edward Lee, jr.	"	–	12	
A. B. Venable,	"	–	10	
John Gordon,	"	–	10	
Anthony Smith,	Corporal,	–	9	
Samuel Brister,	"	–	10	
Edmund Parish,	"	–	13	
Matthew Davidson,	"	–	12	
Cad. W. Archer,	Private,	–	10	
John Allison,	"			
Daniel E. Allen,	"	–	4	
John H. Brewer,	"	–	7	
John H. Booth,	"	–	13	
Robert Brister,	"	–	7	
Jesse Bendall,	"			
John H. Brown,	"	–	11	
John Brown,	"	–	11	
William Boswell,	"			
Henry Chieves,	"	–	11	
Robert Cocke,	"	–	7	
Levy Carpenter,	"	–	10	
Jesse L. Dupuy,	"	–	2	
Daniel Dodson, jr.	"	–	9	
Lewis B. Dunn,	"	–	11	
John A. Ezell,	"	–	12	
Henry Elliott,	"			
James Ennis,	"	–	11	
Daniel Foster,	"	–	10	
Francis Follett,	"			
Christopher Ford,	"	–	10	
William W. Fernando,	"	–	9	
Edmund Folks,	"	–	6	
Henry P. Guthrie,	"	–	12	
James L. Gilliam,	"	–	10	
Joseph Gray,	"	–	12	
Alexander Gordon,	"	–	10	
Riland Geiter,	"	–	11	
Samuel Hinton,	"	–	12	
David A. Ivy,	"	–	12	
Barksdale Jefferson,	"	–	13	
Frederick Jones,	"	–	12	
George H. Jones,	"	–	6	
John Lantrip,	"	–	13	
George K. Lee,	"	–	7	

NAMES.	RANK.	TIME OF SERVICE.		REMARKS.
		Months.	Days.	
Theodorick Lone, - -	Private,	—	5	
Robert Leath, - -	"	—	9	
Joseph H. Lee, - -	"	—	9	
Lewis Maury, - -	"	—	6	
Benjamin Mattox, - -	"	—	10	
Jones Mitchell, - -	"	—	12	
Benjamin May, - -	"	—	12	
John F. May, - -	"	—	13	
Richard May, - -	"	—	12	
Thomas Murphy, - -	"	—	13	
David Maben, - -	"	—	4	
John Owen, - -	"	—	9	
Chichester Owen, - -	"	—	5	
Williams Pace, - -	"	—	10	
Samuel Pete, - -	"	—	7	
James Prentice, - -	"	—	12	
George Roberts, - -	"	—	11	
William Smith, - -	"	—	12	
James Smith, - -	"	—	11	
Richard F. Taylor, -	"			
Henry Tucker, - -	"	—	11	
John Tracy, - -	"	—	11	
Claiborne Vaughan, -	"	—	9	
George Wise, - -	"	—	11	
Samuel Woodcock, -	"	—	10	
John Wright, jr. - -	"	—	12	
William Wilkinson, -	"	—	8	
Thomas Watkins, - -	"	—	10	
John Williams, - -	"	—	7	

MUSTER ROLL

Of Lieutenant Benjamin Clark's Company of the Sixteenth Regiment, Virginia Militia, commanded by Lieutenant Colonel Aylette Waller, in Service from 22d July to 17th August, 1814.

NAMES.	RANK.	TIME OF SERVICE.		REMARKS.
		Months.	Days.	
Benjamin Clark,	Lieutenant,	–	26	
Hugh M. Patton,	Ensign,	–	26	
Samuel Howerson,	Sergeant,	–	26	
John B. Jenkins,	"	–	26	
Elias E. Buckner,	"	–	26	
Charles Jones,	"	–	26	
Isaac West,	Corporal,	–	26	
E. L. Waring,	"	–	26	
Horace B. Hill,	"	–	26	
Darling Anderson,	"	–	26	
John Alsop,	Private,	–	26	
Benjamin Bramhall,	"	–	26	
Thomas R. Blackburne,	"	–	26	
Wm. G. Bronaugh,	"	–	26	
Wm. Burton,	"	–	26	
John Brown,	"	–	26	
Munson Curtis,	"	–	26	
John R. Cotton,	"	–	26	
Owen W. Colson,	"	–	26	
Lewis Courtney,	"	–	26	
David Curtis,	"	–	26	
John Cox,	"	–	26	
Styles P. Curtis,	"	–	26	
Lindsey Daniel,	"	–	26	
Amos Denormandie,	"	–	26	
Reubin Daniel,	"	–	26	
Cornelius Davis,	"	–	26	
Spencer S. Doggett,	"	–	26	
James Dawnton,	"	–	26	
Robert Deadman,	"	–	26	
John Edwards,	"	–	26	
Thos. Ferneyhough,	"	–	26	
John Ferrel,	"	–	26	
Jacob Gore,	"	–	26	
David Goldsby,	"	–	26	
Bartlett Guthrie,	"	–	26	
Walter Gimbo,	"	–	26	
John Grotz,	"	–	26	
Charles Geyer,	"	1	2	
William Howard, jr.	"	–	26	
Samuel C. Hooten,	"	–	26	
William R. Head,	"	–	26	
Benjamin Johnson,	"	–	26	
Isaac Jones,	"	–	26	
Ashton Johnston,	"	–	7	
Stapleton Lipscomb,	"	–	26	
Benjamin Lewis,	"	–	26	
Wm. L. Lewis,	"	–	26	

NAMES.	RANK.	TIME OF SERVICE.		REMARKS.
		Months.	Days.	
Jacob Laughlin, - -	Private,	—	26	
Robinson Morton, - -	"	—	26	
Graves P. Matthews, - -	"	—	26	
George Milna, - -	"	—	26	
Charles Martin, - -	"	—	26	
Benjamin Murray, - -	"	—	26	
Thomas Mitchell, - -	"	—	26	
Austin Melna, - -	"	—	26	
James Maning, - -	"	—	26	
Edwin D. Meredith, - -	"	—	26	
Spotswood Pumphrey, -	"	—	26	
William Pinkard, - -	"	—	26	
Josiah Richardson, - -	"	—	26	
Richard Ratcliff, - -	"	—	26	
Jacob Reader, - -	"	—	26	
John Richards, - -	"	—	26	
John Robinson, - -	"	—	26	
William K. Snider, - -	"	—	26	
James Stonnel, - -	"	—	26	
James Scofield, - -	"	—	26	
Philemon Samuel, - -	"	—	26	
George Stairs, -	"	—	26	
John Stevens, - -	"	—	26	
William A. Spooner, - -	"	—	26	
Zephaniah Turner, - -	"	—	26	
John Tupman, - -	"	—	26	
Keeling Terril, - -	"	—	26	
William Timberlake, - -	"	—	26	
Charles Thornton, - -	"	—	26	
William Thompson, - -	"	—	26	
Joseph Williams, - -	"	—	26	
Thomas Wren, - -	"	—	26	
John Watts, - -	"	—	26	
Samuel Washington, - -	"	—	26	
Meredith Yeatman, - -	"	—	26	

MUSTER ROLL

Of Lieutenant James Clarke's Company of the Twenty-third Regiment, Virginia Militia, in the County of Chesterfield, called into actual Service under general orders, from the 18th to the 24th March, and from the 26th June to the 2d July, in the year 1813.

NAMES.			RANK.	TIME OF SERVICE.		REMARKS.
				Months.	Days.	
James Clarke, jun'r,	-	-	Lieutenant,	–	14	
Isaac Davis,	-	-	Ensign,	–	14	
Young Pomroy,	-	-	Sergeant,	–	12	
Robt. R. Miller,	-	-	"	–	13	
Thomas Winfree,	-	-	"	–	14	
Wash. Weisiger,	-	-	"	–	7	
James Caskie,	-	-	Corporal,	–	14	
Thomas Smith,	-	-	"	–	7	
William Bradshaw,	-	-	"	–	7	
Ro. Dainsworth,	-	-	"	–	7	
James Long,	-	-	"	–	7	
James Gray,	-	-	"	–	3	
James B. Hooper,	-	-	"	–	7	
Ro. Ainsworth,	-	-	Private,	–	3	
Thomas Brackett,	-	-	"	–	7	
W. Brackett,	-	-	"	–	7	
Isaac Burnard,	-	-	"	–	14	
John Bunoff,	-	-	"	–	7	
W. B. Clarke,	-	-	"	–	10	
Ro. Clarke,	-	-	"	–	14	
M. Elam,	-	-	"	–	7	
And. Fare,	-	-	"	–	12	
Jno. Gilchrist,	-	-	"	–	14	
Nich. Garden,	-	-	"	–	10	
P. E. Graves,	-	-	"	–	7	
James Gray,	-	-	"	–	7	
John Hobson,	-	-	"	–	10	
J. B. Hooper,	-	-	"	–	7	
Jno. Jenkins,	-	-	"	–	7	
Edw'd Johnston,	-	-	"	–	9	
Stephen Johnston,	-	-	"	–	12	
James Long,	-	-	"	–	7	
Wm. Long,	-	-	"	–	7	
C. McRae,	-	-	"	–	7	
H. Moody,	-	-	"	–	14	
B. S. Morrison,	-	-	"	–	10	
Nicholas Mills,	-	-	"	–	14	
P. Michaels,	-	-	"	–	9	
Hugh M. Miller,	-	-	"	–	6	
Ro. D. Murchie,	-	-	"	–	14	
Daniel McLeod,	-	-	"	–	3	
Stephen Punkey,	-	-	"	–	14	
Wm. A. Patterson,	-	-	"	–	7	
Bev. Randolph,	-	-	"	–	14	
Edm'd Rudford,	-	-	"	–	7	
Tarlton Saunders,	-	-	"	–	8	
Jno. Scott,	-	-	"	–	14	

NAMES.			RANK.	TIME OF SERVICE.		REMARKS.
				Months.	Days.	
Sam'l Sizer,	-	-	Private,	—	13	
John Spencer,	-	-	"	—	14	
Sam'l Taylor,	-	-	"	—	14	
Thos. Vaden,	-	-	"	—	10	
J. Winfree,	-	-	"	—	9	
Ro. Warren,	-	-	"	—	14	
W. Weisiger,	-	-	"	—	7	
Ro. Weisiger,	-	-	"	—	7	
Jno. Weisiger,	-	-	"	—	14	
Daniel Weisiger,	-	-	"	—	12	
Mansfield Watkins,	-	-	"	—	12	
James Willet,	-	-	"	—	14	
James W. Winfree,	-	-	"	—	3	

MUSTER ROLL

Of Lieutenant Philmer Clark's Company of the Sixty-eighth Regiment, Virginia Militia, in the Service of the United States, from the 12th August to the 2d September, and from the 1st November to the 3d December, in the year 1814.

NAMES.		RANK.	TIME OF SERVICE.		REMARKS.
			Months.	Days.	
Philmer Clark,	- -	Lieutenant,	1	21	
William Whitaker,	- -	"	1	23	
Bennett Kirby,	- -	Sergeant,	—	21	
Thomas Wade,	- -	"	—	21	
John Paterson,	- -	"	1	23	
George Dudgeon,	- -	"	1	2	
William Gibb,	- -	"	1	2	
Benj. Hansford,	- -	"	—	21	
Francis Tone,	- -	Corporal,	—	21	
Cuthbert Hubberd,	- -	"	—	21	
Richard Wynne,	- -	"	—	21	
Thomas Presson,	- -	"	1	2	
James Guthrie,	- -	"	1	2	
Thomas Valentine,	- -	"	1		
John Brooks,	- -	Fifer,	—	27	
James Chadick,	- -	"	—	18	
Dick,	- -	Drummer,	—	21	
John C. Ashlock,	- -	Private,	1	1	
George Booth,	- -	"	—	21	
William Buffin,	- -	"	—	21	
Glanvil Booth,	- -	"	—	20	
John Booth,	- -	"	—	26	
Lewis Brown,	- -	"	—	17	
Hays Burcher,	- -	"	—	17	
Allen Chapman,	- -	"	—	20	
Thomas Dod,	- -	"	1	1	
John T. Earnest,	- -	"	1	1	
George Earnest,	- -	"	—	21	
Thomas Hughs,	- -	"	—	21	
James Hay,	- -	"	—	20	
John Hansford,	- -	"	—	20	
Charles Hansford,	- -	"	—	21	
William Hubbard,	- -	"	—	21	
Rowland Jones,	- -	"	—	21	
Robert Jackson,	- -	"	1		
Richard Jackson,	- -	"	1		
James Kerr,	- -	"	—	21	
Robert Lark,	- -	"	—	23	
John Lee,	- -	"	—	21	
Robert Lester,	- -	"	—	21	
Joshua Lester,	- -	"	—	18	
Charles Moore,	- -	"	—	20	
Merit Moore,	- -	"	—	18	
James McKendree,	- -	"	—	20	
Thomas Orrill,	- -	"	—	23	
John Perrin,	- -	"	1	2	
Thomas Patrick,	- -	"	—	21	
James Provoo,	- -	"	—	21	

NAMES.	RANK.	TIME OF SERVICE.		REMARKS.
		Months.	Days.	
Thomas Presson, - -	Private,	–	20	
Edward Roe, - -	"	1	2	
Jacob Roe, - -	"	–	20	
William Richards, - -	"	–	21	
James Roan, - -	"	–	20	
John T. Stokes, - -	",	–	21	
James Scillan, - -	"	–	21	
Caleb Smith, - -	"	1	2	
John Timson, - -	"	1	2	
James Taylor, - -	"	–	16	
John Vail, - -	"	–	20	
James Ware, - -	"	–	21	
John Wynne, - -	"	–	21	
Benjamin Wollow, - -	"	–	21	

MUSTER ROLL

Of Captain Samuel Clarke's Company of Infantry of the Twenty-third Regiment, Virginia Militia, in the County of Chesterfield, called into actual Service from 18th to 29th March, from the 27th to the 28th June, and from the 30th June to 2d July, in the year 1813.

NAMES.	RANK.	TIME OF SERVICE.		REMARKS.
		Months.	Days.	
Samuel Clarke,	Captain,	—	18	
Peter Clarke,	Lieutenant,	—	16	
Archibald Newby,	Ensign,	—	15	
Jeremiah Clarke,	Sergeant,	—	17	
Josiah Baugh,	"	—	17	
Thomas Belcher,	"	—	17	
John Woodfin,	"	—	17	
John Andrews,	Private,	—	17	
Peter Ashbrook,	"	—	5	
Admiral Brooks,	"	—	17	
William Baugh,	"	—	13	
Jeremiah Baugh,	"	—	13	
Martin Brooks,	"	—	17	
Peter Baugh,	"	—	17	
Abner Baugh,	"	—	17	
Henry Blankenship,	"	—	17	
Hatcher Clarke,	"	—	17	
Gardner Clarke,	"	—	17	
Charles Clarke,	"	—	17	
Ezekiel Davis,	"	—	17	
Pleasant Ellett,	"	—	13	
Moses Fergusson,	"	—	17	
John Fergusson,	"	—	17	
Thomas Fergusson,	"	—	17	
Gardner Fowler,	"	—	17	
Jesse Fergusson,	"	—	2	
Jesse Gill,	"	—	17	
Robert Lockett,	"	—	17	
Richard Loving,	"	—	17	
Andrew Laprade,	"	—	17	
Walthall Lockett,	"	—	12	
James Maxley,	"	—	12	
William Newby, sen'r.	"	—	17	
John Newby,	"	—	17	
William Newby, jr.	"	—	17	
Claibourne Nunnally,	"	—	17	
Nelson Newby,	"	—	17	
James Newby,	"	—	3	
Levi Puckett,	"	—	17	
John Perdue,	"	—	17	
Thomas Perdue,	"	—	17	
Labourn Puckett,	"	—	17	
Isham Puckett,	"	—	11	
Rowlett Patram,	"	—	17	
Shadrack Perdue,	"	—	11	
Rowling Puckett,	"	—	11	
Littleberry Perdue,	"	—	11	
Enoch Roberts,	"	—	17	

NAMES.			RANK.		TIME OF SERVICE.		REMARKS.
					Months.	Days.	
Bedford Traylor,	-	-	Private,		–	17	
Henry Vest.	-	-	"		–	17	
Obadiah Vest,	-	-	"	⟨	–	13	
John Wyatt,	-	-	"		–	17	
Peter Winfree.	-	-	"		–	14	
Ransom Wyatt,	-	-	"		–	11	

Ensign Matthew Clay's Detachment—at Charles City Courthouse.

NAMES.	RANK.	TIME OF SERVICE.		REMARKS.
		Months.	Days.	
John Dewberry, - -	Corporal.	–	14	
Arch'd Palmer, - -	"	–	17	
James Burnett, - -	Private,	–	–	Deserted 20 Dec. 1814.
Vincent Burch, - -	"	–	–	" 24 " "
Edward Cole, - -	"	–	17	
Jesse Foard, - -	"	–	17	
John Hazelwood, - -	"	–	26	
Arch'd Jones, - -	"	–	14	Died 25 Dec. 1814.
John Johnson, - -	"	–	16	
Duncan King, - -	"	–	17	
John Miller, - -	"	–	17	
William Pearson, - -	"	1		
John Palmer, - -	"	1		
John Still, - -	"	–	18	
Henry Simmons, - -	"	–	17	
Isaac Saunders, - -	"	–	–	Deserted Dec. 20, 1814.
John Trammil, - -	"	–	17	
James O. Tucker, - -	"	–	17	
John Walker, - -	"	–	–	Deserted 20 Dec. 1814.
Stephen Walker, - -	"	–	–	" " "

(For rest of this company, see publication of Pay Rolls.)

MUSTER ROLL

Of Captain John F. Cocke's Company of the One Hundred and Second Regiment, Virginia Militia, in the County of Powhatan, called into actual Service under the general orders of the 26th August, from the 28th August to the 16th September, in the year 1814.

NAMES.	RANK.	TIME OF SERVICE.		REMARKS.
		Months.	Days.	
John F. Cocke,	Captain,	–	19	
Will. J. Harris,	Lieutenant,	–	19	
Charles W. Lewis,	"	–	19	
Henry Booker,	Cornet,	–	19	
Edmond Saunders,	Sergeant,	–	19	
John H. Price,	"	–	19	
Thomas Jordan,	"	–	19	
William Nunnally,	"	–	19	
Isaac N. Cardozo,	Corporal,	–	19	
Henry Whitlocke,	"	–	19	
Jesse Owen,	"	–	19	
William Baugh,	"	–	19	
Richard Adams,	Private,	–	19	
Willi. C. Adams.	"	–	19	
Richard W. Atkinson,	"	–	19	
Peter E. Bentley,	"	–	19	
James R. Bentley,	"	–	19	
Daniel Bagby,	"	–	19	
Jordan Ballew,	"	–	19	
Richard Bass,	"	–	19	
Jacob W. Branch,	"	–	19	
Joseph Brackett,	"	–	19	
William A. Cocke, jr.	"	–	19	
Abraham N. Cardozo,	"	–	19	
Rich'd Crump,	"	–	19	
Moses N. Cardozo,	"	–	19	
David N. Cardozo,	"	–	19	
Gater Clarke,	"	–	19	
Isham W. Clements,	"	–	19	
Josiah Cosby,	"	–	19	
Smith Cocke,	"	–	15	
William F. Carter,	"	–	2	
John S. Deane,	"	–	19	
John Elam,	"	–	19	
Richard Elam,	"	–	19	
Pleasant Farley,	"	–	19	
James Faris.	"	–	19	
James Forsel.	"	–	19	
Robert French,	"	–	19	
Henry Gordon,	"	–	19	
William Goodman,	"	–	19	
John O. Gilori,	"	–	19	
John Gordon,	"	–	19	
James M. Hanes,	"	–	19	
William M. Heth,	"	–	19	
John Johnson,	"	–	19	

NAMES.	RANK.	TIME OF SERVICE.		REMARKS.
		Months.	Days.	
William Lewis,	Private,	–	19	
Edw'd Moseley,	"	–	19	
Edw'd Munford,	"	–	19	
Thomas Moore,	"	–	19	
Claiborne Mays,	"	–	19	
Edw'd Mye,	"	–	19	
Thomas Merryman,	"	–	19	
William C. Netherland.	"	–	19	
Bennett Povall.	"	–	19	
Robert Pleasants,	"	–	19	
John T. Pleasants,	"	–	19	
William Sublett,	"	–	19	
William Swann,	"	–	19	
George Swann,	"	–	19	
Samuel Swann, sr.	"	–	19	
Samuel Swann, jr.	"	–	19	
John Swann,	"	–	19	
Elijah Smith,	"	–	19	
George Stratton,	"	–	19	
Littleberry Stegar,	"	–	19	
Thomas Smith,	"	–	19	
Ro. H. Saunders,	"	–	9	
Warren M. Seay,	"	–	19	
Richard Snead,	"	–	19	
Martin Tucker,	"	–	19	
Peyton Tucker,	"	–	19	
Charles Taylor,	"	–	19	
J. D. Turpin,	"	–	19	
William Tompkins,	"	–	15	
William Utley,	"	–	19	
Joseph Woodson,	"	–	19	
Thomas Wilkinson,	"	–	19	
William Wellburn,	"	–	19	
John Whitlocke,	"	–	19	
Stephen D. Watkins,	"	–	19	

MUSTER ROLL

Of Captain Thomas Cockes' Company of the Seventy-first Regiment, Virginia Militia, commanded by Lieutenant Colonel William Allen, called into actual Service from 30th June to 10th July, in the year 1813.

NAMES.	RANK.	TIME OF SERVICE.		REMARKS.
		Months.	Days.	
Thomas Cockes,	Captain,	–	11	
William Scammell,	Lieutenant,	–	11	
Michael Holt,	Ensign,	–	11	
Jonathan Ellis,	Sergeant,	–	10	
William J. Cokes.	"	–	10	
James Clinch,	"	–	10	
Moody Emory,	"	–	10	
Christopher Rispes,	Corporal,	–	10	
Joel Savage,	"	–	10	
John Write,	"	–	10	
Robert Moring,	"	–	10	
Thomas Barham,	Private,	–	10	
James Bennett,	"	–	10	
Thomas W. Bage,	"	–	10	
James Barham,	"	–	5	
Thomas Clinch,	"	–	10	
Thomas E. Cosby,	"	–	10	
Samuel Cokes,	"	–	10	
William M. Davis,	"	–	10	
Wila Davis,	"	–	10	
Nicholas T. Davis,	"	–	10	
Mark Davis,	"	–	10	
John Emery,	"	–	10	
John M. Galt,	"	–	10	
James Holt,	"	–	4	
Robert B. Hunnicutt.	"	–	10	
Henry Judkins,	"	–	10	
Edwin James,	"	–	10	
William Ingram,	"	–	10	
John H. Judkins,	"	–	10	
Benjamin King,	"	–	10	
John Lane,	"	–	10	
Thomas Lane,	"	–	10	
Benjamin Newsum,	"	–	10	
Randolph H. Price,	"	–	10	
Wiatt Philips,	"	–	10	
Nathaniel Price,	"	–	10	
Allen Porter,	"	–	10	
James Rowell,	"	–	4	
Joseph Rainey,	"	–	6	
John Riggan,	"	–	10	
Ira Riggan,	"	–	10	
Francis Riggan,	"	–	10	
Benjamin Riggan,	"	–	10	
Thomas J. Ryland,	"	–	10	
John Rispess,	"	–	10	
James Ryland,	"	–	10	
Burwell Savage,	"	–	10	

NAMES.			RANK.	TIME OF SERVICE.		REMARKS.
				Months.	Days.	
Edwin Seward,	-	-	Private,	–	10	
Doila Savage,	-	-	"	–	10	
John Seward,	-	-	"	–	10	
John Tines,	-	-	"	–	10	
Willis Turner,	-	-	"	–	10	
Mark Warren,	-	-	"	–	10	

MUSTER ROLL

Of Captain William Cock's Troop of Cavalry of the First Regiment, Virginia Militia, in the County of Campbell, called into actual Service under the general orders of the 26th August, from 30th August to 20th September, in the year 1814.

NAMES.	RANK.	Months.	Days.	REMARKS.
William Cock,	Captain,	–	5	
Thomas Hunter,	Lieutenant,	–	11	
Richard Jones,	Ensign,	–	21	
John Rosser,	Sergeant.	–	21	
William W. Williams,	"	–	21	
William Hunter,	"	–	21	
Hillroy Talbot,	"	–	21	
Charles Martin,	Corporal,	–	21	
Thomas Williams.	"	–	21	
Thomas Matthews,	"	–	21	
Thomas Hamlet,	"	–	21	
Alexander Barker.	Private,	–	21	Sub. for Jas. Shannon.
John Cock,	"	–	21	
Thomas Crawford,	"	–	21	
William T. Cobbs,	"	–	21	
Thomas A. Cobbs,	"	–	21	
Simeon Cobbs,	"	–	21	
Thomas Cobbs,	"	–	21	
William W. Cobbs,	"	–	21	
Thomas S. Cheatham,	"	–	21	
Charles Depriest,	"	–	21	Sub. for Wm. Franklin.
James Daniel,	"	–	21	
Josiah Daniel,	"	–	21	
Willis D. Ellett,	"	–	21	
Isaac Foster,	"	–	21	
Larkin Foster,	"			
Michael Hubberd,	"	–	21	
Alfred Hunter,	"	–	21	Sub. for Wm. Jones.
John Hunter,	"	–	21	Sub. for Ro. Hunt.
John M. Jones,	"	–	21	
William F. Jones,	"	–	21	Sub. for Wm. Foster.
Talbot Jones,	"	–	21	Sub. for Jas. Jones.
Jesse Jones,	"	–	21	
William Jones,	"	–	21	
Abraham Irvine,	"	–	21	
Joseph Irvine,	"	–	21	
Asa Jones,	"	–	21	
James U. Irvine,	"	–	21	
Samuel Kitchen,	"	–	21	
Pleasant Kay,	"	–	21	
Michael Leason,	"	–	21	
William Lewis,	"	–	21	Sub. for Wm. Hannah.
Thomas Luster,	"	–	21	
James Maxey,	"	–	21	
Burwell Mason,	"	–	21	Sub. for John Wood.
David McKenny,	"	–	21	Sub. for Pred. Moore.
Luke Matthews,	"	–	21	Sub. for Wm. Hamlet.

NAMES.	RANK.	TIME OF SERVICE.		REMARKS.
		Months.	Days.	
Lewis D. Poindexter, -	Private,	–	21	
David Robertson, - -	"	–	21	
Pleasant Rosser, - -	"	–	21	
James Reynolds, - -	"	–	21	
Jesse Rosser, - -	"	–	21	
William Rosser, - -	"	–	21	
John Shannon, - -	"	–	21	
George J. Stoball, - -	"	–	21	
Richmond Tatum, - -	"	–	21	
Merit Talbott, - -	"	–	21	
John Taiddie, - -	"	–	21	
Pleasant Talbot, - -	"	–	21	
Allen Talbot, - -	"	–	21	
William Vaughan, - -	"	–	21	

MUSTER ROLL

Of Captain Benjamin Cole's Company of Artillery, stationed at Camp Holly Springs, commanded by Major William Armistead.

NAMES.	RANK.	TIME OF SERVICE.		REMARKS.
		Months.	Days.	
Benjamin Cole, - -	Captain,			No time given in this roll, except in the case of Thomas King.
Thompson Ashley, - -	Lieutenant,			
George Thom, - -	"			
Bailey Buckner, - -	Sergeant,			
William F. Thompson, - -	"			
Catlett Pendleton, - -	"			
Robert Green, - -	"			
Edward Green, - -	Corporal,			
Richard C. Gaines, - -	"			
William B. Thornton, - -	"			
Robert Waggoner, - -	"			
William Gaines, - -	Drummer,			
William Wise, - -	Fifer,			
Nimrod Apperson, - -	Matross,			
Joseph Bowen, - -	"			
Thomas Charlton, - -	"			
George Camp, - -	"			
Willis Crump, - -	"			
John Dobbs, - -	"			
Peyton R. Eldridge, - -	"			
George Green, - -	"			
Benjamin Hawkins, - -	"			
Silas Hawkins, - -	"			
Nicholas Hart, - -	"			
Lawson Jones, - -	"			
Thomas King, - -	"	3	22	
Richard P. Menger, - -	"			
John Miles, - -	"			
Pittie Dudley, - -	"			
Thomas C. Powell, - -	"			
Robert Roe, - -	"			
Moses Revell, - -	"			
Larkin Rosson, - -	"			
Abbott Rosson, - -	"			
James Saunders, - -	"			
Nathaniel Saunders, - -	"			
Oliver Sims, - -	"			
John Smith, - -	"			
Henry Smith, - -	"			
Samuel Slait, - -	"			
Gustavus Summersall, - -	"			
Larkin Turner, - -	"			
James Wise, - -	"			
Ignatius Wheeler, - -	"			

(For the rest of this company, see publication of Pay Rolls.)

Captain Hailey Cole's Company—Twenty-third Regiment.

NAMES.	RANK.	TIME OF SERVICE.		REMARKS.
		Months.	Days.	
Hailey Cole, - -	Captain,	–	13	
Thomas Finney, - -	Lieutenant,	–	13	
William Ellis, - -	Ensign,	–	13	
Isham Cheatham, - -	Sergeant.	–	13	
Robert Baugh, - -	"	–	13	
James Folks, - -	"	–	13	
Geo. W. Cole, - -	"	–	13	
Daniel Cheatham, - -	Corporal,	–	16	
Matthew Anderson. - -	Fifer,	–	13	
Peter Archer, - -	Private,	–	9	
William Beasley, - -	"	1		
Richard Bass, - -	"	–	13	
Edward Bass, - -	"	–	13	
Archibald Bass, - -	"	–	9	
Young Beasley, - -	"	–	11	
Thomas Barnes, - -	"	–	11	
Daniel Blankinship, - -	"	–	11	
Henry Beasley, - -	"	–	11	
Richard Beasley, - -	"	–	11	
Henry Bridgwater, - -	"	–	11	
Samuel Cheatham, - -	"	–	13	
Samuel Cashon, - -	"	–	13	
Elam Cheatham, - -	"	–	13	
Joseph Cole, jr. - -	"	–	13	
Joseph Cole, - -	"	1		
John H. Cole, - -	"	–	13	
Jackson Cashon, - -	"	–	9	
Pleasant Cole, - -	"	–	9	
Obadiah Cox, - -	"	–	13	
Francis Cashon, - -	"	–	11	
Josiah Cendry, - -	"	–	29	
Henry Cox, - -	"	–	11	
Fountain Cheatham, - -	"	1	9	
Henry Cheatham, - -	"	1	9	
Charles Elam, - -	"	–	13	
Joel Folks, - -	"	–	13	
John Folks, - -	"	–	9	
William Hill, - -	"	–	11	
Edward Hill, - -	"	–	9	
John Hill, - -	"	–	11	
James Lockett, - -	"	–	11	
Everett Moore, - -	"	–	13	
Haley Moore, - -	"	–	13	
Edward Nunnally, - -	"	–	13	
Elijah Nunnally, - -	"	–	9	
Lewis Puckett, - -	"	–	9	
John Pringle, - -	"	–	11	
Phineas Puckett, - -	"	–	11	
Elijah Rudd, - -	"	–	13	
John W. Rudd, - -	"	–	13	
Jabez Rucks, - -	"	–	9	
John Rudd, sr. - -	"	–	13	
Leonard Rudd, - -	"	–	13	
Hezekiah Rudd, - -	"	–	13	

NAMES.	RANK.	TIME OF SERVICE.		REMARKS.
		Months.	Days.	
Robert Rudd, - -	Private,	—	13	
John Robertson, - -	"	—	13	
Archibald Rudd, - -	"	—	13	
Thomas Roberts, - -	"	—	13	
James H. Spears, - -	"	—	9	
William Talbot, - -	"	—	9	
John Wilkerson, sr. - -	"	—	9	
John Womack. - -	"	—	13	
Mark Wilkerson, - -	"	—	13	
Joseph Wilkerson, - -	"	—	13	
James Wilkerson, - -	"	—	23	
Peter Wilkerson, sr. -	"	—	9	
Peter Wilkerson, jr. -	"	—	9	
John Ware, - - -	"	—	9	
Edward Worsham, - -	"	—	11	

(For rest of this company, see publication of Pay Rolls.)

Captain Robert L. Coleman's Company—Eighth Regiment.

NAMES.	RANK.	TIME OF SERVICE.		ʒ REMARKS.
		Months.	Days.	
John Harden, - -	Private,	1	26	
Watkins Owen, - -	"	–	9	
William Rudder, - -	"	1	22	S. Rudder's sub., 7th Jan. 1815.
George W. Tribble, - -	"	–	13	J. Lavender his sub., 14th Sept'r.

(For rest of this company, see publication of Pay Rolls.)

Captain Cadwallader J. Claibourne's Company—Thirty-ninth Regiment.

NAMES.	RANK.	TIME OF SERVICE.		REMARKS.
		Months.	Days.	
Mathew B. Dyer, - -	Ensign,	–	10	
Nelson Wells, - -	Corporal,	–	10	
Henry Pegram, - -	"	–	10	
Benjamin Andrews, - -	Private,	–	10	
Lynder Andrews, - -	"	–	10	
George Crowder, - -	"	–	10	
Peterson Crowder, - -	"	–	10	
Samuel Chandler, - -	"	–	10	
Edmund Dance, - -	"	–	10	
Benjamin George, - -	"	–	10	
Chesley Hardy, - -	"	–	10	
Joseph Hardy, - -	"	–	10	
Thomas James, - -	"	–	10	
Hamlin E. Spain, - -	"	–	10	
Thomas Trewhatt, - -	"	–	10	
Bedford Wills, - -	"	–	10	
Benjamin Walter, - -	"	–	10	
Edmund Wells, - -	"	–	10	
Edward Washam, - -	"	–	10	
John Watts, - -	"	–	10	
Jerrell Wills, - -	"	–	10	
Thomas Wilbar, - -	"	–	10	

(For rest of this company, see publication of Pay Rolls.)

MUSTER ROLL

Of Captain Thomas Coleman's Company of Infantry of the Sixty-eighth Regiment of Virginia Militia, commanded by Lieutenant Colonel B. Bassett, called into the Service of the United States, from the 28th January to the 15th of February, in the year 1814.

NAMES.	RANK.	TIME OF SERVICE.		REMARKS.
		Months.	Days.	
Thomas Coleman,	Captain,	—	18	
Robert McCandlish,	Lieutenant,	—	18	
Benjamin Seixas,	Ensign,	—	18	
George Piggot,	Sergeant,	—	18	
Lewis Pagaud,	"	—	18	
Thomas Lucas,	"	—	18	
Lewis C. Tyler,	"	—	18	
August Deneufville,	Corporal,	—	18	
John Lucas,	"	—	18	
James Clarke,	"	—	18	
Ro. J. Deneufville,	"	—	13	
John Andrews,	Private,	—	18	
John L. Bryant,	"	—	18	
George Basserer,	"	—	18	
Richard Ball,	"	—	18	
Wm. H. Bassarer,	"	—	15	
Jos. W. Barbour,	"	—	8	
Wm. Broadrib,	"	—	8	
William Bartlet,	"	—	8	
George Brister,	"	—	6	
James Cox,	"	—	18	
Mark Cosby,	"	—	6	
William R. Chaplin,	"	—	18	
John Cooper,	"	—	8	
Hugh Freeman,	"	—	8	
James Lawson,	"	—	18	
Charles Lindsay,	"	—	18	
James Lovely,	"	—	18	
William Mason,	"	—	18	
Jackson Morton,	"	—	18	
Thomas Ortor,	"	—	18	
William Poner,	"	—	7	
William Randolph,	"	—	18	
William Robinson,	"	—	16	
John H. Smith,	"	—	18	
Larkin Smith,	"	—	18	
Thomas M. Seawell,	"	—	18	
Henry H. Shield,	"	—	18	
Robert P. Waller,	"	—	18	
Samuel Williford,	"	—	18	
William Washer,	"	—	18	
Isham,	Drummer,	—	18	
Peter,	Wagoner,	—	15	

Captain William Coleman's Company—Ninetieth Regiment.

NAMES.			RANK.	TIME OF SERVICE.		REMARKS.
				Months.	Days.	
Dennis Enzy,	-	-	Corporal,	1		
James Daily,	-	-	Drum Major,	1		
James Edwards,	-	-	Fife Major,	1		
Lunsford Carter,	-	-	Private,	1	27	
Dennis Ensy,	-	-	"	1		
Jacob Gilliam,	-	-	"	1		
Thomas Gilbert,	-	-	"	1	27	
Wright Robinson,	-	-	"	1		
Walter Williams,	-	-	"	2	27	

(For rest of this company, see publication of Pay Rolls.)

MUSTER ROLL

Of Captain Charles M. Collier's Company of the One Hundred and Fifteenth Regiment, Virginia Militia, in Service from 6th February to 7th July, in the year 1813, and from 27th September to the 18th October, in the year 1814.

NAMES.	RANK.	TIME OF SERVICE.		REMARKS.
		Months.	Days.	
Charles M. Collier, - -	Captain,	6	14	
William Armstead, - -	Lieutenant.	5	1	
John W. Jones, - -	"	—	22	
James Webb, - -	Ensign,	5	23	
Anthony Armistead, - -	Cornet,	—	21	
Robert Seymour, - -	Sergeant,	5	1	
Francis M. Armistead,	"	5	1	
William Sandrum, - -	"	5	1	
Clement Parker, - -	"	5	23	
Thomas L. Nicholson,	"	—	22	
Benjamin West, - -	"	—	22	Henry Robinson substitute for West.
Andrew Bully, - -	"	—	22	
William Langhorne, - -	"	—	21	
Thomas Burnham, - -	"	—	21	
James Parker, - -	Corporal,	5	1	
John Wood, - -	"	5	1	
John Drewry, - -	"	5	23	
William Davis, - -	"	5	1	
Richard Vaughan, - -	"	—	22	
Cary S. Jones, - -	"	—	22	
John Dewbre, - -	"	—	20	
Hieth Wray, - -	"	—	21	
Robert Noel, - -	"	—	21	
James Bluford, - -	Drummer,	5	1	
Jacob Bayley, - -	Fifer,	5	1	
William Bailey, - -	Drummer,	—	22	
Matthew Bains, - -	Private,	5	1	
John Bully, jun'r, - -	"	—	22	
Richard Barron, - -	"	—	22	
William Burge, - -	"	—	21	
John C. Bennet, - -	"	—	21	
Thomas Banes, - -	"	—	21	
William Bushel, - -	"	—	21	
William Backhouse, - -	"	—	21	
James Burk, jr. - -	"	5	1	
William Bean, - -	"	—	21	
Charles Cooper, - -	"			
William Clarke, - -	"	—	—	Substitute for Charles Hopkins
Whiton Crocket, - -	"	—	21	Substitute for Howard Parsons.
James Davis, jr. - -	"	5	1	
William Davis, - -	"	5	22	Substitute for Solomon Powell.
Thomas Dixon, - -	"	—	22	Wm. Budd substitute for Dixon.
Robert Field, - -	"	5	22	

NAMES.	RANK.	TIME OF SERVICE.		REMARKS.
		Months.	Days.	
Jonathan Frazer, - -	Private,	–	22	
Abram Gibbs, - -	"	5	1	
Nat. Giddins, - -	"	–	22	Geo. Randolph sub. for Giddins.
John Gayle, - -	"	–	10	
Will. Howell, - -	"	5	1	
William C. Hicks, - -	"	–	20	Sub. for Jas. Almond.
Stephen Hopkins, - -	"	–	9	
John Harwood, - -	"	–	21	Sub. for Humphrey Harwood.
William S. Ironmonger, -	"	–	22	
John Jenkins, - -	"	5	1	
George Ketler, - -	"	5	1	
William Lewis, - -	"	–	22	
Thomas Lewis, - -	"	–	21	
James M. Landrum, - -	"	–	22	
Thomas Latimer, - -	"	–	21	
George Latimer, - -	"	–	21	
Joshua Mee, - -	"	5	1	
Edward Melson, - -	"	5	23	
Will. S. Mallows, - -	"	5	1	
Robert Marrow, - -	"	5	1	
Josiah Massenburg, -	"	5	1	
George Middleton, - -	"	–	22	
William Melson, - -	"	–	22	
William Marrow, - -	"	–	22	
Merritt Moore, - -	"	–	21	
William Mears, - -	"	–	21	
Thomas Minson, - -	"	–	21	
Christ. K. Needham, -	"	–	20	
James Presson, - -	"	5	1	
James Powell, - -	"	5	1	
Edward Parish, - -	"	5	1	
John Parish, - -	"	5	1	
John S. Parker, - -	"	–	22	
William Perkinton, - -	"	–	22	
William Patrick, - -	"	–	22	
George Phillips, - -	"	–	22	Edward Bennett sub. for Phillips.
Edmond Patrick, - -	"	–	21	
James Phillips, - -	"	–	21	
William Russell, - -	"	–	22	
Wilson H. Skinner, -	"	5	1	
John Sherington, - -	"	5	1	
Thomas Skinner, - -	"	5	1	
John Skinner, - -	"	5	23	James Wood sub. for Skinner.
William Sands, - -	"	5	1	
William Smaw, - -	"	5	1	
Thomas Sands, - -	"	5	1	
William Skinner, - -	"	5	1	
William F. Striger, - -	"	5	1	
Sam'l Seley, - -	"	5	1	
John Seldon, - -	"	–	22	
John Sneed, - -	"	–	15	
Sevin Smith, - -	"	–	21	
Natt. Seburn, - -	"	–	21	Sub. for Roe Boutwell.
William Turnbull, - -	"	–	20	
William Tompkins, -	"	–	22	
Planner Tyler, - -	"	–	22	
Jessey Tenniss, - -	"	–	22	
Charles Thompson, -	"	–	19	
John Wymonth, - -	"	5	1	
John Wilson, - -	"	5	1	
John Wilson, sr. - -	"	–	22	
Robert Wilson, - -	"	–	22	Ro. Seldon for Wilson.
James Wilson, - -	"	–	21	Sub. for Sam. Wills.

MUSTER ROLL

Of Captain Charles Comer's Company, of the Sixty-third Regiment, Virginia Militia, in the service of the State, from 1st July to the 10th of the same month, in the year 1813.

NAMES.	RANK.	TIME OF SERVICE.		REMARKS.
		Months.	Days.	
Charles Comer,	Captain,	–	10	
Wm. E. Rivers,	Lieutenant,	–	10	
James Young,	Ensign,	–	9	
Wm. E. Temple,	Sergeant,	–	10	
Richard H. Muro,	"	–	10	
Jesse Mustleright,	"	–	10	
John Lee,	"	–	10	
Marcus Cook,	Corporal,	–	10	
Laban Ledbetter,	"	–	10	
Epps Leath,	"	–	10	
Robert Ledbetter,	"	–	10	
William Alley,	Private,	–	10	
Reaps Ambrose,	"	–	10	
Wood Burge,	"	–	10	
Littleberry Bonner,	"	–	9	
Wm. Bishop,	"	–	10	
Edmund Bishop,	"	–	10	
Henderson Crowder,	"	–	10	
Wm. Cotton,	"	–	10	
Edward Davenport,	"	–	10	
Frederick Heath,	"	–	10	
Drury Heath,	"	–	10	
Herbert Heath,	"	–	10	
Adam Heath,	"	–	10	
Richard Harwell,	"	–	9	
Armistead Harwell,	"	–	10	
Elijah Harwell,	"	–	10	
Leath Harewell,	"	–	10	
Willis Hall,	"	–	10	
W'mson Kirkland,	"	–	10	
Littleberry Lee,	"	–	10	
Green Lee,	"	–	9	
Jonathan Perkins,	"	–	9	
Nathaniel Ruins,	"	–	10	
John Shands,	"	–	10	
Joshua Temple,	"	–	10	
Charles G. Tatum,	"	–	10	
Frederick Temple,	"	–	10	
James Y. Temple,	"	–	10	
Edwin Temple,	"	–	10	
Robert Temple.	"	–	10	
Pleasant Temple,	"	–	10	
Reuben Tucker,	"	–	10	
Hartwell Tucker,	"	–	9	
Reuben Wright,	"	–	8	

Captain Archer B. Conway's Company—Thirty-ninth Regiment.

NAMES.			RANK.	TIME OF SERVICE.		REMARKS.
				Months.	Days.	
Joseph Fenn.	-	-	Sergeant,	–	9	
Benjamin Black,	-	-	"	–	9	
David Smith,	-	-	Corporal,	–	9	
Thomas Archer,	-	-	Private,	–	9	
William Brister,	-	-	"	–	9	
George Blick,	-	-	"	–	9	
Thomas Durrow,	-	-	"	–	9	
Thomas F. Fenn,	-	-	"	–	9	
William G. James.	-	-	"	–	9	
Thomas Keys,	-	-	"	–	9	
John Michal,	-	-	"	–	9	
James Rideout,	-	-	"	–	9	
Joel Vaughan,	-	-	"	–	9	
Peter Vaughan,	-	-	"	–	9	
Lemuel Vaughan,	-	-	"	–	9	
Herbert L. Vaughan,	-	-	"	–	9	

(For rest of this company, see publication of **Pay Rolls**.)

Captain John B. Cooper's Company—One Hundred and Fiftcenth Regiment.

NAMES.	RANK.	TIME OF SERVICE.		REMARKS.
		Months.	Days.	
John B. Cooper, - -	Captain.	—	3	
John P. Armistead, - -	Lieutenant.	—	3	
Marshall Booker. - -	"	—	3	
Robert Lowry, - -	Cornet.	—	3	
George Malicoat, - -	Sergeant.	—	3	
John Harwood, - -	"	—	3	
Thomas Malicoat, - -	"	—	3	
William Crittenden, -	"	—	3	
William Harwood, - -	Corporal.	—	3	
Thomas Burnham, - -	"	—	3	
James Clements, - -	"	—	3	
John F. Stringe, - -	"	—	3	
Anthony Armstead, - -	Qr. Master.	—	3	
Richard G. Brown, - -	Private.	—	3	
Wm. Banks, - -	"	—	3	
Roger J. Blackburn. - -	"	—	3	
John Bland, - -	"	—	3	
Richard Booker, - -	"	—	3	
William Bushel, - -	"	—	3	
William Cooper, - -	"	—	3	
Henry Crofford, - -	"	—	3	
Robert Cary, - -	"	—	3	
John Drummond, - -	"	—	3	
George Fisher, - -	"	—	3	
Holder Hudgins, - -	"	—	3	
Benjamin Ham, (or How,) -	"	—	3	
Walker Haughthorn, - -	"	—	3	
Calthorpe Howard, - -	"	—	3	
Humphrey Howard, - -	"	—	3	
Edward Latimer, - -	"	—	3	
Thomas Latimer, - -	"	—	3	
Thomas Lowry, - -	"	—	3	
Merit Moore, - -	"	—	3	
James Moss, - -	"	—	3	
Roscow Parsons, - -	"	—	3	
Solomon Powell, - -	"	—	3	
Copeland Pearce, - -	"	—	3	
John Robertson, - -	"	—	3	
James Smilt, - -	"	—	3	
James Wallace, - -	"	—	3	
Mathew Wood, - -	"	—	3	

(For rest of this company, see publication of Pay Rolls.)

Captain Lemuel Cornick's Company—Twentieth Regiment.

NAMES.	RANK.	TIME OF SERVICE.		REMARKS.
		Months.	Days.	
John Cornick,	Lieutenant,	–	21	
Sowell Norris,	Sergeant,	–	15	
Simon Murden.	Corporal,	–	9	
Ezekiel Ewell,	"	–	28	
John Widgen.	"	–	13	
John Lindsay,	Drummer.	–	8	
Joshua Barnes,	Private,	–	27	
James Barnes.	"	–	15	
John Butt,	"	–	12	
Jonathan Bonney,	"	–	9	
John Haynes,	"	–	16	
Wm. T. Keeling,	"	–	27	
James Lamount.	"	–	17	
Simon Murden,	"	–	18	
Charles Norris,	"	–	21	
Jonathan Roberts,	"	–	21	
Thomas Robinson.	"	–	9	
Thomas Scott,	"	–	8	
Smith Stryan,	"	–	8	
Isaac Widgen.	"	–	11	
William B. Wilkins.	"	–	21	

(For rest of this company, see publication of Pay Rolls.)

PAY ROLL

Of Captain Abraham Cowley's Company of Infantry, from the Second Battalion of the Thirty-third Regiment of Virginia Militia, called into Service the 19th and discharged 29th March, 1813.

NAMES.	RANK.	TIME OF SERVICE.		REMARKS.
		Months.	Days.	
Abraham Cowley, - -	Captain,	–	5	
Josiah Gathright. - -	Lieutenant.	–	5	
Philip Faloher, - -	Ensign,	–	5	
Samuel Henry. - -	Sergeant,	–	5	
Henry Negby, - -	"	–	5	
Henry Vaughan, - -	"	–	5	
Bartholomew Martin, -	"	–	5	
James V. Thompson, -	Corporal,	–	5	
William King, - -	"	–	5	
William Beverage, -	"	–	4	
William Straus, -	"	–	5	
Robert Anderson, - -	Private,	–	5	
John W. Allen, - -	"	–	5	
Nelson Anderson. -	"	–	5	
John Beverage, -	"	–	5	
William Banks, - -	"	–	5	
Jesse Britain, - -	"	–	5	
Gideon Bosher, -	"	–	1	
Elisha Bethell, -	"	–	5	
Charles Barker, -	"	–	4	
Nimrod Chience, -	"	–	3	
Samuel Cowley, -	"	–	5	
Pery Clark, - -	"	–	1	
Peter Franklin, - -	"	–	4	
Dudley Gillman, -	"	–	3	
Jno. A. Grant, - -	"	–	5	
Elisha Harwood, -	"	–	5	
John Harlin, -	"	–	5	
Benjamin Haley, -	"	–	5	
Gabriel C. Higgason, -	"	–	5	
Joseph C. Haley, -	"	–	4	
Mitchem Hadkins, -	"	–	1	
William Johnson, -	"	–	5	
John Kemp, -	"	–	4	
David Knight, -	"	–	1	
Mordecai Marks, -	"	–	2	
William New, -	"	–	5	
John Philips, -	"	–	5	
Francis R. Price, -	"	–	5	
Joseph C. Pleasants, -	"	–	5	
John Paul, - -	"	–	5	
Robert Price, -	"	–	3	
Jonathan Quisall, -	"	–	5	
Jno. H. Saunders, -	"	–	4	
William Williams, -	"	–	1	

Captain James Cox's Company—One Hundred and Eleventh Regiment.

NAMES.	RANK.	TIME OF SERVICE.		REMARKS.
		Months.	Days.	
James Cox, - -	Captain,	1	13	
John B. Murphy, - -	Lieutenant,	2	8	
Fleet Cox, - -	Ensign,	2	8	
James Robinson, - -	Sergeant,	2	8	Deserted.
Benedict Lamkin, - -	"	2	8	
William Courtney, - -	"	2	6	
James Bland, - -	"	2	8	
Richard Nott, - -	"	—	12	
Samuel Annandale, - -	Private,	—	28	
Charles S. Askins, - -	"	2	8	
Benjamin Askins, - -	"	2	20	
John C. Askins, - -	"	2	8	
William Askins, - -	"			
Robert Bailey, - -	"	—	22	
Thomas Beale, - -	"	1	11	Deserted.
Henry Beale, - -	"	2	19	
Reuben Brann, - -	"	2	17	
John Beale, - -	"	1	3	
John B. Barbour, - -	"	2	19	
James Brann, - -	"	1	29	
Stephen Bailey, - -	"	—	12	
John Bailey, - -	"	—	11	
James Bland, - -	"	—	12	
Wm. C. Chandler, - -	"	2	8	
Linsey Courtney, - -	"	—	28	
Presley Cox, - -	"	2	15	
George N. Cluskey, - -	"	1	5	
John Carey, - -	"	—	12	
Willis Garner, - -	"	1	15	
Trussell Hall, - -	"	2	8	
Wm. P. Hall, - -	"	—	12	
William Jewel, - -	"	1	7	
Griffin Jeffries, - -	"	2	4	
Richard R. Jackson, - -	"	1	7	
Robert Long, - -	"	2	8	
James M. Lewis, - -	"	2	12	
Nathaniel Lefevre, - -	"	2	5	
Robert Middleton, - -	"	2	8	
Peter K. Morgan, - -	"	—	11	
Daniel Mahany, - -	"	1	5	
John Maguire, - -	"	1	9	Deserted.
Daniel Mealy, - -	"	1		
Robert Murphy, - -	"	1	2	
James W. Nash, - -	"	2	7	
Thomas Pillion, - -	"	2	7	
George Robinson, - -	"	1	1	
Thomas Rowand, - -	"	2	5	
William Rice, - -	"			
George Smith, jr. - -	"	1	9	

NAMES.	RANK.	TIME OF SERVICE.		REMARKS.
		Months.	Days.	
Jeremiah Smith, - -	Private,	1	20	Deserted.
Fleet Self, - -	"	2	8	
John Smith, jr. - -	"	—	11	
Jeremiah Thrift, - -	"	1	13	
John P. Thompson. - -	"	2	6	
Daniel Wherrit, - -	"	—	12	
John Withers. - -	"	—	12	

(For rest of this company, see publication of Pay Rolls.)

MUSTER ROLL

Of Ensign Kenner W. Cralle's Company of Infantry of the Thirty-seventh Regiment, Virginia Militia, commanded by Lieutenant Colonel Thomas D. Downing, in the Service of the United States, from the 1st day of October 1814, when last mustered, to the 31st of December, 1814.

NAMES.	RANK.	TIME OF SERVICE.		REMARKS.
		Months.	Days.	
Kenner W. Cralle,	Ensign,	–	12	
James Oldham,	Sergeant,	–	16	
Meredith Barnes,	"	–	3	
John C. Hudson,	"	–	9	
Vincent Barnes,	"	–	11	
John Kent,	Drummer,	–	22	
Presley Hudson,	Fifer,	–	5	
John Anderson.	Private,	–	14	
George C. Ashburn,	"	–	17	
Richard Bearcroft.	"	–	12	
Mottrom Bearcroft,	"			
Bushrod M. Beacham,	"			
Samuel Barnes.	"	–	16	
Presley Blincoe.	"	–	21	
Daniel W. Beacham,	"			
Richard Bruer,	"	–	12	
Samuel Clarke.	"	–	7	
William R. Fallen,	"	–	12	
William B. Fisher,	"	–	20	
George H. Headley,	"			
Randall Headley,	"			
Richard Holliday,	"			
James Harding,	"			
Samuel Hudson,	"	–	3	Dead.
Matthew Harrison,	"	–	3	
Willis Jones.	"			
Charles Kent,	"			
Richard Knott,	"	–	5	
Vincent Kinkham,	"			
Leroy P. Leland,	"	–	7	
Peter McClanahan,	"			
Richard McClanahan,	"			
Alexander Newsom,	"	–	2	
John Redman,	"	–	–	Dead.
William Rochester,	"	–	17	
Henry Travers, jr.	"	–	14	
Thomas Vanlandingham,	"			
Armistead Vanlandingham,	"			
Samuel Winstead.	"	–	11	
Holland Winstead,	"	–	6	
John Winstead.	"	–	20	
Benjamin R. Williams,	"	–	12	

Captain Z. U. Crittenden's Company—One Hundred and Ninth Regiment.

NAMES.		RANK.	TIME OF SERVICE.		REMARKS.
			Months.	Days.	
Edm'd Henley,	- -	Ensign,	–	12	
James Miller,	- -	Private,	–	4	

(For rest of this company, see publication of Pay Rolls.)

Captain William H. Cousins' Company—Eighty-third Regiment.

NAMES.	RANK.	TIME OF SERVICE.		REMARKS.
		Months.	Days.	
Brooke Duval, - -	Sergeant,	–	5	
Shadrack Alfriend, - -	"	–	5	
John F. Evans, - -	"	–	5	
John Murrell, - -	Corporal,	–	5	
Edward Goode, - -	"	–	5	
Francis Reese, - -	"	–	5	
Alexander G. Hall, - -	Drummer,	–	5	
William Elder, - -	Private,	–	11	
Howell Featherstone, - -	"	–	5	
William Hunnicutt, - -	"	–	5	
Peterson Harper, - -	"	–.	5	
Amas S. Johnson, - -	"	–	21	
Right King, - -	"	–	–	Deserted.
Peter Lamb, - -	"	–	5	
Joseph Nunnally, - -	"	–	–	Deserted.
Clement Old, - -	"	–	5	
Patrick H. Poythress, - -	"	–	5	
Peter Poythress, - -	"	–	5	
John Spain, - -	"	–	5	
John Williams, - -	"	–	5	
Robert West, - -	"	–	5	
Pleasant Wells, - -	"	–	27	Enlisted in U. S. Army.

(For rest of this company, see publication of Pay Rolls.)

MUSTER ROLL

Of Captain Seaton W. Crump's Company of Infantry, from the Fifty-second Regiment of Virginia Militia, in the County of New Kent, called into actual Service from the 28th June to the 13th July, in the year 1813.

NAMES.	RANK.	TIME OF SERVICE.		REMARKS.
		Months.	Days.	
Seaton W. Crump,	Captain,	—	16	
Richard Crump,	Lieutenant,	—	16	
John B. Clopton,	Sergeant.	—	16	
Anderson Crump,	"	—	16	
Benj. Kirningham,	"	—	11	
Thos. Howle,	Corporal,	—	10	
Robert Bullington,	"	—	10	
Joshua Acree,	Private,	—	6	
Benj'n Bradley,	"	—	6	
Fielding Crump,	"	—	6	
Daniel Clarke,	"	—	6	
Jonathan Ellison,	"	—	6	
Wm. Fariss, sen'r.	"	—	10	
Beverley Frayser,	"	—	6	
Thomas Frayser,	"	—	6	
William Fariss, jr.	"	—	6	
James Gary,	"	—	6	
Fras. Gunnell,	"	—	6	
Matthew Higgins,	"	—	10	
Jno. Hazlegrove,	"	—	6	
Wm. Hamlet,	"	—	6	
John Higgins,	"	—	6	
Robert Kent,	"	—	6	
Thos. Martin,	"	—	6	
Dandridge Martin,	"	—	6	
Wm. Martin,	"	—	10	
Joseph Parkinson,	"	—	10	
Wm. Shearman,	"	—	6	
Henry Tyree,	"	—	6	
Edwin Waddill,	"	—	6	

PAY ROLL.

Of Captain John Cunningham's Company.

NAMES.			RANK.	TIME OF SERVICE.		REMARKS.
				Months.	Days.	
Matthew Toler,	-	-	Cornet,	–	22	
Michael Fisher,	-	-	Private,	1		
David Miles,	-	-	"	1		
Charles Machir,	-	-	"	–	22	
Abram Shobe,	-	-	"	–	22	

(For rest of this company, see publication of Pay Rolls.)

Of Captain John Critchlow's Company.

NAMES.	RANK.	TIME OF SERVICE.		REMARKS.
		Months.	Days.	
James Hearn, - -	Private.	–	–	Deserted.
John Johnson. - -	"	2	5	
Matt. Luter, - -	"	–	–	Deserted.
John Meyrick, - -	"	–	–	Deserted.
Council Vick, - -	"	–	26	Enlisted in U. S. service 21st Sept. 1814.

(For rest of this company, see publication of Pay Rolls.)

Captain Henry B. Custis' Company—Second Regiment.

NAMES.			RANK.	TIME OF SERVICE.		REMARKS.
				Months.	Days.	
Henry B. Custis,	-	-	Captain,	..	19	
Willam Custis,	-	-	Lieutenant,	–	22	
Geo. D. Wise,	-	-	"	–	14	
Thomas Edmunds,	-	-	Cornet,	–	22	
Edward Boisnard,	-	-	Sergeant,	–	22	
Thomas Harrison,	-	-	"	–	21	
John Berry,	-	-	"	–	19	
Charles Mason,	-	-	"	–	10	
John Mason,	-	-	"	–	8	
Samuel Justice,	-	-	"	–	15	
Thomas J. Edwards,	-	-	"	–	7	
Edmund Lilliston,	-	-	"	1	4	
William C. White,	-	-	"	–	22	
John Watson,	-	-	"	1	8	
George Drummond,	-	-	Musician,	–	21	
Thomas B. Custis,	-	-	"	–	20	
Elijah Boggs,	-	-	Private,	–	20	
Bowman H. Bailey,	-	-	"	1	6	
George Bull,	-	-	"	–	26	
John Bagwell,	-	-	"	–	28	
Jesse Bonwell,	-	-	"	1	8	
Solomon Bunting,	-	-	"	–	16	
Jacob Bell,	-	-	"			
John C. Copes,	-	-	"	–	19	
Edmund R. Custis,	-	-	"			
Thomas B. Custis,	-	-	"			
William Dix,	-	-	"	–	20	
Severn H. Dakes,	-	-	"	–	29	
William Finney,	-	-	"	2	8	
William Grinalds,	-	-	"	–	21	
Southey Grinalds,	-	-	"	–	21	
James Gibbons,	-	-	"	1		
Leonard Gurney,	-	-	"	–	8	
Michael Higgins,	-	-	"	–	8	
Asa Hickman,	-	-	"	–	22	
William Hayley,	-	-	"	–	11	
Peter Holland,	-	-	"			
Thomas James,	-	-	"	–	17	
Samuel Justice,	-	-	"	–	4	
William Kendall,	-	-	"	1	18	
Ethel Lyon,	-	-	"	–	19	
Alexander McCollom,	-	-	"	–	11	
John Mason,	-	-	"	1	6	
Horace M. Newton,	-	-	"	1	9	
John Poulson,	-	-	"	–	7	
Abel Rodgers,	-	-	"			
William T. Rodgers,	-	-	"	–	28	
William Savage,	-	-	"	–	14	
Nehemiah Stockley,	-	-	"	–	22	
Abel Savage,	-	-	"	1	26	
Wiley J. Twiford,	-	-	"	–	16	
Samuel Teakle,	-	-	"	–	26	

NAMES.	RANK.	TIME OF SERVICE.		REMARKS.
		Months.	Days.	
John B. Upshur, - -	Private,	–	21	
William A. White, - -	"	1	25	
Isaac Wright, - -	"	–	6	
Horace Wright, - -	"	–	G	

(For rest of this company, see publication of Pay Rolls.)

(This Captain's name is spelt Curtis in the index of Pay Rolls.)

PAY ROLL

Of Captain Thomas Custis' Company of Infantry of the Second Regiment, Virginia Militia, from the County of Accomack, called into actual Service under the general orders of the 22d of May, from the 22d of May to the 30th of May, in the year 1813.

NAMES.			RANK.	TIME OF SERVICE.		REMARKS.
				Months.	Days.	
Thomas Custis,	-	-	Captain,	—	9	
Levin S. Joynes,	-	-	Lieutenant,	—	9	
John Bull,	-	-	Ensign,	—	9	
Levin Parker,	-	-	Q. M. S.	—	9	
Levin Ayres,	-	-	Sergeant,	—	9	
William Rice,	-	-	"	—	9	
Dennis Rice,	-	-	"	—	9	
Obed Adams,	-	-	"	—	9	
Elisha Chandler,	-	-	Drummer,	—	9	
William Scott,	-	-	Fifer,	—	9	
Littleton Ayres,	-	-	Private,	—	9	
William C. Adams,	-	-	"	—	9	
Thomas Ayres,	-	-	"	—	9	
Henry Beasly,	-	-	"	—	9	
Charles Booth,	-	-	"	—	9	
Samuel Benson,	-	-	"	—	9	
Elijah Bull,	-	-	"	—	9	
Littleton Chandler,	-	-	"	—	9	
John F. Caharty,	-	-	"	—	9	
George Fleaharty,	-	-	"	—	9	
John Hall,	-	-	"	—	9	
Gilbert Hall,	-	-	"	—	9	
Robert Hall,	-	-	"	—	9	
Stephen Hopkins,	-	-	"	—	9	
Thomas Hurst,	-	-	"	—	9	
John Johnson,	-	-	"	—	9	
Ezekiel Kilman,	-	-	"	—	9	
William Lewis,	-	-	"	—	9	
Edmund Littaston,	-	-	"	—	9	
Samuel Lewis,	-	-	"	—	9	
James Lewis,	-	-	"	—	9	
Robert Lewis,	-	-	"	—	9	
Isaac Mesten,	-	-	"	—	9	
James F. Mesten,	-	-	"	—	9	
Smith Milson,	-	-	"	—	9	
Robert Milson,	-	-	"	—	9	
Abel Mason,	-	-	"	—	9	
Major Rayfield,	-	-	"	—	9	
Spencer Russell,	-	-	"	—	9	
Raymond Rolly,	-	-	"	—	9	
Levin Russell,	-	-	"	—	9	
Tully Snead,	-	-	"	—	9	
Robinson Salisberry,	-	-	"	—	9	
Samuel Singleton,	-	-	"	—	9	
Isaac Snead,	-	-	"	—	9	
Southy Simpson,	-	-	"	—	9	
William Stakes,	-	-	"	—	9	

NAMES.	RANK.	TIME OF SERVICE.		REMARKS.
		Months.	Days.	
William Sharrod, - -	Private,	–	9	
Ruell Sharrod, - -	"	–	9	
Thomas Scott, - -	"	–	9	
Henry L. Wilson, - -	"	–	9	
George West, - -	"	–	9	
Charles Willet, - -	"	–	9	
Robinson West, - -	"	–	9	
Jonathan West, - -	"	–	9	

MUSTER ROLL

Of Captain William P. Custis' Company of the Second Regiment, Virginia Militia, commanded by Lieutenant Colonel Thomas M. Bayly, in the Service of the United States, from the 25th of March to the 28th of the same month, from the 22d May to the 29th, and from the 25th November to the 27th of the same month, in the year 1813.

NAMES.	RANK.	TIME OF SERVICE.		REMARKS.
		Months.	Days.	
William P. Custis,	Captain,	–	15	
Mitchell Chandler,	Lieutenant,	–	15	
William Drummond,	Ensign,	–	15	
Daniel Ardis,	Sergeant,	–	15	
William White,	"	–	15	
Littleton Townsend,	"	–	15	
John S. Cropper,	"	–	15	
Thomas Degare,	Fifer,	–	15	
James Russell,	Drummer,	–	15	
James Ecchellenger,	Q. M. Serg't,	–	12	
Edward Ayres,	Private,	–	15	
William Budd,	"	–	12	
Edward Bell,	"	–	15	
John Bagwell,	"	–	15	
John Budd,	"	–	15	
John Bell,	"	–	8	
Jacob Bell,	"	–	11	
McKule Budd,	"	–	15	
William Bull,	"	–	15	
Robert Barnes,	"	–	15	
Daniel Baker,	"	–	15	
James Bull,	"	–	3	
John Bull, (of Geo.)	"	–	3	
Tully Beasly,	"	–	3	
Elijah Bloxum,	"	–	4	
Savage Copes,	"	–	15	
Thomas Copes,	"	–	12	
Parker Copes,	"	–	15	
John Crowson,	"	–	11	
Laban Chandler,	"	–	3	
George Chandler,	"	–	3	
Thomas B. Custis,	"	–	4	
Richard Drummond,	"	–	12	
Robert Drummond,	"	–	15	
Thomas Fox,	"	–	11	
William Fox,	"	–	15	
John Fox,	"	–	15	
John Guy,	"	–	3	
John Gray,	"	–	8	
William Haney,	"	–	11	
Isaac Hist,	"	–	8	
William Henderson,	"	–	3	
Isaiah Johnson,	"	–	15	
David Jaquish,	"	–	15	
Luther Jaquish,	"	–	15	
John Kelly,	"	–	11	

NAMES.	RANK.	TIME OF SERVICE.		REMARKS.
		Months.	Days.	
William Kendall, - -	Private,			
John Lewis, (of T.) -	"	–	15	
Samuel Lumber, - -	"	–	15	
Andrew Lee, - -	"	–	15	
Nath'l Long, - -	"	–	8	
Luther Mason, (or Sacker,) -	"	–	15	
Charles Mason, - -	"	–	12	
H. M. Newton. - -	"	–	12	
William Powell, - -	"	–	12	
Ignatius Russell, - -	"	–	3	
Charles Ren, - -	"	–	8	
Charles Rice, - -	"	–	4	
Zadock Selby, - -	"	–	12	
Thomas Sharrard. - -	"	–	12	
James Taylor, - -	"	–	15	
James Townsend, - -	"	–	11	
Israel Trader, - -	"	–	11	
Nathaniel Trader, - -	"	–	11	
Parker Trader. - -	"	–	11	
James Twiford, - -	"	–	11	
Samuel Taylor, - -	"			
James Watson, - -	"	–	12	
Isaac West, - -	"	–	4	
Jacob Waterfield, -	"	–	15	
John Watson, (of F.) -	"	–	15	
John L. Watson, - -	"	–	15	
Littleton Watson, - -	"	–	3	
William Willet, - -	"	–	11	
John White, -	"	–	4	

PAY ROLL

Of Captain Cadw. J. Dade's Company of the Twenty-fifth Regiment, Virginia Militia, in the Service from 4th to 12th September, 1814, (four days allowed for travelling home, making it to the 16th September.)

NAMES.			RANK.	TIME OF SERVICE.		REMARKS.
				Months.	Days.	
Cadw. J. Dade,	-	-	Captain,	—	12	
Moore Lurty,	-	-	Lieutenant,	—	12	
James Edwards,	-	-	Ensign,		12	
George M. Cooke,	-	-	"	—	12	
John Dishman,	-	-	Sergeant,	—	12	
Enoch Edwards,	-	-	"	—	12	
Carlton Roe,	-	-	"	—	12	
Richard Crope,	-	-	"		12	
Thomas Payne,	-	-	"	—	12	
Hyram Davis,	-	-	Corporal,	—	12	
Thomas B. Barker,	-	-	"	—	12	
William D. Greer,	-	-	"	—	12	
Thornton A. Price,	-	-	"		12	
Samuel O. Wilkinson,	-	-	"	..	12	
Nath'l W. D. Fox,	-	-	"	—	12	
Samuel Atwell,	-	-	Private,	—	12	
Geo. Armstrong,	-	-	"	—	12	
Thornton Atwell,	-	-	"	—	12	
William Burton,	-	-	"	—	12	
Samuel Botts,	-	-	"	—	12	
Joseph Black,	-	-	"	—	12	
John Bailey,	-	-	"	—	12	
Roger Betty,	-	-	"	—	12	
Geo. Bruce,	-	-	"	—	12	
Richard Curtis,	-	-	"	—	12	
John McColley,	-	-	"	—	12	
Pleasant Clift,	-	-	"	—	12	
Walker Clarke,	-	-	"	—	12	
Josiah Dodson,	-	-	"	—	12	
John Dickerson.	-	-	"	—	12	
Geo. Donaphan,	-	-	"	—	12	
Geo. Enfield,	-	-	"	—	12	
Presley Gill,	-	-	"	—	12	
William P. Gaynes,	-	-	"	—	12	
Benjamin Guey,	-	-	"	—	12	
William Guey,	-	-	"	—	12	
Fielding George,	-	-	"	—	12	
John L. Gubenater,	-	-	"	—	12	
Daniel Garner,	-	-	"	—	12	
James Garner,	-	-	"	—	12	
John Hedgman,	-	-	"	—	12	
Charles T. Hay,	-	-	"	—	12	
Lewis Hall,	-	-	"	—	12	
Benjamin Hayles,	-	-	"	—	12	
William Jett, jr.	-	-	"	—	12	
John Jones, jr.	-	-	"	—	12	
Thomas Inscoe,	-	-	"	—	12	
Benjamin Jones,	-	-	"	—	12	

NAMES.	RANK.	TIME OF SERVICE.		REMARKS.
		Months.	Days.	
Joseph Jones, - -	Private,	–	12	
William Jett, sen'r, - -	"	–	12	
John Jones, sen. - -	"	–	12	
William Johnson, - -	"	–	12	
John Johnson, - -	"	–	12	
James Jones, - -	"	–	12	
Dan'l J, Johnson, - -	"	–	12	
James Lunsford, - -	"	–	12	
John Marquis, - -	"	–	12	
John J. Mussleman, - -	"	–	12	
Jesse Mussleman, - -	"	–	12	
Warner P. Massey, - -	"	–	12	
Reubin Massey, - -	"	–	12	
Powell Massey, - -	"	–	12	
Christopher Marmaduke, -	"	–	12	
Lewis Palmer, - -	"	–	12	
Thomas Patterson, - -	"	–	12	
Alexander Patton, - -	"	–	12	
John Price, - -	"	–	12	
Samuel Potts, - -	"	–	12	
James Pursley, - -	"	–	12	
William Potts, - -	"	–	12	
Reubin Rawlins, - -	"	–	12	
Geo. Rogers, - -	"	–	12	
Williams Rawlins, - -	"	–	12	
James B. Storke, - -	"	–	12	
William T. Sinclair, - -	"	–	12	
John Sabastin, - -	"	–	12	
Dempsey Spelman, - -	"	–	12	
James Stephens, - -	"	–	12	
James Self, - -	"	–	12	
Jno. Spelman, - -	"	–	12	
Jno. N. Tolson, - -	"	–	12	
Thomas Timmons, - -	"	–	12	
John Trussell, - -	"	–	12	
James Thompson, - -	"	–	12	
Thomas Taylor, - -	"	–	12	
William Trigger, - -	"	–	12	
William Thomas, - -	"	–	12	
Thomas B. Truslow, -	"	–	12	
Benj'n Warmsley, - -	"	–	12	
John T. West, - -	"	–	12	
John White, - -	"	–	12	
Henry Wallace, - -	"	–	12	
Isaac Wood, - -	"	–	12	
James West, - -	"	–	12	
Servant Lloyd,	"		12	

Captain William Daney's Company—First Regiment.

NAMES.			RANK.	TIME OF SERVICE.		REMARKS.
				Months.	Days.	
William W. Allen,	-	-	Private,	—	10	
Michael Davis,	-	-	"	—	25	Transferred to artillery.
John J. Hinton,	-	-	"	—	25	" "
Benjamin Jones,	-	-	"	—	11	
Abel Nanny,	-	-	"	—	9	
William Richardson,	-	-	"	—	9	
Hiram Roof,	-	-	"	—	23	" "
Bartholomew Spence,		-	"	—	—	Deserted.
William Southern,	-	-	"	—	—	" "
Thomas Stovall,	-	-	"	—	—	" "
Johnson Thomas,	-	-	"	—	28	Enlisted in U. S. service.
Allen Thomas,	-	-	"	—	9	
Joseph Wallis,	-	-	"	—	28	Transferred to artillery.

(For rest of this company, see publication of Pay Rolls.)

MUSTER ROLL

Of Captain James Daniel's Company of Virginia Militia, from the Thirtieth Regiment, commanded by Major Reubin Tankersley, in the Service of the State of Virginia, from the 3d to the 9th of December, 1814, also in the One Hundred and Eleventh Regiment, commanded by Lieutenant Colonel Richard E. Parker, in the Service of the United States, from 24th of July to the 25th of September, 1814.

NAMES.	RANK.	TIME OF SERVICE.		REMARKS.
		Months.	Days.	
James Daniel, - -	Captain,	2	7	
William G. Maury, - -	Ensign,	2	6	
Armstrong McKinney, -	Lieutenant,		23	
Samuel Chapman, - -	Sergeant,	2		
John Robinson, - -	"	2	7	
William Robinson, - -	"	2	7	
Thomas Sale, - -	"	2	1	
William Reamey, - -	"	—	23	
Alvin Saunders, - -	"	2	1	
Philip Green, - -	Corporal,	2	7	
Thomas Bland, - -	"	2	7	
Geo. Chapman, - -	"	2	7	
Roy McCou, - -	"	2	1	
Byrd Anderson, - -	"	2	1	
Churchil Blackburn, - -	Private,	2	1	
Philip Beazeley, - -	"	2	1	
Edmond Beazeley, - -	"	2	6	
Robert Brewer, - -	"	—	23	
John Barker, - -	"	—	23	
Joseph Barker, - -	"	—	23	
Daniel Barker, - -	"	—	23	
Christopher Beazeley, -	"	—	5	
Thomas Clayton, - -	"	2	6	
Joseph Carter, - -	"	2	6	
Philip Carter, - -	"	2	6	
James B. Carter, - -	"	—	22	
Hayman Chandler, - -	"	2	5	
William Coats, - -	"	—	23	
John Curley, - -	"	—	23	
Alexander Chapman, - -	"	—	4	
John Drake, - -	"	—	23	
John B. Deatley, - -	"	—	23	
John Deatley, - -	"	—	23	
Philip Dishman, - -	"	—	23	
Achilles B. Foster, - -	"	—	5	
William Fisher, - -	"	—	5	
Samuel Grymes, - -	"	—	5	
William Garrett, - -	"	—	6	
James J. Garrett, - -	"	2	6	
James Gutridge, - -	"	—	23	
Joseph Gwaphmy, - -	"	2	1	
Geo. Green, - -	"	—	23	
Whiten Green, - -	"	—	23	
Thomas Howard, - -	"	2	5	
William Howard, - -	"	2	5	

NAMES.	RANK.	TIME OF SERVICE.		REMARKS.
		Months.	Days.	
Thomas Haynes, - -	Private,	2	5	
William Hudsen, - -	"	2	5	
John Hays, - -	"	–	25	
Joseph Harrison, - -	"	–	25	
Taliaferro Jett, - -	"	–	23	
William J. Jett, - -	"	–	23	
Weadon Jett, - -	"	–	23	
Abner James, - -	"	–	23	
John Keesee, - -	"	2	6	
Robert Lumpkin, - -	"	2	1	
Joseph Lumpkin, - -	"	2	6	
Pittman Levin, - -	"	2	1	
Thomas Levin, - -	"	2	1	
John Long, - -	"	2	1	
Thomas Loving, - -	"	–	5	
Simon Miller, - -	"	2	6	
Geo. McKinney, - -	"	–	23	
William McKinney. - -	"	–	23	
Thomas McKinney, - -	"	–	23	
John Mitchell, - -	"	–	23	
James McDaniel, - -	"	–	23	
Richard H. Micou, - -	"	–	6	
Samuel Noel, - -	"	2	1	
James Noel, - -	"	–	6	
Lofty Oliff, - -	"	–	23	
Elijah M. Oliff, - -	"	–	23	
Reubin Owens, - -	"	–	23	
Levi Parker, - -	"	2	6	
Thomas Puller, - -	"	2	6	
John Pettis, - -	"	2	6	
Fielding Pettis, - -	"	2	6	
Edmond Prewett, - -	"	2	5	
John Peed, - -	"	2	1	
John Pare, - -	"	–	5	
John Pursley, - -	"	–	23	
Fleming Pittman, - -	"	–	5	
Thomas Pegg, - -	"	–	23	
George Quesinberry, - -	"	–	23	
James Reamy, - -	"	–	23	
Edmond Reynolds, - -	"	–	16	
John F. Reynolds, - -	"	2	6	
Atwell Samuel, - -	"	2	1	
Anthony Sale, - -	"	2	6	
Geo. W. Slaughter, - -	"	2	6	
Geo. Spillman, - -	"	–	23	
William Spillman, - -	"	–	23	
Silas Short, - -	"	–	23	
Abram Selby, - -	"	–	23	
William T. Saunders, - -	"	–	23	
Benjamin Sims, - -	"	–	23	
Richard Turner, - -	"	–	16	
Benjamin Thomas, - -	"	–	23	
Edmond Verlander, - -	"	–	16	
John Waters, - -	"	2	5	
Richard Waters, - -	"	–	23	

MUSTER ROLL

Of Lieutenant William Dardin's Company of Infantry, Virginia Militia, in the Twenty-ninth Regiment, commanded by Major Joseph W. Ballard, in the Service from 24th June to the 13th day of July, 1813.

NAMES.	RANK.	TIME OF SERVICE.		REMARKS.
		Months.	Days.	
William Darden,	Lieutenant,	–	20	
John M. Eley,	Ensign,	–	20	
Benjamin Powell,	Sergeant,	–	17	
Allen Guy,	"	–	19	
John Watkins,	"	–	16	
Stephen Johnson,	"	–	20	
Henry Johnson,	Corporal,	–	19	
William McClenny,	"	–	19	
William Taylor,	"	–	20	
Jacob H. Duck,	"	–	19	
Lebanah Butler,	Private,	–	17	
James Butler,	"	–	16	
Samuel Blann,	"	–	20	
Jethro Butler,	"	–	18	
Robert Butler,	"	–	20	
Allen Butler, sr.	"	–	20	
Allen Butler, jr.	"	–	16	
Benjamin Butler,	"	–	16	
Elias Beal,	"	–	16	
Littleton A. Coan,	"	–	16	
Willis Carr,	"	–	20	
Nathaniel Carr,	"	–	19	
John Carr,	"	–	19	
Eley Crumpler,	"	–	19	
William Duck,	"	–	19	
Hardy Darden,	"	–	19	
Jessee Duck,	"	–	19	
Dempcy Duck,	"	–	19	
Holland Darden,	"	–	19	
Willis Duck,	"	–	19	
Aziza Darden,	"	–	19	
William English,	"	–	19	
Nathan English,	"	–	19	
Benjamin Glover,	"	–	19	
Willis Haynes,	"	–	19	
Elisha Holland,	"	–	19	
Benjamin Holland,	"	–	19	
William Johnson,	"	–	20	
Jonney Johnson,	"	–	19	
Eley Johnson,	"	–	19	
Allen Jenkins,	"	–	19	
Gale Johnson,	"	–	13	
Allen Jones,	"	–	13	
Wiley Jenkins,	"	–	13	
Wade Mountford,	"	–	13	
William Mountford,	"	–	13	
Edward Outland,	"	–	13	
Matthew Pope,	"	–	13	

NAMES.			RANK.	TIME OF SERVICE.		REMARKS.
				Months.	Days.	
Daniel Pope,	-	-	Private,	–	13	
James Rhoades,	-	-	"	–	13	
Andrew Redd,	-	-	"	–	13	
Willis Roberson,	-	-	"	–	13	
Jesse Spivey,	-	-	"	–	20	
Charles Stephens.	-	-	"	–	19	
Allen Spivey,	-	-	"	–	19	
Stephen Spivey,	-	-	"	–	19	
Joseph Saunders,	-	-	"	–	19	
Stephen Turner,	-	-	"	–	20	
Jacob Turner,	-	-	"	–	20	
Jordan Turner.	-	-	"	–	19	
John Turner,	-	-	"	–	19	
Richard Turner,	-	-	"	–	20	
Eley Turner.	-	-	"	–	19	
James Watkins.	-	-	"	–	20	
Jack Whitehead,	-	-	"	–	19	
Dempcy Whitehead,	-	-	"	–	20	
John Wilson.	-	-	"	–	19	
Benjamin Watkins,	-	-	"	–	19	

Captain Samuel Davis' Company—Twenty-fifth Regiment.

NAMES.	RANK.	TIME OF SERVICE.		REMARKS.
		Months.	Days.	
John Berry, - -	Private.	1	15	
William Berry, - -	"	–	26	Deserted.
William Humphreys. - -	"	1	6	"
John Mardens, sen. - -	"			
Ewell Owens, - -	"			
Thomas Rose, - -	"	1	6	"
John Sacry, - -	"	1	–	"
Richard Steel, - -	"	–	25	
George White, - -	"	–	16	

(For rest of this company, see publication of Pay Rolls.)

MUSTER ROLL

Of Captain Elliott Dejarnatt's Company of Infantry, of the Thirtieth Regiment, commanded by Major Reubin Tankersley, in the Service of the State of Virginia, from the 3d to the 9th December, 1814.

NAMES.	RANK.	TIME OF SERVICE.		REMARKS.
		Months.	Days.	
Elliott Dejarnatt,	Captain,	—	7	
William Kidd,	Lieutenant,	—	7	
Lewis Madison,	Ensign,	—	7	
William G. Pemberton,	Sergeant,	—	7	
John P. Walden,	"	—	7	
Thomas Berry,	"	—	7	
John M. Gray,	"	—	7	
William Dillard,	Corporal,	—	7	
William Robinson,	"	—	7	
Henry Clift,	"	—	7	
Theophilus F. Green,	"	—	7	
Dudley Hall,	Musician,	—	7	
William Taylor,	"	—	7	
Allen Beazley,	Private,	—	7	
Arculas Beckan,	"	—	7	
Robert Brooks,	"	—	7	
John Baylor,	"	—	7	
Washington Beazley,	"	—	7	
Philip Brooks,	"	—	7	
John Cecile,	"	—	7	
John Donahoe,	"	—	7	
Jesse Dillard,	"	—	7	
James Elliott,	"	—	7	
Edmond Fortune,	"	—	7	
Chany Gatewood,	"	—	4	
Bloxham Hord,	"	—	3	
Joel Hill,	"	—	7	
John Jones,	"	—	7	
Diggs Luck.	"	—	7	
Robert L. Parker,	"	—	7	
James Pare,	"	—	7	
John Scantland,	"	—	7	
James Southworth,	"	—	7	
John Searls,	"	—	7	
John Seal,	"	—	7	
David Seal,	"	—	7	
Thomas Taylor, sr.	"	—	7	
Thomas Taylor, jr.	"	—	7	
Henry Taylor,	"	—	7	
Major Taylor, jr.	"	—	7	

MUSTER ROLL

Of Captain Larkin Deshazo's Company of the Ninth Regiment, Virginia Militia, commanded by Lieutenant Colonel William Boyd, in the Service from the 2d to the 10th December, 1814.

NAMES.			RANK.	TIME OF SERVICE.		REMARKS.
				Months.	Days.	
Larkin Deshazo,	-	-	Captain,	–	9	
Baylor Walker,	-	-	1st Lieutenant,	–	9	
Alex'r Cambell,	-	-	Ensign,	–	9	
Lewis Howerton,	-	-	Sergeant,	–	9	
Thomas Nubill,	-	-	"	–	9	
Richard Watkins,	-	-	"	–	9	
William S. Nunn,	-	-	"	–	9	
Thomas Cleavely,	-	-	Corporal,	–	9	
Edmond Price,	-	-	"	–	9	
Temple Walker,	-	-	"	–	9	
Acre Chaney,	-	-	Private,	–	9	
Reubin Basket,	-	-	"	–	9	
Wily Brown,	-	-	"	–	9	
James Brown,	-	-	"	–	9	
Jacob Blake,	-	-	"	–	9	
Thomas Crane,	-	-	"	–	9	
Peyton Crane,	-	-	"	–	9	
Larkin Deshazo, jr.	-	-	"	–	9	
William Griffith,	-	-	"	–	9	
Sawyer B. Griffith,	-	-	"	–	9	
William Hill,	-	-	"	–	9	
William Jones,	-	-	"	–	9	
Thomas Mitchell,	-	-	"	–	9	
Robt. Mann,	-	-	"	–	9	
Robert Prince,	-	-	"	–	9	
Leroy Read,	-	-	"	–	9	
Fleming Read,	-	-	"	–	9	
Francis W. Terry,	-	-	"	–	9	
Robert Temple,	-	-	"	–	9	
Robt. Veilander,	-	-	"	–	9	
Baylor Wheely,	-	-	"	–	9	
William Whayne,	-	-	"	–	9	

Captain Joseph Deshield's Company—Fourth Regiment.

NAMES.			RANK.	TIME OF SERVICE.		REMARKS.
				Months.	Days.	
Horner Webb,	-	-	Sergeant.	–	15	
Matthew Neale,	-	-	"	1	3	
Eppa Dawson,	-	-	Private.	–	20	
John Dawson,	-	-	"	–	8	
Thomas L. Elmore,	-	-	"	–	24	
Elisha H. Gill,	-	-	"	–	8	
Thomas Haydon,	-	-	"	–	29	
Valentine Harcum,	-	-	"	–	12	
Hollen Haynie, sen'r,	-	-	"	1	14	
Samuel McCurdy,	-	-	"	–	3	
William Pickring,	-	-	"	–	14	
Jeduthan Pitman,	-	-	"	–	6	
George H. Pope,	-	-	"	–	11	
Daniel Pitman,	-	-	"	–	28	
George K. Rains,	-	-	"	–	8	
Haynie Wilkins,	-	-	"	–	10	
Chichester Walker,	-	-	"	–	24	
Joseph C. Williams,	-	-	"	–	10	
Thomas Walker, jr.	-	-	"	–	14	
Horner Webb,	-	-	"	–	9	
Samuel Webb,	-	-	"	–	8	
Vincent Webb,	-	-	"	–	8	
Samuel Day,	-	-	Servant,	1	6	
Dennis,	-	-	"	2	6	

(For rest of this company, see publication of Pay Rolls.)

MUSTER ROLL

Of Captain David Dick's Company of the Twenty-ninth Regiment, Virginia Militia, commanded by Lieutenant Colonel Francis M. Boykin, in the Service of the State of Virginia, from the 28th August to the 13th September, 1814.

NAMES.	RANK.	Months.	Days.	REMARKS.
David Dick,	Captain,	–	16	
Joseph Godwin,	Lieutenant,	–	16	
John M. Eley,	"	–	16	
Henry W. Applewhaite,	Ensign,	–	16	
William Lightfoot.	Sergeant,	–	16	
Thomas Marshall,	"	–	16	
John Smilley,	"	–	16	
Willis Williams,	"	–	16	
Davis Gray,	Corporal.	–	16	
Davis Bullock,	"	–	16	
Holland Butler,	"	–	16	
Robert Gale,	"	–	16	
Hezekiah Bracey,	Fifer,	–	16	
Pleasants Casey,	Drum Major,	–	16	
Zachariah Atkins,	Private,	–	16	
Henry Atkinson,	"	–	15	Detached from Captain Kello's Company.
William G. Britt,	"	–	15	" " "
Richard Bradshaw,	"	–	15	" " "
John Bryant,	"	–	15	" " "
Rix Beale,	"	–	16	
Richard Bowden,	"	–	16	
Samuel Bagrall,	"	–	16	
Henry Bagrall,	"	–	16	
John Bracey,	"	–	16	
Thomas McClainey,	"	–	16	
William Carbill,	"	–	16	
Barton Chitty,	"	–	15	" " "
John Crumpler,	"	–	15	" " "
Nathaniel Channel,	"	–	15	" " "
Pitt Cooke,	"	–	16	
John Clayton,	"	–	16	
Jonathan Coggin,	"	–	16	
Josiah Corbell,	"	–	16	
Henry Davis,	"	–	16	
George Dixon,	"	–	16	
George Davis,	"	–	16	
Mills Doyle,	"	–	15	" "
Jonas Edwards,	"	–	16	
Emanuel Edwards,	"	–	16	
Jonas Edwards,	"	–	16	
James Flake,	"	–	16	
Willis Fulyhan,	"	–	16	
William Foster,	"	–	16	
John Fitchene,	"	–	16	
John Foster,	"	–	15	" " "
James Foster,	"	–	15	" " "
Willis Garner,	"	–	16	

NAMES.			RANK.	TIME OF SERVICE.		REMARKS.
				Months.	Days.	
Thomas Garner,	-	-	Private,	—	16	
Andrew Gale,	-	-	"	—	16	
Mills Godwin,	-	-	"	—	16	
William Goodrich,	-	-	"	—	16	
John Gray,	-	-	"	—	16	
Thomas Hampton,	-	-	"	—	16	
James Hall,	-	-	"	—	16	
Thomas Hall,	-	-	"	—	16	
John Hall,	-	-	"	—	16	
James F. Hall,	-	-	"	—	16	
Gilliam Hatchett,	-	-	"	—	16	
Thomas Hardy,	-	-	"	—	16	
Willis Johnson,	-	-	"	—	16	
Robert Johnson,	-	-	"	—	16	
Thomas Ivey,	-	-	"	—	15	Detached from Capt.
Joseph Joyner,	-	-	"	—	15	Kello's company " " "
Carter H. Lundy,	-	-	"	—	15	" " "
John Marshall,	-	-	"	—	16	
John Murphy,	-	-	"	—	16	
Nathan Murphy,	-	-	"	—	16	
Samuel Matthews,	-	-	"	—	16	
James Mitchell,	-	-	"	—	16	
Drewry Mints,	-	-	"	—	16	
Thomas Minton,	-	-	"	—	16	
John Minton,	-	-	"	—	16	.
Wilson Murry,	-	-	"	—	16	
William Nicholson,	-	-	"	—	16	
David Neloney,	-	-	"	—	16	
John Nestor,	-	-	"	—	16	
James Nance,	-	-	"	—	15	" " "
Henry Pitt,	-	-	"	—	16	
John Pitt,	-	-	"	—	16	
Edward Price,	-	-	"	—	16	
William Powell,	-	-	"	—	16	
Willis Powell,	-	-	"	—	16	
Joseph Powell,	-	-	"	—	16	
Richard Parr,	-	-	"	—	16	
Thomas Powell,	-	-	"	—	16	
Edmond Pitt,	-	-	"	—	16	
Peter Peck,	-	-	"	—	16	
Hartwell Pate,	-	-	"	—	15	" " "
Anselm Renn,	-	-	"	—	15	" " "
Wilson Shivers,	-	-	"	—	16	
John Shivers,	-	-	"	—	16	
Geo. Shivers,	-	-	"	—	16	
Jordan Stephens,	-	-	"	—	16	
Richard Simmons,	-	-	"	—	15	" " "
Willis Turner,	-	-	"	—	16	
Newsom Turner,	-	-	"	—	16	
Joseph Turner,	-	-	"	—	16	
Geo. Turner,	-	-	"	—	16	
Joseph Turner, jr.	-	-	"	—	16	
Wiley Turner,	-	-	"	—	16	
Joseph Villines,	-	-	"	—	16	
John Villines,	-	-	"	—	16	
Matthew Westray,	-	-	"	—	16	
John Westray,	-	-	"	—	16	
Zachariah Womble,	-	-	"	—	16	
Stephen Whilley,	-	-	"	—	16	
Geo. Williams,	-	-	"	—	15	" " "
John Younger,	-	-	"	—	16	

Captain Bailey Digges' Company—Sixty-first Regiment.

NAMES.			RANK.	TIME OF SERVICE.		REMARKS.
				Months.	Days.	
William Thomas,	-	-	Lieutenant.	—	4	
Booker Miller,	-	-	Sergeant,	—	6	
Weston Brooks,	-	-	"	—	2	
George K. Brooks,	-	-	Private.	—	2	
Arch'd Brownley,	-	-	"	—	4	
Joshua Brooks,	-	-	"	—	8	
Augustine Digges, jr.		-	"	—	29	
Cole Digges,	-	-	"	—	2	
Isaac Foster,	-	-	"	—	9	
James Foster,	-	-	"	—	2	
Abraham Forrest,	-	-	"	—	2	
William Garrett,	-	-	"	—	4	
Lewis Hudgin,	-	-	"	—	9	
Bailey Hudgin, ·	-	-	"	—	2	
James G. Hudgin,	-	-	"	—	24	
Matt. Hopkins,	-	-	"	—	2	
John Hunley,	-	-	"	—	5	
Thomas James,	-	-	"	—	4	
Josiah Minter,	-	-	"	—	5	
Armistead Miller,	-	-	"	—	4	
Joshua Morgan,	-	-	"	—	4	
Elias Pugh, -	-	-	"	—	5	
Thomas Ripley.	-	-	"	—	10	
Isaac Smith,	-	-	"	—	5	
Richard Singleton.		-	"	—	4	
James Thomas,	-	-	"	—	4	
Daniel Turner,	-	-	"	—	4	
Joseph White,	-	-	"	—	5	

(For rest of this company, see publication of Pay Rolls.)

Captain Henry Digges' Company—Sixty-first Regiment.

NAMES.	RANK.	TIME OF SERVICE.		REMARKS.
		Months.	Days.	
John Ashbury, - -	Private,	–	28	
John Anderton, (of Wm.) -	"	–	24	
John B. Anderton, - -	"	1	6	
Isaac Brownley, - -	"	1	10	
Robert Callis, - -	"	–	1	
John Dunn, - -	"	–	10	
Mary Dunn, - -	"	–	6	
William Dunbar, - -	"	–	22	
George E. Dudley, - -	"	–	12	
Michael Drisgale, - -	"	–	3	
Daniel Fitchett, - -	"	–	22	
Thomas Fitchett, - -	"	–	11	
Caleb H. Green, - -	"	–	28	
Miles Gayle, - -	"	–	27	
Joshua Gayle, - -	"			
Caleb Hunley, - -	"			
James McBride, - -	"	–	19	
Robert Minor, - -	"	–	17	
Jesse Mitchem, - -	"	–	9	
William Robins, - -	"	–	23	
Thomas Robins, - -	"	–	3	
Thomas Ransone, - -	"	–	2	
Seymour Shackleford, -	"	–	7	
James Sprat, - -	"	–	3	
Hunley Thomas, - -	"	4	20	
James Williams, - -	"	1	4	
Joseph White, - -	"	1	10	

(For rest of this company, see publication of Pay Rolls.)

MUSTER ROLL

Of Captain Levi Dix's Company of the Ninety-ninth Regiment, Virginia Militia, commanded by Lieutenant Colonel Charles Bagwell, in the Service of the United States, from 28th May to the 2d June, 1813, and from 9th to the 12th September, 1814.

NAMES.	RANK.	TIME OF SERVICE.		REMARKS.
		Months.	Days.	
Levi Dix, - - -	Captain,	–	10	
John S. Bundick, - -	Lieutenant,	–	10	
James Ailworth, - -	Ensign,	–	10	
William Copes, - -	Sergeant,	–	6	
Raymond Taylor, - -	"	–	8	
Southy Grinalds, - -	"	–	10	
Isaac Dix, jr. - -	"	–	10	
John B. Burton, - -	"	–	4	
James Powell, - -	"	–	4	
William Bundick, - -	"	–	10	
Spencer Bull, - -	Corporal,	–	10	
Robert Broadwater, - -	"	–	10	
Richard Bloxom, - -	"	–	4	
William Barnes, - -	"	–	8	
Elijah Hickman, - -	"	–	6	
Robert Hickman, - -	"	–	10	
John Sterling, - -	"	–	6	
Ephraim Vessells, - -	"	–	10	
Geo. Dix, - - -	Fifer,	–	6	
Revell Dix, - - -	"	–	4	
Geo. West, - - -	Drummer,	–	10	
James Berry, - - -	Private,	–	10	
Preson Baker, - -	"	–	8	
Robert Chanock, - -	"	–	8	
Evander Cameron, - -	"	–	10	
Thomas Churn, - -	"	–	8	
James Davis, - -	"	–	8	
Isaac Dix, sr. - -	"	–	8	
Dennis Gray, - -	"	–	10	
James Gray, - -	"	–	4	
John Hickman, - -	"	–	10	
Stephen Hickman, - -	"	–	8	
Thomas Hickman, - -	"	–	8	
Solomon Lewis, - -	"	–	8	
Geo. Lilleston, - -	"	–	8	
John Lewis, sr. - -	"	–	8	
John Lewis, (of Jno.) -	"	–	6	
Isaac Lewis, - -	"	–	6	
William Matthew, - -	"	–	10	
Joseph Melson, - -	"	–	8	
William Moore, - -	"	–	10	
James Melson, - -	"	–	10	
John Only, - - -	"	–	10	
Elijah Parks, - -	"	–	10	
Edmund Parks, - -	"	–	8	
Raymond Parks, - -	"	–	8	
Geo. Pettit, - -	"	–	8	
William Powell, - -	"	–	2	

NAMES.			RANK.	TIME OF SERVICE.		REMARKS.
				Months.	Days.	
Peter Parks,	-	-	Private,	—	2	
Andrew Russell,	-	-	"	—	8	
Raymond Riley,	-	-	"	—	8	
Henry Riley,	-	-	"	—	10	
Reubin Rodgers,	-	-	"	—	6	
Charles Rew,	-	-	"	—	2	
Levin Shreaves,	-	-	"	—	10	
Geo. M. Snead,	-	-	"	—	2	
Reubin Simpson,	-	-	"	—	2	
Robert Savage,	-	-	"	—	2	
Southey Taylor,	-	-	"	—	8	
Major Taylor,	-	-	"	—	8	
John B. Taylor,	-	-	"	—	8	
Bagwell Taylor,	-	-	"	—	8	
Major Turnell,	-	-	"	—	2	
William Vessells,	-	-	"	—	10	
Thomas Vessells,	-	-	"	—	2	
John West,	-	-	"	—	8	
Geo. White,	-	-	"	—	10	
Thomas White.	-	-	"	—	8	
James Wright,	-	-	"	—	8	
John Wright,	-	-	"	—	8	
Nathaniel West,	-	-	"	—	2	
Dennis Wright,	-	-	"	—	2	

MUSTER ROLL

Of Captain Jesse Dold's Troop of Cavalry from the Ninety-third Regiment, Virginia Militia, commanded by Major J. Woodford, in the Service from 1st September to the 12th November, 1814.

NAMES.	RANK.	TIME OF SERVICE.		REMARKS.
		Months.	Days.	
Jesse Dold,	Captain,	2	11	
Matthew Link,	Lieutenant,	2	11	
Robert Brown,	"	1	24	
Jacob Clingimpeel,	"	2	11	
J. T. Whitcomb,	Sword Master.	2	11	
James M. Beard,	Sergeant,	2	11	
Andrew Grove,	"	2	11	
John Tate,	"	2	11	
Robert Guy,	"	2	11	
John Garrison,	Corporal,	2	11	
David Cunningham,	"	2	11	
James Scott,	"	2	11	
Adam Grove,	"	2	11	
John Argenbright,	Private,	2	11	
Samuel Armstrong,	"	2	11	
Theoderick Argenbright,	"	2	11	
Thomas Adam,	"	2	11	
Thomas Brown,	"	2	11	
Geo. Baylor,	"	2	11	
Robert Beard,	"	2	11	
Joseph Blan,	"	2	11	
Jacob Baylor,	"	2	11	
Joseph Brubeck,	"	2	11	
Christian Beard,	"	2	11	
James Buckhanan,	"	2	11	
John Brownlee,	"	2	11	
William Brown,	"	2	11	
Geo. Bozwell,	"	2	11	
John Becton,	"	2	11	
James Cunningham,	"	2	11	
John Caldwell,	"	2	11	
David Caldwell,	"	2	11	
Enoch Churchman,	"	2	11	
John Churchman,	"	2	11	
Alexander Cunningham,	"	2	11	
Josiah Cushing,	"	2	11	
John Dunlap,	"	2	11	
Hervey Drawbond,	"	2	11	
David Donaldson,	"	2	11	
Philip Engleman,	"	2	11	
Abraham Engleman,	"	2	11	
Peter Engleman,	"	2	11	
Robert Grass,	"	2	11	
John Grass,	"	2	11	
James Glendie,	"	2	11	

NAMES.	RANK.	TIME OF SERVICE.		REMARKS.
		Months.	Days.	
Peter Grabbart, - -	Private,	1	3	
Benjamin Gregary, -	"	2	11	
William Gray, - -	"	2	11	
Anderson Grubs, - -	"	2	11	
Jacob Hayberger, sen. -	"	2	11	
Frederick Hanger, - -	"	2	11	
Peter Hanger, - -	"	2	11	
John Hawke, - -	"	2	11	
Henry Hicks, - -	"	2	11	
Jacob Hayberger, jr. -	"	2	11	
Jacob Hanger, - -	"	2	11	
Edward Herzer, - -	"	2	11	
Geo. Hanger, - -	"	2	11	
Wilson B. Harper, - -	"	2	11	
Benjamin Imboden, - -	"	2	11	
Matthew Jamison, - -	"	1	11	
Peter Lower, - -	"	2	11	
John Lower, - -	"	2	11	
Linsey Lilley, - -	"	2	11	
Samuel Lightner, - -	"	2	11	
Simon Loop, - -	"	2	11	
William McComb, - -	"	2	11	
John Mollette, - -	"	2	11	
William Marshall, - -	"	2	11	
Thomas Mitchel, - -	"	2	11	
Henry A. McCarmac, -	"	2	11	
John Patton, - -	"	2	11	
Littleton H. Parham, -	"	2	11	
Thomas Puce, - -	"	–	1	
Alexander Parris, - -	"	2	11	
John Robertson, - -	"	2	11	
Robert Russell, - -	"	2	11	
Peter Rush, - -	"	2	11	
Samuel Steele, - -	"	2	11	
John Swink, - -	"	2	11	
James Short, - -	"	2	11	
James Steele, - -	"	2	11	
Jacob Serber, - -	"	2	11	
John Tobbert, - -	"	2	11	
John T. Cluff, - -	"	2	11	
Daniel Waseman, - -	"	2	11	
Robert Wilson, - -	"	2	11	
Jamison Cockran, - -	"	2	11	
Robert McPhuters, - -	"	2	11	
James Loftas, - -	"	2	11	
James Waldrip, - -	"	2	11	
Matthew Marshall, - -	"	2	11	
Philip Johnson, - -	"	2	11	

Captain Samuel Downing's Company—Thirty-seventh Regiment.

NAMES.	RANK.	TIME OF SERVICE.		REMARKS.
		Months.	Days.	
Lindsay Davis, - -	Sergeant.	–	15	
Samuel Berry.	"	–	6	
Hiram Davis, - -	"	–	3	
William Dountain, - -	Corporal.	–	15	
John Blundon, - -	Private.	–	14	
William Bridgman, - -	"	–	9	
Richard Cornish, - -	"	–	13	
Griffin Edwards, - -	"			
Joseph L. Edwards, - -	"			
William France, - -	"	–	27	
Charles France, - -	"	–	8	
Jesse Haynie, - -	"	–	9	
Rodham Haynie, - -	"	–	15	
John Haynie, - -	"	1	14	
Lee P. Harcum, - -	"	–	12	
Ellis Hudnall, - -	"	–	3	
William Hughlett, - -	"	–	9	
Richard Leader, - -	"	–	12	
John W. Mitchell, - -	"	–	14	
Charles Moore, - -	"	–	12	
James Power. - -	"	–	22	
Mottrom Pickaren, - -	"	–	19	
Hiram Smither, - -	"	–	18	
James Throp, - -	"			
Tarpley Watts, - -	"	–	17	
William Wood, - -	"	–	3	
John F. Williams, - -	"	1	8	
Robert Williams, - -	"	–	9	
Giles Webb, - -	"	–	15	

(For the rest of this company, see publication of Pay Rolls.)

MUSTER ROLL

Of Lieutenant Joseph Doulin's Company, from the Thirty-seventh Regiment, Virginia Militia, commanded by T. D. Downing, Commandant of the Regiment, in the Service from 1st October, 1814, to 1st January, 1815.

NAMES.	RANK.	TIME OF SERVICE.		REMARKS.
		Months.	Days.	
Joseph Doulin,	Lieutenant,	–	25	
Shaply N. Waddy,	Ensign,	–	7	
Thomas Keeve,	1st Sergeant,	–	4	
Geo. W. Ball,	"			
Richard Morrison,	"	–	7	
Linsey Davis,	"	–	6	
Hiram Carbell,	1st Corporal,	–	7	
John Nelms,	"			
Clemm Doged,	"	–	17	
John Berry,	"			
William Bridgman,	Private,	–	15	
Wade G. Beatley,	"	–	8	
William B. Beatley,	"	–	8	
Samuel Blundon,	"			
Thomas Conway,	"	–	9	
William Corbell,	"	–	7	
Samuel Cockarill,	"			
Crew Eaden,	"			
Geo. Edwards,	"		6	
Winder Eleston,	"			
John S. Eleston,	"	–	5	
Griffin Edwards,	"	–	11	
Eli Gill,	"	–	11	
Eles Gill,	"	–	6	
Elisha H. Gill,	"	–	16	
Thomas Hudnall,	"	–	7	
Thomas Hudson,	"	–	5	
Onesephus Harvey,	"	–	7	
John Hull,	"			
Thomas G. Hull,	"	–	14	
William Jones,	"			
John Lonsdell,	"	–	16	
John Moore,	"	–	2	
William B. Nelms,	"			
Hiram Nelms,	"			
Geo. R. Rains,	"			
William Webb,	"	–	19	
Vincent Webb,	"	–	16	
Samuel Webb,	"	–	12	
John Watts,	"	–	3	
William Wildey,	"			
Henry Waren,	"	–	1	
Martin Williams,	"	–	3	
William Wilkins,	"	–	3	
Walter Anderson,	"	–	2	
Geo. Hays,	"	–	1	

MUSTER ROLL

Of Captain Allen S. Dozier's Company of the One Hundred and Eleventh Regiment, Virginia Militia, Westmoreland County, commanded by Major William Nelson, in the Service from 36th of October to the 17th of November, 1813.

NAMES.	RANK.	TIME OF SERVICE.		REMARKS.
		Months.	Days.	
Allen S. Dozier, - -	Captain,	–	18	
Stephen Bailey, - -	Lieutenant,	–	18	
James English, - -	Ensign,	–	18	
Charles Scott, - -	Sergeant.	–	15	
Peter P. C. Straughan, -	"	–	15	
Solomon S. Hunt, - -	"	–	14	
Henry Parker, - -	"	–	14	
Thomas Palmer, - -	Corporal,	–	15	
John Pope, - -	"	–	14	
Geo. Brinnon, - -	"	–	14	
Charles C. Rice, - -	"	–	14	
John Elmore, - -	Private,	–	14	
William Roberson, -	"	–	12	
Murdock Murphy, - -	"	–	2	
William Butler, - -	"	–	6	
Geo. Butler, - -	"	–	14	
Joseph Elmore, - -	"	–	14	
William Gawen, - -	"	–	13	
James Brann, - -	"	–	14	
William Pillion, - -	"	–	12	
James Potter. - -	"	–	9	
Geo. N. McCluskey, - -	"	–	15	
Corbin Straughan, - -	"	–	2	
Charles Cullahan, - -	"	–	14	
Richard Atwell, - -	"	–	15	
Thomas Brown, - -	"	–	13	
Edmund Elmore, - -	"	–	15	
Thomas Gregory, - -	"	–	12	
John Gregory, - -	"	–	12	
Randal Kirk, - -	"	–	10	
John Crenshaw, - -	"	–	9	
Geo. B. Danks, - -	"	–	15	
James Jett, - -	"	–	15	
William Burnett, - -	"	–	14	
Geo. Curlis, - -	"	–	4	
Clark Short, - -	"	–	5	
James B. Stephens, - -	"	–	15	
Ludwell Nash, - -	"	–	11	
James Kirk, - -	"	–	12	
Thomas King, - -	"	–	2	
Jeremiah McCluster, - -	"	–	15	
Richard Coleman, - -	"	–	15	
Dosier Garner, - -	"	–	7	
Richard Burwell, - -	"	–	9	
James Nash, - -	"	–	11	
Ira Jones, - -	"	–	11	
Elliott S. Minor, - -	Videt,	–	15	

MUSTER ROLL

Of Captain James Dozier's Company, from the One Hundred and Eleventh Regiment, commanded by Major William Nelson, in the Service from the 15th to the 22d July, 1813.

NAMES.	RANK.	TIME OF SERVICE.		REMARKS.
		Months.	Days.	
James Dozier,	Captain,	–	9	
William Franklin,	Lieutenant,	–	8	
Meredith M. Marmaduke,	Ensign,	–	8	
William S. Sandford,	Sergeant,	–	8	
Joseph Dozier,	"	–	8	
Newman B. Jackson,	"	–	8	
Edward Porter,	"	–	8	
William Sanford, sen.	Private.	–	3	
Vincent Marmaduke,	"	–	2	
William Sanford, jr.	"	–	2	
Thomas Doleman,	"	–	8	
William Barrott,	"	–	8	
Thomas W. Clark,	"	–	6	
Andrew Montgomery,	"	–	4	
Simon Robinson,	"	–	7	
James Lampkin,	"	–	7	
John Norwood, jr.	"	–	4	
Levi Bryant,	"	–	8	
Jeremiah Sandford,	"	–	7	
William Rowles,	"	–	8	
Henry Brawner,	"	–	8	
Thomas Hutchins,	"	–	8	
Joel Crask,	"	–	8	
John Wroe,	"	–	7	
Geo. Coats,	"	–	4	
Fleet Lampkin,	"	–	2	
Moses Chilley,	"	–	7	
Josiah Hazzard,	"	–	3	
James Crask,	"	–	8	
William Anthony.	"	–	8	
John Mothershead,	"	–	8	
Boin Bashaw,	"	–	8	
William Marmaduke,	"	–	7	
James Rowles,	"	–	8	
Richard Caddeen,	"	–	8	
Ransdell Pegg,	"	–	8	
Thomas W. Hallbrooks,	"	–	8	
James Bashaw,	"	–	8	
John Barrott,	"	–	4	
James Montgomery,	"	–	3	
Samuel Templeman, jr.	"	–	8	
William Dillard,	"	–	2	

MUSTER ROLL

Of Captain John P. Drummond's Company of the Ninety-ninth Regiment, Virginia Militia, under the orders of Lieut. Col. Charles Bagwell, in the Service of the United States, from the 4th to the 10th of June, 1814.

NAMES.	RANK.	TIME OF SERVICE.		REMARKS.
		Months.	Days.	
John P. Drummond, - -	Captain,	–	7	
William Dunen, - -	Lieutenant,	–	5	
William Drummond, -	2d "	–	7	
James Northom, - -	Sergeant,	–	7	
Levin Drummond, - -	"	–	7	
William Northom, - -	"	–	5	
Noah Drummond, - -	"	–	7	
Geo. Northom, - -	"	–	5	
John Bayley, - -	Corporal,	–	5	
Elijah Bayley, - -	"	–	5	
John Marchel, - -	"	–	5	
Edmund Duncan, - -	"	–	5	
William Aleworth, - -	Fifer,	–	5	
James Jestis, - -	Drummer,	–	5	
Jacob Andrews, - -	Private,	–	5	
John Bayley, jr. - -	"	–	4	
James Bayley, - -	"	–	5	
John F. Bayley, - -	"	–	5	
Colmore Bird, - -	"	–	5	
Jacob Bird, - -	"	–	5	
William Christopher, - -	"	–	5	
Geo. Croswell, - -	"	–	5	
Elis Chesser, - -	"	–	5	
John Christopher, - -	"	–	5	
William Christopher, jr. -	"			
Ephraim Chesser, - -	"	–	5	
Pernel Chesser, - -	"	–	5	
William Chesser, - -	"	–	5	
Henry Chesser, - -	"			
Edmond Crosswell, - -	"	–	5	
James Chessor, - -	"			
Jessee Duncan, - -	"			
Meshack Duncan, - -	"	–	3	
James Delastatius, - -	"	–	5	
Spencer Drummond, - -	"	–	5	
Richard Hart, - -	"			
James Hoffmond, - -	"	–	5	
Leven Hammond, - -	"	–	5	
John Hull, - -	"	–	5	
Michael Hancock, - -	"	–	5	
Jessey Kelley, - -	"	–	5	
Elijah Lucas, - -	"	–	5	
Sathy Lucas, - -	"	–	5	
Samuel Marshall, - -	"	–	5	
Isaac Marshall, - -	"	–	5	
Robert Marshall, - -	"	–	5	
Sampson Marshall, - -	"	–	5	
Geo. Martin, - -	"	–	5	

NAMES.			RANK.	TIME OF SERVICE.		REMARKS.
				Months.	Days.	
Henry Marshall,	-	-	Private,	–	5	
James Martin,	-	-	"			
Ezekiel Ross,	-	-	"			
Noah Small,	-	-	"	–	5	
William Smart,	-	-	"			
James Taylor,	-	-	"	–	5	
John Thornton,	-	-	"	–	5	
William Trador,	-	-	"	–	5	
Nathaniel Tilon,	-	-	"			
Eshmond Trador,	-	-	"			
Shadrack Warrington,	-	-	"	–	5	
Henry Whaley,	-	-	"	–	5	

MUSTER ROLL

Of Captain David Duke's Company of the Fifty-ninth Regiment, Virginia Militia, commanded by Lieut. Col. J. Riddick, jr., in the Service from the 1st to the 16th day of May, 1813.

NAMES.	RANK.	TIME OF SERVICE.		REMARKS.
		Months.	Days.	
David Duke,	Captain,	—	16	
Benj'n Goodman,	Lieutenant,	—	16	
Abraham Raby,	Fifer,	—	16	
Samuel Bartlett,	Private,	—	16	
Samuel Bird,	"	—	16	
Jacob Butler,	"	—	16	
David Beasley,	"	—	16	
Elias Daughtery,	"	—	16	
Benj. Darden,	"	—	12	
Elvin Franklin,	"	—	16	
Henry Holland,	"	—	16	
Kader Harrell,	"	—	16	
Jethro Holland,	"	—	16	
Jeremiah Holland,	"	—	12	
Howell Hedgbeth,	"	—	16	
Andrew Jones,	"	—	16	
Jonas Lawrence,	"	—	13	
Nathaniel Norfleet,	"	—	16	
Christopher Norfleet,	"	—	16	
Willis Parker,	"	—	16	
Jesse Parker,	"	—	16	
Asa Wiggins,	"	—	16	
Ethelied Wilkins,	"	—	16	

MUSTER ROLL

Of Lieutenant James Dunn's Company of the Sixth Regiment, Virginia Militia commanded by Colonel A. Ritchie, in the Service of the United States, from the 1st to the 9th December, 1814.

NAMES.		RANK.	TIME OF SERVICE.		REMARKS.
			Months.	Days.	
James Dunn,	- -	Lieutenant,	—	9	
Henry C. Howerton,	-	Ensign,	—	9	
Henry Dunn,	- -	Sergeant,	—	9	
Isaac Fisher,	- -	"	—	9	
John Cauthorn,	- -	"	—	2	Was appointed from the 1st to 7th, then was made Sergeant.
John Bush,	- -	Corporal,	—	16	
Gabrell Davis,	- -	"	—	16	
Travis Brezendine,	- -	"	—	16	
Moten Armstong,	- -	Private,	—	2	
James Brizendine,	- -	"	—	15	
William Griggs,	- -	"	—	16	
John Gert,	- -	"	—	16	
John Taylor,	- -	"	—	16	
Leary Taylor,	- -	"	—	16	Or Leroy.

MUSTER ROLL

Of Captain John Dunn's Company, from the One Hundred and Fifteenth Regiment, Virginia Militia, Warwick County, commanded by the Lieutenant Colonel of the Regiment, in Service from the 26th day of June to the 7th July, and from 13th March to 3d April, 1813.

NAMES.	RANK.	TIME OF SERVICE.		REMARKS.
		Months.	Days.	
John Dunn, - - -	Captain,	1	2	
William Langham, - -	Lieutenant,	1	2	
Hinde B. Dunn, - -	Ensign,	1	2	
Peter Garrow, - -	Sergeant,	1	2	
Matthew Drewry, - -	"	1	2	
Thomas Drewry, - -	"	1	2	
John Leweling, - -	"	1	2	
Richard Dunn, - -	Corporal,	1	2	
Samuel McIntosh, - -	"	1	2	
John Young, - -	"	1	2	
William Diggs, - -	"	1	2	
Thomas Wood, - -	Drummer,	1	2	
John Watkins, - -	Fifer,	1	2	
John Burnham, - -	Private,	1	2	
Levi Buchan, - -	"	1	2	
Lackey Burnham, - -	"	1	2	
John Bendall, - -	"	1	2	
Jacob Babcock, - -	"	—	11	
John Cary, - -	"	—	11	
William Crutchfield, -	"	—	11	
Robert Drewry, - -	"	1	2	
Robert Dunn, - -	"	1	2	
Dolphin Drewry, - -	"	1	2	
Thomas R. Dunn, - -	"	—	21	
Richard Drewry, - -	"	1	2	
William Garron, - -	"	1	2	
James Gilbert, - -	"	1	2	
Edward Gisburn, - -	"	1	2	
Richard Jones, - -	"	1	2	
John Jones, - -	"	1	2	
Edward Lee, - -	"	1	2	
William Mallicote, - -	"	1	2	
John Moore, - -	"	1	2	
James Noblin, - -	"	—	21	
Samuel Noblin, - -	"	—	11	
Thomas Presson, - -	"	1	2	
Thomas Parker, - -	"	1	2	
William Parker, - -	"	1	2	
Hinde Russell, - -	"	1	2	
John S. Russell, - -	"	1	2	
Peter Ridley, - -	"	1	2	
Garrard Ridley, - -	"	1	2	
Samuel Wilson, - -	"	1	2	
William Young, - -	"	1	2	

Captain James Dunington's Company—at Camp Holly.

NAMES.	RANK.	TIME OF SERVICE.		REMARKS.
		Months.	Days.	
James Dunington, - -	Captain,			
Peter Dudley, - -	1st Lieutenant,			
William B. Lynch, - -	2d "			
John Robinson, - -	Sergeant,			
Edmund B. Norrell, - -	"			
Samuel Garland, - -	"			
James Benligh, - -	"			
William Martin, - -	Corporal,			
Christopher Fowler, - -	"			
Robert Thurman, - -	"			
French S. Gray, - -	"			
Benjamin Crenshaw, - -	Drummer,	1		
John Y. Johnson, - -	"	4		
John F. Lamb, - -	Private,	1		
David Campbell, - -	Matross,			
John Mays, - -	"			
Fielding Bradford, - -	"			
Isham Puckett, - -	"			
David F. Mason, - -	"			
Joseph Mays, - -	"			
John N. Anderson, - -	"			
Hezakiah Ellis, - -	"			
Littleton Rose, - -	"			
Nathan B. Harmon, - -	"			
Aaron Williams, - -	"			
Spelly Lee, - -	"			
Daniel Young, - -	"			
Hugh M. Rose, - -	"			
Joseph E. Royall, - -	"			
John McAllester, - -	"			
Isaac Gregory, - -	"			
John Reed, - -	"			
Gideon Mitchell, - -	"			
John Davis, - -	"			
Geo. Mettart, - -	"			
Netherland Tait,	"			
John B. Roy, - -	"			
John Vaister, - -	"			
Harrison Robinson, - -	"			
Nicholas C. Horsley, - -	"			
Robert Gray, - -	"			
William Doyle, - -	"			
James Walferford, - -	"			
Pleasant Parter, - -	"			
James D. Askins, - -	"			
Harden D. Murrell, - -	"			
Cornelius Pierce, - -	"			
Peter E. Booker, - -	"			
John Mattox, - -	Driver,			
William M. Rieves, - -	Matross,			
John H. Norman, - -	"			
John Strong, - -	"			
James T. Wright, - -	"			
Edmond Watt, - -	"			

NAMES.	RANK.	TIME OF SERVICE.		REMARKS.
		Months.	Days.	
Charles G. Cobbs, - -	Matross,			
David Smith, - -	Driver,			
John Y. Johnson, - -	"			

(For rest of this company, see publication of Pay Rolls.)

Captain Matthew H. Dunton's Company—Twenty-seventh Regiment.

NAMES.	RANK.	TIME OF SERVICE.		REMARKS.
		Months.	Days.	
Jno. D. Turpin, - -	Lieutenant,	–	11	
Anthony Bell, - -	Sergeant,	–	11	
John Pritlove, - -	"	–	11	
Kendall J. Belote, - -	Private,	–	11	
Patrick Benson, - -	"	–	11	
Samuel Dalby, - -	"	–	11	
Laban Johnson, - -	"	–	11	
James Johnson, - -	"	–	11	
Bowdoin Hamilton, - -	"	1		
Jno. W. Kendall, - -	"	–	11	

(For rest of this company, see publication of Pay Rolls.)

MUSTER ROLL

Of Captain Daniel Duval's Company of the Thirtieth Regiment, Virginia Militia, commanded by Major Tankersley, in the Service of the State from the 5th to the 9th day of December, 1814.

NAMES.	RANK.	TIME OF SERVICE.		REMARKS.
		Months.	Days.	
Dan'l Duval,	Captain.	–	5	
John C. Boxley,	Lieutenant,	–	4	
Madison Dillard,	Sergeant,	–	5	
William Skinner,	"	–	5	
Moseley M. Mullin,	"	–	5	
Absalom Standley,	"	–	5	
Samuel Alsop,	Private,	–	5	Substitute for Wm. Alport.
John Alsop,	"	–	4	
John Battaile,	"	–	5	
Robert Child,	"	–	5	
John Conway,	"	–	4	
Thomas Dillard,	"	–	5	
Horace Johnson,	"	–	5	
Stanfield Jones,	"	–	5	
Thomas Knox,	"	–	5	
Turner Lawson,	"	–	5	
William Long,	"	–	5	
James Mullin,	"	–	5	
Benjamin Pilcher,	"	–	5	
Keeling Row,	"	–	5	
Richard Wyatt,	"	–	5	Substitute for Geo. T. Todd.
Peter Thornton,	"	–	5	
Charles Thornton,	"	–	5	
Alexander Williamson,	"	–	5	

Captain Langley B. Eddins' Company—Sixty-first Regiment.

NAMES.			RANK.	TIME OF SERVICE.		REMARKS.
				Months.	Days.	
Humphrey Hunley,	-	-	Drummer,	–	6	
John Plummer,	-	-	Fifer,	–	6	
Ralph Armistead,	-	-	Private,	–	6	
John Adams,	-	-	"	–	5	
Thomas Bassett,	-	-	"	–	8	
Thomas Billups,	-	-	"	–	13	
George Brown,	-	-	"	–	6	
Thomas Bailey,	-	-	"	–	6	
John S. Clayton,	-	-	"	–	5	
William Drisgel,	-	-	"	–	5	
Richard Dudley,	-	-	"	–	9	
Thomas Eddins,	-	-	"	–	8	
Joseph Eaton,	-	-	"	–	5	
Thomas Forrest,	-	-	"	–	18	
Herod Foster,	-	-	"	–	16	
Joseph Foster,	-	-	"	–	16	
Joshua Foster,	-	-	"	–	21	
Abram Foxwell,	-	-	"	–	10	
John Hudgin,	-	-	"	–	24	
Richard James,	-	-	"	–	7	
John R. Lewis,	-	-	"	–	6	
Hiram Morgan,	-	-	"	–	23	
John Morgan,	-	-	"	–	6	
Matthew Pickett,	-	-	"	–	6	
Absalom Sadler,	-	-	"	–	14	
Isaac Sadler,	-	-	"	–	16	
William Smith,	-	-	"	–	6	
Henry Sadler,	-	-	"	–	5	
Absalom Sadler,	-	-	"	–	5	
Robert Sampson,	-	-	"	–	6	
William Teakle,	-	-	"	–	2	
James White,	-	-	"	–	6	
Thomas Willis,	-	-	"	–	6	

(For rest of this company, see publication of **Pay Rolls**.)

MUSTER ROLL

Of Captain Henry Edmunds' Company of the Sixty-sixth Regiment, Virginia Militia, from the County of Brunswick, called into actual Service under the general orders of the 28th June, from the 4th to the 6th July, in the year 1813.

NAMES.	RANK.	TIME OF SERVICE.		REMARKS.
		Months.	Days.	
Henry Edmunds,	Captain,	–	3	
John Juda,	Lieutenant,	–	3	
Thomas Meredith,	Ensign,	–	3	
Benj. Jones,	Sergeant,	–	3	
Obadiah Stith,	"	–	3	
Braxton Nursome,	"	–	3	
Thomas Crook,	"	–	3	
James Smith,	"	–	3	
Josiah Nolley,	"	–	3	
Richard Morris,	Drummer,	–	3	
Anderson Johnson,	Fifer,	–	3	
Elisha Abernethy,	Private,	–	3	
John Abernethy,	"	–	3	
William Black,	"	–	3	
Nathaniel Bass,	"	–	3	
Joel Baugh,	"	–	3	
Benj. H. Bass,	"	–	3	
Veries Browne,	"	–	3	
James Brintte,	"	–	3	
Sterling Briggs,	"	–	3	
William Buckner,	"	–	3	
Benj. Bennett,	"	–	3	
George Crooke,	"	–	3	
Nicholas Daniel,	"	–	3	
James Eldridge,	"	–	3	
Matthew Edwards,	"	–	3	
Allen Floyd,	"	–	3	
Frederick Hawthorne,	"	–	3	
Wm. W. Harper,	"	–	3	
John House,	"	–	3	
Freeman Jordan,	"	–	3	
David Jackson,	"	–	3	
William Johnson,	"	–	3	
John Kirkland,	"	–	3	
Wm'son Kirkland,	"	–	3	
Micajah Lane,	"	–	3	
Jessee Matthews,	"	–	3	
James Manly,	"	–	3	
Growner Ower,	"	–	3	
John L. Penington,	"	–	3	
Wm. Redcoat,	"	–	3	
William Rainely,	"	–	3	
Benj. Rawlings,	"	–	3	
Daniel Rawlings,	"	–	3	
John Slate,	"	–	3	
Samuel Sims,	"	–	3	
Wm'son Smith,	"	–	3	

NAMES.	RANK.	TIME OF SERVICE.		REMARKS.
		Months.	Days.	
Sterling Thacker, - -	Private.	–	3	
Banister Tomason, - -	"	–	3	
Wm. Taylor, - -	"	–	3	
Wm. Vaughan, - -	"	–	3	
Robert Vaughan, - -	"	–	3	
John R. Williams. - -	"	–	3	

Captain John C. Edrington's Company—Forty-fifth Regiment.

NAMES.	RANK.	TIME OF SERVICE.		REMARKS.
		Months.	Days.	
John C. Edrington, - -	Captain,	1	7	
James Walker, - -	Lieutenant,	–	9	
James Waller, - -	"	–	28	
George M. Cook, - -	Ensign,	–	15	
Aaron H. Ball, - -	"	–	28	
Joel T. Doniphan, - -	"	–	21	
Walter Hose, - -	Sergeant,	–	17	
Walter Williams, - -	"	1	27	
James Homes, - -	"	–	9	
Joel Holding, - -	"	–	9	
Benjamin Williams, - -	"	1	26	
John P. Williams, - -	"	–	28	
Noah Read, - -	"	–	23	
Thomas Crop, - -	"	–	21	
Joel Harding, - -	"	–	8	
Thomas Worman, - -	Corporal,	–	9	
Charles Williams, - -	"	–	17	
John Williams, - -	"	–	9	
Benj. Williams, jr. - -	"	–	9	
Allen W. Norman, - -	"	–	21	
Thomas Norman, - -	"	–	8	
Benj. Ashby, - -	"	1	18	
William H. Tyler, - -	"	–	28	
Rowza Peyton, - -	"	–	28	
Samuel Geter, - -	"	–	21	
Thomas Burton, - -	"	–	21	
John Starke, - -	"	–	28	
Augustus Shelton, - -	Musician,	–	17	
Cilas Edwards, - -	"	–	17	
Benjamin Ashby, - -	Private,	–	9	
James Atchison, - -	"	–	17	
Philip Alexander, - -	"	1	4	
James Armstrong, - -	"	2		
Robert Allen, - -	"	–	25	
James Armstrong, jr. - -	"	1	2	
William Abbott, - -	"	2	14	
John Ashby, - -	"	1	4	
Willis Brown, - -	"	–	17	
Rhodin Bridgman, - -	"	–	9	
Henry Bloxton, - -	"	–	9	
Joseph Briant, - -	"	–	29	
Thomas Bickett, - -	"	–	9	
Ephraim Brown, - -	"	–	17	
Abraham Bowling, - -	"	–	9	
George Bowling, - -	"	–	17	
George Brent, - -	"	–	17	
Richard Beckwith, - -	"	–	21	
William Briant, - -	"	–	21	

NAMES.	RANK.	TIME OF SERVICE.		REMARKS.
		Months.	Days.	
John M. Butler, - -	Private,	–	21	
William Billingsly, - -	"	–	16	
Clement Billingsly, - -	"	–	16	
Ire Burton, - -	"	–	16	
William Bettis, - -	"	–	16	
Charles Bowling, - -	"	–	13	
James Bowling, - -	"	–	11	
William Brumley, - -	"	–	11	
Rodham Berryman, - -	"	–	8	
Thomas Bethel, - -	"	–	8	
Elijah Bowling, - -	"	–	8	
John Colier, - -	"	–	9	
Bryant Chadwell, - -	"	1	27	
Jeremiah Carter, - -	"	3	1	
William Carter, - -	"	–	17	
Joseph Carter, - -	"	–	17	
John Colvin, - -	"	1	18	
Thomas Curtis, - -	"	1	4	
John Curtis, - -	"	–	21	
William Chilton, - -	"	–	21	
Benjamin Corbin. - -	"	–	19	
Peter Cox. - -	"	–	19	
Carnick Cox. - -	"	–	16	
George Cokely, - -	"	–	15	
James Carpenter, - -	"	1	26	
Samuel Cox, - -	"	–	15	
John Christie, - -	"	–	7	
William Dent, - -	"	1	27	
Thomas Davis, - -	"	–	21	
Walter R. Daniel, - -	"	–	18	
Henry Dillion, - -	"	–	18	
William Daffin, - -	"	–	21	
Thomas Edwards, - -	"	1	6	
William Edwards, - -	"	1	14	
Cilas Edwards, - -	"	–	28	
Thomas Franklin, - -	"	1	7	
Charles Franklin, - -	"	–	28	
Bailey Fritter, - -	"	1	16	
Ephraim Fritter, - -	"	–	25	
George B. Fant, - -	"	–	21	
Robert Fennel, - -	"	–	16	
Arthur R. Fitzhugh, - -	"	1	11	
Jonathan Finnel, - -	"	–	21	
Daniel Fines, - -	"	–	18	
John Fines, - -	"	–	18	
Charles Fox, - -	"	–	21	
George Ferguson, - -	"	–	14	
Charles C. Franklin, - -	"	–	19	
John Garrison, - -	"	1	25	
Jesse Garrison, - -	"	1	25	
Robert Gallahan, - -	"	–	17	
John Gallahon, - -	"	1	25	
George Green, - -	"	–	17	
William Gregory, - -	"	–	17	
Moses Garrison, - -	"	2	4	
Ralph Griffith, - -	"	1	6	
Benj. Guy, - -	"	1	2	
Benj. Groves, - -	"	–	15	
Geo. Homes, - -	"	2	13	
Fielding Hudson, - -	"	–	9	
William Horton, - -	"	–	17	
Samuel Hobday, - -	"	–	17	
Willis Harrel, - -	"	1	7	
Geo. W. Hore, - -	"	1	16	

NAMES.	RANK.	TIME OF SERVICE.		REMARKS.
		Months.	Days.	
Francis Hewitt,	Private,	—	21	
James Homes,	"	—	20	
William Hewitt,	"	—	21	
Thomas P. Harrison,	"	—	16	
John Holloday,	"	—	13	
Peter Jett,	"	—	21	
James Jones,	"	—	13	
William T. Jones,	"	—	13	
Jilcent Jett,	"	—	21	
James Jackson,	"	—	8	
Uriah Knight,	"	1	10	
John Knight,	"	—	17	
Barnett Kendall,	"	1	21	
Elijah Knight,	"	2	3	
John F. Kemper,	"	—	17	
Travis Kendall,	"	—	9	
James Knight,	"	1	16	
John Limbrick,	"	1	2	
Robert Laing,	"	—	29	
Edward Lowe,	"	2	3	
Jerrard Lomax,	"	2	6	
Richard Lomax,	"	2	8	
Vincent Limbrick,	"	—	21	
James Leach,	"	—	21	
James Limbrick, sr.	"	—	21	
William Lowery,	"	—	21	
James Limbrick, jr.	"	—	21	
William Lunsford,	"	—	17	
John Leach,	"	—	16	
John Laing,	"	—	15	
Cilas Leach,	"	—	11	
John Miflin,	"	1	29	
Sanford Miflin,	"	—	17	
James Miflin,	"	1	7	
John Moncure, jr.	"	—	9	
Edwin C. Moncure,	"	—	9	
John J. Massoman,	"	—	17	
Charles Miflin,	"	—	23	
Thomas McGuire,	"	—	21	
Daniel Monroe,	"	—	8	
Matt. Norman,	"	—	17	
Thomas Norman,	"	1	26	
Rowzee Peyton,	"	—	9	
William F. Phillips,	"	—	17	
Reuben Payne,	"	—	17	
Lewis Payne,	"	—	17	
Led. G. Payne,	"	1	16	
William Payne,	"	—	19	
Burkett Pratt,	"	—	21	
James Peyton,	"	—	14	
Thomas Peyton,	"	—	11	
Daniel Rills,	"	—	9	
Alexander G. Ratcliffe,	"	1	26	
Noah Read,	"	—	28	
Richard Randall,	"	—	22	
Francis Rollow,	"	—	21	
James Robertson,	"	—	21	
James Richards,	"	—	15	
Barnett Stewart,	"	—	17	
James Sorrel,	"	—	9	
Solomon Shackleford,	"	1	27	
Schila Shackleford,	"	1	7	
Rodney Sullivant,	"	—	24	
Thomas Stewart,	"	1	1	

NAMES.	RANK.	TIME OF SERVICE.		REMARKS.
		Months.	Days.	
Armstead Southard, - -	Private,	–	21	
Benj. Sullivant, - -	"	–	21	
James Spilman, - -	"	–	21	
James Sullivant, - -	"	–	21	
James M. Smith, - -	"	–	17	
Thomas Starke, - -	"	–	21	
Daniel Simms, - -	"	–	11	
Benjamin Simms, - -	"	–	10	
Bayley W. Starke, - -	"	–	8	
John Starke, - -	"	–	28	
Charles Stewart, - -	"	–	9	
William H. Tyler. - -	"	–	7	
Robert Tambs, - -	"	–	21	
Fielding Tolson, - -	"	–	21	
William Templeman. - -	"	–	12	
Benjamin Williams, sen'r, -	"	–	9	
Charles Williams, - -	"	–	20	
James Williams, - -	"	–	21	
Benjamin Wamsly. - -	"	–	21	

(For rest of this company, see publication of Pay Rolls.)

MUSTER ROLL

Of Brice Edwards' Company of Riflemen, of the Sixty-fourth Regiment, Virginia Militia, in the County of Henry, called into Service under the general orders of the 26th August, from the 11th to the 23d day of September, in the year 1814.

NAMES.	RANK.	Months.	Days.	REMARKS.
Brice Edwards,	Captain,	–	13	
John Edwards,	Lieutenant,	–	13	
Spencer Hunt,	Ensign,	–	13	
Chiles Edwards,	1st Sergeant,	–	13	
George Egelton,	"	–	13	
Cuthbert Cheeley,	"	–	13	
John L. Foster,	"	–	13	
Taphner Hailey,	Corporal,	–	13	
Gideon Northcutt,	"	–	13	
David Bryant,	"	–	13	
Adam Thomason,	"	–	13	
James Arnold,	Private,	–	13	
Bazel Burch,	"	–	13	
Edmund Bryant,	"	–	13	
Elijah Baize,	"	–	13	
David Burton,	"	–	13	
Simpson Cheshead,	"	–	13	
Walker Carter,	"	–	13	
James Clark,	"	–	13	
Isaac Clark,	"	–	13	
Edmund Davis,	"	–	13	
James Devin,	"	–	13	
John Dickerson,	"	–	13	
John Devin,	"	–	13	
Thomas Dickerson,	"	–	13	
Henry Edwards,	"	–	13	
Joseph Edwards,	"	–	13	
Ambrose B. Edwards,	"	–	13	
Joseph Egelton,	"	–	13	
Thomas Egelton,	"	–	13	
James Foster,	"	–	13	
George Fluman,	"	–	13	
Charles Grigg,	"	–	13	
Nathan Hill,	"	–	13	
James Hailey,	"	–	13	
Edward Hailey,	"	–	13	
Thomas Hailey,	"	–	13	
Reuben Hankins,	"	–	13	
Edward Hunt,	"	–	13	
John Hunley,	"	–	13	
James Lawrence,	"	–	13	
Henry Lawrence,	"	–	13	
Jesse Martin,	"	–	13	
Joseph Martin,	"	–	13	
Elijah Pedigo,	"	–	13	
Edward Poston,	"	–	13	
Solomon Poston,	"	–	13	

NAMES.	RANK.	TIME OF SERVICE.		REMARKS.
		Months.	Days.	
James Robertson, - -	Private,	–	13	
Jesse Simpson, - -	"	–	13	
George Solmons, - -	"	–	13	
Joseph Thomason, - -	"	–	13	
James Taylor, - -	"	–	13	
John Woodall, - -	"	–	13	
Henry Wyatt, - -	"	–	13	
Baker Wells, - -	"	–	13	
Nathan Woodall, - -	"	–	13	
Berriman Wells, - -	"	–	13	
Peyton Wells, - -	"	–	13	
Reuben Wells, - -	"	–	13	
John P. Wyatt, - -	"	–	13	
Craven Wyatt, - -	"	–	13	
Solomon Washington, -	"	–	13	

MUSTER ROLL

Of Captain Daniel Eppes' Company of the Sixty-second Regiment, Virginia Militia, from the County of Prince George, commanded by Colonel Miles Selden, called into actual Service from the 28th June to the 9th July, in the year 1813.

NAMES.	RANK.	TIME OF SERVICE.		REMARKS.
		Months.	Days.	
Daniel Eppes,	Captain,	–	12	
Peter Eppes,	Lieutenant,	–	12	
Wilkin C. Andrews,	Sergeant,	–	12	
William Ferguson,	"	–	12	
Amans Livesay,	"	–	12	
Wm. House,	"	–	12	
Lemuel Hunnick,	Corporal,	–	12	
Robert Folks,	"	–	12	
John Richard,	"	–	12	
Daniel Livesay,	"	–	12	
James Eppes,	Drummer,	–	12	
William Leigh,	Fifer,	–	12	
Richard Bishop,	Private,	–	–	Deserted.
Wm. Cornnith,	"	–	12	
James Daniel,	"	–	12	
Edmond Eppes,	"	–	12	
John Edward,	"	–	12	
Hamlin Eppes,	"	–	12	
John Eppes, jr.	"	–	12	
Armstead Goalden,	"	–	12	
John Hawkes,	"	–	12	
John Hoast,	"	–	12	
David Heath,	"	–	5	
Benjamin Heath,	"	–	11	
Jesse Heath,	"	–	11	
William Hadden,	"			
George Livesay,	"	–	12	
William Lynch,	"	–	12	
James Livesay,	"	–	11	
John Mugee,	"	–	29	
Michael Madden,	"	–	12	
William Patton,	"	–	10	
William Pentiman,	"	–	12	
Charles Russell,	"	–	6	
Collen Shuffield,	"	–	12	
Wilkins Stainback,	"	–	12	
Paschal Shuffield,	"	–	12	
Josiah Tilmarsh,	"	–	12	
Wm. Vaughan,	"	–	12	
Samuel Vaughan,	"	–	12	
John Wood,	"	–	12	
Robt. Williams,	"	–	12	
Alexander Wilson,	"	–	12	
Ambrose Wilkins,	"	–	12	

(For rest of this company, see publication of Pay Rolls.)

Captain Triplett T. Estis' Company—Eighth Regiment.

NAMES.	RANK	TIME OF SERVICE.		REMARKS.
		Months.	Days.	
John Stephens,	Lieutenant,	–	8	
Thomas Jarmon,	"	–	12	
Andrew McKee,	"	–	12	
Milton Payne,	Ensign,	–	14	
John B. Hurt,	Drummer,	–	8	
William Armistead,	Private,	–	8	
James Armistead,	"	–	8	
David Austin,	"	–	9	
Bennett Austin,	"	1	7	Sub. for Trevillian, 18th January.
John Broadway,	"	–	8	
John Boatwright,	"	–	8	
John Conner,	"	–	8	
Robert Chumleigh,	"	–	8	
John T. Duke,	"	–	8	
Charles Downey,	"	–	8	
Pleasant Goulden,	"	–	8	
James Gray,	"	–	11	
John Hughs,	"			
John Hudson,	"	–	8	
William Jackson,	"	–	8	
Walter Key,	"	2		
William Lenedue,	"	–	8	
James Marr,	"	1	15	Sub. for M. Bowell, 10th January.
James Miller,	"	1	21	Sub. for L. Catlett, 4th January.
John C. Montague,	"	1	14	Sub. for J. Robinson, 11th January.
Jas. B. Medley,	"	–	8	
Wm. D. Nash,	"	–	8	
Presley Nash,	"	–	8	
Thomas P. O'Brien,	"	–	8	
Spencer Sharp,	"	–	8	
Robert L. Smith,	"	–	16	Promoted to ensign.
John Thomas,	"	1	17	Sub. for Jas. Thomas, 8th January.
Uriah Willard,	"	–	8	
Jacob Wyman,	"	–	6	Michael Markwood his sub. 4th September.
Matt. Wingfield,	"	4	2	Dora Wheat his sub., 31st December.
Wm. Wingfield,	"	3	27	

MUSTER ROLL

Of Captain Richard Evans' Company of Light Infantry of the Sixth Regiment, Virginia Militia, called into Service by Lieutenant Colonel John Daingerfield, from the 6th to the 15th of April, in the year 1813.

NAMES.	RANK.	TIME OF SERVICE.		REMARKS.
		Months.	Days.	
Richard Evans,	Captain,	–	10	
James Dunn,	Lieutenant,	–	10	
Henry C. Howerton,	Ensign,	–	10	
George Troble,	Sergeant,	–	10	
Isaac Fisher,	"	–	10	
William Ladler,	"	–	10	Or Sadler.
Thomas Coats,	"	–	10	
William George,	Corporal,	–	10	
Isaac Brooks,	"	–	10	
Sudy Treble,	"	–	10	
Henry Haile,	"	–	10	
James Boughton,	Private,	–	10	
Lewis Boughton,	"	–	10	
Travis Brizendine,	"	–	10	
John Bush,	"	–	10	
George Brooks,	"	–	10	
Samuel Brocks,	"	–	10	
Beverley Carroll,	"	–	10	
John Carter,	"	–	10	
John Codington,	"	–	10	
Melvin Dozer,	"	–	10	
Gabriel Davis,	"	–	10	
John Dunn,	"	–	10	
Godfrey Davis,	"	–	10	
John Downey,	"	–	10	
James Evans,	"	–	10	
Thomas Eylett,	"	–	10	
Travis Gatewood,	"	–	10	
William Greggs,	"	–	10	
John Gist,	"	–	10	
Thomas Hunley, jr.	"	–	10	
Richard S. Haile,	"	–	10	
Richard Jones,	"	–	10	
Anderson Jeffries,	"	–	10	
James McEndry,	"	–	10	
Major Oaks,	"	–	10	
Philip Orrill,	"	–	10	
Leroy Taylor,	"	–	10	
Lewis Waldon,	"	–	10	
Bernard Williamson,	"	–	10	

MUSTER ROLL

Of Captain Thomas Evans' Troop of Cavalry, of the Sixth Regiment, Virginia Militia, called into Service by the orders of Lieutenant Colonel John Daingerfield, at different periods in the years 1813 and 1814.

NAMES.	RANK.	TIME OF SERVICE.		REMARKS.
		Months.	Days.	
Thomas Evans, - -	Captain,	1	1	
Thomas L. Latane, - -	Lieutenant,	–	25	
James Upshaw, - -	"	–	25	
Thomas Dix, - -	Cornet,	–	25	
Thomas St. John, - -	Sergeant,	–	25	
Edmond Mickleborough, -	"	–	25	
Dandridge Pitts, - -	"	–	16	
Henry Waring, - -	"	–	25	
Bevin D. Pitts, - -	"	–	9	
William Clark, - -	"	–	6	
Lewis G. Upshaw, - -	Corporal,	–	25	
Edwin Clements, - -	"	–	25	
John Beazly, - -	"	–	25	
Jesse Gouldman, - -	"	–	23	
Perkins Armstrong, - -	Private,	–	27	
Anderson Allen, - -	"	–	16	
Thomas Allen, - -	"	–	23	
John Atkinson, - -	"	–	25	
Major J. Boughan, - -	"	–	16	
Thomas Blackburn, - -	"	–	25	
William Blackburn, - -	"	–	25	
John B. Burke, - -	"	–	16	
John Boughan, - -	"	–	16	
Chaney Brizendine, - -	"	–	25	
Richard Beazley, - -	"	–	9	
Henry H. Boughan, - -	"	–	9	
William Broock, - -	"	–	9	
John Bohannan, - -	"	–	4	
Thomas Coghill, - -	"	–	25	
Wm. S. S. Clements, -	"	–	25	
William Crittenden, - -	"	–	25	
Samuel Croxton, - -	"	–	25	
William Clark, - -	"	–	16	
Nathaniel Crow, - -	"	–	25	
John Croxton, - -	"	–	25	
Smallwood Coghill, - -	"	–	25	
James Clark, - -	"	–	25	
James Clark, jr. - -	"	–	16	
James P. Clarke, - -	"	–	9	
Edward Covington, - -	"	–	6	
Richard Croxton, - -	"	–	3	
Edward G. Davis, - -	"	–	25	
John Downey, - -	"	–	25	
Thomas Dennett, - -	"	–	25	
James Dix, - -	"	–	18	
Leroy Evans, - -	"	–	25	
William B. Evans, - -	"	–	25	
Richard Evans, - -	"	–	9	

NAMES.	RANK.	TIME OF SERVICE.		REMARKS.
		Months.	Days.	
Thomas B. W. Gray,	Private,	–	25	
William Gatewood,	"	–	25	
Thomas Greenwood,	"	–	25	
George T. Greenwood,	"	–	25	
Muscoe Garnett,	"	–	16	
Burkett Gray,	"	–	25	
William H. Hill,	"	–	9	
Ransdall Hill,	"	–	9	
Nathaniel Herbert,	"	–	9	
Richard Jones,	"	–	25	
Thomas Jesse, jr.	"	–	25	
Henry Kerchevall,	"	–	25	
Richard Kay,	"	–	25	
John Lee,	"	–	6	
Charles A. L. Lewis,	"	–	16	
Warner Lewis,	"	–	9	
John Macow,	"	–	9	
Lewis Munday,	"	–	9	
Amos Newhall,	"	–	25	
George Newbill,	"	–	22	
James Newbill,	"	–	25	
Philip Pilkerton,	"	–	25	
Samuel C. Parker,	"	–	25	
Washington H. Purkins,	"	–	25	
Edmund Pilkerton,	"	–	25	
Alexander Parker,	"	–	9	
Edward Rouze,	"	–	9	
James Reynolds,	"	–	9	
Lewis Rouze,	"	–	12	
Fielding Sale,	"	–	9	
Walker Strent,	"	–	9	
Thomas Strent,	"	–	9	
George A. Steptoe,	"	–	10	
Frederick Tinsbloom,	"	–	16	
John S. Thruston,	"	–	16	
Taswell Upshaw,	"	–	9	
Wm. T. Upshaw,	"	–	25	
John Waring,	"	–	25	
Lewis Walden,	"	–	16	
Robt. P. Waring,	"	–	16	
Horace Waring,	"	–	9	

MUSTER ROLL

Of Captain George H. Ewell's Company, of the Ninety-ninth Regiment, Virginia Militia, called into actual Service of the United States, under general orders of Lieutenant Charles Bagwell, from 1st to 6th June, 1813.

NAMES.	RANK.	TIME OF SERVICE.		REMARKS.
		Months.	Days.	
George H. Ewell,	Captain,	—	6	
Sebastian Cropper,	Lieutenant,	—	6	
Robert Young,	Sergeant,	—	3	
William Young,	"	—	2	
Solomon Ewell,	"	—	5	
Richard Justice,	"	—	4	
John Kelman,	Corporal,	—	4	
Michael Landon,	"	—	6	
Stephen Mitchell,	"	—	4	
Richard Taylor,	"	—	6	
John Heart,	Drummer,	—	6	
John Wessels,	Fifer,	—	6	
Teackle Annis,	Private,	—	6	
William Annis,	"	—	6	
Curtis Annis,	"	—	5	
George Baker,	"	—	6	
Arthur Barnes,	"	—	6	
Thomas Barnes,	"	—	3	
Parker Barnes,	"	—	4	
Richard Christopher,	"	—	6	
James Coloncy,	"	—	4	
Dennis Clayton,	"	—	1	
Jesse Clayton,	"	—	1	
Geo. Clayton,	"	—	1	
Geo. Ewell,	"	—	6	
William Ewell,	"	—	4	
James Gooter,	"	—	6	
Isaiah Justice,	"	—	4	
Edward Kelman,	"	—	6	
Charles Kelman,	"	—	6	
Thomas Kelman,	"	—	6	
Samuel Kelman,	"	—	5	
James Lewis,	"	—	6	
William Lewis,	"	—	3	
Custis Lewis,	"	—	4	
Revell Lewis,	"	—	4	
John Lewis,	"	—	4	
John Lewis,	"	—	4	
Samuel Marshall,	"	—	4	
Major Mason,	"	—	6	
John Parks,	"	—	4	
Isaac Russell,	"	—	6	
Thomas Russell,	"	—	6	
Elijah Russell,	"	—	4	
John Shreves,	"	—	4	
Major Taylor,	"	—	6	
William Taylor,	"	—	3	
Thomas Thornton,	"	—	5	

NAMES.			RANK.	TIME OF SERVICE.		REMARKS.
				Months.	Days.	
Jacob Thorns,	-	-	Private,	–	6	Or Thoins.
Robert Taylor,	-	-	"	–	5	
Southey Taylor,	-	-	"	–	3	
James Taylor,	-	-	"	–	6	
William Thornton,	-	-	"	–	6	
David Thornton,	-	-	"	–	3	
James Treham,	-	-	"	–	4	
James Thornton,	-	-	"	–	1	
Custis Wessels,	-	-	"	–	6	
Thomas Wessels,	-	-	"	–	5	
Isaac Wessels,	-	-	"	–	6	
William Wessels,	-	-	"	–	3	
John West,	-	-	"	–	4	

Page 313

MUSTER ROLL

*Of Captain John Fariss' Company of the One Hundred and Seventeenth Regiment, Virginia Militia, Campbell County, in the Service from 30th **August to** the 15th September, 1814.*

NAMES.	RANK.	Months.	Days.	REMARKS.
John Fariss,	Captain,	–	16	
Richard Clark.	Lieutenant,	–	16	
Samuel Weaver,	Ensign,	–	16	
Ben. W. S. Cabell,	"	–	6	
William Thompson,	Qr. M. Serg't,	–	6	
Edmund W. Walker,	Sergeant,	–	16	
William Weaver,	"	–	6	
John Stratton,	"	–	6	Robt. Hunter sub.
Daniel Evans,	"	–	6	
Sampson Woodall,	Drummer,	–	16	
William Arrington.	Private,	–	6	R. Hunter sub.
Francis Armistead,	"	–	6	
Alexander Asher,	"	–	6	
John Brooks,	"	–	16	
Zachariah Brooks,	"	–	16	
William L. Burks,	"	–	6	Sub. for Thomas Burnett.
Thomas Burnett,	"	–	10	
Charles Burnett,	"	–	10	
William Carville,	"	–	16	Or Carwiles.
Zack. Carville,	"	–	10	Or Carwiles.
Absalom Dudley,	"	–	16	
Robert Elliott,	"	–	6	
William Fariss,	"	–	16	
Francis Fariss,	"	–	16	
Francis Grinstone.	"	–	6	
Elijah Garrett,	"	–	16	
Elijah Garvine.	"	–	6	
Thomas Holt,	"	–	6	
John Hazelwood,	"	–	16	
Edmund Haley,	"	–	16	
William Hamersley.	"	–	16	Sub. for John Stratton.
Archibald Jennings,	"	–	6	
Thomas Kitchen,	"	–	6	
John McCormick,	"	–	16	
William Mayberry,	"	–	16	
William G. Moore,	"	–	6	
Willis Martin,	"	–	6	
Benjamin Martin,	"	–	6	
William Mann,	"	–	6	
Samuel Martin,	"	–	6	
Robert D. Nash,	"	–	16	
David Perdew,	"	–	6	
David Patterson,	"	–	6	Chas. Burnett sub. for D. Patterson.
Martin O. Harrow,	"	–	6	
John Ray,	"	–	6	
John Reynolds,	"	–	16	

NAMES.	RANK.	TIME OF SERVICE.		REMARKS.
		Months.	Days.	
Archibald Robertson, - -	Private,	–	6	
Joseph Scott, - -	"	–	6	
John Still, - -	"	–	16	
James Shearer, - -	"	–	6	
Walter Taylor, - -	"	–	16	
David Terrence, - -	"	–	6	
Chesley Taylor, - -	"	–	6	
James Taylor, - -	"	–	6	
Robert Wright, .. -	"	–	10	

Captain John Field's Company—Eighth Regiment.

NAMES.			RANK.	TIME OF SERVICE.		REMARKS.
				Months.	Days.	
William Wood,	-	-	Ensign,	–	8	
Thomas Gooch,	-	-	"	–	13	
Joseph Field.	-	-	Corporal,	–	17	
John Darneall,	-	-	Private,	–	8	Holman Snead his sub.
Elisha Davis,	-	-	"	–	10	Hugh Hillis his sub.
Thomas Daniel,	-	-	"	–	12	Gustavus Ware his sub.
Thomas Hulett,	-	-	"	2	13	Sub for A. Old.
Skyler Moon,	-	-	"	–	22	
Francis Tinnell.	-	-	"	3	12	Sub for D. Hicks.

(For rest of this company, see publication of Pay Rolls.)

Captain William Field's Company—Twenty-first Regiment.

NAMES.			RANK.	TIME OF SERVICE.		REMARKS.
				Months.	Days.	
Thomas Dunston,	-	-	Private,	–	23	
John Edwards,	-	-	"	–	17	
Thomas Edwards,	-	-	"	–	28	
T. Q. Kinningham,	-	-	"	–	7	
Francis Robins,	-	-	"	–	7	
James E. West,	-	-	"	–	25	

(For rest of this company, see publication of Pay Rolls.)

Captain Walter L. Fontaine's Company—Eighth Regiment.

NAMES.			RANK.	TIME OF SERVICE.		REMARKS.
				Months.	Days.	
John Dunnivant,	-	-	Private,	1	23	Sub. for Jno. S. Duke.
Sherwood Kidd,	..	.	..	—	24	
George B. Minor.	-	.	..	1	17	Sub. for John Fulkes.
James Rowsey,	-	-	..	5	18	

(For rest of this company, see publication of Pay Rolls.)

Captain Thomas Faulkner's Company—Ninth Regiment.

NAMES.	RANK.	TIME OF SERVICE.		REMARKS.
		Months.	Days.	
Thomas Faulkner,	Captain,	—	18	
James G. Row,	Lieutenant,	—	8	
James H. Henry,	Ensign,	—	9	
Thomas F. Spencer,	"	—	5	
Elias Williams,	Or. Sergeant,	—	9	
John Hundley,	"	—	9	
Geo. Hoomes,	Sergeant,	—	9	
Dangerfield Bowden,	"	—	18	
John Ware,	"	—	9	
John L. Marshall,	"	—	9	
William Adams,	Private,	—	9	
Robert Boyd,	"	—	9	
Thomas Boyd,	"	—	9	
John Burch,	"	—	18	
John Bew,	"	—	18	
Christopher Bew,	"	—	9	
Sterling Burch,	"	—	8	
Braxton Bird,	"	—	5	
Baylor Cardwell,	"	—	9	
James B. Cardwell,	"	—	9	
Robert Cardwell,	"	—	18	
Richard E. Cardwell,	"	—	9	
William Cooper,	"	—	9	
John Cook,	"	—	18	
William Crouch,	"	—	9	
William Colley,	"	—	9	
John Cardwell,	"	—	6	
Thomas Drew,	"	—	9	
John Dalby,	"	—	9	
Anderson Davis,	"	—	18	
Thomas Eubank,	"	—	9	
Geo. Eubank,	"	—	5	
John W. Fleet,	"	—	9	
Robert Garratt, jr.	"	—	9	
Henry Gray,	"	—	9	
Thomas Hart,	"	—	9	
Thomas Huggett,	"	—	9	
John Hundley,	"	—	9	
James Henderson,	"	—	18	
Robert Jordan,	"	—	18	
John Kidd,	"	—	18	
William R. Milby,	"	—	15	
Robert Thruston,	"	—	18	
Hardy South,	"	—	6	
John Southgate,	"	—	6	
Beubin Ware,	"	—	18	
William Walton,	"	—	9	
Leonard Williams,	"	—	9	

(For rest of this company, see publication of Pay Rolls.)

MUSTER ROLL

Of Captain Moses Fentress's Company of the Twentieth Regiment, Virginia Militia, commanded by Lieutenant Colonel James Robinson, in the Service of the United States, from the 5th to 13th February, from 10th to 15th March, and from 24th to 29th September, 1813.

NAMES.	RANK.	TIME OF SERVICE.		REMARKS.
		Months.	Days.	
Moses Fentress,	Captain,	—	15	
Henry Lewis,	Lieutenant,	—	15	
Benjamin Cason,	Ensign,	—	15	
Thomas Harrison,	Sergeant,	—	15	
Thomas Henley,	"	—	15	
John Harrison,	"	—	15	
John James,	"	—	10	
William B. Day,	Corporal,	—	15	
Peter Whitehurst,	"	—	9	
Thomas Woodhouse,	"	—	10	
Hilley Brown,	"	—	15	
Simon M. Etheredge,	"	—	5	
William Axstead,	Private,	—	5	
James Brown,	"	—	15	
William Brown,	"	—	10	
Thomas Brown,	"	—	15	
Peter Brown,	"	—	15	
Hilley Cason,	"	—	10	
Joshua Cannon,	"	—	10	
John Fentress, sr.	"	—	13	
William Fentress,	"	—	13	
John Fentress, jr.	"	—	10	
Peter Fentress,	"	—	15	
Willoughby Flanagan,	"	—	15	
Robert Holmes,	"	—	15	
Emperor James,	"	—	15	
Edward Kays,	"	—	15	
Willis Langley,	"	—	15	
Reubin Land,	"	—	10	
Henry Land,	"	—	5	
Henry Liggatt,	"	—	10	
William McClanen,	"	—	10	
Joshua McClanen,	"	—	15	
Demcey McClanen,	"	—	15	
Thomas McClanen,	"	—	10	
John Malbone,	"	—	10	
Abner Malbone,	"	—	12	
Batson Malbone,	"	—	15	
Jessee Malbone,	"	—	10	
William Moore,	"	—	15	
Tulley Moore,	"	—	10	
James Moore,	"	—	5	
William Newman,	"	—	15	
Etheridge M. Simon,	"	—	10	
James Simpson,	"	—	5	

NAMES.	RANK.	TIME OF SERVICE.		REMARKS.
		Months.	Days.	
Robert Ward, - -	Private.	–	15	
Jeremiah Woodhouse, -	"	–	15	
Lancaster Woodhouse, -	"	–	15	
James Woodhouse, - -	"	–	5	
Benjamin Homes, - -	"	–	5	

MUSTER ROLL

Of Captain John Finney's Troop of Cavalry, from the Second Regiment, Virginia Militia, Accomack County, in the Service from the 18th to 25th March, and from 22d May to 2d June, 1813.

NAMES.	RANK.	TIME OF SERVICE.		REMARKS.
		Months.	Days.	
John Finney, - -	Captain,		19	
Leven E. Parker, - -	1st Lieutenant,	–	13	
Geo. D. Wise, - -	2d "	–	19	
William Curtis, - -	Cornet,	–	11	
Thomas Edwards, - -	Sergeant,	–	12	
Edward R. Boisman, -	"	–	12	
Samuel Justice, - -	"	–	12	
John Poulson, - -	Private,	–	11	
Thomas R. Riley, - -	"	–	11	
Alexander McColm, - -	"	–	11	
Michael Higgins, - -	"	–	11	
William Slocomb, - -	"	–	11	
Elias Joynes, - -	"	–	12	
Elijah Boggs, - -	"	–	12	
Severn Young, - -	"	–	11	
Ethel Lyon, - -	"	–	10	
William Finney, - -	"	–	12	
Bowman H. Bailey, - -	"	–	12	
William E. Curtis, - -	"	–	12	
Henry B. Curtis, - -	"	–	11	
William T. Rogers, - -	"	–	11	
Abel Rogers, - -	"	–	7	
William Grinalds, - -	"	–	12	
John B. Upshur, - -	"	–	11	
Abel Savage, - -	"	–	7	
Asa Hickman, - -	"	–	7	
John C. Copes, - -	"	–	12	
John Cropper, - -	"	–	12	
Thomas B. Curtis, - -	"	–	12	
William Savage, - -	"	–	12	
John Vandyke, - -	"	–	7	
William B. Addison, - -	"	–	7	
John Read, - -	"	–	7	
Geo. Drummonds, - -	"	–	–	The remainder of the men joined this company, but performed duty in the companies to which they formerly belonged.
Thomas Harrison, - -	"			
Horace M. Newton, - -	"			
Southey Grinalds, - -	"			
Wiley J. Twiford, - -	"			
John Perry, - -	"			
John A. Bundsick, - -	"			
William E. Wise, - -	"			
Isaiah E. Wise, - -	"			
Charles Mason, - -	"			
Thomas James, - -	"			

MUSTER ROLL

Of Captain Benjamin Fisher's Company of Virginia Militia, from Sixth Regiment, commanded by Lieutenant Colonel John Dangerfield, in the Service from the 5th to the 7th of April, 1813.

NAMES.	RANK.	TIME OF SERVICE.		REMARKS.
		Months.	Days.	
Benjamin Fisher, - -	Captain,	—	3	
William C. Latane, - -	Lieutenant,	—	3	
John Clarkston, - -	Sergeant,	—	3	
Fielding S. Crow. - -	"	—	3	
Richard Ball, sen. - -	"	—	3	
Geo. Wright, - -	"	—	3	
Carter Moody, - -	Corporal,	—	3	
Carter Ball, - -	"	—	3	
John Sherdock, - -	"	—	3	
Churchill Ball, - -	Private,	—	3	
Lewis Gatwood, - -	"	—	3	
Joseph Clarkson, - -	"	—	3	
Robert W. Dunn, - -	"	—	3	
Alexander Elliott, - -	"	—	3	
Spencer Moody, - -	"	—	3	
Richard Marriner, - -	"	—	3	
James Marriner, - -	"	—	3	
Lewis Dix, - -	"	—	3	
Thomas Wright, - -	"	—	3	
Jamison Moody, - -	"	—	3	
Vincent Dyke, - -	"	—	3	
Joseph Burnett, - -	"	—	3	
Martin Coleman, - -	"	—	3	
Henry W. Latane, - -	"	—	3	
John Brown, - -	"	—	3	
Warner Lewis, - -	"	—	3	
John Bohannan, - -	"	—	3	
Robert Elliott, - -	"	—	3	
Reubin Sale, - -	"	—	3	
Joseph Lewis, - -	"	—	3	
Richard Barefoot, - -	"	—	3	
Thomas Minter, - -	"	—	3	
James Coleman, - -	"	—	3	
Richard Jones, - -	"	—	3	
Joseph Minter, - -	"	—	3	
John Waring, - -	"	—	3	
David Roper, - -	"	—	3	
Charles Minter, - -	"	—	3	

Captain James Fisher's Company—Sixty-sixth Regiment.

NAMES.			RANK.	TIME OF SERVICE.		REMARKS.
				Months.	Days.	
Kinchea Mabry,	-	-	Sergeant,	–	27	
Beverley B. Burge,	-	-	Private,	–	27	
Richard Ezell,	-	-	"	–	28	
John Hall,	-	-	"	–	27	
Henry House,	-	-	"	–	7	Josiah Fuqua sub.
Kindred Jackson.	-	-	"	–	20	
Jesse Lewis,	-	-	"	–	26	
Robert Lanier.	-	-	"	–	27	
Lewis Mays,	-	-	"	–	29	
Thomas Manning,	-	-	"	–	28	
William Noble,	-	-	"	–	26	
Edmund Short,	-	-	"	–	27	

(For rest of this company, see publication of Pay Rolls.)

Captain William H. Fitzhugh's Company—Forty-fifth Regiment.

NAMES.			RANK.	TIME OF SERVICE.		REMARKS.
				Months.	Days.	
William H. Fitzhugh,	-	-	Captain,	–	9	
Geo. Walker,	-	-	Lieutenant,	–	9	
Archibald Rollow,	-	-	Ensign,	–	18	
Geo. M. Cooke,	-	-	"	–	28	
Thomas M. Martin,	-	-	Sergeant,	–	9	
William Broomly,	-	-	"	–	9	
James Hewett,	-	-	"	–	18	
Allen W. Norman,	-	-	"	–	9	
Alexander Hay,	-	-	Corporal,	–	18	
Richard Rendale,	-	-	"	–	18	
Thornton Skidmore,	-	-	"	–	18	
Geo. Cox,	-	-	"	–	9	
John R. Fitzhugh,	-	-	"	–	28	
Philip Alexander,	-	-	Private,	–	9	
Thomas Berry,	-	-	"	–	18	
John Berry,	-	-	"	–	18	
Richard Berry,	-	-	"	–	18	
James Bustlee,	-	-	"	–	18	
William Bates,	-	-	"	–	28	
Jessee Berry,	-	-	"	–	28	
Eli Barbee,	-	-	"	–	28	
Thornton Curtis,	-	-	"	–	9	
Cary Cox,	-	-	"	–	9	
James Coakley,	-	-	"	–	9	
Lemuel Cox,	-	-	"	–	18	
John Cooke,	-	-	"	–	9	
Newton Cox,	-	-	"	–	28	
Joseph Cary,	-	-	"	–	28	
Edmond Dishman,	-	-	"	–	18	
Walter Daniel,	-	-	"	–	9	
William Edwards,	-	-	"	–	9	
John Fletcher,	-	-	"	–	9	
Travers Fritter,	-	-	"	–	28	
John Gollahorn,	-	-	"	–	9	
William Green,	-	-	"	–	9	
William Gollahorn,	-	-	"	–	9	
Ralph Griffith,	-	-	"	–	9	
Thomas Gillihore,	-	-	"	–	18	
Thomas Graves,	-	-	"	–	9	
Benjamin Groves,	-	-	"	–	18	
James Green,	-	-	"	–	18	
Joel Gray,	-	-	"	–	28	
Peter Grigsby,	-	-	"	–	5	
William Holsday,	-	-	"	–	9	
James Holsday,	-	-	"	–	18	
James Hedgman,	-	-	"	–	9	
Geo. G. Hedgman,	-	-	"	–	18	
John Holsday,	-	-	"	–	9	
James Hefferlin,	-	-	"	–	28	
Geo. Jones,	-	-	"	–	18	
William Jett,	-	-	"	–	9	
Allen Jones,	-	-	"	–	9	
Joseph Jones,	-	-	"	–	9	
Thomas F. Knox,	-	-	"	–	18	

NAMES.		RANK.	TIME OF SERVICE.		REMARKS.
			Months.	Days.	
John Laing,	- -	Private,	–	18	
Alex'r Laing,	- -	"	–	9	
John Leitch,	- -	"	–	16	
James Mountjoy,	- -	"	–	9	
Thomas Morton,	- -	"	–	9	
James Newton,	- -	"	–	9	
James Peyton,	- -	"	–	9	
William Powell,	- -	"	–	18	
John S. Phillips,	- -	"	–	28	
Joel Rose, -	- -	"	1	16	
William Randall,	- -	"	–	9	
Richard Randall,	- -	"	–	28	
Jessee Randall,	- -	"	–	28	
Henry Rose,	- -	"	–	28	
Rodney Sullivant,	- -	"	–	9	
William Snelling,	- -	"	–	9	
James Stewart,	- -	"	–	9	
George Stone,	- -	"	–	9	
James Southard,	- -	"	–	18	
Abram Sullivant,	- -	"	–	18	
Thornton Skidmore,	-	"	–	28	
William Southard,	-	"	–	28	
Armistead Southard,	-	"	–	28	
John Truslaw,	- -	"	–	9	
William Tissley,	- -	"	–	18	
Robert Tombs,	- -	"	–	18	
Daniel Wamsley,	- -	"	–	28	

(For rest of this company, see publication of Pay Rolls.)

PAY ROLL

Of Captain William Fleming's Troop of Cavalry, from the Third Regiment, Virginia Militia, in the Service of the United States, from the 2d to 21st of September, 1814.

NAMES.		RANK.	TIME OF SERVICE.		REMARKS.
			Months.	Days.	
William Fleming,	- -	Captain,	–	21	
Geo. Rodgers,	- -	1st Lieutenant,	–	21	
Em'l Harris,	- -	2d "	–	21	
William Evans,	- -	Cornet,	–	21	
Stephen C. Farrar,	- -	Sergeant,	–	21	
John Dunlop,	- -	"	–	21	
Robert Filson,	- -	"	–	21	Or Fitson.
Mark Evans,	- -	"	–	21	
Hugh Dempsey,	- -	Corporal,	–	21	
Geo. Short,	- -	"	–	21	
Sam'l Harris,	- -	"	–	21	
William Fog,	- -	"	–	21	
James Bolinger,	- -	Private,	–	21	
Randal Abshire,	- -	"	–	21	
John Burnes,	- -	"	–	21	
James Blair,	- -	"	–	21	
Thomas Banday,	- -	"	–	21	
Joseph Black,	- -	"	–	21	
Hezekiah Brown,	- -	"	–	21	
Horatio Belt,	- -	"	–	21	
Henry Blackwell,	- -	"	–	21	
John Blackwell,	- -	"	–	21	
Aquila Combs,	- -	"	–	21	
Thomas Combs,	- -	"	–	21	
Jacob Coon,	- -	"	–	21	
Sam'l Cunningham,	- -	"	–	21	
Joseph Cook,	- -	"	–	21	
Alexander Davis,	- -	"	–	21	
John Day,	- -	"	–	16	
David Ferguson,	- -	"	–	21	
Michael Fisher,	- -	"	–	21	
Joseph Graves,	- -	"	–	21	
Sam'l Garwood,	- -	"	–	21	
John Hannah,	- -	"	–	21	
Lewis Harvey,	- -	"	–	11	He was appointed wagon master in the 3d brigade.
Benjamin Horne,	- -	"	–	21	
Allen Jones,	- -	"	–	21	
Samuel Jackson,	- -	"	–	21	
Abraham Kesler,	- -	"	–	21	
William Lee,	- -	"	–	21	
Jonathan Mason,	- -	"	–	21	
John Murray,	- -	"	–	21	
Joseph Middlecoff,	- -	"	–	21	
John Martin,	- -	"	–	21	
Thomas McCrey,	- -	"	–	21	
Andrew McCrery,	- -	"	–	21	

NAMES.	RANK.	TIME OF SERVICE.		REMARKS.
		Months.	Days.	
John McCrery, - -	Private,	—	21	
John McCoy, - -	"	—	21	
John Noftsinger, - -	"	—	21	
Abram Powell, - -	"	—	21	
Joseph Peck, - -	"	—	21	
John Riddle, - -	"	—	21	
Lewis Rudisill, - -	"	—	21	
Michael Rightsman, - -	"	—	21	
Daniel Rightsman, - -	"	—	21	
Samuel Richardson, - -	"	—	21	
Thomas Stephen, - -	"	—	21	
Nathaniel Solesburg, - -	"	—	21	
John Shepard, - -	"	—	21	
Absalom Smith, - -	"	—	21	
Robert Scott, .. -	"	—	21	
Abraham Staley, - -	"	—	21	
John Terry, - -	"	—	21	
John Thomisen, - -	"	—	21	
Christian Uring, - -	"	—	21	
Peter Vineyard, - -	"	—	21	
Moses Wright, - -	"	—	21	
James Wilson, - -	"	—	21	
William Whetten, - -	"	—	21	

MUSTER ROLL

Of Captain Daniel Flournoy's Company of Virginia Militia, from the Twenty-third Regiment, Chesterfield County, commanded by Colonel William Brown, in the Service from the 18th to the 30th March, from 26th to 28th June, and from 30th June to 2d July, 1813.

NAMES.	RANK.	TIME OF SERVICE.		REMARKS.
		Months.	Days.	
Daniel Flournoy,	Captain,	–	18	
Abram S. Woodridge,	Lieutenant,	–	18	Or Wooldridge.
Edward H. Mosley,	Ensign,	–	18	
Francis Watkins,	Sergeant,	–	18	
John Crump,	"	–	18	
John Roper,	"	–	18	
Berkley Elam,	"	–	18	
Anderson Johnson,	Private,	–	18	
Ephraim Miles,	"	–	18	
Bartholomew Kidds,	"	–	18	
John Stainford,	"	–	18	
Phineas Clay,	"	–	18	
Solomon Godsey,	"	–	18	
Carrington Simpson,	"	–	18	
Richard W. Michaux,	"	–	18	
Langhorn Simpson,	"	–	18	
Joseph Flournoy,	"	–	18	
Joshua Powell,	"	–	18	
Hezekiah Thurman,	"	–	18	
Spencer Hancock,	"	–	18	
James Alsop,	"	–	18	
Wade McGruder,	"	–	18	
Cheatham Lockett,	"	–	18	
James Adkinson,	"	–	18	
Jesse Snelling,	"	–	18	
Jacob A. Flournoy,	"	–	18	
John Elliott,	"	–	18	
Joseph H. Walker,	"	–	18	
Jeremiah Fowler,	"	–	18	
Milton Cary,	"	–	18	
William Howard,	"	–	18	
Landa Hopkins,	"	–	18	
Royal Martin,	"	–	18	
Forest Flournoy,	"	–	18	
Daniel Taylor,	"	–	18	
Nelson Flournoy,	"	–	18	
Elisha Keen,	"	–	18	
Peter F. Farrow,	"	–	18	
Anthony Taylor,	"	–	18	
Benjamin Burton,	"	–	18	
Thomas Taylor,	"	–	18	
Seth W. Flournoy,	"	–	18	
Jacob Alpine,	"	–	18	
Hickerson Hancock,	"	–	18	
John Baugh,	"	–	18	

NAMES.	RANK.	TIME OF SERVICE.		REMARKS.
		Months.	Days.	
James Hubbard, - -	Private,	–	18	
Robert Hoskins, - -	"	–	18	
Cyrus Powell, - -	"	–	2	
Obadiah Lockett, - -	"	–	2	
Arch'd. L. Wooldridge, -	"	–	2	
Jeremiah Wooldridge, -	"	–	2	
William T. Johnson, - -	"	–	13	

MUSTER ROLL

Of Lieutenant John Floyd's Company of Mounted Riflemen, attached to the Seventy-fifth Regiment, Virginia Militia, in the Service of the State of Virginia, from the 5th to 24th September, 1814.

NAMES.	RANK.	TIME OF SERVICE.		REMARKS.
		Months.	Days.	
John Floyd, - -	Lieutenant,	–	19	
James Barnet, - -	Sergeant,	–	19	
Robert Craigg, - -	Private,	–	19	
Walton Crockett, - -	"	–	19	
Henry Edmundson, - -	"	–	19	
Hugh Gibson, - -	"	–	19	
Robert Goodson, - -	"	–	19	
Joseph King, - -	"	–	19	
William Inglish, - -	"	–	19	
Samuel Lucus, - -	"	–	19	
Dennis Preleman, - -	"	–	19	
Cyrus Robertson, - -	"	–	19	
Alexander H. Robertson, -	"	–	19	
James Rogers, - -	"	–	19	
Hamilton Wade, - -	"	–	19	
William Walker, - -	"	–	19	
Thomas Walnson, - -	"	–	19	

MUSTER ROLL

Of Captain William Folke's Company, from the Fifty-second Regiment, Virginia Militia, commanded by Lieut. Col. John H. Christian, in the Service from the 28th June to the 13th July, 1813.

NAMES.	RANK.	TIME OF SERVICE.		REMARKS.
		Months.	Days.	
William Folkes,	Captain,	—	16	
Robert W. Irby,	Lieutenant,	—	16	
Tyler Hardyman,	Ensign,	—	16	
Edward Carter,	Sergeant,	—	16	
William Bradley,	"	—	16	
Edward Christian,	"	—	16	
Geo. W. Pendleton,	"	—	16	
Matthew Hobson,	Corporal.	—	16	
James H. Ware,	"	—	16	
Thomas Stagg,	"	—	16	
Thomas Bradley,	" .	—	16	
William Irby,	Private,	—	16	
Matthew Shields,	"	—	16	
Elisha Folks,	"	—	16	
Robert Phillips,	"	—	16	
William Drake,	"	—	16	
Elijah Roach,	"	—	16	
Giles Ruffin,	"	—	16	
Henry Fuqua,	"	—	16	
Littleton Roach,	"	—	16	
Robert C. Willis,	"	—	16	
Peyton Gill,	"	—	16	
Joshua Fuqua,	"	—	16	
Collier Pearman,	"	—	16	
Josh. Folkes,	"	—	16	
John M. Wills,	"	—	16	
Fauntleroy Pearman,	"	—	16	
Thos. Otey,	"	—	16	
Patrick Pearman,	"	—	16	
Joseph Jackson,	"	—	16	
John Minson,	"	—	16	
Joel Hamlet,	"	—	16	
Arch'd Holt,	"	—	16	
John Roache,	"	—	16	
John H. Phillips,	"	—	16	
Thomas Hewlett,	"	—	16	
Littleton Bradley,	"	—	16	
Caleb Farell,	"	—	16	
Thomas Dewling,	"	—	16	
Thomas Hamlet,	"	—	16	
William Cockram,	"	—	16	
Charles Peterson,	"	—	16	
William H. Wills,	"	—	16	
Braxton Gill,	"	—	16	

Captain Boaz Ford's Company—Seventh Regiment.

NAMES.	RANK.	TIME OF SERVICE.		REMARKS.
		Months.	Days.	
Guthrey Morris, - -	Ensign,	–	10	
John Magu, - -	Sergeant.	2		
Charles Call, - -	Fifer,	–	9	Prom'd fife major 7th regiment,
Minor Alexander, - -	Private.	2	14	Sub. for George Anderson—Deserted 23 December, 1814.
John Branson, - -	··			
Micajah Burton, - -	··			
John Bibe, - -	··	–	11	
Wm. H. Grizzle, - -	··			
Wm. Holman, - -	··			
Jas. Harris, - -	··			
Daniel King, - -	··	–	29	
Richard Minor, - -	··	2	3	Sub. for P. Howell—Deserted 23 December, 1814.
Edward Maxey, - -	··			
Samuel Scruggs, - -	··			

(For rest of this company, see publication of Pay Rolls.)

Captain Thomas E. Fortune's Company—Second Regiment.

NAMES.	RANK.	TIME OF SERVICE.		REMARKS.
		Months.	Days.	
Thomas E. Fortune, - -	Captain,	2	3	
Charles Perrow, - -	Lieutenant,	2	3	
Elisha Fortune, - -	"	2	3	
Austin Seay, - -	Sergeant.	2	3	
John M. Alexander, - -	"	2	3	
Narborne B. Powell, -	"	2	3	
Burwell Seay, - -	Corporal,	2	3	
Samuel Phillips, -	"	2	3	
Benjamin Fortune, -	"	2	3	
James Bibb. -	"	2	3	
Joseph McCaleb, - -	Drummer,	2	3	
John Allen, - -	Private,	2	3	
Nelson Burnett. - -	"	2	3	
William Bibb, - -	"	2	3	
John Butler, - -	"	2	3	
William Crisp, - -	"	2	3	
Samuel Denny, - -	"	2	3	
William Davis, - -	"	2	3	
William Dowden, -	"	2	3	
Zachariah Drummond, -	"	2	3	
Jessee Fortune, -	"	2	3	
Meredith Fortune, - -	"	2	3	
Doctor Griffin, - -	"	2	3	
Richard Harvie. - -	"	2	3	
Collin Harrison. - -	"	2	3	
Powell Hawkins, - -	"	2	3	
John J. Hatch, - -	"	2	3	
Zachariah Jones, - -	"	2	3	
William Kenney, - -	"	2	3	
William Lavender, - -	"	2	3	
Mexen Loving, - -	"	2	3	
John D. Layne, - -	"	2	3	
Henry McCarty, - -	"	2	3	
William Moody, - -	"	2	3	
William Millon. - -	"	2	3	
George Martin, - -	"	2	3	
Lewis Mallory, - -	"	2	3	
Bennett Nally, - -	"	2	3	
Fleming Ponten. - -	"	2	3	
Thomas Ponten, - -	"	2	3	
Daniel Perrow, - -	"	2	3	
Burwell Rives, - -	"	2	3	Sub. for Lawrence Gianini.
Henry Roberts, - -	"	2	3	
John Richards. - -	"	2	3	
Benjamin Wilson, - -	"	2	3	
James Willis, jr. - -	"	2	3	
John Wright, - -	"	2	3	
Nelson Wright, - -	"	2	3	

(For rest of this company, see publication of Pay Rolls.)

Captain Peter Foster's Company—Sixty-first Regiment.

NAMES.	RANK.	TIME OF SERVICE.		REMARKS.
		Months.	Days.	
Ralph Armistead, - -	Ensign,	–	12	
Richard Foster, - -	Sergeant.	–	13	
Bassett Brownley. - -	Corporal.	–	13	
John Hayes, - -	"	–	9	
William Foster, - -	"	–	28	
James Brownley. - -	"	–	26	
Robert Parrott, - -	"	–	26	
Jeremiah Parrish, - -	"	–	21	
William Amiss. - -	Private.	1		
Thomas Ashbury, - -	"	–	28	
John Ashbury, - -	"	–	28	
Thomas Anderton. - -	"	–	10	
Francis Armistead, - -	"	–	13	
Conrad Booze, - -	"	–	2	
Robert Dawson, - -	"	–	10	
Henry Dunn, - -	"	–	21	
Daniel Downs, - -	"	–	22	
William Dunbar, - -	"	–	21	
Bailey Digges, - -	"	–	19	
John Evans, - -	"	–	18	
Thomas Evans, jr. - -	"	–	11	
Thomas Eaton. - -	"	–	21	
John Gayle, - -	"	–	28	
John Green. - -	"	–	13	
Robert Hudgin. - -	"	–	13	
James Hunley, - -	"	–	10	
George D. Iverson. - -	"	–	24	
Armistead Manning, - -	"	–	27	
John Morris, - -	"	–	21	
John Matthews, - -	"	–	2	
John Machen, - -	"	–	13	
William Morgan. - -	"	–	8	
Samuel Owen, - -	"	–	13	
Charles E. Owen, - -	"	–	13	
James Peed, - -	"	–	24	
Jeremiah Parrish, - -	"	–	1	
Whitney Perkins, - -	"	–	20	
James Spratt, - -	"	–	10	
Seymour Shackleford, - -	"	–	21	
William Simmons, - -	"	–	12	
Robert Thomas, - -	"	–	28	
Hunley Thomas, - -	"	–	13	
Edw'd White, - -	"	–	26	
Absalom White, - -	"	–	27	
Robert White, - -	"	–	27	
Davis White, - -	"	–	13	
Joseph White, - -	"	–	13	
Gregory Williams, - -	"	–	21	
Charles White, - -	"	–	26	

(For rest of this company, see publication of Pay Rolls.)

Captain James H. Fox's Company—Sixteenth Regiment.

NAMES.	RANK.	TIME OF SERVICE.		REMARKS.
		Months.	Days.	
Thomas Pritchett, - -	Lieutenant,	–	26	
Robert Wigglesworth, -	"	–	12	
Thomas N. Grymes, - -	Ensign,	–	12	
John Chancellor, - -	Sergeant,	–	26	
Robert Layton, - -	"	–	26	
Charles Phillips, - -	"	–	12	
Thomas Beverley, - -	"	–	12	
James Mason, - -	"	–	12	
Thomas Jenkins, , -	"	–	12	
Thomas Stewart, - -	Corporal,	–	26	
Curtis Pendleton, - -	"	–	26	
Benjamin Turner, - -	"	–	26	
Thomas Duerson, - -	"	–	12	
Elijah Partlow, - -	"	–	12	
David W. Hackney, - -	"	–	12	
William Crawford, - -	"	–	12	
Francis Pervis, - -	"	–	12	
Thomas Apperson, - -	Private,	–	26	
Kemp Adams, - -	"	–	26	
John Aylett, - -	"	–	12	
Hezekiah Acres, - -	"	–	12	
Bernard Andrews, - -	"	–	12	
Thomas Adams, - -	"	–	12	
Thomas A. Acres, - -	"	–	12	
Thomas Backster, - -	"	–	26	
James Ballard, - -	"	–	26	
John Ballard, - -	"	–	26	
William Brimer, - -	"	–	26	
Richard Bullard, - -	"	–	26	
Thomas Bullock, - -	"	–	12	
John Birum, - -	"	–	12	
Jesse Barnett, - -	"	–	12	
Fontain Bell, - -	"	–	12	
John Bullock, - -	"	–	12	
William Blaydes, - -	"	–	12	
John Brown, - -	"	–		
William Charters, - -	"	–	26	
Thomas Curtis, - -	"	–	26	
Hervy Chandler, - -	"	–	26	
Thomas Carter, - -	"	–	26	
Walker Clayton, - -	"	–	26	
Cecelius Calvert, - -	"	–	26	
William Carter, - -	"	–	26	
Robert B. Chew, - -	"	–	26	
John Cason, - -	"	–		
William Chaisley, - -	"	–	21	
James C. Crawford, - -	"	–	12	
Larkin Downer, - -	"	–	26	
James Dabney, - -	"	–	12	
Isaac Donerly, - -	"	–	12	
Garland Dillard, - -	"	–	12	

NAMES.	RANK.	TIME OF SERVICE.		REMARKS.
		Months.	Days.	
Richard Estis, - -	Private,	–	26	
Jacob England, - -	"	–	26	
Berkeley Estis, - -	"	–	26	
Moses Estes, - -	"	–	12	
Thomas Epperson, - -	"	–	21	
Washington Fletcher, - -	"	–	26	
Nicholas Fisher, - -	"	–	26	
Richard R. Furish, - -	"	–	12	
James Fagg, - -	"	–	12	
Joseph Fagg, - -	"	–	12	
William Fisher, - -	"	–	12	
James French, - -	"			
John Grady, - -	"	1	17	
Pumphrey Gooch, - -	"	–	26	
Henry Goss, - -	"	–	12	
Sym. B. Goodloe, - -	"	–	3	
Thomas Haney, - -	"	–	26	
John Hawkins, - -	"	–	26	
Abner Haydon, - -	"	–	26	
James Hyles, - -	"	–	21	
James Hoard, - -	"	–	7	
Francis Hogin, - -	"	–	12	
Robert Hackney, - -	"	–	12	
Galin Hodges, - -	"	–	12	
George Henage, - -	"	–	12	
Lawson Hopkins, - -	"	–	12	
Robert Humphreys, - -	"	–	12	
Freeding Hackney, - -	"	–	5	
Archibald Hiles, - -	"	–	21	
William Jones, : -	"	–	26	
Edward Jones, - -	"	–	26	
Richard Jones, - -	"	–	26	
John L. Jones, - -	"	–	12	
Isaac Jones, - -	"	–	6	
Thomas C. Kemp, - -	"			
Henry Kennedy, - -	"	–	12	
James Kurnell, - -	"	–	12	
William Lewis, - -	"	–	20	
James Level, - -	"	–	12	
Garland Liveley, - -	"	–	12	
Chillion Liveley, - -	"	–	12	
John Matthews, - -	"	–	26	
James McDorman, - -	"	–	26	
Golder Martin, - -	"	–	12	
Thomas Minor, jr. - -	"	–	12	
Thomas Moore, - -	"	–	12	
John Moxley, - -	"	–	12	
George Morning, - -	"	–	12	
James Manning, - -	"	–	12	
John Newton, - -	"			
Thomas Noland, - -	"	–	12	
Richard C. Overton, - -	"	–	21	
John T. Owens, - -	"	–	12	
Thomas Palmer, - -	"	–	26	
John G. Peyton, - -	"	–	12	
Rice Pendleton, - -	"	–	26	
Stark Perks, - -	"	–	12	
David Porke, - -	"	–	12	
George Peyton, - -	"	–	12	
Winslow Rogers, - -	"	–	26	
William Rogers, - -	"	–	21	
Sam'l. J. Ragling, - -	"	–	12	
Thomas Ratcliff, - -	"	–	12	
Thomas Stewart, - -	"	–	26	

NAMES.	RANK.	TIME OF SERVICE.		REMARKS.
		Months.	Days.	
William Simpson, - -	Private,	–	26	
Robert Stewart, - -	"	–	26	
Rice W. Schooler, - -	"	–	26	
Richard Sorrel, - -	"	–	26	
John Stewart, - -	"	–	26	
John Sorrel, - -	"	–	12	
Garnett Smith, - -	"	–	12	
Richard Sale, - -	"	–	12	
William Sindal, - -	"	–	21	
Moses Sturd, - -	"	–	12	
Henry Smith, - -	"	–	12	
Burnley Smith, - -	"	–	12	
Carter Sorrel, - -	"	–	12	
William Spindle, - -	"	–	12	
Richard Tyler, - -	"	–	12	
William Thomas, - -	"	–	12	
William Tompkins, - -	"	–	12	
George Tolson, - -	"	–	12	
Joseph Tate, - -	"	–	12	
Philip Thornton, - -	"	–	12	
James Trewell, - -	"	–	12	
Henry Tyler, - -	"	–	12	
John Wallace, - -	"	–	26	
Augustine Webber, - -	"	–	26	
Robert Whorton, - -	"	–	26	
Thomas Waller, - -	"	–	21	
Benjamin Wilcher, - -	"	–	12	
William Wilson, - -	"	–	12	
Hezekiah Wafle, - -	"	–	12	
Joseph Wilson, - -	"	–	12	
Callum Wigglesworth, -	"	–	12	
William White, - -	"	–	12	
John Young, - -	"	–	12	
Paul Yates, - -	"	–	12	

(For rest of this company, see publication of Pay Rolls.)

MUSTER ROLL

Of Captain John Fraser's Company, from the Eighty-third Regiment, Virginia Militia, commanded by Lieutenant Colonel James Scott, in the Service from the 1st to the 6th July, 1813.

NAMES.	RANK.	TIME OF SERVICE.		REMARKS.
		Months.	Days.	
John Fraser,	Captain,	–	6	
James G. Young,	Lieutenant.	–	6	
Allen Thweatt,	Ensign,	–	6	
Lewis Meredith,	Sergeant,	–	6	
Thomas Lewis,	"	–	6	
William Reames,	"	–	6	
Abraham Spain,	"	–	6	
Peter M. Ledbetter,	Corporal,	–	6	
Francis Dabney,	"	–	6	
David Pilkington,	"	–	6	
Thomas Rollins,	"	–	6	
Henry Chandler,	Private,	–	6	
John Gee,	"	–	6	
John Crowder,	"	–	6	
Edmond Grigg,	"	–	6	
William Chandler,	"	–	6	
William A. Meredith,	"	–	6	
Robert Gee,	"	–	6	
Peter Elder,	"	–	6	
Samuel S. Wells,	"	–	6	
William Harper,	"	–	6	
Joseph B. Cornwall,	"	–	6	
Wesley Williamson,	"	–	6	
Richard Allen,	"	–	6	
John Thweat,	"	–	6	
Coleman Wells,	"	–	6	
William Wells,	"	–	6	
Sterling Overbey,	"	–	6	
Vines C. Williams,	"	–	6	
John Coleman,	"	–	6	
Daniel Elder,	"	–	6	
Buckner Kirkland,	"	–	6	
William Cox,	"	–	6	
Gardner Ledbetter,	"	–	6	
Williams Reames, sen.	"	–	6	
John Robertson,	"	–	6	
Sandf'd Coleman,	"	–	6	
Hamilton Williamson,	"	–	6	
Thomas Rivers,	"	–	6	
Gabriel Baughan,	"	–	6	
William Ledbetter,	"	–	6	
William Lewis,	"	–	6	
Grief Slaughter,	"	–	6	
Peter Vaughan,	"	–	6	
Edward Clay,	"	–	6	
John Still,	"	–	6	
Geo. W. Still,	"	–	–	On duty at Norfolk.
Jeremiah Browder,	"	–	–	" "

NAMES.	RANK.	TIME OF SERVICE.		REMARKS.
		Months.	Days.	
Jeremiah Still, - -	Private,	–	–	On duty at Norfolk.
Dr. John Robertson, -	"	–	–	" "
James Wallace, - -	"	–	–	" "
William McConnell, -	"	–	–	" "
John Clemonds, - -	"	–	–	" "
Thomas Grant, - -	"	–	–	" "

Captain William J. Freeland's Company—Seventh Regiment.

NAMES.			RANK.	TIME OF SERVICE.		REMARKS.
				Months.	Days.	
James Carroll.	-	-	Private,	–	–	Deserted.
Thomas Hood,	-	-	"	–	17	
Rezin S. Porter,	-	-	"	–	8	
Nelson Patterson,	-	-	"	–	13	
Nelson Shelton,	-	-	"	–	4	
David Thompson,	-	-	"	–	16	
William Wade,	-	-	"			

(For rest of this company, see publication of Pay Rolls.)

PAY ROLL

Of Captain Thomas Friend's Company, from Thirty-third Regiment, Virginia Militia, in the Service from 19th to 29th March, 1813.

NAMES.	RANK.	TIME OF SERVICE.		REMARKS.
		Months.	Days	
Thomas Friend, - -	Captain,	—	5	
Francis Pearil, - -	Lieutenant,	—	4	
Edward Marable. - -	Ensign,	—	3	
Richard Turpin, - -	Sergeant,	—	5	
Collin Adams, - -	Private,	—	5	
John Williams, - -	"	—	5	
James Jourdan, - -	"	—	5	
Rowland Hampton, - -	"	—	4	
Archer Johnson, - -	"	—	5	
Samuel Williams. - -	"	—	4	
Braxton Redford, - -	"	—	5	
William Clarke, - -	"	—	5	
Spotswood Bradey, - -	"	—	4	
William Giles, - -	"	—	3	
Morgan Pearce - -	"	—	5	
Edward Enroughty, - -	"	—	4	
Major Johnson, - -	"	—	5	
Bernard Redford, - -	"	—	4	
Thomas Berry, - -	"	—	5	
William Carter, - -	"	—	5	
Josiah Bulington, - -	"	—	5	
John Breeding, - -	"	—	5	
Richard Williams, - -	"	—	4	
William Hampton, - -	"	—	4	
Charles Breeding, - -	"	—	5	
Robert Bradley, - -	"	—	5	
William B. Crumpton, - -	"	—	5	
Josiah Throgmorton, - -	"	—	3	
Sam'l Ball, - -	"	—	5	
William Hix, - -	"	—	5	
Andrew Redford, - -	"	—	3	
Edward Cox, - -	"	—	4	
Pleasant Jourdan, - -	"	—	4	
Edward Moody, - -	"	—	4	
Edward Marable, - -	"	—	2	

MUSTER ROLL

Of Captain Thomas Fristoe's Company, from Forty-fifth Regiment, Virginia Militia, commanded by Lieutenant Colonel S. Peyton, in the Service from the 16th to 24th July, 1813.

NAMES.	RANK.	TIME OF SERVICE.		REMARKS.
		Months.	Days.	
Thomas Fristoe,	Captain,	–	8	
Jer'h B. Templeman,	Lieutenant,	–	8	
Nathaniel P. Williams,	Ensign.	–	8	
William Fristoe,	Sergeant.	–	8	
John Harding,	"	–	8	
Presley Gill,	"	–	8	
Francis Jackson,	"	–	8	
Cuthbert Million,	Corporal.	–	8	
Joseph Ashby,	"	–	8	
William Maiguess,	"	–	8	
Daniel Simmons,	"	–	8	
William Breadwell,	Private.	–	8	
Samuel Botts,	"	–	8	
Richard Bredwell,	"	–	8	
Brook Barker,	"	–	8	
John Bredwell,	"	–	8	
James Bowling,	"	–	8	
Geo. Burrough,	"	–	8	
Bailey Bell,	"	–	8	
William Bowling.	"	–	8	
William Bettice,	"	–	8	
John Cloe,	"	–	8	
Rolley Cooper,	"	–	8	
Benjamin Carney.	"	–	8	
James Chapman,	"	–	8	
John Chrisley,	"	–	8	
Richard Curtice,	"	–	8	
Geo. Curtice,	"	–	8	
Clement Dawson.	"	–	8	
Josias Dodson,	"	–	8	
Lewis Dickinson,	"	–	8	
Geo. Duilton,	"	–	8	
James Ford,	"	–	8	
Heland Fare,	"	–	8	
Geo. Garrison,	"	–	8	
William P. Gaines,	"	–	8	
Aaron Garrison,	"	–	8	
Alexander Garrison,	"	–	8	
Nathaniel Gaines,	"	–	8	
Thomas Graves,	"	–	8	
Thomas Henry,	"	–	8	
William Harding,	"	–	8	
Cuzeby Kees,	"	–	8	
Elijah Million,	"	–	8	
John McColley,	"	–	8	
John McFee,	"	–	8	
Geo. H. Tolsen,	"	–	8	

NAMES.			RANK.	TIME OF SERVICE.		REMARKS.
				Months.	Days.	
Joseph Tissen,	-	-	Private,	–	8	
James Tyson,	-	-	"	–	8	
Jessee Turner,	-	-	"	–	8	
James Brannutt,	-	-	"	–	8	
Daniel Tims, sen'r,	-	-	"	–	8	
Byram Harding,	-	-	"	–	8	
Allen Way,	-	-	"	–	8	
John Way,	-	-	"	–	8	

MUSTER ROLL

Of Captain Robert Gamble's Troop of Cavalry, from the 19th Regiment, Virginia Militia, commanded by Lieutenant Colonel John Ambler, in the Service of the United States, at different periods in the years 1813, and 1814.

NAMES.			RANK.	TIME OF SERVICE.		REMARKS.
				Months.	Days.	
Robert Gamble,	-	-	Captain,	2	15	
Alexander Fulton,	-	-	1st Lieutenant.	1	20	
Benjamin Shepard,	-	-	2d "	–	27	
James Sheppard,	-	-	2d "	1	18	
Jacq'ne B. Harvie,	-	-	Cornet,	–	27	
Richard Randolph,	-	-	"	1	18	
John B. Hillard,	-	-	S. Master,	–	27	
Thomas Burton,	-	-	Q. M. Serg't,	–	27	
William Bootright,	-	-	Sergeant,	–	27	
Reuben Johnston,	-	-	"	1	13	
Thomas Guy,	-	-	"	–	27	
Thomas Diddep,	-	-	"	–	27	
James H. Lynch,	-	-	"	1	18	
Gabriel Ralston,	-	-	"	1	18	
James Currie,	-	-	"	1	13	
William Randolph,	-	-	Corporal,	1	18	
Macon Green,	-	-	"	1	18	
Henry Heath,	-	-	"	–	16	
James Seldon,	-	-	"	1	8	
Thomas H. Harris,	-	-	"	–	27	
Peter Chevallie,	-	-	"	–	27	
Hull Melson,	-	-	"	–	27	
John Woodfin,	-	-	"	–	27	
Theodorick,	-	-	Trumpeter,	1	13	
Frank Washington,	-	-	"	1	2	
Jedediah Allen,	-	-	Private,	2	15	
Spencer Alvis,	-	-	"	–	27	
P. Aylett,	-	-	"	1	2	
Thomas Bohannon,	-	-	"	2	15	
John Burton,	-	-	"	2	15	
Richard Brooks,	-	-	"	1	20	
William Burksdale,	-	-	"	–	27	
Thomas Burton,	-	-	"	1	18	
William Bootwright,	-	-	"	1	16	
Reubin Burton,	-	-	"	1	18	
J. D. Brown,	-	-	"	1	16	
J. Buckner,	-	-	"	2	1	
James Currie,	-	-	"	–	27	
Charles Childree,	-	-	"	2	15	
B. F. Cocke,	-	-	"	2	13	
John Craddock,	-	-	"	–	27	
William Colquahoon,	-	-	"	–	2	
Joel Colice,	-	-	"	–	27	
Richard Crouch,	-	-	"	–	27	
Peter Chevallie,	-	-	"	1	5	
John Collins,	-	-	"	1	18	
Richard Darrington,	-	-	"	–	2	

NAMES.	RANK.	TIME OF SERVICE.		REMARKS.
		Months.	Days.	
J. F. Dennis,	Private,	2	15	
James Dick,	"	1	20	
Martin Drury,	"	2	15	
William Dupriest,	"	1	3	
John Dove,	"	–	27	
David Dorrington.	"	2	8	
William Derrough,	"	1	18	
Edward C. Davis,	"	1	18	
William Dornin,	"	–	6	
John S. Ellis,	"	2	15	
Francis Ellis,	"	1	18	
Samuel Frazer,	"	2	15	
Thomas Foster,	"	1	13	
William Frost,	"	–	6	
W. H. Fitzhugh,	"	1	2	
Mucon Green,	"	–	27	
William Good,	"	1	13	
James Gwathmey,	"	1	13	
John Gatewood,	"	1	12	
Thomas Guy,	"	1	18	
John Gunn,	"	1	12	
George Hendree,	"	–	27	
Geo. M. Hopkins,	"	–	27	
Charles Hay,	"	2	15	
Thomas H. Harris,	"	1	12	
John B. Hillard,	"	–	16	
J. Harwood,	"	–	10	
J. B. Harvey,	"	–	16	
J. Haynes,	"	1	2	
R. Harwood,	"	1	2	
Lightfoot Janney,	"	1	16	
Ambrose Jenkins,	"	–	16	
P. W. Jackson,	"	–	12	
Robert K. Jones,	"	–	25	
Nichl's Kimbrough,	"	1	12	
Caleb Lownes,	"	1	3	
Jacob Lyon,	"	2	13	
James Lynch,	"	2	13	
William Lambert,	"	–	6	
William Mann,	"	2	15	
Jo. H. Mays,	"	2	15	Or Mayo.
Elijah Marquis,	"	2	15	
Wade Mosby, jr.	"	–	27	
William Miller,	"	1	12	
James Morris,	"	1	18	
John McAllister,	"	1	18	
Nath'l Nelson,	"	1	18	Or James.
Hall Neilson,	"	–	10	
Geo. Pickett,	"	1	20	
Mann Page,	"	–	27	
William B. Page,	"	1	17	
Francis Pratte,	"	1	18	
Whitley Preston.	"	1	18	
Thos. H. Puryear,	"	–	10	
G. Payne,	"	1	2	
William Randolph,	"	–	27	
Gabriel Ralston,	"	–	27	
Jas. B. Roddy,	"	1	13	
Isaac Raphael,	"	–	27	
Wm. B. Randolph,	"	–	27	
William Richardson, jr.	"	2	15	
John M. Redford,	"	1	18	
Timothy Redmond,	"	1	18	
P. Roane,	"	1	2	

NAMES.	RANK.	TIME OF SERVICE.		REMARKS.
		Months.	Days.	
James Selden, - -	Private,	–	27	
John Strother, - -	"	1	7	
John Stagg, - -	"	2	5	
Walter Shelton, - -	"	1	3	
John Schermerhorn, -	"	1	3	
Lenews Smith, - -	"	1	13	
N. Smith, - -	"	1	5	
John S. Shelton, - -	"	2	15	
John Shippard, - -	"	1	5	
Robert Smith, - -	"	1	18	
P. Shevallia, - -	"	1	2	Or Chevallie.
M. Smith, - -	"	1	2	
Saml. II. Smith, - -	"	–	6	
Claiborne Thomas, - -	"	1	14	
Henry Tompkins, - -	"	2	15	
John Taylor, - -	"	–	18	
James Talley, - -	"	1	13	
Ezra Talmadge, - -	"	1	13	
William Temple, - -	"	1	18	
Thomas Watson, - -	"	2	15	
Nathaniel White, - -	"	2	15	
John Watson, - -	"	2	9	
Daniel Warwick, - -	"	1	13	
John Woodfin, - -	"	1	12	
James Whitlock, - -	"	1	18	
Thomas Williams, - -	"	–	6	
Isaac Webster, - -	"	1	8	
Thomas Underwood, -	"	1	8	

Captain John Gannaway's Company—Eighth Regiment.

NAMES.			RANK.	TIME OF SERVICE.		REMARKS.
				Months.	Days.	
Drury Woodson,	-	-	Ensign,	–	16	
John Sanders,	-	-	Corporal,	–	28	
Allen Bailey,	-	-	Private,	–	–	Reuben Chadoin his sub.
William Bryant,	-	-	"	–	–	Transferred to Captain Fontaine.
William Brown,	-	-	"	–	25	Josiah Trent his sub.
Thos. Bondurant,	-	-	"	2	14	
Reuben Chadoin,	-	-	"	–	–	Sub. for A. Baily transferred to Capt. Fontaine.
David Crews,	-	-	"	–	–	Transferred to Captain Fontaine.
George A. Duncan,	-	-	"	–	–	" " "
Samuel Finley,	-	-	"	–	24	
Charles Gunter,	-	-	"	–	12	
Thomas Hudgins,	-	-	"	–	–	" " "
William Hatcher,	-	-	"	–	–	" " "
Nat. Hawkins,	-	-	"	–	27	Sub. for James Mayo.
Samuel F. Moses,	-	-	"	–	14	
Joseph Martin,	-	-	"	–	17	
Charles E. Rice,	-	-	"			
Ben. Staton,	-	-	"	–	14	
William Scruggs,	-	-	"	–	–	Transferred to Captain Fontaine.
John Toney,	-	-	"	–	–	" " "
Rawleigh Tapscott,	-	-	"	–	14	
John Turner,	-	-	"			
James Woody,	-	-	"			
John Walton,	-	-	"	–	23	
Samuel Wright,	-	-	"	–	17	

(For rest of this company, see publication of Pay Rolls.)

MUSTER ROLL

Of Reubin M. Garnett's Company, from the Ninth Regiment, Virginia Militia, commanded by Lieutenant Colonel William Boyd, in the Service of the United States, from the 2d to the 10th December, and from 10th to the —, 1814.

NAMES.	RANK.	TIME OF SERVICE.		REMARKS.
		Months.	Days.	
Reuben M. Garnett, - -	Captain,	—	19	
Joseph Pollard, - -	Lieutenant,	—	19	
Baylor Walker, - -	2d "	—	10	
Alex'r Cambell, - -	Ensign,	—	10	
Richard Taliaferro, -	2d "	—	10	
Charles Hutchason, - -	"		9	
Thomas Dudley, - -	Sergeant,		9	
James Gresham, - -	"	—	19	
Phill Pitts, - -	"	—	10	
William Bland, - -	"	—	10	
G. W. Gatewood, -	"	—	8	
Elijah Schools, -	"	—	9	
William Eubank, - -	Corporal,	—	9	
Silas Cook, - -	"	—	9	
Nath'l Jeffries, - -	"	—	9	
Gabriel Dix, - -	"	—	10	
Gouldman Parker, - -	"	—	10	
William Brown, - -	Drummer,	—	10	
Richard Alexander, - -	Private,	—	10	
Robt. S. Anderson, - -	"	—	10	
John Burch, - -	"	—	10	
Robert Buskley, - -	"	—	10	
William Bynes, - -	"	—	10	John Dix substitute for W. Bynes.
Ambrose Bland, - -	"	—	10	
Wiley Brown, - -	"	—	10	David Terry substitute for W. Brown.
Beverly Broaddus, -	"	—	10	
Edward Boulware, -	"	—	10	
John Cocke, -	"			
Richard Carlton, sen.	"		10	
John Caltom, -	"	—	10	Or Carlton.
Charles Colly, -	"	—	10	
Isaiah Clegg, -	"	—	10	
Laban Clegg, -	"	—	10	
Zachariah Collier, -	"	—	10	
William Crouch, -	"	—	10	
Richard Carlton, jr. -	"	—	10	
Isaac Carlton, -	"	—	10	Jno. G. Hays' substitute.
Joseph Collier, jr. -	"	—	10	
William Currie, -	"	—	10	
Christopher Carlton, -	"	—	10	
John Collier, -	"	—	10	
Matthew Cox, -	"	—	10	
Presley Chenault, -	"	—	9	
William Dillard, No. 1, -	"	—	10	
William W. Dillard, No. 2, -	"	—	10	

NAMES.	RANK.	TIME OF SERVICE.		REMARKS.
		Months.	Days.	
Richard Dudley, - -	Private,	—	10	
Obadiah Fogg, - -	"	—	10	
John Gardner, - -	"			
John Gatewood, - -	"			
Thomas Graves, jr. - -	"	—	19	
Sawyer B. Griffitt, - -	"	—	10	Patrick Gleason sub. for S. R. Griffit.
William Gatewood, - -	"	—		
Philip Golden, - -	"	—	9	
Joseph Greenstead, - -	"	—	9	
Rivington Garnett, - -	"	—	9	
William Hill, - -	"	—	10	
Thomas Harper, - -	"	—	19	
James Harper, - -	"	—	10	
John Hart, - -	"	—	10	Thos. Sears sub. for J. Hart.
James Henderson, - -	"	—	10	
William Ireson, - -	"			
John Kidd, - -	"	—	10	Wm. Stuart sub. for J. Kidd.
Robt. T. Kauffman, - -	"	—	10	
Thomas Kay, - -	"	—	19	
Henry Lumpkin, - -	"	—	10	John W. Watkins sub. for H. Lumpkin.
John Lambeth, - -	"	—		
Jacob Lumpkin, - -	"	—	10	
Pleasant Langham, - -	"	—	2	
Josiah Lovern, - -	"	—	2	
John Lovern, - -	"	—	2	
Churchill Lovern, - -	"	—	2	
James Lovern, - -	"	—	2	
Geo. Lovern, - -	"	—	2	
Lewis Munday, - -	"	—	18	
Andrew Mahon, - -	"	—	10	
William Minor, - -	"	—	10	
Thomas Mitchell, - -	"	—	10	
John Mitchell, - -	"	—	10	
William Muire, - -	"	—	10	John Dillard sub. for W. Muire.
Richard Marshall, - -	"	—	10	
Benj. Newcomb, - -	"	—	10	
James Newhill, - -	"	—	10	
James H. Prince, - -	"	—	10	
Thomas Pitts, - -	"	—	5	
Younger Pitts, - -	"	—	5	
Elijah Parker, - -	"	—	5	
Major Roane, - -	"	—	10	James Wright sub. for Major Roane.
Powell Reynolds, - -	"	—	5	
Richard Stone, - -	"	—	10	
Thomas Schools, sen. - -	"	—	17	
John Schools. - -	"	—	15	
Joseph Stuart, - -	"	—	10	Major Harper sub. for J. Stuart.
Augustine Smith, - -	"	—	10	Lewis Williams substitute for A. Smith.
Taliaferro Schools, - -	"	—	17	
Edward Smith, - -	"	—	10	
Thomas Schools, jr. - -	"	—	17	
Leonard Stevens, - -	"	—	10	
Uriah Schools. - -	"	—	5	
Samuel Thurston, - -	"	—	10	
Carter Taylor, - -	"	—	6	
Christopher Taylor, - -	"	—	12	

NAMES.			RANK.	TIME OF SERVICE.		REMARKS.
				Months.	Days.	
Robert Tignor,	-	-	Private,	–	15	
John Turner,	-	-	··	–	15	
Lemuel Thurston.	-	-	··	–	10	
Francis W. Terry,	-	-	··	–	10	
William W. Wayne,	-	-	··	–	10	
Geo. Walton,	-	-	··	–	10	
Reubin Wilson.	-	-	··	–	10	
John Williams,	-	-	··	–	10	
John A. Ware.	-	-	··	–	10	
William T. Ware.	-	-	··	–	10	

MUSTER ROLL

Of Captain William Garnett's Company, of the Sixth Regiment, Virginia Militia, commanded by Lieutenant Colonel Archbold Ritchie, in the Service of the United States, from the 1st to the 9th December, 1814.

NAMES.	RANK.	TIME OF SERVICE.		REMARKS.
		Months.	Days.	
William Garnett, - -	Captain,	—	9	
Thomas W. Hill, - -	Lieutenant,	—	9	
Paul Micou, - -	Ensign,	—	8	
John Long. - -	Sergeant,	—	9	
Edward Jones, - -	"	—	9	
Thomas H. Pitts, - -	"	—	8	
Meredith Murry, - -	"	—	9	
John Gray. - -	"	—	9	
John S. Garrett, - -	Corporal,	—	9	
Josiah Minter, - -	"	—	9	
Thomas Jones, - -	"	—	9	
Richard Clarkson, - -	"	—	9	
Edwin Ball, - -	Private,	—	9	
Richard Ball, - -	"	—	9	
Harrison Ball, - -	"	—	9	
Alexander S. Bohannon, -	"	—	9	
Curtis Ball, - -	"	—	9	
Lewis D. Brooks, - -	"	—	9	
Dabney Brooks, - -	"	—	9	
John H. Brigantine, -	"	—	9	
Benj'n Clarkson, - -	"	—	9	
Joseph Clarkson, - -	"	—	9	
Burklet Clark, - -	"	—	9	
Thomas Covington, - -	"	—	9	
James Coleman, - -	"	—	9	
John Clarke, - -	"	—	9	
David Dishman, - -	"	—	9	
Gregory Bennet, - -	"	—	9	
Jackson H. Dunn, - -	"	—	9	
Robert W. Dunn, - -	"	—	9	
Vincent Dyke, - -	"	—	9	
Jackson Dyke, - -	"	—	9	
Alexander Elliott, - -	"	..	9	
Lewis Fisher, - -	"	—	9	
William N. Fogg, - -	"	—	9	
Churchill Fidler, - -	"	—	9	
Richard Gouldman, - -	"	—	9	
Philip E. Gatewood, -	"	—	9	
Garrett Greentreat, -	"	—	9	
Spencer Graves, - -	"	—	9	
John M. Garrett, - -	"	—	3	
Thomas Halbert, - -	"	—	9	
Richard T. Hale, - -	"	—	9	
Charles Hill, - -	"	—	3	
Philip E. Jones, - -	"	—	9	
James Kay, - -	"	—	9	
James Loyal, - -	"	—	9	
Roderick Lumpkin, -	"	—	9	

NAMES.	RANK.	TIME OF SERVICE.		REMARKS.
		Months.	Days.	
Henry W. Latie, - -	Private,	–	2	
Larkin Moody, - -	"	–	9	
Jamison Moody, - -	"	–	9	
John Martin, - -	"	–	9	
Thomas Munday, - -	"	–	9	
Johnson Munday, - -	"	–	9	
Lewis Noel, - -	"	–	9	
Muscoe Noel, - -	"	–	9	
Edwin Noel, - -	"	–	9	
Oswald Noel, - -	"	–	2	
Thomas Pitts, - -	"	–	4	
Geo. R. Pitts, - -	"	–	9	
Leonard Sale, - .	"	–	9	
Reubin Sale, - -	"	–	9	
Jeremiah Shotwell, - -	"	–	9	
Sthreshley Stokes, - -	"	–	9	
Brooking Stokes, - -	"	–	9	
Sthreshley Taylor, - -	Surgeon,	–	2	
William Younger, - -	Private,	–	9	

MUSTER ROLL

Of Captain James Garrison's Company—Second Regiment.

NAMES.	RANK.	TIME OF SERVICE.		REMARKS.
		Months.	Days.	
Charles Wharton,	Sergeant,	–	7	
Thomas Floyd,	Corporal,	1	9	
John Tully,	Drummer,	–	7	
Abel Bradford,	Fifer,	–	7	
Thomas Bull,	Private.	–	7	
Wm. Burton,	"	–	23	
Wm. R. Bunting,	"	–	7	
Hancock Belote,	"	–	5	
Zoro. Chandler,	"	–	7	
William Charn,	"			
William Cobb,	"	–	7	
Caleb Elliott,	"	–	7	
John Edwards,	"	–	7	
Charles East,	"	–	5	
Thomas Floyd,	"	–	13	
Joseph Gunter,	"			
John Hutchins,	"	–	7	
Jesse Harrison,	"	–	7	
William Harmon,	"	–	7	
James Kelley,	"			
William Kellam,	"	–	7	
Levin James,	"	–	15	
Richard Leuce,	"	–	7	
Isaac Leuce,	"	–	7	
Thomas Leuce, jr.	"	–	5	
Thomas Leuce, sr.	"	–	7	
William Lingar,	"	–	18	
Revel Mears,	"	–	7	
Jesse Martin,	"	1		
Saccor Philips,	"			
Darius Poulson,	"	1	16	
Jesse Revelle,	"	–	8	
William Wharton,	"			
Levin White,	"	–	8	
Lot Ward,	"	–	7	
Anthony Young,	"	–	8	

(For rest of this company, see publication of Pay Rolls.)

Captain Alexander Gibbs' Company—Twenty-third Regiment.

NAMES.	RANK.	TIME OF SERVICE.		REMARKS.
		Months.	Days.	
Alexander Gibbs, - -	Captain,	–	17	
Peter Gill, - -	Lieutenant,	–	17	
William H. Vaden, - -	Ensign,	–	17	
John H. Cole, - -	Q. S.	–	20	
Daniel Brown, - -	Sergeant,	–	17	
Thomas Rowlett, - -	"	–	17	
Abner Tolley, - -	"	–	17	
Aaron Marsh, - -	"	–	17	
Edmund Belcher, - -	Private,	–	3	
William Andress, - -	"	–	17	
Adam Andress, - -	"	–	17	
William Allen, - -	"	–	17	
Joseph Andress, - -	"	–	17	
Bullard Andress, - -	"	–	17	
Erasmus Andress, - -	"	–	17	
Peter Archer, - -	"	–	13	
Ephraim Blankenship, - -	"	–	17	
Isham Belcher, jr. - -	"	–	17	
Alexander Brown, - -	"	–	17	
Daniel P. Berry, - -	"	–	17	
Abel Browman, - -	"	–	2	
Edmund Belcher, - -	"	–	17	
Archer Bott, - -	"	–	12	
Gabriel Broodie, - -	"	–	14	
James Blankenship, - -	"	–	15	
Jacob Bennette, - -	"	–	14	Substituted by P. T. Farrar.
William Beasly, - -	"	–	13	
William Bragg, - -	"	–	13	
Fleming Bowles, - -	"	–	13	
Francis Cashon, - -	"	–	13	
Francis Chatham, - -	"	–	13	
Joshua Coudre, - -	"	–	13	
John Davis, - -	"	–	17	
Robert Davis, - -	"	–	17	
James Deaton, - -	"	–	17	
John Dyre, - -	"	–	14	
John Dishman, - -	"	–	17	
Daniel Dishman, - -	"	–	17	
William Drummond, - -	"	–	5	
Isham Evans, - -	"	–	17	
David Evans, - -	"	–	17	
George B. Greenhow, - -	"	–	17	
Good Gill, - -	"	–	17	
Allen Granger, - -	"	–	17	
Daniel Gill, - -	"	–	17	
Benjamin Gates, - -	"	–	5	
William Gill, - -	"	–	5	
Temple Gates, - -	"	–	17	
James Howlett, - -	"	–	17	
John G. Hayes, - -	"	–	15	
Jeremiah Holby, - -	"	–	27	Substituted by David T. Butler.
James Lynch, - -	"	–	2	

NAMES.	RANK.	TIME OF SERVICE.		REMARKS.
		Months.	Days.	
Claiborne Loyal, - -	Private,	–	2	
Robert Mall, - -	"	–	17	
Cain Mann, - -	"	–	17	
Tary Mate, - -	"	–	17	Or Irby.
James McGee, - -	"	–	24	Substituted by Claiborne Royal.
Isham Male, - -	"			
Isham Mall, - -	"	–	15	
David Nunney, - -	"	–	17	
Robert Partin, - -	"	–	17	
Mufford Perkinson, - -	"	–	17	
Dennis Parten, - -	"	–	2	
Perkinson Peter, - -	"	–	2	
William Rowlett, jr. - -	"	–	17	
William Rowlett, - -	"	–	17	
Claiborne Royal, - -	"	2	12	
Richard Spain, - -	"	–	17	
Austin Spears, - -	"	–	13	
John Styles. - -	"	–	8	Sub. Wm. Traylor.
James B. Simms, - -	"	–	13	
Ewin Traylor, - -	"	–	17	
Thomas Traylor, - -	"	1	17	Sub. by John Drummond.
Archer Traylor, - -	"	–	24	Sub. by Geo. Greenhow.
Joseph Traylor, - -	"	–	5	
William Traylor, - -	"	–	28	
Archer Totley, - -	"	–	17	
William Vaden, - -	"	–	17	
Isham Vaden, - -	"	–	5	
Randal Wyatt, - -	"	–	17	
Dickerson Wells, - -	"	–	17	
Lodick Wilson, - -	"	–	17	
William Wyatt, - -	"	–	17	

(For rest of this company, see publication of Pay Rolls.)

Captain Matthew Gibbs' Company—Twenty-first Regiment.

NAMES.	RANK.	TIME OF SERVICE.		REMARKS.
		Months.	Days.	
Francis S. Wiatt,	Corporal,			
Bowden Newcomb,	"	–	–	Joined the troop of
Hugh G. Billups,	Private,	–	14	horse.
Charles Blake,	"	–	8	
Thomas Collier,	"	–	6	
James Dutton,	"	–	16	
Richard Dutton,	"	–	22	
Bartlett Edwards,	"	–	9	
Samuel G. Fauntleroy,	"			
James Hibble,	"	1	9	
Lewis Hibble,	"	–	17	
George Norton,	"			
Thomas Norton,	"			
James Wiatt,	"			
James E. West,	"	–	16	
William Wiatt,	"			
William Young,	"			

(For rest of this company, see publication of Pay Rolls.)

MUSTER ROLL

Of Captain Joseph R. Gilbert's Company, from Thirty-sixth Regiment, Virginia Militia, commanded by Lieutenant Colonel Enoch Rennoe, in the Service from 20th to 26th July, 1813, and from 24th to 30th August, 1814.

NAMES.	RANK.	TIME OF SERVICE.		REMARKS.
		Months.	Days.	
Joseph R. Gilbert,	Captain,	—	12	
William Dawe,	Lieutenant,	—	6	
William Brundige,	"	—	6	
William French,	Ensign,	—	6	
Samuel Adams,	"	—	6	
William Colquhoun,	Sergeant,	—	6	
Henry M. Smoote,	"	—	6	
William C. Williams,	"	—	6	
Jon'a C. Gibson,	"	—	6	
Judah Lord,	"	—	6	
Thomas F. Tebbs,	"	—	4	Transferred to the staff 28th Aug. 1814.
Geo. F. Huber,	"	—	6	
Lemuel M. Hedger,	Corporal,	—	6	
Bayly Taylor,	"	—	6	
Francis Purnell,	"	—	6	
David Moore,	"	—	6	
Wansford Evans,	"	—	6	
James D. Bohannon,	"	—	6	
John S. Harrison,	"	—	6	
Robert Alexander,	Private,	—	12	
Richard Allen,	"	—	6	
Willis Athey,	"	—	6	
Hugh Adie,	"	—	6	
Levi Athey,	"	—	6	
Zachariah Allen,	"	—	6	
Spencer Bird,	"	—	6	
James Bradley,	"	—	6	
Henry Brawner,	"	—	6	
Jessee Bobo,	"	—	6	
Samuel Boswell,	"	—	6	
Silvanus Crosby,	"	—	6	
William Cannon,	"	—	6	
Larkin Carr,	"	—	6	
William Carter,	"	—	6	
James Curry,	"	—	4	
James Chick,	"	—	6	
William Carney,	"	—	6	
Daniel Cole,	"	—	6	
Thomas Cocke,	"	—	11	
Alexander Crosby,	"	—	6	
Charles Cook,	"	—	6	
John Carney,	"	—	6	
Charles Calhoun,	"	—	6	
Charles G. Cannon,	"	—	6	
John Crismond, jr.	"	—	6	
Jessee Davis,	"	—	6	
Hugh C. Davis,	"	—	6	

NAMES.	RANK.	TIME OF SERVICE.		REMARKS.
		Months.	Days.	
Richard Dunnington, -	- Private,	–	6	
David Davis,	"	–	6	
Charles Edrington, -	"	-	6	
William Evans, -	"	–	6	
Robert Forgie, -	"	–	12	
Matthew Guy, -	"	–	6	
Hezekiah Gray, -	"	–	11	
Townly Gray, -	"	–	6	
John P. Harrison, -	"	–	6	
Walter Harrison, -	"	–	6	
Zacheus Holliday, -	"	–	6	
Cuthbert V. Harrison, -	"	–	6	
Philip Harrison, -	"	–	6	
Thomas W. Hewett, -	"	–	6	
James Jordan, -	"	–	6	
Thomas Johnston, -	"	–	6	
Robert Keys, -	"	–	6	
John Keys, -	"	–	6	
Archibald Lawson, -	"	–	12	
John Landsdown, -	"	–	6	
Joseph B. Linebough, -	"	–	6	
Thomas Lawson, -	"	–	6	
William Moore, -	"	–	6	
Isaac Murphy, -	"	–	6	
Geo. Maddox, -	"	–	6	
James Merchant, -	"	–	6	
Thomas Montgomery, -	"	–	6	
William Phillips, -	"	–	6	
William Patterson, -	"	–	6	
Arthur S. Robertson, -	"	–	6	
Alexander P. Ralls, -	"	–	6	
Peyton Reid, -	"	–	6	
William Rennoe, -	"	–	6	
John Stroke, jr, -	"	–	6	
Wilford D. Sidebotham, -	"	–	6	
James Smith, -	"	–	6	
Lemuel Stone, -	"	–	6	
Jessee Sincox, -	"	–	6	
William Smithers, -	"	–	6	
George Scott, -	"	–	6	
Henry Tasker, -	"	–	6	
Thomas F. Tibbs, -	"	–	6	
Charles Thomas, -	"	–	6	
Thomas Tomlin, -	"	–	6	
John H. W. Wardie, -	"	–	6	
James Watson, -	"	–	6	
Eliflett Umberfield, -	"	–	6	
Nicholas Young, -	"	–	6	

Captain John Gilkeson's Company—Fifty-first Regiment.

NAMES.			RANK.	TIME OF SERVICE.		REMARKS.
				Months.	Days.	
Daniel Harshbarger,	-	-	Corporal,	–	18	
Michael Comer,	-	-	Private,	–	24	
Jesse Fleming,	-	-	"	–	23	
Stephen George,	-	-	"	–	23	
Alexander Gordon,	-	-	"	–	21	
Jeremiah Mahanie,	-	-	"	1	14	
Thomas Martin,	-	-	"	–	4	
David Moore,	-	-	"	–	23	
William Settles,	-	-	"	–	10	
Joseph Whitson,	-	-	"			

(For rest of this company, see publication of Pay Rolls.)

Captain Hugh B. Gwyn's Company—Twenty-first Regiment.

NAMES.			RANK	TIME OF SERVICE.		REMARKS.
				Months.	Days.	
Overton Seawell,	-	-	Lieutenant,	—	8	
Vincent Hudson.	-	-	Fifer,	—	3	
William Hudson,	-	-	Drummer,	—	3	
Leroy Bristow,	-	-	Private,	—	18	
James Fleming.	-	-	"	—	24	
William Fleming.	-	-	"	—	17	
John Figg,	-	-	"	—	5	
John L. Gussett.	-	-	"	—	18	
John Rowe,	-	-	"	—	7	

(For rest of this company, see publication of Pay Rolls.)

MUSTER ROLL

Of Captain John W. Gill's Company, from the Twenty-third Regiment, Virginia Militia, Chesterfield County, commanded by Lieutenant Colonel William Brown, in the Service from the 17th to 29th March, from 26th to 28th June, and from 1st to 2d July, 1813.

NAMES.	RANK.	TIME OF SERVICE.		REMARKS.
		Months.	Days.	
John W. Gill, - -	Captain,	–	7	
William Dyson, - -	Lieutenant,	–	7	
Thomas J. Bragg, - -	Ensign,	–	7	
Samuel D. Davis, - -	1st Sergeant,	–	7	No. 1, and under Capt. Weisiger 3 days.
Robert V. Fogg, - -	"	–	7	
William Evans, - -	"	–	7	
John Evans, - -	"	–	7	
Fielding Archer, - -	Private,	–	7	
William Archer, - -	"	–	7	
Mark Andrews, - -	"	–	5	
Bartlett Andrews, - -	"	–	3	
William Berry, - -	"	–	7	
Arthur Burton, - -	"	–	7	
Abram Blankenship, - -	"	–	5	
Abraham Burton, - -	"	–	4	
William Britton, - -	"	–	7	
Henry Britton, - -	"	–	7	
Gabriel Bocciard, - -	"	–	7	
Jessee Brown, - -	"	–	7	
Charles Burton, - -	"	–	7	
Daniel Blankenship, - -	"	–	7	
Robert Bashall, - -	"	–	2	
John Burton, - -	"	–	4	
Thomas Britton, - -	"	–	5	
John Britton, - -	"	–	3	
James Clardy, - -	"	–	7	
Lodwick Covington, - -	"	–	7	
John Cozins, - -	"	–	7	
William Cozins, - -	"	–	3	
John Dance, - -	"	–	7	
Edward Dance, - -	"	–	7	
William Dance, jr. - -	"	–	7	
Thomas Dance, - -	"	–	7	
William Dance, sr. - -	"	–	5	
John W. Davis, - -	"	–	3	
Thomas Eanes, - -	"	–	4	
Parker G. Ervin, - -	"	–	7	
James Franklin, - -	"	–	7	
Jessee Franklin, - -	"	–	7	
Robert Gill, - -	"	–	7	
John Gill, - -	"	–	7	
Alexander Gibbs, - -	"	–	7	
Peter Gill, - -	"	–	7	
Edward Griffin, - -	"	–	7	
Thomas Gill, - -	"	–	7	
Peter D. Gibbs, - -	"	–	3	

NAMES.	RANK.	TIME OF SERVICE.		REMARKS.
		Months.	Days.	
Henry Haxall, - -	Private,	–	3	
John Mann, - -	"	–	5	
William McKean, - -	"	–	7	
Fielding Purkinson, - -	"	–	7	
Wilson Purkinson, - -	"	–	7	
Thomas Purkinson, - -	"	–	7	
Worsham Purkinson, - -	"	–	7	
John A. Pride, - -	"	–	7	
William Reams, - -	"	–	7	
Daniel Reams. - -	"	–	7	
Benjamin Smith. - -	"	–	7	
John Stiles, - -	"	–	7	
William Stiles. - -	"	–	5	
Geo. Traylor, - -	"	–	7	
Arch'd. Traylor, - -	"	–	7	
Thomas Tolly, - -	"	–	7	
William B. Tunstill, - -	"	–	3	
Thomas Varner, - -	"	–	7	
Ephraim Wilson, - -	"	–	7	
John Whiteford, - -	"	–	7	
Thomas Wyatt, - -	"	–	5	
Edmund Wells, - -	"	–	5	
Joseph Whiteford, - -	"	–	3	
Thomas Jones, - -	"	–	7	

MUSTER ROLL

Of Captain Geo. Glasscock's Troop of Cavalry, of the One Hundred and Eleventh Regiment, commanded by Lieutenant Colonel Rich'd E. Parker, in the Service of the United States, from the 16th of August to the 25th September, 1814.

NAMES.	RANK.	TIME OF SERVICE.		REMARKS.
		Months.	Days.	
Geo. Glasscock,	Captain,	1	9	
Josiah Hazzard,	1st Lieutenant,	–	16	
William Y. Sturman,	2d "	1	9	
Richard B. Hut,	Cornet,	1	9	
David Greenlaw,	Sergeant,	–	24	
Spencer Miller.	"	1	9	
William Johnson,	"	1	9	
John Hunter,	"	1	9	
William Anderson,	Private,	1	9	
Thomas M. Bragg,	"	1	9	
James Bruce,	"	1	9	
Richard Bayn,	"	1	9	
John Bayn,	"	1	9	
Philip A. J. Crabb,	"	1	9	
Richard Coleman,	"	1	9	
Hudson Connellee,	"	1	8	
James Coats,	"			
Thornton Connellee,	"	1	9	
Austin Dozier,	"	1	9	
William Dillard,	"	1	9	
William Gawn,	"	1	9	
John T. Hallbrooks,	"	1	9	
Octavius Harvey,	"	1	9	
Warner Hudson,	"	1	9	
Lewis Hammock,	"	1	9	
James H. Jenkins,	"	1	9	
Nath'l King,	"	1	9	
Dozier Lyell,	"	1	9	
James Lamkin,	"	1	9	
Thomas Miller,	"	1	9	
William Morgan,	"	1	9	
Thomas Muse,	"	1	9	
James Motgomery,	"	–	21	
Samuel Mothershead,	"	1	9	
Andrew Montgomery,	"	1	9	
Richard Motley,	"	1	9	
Henry Maskell,	"	1	9	
Ludwell Nash,	"	1	9	
Bennett Night,	"	1	4	
Edward Porter,	"	1	8	
John Potter,	"	1	9	
Joshua Reamy,	"	1	9	
Robert Ralph,	"	1	9	
Mayer Roley,	"	1	8	
John Sanford,	"	1	9	
Benj'n P. Smith,	"	1	6	
Zachariah Scott,	"	1	9	
Henry Sims,	"	1	4	

Captain Richard M. Glasscock's Company—Second Regiment.

NAMES.			RANK.	TIME OF SERVICE.		REMARKS.
				Months.	Days.	
Jeremiah Alderson,	-	-	Private,			
William Bryant,	-	-	"			
William H. Brooks,	-	-	"	–	29	
John Bryant,	-	-	"	–	13	
Frederick Boothe,	-	-	"	–	24	
Thomas Barnes,	-	-	"			
John N. Chinn,	-	-	"			
George Curtis,	-	-	"			
William Downman,	-	-	"			
Francis Douglass,	-	-	"			
Thomas Dobson,	-	-	"	–	13	
Thomas Glasscock,	-	-	"	–	5	
James Hornsby,	-	-	"			
William H. Hall,	-	-	"	–	9	
John Marks,	-	-	"	–	9	
Pierce B. Mozingo,	-	-	"	–	9	
George Newman,	-	-	"	–	4	
Gabriel Perkins,	-	-	"	–	2	
Samuel Pritchett,	-	-	"	–	13	
Thomas Swann,	-	-	"	–	25	
George N. Stoneham,	-		"	–	12	

(For rest of this company, see publication of Pay Rolls.)

MUSTER ROLL

Of Captain William Goff's Company, from the Twenty-third Regiment, Virginia Militia, commanded by Lieutenant Colonel William Brown, in the Service from the 24th to 30th March, from 26th to 28th June, and from 30th June to 2d July, 1813.

NAMES.	RANK.	TIME OF SERVICE.		REMARKS.
		Months.	Days.	
William Goff,	Captain,	–	11	
John Lora,	Lieutenant,	–	11	Or Lura.
James Ford,	Ensign,	–	11	
Thomas Ball,	Sergeant,	–	6	
G. N. Brichan,	"	–	6	
Thomas Drake,	"	–	11	
Bennet Goode,	"	–	11	
Branch Turner,	"	–	5	
Thomas A. Brookin,	"	–	11	
Robert H. Adams,	"	–	11	
Joseph C. Adkins,	"	–	11	
Robert Adams,	"	–	11	
John Anderson,	"	–	5	
John Anderson,	"	–	2	
Samuel Brooks,	"	–	6	
G. W. Branch,	"	–	11	
William Britervill,	"	–	6	Or Britewell.
John Brooks,	"	–	11	
Levin H. Boles,	"	–	5	
John Benereff,	"	–	5	
Charles Buckan,	"	–	5	
John Banony,	"	–	3	
Charles Cunleff,	"	–	11	
Frs. Cheatham,	"	–	11	
John W. Dandridge,	"	–	11	
Henry Hobson.	"	–	5	
John Handcock,	"	–	5	
Lewis Jeffries,	"	–	11	
Jacob Lora,	"	–	11	
William Lora,	"	–	6	
Wilson Lane,	"	–	6	
Drury L. Luckadoe,	"	–	11	
David Luckadoe,	"	–	5	
Riley Moore,	"	–	6	
John McCollum,	"	–	11	
John Norman,	"	–	6	
Samuel Nelson,	"	–	11	
John L. Pleasants,	"	–	11	
William Paul.	"	–	11	
Austin Pourtor,	"	–	6	
Austin Paul,	"	–	5	
John Rozell.	"	–	5	
John Rockp'd,	"	–	5	
Turner Sharp,	"	–	11	
Samuel Short,	"	–	11	
John Simpson,	"	–	11	
James Short,	"	–	11	

NAMES.	RANK.	TIME OF SERVICE.		REMARKS.
		Months.	Days.	
John Simpson, - -	Private,	–	6	
William Simpson, - -	"	–	5	
Henry Sumpter, - -	"	–	5	
Josiah Taylor, - -	"	–	11	
John S. Vauhan, - -	"	–	11	Or Vaughan.
Walter S. Winfree, - -	"	–	11	
Frs. Watkins, - -	"	–	5	
John Fowler, - -	"	–	5	
John R. Olders, - -	"	–	5	

Captain Southy Goffigon's Company—Twenty-seventh Regiment.

NAMES.	RANK.	TIME OF SERVICE.		REMARKS.
		Months.	Days.	
Southy Goffigon, - -	Captain,	–	9	
Walter Luke, - -	Lieutenant,	–	9	
John Williams, - -	Ensign,	–	9	
James Spady, - -	Sergeant,	–	9	
William Tyson, - -	"	–	9	
Thos. Nottingham, - -	"	–	9	
John Spady, - -	"	–	9	
Abram Costin, - -	"	–	10	
Laban Kelly, - -	"	–	10	
Levi Wingate, - -	Drummer,	–	15	
John Anderson, - -	Private,	–	5	
Nat. Burris, - -	"	–	9	
John F. Belote, - -	"	–	10	
Nath'l Bishop, - -	"	–	27	
Charles Begg, - -	"	–	9	
John Bishop, - -	"	–	9	
James Clay, - -	"	–	10	
Francis Costin, - -	"	–	5	
Lewis Copes, - -	"	–	5	
Robert Clagg, - -	"	–	9	Or Clegg.
Robertson Custis, - -	"	–	9	
William Dixon, - -	"	–	7	
Thomas Downes, - -	"	–	27	
Eli Dowly, - -	"	–	9	
Geo. Esham, jr. - -	"	–	9	
James Fisher, - -	"	–	27	
Samuel Floyd, - -	"	–	17	
William Floyd, sen. - -	"	–	9	
Shepp'd Floyd, - -	"	–	9	
Luke Griffith, - -	"	1	27	
Littleton Griffith, - -	"	–	10	
Thomas Hamby, - -	"	–	8	
William Hallett, - -	"	–	10	
Seth Harrison, - -	"	–	9	
Nath'l Jones, - -	"	–	15	
Tackle Jacob, - -	"	–	9	
James Jones, - -	"	–	9	
Abraham Moore, - -	"	–	9	
Joseph Nottingham, - -	"	–	9	
Thomas L. Nolin, - -	"	–	9	
Thomas Nottingham, - -	"	–	10	
John Nelson, - -	"	–	10	
John Parsons, - -	"	–	8	
Geo. Parroll, - -	"	–	9	
William Richardson, - -	"	–	9	
Thomas B. Snead, - -	"	–	9	
Thomas Speakman, - -	"	–	9	
William Stockly, - -	"	–	9	
Levin Scott, - -	"	–	9	
Geo. Scott, (of Geo.) - -	"	–	9	
William Trost, - -	"	–	9	
Daniel Wingate, - -	"	–	9	
Severn Wilkins, - -	"	–	9	
Patrick Warren, - -	"	–	9	
Thomas Wingate, - -	"	–	14	

NAMES.	RANK.	TIME OF SERVICE.		REMARKS.
		Months.	Days.	
Severn Wingate, - -	Private.	–	9	
Sam'l S. Williams, - -	"	–	9	
Samuel Williams, - -	"	–	9	
John Wilkins, (of Wm.) -	"	–	9	
Zorobabel Wills, - -	"	–	9	
Hillary Warren, - -	"	–	10	
William Wingate, - -	"	–	15	
William Wilson, jr. - -	"	1	7	
Southy Wingate, - -	"	–	10	
James Wilson, - -	"	–	17	
Seve Wilkins, - -	"	–	22	
Joadkin Wilkins, - -	"	–	22	
Thomas Vickhouse, - -	"	1	9	

(For rest of this company, see publication of Pay Rolls.)

Captain Benjamin Goode's Company—Twenty-third Regiment.

NAMES.	RANK.	TIME OF SERVICE.		REMARKS.
		Months.	Days.	
Benjamin Goode,	Captain,		17	
William Blankenship,	Lieutenant,	–	17	
Henry Cox,	Ensign,	–	17	
John Cheatham,	Sergeant,	–	17	
John Robertson,	"	–	17	
Joseph Wilkerson,	"	–	17	
Spencer Wooldridge,	"	–	17	
Thomas Anderson,	Private,	–	17	
William Anderson,	"	–	17	
Jacob Andrews,	"	–	17	
John Ashborne,	"	–	17	
Edward Anderson,	"	–	15	
Thomas Branch,	"	–	17	
Benjamin Branch,	"	–	17	
Geo. Bailey,	"	–	17	
Thomas Branch, jr.	"	–	17	
Thomas Bass,	"	–	17	
Lenevas Bass,	"	–	17	
Miles Branch,	"	–	15	
Matthew H. Branch,	"	–	17	
Robert F. Branch,	"	–	17	
Henry Beazley,	"	–	13	
Robert Bass,	"	–	2	
Henry Branch,	"	–	2	
William Dunevant,	"	–	17	
Haley Dunevant,	"	–	17	
Henry Dillon,	"	––	17	
Buckner Eans,	"	–	12	
Forrest Flournoy,	"	–	15	
John Fuqua,	"	–	17	
King Fowler,	"	–	17	
Murck Goode,	"	––	17	
Tapley Goode,	"	–	17	
Isham Graves,	"	–	17	
Thomas Gibbs,	"	–	17	
John Goode,	"	–	17	
Francis Goode,	"	–	17	
Pleasant Gordon,	"	–	17	
Elijah Gresham,	"	–	17	
Edward Goode,	"	–	15	
John Hill,	"	–	17	
Thomas Hix,	"	–	26	
James Moore,	"	–	3	
Thomas Morriss,	"	–	17	
Pleasant H. Mann,	"	–	17	
James McDowell,	"	–	17	
Zachariah Puckett,	"	–	17	
John Pinchback,	"	–	17	
Bartholomew Perduc,	"	–	17	
Francis Patram,	"	–	17	
Benjamin Patram,	"	–	15	
John Rison,	"	–	17	

NAMES.	RANK.	TIME OF SERVICE.		REMARKS.
		Months.	Days.	
Henry W. Robertson, -	Private,	–	17	
John Rowlett, - -	"	–	17	
William Rowlett, - -	"	–	17	
Daniel Stringer, - -	"	–	17	
Elijah Smith, - -	"	–	17	
Robert Stokes, - -	"	–	15	
William Sadler, - -	"	–	17	
Thomas B. Thweatt, - -	"	–	17	
John Turpin, - -	"	–	17	
Benjamin Watkins, - -	"	–	17	
Samuel Wilkerson, - -	"	–	17	
Edward Wanderson, - -	"	–	2	
Jessee Cashion, - -	"	–	17	
William Coats, - -	"	–	17	
Thomas Cheatham, - -	"	–	17	
Shadrack Clarke, - -	"	–	15	

(For rest of this company, see publication of Pay Rolls.)

MUSTER ROLL

Of Captain Edward O. Goodwin's Company, from the Thirty-ninth Regiment, Virginia Militia, Dinwiddie County, commanded by Major J. G. Wilder, in the Service from the 1st to the 6th July, 1813.

NAMES.	RANK.	TIME OF SERVICE.		REMARKS.
		Months.	Days.	
Edward O. Goodwin,	Captain,	–	6	
Littleberry Burge,	Lieutenant,	–	6	
Littleberry Butterworth.	Ensign,	–	6	
Philip Shelly,	Sergeant,	–	6	
John W. M. Kerby,	"	–	6	
Henry Moody,	"	–	6	
Joshua Blick,	"	–	6	
Claiborne Seymour,	Corporal,	–	6	
John Todd,	"	–	6	
Aaron Granger.	"	–	6	
William Harrison,	"	–	6	
John Archer,	Private,	–	6	
James Aldridge,	"	–	6	
Green W. Burge,	"	–	6	
Stith Butterworth,	"	–	6	
John Butterworth,	"	–	6	
Solomon Day,	"	–	6	
Josiah Farlow,	"	–	6	
Peterson Haddon,	"	–	6	
Pleasant Haddon,	"	–	6	
Littleberry Haddon,	"			
Jordan Hargrave,	"	–	6	
Jessee Heath,	"	–	6	
Gregory Johnson,	"	–	6	
Uriah Jones,	"	–	6	
Roger A. Jones,	"	–	6	
John Kerby,	"	–	6	
John Kirkland,	"	–	6	
William Morriss,	"	–	6	
Baker Perkins, sr.	"	–	6	
Thomas Parkham,	"	–	6	
Wright Perkins,	"	–	6	
David Perkins,	"	–	6	
Baker Perkins, jr.	"	–	6	
Joel Rosser,	"	–	6	
Wiley Rosser,	"	–	6	
Wright Rosser,	"	–	6	
Francis Smith,	"	–	6	
John Smith,	"	–	6	
James Turner,	"	–	6	

Captain Benjamin Graves' Company—Twenty-third Regiment.

NAMES.	RANK.	TIME OF SERVICE.		REMARKS.
		Months.	Days.	
Benjamin Graves,	Captain,	1	14	
Edward Nunnalley,	Lieutenant,	1	14	
Henry Waltham,	Ensign,	1	14	
Edward Anderson,	Sergeant,	1	14	
John Lafon,	"	–	11	
Jessee Coghill,	"	1	14	
William Chapple,	"	1	3	
Henry Farmer,	"	–	11	
Henry Elliott,	Corporal,	1	14	
Henry Winfree,	"	1	3	
Willi. Jackson,	"	1	14	
Thomas Gregory,	"	–	11	
Archbold Blankenship,	"	1	14	
Edward B. Archer,	Private.	1	14	
Richard H. Archer,	"	–	11	
William Bragg, jr.	"	1	14	
John Bowman,	"	1	14	
Jessee W. Busten,	"	1	14	
Thos. Brintle,	"	1	3	
Edmond Burton,	"	1	14	
Matthew H. Branch,	"	1	3	
Edw'd W. Bass,	"	–	11	
Christopher M. Bass,	"	1	3	
Thomas Clayton,	"	1	14	
John Clayton,	"	–	11	
Reubin Cole,	"	1	14	
Sherard Crostick,	"	2	4	
William Chappel,	"	–	11	
William Crostick,	"	–	11	
Philip Coghill,	"	–	11	
Ellison Clarke,	"	1	14	
Spencer Chalkley,	"	1	3	
Richard W. Crouch,	"	1	3	
Willi. Q. Dunevant,	"	1	14	
Asa Drereal,	"	1	3	
John W. Edwards,	"	1	14	
John Evans,	"	–	11	
Pleasant Elliott,	"	1	3	
Thomas Evans,	"	1	3	
Daniel Furguson,	"	1	14	
Newby Furguson,	"	–	11	
Thomas Franklin,	"	1	14	
Asa Furguson,	"	1	14	
Abner Farmer,	"	1	14	
James Furgason,	"	–	11	
Pleasant Farmer,	"	1	10	
Eben Farmer,	"	1	14	
John Freeman,	"	–	11	
Daniel Ford,	"	–	11	
Stephen Farmer,	"	1	14	
John Fuqua,	"	1	3	
Joseph Gill,	"	1	14	
Thos. Gregory,	"	1	3	
Thos. J. Gordon,	"	–	27	

NAMES.	RANK.	TIME OF SERVICE.		REMARKS.
		Months.	Days.	
Geo. Harrison, - -	Private,	1	14	
Christopher Hudson, -	"	1	3	
William Jackson, - -	"	1	14	
Atwell Lafon, - -	"	1	3	
John Martin. - -	"	1	14	
Francis O. Markham, -	"	1	3	
Thomas H. Mann, - -	"	—	11	
Baker Miles, - -	"	—	11	
Abner Mewby, - -	"	—	11	
David Moore, - -	"	—	7	
Benjamin Moody, - -	"	—	11	
Abraham Newby, - -	"	1	14	
John Nunnally, - -	"	1	14	
Edward Nunnally, - -	"	—	11	
Thomas Pride, - -	"	1	14	
Littleby Perdue, - -	"	1	3	
Sylvester Plumb, - -	"	1	3	
John Perdue, sen. - -	"	—	11	
John Rattell. - -	"	1	14	
Thomas Shell, - -	"	1	14	
Geo. Soller, - -	"	1	3	
John Smith, - -	"	1	14	
Thomas Saddler, - -	"	—	11	
Lewis Senan, - -	"	—	11	
Isham Traylor, - -	"	1	14	
John Truman, - -	"	1	3	
Thomas T. Totty, - -	"	1	3	
Thomas W. Traylor, -	"	1	3	
Bedford Traylor, - -	"	1	3	
Daniel Vaden. - -	"	1	3	
Martial Vaden, - -	"	1	3	
Michael Wells, - -	"	1	14	
Daniel Wilkerson, - -	"	1	3	
Thomas Wilkins, - -	"	1	3	
Baker Wells, - -	"	1	3	
Miles Watkins, - -	"	1	3	
Daniel Wilkerson, - -	"	—	11	
Henry Walthall, - -	"	—	11	
Thomas Wilkerson, - -	"	—	11	
Nelson Winfree, - -	"	—	11	

(For rest of this company, see publication of Pay Rolls.)

MUSTER ROLL

Of Ensign Edmund V. Graves' Company, from the Fifty-second Regiment, Virginia Militia, New Kent County, commanded by Lt. Col. John H. Christian, in the Service from the 28th June to 13th July, 1813.

NAMES.	RANK.	TIME OF SERVICE.		REMARKS.
		Months.	Days.	
Edmund V. Graves, - -	Ensign,	—	16	
William Cook, - -	Sergeant,	—	16	
Gidethan Gibson, - -	"	—	16	
William H. Varden, - -	"	—	16	
Jas. Otey, - -	"	—	16	
Thos. Morriss, - -	Corporal,	—	16	
Henry Curt, - -	"	—	16	
John Davis, - -	"	—	16	
James Clopton, - -	"	—	16	
Charles Binns, - -	Private,	—	16	
John Bailey, - -	"	—	16	
William G. Bowes, - -	"	—	16	
Robert W. Crump, - -	"	—	16	
Beverly Crump, - -	"	—	16	
James Evins, - -	"	—	16	
Manly P. Gower, - -	"	—	16	
Richard Gawthmey, - -	"	—	16	
Edward W. Hockaday, - -	"	—	16	
Stephen H. Lacy, - -	"	—	16	
William Moss, - -	"	—	16	
Daniel Morris, - -	"	—	16	
Caleb Martin, - -	"	—	16	
Richard H. Muex, ' - -	"	—	16	
John Pollard, - -	"	—	16	
Edward Richardson, - -	"	—	16	
William Roper, - -	"	—	16	
William Roberts, - -	"	—	16	
John Roper, - -	"	—	16	
Richard L. Smith, - -	"	—	16	
Clement Taylor, - -	"	—	16	
John Walker, - -	"	—	16	
Gideon Wade, - -	"	—	16	
William Woodward, - -	"	—	16	

MUSTER ROLL

Of Captain George W. Graves' Company of the Thirtieth Regiment, Virginia Militia, commanded by Major Reubin Tankersly, in the Service of the State from the 3d to the 9th December, 1814.

NAMES.	RANK.	TIME OF SERVICE.		REMARKS.
		Months.	Days.	
Geo. W. Graves, - -	Captain,	–	6	
Edmund Taylor, - -	Ensign,	–	6	
Joseph Sale, - -	Sergeant,	–	6	
William P. Jessee, -	"	–	4	
Ray Micou, - -	"	–	5	
James Thompson, - -	"	–	5	
Walter Bowie, - -	Corporal,	–	4	
Robert Chapman, - -	"	–	4	
John Pittman, - -	"	–	6	
John Miller, - -	"	–	6	
Nelson Beazley, - -	Private,	–	5	
Armstead Beazley, - -	"	–	5	
John Covington, - -	"	–	6	
Thomas Covington, - -	"	–	6	
Thomas Doggett, - -	"	–	3	
John Fortune, - -	"	–	5	
James Frawner, - -	"	–	5	
Staten Frawner, - -	"	–	5	
Joseph Frawner, - -	"	–	3	
John Gravett, - -	"	–	4	
Robert Hall, - -	"	–	5	
William Hall, - -	"	–	4	
Thomas Jones, - -	"	–	4	
Charles S. Jones, - -	"	–	4	
John Jones, - -	"	–	2	
Burkett Jett, - -	"	–	5	
Barnes Lawson, - -	"	–	4	
Willis Lawson, - -	"	–	3	
Archibald Murer, - -	"	–	4	
Benjamin Murer, - -	"	–	5	
Richard Malone, - -	"	–	5	
Dixon Morgan, - -	"	–	4	
Dandridge G. Pittman, -	"	–	6	
James Reynolds, - -	"	–	6	
John Ray, - -	"	–	5	
Geo. W. Samuel, - -	"	–	6	
William Sanders, - -	"	–	4	
Geo. Taylor, - -	"	–	4	
Reubin Taylor, - -	"	–	4	
James H. White, - -	"	–	5	
John White, - -	"	–	5	

Captain John P. Gray's Company—Ninety-first and One Hundredth Regiments.

NAMES.			RANK.	TIME OF SERVICE.		REMARKS.
				Months.	Days.	
William Calvert,	-	-	Private,	–	14	
Joseph Fuqua,	-	-	"	–	14	
William Fuqua,	-	-	"	–	14	
Wilson Meador,	-	-	"	3	2	
Jeremiah Meador,	-	-	"	–	15	
Rowley Reese,	-	-	"	–	15	

(For the rest of this company, see publication of Pay Rolls.)

MUSTER ROLL

Of Captain William F. Gray's Company, from the Thirtieth Regiment, Virginia Militia, Caroline County, in the Service from the 16th to 27th July, 1813; also from Sixteenth Regiment, commanded by Lieutenant Colonel Aylett Waller, in the Service of the United States from the 29th August to 22d September, 1814.

NAMES.	RANK.	Months.	Days.	REMARKS.
William F. Gray,	Captain,	1	2	
Charles L. Johnson,	Lieutenant,	–	11	
Claiborne Wiglesworth,	"	–	24	
Benjamin Clarke,	"	–	24	
Peter Lucas,	"	–	24	
Robert Hildrup,	Sergeant,	–	12	
John Summerson,	"	–	12	
Richard Sale, jr.	"	–	12	
Watts Parker,	"	–	12	
James W. Blair,	"	–	24	
James Williams,	"	–	24	
John Ledwidge,	"	–	24	
Thomas N. Berkley,	"	–	24	
John Harrison,	"	–	24	
Richard B. Thornton,	Corporal,	–	24	
Charles Jones,	"	–	24	
Geo. P. Shepard,	"	–	24	
Reubin Stevens,	"	–	24	
Henry W. Ashton,	Private,	–	24	
John Alsop,	"	–	24	
Vivian Ashby,	"	–	24	
James Atchison,	"	–	24	
Lewis Andrew,	"	–	24	
John Banks,	"	–	24	
Gray Bolware,	"	–	12	
Walter Bowie,	"	–	12	
Linsey Boulware,	"	–	12	
Baylor Banks,	"	–	24	
Richard T. Banks,	"	–	24	
George Baggott,	"	–	24	
George Brent,	"	–	24	
Thomas Ball,	"	–	24	
Nathaniel Brown,	"	–	2	
William Burton,	"	–	24	
Thomas Bloxton,	"	–	24	
John W. Beedle,	"	–	24	
Benjamin Bramhull,	"	–	24	
John Brown, jr.	"	–	24	
Waller L. Brightwell,	"	–	24	
Seth Barton,	"	–	18	
Spencer M. Carter,	"	–	12	
William Carrack,	"	–	12	
Charles Carter,	"	–	12	
Smallwood Cogbill,	"	–	12	
James Cooke,	"	–	24	
Viomany Carter,	"	–	24	
William Cox,	"	–	24	

NAMES.	RANK.	TIME OF SERVICE.		REMARKS.
		Months.	Days.	
Daniel Curtis, - -	Private,	–	24	
Munsen Curtis, - -	"	–	24	
Stiles P. Curtis, - -	"	–	24	
Jeremiah Covert, - -	"	–	24	
P. E. Cady, - -	"	–	24	
Spencer S. Doggett, - -	"	–	24	
Robert Dearman, - -	"	–	24	
Thomas J. Denison, - -	"	–	24	
John Duerson, - -	"	–	24	
Alsop Y. Daniel, - -	"	–	24	
Joseph Dennis, - -	"	–	12	
John Dearson, - -	"	–	12	
Thomas Douglass, - -	"	–	12	
Geo. Doggett, - -	"	–	12	
Thomas Edmonson, - -	"	–	12	
Robert French, - -		–	9	
Jacob Gore, - -	"	–	24	
Charles Goodwin, - -	"	–	11	
David Goldsby, - -	"	–	24	
John Green, - -	"	–	20	
Benjamin Gilbert, - -	"	–	16	
James Gray, - -	"	–	12	
Joseph Gatewood, - -	"	–	12	
John Goldsmith, - -	"	–	12	
Peter Hord, - -	"	–	24	
James Harrison, - -	"	–	24	
William Howard, jr. - -	"	–	24	
Charles R. Hall, - -	"	–	24	
James D. Harrison, - -	"	–	24	
Henry Hill. - -	"	–	12	
Henry Jones, - -	"	–	13	
Jeremiah Johnson, - -	"	–	12	
John Lawson, - -	"	–	24	
Robert C. Lipscomb, - -	"	–	24	
John Lewis, - -	"	–	24	
James Long, - -	"	–	24	
Geo. Lewis, - -	"	–	15	
John Lightburn, - -	"	–	12	
Ralph Lomax, - -	"	–	12	
John Lufoe, - -	"	–	12	
Henry Lucas, - -	"	–	12	
William Lawson, - -	"	–	12	
John H. Micou, - -	"	–	12	
John Massey, - -	"	–	12	
Benjamin Murrow, - -	"	–	12	
William Miller, - -	"	–	12	
Philip Major, - -	"	–	24	
John Morgan, - -	"	–	24	
Thompson Murrin, - -	"	–	24	
Thomas Mitchell, - -	"	–	24	
Joseph Mitchell, - -	"	–	24	
Thomas Minor, - -	"	–	24	
John Minor, - -	"	–	24	
William Martin, - -	"	–	24	
Graves P. Matthew, - -	"	–	24	
Hugh Nelson, - -	"	–	24	
Henry Nicleson, - -	"	–	24	
Thornton Norwood, - -	"	–	20	
John Noble, - -	"	–	24	
William Proctor, - -	"	–	24	
William Payne, - -	"	–	24	
Will. Pinkard, - -	"	–	24	
Benjamin Plunkett, - -	"	–	24	
Geo. Patton, - -	"	–	24	

NAMES.	RANK.	TIME OF SERVICE.		REMARKS.
		Months.	Days.	
Jessee Perry, - -	Private,	—	24	
Robert C. Patrick, - -	"	—	24	
John Parker, - -	"	—	12	
Samuel Parks, - -	"	—	12	
Richard Phillips, - -	"	—	12	
Robert Pane, - -	"	—	12	
John Pitman, - -	"	—	12	
Frederick Pensaboom, -	"	—	12	
William Phillips, - -	"	—	12	
Henry Ramsay, - -	"	—	12	
John Ray, - -	"	—	12	
Benjamin Rolins, - -	"	—	24	
Josiah Richardson, - -	"	—	24	
John Robertson, - -	"	—	24	
James Renard, - -	"	—	24	
Geo. D. Starke, - -	"	—	24	
Wm. K. Snyder, - -	"	—	24	
John L. Shaltice. - -	"	—	24	
Geo. Stairs, - -	"	—	24	
Gerard Simpson, - -	"	—	24	
Philemon Samuel, - -	"	—	24	
Jabez M. Scantland, - -	"	—	12	
John Stevens, - -	"	—	24	
Richard Summerson, - -	"	—	12	
William Shaddock, - -	"	—	12	
Charles Saunders, - -	"	—	12	
William Summerson, - -	"	—	12	
Hipkins Summerson, - -	"	—	12	
Philip Tutt, - -	"	—	24	
Charles Thornton, - -	"	—	24	
Zephaniah Turner, - -	"	—	24	
William Thompson, - -	"	—	24	
William Timberlake, - -	"	—	24	
Nicholas Thornton. - -	"	—	24	
James B. Timberlake, -	"	—	12	
John Taylor, - -	"	—	12	
Edward B. Victor, - -	"	—	24	
William T. Williams, - -	"	—	24	
Harris Walker, - -	"	—	24	
James A. Waddle, - -	"	—	24	
Isaac West. - -	"	—	24	
John T. Wilson, - -	"	—	24	
Joseph Williams, - -	"	—	24	
Thomas Wright, - -	"	—	24	

MUSTER ROLL

Of Videttes, from the Fourteenth Regiment, Westmoreland County, ordered into Service by Major William Nelson, in July, 1813.

NAMES.			RANK.	TIME OF SERVICE.		REMARKS.
				Months.	Days.	
David Greenlaw,	-	-	—	—	11	
Baldwin M. Lee,	-	-	—	—	9	
Robert G. Robb,	-	-	—	—	9	
James Miller,	-	-	—	—	9	
Richard T. Brown,	-	-	—	—	7	
John W. Jones,	-	-	—	—	7	
James Montgomery,	-	-	—	—	7	
Alpha Shaw,	-	-	—	—	7	
Henry D. Storke,	-	-	—	—	7	
Charles White,	-	-	—	—	7	
Robert F. Ralf,	-	-	—	—	7	
Joseph Fox,	-	-	—	—	9	

Captain William Grigg's Company—First Regiment.

NAMES.	RANK.	TIME OF SERVICE.		REMARKS.
		Months.	Days.	
Benjamin Walker, - -	Sergeant,	–	16	
Delbridge Dennison, -	Private,	–	15	

(For rest of this company, see publication of Pay Rolls.)

MUSTER ROLL

Of Captain John Gregory's Company, from the Twenty-third Regiment, Virginia Militia, commanded by Lieutenant Colonel William Brown, in the Service from 18th to 29th March, from 27th to 28th June, and from 1st to 2d July, 1813.

NAMES.	RANK.	TIME OF SERVICE.		REMARKS.
		Months.	Days.	
John Gregory,	Captain,	—	15	
Arch'd Franklin,	Lieutenant,	—	15	
Thomas Graves,	Ensign,	—	15	
Martin Newby,	Sergeant,	—	15	
James Newby,	"	—	11	
Thomas Fendley,	"	—	15	
Reuben Bottoms,	"	—	15	
Nath'l Newby,	"	—	11	
Robert Belcher,	"	—	14	
Benj. V. Jackson,	"	—	14	
Martin Adkins,	Private,	—	15	
Edmond Adkins,	"	—	15	
Geo. Adkins,	"	—	15	
William Adkins,	"	—	15	
David Adkins,	"	—	15	
Robert P. Archer,	"	—	15	
Geo. S. Anthony,	"	—	15	
John Beasley,	"	—	15	
Wilson Branch,	"	—	15	
Ezekiel Bowman,	"	—	15	
Branch Blankinship,	"	—	15	
Martin Costley,	"	—	15	
John P. Crump,	"	—	15	
Charles Graves,	"	—	15	
Wm. Haden,	"	—	2	
Zach. Hatcher,	"	—	15	
Edward Hatcher,	"	—	15	
David Hancock,	"	—	4	
Jeremiah Jackson,	"	—	15	
Henry Newby,	"	—	15	
Matthew Newby,	"	—	15	
Stephen Perdue,	"	—	15	
John Perry, jr.	"	—	15	
Hezekiah Smith,	"	—	15	
William Smith,	"	—	15	
Alexander Smith,	"	—	15	
Thomas Smith,	"	—	15	
Isham Smith,	"	—	15	
Granvill Smith,	"	—	15	
Valentine Smith,	"	—	15	
John Smith,	"	—	15	
John Taylor, sr.	"	—	15	
Stephen Turner,	"	—	15	
William Vaden,	"	—	15	
Clem. Watkins,	"	—	15	
Joshua White,	"	—	15	
Henry Woodcock,	"	—	15	
Marvil Winfree,	"	—	15	
Haley Ferguson,	"	—	15	
Felix Ferguson,	"	—	15	
David Franklin,	"	—	15	

MUSTER ROLL

Of Ensign Thomas Gresham's Company, of the Ninth Regiment, Virginia Militia, commanded by Lt. Col. William Boyd, in the Service from the 2d to the 10th December, 1814.

NAMES.	RANK.	TIME OF SERVICE.		REMARKS.
		Months.	Days.	
Thomas Gresham,	Ensign,	—	10	
Isham Bagby,	Sergeant,	—	10	
John Gresham,	"	—	10	
Wm. C. Courtney,	"	—	10	
Andrew C. Browne,	Corporal,	—	10	
Thomas Durham,	"	—	10	
Thomas Clarke,	"	—	10	
Samuel Jeffries,	"	—	10	
Churchil Brumley,	Private,	—	10	
Major Brooks,	"	—	10	
Thomas Brumley,	"	—	10	
Edward C. Boulware,	"	—	10	
John Bagby, jr.	"	—	10	
James Carlton,	"	—	10	
Matth. Cox,	"	—	10	
Geo. Foster,	"	—	10	
John Griffith, sen'r,	"	—	10	
Ro. T. Kauffman,	"	—	10	
Jacob Lumpkin,	"	—	10	
Thomas Mitchell,	"	—	10	
John Mitchell,	"	—	10	
Philip Prince,	"	—	10	
Reuben Smith,	"	—	10	
Edmund Smith,	"	—	10	
Robert Simco,	"	—	10	
Edmond Stone,	"	—	10	
Augustin Smith,	"	—	10	
Philip Wright,	"	—	10	
Thomas Walton,	"	—	10	

MUSTER ROLL

Of Captain Simmons Gwaltney's Company, attached to the Twenty-ninth Regiment, Virginia Militia, commanded by Major Joseph W. Ballard, in the Service from 23d June to the 13th July, 1813.

NAMES.	RANK.	TIME OF SERVICE.		REMARKS.
		Months.	Days.	
Simmons Gwaltney, - -	Captain,	—	21	
Josiah Holleman, -	Lieutenant,	—	21	
Dawson Delk, - -	Ensign,	—	21	
Jordan Holleman, - -	Sergeant,	—	21	
Thomas Dews, -	"	—	21	
Edwin Delk, - -	"	—	20	
Joseph Coper, - -	"	—	21	
Jonathan Holleman, - -	Corporal,	—	18	
John B. Lane, -	"	—	18	
Littleberry Delk, - -	"	—	21	
Jordan W. Stingfield, -	"	—	21	
Thomas Wiley, - -	Drummer,	—	21	
Samuel Addison, - -	Private,	—	21	
Anthony Addison, - -	"	—	20	
John Addison, -	"	—	21	
Benj'n Brock, - -	"	—	21	
Thomas Bell, - -	"	—	21	
Robert Brock, -	"	—	21	
Elpenkston Betts, - -	"	—	18	
John Cofer, - -	"	—	21	
John Cruse, - -	"	—	21	
Joseph J. Crocker, - -	"	—	21	
Henry Calcut, - -	"	—	21	
William Cofer, - -	"	—	21	
Moody Cofer, - -	"	—	10	
Jeremiah Delk, - -	"	—	21	
Alfred Dews, - -	"	—	21	
Samuel Flake, - -	"	—	21	
Joseph Fiveash, - -	"	—	21	
Willis Flake, - -	"	—	21	
Thomas Flake, - -	"	—	21	
Natha'l Gwaltney, - -	"	—	21	
William Gray, - -	"	—	21	
James Gray, - -	"	—	18	
John S. Gwaltney, - -	"	—	21	
Benj'n Hicks, - -	"	—	21	
Thomas Harrison, - -	"	—	21	
John Harriss, - -	"	—	21	
Samuel Harriss, - -	"	—	18	
Joel Halloway, - -	"	—	21	
David Holloway, - -	"	—	14	
John Jones, - -	"	—	21	
Harbert Jones, - -	"	—	21	
Dawson Moody, - -	"	—	21	
Thomas Pitman, - -	"	—	21	

NAMES.			RANK.	TIME OF SERVICE.		REMARKS.
				Months.	Days.	
Benj'n Pitman,	-	-	Private,	–	21	
James Stallings,	-	-	"	–	21	
Martin Stallings,	-	-	"	–	21	
Joseph Stroud,	-	-	"	–	17	
Edwin Wombley,	-	-	"	–	18	
Edwin White,	-	-	"	–	18	
Wm. Wilson White,		-	"	–	21	

MUSTER ROLL

Of Captain Robert G. Hail's Company, from the Sixth Regiment, Virginia Militia, commanded by Lieut. Col. Archibald Ritchie, in the Service of the United States from the 5th to 7th of April 1813, and from the 1st to 9th December, 1814.

NAMES.			RANK.	TIME OF SERVICE.		REMARKS.
				Months.	Days.	
Robert G. Hail,	-	-	Captain,	–	11	
Winter Bray,	-	-	Ensign,	–	11	
Wm'son Foster,	-	-	Sergeant,	–	11	
William R. Boulware,	-	-	"	–	2	
Griffin Harper,	-	-	"	–	2	
John Games,	-	-	"	–	11	
Richard Cogbill,	-	-	"	–	9	
Abner Brizendine,	-	-	"	–	9	
Fielding S. Crow,	-	-	"	–	9	
Joseph Harper,	-	-	Corporal,	–	11	
Rew. Coleman,	-	-	"	–	11	
Jos. Hester,	-	-	"	–	2	
Abraham Brizendine,	-	-	"	–	11	
Robert Samuel,	-	-	"	–	9	
James Trible,	-	-	"	–	9	
Edward Parker,	-	-	"	–	9	
Obediah Alexander,	-	-	Private,	–	9	
Ambrose Armstrong,	-	-	"	–	9	
William Bispan,	-	-	"	–	9	
William Brizendine,	-	-	"	–	9	
Geo. Brooks,			"	–	9	
William Breedlove,	-	-	"	–	9	
Robert Brooks,	-	-	"	–	9	
William Beazley,	-	-	"	–	9	
Henry Brown,	-	-	"	–	9	
James Brizendine,	-	-	"	–	9	
John Bellfield,	-	-	"	–	2	
Richard Barnes,	-	-	"	–	2	
Benjamin Blake,	-	-	"	–	2	
John Crow, jr.			"	–	9	
Richard Collins,	-	-	"	–	9	
John Crow, sen'r,	-	-	"	–	9	
Richard Coats,	-	-	"	–	9	
Godphrey Corthom,	-	-	"	–	9	
John Chamberlain,	-	-	"	–	9	
Green Coleman,	-	-	"	–	11	
Moses Crow,	-	-	"	–	2	
John Clark,	-	-	"	–	2	
E. Clements,	-	-	"	–	2	
William Coleman,	-	-	"	–	2	
William Davis,	-	-	"	–	9	
Irvin Davis,	-	-	"	–	9	
Thomas Durham,	-	-	"	–	9	
Samuel Doggins,	-	-	"	–	9	
Tundy Dix,	-	-	"	–	9	
Geo. Davis,	-	-	"	–	2	
Lewis Davis,	-	-	"	–	2	
Greenwood Fisher,	-	-	"	–	9	

NAMES.			RANK.	TIME OF SERVICE.		REMARKS.
				Months.	Days.	
John Greenwood,	-	-	Private,	—	9	
Isaac Greenwood,	-	-	"	—	9	
Philip Griggs,	-	-	"	—	9	
William Graves,	-	-	"	—	11	
Ewen Goode,	-	-	"	—	9	
Th. Gatewood,	-	-	"	—	2	
William Gatewood,	-	-	"	—	2	
Th. Gatewood,	-	-	"	—	2	
James Gatewood,	-	-	"	—	2	
Th. Gresham,	-	-	"	—	2	
Major Hodges,	-	-	"	—	9	
James Howerton,	-	-	"	—	9	
Philip Howerton,	-	-	"	—	9	
Thomas Hodges,	-	-	"	—	9	
R. B. Hunt,	-	-	"	—	2	
Mourning Johnson,	-	-	"	—	11	
John Long,	-	-	"	—	2	
Hunly Moody,	-	-	"	—	11	
John L. Marye,	-	-	"	—	6	
James Mackandre,	-	-	"	—	9	
Elijah McKann,	-	-	"	—	9	
Thomas Marbow,	-	-	"	—	9	
B. Meadows,	-	-	"	—	2	
John Micou,	-	-	"	—	2	
James Owen,	-	-	"	—	9	
Geo. Perkins,	•	-	"	—	9	
Edward Rose,	-	-	"	—	9	
Stephen Rodney,	-	-	"	—	2	
Allen D. Smith,	-	-	"	—	9	
William Sheppard,	-	-	"	—	9	
E. Sheppard,	-	-	"	—	2	
John Taylor,	-	-	"	—	9	
Luay Taylor,	-	-	"	—	9	Or Leroy.
John Townley,	-	-	"	—	9	
Ludy Trible,	-	-	"	—	9	
Geo. Trible,	-	-	"	—	9	
John Tucker,	-	.	"	—	9	
Benjamin Tucker,	-	-	"	—	9	
Th. Turner,	-	-	"	—	2	
Jas. Williamson,	-	-	"	—	9	
Upton Williamson,	-	•	"	—	9	
Robert Wire,	-	-	"	—	2	
H. Woodward,	-	-	"	—	9	
Godphrey Young,	-	-	"	—	9	
William T. Upshaw,	-	-	"	—	2	
L. G. Upshaw,	-	•	"	—	2	

MUSTER ROLL

Of Captain Thomas Hall's Company of Infantry, of the Twenty-first Regiment, Virginia Militia, in Gloucester County, commanded by Lieutenant Colonel William Jones, in the Service of the United States, at different periods during the years 1813, and 1814.

NAMES.	RANK.	TIME OF SERVICE.		REMARKS.
		Months.	Days.	
Thomas Hall, - -	Captain,	3	4	
Catesby Jones, - -	Lieutenant,	–	11	
Matthew Gibbs, - -	"	2	23	
Henry L. Nuttall, - -	Ensign,	2	28	
Horatio G. Howard, · -	"	–	11	
Lewis Enos, - -	Sergeant,	1	28	Attached to Captain Thruston.
Thomas Glass, - -	"	2	4	
James Crewdson, - -	"	–	19	Joined artillery comp'y.
James W. Howard, - -	"	–	6	
John C. Dare, - -	"	2	23	
John Wood, - -	"	2	4	
James Miller, - -	"	2	15	
Francis Thornton, - -	"	1		
William Urie, - -	Corporal,	1	28	
Charles Blake, - -	"	1	6	
John Stubbs, - -	"	3	4	
Thomas Chapman, jr. -	"	1	6	
Absalom Moore, - -	"	1	28	
Thos. Davis, - -	"	–	27	
Warner Enos, - -	"	1	21	
John Hall, - -	"	2	4	
John Wood, - -	"	1		
William Hudson, - -	Drummer,	1	3	
Vincent Hudson, - -	Fifer,	1	3	
James Acra, - -	Private,	1	28	
John Adams, - -	"	–	29	
Leonard Bohannon, - -	"	–	29	
Leroy C. Bridget, - -	"	1	22	
Thomas Boram, - -	"	–	14	
George Bush, - -	"	–	28	
Thomas Bridges, - -	"	–	18	
Leroy Bustor, - -	"	–	5	
Robinson Bridges, - -	"	1	6	
Thomas Blake, - -	"	–	28	
John Blake, - -	"	–	28	
Ambrose Bohannan, - -	"	1	6	
James Coleman, - -	"	3	10	
William Carney, - -	"	1	16	
Richard Coleman, - -	"	3	10	
Thomas Collier, - -	"	1	6	
Thomas Chapman, sen. -	"	1	6	
Lewis Dutton, - -	"	2	22	
John B. Dame, - -	"	–	16	
Theophilus Dame, - -	"	–	16	
Nelson Deagle, - -	"	–	29	
Warner Enos, - --	"	1		

NAMES.		RANK.	TIME OF SERVICE.		REMARKS.
			Months.	Days.	
George Enos,	- -	Private,	2	28	
Samuel Enos,	- -	"	1	22	
Lewis Fletcher,	- -	"	–	16	
George B. Fields,	- -	"	–	7	
Thomas Glass,	- -	"	1		
Thomas Goulder,	- -	"	–	11	
Christopher Gayle,	- -	"	2	20	
John M. Gayle, -	- -	"	1	1	
William German,	- -	"	1	6	
Tunstel German.	- -	"	–	25	
Edmund Hobday,	- -	"	2	21	
John Hall,	- -	"	1		
Francis Hall,	- -	"	3	4	
Houlder Hudgins,	- -	"	1	2	
Thomas Hull,	- -	"	–	11	
James Hull,	- -	"	–	11	
James Hall,	- -	"	2	23	
Charles Hobday,	- -	"	1	17	
Anthony D. Haynes, -	- -	"	–	29	
George Haynes,	- -	"	–	18	
William Hardy,	- -	"	–	25	
Warner Hall,	- -	"	–	16	
Richard Haynes,	- -	"	1	6	
John Hopkins,	- -	"	1	6	
James Hibble,	- -	"	–	13	
Henry Hall,	- -	"	–	25	
John Howlett,	- -	"	–	16	
Reuben Ison,	- -	"	1	10	
Thomas Jarvis,	- -	"	2	21	
Edward Jarvis,	- -	"	–	19	Joined artillery.
Robert Jackman,	- -	"	–	28	
Thomas Jackman,	- -	"	1	6	
Richard C. Jones,	- -	"	–	29	
Peter Kemp,	- -	"	1		
George Kemp,	- -	"	1	6	
Charles King,	- -	"	–	29	
John Lewis,	- -	"	1	28	
William Lutwyche,	- -	"	1	22	
Henry Lewis,	- -	"	1	6	
Adderson Morriss,	- -	"	2	21	
John Minor,	- -	"	3	4	
Joel Mitcham,	- -	"	1	28	
James Miller,	- -	"	–	19	
Thomas Muire,	- -	"	–	16	
Matthias Moughon, -	- -	"	1	6	
William Massenburg,		"	–	29	
Robert Mitcham,	- -	"	–	7	
James Oliver,	- -	"	–	13	
Ambrose Oliver,	- -	"	–	29	
James B. Purcell,	- -	"	3	4	
John Purcell,	- -	"	3	12	
John Pointer,	- -	"	–	19	Joined artillery.
James P. Purcell,	- -	"	–	11	
Robert Purcell,	- -	"	–	10	
Thomas Purcell,	- -	"	1	25	
John Philpotts,	- -	"	2	4	
Paul Philpotts,	- -	"	–	16	
William Powell,	- -	"	–	16	
James Powers,	- -	"	1	6	
Julian Pallister,	- -	"	–	5	
William Proctor,	- -	"	1	6	
William Ransone,	- -	"	–	19	Joined artillery.
Robert Ransone,	- -	"	–	19	
Armstead Robins,	- -	"	–	2	

NAMES.	RANK.	TIME OF SERVICE.		REMARKS.
		Mouths.	Days.	
William D. Stubbs, - -	Private,	1		
William Smith, - -	"	1		
Anthony Saunders, - -	"	–	11	
Simeon Stubblefield, - -	"	2	23	
Samuel Stubbs, - -	"	–	19	
William Smith, - -	"	2	4	
John Stubblefield, - -	"	–	8	
Laurence Stubbs, -	"	1	22	
James Soles, -	"	1	6	
John Soles, - -	"	1	6	
Leonard Stephens, - -	"	–	11	
Dawson Soles, - -	"	–	23	
Thomas Trevillian, - -	"	1	22	
Francis Thornton, - -	"	1	6	
William Tomlinson, - -	"	–	13	
William Washer, - -	"	2	4	
Isaac Walton, - -	"	2	4	
James West, - -	"	–	16	
William Wilkins, .. -	"	–	16	
James Ware, - -	"	–	12	

MUSTER ROLL

Of Captain And. Hamilton's Company, from the Forty-eighth Regiment, Virginia Militia, in the Service from the 1st to 12th Sept. 1814.

NAMES.			RANK.	TIME OF SERVICE.		REMARKS.
				Months.	Days.	
And. Hamilton,	-	-	Captain,	–	12	
Nathl. Burwell,	-	-	Lieutenant,	–	12	
John M. Bowyer,	-	-	"	–	12	
Alfred Lackland,	-	-	Cornet,	–	12	
Strother Bowyer,	-	-	Sergeant,	–	12	
James L. Turner,	-	-	"	–	12	
Joseph Gaunt,	-	-	"	–	12	
And'a Persinger,	-	-	"	–	12	
Robert Keyle,	-	-	Corporal,	–	12	
John Henry Denis,	-	-	"	–	12	
Haynes Holoway,	-	-	"	–	12	
Robert H. Calahon,	-	-	"	–	12	
John Anderson,	-	-	Private,	–	12	
James Anderson,	-	-	"	–	12	
Robert Allen,	-	-	"	–	12	
John Badows,	-	-	"	–	12	
John Brough,	-	-	"	–	12	
John Beale,	-	-	"	–	12	
Granvill Coldwell,	-	-	"	–	12	
David Camper,	-	-	"	–	12	
Samuel Carpenter,	-	-	"	–	12	
Allen Cardon.	-	-	"	–	12	
William H. Cartmill,	-	-	"	–	12	
Daniel Craft.	-	-	"	–	12	
Thomas Dodd,	-	-	"	–	12	
William Dodd,	-	-	"	–	12	
Dubartis Dempry,	-	-	"	–	12	
Jacob Fleagar,	-	-	"	–	12	
Adam Fisor,	-	-	"	–	12	
James Fevry.	-	-	"	–	12	
Hamilton Gilbreath,	-	-	"	–	12	
William Henderson,	-	-	"	–	12	
William Hamilton,	-	-	"	–	12	
Samuel Howard,	-	-	"	–	12	
Elijah Howard,	-	-	"	–	12	
Edward Howard,	-	-	"	–	12	
David Hatch,	-	-	"	–	12	
David Homes,	-	-	"	–	12	
James Jourdan,	-	-	"	–	12	
John Kimberton,	-	-	"	–	12	
James Kenny,	-	-	"	–	12	
Geo. Lemon,	-	-	"	–	12	
Geo. Lenkinoger,	-	-	"	–	12	
Thomas Loffle,	-	-	"	–	12	
Henry Miller,	-	-	"	–	12	
Michael Mallow,	-	-	"	–	12	
Geo. Newman.	-	-	"	–	12	
Jonathan Newman,	-	-	"	–	12	

NAMES.	RANK.	TIME OF SERVICE.		REMARKS.
		Months.	Days.	
Peter Nace, - -	Private,	—	12	
John Preston, - -	"	—	12	
Robert Patterson, - -	"	—	12	
John Prank, - -	"	—	12	
Daniel Prank, - -	"	—	12	
Joseph Pool, - -	"	—	12	
Joseph Pininger, - -	"	—	12	
Moses Pininger, - -	"	—	12	
John Pininger, - -	"	—	12	
Adam Pininger, - -	"	—	12	
Geo. Painter, - -	"	—	12	
John Pulling, - -	"	—	12	
Joseph Rodgers, - -	"	—	12	
Bastan Ray, - -	"	—	12	
William Rose, - -	"	—	12	
Nicholas Shirky, - -	"	—	12	
Patrick Shirky, - -	"	—	12	
Matthias Wrick, - -	"	—	12	
James Wrick, - -	"	—	12	
John Williams, - -	"	—	12	
James Wood, - -	"	—	12	
Thomas Whitehall, - -	"	—	12	

MUSTER ROLL

Of Captain Geo. Hamilton's Company, from the Sixteenth Regiment, Virginia Militia, commanded by Lieutenant Colonel Aylett Waller, in the Service from the 24th July to 17th August, 1814.

NAMES.	RANK.	TIME OF SERVICE.		REMARKS.
		Months.	Days.	
Geo. Hamilton,	Captain,	–	25	
Geo. M. Buckner.	Lieutenant,	–	25	
John Minor.	Ensign,	–	25	
Thomas Jenkins,	Sergeant,	–	25	
Charles Philips,	"	–	25	
John Proctor,	"	–	25	
Benjamin Plunket,	"	–	25	
Burwell Leavill,	Corporal,	–	25	
James Owens,	"	–	25	
William L. Spotswood,	"	–	25	
Francis Purvis,	"	–	25	
William Alsop.	Private,	–	25	
Solomon Adams,	"	–	23	
John Abbott,	"	–	25	
Abener Bullock,	"	–	25	
John Bullock,	"	–	25	
James Bullock,	"	–	25	
Thomas Bullock, jr.	"	–	25	
Jessee Barnett,	"	–	25	
William Bruin,	"	–	25	
Eley Bartley,	"	–	25	
Thomas Callet,	"	–	25	
Baizel Carnahan,	"	–	25	
William Coventon,	"	–	25	
James Dabny,	"	–	25	
William Dabny,	"	–	25	
Daniel Dilliard,	"	–	10	
Bland Dangerfield,	"	–	25	
Robert Elliott,	"	–	22	
John Ferneyhough, jr.	"	–	25	
Richard R. Farish,	"	–	25	
Dade Fountalow,	"	–	25	
Henry Gross,	"	–	25	
Joseph Gross,	"	–	25	
Lawson Hopkins,	"	–	25	
Francis Hogan,	"	–	25	
Robert Hackney,	"	–	25	
James Haslip,	"	–	25	
Benjamin Jones,	"	–	25	
John Jones,	"	–	25	
William Jones,	"	–	25	
John Mordes,	"	–	25	
John Moxley,	"	–	25	
John Molin,	"	–	25	
Jonathan Newton,	"	–	25	
John Owens,	"	–	25	
Jessee Petty,	"	–	25	
William Richardson,	"	–	25	

NAMES.	RANK.	TIME OF SERVICE.		REMARKS.
		Months.	Days.	
Robert Stevens, - -	Private,	–	25	
Joseph Steward, - -	"	–	15	
James Stevens, - -	"	–	25	
John Sorrell, - -	"	–	25	
William Shadock, - -	"	–	25	
Richard Sale, - -	"	–	25	
Moses Steward, - -	"	–	25	
John Tombs, - -	"	–	25	
John Williams, - -	"	–	25	
Benjamin Wilcher, -	"	–	25	
Hezekiah Waple, - -	"	–	25	
Randal, - - -	Wagoner,	–	4	
Alfred Dean, - -	"	–	14	
James Minor, - -	"	–	6	

Captain Joseph Hannah's Company—One Hundred and Twenty-first Regiment.

NAMES.			RANK.	TIME OF SERVICE.		REMARKS.
				Months.	Days.	
Frederick Walker,	-	-	Corporal,	2	20	
Christopher Alburn,	-	-	Private,	–	20	
John Clarke,	-	-	"	1	14	
George Hellindollar,		-	"	–	14	
Josiah Molden,	-	-	"	–	17	
David Overhain,	-	-	"	1	15	
David Roy,	-	-	"	–	22	
David Smith.	-	-	"			

(For rest of this company, see publication of Pay Rolls.)

Captain Horatio G. Harwood's Company—Twenty-first Regiment.

NAMES.	Rank.	TIME OF SERVICE.		REMARKS.
		Months.	Days.	
James Dutton, - -	Private,	–	15	
Richard Dutton, - -	"	–	1	
John Edwards, - -	"	–	27	
Sam'l G. Fauntleroy, - -	"	–	7	
William Fields, - -	"	–	16	
James E. West, - -	"	–	21	
William Young. - -	"		22	

(For rest of this company, see publication of Pay Rolls.)

MUSTER ROLL

Of Captain Elijah Harding's Company, from the Forty-fifth Regiment, Virginia Militia, Stafford County, commanded by Lieutenant Colonel Samuel H. Peyton, in the Service from the 22d July to 18th August, 1814.

NAMES.	RANK.	TIME OF SERVICE.		REMARKS.
		Months.	Days.	
Elijah Harding, - -	Captain,	–	28	
William McQuter, - -	Lieutenant,	–	28	
John Ross, - -	Ensign,	–	28	
Barbly Dawson, - -	Sergeant,	–	28	
Edmond Holmes, - -	"	–	28	
Joseph Holmes, - -	"	–	28	
Harrison Bradshaw, - -	"	–	28	
Joel Harding, - -	Corporal,	–	28	
William B. Billingsby, -	"	–	28	
Selim F. G. Phillips, -	"	–	28	
Clement T. Billingsby, -	"	–	28	
James Atchison, - -	Private,	–	28	
Westley Brodwell, -	"	–	28	
James Butler, - -	"	–	28	
Lamth Barbee, - -	"	–	28	
John Beach, - -	"	–	28	
James Brown, - -	"	–	28	
Peter Beach, - -	"	–	28	
Thomas Berry, - -	"	–	28	
William Corwin, - -	"	–	28	
Champ Corwin, - -	"	–	28	
William Cox, - -	"	–	28	
Mason Corbin, -	"	–	28	
Benjamin Corbin, -	"	–	28	
Joel Faut, - -	"	–	28	
Strother Ficklin, - -	"	–	28	
Bailey Frither, - -	"	–	28	
John Gough, - -	"	–	28	
James Garrison, - -	"	–	28	
Jessee Gray, - -	"	–	25	
William B. Gordon, - -	"	–	28	
Nathan Holloway, - -	"	–	28	
James Hawkins, - -	"	–	28	
Charles Humpries, - -	"	–	23	
Lewis Hall, - -	"	–	28	
William Hefflin, - -	"	–	28	
Noah Jones, - -	"	–	28	
Thomas Jones, - -	"	–	28	
William Kendall, - -	"	–	28	
Ranson Knight, - -	"	–	28	
Bailey Knight, - -	"	–	28	
Joshua Kendall, - -	"	–	28	
Nelson Mason, - -	"	–	28	
Charles Martin, - -	"	–	28	
James Mason, - -	"	–	28	
Lawson Patterson, -	"	–	28	
Ely Patterson, - -	"	–	28	
Auron Patterson,	"	–	28	

NAMES.	RANK.	TIME OF SERVICE.		REMARKS.
		Months.	Days.	
Thomas Stroke, - -	Private,	–	28	
Harrison Smith, - -	"	–	28	
James N. Steward, - -	"	–	28	
William T. Sinclair, - -	"	–	28	
William Tharp, - -	"	–	28	
John B. Taylor, - -	"	–	28	
James Tharp, - -	"	–	28	
Thomas Timmons, - -	"	–	28	
Richard Tharp, - -	"	–	28	
Thomas Waters, - -	"	–	28	

Captain Walter Harnbaugh's Company—Ninety-seventh Regiment.

NAMES.	RANK.	TIME OF SERVICE.		REMARKS.
		Months.	Days.	
Stephen George, • -	Private,	1	10	

(For rest of this company, see publication of Pay Rolls.)

Captain Robert Hook's Company—Fifty-eighth Regiment.

NAMES.	RANK.	TIME OF SERVICE.		REMARKS.
		Month.	Days.	
Robert Martin, - -	Corporal.	–	20	
Henry N. Carroll, - -	Private.	–	21	
R. S. Emmett, - -	"	–	10	
Daniel O. Hannagan, -	"	–	22	
Joseph Holland, - -	"	–	19	Joined Capt. Hooke's company.

(For rest of this company, see publication of Pay Rolls.)

MUSTER ROLL

Of Captain Fred. Harris' Troop of Cavalry, from the —— Regiment, Virginia Militia, commanded by Lieutenant Colonel Thomas M. Randolph, in the Service of the United States, from the 30th August to 14th September, 1814.

NAMES.	RANK.	TIME OF SERVICE.		REMARKS.
		Months.	Days.	
Fred. Harris, - -	Captain,	–	19	
John Jones, - -	Lieutenant,	–	19	
William Crawford, - -	"	–	19	
Lewis Sherley, - -	Cornet,	–	19	
Jas. F. Nichie, - -	Sergeant,	–	19	Or Michie.
Jno. W. Cowherd, - -	"	–	19	
Jas. L. Crawford, - -	"	–	19	
Richard Hollins, - -	"	–	19	
Richard W. Muntto, - -	"	–	19	
William Fortune, - -	Corporal,	–	19	
William H. Parrington, -	"	–	19	
Sol. W. Nelson, - -	"	–	19	
William Cole, - -	"	–	19	
Lewis Shisbee, - -	"	–	19	Or Shislee.
Joseph Andrews, - -	Private,	–	16	
James Bibb, - -	"	–	19	
John Biggars, - -	"	–	19	
John Bibb, - -	"	–	16	
Robert Broadus, - -	"	–	16	
Samuel Baker, - -	"	–	16	
Abner Barnley, - -	"	–	19	
William Bird, - -	"	–	19	
John T. Chiles, - -	"	–	19	
Samuel Cole, jr. - -	"	–	19	
William Cooper, jr. - -	"	–	19	
John Cole, - -	"	–	19	
James Cowherd, - -	"	–	19	
John H. Cosby, - -	"	–	18	
John Carpenter, - -	"	–	18	
Edward Downing, - -	"	–	19	
John Dunn, - -	"	–	19	
William Dickerson, - -	"	–	16	
John Estes, - -	"	–	16	
Richard C. Eggleston, -	"	–	19	
John Fielding, - -	"	–	16	
William Goodwin, - -	"	–	19	
Overton Gooch, - -	"	–	19	
Flewry Garrett, - -	"	–	18	
Ashton Garrett, - -	"	–	18	
David Gray, - -	"	–	15	
James Gunter, jr. - -	"	–	15	
Arch'd Hutcherson, - -	"	–	19	
Robert Hollins, - -	"	–	18	
Benj'a M. Harris, - -	"	–	18	
William Hughson, - -	"	–	18	
Jessee Hunter, - -	"	–	18	
Thos. Harris, - -	"	–	18	
Benjamin Hoard, - -	"	–	15	
William L. Hoard, - -	"	–	18	

NAMES.	RANK.	TIME OF SERVICE.		REMARKS.
		Months.	Days.	
Collin Johnson,	"	–	15	
Alexander Levi,	"	–	16	
Moses Lipscomb,	"	–	18	
Tandy Lewis,	"	–	10	
Matthew Michie,	"	–	18	
James Melton,	"	–	18	
Geo. McGehee,	"	–	18	
William Meredith,	"	–	18	
Oswald McGehee,	"	–	17	
Joseph Perkins,	"	–	18	
Nelson Parrish,	"	–	18	
William Poindexter.	"	–	18	
Samuel Philips,	"	–	18	
John Poindexter,	"	–	18	
James Peters,	"	–	18	
Daniel Perkins,	"	–	17	
Achilles Smith,	"	–	18	
Francis Smith,	"	–	18	
John Swift, jr.	"	–	17	
Edward Swift,	"	–	18	
Geo. Thomasson,	"	–	18	
James Timberlake,	"	–	18	
Alexander Trice,	"	–	18	
Champ Terry,	"	–	18	
Geo. Vest,	"	–	17	
Benjamin Waddy,	"	–	18	
Reuben Watkins,	"	–	18	
William Wash, jr.	"	–	18	
Garl'd T. Waddy,	"	–	17	
James Wood,	"	–	7	

PAY ROLL

Of Captain James Harrison's Company, from the Twentieth Regiment, Virginia Militia, commanded by Lieutenant Colonel James Robinson, in the Service of the United States, from 2d to 18th February, from 10th to 15th March, and from 17th to 21th September, 1813.

NAMES.	RANK.	TIME OF SERVICE.		REMARKS.
		Months.	Days.	
James Harrison,	Captain,	–	19	
Reuben Lovett,	Lieutenant,	–	13	
Andrew Land,	Ensign,	–	17	
Charles Hartley,	Sergeant,	–	21	
Edmond Garrison,	"	–	7	
Solomon Capps,	"	–	19	
John Shipps,	"	–	21	
Adam Lovett,	Corporal,	–	21	
Erasmus Capps,	"	–	19	
James Capps,	"	–	8	
Joel Waterman,	"	–	6	
Andrew Baits,	Private,	–	13	
Erasmus Ballance,	"	–	13	
Joel Bonney,	"	–	7	
Moses Bonney,	"	–	7	
William Bonney,	"	–	13	
Ancil Capps,	"	–	22	
Dennis Capps,	"	–	13	
David Capps, sr.	"	–	21	
David Capps, jr.	"	–	21	
Enoch Capps,	"	–	21	
Elijah Capps,	"	–	7	
Hillary Capps,	"	–	7	
John Capps, jr.	"	–	15	
John Capps, sr.	"	–	7	
James Capps,	"	–	7	
Kader Capps,	"	–	21	
William Capps,	"	–	25	
Jessee Capps, sr.	"	–	14	
Jessee Capps, jr.	"	–	8	
James Cupper,	"	–	7	
Willoughby Cupper,	"	–	7	
William Cox,	"	–	21	
William Cornvill,	"	–	6	
Benjamin Cox,	"	–	6	
Horatio Davis,	"	–	21	
James Davis,	"	–	21	
James Dawby,	"	–	6	
Jessee Dandage,	"	–	14	
James Dyer,	"	–	21	
Jessee Dawby,	"	–	21	
Moses Dyer,	"	–	13	
William Dyer,	"	–	15	
Charles Dyer,	"	–	14	
Henry Franklin,	"	–	13	
Reuben Fountain,	"	–	21	
Benjamin Holmes,	"	–	8	

NAMES.	RANK.	TIME OF SERVICE.		REMARKS.
		Months.	Days.	
Hillary Moore, - -	Private.	–	13	
Tully Smith, - -	"	–	13	
John Smith, - -	"	–	6	
Henry Shurwood, - -	"	–	6	
Stephen Shurwood, - -	"	–	8	
Daniel Whitehurst, - -	"	–	21	
Joel Waterman, - -	"	–	13	
Joshua Whitehurst, - -	"	–	21	
Obed. Whitehurst, - -	"	–	21	
Tully Whitehurst, - -	"	–	13	
Willoughby Whitehurst, -	"	–	21	
Joseph Waters, -	"	–	14	

MUSTER ROLL

Of Captain Robert Harrison's Company, from the Sixty-second Regiment, Virginia Militia, Prince Edward County, commanded by Lieutenant Col. Miles Selden, in the Service from the 27th June to 9th July, from 14th August to 14th October, and from 14th October to 6th November, 1813.

NAMES.	RANK.	TIME OF SERVICE.		REMARKS.
		Months.	Days.	
Robert Harrison, - -	Captain,	3	8	
William E. Rieves, - -	Lieutenant,	2	25	
Joseph Glover, - -	"	—	13	
Richard Marks, - -	Ensign,	3	8	
Joel Titmash, - -	Qr. Sergeant,	2	25	
Frederick Ragsdale, - -	Sergeant,	3	8	
Thomas Adams, - -	"	3	8	
Henry Gee, - -	"	2	25	
Edmund Wilkins, - -	"	3	8	
Robert Mattox, - -	"	—	13	
Ephraim Heath, - -	"	—	13	
Samuel Fenqua, - -	Corporal,	2	25	
Thomas H. Allen, - -	"	2	25	
Jesse Musslewhite, - -	"	2	25	
David Simmons, - -	"	—	25	
William Backley, - -	"	—	13	
William H. Stainback, - -	"	—	13	
Samuel Donoldson, - -	"	—	13	
Samuel Wammack, - -	Drummer,	2	25	
Stephen Andrews, - -	Fifer,	2	25	
Jeremiah Aldridge, - -	Private,	2	25	
William Adams, - -	"	—	13	
Samuel Adams, - -	"	—	13	
Robert Brockwell, - -	"	2	25	
Luke Burnet, - -	"	3	8	
Joseph Blackey, - -	"	2	25	
William Bonner, - -	"	2	25	
William Bratton, - -	"	2	25	
William H. Bassarer, - -	"	2	25	
Samuel Brockwell, - -	"	—	13	
Peter W. Brockwell, - -	"	2	25	
Robert Cunnings, - -	"	2	25	
John Cryder, - -	"	3	8	
James Comer, - -	"	3	8	
Eppes Cryder, - -	"	—	12	
Hampton Eppes, - -	"	2	25	
James Eppes, - -	"	2	25	
William Eppes, - -	"	2	25	
John Edwards, - -	"	2	25	
Josiah Feuqua, - -	"	2	25	
Benjamin Fenner, - -	"	2	25	
Henry Fisher, - -	"	—	12	
Thomas Grasswit, - -	"	2	25	
James Goulder, - -	"	2	25	
Francis Grammer, - -	"	2	25	
William Galt, - -	"	2	25	
Samuel Galt, - -	"	—	13	

NAMES.	RANK.	TIME OF SERVICE.		REMARKS.
		Months.	Days.	
Edmund Goulder, - -	Private,	2	25	
Geo. Grasswell, - -	"	2		
Joshua Grammer, - -	"	3	8	
Hartwell Heath, - -	"	2	25	
Hartwell Hackneday, - -	"	2	25	
John Hamlin, jr. - -	"	2	25	
Collin L. Hobbs, - -	"	2	25	
Carter Harrison, - -	"	2	25	
William H. Hobbs, - -	"	—	11	
Edmund Harrison, - -	"	—	13	
William Lece, - -	"	2	25	
Wille Livesay, - -	"	2	25	
William L. Lanier, - -	"	—	13	
Littleberry Murray, - -	"	2	25	
William Moore, - -	"	3	8	
John Murphy, - -	"	—	13	
Thomas McCann, - -	"	3	5	
John Moore, - -	"	—	11	
Rolin New, - -	"	—	13	
Joseph Philips, - -	"	2	25	
Edmund Ruffin, - -	"	—	13	
Drury A. Proctor, - -	"	—	13	
Jones Stephens, - -	"	2	25	
Colin Sheffield, - -	"	2	25	
Peyton Stainback, - -	"	2	25	
William Stephens, - -	"	2	25	
Peter Stainback, - -	"	2	25	
John Stevens, - -	"	—	13	
Samuel Sheffield, - -	"	—	13	
David Simmons, - -	"	—	13	
Samuel P. Snipes, - -	"	—	13	
John Snipes, - -	"	—	5	
Joseph Titmash, - -	"	2	25	
John Tyre, - -	"	—	13	
Thomas Travis, - -	"	—	10	
Nathaniel Wamack, - -	"	2	25	
Nathan Williamson, - -	"	2	25	
Waller Warthen, - -	"	2	25	
James Warthen, - -	"	2	25	
Herbert Williams, - -	"	—	25	
David Williams, - -	"	—	13	
Alexander Wilson, - -	"	2	25	

MUSTER ROLL

*Of Captain William H. Harrison's Company, from the Sixty-second **Regiment**, Virginia Militia, in the Service from the 31st August to 13th September, 1814.*

NAMES.	RANK.	TIME OF SERVICE.		REMARKS.
		Months.	Days.	
William H. Harrison, - -	Captain,	–	14	
Richard Marks. - -	Lieutenant,	–	14	
Barker Andrews, - -	Ensign,	–	–	On duty at **Norfolk.**
Joel Titcash, -	Sergeant,	–	11	
Robert Mattox, - -	"	–	14	
Edmund Wilkins, - -	"	–	14	
Geo. Grapwell, - -	"	–	14	
Samuel Fenqua, -	Corporal,	–	14	
Wm'son W. Wamack,	"	–	14	
Amos Livesay, -	"	–	11	
Edmond Whitmore, -	"	–	14	
Samuel Wamack, -	Drummer,	–	14	
William Bishop, -	Fifer,	–	14	
Thomas H. Allen, -	Private,	–	14	
Evans Andrews, -	"	–	14	
James Bradley, - -	"	–	14	
Luke Burnett, - -	"	–	14	
Nathan Bishop, - -	"	–	14	
James Bishop, - -	"	–	14	
Robert Rrockwell, -	"	–	14	
Edward Branch, jr. -	"	–	14	
William Beckley, -	"	–	14	
Joseph Beckley, - -	"	–	–	" "
Thomas Coleman, -	"	–	14	
Samuel Donaldson, -	"	–	14	
John Edwards, -	"	–	14	
Wilie Epes, - -	"	–	14	
Hamlin Epes, - -	"	–	14	
Josiah Fenqua, - -	"	–	14	
Edward Finney, -	"	–	14	
Thomas Grapwell, -	"	–	11	
William Gary. - -	"	–	11	
William Galt. - -	"	–	14	
William Hamlin, - -	"	–	14	
William Hackney. -	"	–	14	
Throa'h P. Harrison, -	"	–	14	
Hartwell Heath, - -	"	–	14	
John Hamlin, -	"	–	14	
Collen L. Hobbs, -	"	–	–	" "
Allen Hobbs, - -	"	–	–	" "
William Hall, - -	"	–	–	" "
William C. Hobbs, -	"	–	–	" "
John J. Hatch, - -	"	–	14	
Edmund Harrison, -	"	–	14	
Samuel Harrison, -	"	–	14	
Thomas Hall, - -	"	–	–	" "
John Hoest, - -	"			
Braxton Harrison, -	"			
Collen Harrison, - -	"	–	14	
William Hobbs, - -	"	–	14	

NAMES.	RANK.	TIME OF SERVICE.		REMARKS.
		Months.	Days.	
Zachariah Harrison, - -	Private,	–	14	
John H. Janison, - -	"	–	14	
William Lee, - -	"	–	–	On duty at Norfolk.
William S. Lanier, - -	"	–	14	
Macky McHann, - -	"	–	14	
Henry S. Maring, - -	"	–	14	
William Moore, - -	"	–	14	
Henry C. Machen, - -	"	–	14	
Thomas McHann, - -	"	–	14	
Thomas Machen, - -	"	–	14	
Bolling New, - -	"	–	14	
Wilie Poythress, - -	"	–	14	
John Pitts, - -	"	–	14	
John W. Roberts, - -	"	–	14	
William Stainback, - -	"	–	14	
Jones Stevens, - -	"	–	14	
Peyton Stainback, - -	"	–	14	
Joseph Stevens, - -	"	–	14	
Hamlin Stevens, - -	"	–	14	
Hezekiah Sheffield, - -	"	–	14	
Samuel P. Snips, - -	"	–	14	
John Titmash, - -	"	–	14	
James Thwratt, - -	"	–	14	
Natha'l Wamack, - -	"	–	14	
Zachariah Williams, - -	"	–	14	
James Williams, jr. - -	"	–	14	
Grief Williams, - -	"	–	14	
Wyatt Williams, - -	"	–	14	
Alexander Wilson, - -	"	–	14	
John D. Wood, - -	"	–	14	
Richardson Williams, -	"	–	14	

MUSTER ROLL

Of Captain John Hart's Troop of Cavalry, from Thirty-ninth Regiment, Virginia Militia, commanded by Major General John Pegram, in the Service of the United States, from 23d to 30th March, and from 18th to 23d May, from 30th June to 12th July, and from 30th August to 13th September, 1813.

NAMES.	RANK.	TIME OF SERVICE.		REMARKS.
		Months.	Days.	
John Hart,	Captain,	1	1	
Christopher Jones,	Lieutenant,	–	17	
Benjamin Edwards,	"	–	17	
Benjamin Bragg,	Lt. and Cornet.	–	29	
John B. Bott,	Lt. and Surg.	–	29	
Baker Pegram, jr.	Sergeant,	–	17	
Dandridge Spotswood,	"	–	29	
John Boast,	"	1	8	
James Boyle,	"	–	17	
H. F. McKenna.	"	–	14	
Joshua Whitcomb,	"	1	5	
Geo. N. Belscher,	"	1	5	
Richard Toser,	"	–	17	
William Gilmore,	Corporal,	–	23	
William Young,	"	1	2	
Robert Spotswood,	"	1	2	
Bartley Weeks,	"	1	2	
A. S. Nanstedlor,	"	1	2	
Emor Harland,	"	1	2	
Stephen G. Wells,	Brig. M.	–	15	
Peyton Lynch,	Farrier,	–	9	
Randolph Johnson,	Trumpeter,	1	2	Transferred to Captain Pryor's Troop, 13th September.
John Andrews,	Private,	–	28	" " "
Thomas Aldridge,	"	–	15	" " "
William Bowden,	"	1	2	" " "
Edmund Burchett,	"	1	8	" " "
Zachariah Brewer,	"	1	8	" " "
John Butterworth,	"	–	15	" " "
James Boyle,	"	–	15	" " "
Richard Bate,	"	–	15	
James G. Caldwell,	"	–	15	
Samuel R. Caldwell,	"	–	15	
John Clark,	"	–	17	
Benjamin Curtis,	"	–	23	
Samuel Crawford,	"	–	15	" " "
John W. Dennist,	"	1	2	" " "
John Dijernett,	"	–	8	" " "
Jessee L. Dupee,	"	–	15	" " "
John R. Daniel,	"	–	15	" " "
Henry M. Didlark,	"	–	15	
Benjamin Dumas,	"	–	13	
Robert Elam,	"	1	2	" " "
Allen Finn,	"	1	2	" " "
William Griffin,	"	1	2	
Thomas E. Gray,	"	–	26	" " "

NAMES.	RANK.	TIME OF SERVICE.		REMARKS.
		Months.	Days.	
Edmond Heath, - -	Private,	–	15	
C. F. Jones, - -	"	–	15	Transferred to Captain Pryor's Troop, 13th September.
Walker Jones, - -	"	1	2	" " "
Lyne S. Kemp, - -	"	1	2	" " "
John Kirkland, - -	"	–	15	" " "
Thomas Lewis, - -	"	1	2	" " "
William Lownes, - -	"	1	2	" " "
Thomas T. Morgan, - -	"	–	25	" " "
Arch'd Moore, - -	"	–	15	" " "
Matthew Mahen, - -	"	1	2	" " "
Richard McKae, - -	"	–	15	
Hugh F. McKenna, - -	"	–	17	
Edward H. Pegram, - -	"	1	2	" " "
Frederick J. Redfield, -	"	1	2	" " "
Milton Rose, - -	"	1	2	" " "
Joseph Rowlett, - -	"	–	26	" " "
William Robertson, jr. -	"			
Edwin Ragsdale, - -	"	–	13	
Edward Stokes, - -	"	1	2	" " "
John Stiles, - -	"	1	2	" " "
L. G. Simmson, - -	"	–	15	" " "
David Smith, - -	"	–	15	" " "
Robert Snelson, - -	"	1	2	
David Shelley, - -	"	–	26	
John B. Strachan, - -	"	–	17	
Benjamin Tucker, - -	"	1	3	
Riley Tisdale, - -	"	–	4	
Thomas P. Vial, - -	"	–	17	
David Vaughan, - -	"	–	17	
Hunt Wyatt, - -	"	–	4	
Henry Wilkinson, - -	"	1	4	" " "
Robert Wilkins, - -	"	–	15	" " "
Edmond Wells, - -	"	–	15	" " "
William Wallace, - -	"	–	15	" " "
John Walker, - -	"	–	15	

MUSTER ROLL

*Of Sergeant Henry Harvey's Detachment, from Second Regiment, Virginia Mi-
litia, commanded by Lieutenant Colonel Thos. M. Bailey, in the Service of the
United States, from the 5th September to 5th October, and from 5th October
to 5th November, 1814.*

NAMES.		RANK.	TIME OF SERVICE.		REMARKS.
			Months.	Days.	
Henry Harvey,	- -	Sergeant,	2		
John Bull, -	- -	Private,	2		
John S. Cropper,	- -	"	2		
John Edwards,	- -	"	2		
Richard Lewis,	- -	"	2		
Nathaniel Lang,	- -	"	1		
Spencer Fletcher,	- -	"	1		
Isaac Snead,	- -	"	1		

Captain *William Harwood's Company—Twenty-first Regiment.*

NAMES.	RANK.	TIME OF SERVICE.		REMARKS.
		Months.	Days.	
William Harwood, - -	Captain,	–	29	
Horatio G. Harwood, -	Lieutenant,	1	2	
Thomas C. Amory, - -	Ensign,	1	2	
Edward Brooking, - -	Sergeant,	1	21	
Henry Sears -	"	–	29	
Isaac Brooke, - -	"	1	1	
James Dillard, - -	"	1	1	
William Newcomb, - -	Corporal,	–	2.	
John Minor, - -	"	–	2.	
James Miller, - -	"	1	1	
John Kemp, - -	"	–	27	
William Edwards, - -	"	–	19	
William Acra, - -	Private,	1	1	
Jacob Acra, - -	"	–	9	
Benjamin Brooklin, -	"	1	17	
John A. Brister, - -	"	–	21	
Cary Booker, - -	"	1	17	
Bivion Brooking, - -	"	–	29	
Samuel Brooking, - -	"	–	15	
William Brooking, -	"	–	3	
Benjamin Booker, -	"	–	17	
John Coats, - -	"	–	24	
Jonathan Coats, - -	"	–	16	
Thomas Dutton, - -	"	1	11	
James Dutton, - -	"	1	2	
Henry Dutton, - -	"	–	28	
William Dudley, - -	"	1		
James Dutton, jr. - -	"	–	19	
Warner Dunston, - -	"	–	10	
Richard Dutton, - -	"	1	13	
Thomas Dunston, - -	"	–	29	
Pauldin Drummond, -	"	–	24	
William O. Dear, - -	"	–	6	
Carlton Eubank, - -	"	–	17	
Natt. Hall, - -	"	1		
Geo. Hibble, - -	"	1	14	
James Hibble, - -	"	–	10	
James Hart, - -	"	1	16	
Geo. Haynes, - -	"	1	11	
William Hall, - -	"	–	29	
John Howlett, - -	"	–	28	
John B. Hall, - -	"	–	26	
Natt. Kemp, - -	"	–	27	
John Kemp, - -	"	–	19	
Robert G. Kemp, - -	"	–	3	
John Lawson, - -	"	–	25	
William Lambert, - -	"	1	10	
Ch. Lawson, - -	"	–	3	
Thomas Mason, - -	"	–	14	
John Mason, - -	"	–	27	
Jas. Miller, - -	"	–	3	
George Norton, - -	"			
Bowden Newcomb, - -	"	1	1	

NAMES.			RANK.	TIME OF SERVICE.		REMARKS.
				Months.	Days.	
William Padgett,	-	-	Private,	–	14	
Thomas Pierce,	-	-	"	1	11	
Richard Padget,	-	-	"	–	8	
William Roane,	-	-	"	–	20	
John Rowe,	-	-	"	1	18	
Thomas Roane,	.	-	"	–	21	
Major Roane,	-	-	"	1	6	
James Roy,	-	-	"	–	27	
William Rilie,	-	-	"	–	3	
Thomas Sears,	-	-	"	1	14	
James B. Sheppard,	-	-	"	1	14	
William Snow,	-	-	"	1	1	
Henry Stalker,	-	-	"	–	25	
John Sheppard,	-	-	"	–	29	
William Sears.	-	-	"	–	19	
Edward Waller,	-	-	"	–	11	
James Wiatt,	-	-	"	–	28	
John Wilkins,	-	-	"	1		
William Walden,	-	-	"	–	20	
Francis C. Wiatt,	-	-	"	–	11	
John Walker.	-	-	"	–	23	
James C. West,	-	-	"	–	20	
William Wiatt,	-	-	"	–	8	
Overton Wiatt,	-	-	"	–	8	
John R. Wiatt,	-	-	"	–	24	
Isaac Wilcox,	-	-	"	–	13	
Seaton Wiatt,	-	-	"			
William Young,	-	-	"	–	16	
Carlton Ubank,	-	-	"	–	19	
Seaton Wiatt,	-	-	"	–	3	
William O. Deen,	-	-	"			

(For rest of this company, see publication of Pay Rolls.)

MUSTER ROLL

Of Captain John Hazelwood's Company, from the Sixty-eighth Regiment, Virginia Militia, commanded by Lieutenant Colonel Burwell Bassett, in the Service of the United States, from the 6th to 15th February, 1814.

NAMES.	RANK.	TIME OF SERVICE.		REMARKS.
		Months.	Days.	
John Hazelwood,	Captain	–	10	
Richard A. Green,	Ensign.	–	10	
John Hankins,	Sergeant.	–	10	
Robert Morriss,	"	–	10	
Martin F. Martin,	"	–	10	
Geo. Thomas,	"	–	10	
John Tyree,	Corporal.	–	10	
William Martin,	"	–	10	
William Brown,	"	–	10	
Francis Pierce,	"	–	8	
Thomas Austin,	Private,	–	10	
William Curle,	"	–	10	
Richard Farthing,	"	–	10	
William Hazelwood,	"	–	10	
Fielding Harwood,	"	–	4	
Geo. James,	"	–	10	
Chesley Jones,	"	–	10	
John Jennings,	"	–	10	
John M. Jones,	"	–	10	
Allen Jones,	"	–	10	
William Jennings,	"	–	2	
John Jones,	"	–	2	
John Marsh,	"	–	4	
John Martin,	"	–	4	
James Shelburn,	"	–	10	
Isaac Saunders,	"	–	10	
William B. Taylor,	"	–	4	
Bollen Vaughan,	"	–	4	
John Woodward,	"	–	4	
Geo. Wills,	"	–	4	
Benjamin Walls,	"	–	4	

Captain John Hathaway's Company—Ninety-second Regiment.

NAMES.			RANK.	TIME OF SERVICE.		REMARKS.
				Months.	Days.	
Thomas Biscoe,	-	-	Private,	—	5	
Thomas Carter,	-	-	"	—	24	
Robert Daniel,	-	-	"	1		
Alexander Hazard,	-	-	"	—	24	
John Hubbard,	-	-	"	—	7	
James Hayme,	-	-	"	—	10	
Thaddeus Mitchell,	-	-	"	—	20	
William Sutton,	-	-	"	—	5	
Samuel Stoneham,	-	-	"	—	4	
Thomas Thrall,	-	-	"	—	5	
William Watts,	-	-	"	—	2	
George Webb,	-	-	"	—	10	

(For rest of this company, see publication of Pay Rolls.)

MUSTER ROLL

Of Captain James Hayes' Company, from the Thirty-sixth Regiment, Virginia Militia, in the Service of the State of Virginia, from the 1st to 7th August, and from 24th August to 7th September, 1814.

NAMES.	RANK.	TIME OF SERVICE.		REMARKS.
		Months.	Days.	
James Hayes, - -	Captain,	—	22	Transferred to the staff and acting adjutant to the regiment.
Alfred C. Hayes, -	Lieutenant,	—	22	
William J. Colquhoun, -	Ensign,	—	22	
Henry M. Smoot, -	Sergeant,	—	7	
Anderson Boughton, -	"	—	22	
John B. Cannon, -	"	—	22	
John Bland, -	"	—	14	
Joseph Palmer, -	"	—	14	
Robert Forgie, -	Corporal,	—	7	
James Merchant, -	"	—	7	
Samuel Boswell, -	"	—	14	
Geo. Boswell, -	"	—	14	
William Boswell, -	"	—	14	
William H. Duvall, -	"	—	14	
Daniel Boyd, -	"	—	7	
Richard Calvert, -	Musician,	—	22	
Gustavus Maschett,	"	—	14	
Augustine Athey, -	Private,	—	22	
Horatio Athey, -	"	—	22	
Willis Athey, -	"	—	22	Substitute for Josiah Athey.
Robert Alexander, -	"	—	7	
Jessee Bobo, -	"	—	22	
John Bramel, sen. -	"	—	22	
John Bramel, jr. -	"	—	22	
Samuel Bozel, -	"	—	7	
Geo. Bozel, -	"	—	7	
William Bozel, -	"	—	7	
John Bland, -	"	—	7	
Alphus M. Clark, -	"	—	22	
William Calvert, -	"	—	14	
Geo. Cornwell, -	"	—	14	
James Carter, -	"	—	14	
Bland Currie, -	"	—	22	
Peter Cockrell, -	"	—	15	
John Cornwell, -	"	—	22	
John Duvall, -	"	—	22	
William H. Duvall, -	"	—	7	
Joseph Dunaway, -	"	—	7	
Highly Fayre, -	"	—	7	
John Guy, -	"	—	14	
Aaron Gray, -	"	—	22	
William Harris, -	"	—	22	
Thomas Harris, -	"	—	7	
Corbin Hale, -	"	—	8	
Geo. Hutchison, -	"	—	22	

NAMES.	RANK.	TIME OF SERVICE.		REMARKS.
		Months.	Days.	
Allison Johnston, - -	Private,	—	15	Joined the cavalry.
Starlin Jones, - -	"	—	15	
Richard Johnston, - -	"	—	22	
Gustavus Jones, - -	"	—	22	
Elias King, - -	"	—	14	Joined the cavalry.
Joseph B. Linehough, - -	"	—	15	
Solomon W. Mallory, - -	"	—	22	
Walter Maddox, - -	"	—	22	
Keland Moss, - -	"	—	22	
Geo. Maddox, - -	"	—	8	
Barnaby Purnell, - -	"	—	22	
Jessee Pilcher, - -	"	—	7	
James Risen, - -	"	—	22	
Vincent Stonnell, - -	"	—	22	
Alexander Sincox, - -	"	—	14	
Charles Shaw, - ?	"	—	22	
Richard Stonnell. - -	"	—	22	
Frederick Stiff, - -	"	—	22	
Wilf'd D. Sidebottom, -	"	—	7	
Matthew M. Smoot, - -	"	—	7	
Thomas Tomlin, - -	"	—	14	
John Warden, - -	"	—	14	
Henry West, - -	"	—	22	

MUSTER ROLL

Of Captain Samuel Henderson's Company, from the Ninety-ninth Regiment, Virginia Militia, commanded by Lieutenant Colonel Charles Bagwell, in the Service of the United States from the 7th to 11th June, 1814.

NAMES.	RANK.	TIME OF SERVICE.		REMARKS.
		Months.	Days.	
Samuel Henderson, - -	Captain,	–	5	
William Welbourn, - -	Lieutenant,	–	2	
Charles S. Piper, - -	Ensign,	–	2	
William Johnson, - -	Sergeant,	–	2	
John Marshall, - -	"	–	2	
Lemuel Henderson, - -	"	–	2	
James W. Melvin, - -	"	–	2	
Henry Taylor, - -	Musician,	–	2	
Thomas Collins, - -	"	–	2	
James Alexander, - -	Private.	–	4	
Thomas Alexander, -	"	–	4	
Edward Ardis, - -	"			
James Benson, - -	"	–	2	
Henry Broadwater, - -	"			
Nathaniel Benson, - -	"	–	2	
David K. Baker, - -	"	–	2	
John Collins, (of Jno.) -	"	–	2	
Skinner Collins, - -	"	–	2	
Benjamin Cluff, - -	"	–	2	
John Collins, (of Geo.) -	"	–	2	
Handy Davis, - -	"	–	2	
James Harges, - -	"	–	2	
Thomas Harges, - -	"	–	2	
Thompson Holmes, - -	"			
Caleb Johnson, - -	"	–	2	
Robert Knox, - -	"	–	2	
Levin Mariner, - -	"	–	2	
Daniel J. Marshall, - -	"	–	2	
William Mills, - -	"	–	2	
Littleton Nock, - -	"	–	2	
William Phaget, - -	"	–	2	
Fisher Richardson, - -	"	–	2	
Geo. Read, - -	"	–	2	
James Taylor, - -	"			
Nehemiah Taylor, - -	"	–	2	
Henry Taylor, - -	"	–	2	
Littleton Trador, - -	"	–	2	
Justice Truit, - -	"	–	2	
Levin Tendle, - -	"	–	2	
Levin Townsend, - -	"	–	2	
Charles Tunnell, - -	"	–	2	
James Wilbourn, - -	"	–	2	
David Wilbourn, - -	"	–	2	
James Whealton, - -	"	–	2	
John Whealton, - -	"	–	2	
James Wolridge, - -	"	–	2	
Thomas D. Wilbourn, -	"	–	2	

Captain William Henderson's Company—Second Regiment.

NAMES.	RANK.	TIME OF SERVICE.		REMARKS.
		Months.	Days.	
Edmund Roberts, - -	Sergeant,	–	8	
Hillary B. Stringer, - -	Corporal,	–	6	
Abel Walter, - -	"	–	24	
Robert Mears, - -	"	–	8	
Thos. Fosque, - -	"	–	8	
Elijah Floyd, - -	"	–	8	
Edm'd Cropper, - -	"	–	8	
James S. Benson, - -	Fifer,	–	18	
Edw'd Hutchinson, - -	Drummer,	–	10	
Major Ames, - -	Private,	–	10	
George Ardis, - -	"	–	10	
James S. Benson, - -	"	–	27	
John Bouwell, - -	"	–	24	
Agrippa Bell, - -	"	–	6	
Dudley P. Brown, - -	"	1	10	
Levin Beach, - -	"	–	8	
Edw'd Bailey, - -	"			
Wm. Bell, - -	"	–	16	
Thomas Churn, - -	"	–	14	
Edm'd Cropper, - -	"	1	16	
Richard East, - -	"	–	16	
James Erwin. - -	"	1	6	
Thomas Fosque, - -	"	1	16	
Elijah Floyd, - -	"	1	10	
Benj. Floyd, - -	"	–	16	
Edm'd Garritson, - -	"	–	6	
Wm. Garritson, - -	"	–	6	
Richard Hickman, - -	"	–	6	
James Harrison, - -	"	1	10	
Thos. Harrison, - -	"	–	5	
Robert Mears, - -	"	–	29	
Arthur D. Michael, - -	"	–	8	
Arthur Powell, - -	"	–	6	
Jas. Richardson, - -	"	–	6	
Francis Roberts, - -	"	–	16	
Richard Rogers, - -	"	–	6	
William Stakes, - -	"	–	8	
James Savage, - -	"	–	5	
Wm. F. Savage, - -	"	–	24	
George Smith, - -	"	–	16	
William Watson, - -	"	–	6	
Abel Walter, - -	"	1		
Jacob Watson. - -	"	–	6	

(For rest of this company, see publication of Pay Rolls.)

Captain William Henderson's Company—Thirty-seventh Regiment.

NAMES.	RANK.	TIME OF SERVICE.		REMARKS.
		Months.	Days.	
Daniel W. Beacham, - -	Lieutenant,	1	3	
Samuel Dawson, - -	Corporal,	–	10	
Haynie Ashburn, - -	Private,	–	23	
Stephen Brann, - -	"	–	16	
Richard Brooks, - -	"	–	16	
Samuel Clarke, - -	"	–	16	
Pemberton Cloughton, -	"	1	10	
Linzey T. Dawson, - -	"	–	17	
John Hardwick, - -	"	–	5	
Benj. R. Heale, - -	"	–	3	
William L. Self, - -	"	–	12	
David J. Tellis, - -	"	–	12	
Thomas Whittington, -	"	–	13	

(For rest of this company, see publication of Pay Rolls.)

MUSTER ROLL

Of Captain William Henley's Company, from the Thirty-third Regiment, Virginia Militia, Henrico County, commanded by Lieutenant Colonel John Mayo, in the Service from the 19th to 29th March, 1813.

NAMES.	RANK.	TIME OF SERVICE.		REMARKS.
		Months.	Days.	
William Henley, - -	Captain,	–	10	
John Thomasson, - -	Lieutenant,	–	10	
Thomas Willis, - -	Ensign.	–	10	
Peter Cottrell, jr. - -	Sergeant,	–	10	
Jesse Harlow, - -	"	–	10	
Reuben Cottrell, - -	"	–	10	
John Jude, - -	"	–	10	
John Harlow, - -	Drummer,	–	10	
Dabney Cawthorn, - -	Fifer,	–	10	
Benjamin Duvall, - -	Private,	–	10	
Leon'd Henly, - -	"	–	10	
John Lacey, - -	"	–	10	
Jones Tyler, - -	"	–	10	
James Haweton, - -	"	–	10	
John Miller, - -	"	–	10	
John Harlow, - -	"	–	10	
Joseph Holman, - -	"	–	10	
John Alley, - -	"	–	10	
Allen Tyler. - -	"	–	10	
Zachariah McGruder, - -	"	–	10	
John Guine, - -	"	–	10	
Thomas Wade, - -	"	–	10	
Daniel H. Thacker, - -	"	–	10	
Zachariah Ford, - -	"	–	10	
Richard Wade, - -	"	–	10	
Fleming Ford, - -	"	–	10	
Richard C. Gilliam, - -	"	–	10	
Elisha Wade, - -	"	–	10	
Henry Baughan, - -	"	–	10	
David Hughes. - -	"	–	1	
Ambrose Hutcherson, - -	"	–	10	
James Lawrence, - -	"	–	10	
Peter Flesher, - -	"	–	10	
Austin Ford, - -	"	–	10	
John Flesher, - -	"	–	10	
Joseph Webber, - -	"	–	7	
Tilman Tacker, - -	"	–	10	
Elijah Miller, - -	"	–	10	
William Miller, - -	"	–	10	
Joseph Bowles, - -	"	–	10	
William M. Burton, - -	"	–	10	
Robert Jennings, - -	"	–	10	
John Fandry, - -	"	–	5	
Richard Butler, - -	"	–	10	
Joseph Baughan, - -	"	–	10	
Michael Johnson, - -	"	–	10	
Miles Wade, - -	"	–	10	
Nathl. Harlow, - -	"	–	10	

MUSTER ROLL

Of Captain Harry Heth's Troop of Cavalry, from the First Regiment, Virginia Militia, Chesterfield County, commanded by Lieutenant Colonel William Brown, in the Service from the 8th February to 3d March, from 27th to 29th June, and from 30th June to 1st July, 1813.

NAMES.	RANK.	TIME OF SERVICE.		REMARKS.
		Months.	Days.	
Harry Heth.	Captain,	1	1	
James Scott,	Lieutenant,	–	26	
Branch Cheatham,	"	1	1	
P. F. Smith,	"	–	5	
Harry Randolph,	Cornet,	–	26	
John Cobbs,	"	1	1	
Zachariah Brooks,	Qr. M. S.	1	1	
Peter McCary,	Sergeant,	1	1	
Edward D. Diggs,	"	1	1	
Robert Harris,	"	1	1	
William Winfree,	"	1	1	
Peter T. Smith,	Corporal,	–	26	
Matthew Burfoot,	"	1	1	Promoted to Corporal since 3d March 1813.
Thomas Partor,	"	1	1	
Samuel Woody,	"	–	5	
John Archer,	"	–	5	
Thomas Graves,	"	1	1	
—— Randolph,	Trumpeter,	–	24	
John Archer,	Private,	–	26	
Daniel Belcher,	"	–	26	
William Bradshaw,	"	–	5	
Thomas Ball,	"	–	5	
Arch'd Botts,	"	–	5	
John Clark,	"	1	1	
Is. Cunningham,	"	–	5	
James Flornoy,	"	1	1	
Thomas Farris,	"	1	1	
Arch'd Flornoy,	"	1	1	
Kennon Giles,	"	1	1	
Fendall Gregory,	"	–	26	
Matthew Graves,	"	–	26	
Robert Graham,	"	–	5	
Peter E. Graves,	"	–	3	
Nicho. Gordon,	"	–	5	
Henry Hancock,	"	1	1	
William Hancock,	"	1	1	
Egbert Harris,	"	1	1	
Higgason Hancock,	"	–	26	
Patrick Harris,	"	1	1	
Edward Johnson,	"	–	5	
John Johnson,	"	–	5	
Thomas Kearns,	"	1	1	
James Kelton,	"	1	1	
Francis Lockett,	"	–	26	
Everitt Moore,	"	–	26	
Jacob Michaels,	"	1	1	

NAMES.	RANK.	TIME OF SERVICE.		REMARKS.
		Months.	Days.	
Allen McRae, - -	Private,	1	1	
John B. Mehone, - -	"	—	26	
Collin McRae, - -	"	—	5	
John B. Morrisett, - -	"	—	5	
William Martin, - -	"	—	5	
Dan'l Pelcher, - -	"	—	5	
Joseph Price, - -	"	—	5	
William Patterson, - -	"	—	5	
H. Randolph, - -	"	—	5	
Robert Sanders, - -	"	1	1	
Theoderick Smith, - -	"	1	1	
Jordan Smith, - -	"	1	1	
Sam'l L. Sanders, - -	"	—	5	
Thomas Taylor, - -	"	—	5	
Obediah Winfree, - -	"	1	1	
Valentine Winfree, - -	"	—	26	
John Worsham, -	"	—	2	

Captain John C. Hill's Company—First Regiment.

NAMES.	RANK.	TIME OF SERVICE.		REMARKS.
		Months.	Days.	
John C. Hill, - -	Captain,	–	14	
Thomas Rowlett, - -	Lieutenant,	–	14	
William Booker, - -	"	–	14	
Ferguson Farmer, - -	Ensign,	–	14	
Robert Pescud, - -	"	–	14	
Thomas Powell, - -	Or. Sergeant,	–	14	
Rame Chastain, - -	Q. M. Serg't,	–	14	
Marshall Fariss, - -	Sergeant,	–	14	
James P. Hill, - -	"	–	14	
Robert Dickers, - -	"	–	14	
Joseph Jones, - -	"	–	14	
Anderson Nunally, - -	Corporal,	–	14	
James Allen, - -	"	–	14	
Peter R. Dunnavant, - -	"	–	14	
John Vest. - -	"	–	14	
Thomas W. Vaughan, -	Fifer,	–	14	
Richard Allen, - -	Private,	–	14	
William Bragg, - -	"	–	14	
Bartlett Baugh, - -	"	–	14	
James Booker, - -	"	–	14	
Bernard Brivill, - -	"	–	14	
Littleton E. Belcher, -	"	–	14	
William Butler, - -	"	–	14	
Samuel Bridgewater, -	"	–	14	
William Clayborne, - -	"	–	14	
Spencer Chandler, - -	"	–	14	
John L. Cowardin. - -	"	–	14	
Rowlett Dearen, - -	"	–	14	
Francis Dunevant, - -	"	–	14	
John Dunevant, - -	"	–	14	
John Dunkin, - -	"	–	14	
Royall Fergason, - -	"	–	14	
John Furley, - -	"	–	14	
John Frith, - -	"	–	14	
Micajah French, - -	"	–	14	
Jessee Franklin, - -	"	–	14	
Lewis Goodwin, - -	"	–	14	
William B. Giles, - -	"	–	14	
Henry Garrett, - -	"	–	14	
Walter L. Garrett, - -	"	–	14	
Thomas Hudson, - -	"	–	14	
Walter B. Hughes, - -	"	–	14	
William Howlet, - -	"	–	14	
Osborne Jones, - -	"	–	14	
John Lynch, - -	"	–	14	
Jacob A. Lockett, - -	"	–	14	
Wm. Meglafon, - -	"	–	14	
John Marshall, - -	"	–	14	
Daniel J. Mayes, - -	"	–	14	
John McLaren, - -	"	–	14	
Littleberry Neal, - -	"	–	14	
Francis Pride, - -	"	–	14	
Anderson Pride, - -	"	–	14	
Francis Powell, - -	"	–	14	

NAMES.	RANK.	TIME OF SERVICE.		REMARKS.|
		Months.	Days.	
Laban Pitchford, - -	Private,	–	14	
Isaac Pollard, - -	"	–	14	
John Rayborne, - -	"	–	14	
Wm'son D. Sears, - -	"	–	14	
James C. Stranger, - -	"	–	14	
Peter D. Sublett, - -	"	–	14	
John Smith, - -	"	–	14	
William Timberlake, -	"	–	14	
William H. Vaughan, -	"	–	14	
William Werks, - -	"	–	14	
William Waldrop, - -	"	–	14	

(For rest of this company, see publication of Pay Rolls.)

MUSTER ROLL

Of Captain Robert Hill's Company, from the Sixth Regiment, Virginia Militia, commanded by Lieutenant John Dangerfield, in the Service from 5th to 8th of April, 1813.

NAMES.	RANK.	TIME OF SERVICE.		REMARKS.
		Months.	Days.	
Robert Hill,	Captain,	—	4	
William C. Latane,	Lieutenant,	—	2	
Johnson Munday,	Ensign,	—	3	
Thomas Clarkson,	Sergeant,	—	4	
Edmond Jones,	"	—	4	
Lewis Hoard,	"	—	2	
Richard B. Hutt,	"	—	2	
Richard N. Callis,	Corporal,	—	2	
Fielding S. Crow,	"	—	2	
Lewis Munday,	"	—	2	
Richard Coghill,	Private,	—	2	
William Clark,	"	—	2	
Goldman Carter,	"	—	2	
Moses Crow,	"	—	2	
William Coleman,	"	—	2	
James Colimas,	"	—	2	
William Burfoot,	"	—	1	
Churchill Ball,	"	—	2	
Robert Ball,	"	—	2	
Carter Ball,	"	—	2	
William B. Boulware,	"	—	2	
Motta Ball,	"	—	2	
Philip Baston,	"	—	2	
Lewis Brown,	"	—	2	
Lewis Davis,	"	—	2	
Jack Dyke,	"	—	2	
Alexander Elliott,	"	—	2	
Theophilus Farer,	"	—	2	
Wm. H. Falconner,	"	—	2	
Major Fogg,	"	—	3	
Wm. W. Fogg,	"	—	1	
John S. Garrett,	"	—	1	
Lewis Gatewood,	"	—	1	
Reuben Garrett,	"	—	2	
Philip Gatewood,	"	—	2	
William Games,	"	—	2	
William Gatewood,	"	—	2	
Garnett Grunstead,	"	—	2	
Daniel Goldmon,	"	—	2	
William Garrett,	"	—	2	
William Halbert,	"	—	2	
John T. Hill,	"	—	2	
Joseph Hester,	"	—	2	
Joseph Harper,	"	—	2	
William Hill,	"	—	2	
Joseph Hill,	"	—	2	
Orison Ingram,	"	—	2	
John Mahon,	"	—	1	

NAMES.			RANK.	TIME OF SERVICE.		REMARKS.
				Months.	Days.	
Paul Micome,	-	-	Private,	–	2	
Joseph Minter,	-	-	"	–	2	
Thomas Minter,	-	-	"	–	2	
Spencer Moody,	-	-	"	–	2	
Barton Minter,	-	-	"	–	2	
Moscoe Noel,	-	-	"	–	2	
Edmond Noel,	-	-	"	–	1	
Devald Noel,	-	-	"	–	1	
Austin Oliver,	-	-	"	–	2	
Samuel Parker,	-	-	"	–	2	
Warren Parker,	-	-	"	–	2	
Andrew Runolds,	-	-	"	–	2	
Henry Rouse,	-	-	"	–	2	
Walker Roy,	-	-	"	–	2	
Stephen Rodden,	-	-	"	–	2	
David Roper,	-	-	"	–	2	
Brooking Stokes,	-	-	"	–	1	
Fielding Sale,	-	-	"	–	2	
John Smither,	-	-	"	–	2	
William Smither,	-	-	"	–	2	
Stresley Stokes,	-	-	"	–	2	
Robert Samuels,	-	-	"	–	2	
William Sullivan,	-	-	"	–	2	
Larkin Shaddock,	-	-	"	–	2	
John Sherwood,	-	-	"	–	2	
John Thomas,	-	-	"	–	2	
William D. Thomas,	-	-	"	–	2	
Streshley Taylor,	-	-	"	–	2	
Thomas Turner,	-	-	"	–	2	
Boulware Vauter,	-	-	"	–	2	
Robert Wire,	-	-	"	–	2	

Captain Thomas Hill's Company—Forty-fifth Regiment.

NAMES.	RANK.	TIME OF SERVICE.		REMARKS.
		Months.	Days.	
Thomas Hill, - -	Captain,	–	4	
Thomas Jones, - -	Lieutenant,	–	4	
Robert Beanly, - -	"	–	4	Or Beatty
Christopher Blackburne, -	Cornet,	–	4	
James Patton, - -	Sergeant,	–	4	
Thomas James, - -	"	–	4	
Philemon Heath, - -	"	–	4	
William R. Ensor, - -	"	–	4	
Thomas T. Cooper, - -	Corporal,	–	4	
William Patton, - -	"	–	4	
John A. Starke, - -	"	–	4	
Bennett Harding, - -	"	–	6	
Thomas G. McCoy, - -	Trumpeter,			
James Blackburn, - -	Private,	–	4	
Moses Batterly, - -	"	–	4	
Thomas Custice, - -	"	–	4	
Geo. Garnett, - -	"	–	4	
John Hill, - -	"	–	6	
Alexander Heflin, - -	"	–	4	
Richard Hill, - -	"	–	4	
John Hylin, - -	"	–	4	
James Hylin, jr. - -	"	–	4	
John Heflin, - -	"	–	2	
Jeremiah Hoomes, - -	"	–	5	
Robert Kendall, - -	"	–	4	
Rowzee Lackam, - -	"	–	4	
Gerard Lomax, - -	"	–	6	
Mason G. McCay, - -	"	–	4	
Lewis G. Martin, - -	"	–	7	
James Mouroe, - -	"	–	4	
John Patton, - -	"	–	4	
Joseph Reed, - -	"	–	4	
Jessee Reed, - -	"	–	5	
William Randal, - -	"	–	2	
James Shelkett, - -	"	–	5	
John Sbelkett, - -	"	–	4	
John A. Simms, - -	"	–	4	
Mourning Smith, - -	"	–	6	
Abner Schooler, - -	"	–	4	
Francis Smith, - -	"	–	4	
William Smith, - -	"	–	5	
Jessee Turner, - -	"	–	4	
William Turner, - -	"	–	4	
Alexander Turner, - -	"	–	9	
William Randall, - -	"	–	4	
Joseph Nelson, - -	"	–	4	
William Young, - -	"	–	4	
John Cooper, - -	"	–	27	
Thomas Congers, - -	"	–	8	
Stephen Ensor, - -	"	–	27	
Charles Humphrey, - -	"	–	27	
Mark Harding, - -	"	–	27	
Lewis Harding, - -	"	–	27	
Harrison Harding, - -	"	–	27	
Jessee Holloway, - -	"	–	27	
John E. Hewitt, - -	"	–	27	

NAMES.			RANK.	TIME OF SERVICE.		REMARKS.
				Months.	Days.	
Urllin Jones,	-	-	Private,	—	27	
John E. Kendall,	-	-	"	—	27	
Geo. Latham,	-	-	"	—	27	
Charles Lewis,	-	-	"	—	27	
Jas. Latham,	-	-	"	—	27	
William W. Robertson,	-	-	"	—	27	
Lawson Schooler,	-	-	"	—	27	
John Smith,	-	-	"	—	23	
Geo. Stripling,	-	-	"	—	17	
Bailey H. Starke,	-	-	"	—	27	
Thos. Wilson,	-	-	"	—	27	
Thomas Watson,	-	-	"	—	27	
Lincefield Young,	-	-	"	—	15	

(For rest of this company, see publication of Pay Rolls.)

MUSTER ROLL

Of Captain John Hix's Company, from the Twenty-third Regiment, Virginia Militia, Chesterfield County, commanded by Colonel William Brown, in the Service from 18th to 30th March, and from 27th to 28th June, in the year 1813.

NAMES.	RANK.	TIME OF SERVICE.		REMARKS.
		Months.	Days.	
John Hix,	Captain,	–	14	
William Elliott,	Lieutenant,	–	14	
Green Hancock,	Ensign,	–	14	
Samuel Hancock,	Sergeant,	–	14	
John Snelling,	"	–	14	
John B. Morrissett,	"	–	14	
Charles Lockett,	"	–	14	
John Ashland,	Private,	–	2	
John Brummatt,	"	–	14	
Thomas Bottoms,	"	–	14	
Samuel Bowels,	"	–	14	
Elias Brooks,	"	–	14	
Anderson Bowles,	"	–	2	
Lewing Bowles,	"	–	12	
Higgason Cox,	"	–	14	
Charles Cunliff,	"	–	14	
William Ellison,	"	–	2	
James Ellison,	"	–	12	
Daniel Furcrum,	"	–	14	
Cornelius Furcrum,	"	–	14	
Josiah Flournoy,	"	–	14	
John Furgason,	"	–	14	
Obediah Hix,	"	–	14	
Thomas Hix,	"	–	14	
William Hix,	"	–	2	
Francis Hix,	"	–	12	
John Hopkins,	"	–	12	
James Harding,	"	–	12	
John Johnson,	"	–	14	
William Johnson,	"	–	12	
Samuel Lockett,	"	–	14	
James Moore,	"	–	14	
Neal McLane,	"	–	14	
Robt. McClure,	"	–	12	
Peter Perdure,	"	–	14	
Barnard Roberts,	"	–	14	
Oliver Roberts,	"	–	12	
Richard Sowell,	"	–	14	
Thomas Snellings,	"	–	14	
William Swhatt,	"	–	14	
Edmond Saprad,	"	–	14	
Samuel Short,	"	–	14	
John Strange,	"	–	2	
John Sabarrear,	"	–	12	
Richard Sizer,	"	–	12	
James O. Sandrum,	"	–	12	
Robert M. Tyre,	"	–	2	

NAMES.	RANK.	TIME OF SERVICE.		REMARKS.
		Months.	Days.	
John B. Taylor,	Private,	–	14	
Josiah Taylor,	"	–	12	
James Trasher,	"	–	12	
Hudson Thomas,	"	–	12	
James Williams,	"	–	14	
Edmond Wooldridge,	"	–	14	
Henry Williams,	"	–	14	
Thomas Williams,	"	–	14	
Martin Wooldridge,	"	–	2	

MUSTER ROLL

Of Captain James Hodges' Company, from the Fifty-ninth Regiment, Virginia Militia, commanded by Lieutenant Colonel Josiah Riddick, in the Service from the 18th March to 2d April, 1813.

NAMES.	RANK.	TIME OF SERVICE.		REMARKS.
		Months.	Days.	
James Hodges, - -	Captain,	1	14	
Caleb Jones, - -	Lieutenant,	–	14	
Moses Williams, - -	Ensign,	–	14	
Thomas Dixon, - -	Sergeant,	–	14	
Archbold Jordan, - -	"	–	14	
John Pinner, - -	"	–	14	
James C. Godwin, - -	"	–	14	
James B. Williamson, - -	Corporal,	–	14	
Densy Lassiter, - -	"	–	14	
William Price, - -	"	–	14	
Ro. Riddick, - -	"	–	14	
Josiah Archer, - -	Private,	–	14	
John Aires, - -	"	–	14	
Elijah Bull, - -	"	–	14	
Geo. Bartley, - -	"	–	14	
James Byrd, - -	"	–	14	
Daniel Baker, - -	"	–	14	
James Brother, - -	"	–	14	
William Bailey, - -	"	–	14	
John Brown, - -	"	–	14	
Josiah Cutcher, - -	"	–	14	
David Cutcher, - -	"	–	14	
Slaughter Coffield, - -	"	–	14	
Thomas M. Coffield, - -	"	–	14	
Thomas M. Cowling, - -	"	–	14	
Ro. Clayton, - -	"	–	14	
Jordon Denson, - -	"	–	14	
Whitmiel Duke, - -	"	–	14	
John Denson, - -	"	–	14	
John Foster, - -	"	–	14	
William Foster, - -	"	–	14	
Jordan Frost, - -	"	–	14	
William Godwin, - -	"	–	14	
Maj. Guy, - -	"	–	14	
John Godwin, - -	"	–	14	
Ambrose Hill, - -	"	–	14	
Jesse Hodges, - -	"	–	14	
James Hines, - -	"	–	14	
Geo. Harrison, - -	"	–	14	
James Harris, - -	"	–	14	
Elihue Hedgpeth, - -	"	–	14	
Benjamin Harrison, - -	"	–	14	
Samuel Hale, - -	"	–	14	
James Hudson, - -	"	–	14	
Jordon Howell, - -	"	–	14	
Elisha Hornsbury, - -	"	–	14	
Anthony G. Johnson, - -	"	–	14	

NAMES.	RANK.	TIME OF SERVICE.		REMARKS.
		Months.	Days.	
Anthony Jones,	Private,	–	14	
James Johnson,	"	–	14	
John Lawrence,	"	–	14	
Robert Lassiter,	"	–	14	
John Minton,	"	–	14	
James Milby,	"	–	14	
Stephen Nelms, sr.	"	–	14	
David Nelms,	"	–	14	
Stephen Nelms, jr.	"	–	14	
John Newton,	"	–	14	
John Oliver,	"	–	14	
James Pitt,	"	–	14	
Matthew Powell,	"	–	14	
John S. Parnall,	"	–	14	
William Pinner,	"	–	14	
James Pinner,	"	–	14	
John Pinner, (of Mason,)	"	–	14	
William Rountree,	"	–	14	
Joseph Sanders,	"	–	14	
Henry Small,	"	–	14	
Jethro Spivey,	"	–	14	
Thomas Stokeley,	"	–	14	
Miles Tinnington,	"	–	14	
Thomas Weatherly,	"	–	14	
Thomas Wilkins,	"	–	14	
Rutland Watson,	"	–	14	
Joshua Whitfield,	"	–	14	
Willis Wilkinson,	"	–	14	

Captain Daniel Hoffman's Company—Eighth Regiment.

NAMES.			RANK.	TIME OF SERVICE.		REMARKS.
				Months.	Days.	
James Johnston,	-	-	Lieutenant,	1	11	
Arthur L. Burks,	-	-	Private,	1	11	
Robert Bradley,	-	-	"	–	22	
John Campbell,	-	-	"	–	18	
Benjamin Ford,	-	-	"	1	11	
Joseph Ford,	-	-	"	1	11	
John Feran,	-	-	"	–	28	
William Gaw,	-	-	"	–	27	
William Law,	-	-	"	–	26	
William Moore,	-	-	"	–	18	
John Marshall,	-	-	"	–	19	
Frederick Painter,	-	-	"	2	25	
William Spence,	-	-	"	–	25	
Robert Sims,	-	-	"	1	11	
James Stoops,	-	-	"	1	18	Or Hoops.
Charles Wright,	-	-	"	–	27	Or Right.

(For rest of this company, see publication of Pay Rolls.)

Captain Lewis Holladay's Company—Sixteenth Regiment.

NAMES.			RANK.	TIME OF SERVICE.		REMARKS.
				Months.	Days.	
Lewis Holladay,	-	-	Captain,	–	27	
John Hailey,	-	-	Sergeant,	–	27	
John Puckett,	-	-	"	–	27	
John Pulliam,	-	-	"	–	27	
John G. Lawrence,	-	-	"	–	5	Joined artillery 29th August.
James Eatherton,	-	-	Corporal,	–	9	
Thomas Andrews,	-	-	"	–	27	
Richard Pruett,	-	-	"	–	27	
Nathaniel Anderson,	-	-	Private,	–	27	
Garland Anderson,	-	-	"	–	27	
Dabney Brooks,	-	-	"	–	27	
Overton Brooks,	-	-	"	–	27	Substitute for Malcolm Hart.
William B. Coleman,	-	-	"	–	15	
Robert G. Coleman,	-	-	"	–	14	
James L. Crawford,	-	-	"	–	27	Substitute for James Eatherton.
Garland Dillard,	-	-	"	1	6	
Thomas Duerson, jr.	-	-	"	1	6	
John Eatherton,	-	-	"	–	27	
John L. Jones,	-	-	"	–	9	Substitute for Chas. W. Whitis.
Curtis Luck,	-	-	"	–	27	Substitute for Benj. Cason.
John Lewis,	-	-	"	–	27	
John Lawrence,	-	-	"	–	23	
Tarlton B. Luck,	-	-	"	–	27	
Tarlton Luck,	-	-	"	–	27	
Ira Lipscomb,	-	-	"	–	27	
George Penn,	-	-	"	–	27	
Benj. Rawlings,	-	-	"	–	27	
Samuel Ragland,	-	-	"	–	9	Substitute for David Allen.
Burnley Smith,	-	-	"	–	27	Substitute for David Allen.
Zachery Sandridge,	-	-	"	–	27	
Carey Smith,	-	-	"	–	27	
Richard Tyler,	-	-	"	1	3	
John Tyler,	-	-	"	–	27	
Callum Wigglesworth,	-	-	"	–	9	Substitute for Henry Duerson.
William Wilson,	-	-	"	–	4	Substitute for Wm. B. Coleman.
William Wrenn,	-	-	"	–	27	
Edward Wrenn,	-	-	"	–	27	
Benjamin Waller,	-	-	"	–	27	

(For rest of this company, see publication of Pay Rolls.)

MUSTER ROLL

Of Captain Joseph J. Holland's Company, attached to the Twenty-ninth Regiment, Virginia Militia, commanded by Major Joseph W. Ballard, in the Service from the 25th June to 10th July, 1813.

NAMES.	RANK.	TIME OF SERVICE.		REMARKS.
		Months.	Days.	
Joseph J. Holland, - -	Captain,	–	15	
Jones Griffin, - -	Lieutenant,	–	15	
Henry Daughtrey, - -	Ensign,	–	15	
Miles Daughtrey, - -	Sergeant,	–	15	
James N. Council, - -	"	–	15	
Solomon Darden, - -	"	–	15	
Joseph Duck, - -	"	–	15	
Edwin Daughtrey, - -	Corporal,	–	15	
David Corbit, - -	"	–	15	
Matthew Carr, - -	"	–	15	
Abraham Holland, - -	"	–	15	
Dempcy Beal, - -	Fifer,	–	15	
Jacob Beal, - -	Drummer,	–	15	
William Beal, - -	Private,	–	15	
Jacob Bradshaw, - -	"	–	15	
Britain Beal, - -	"	–	15	
Daniel Beal, - -	"	–	15	
Jacob Beal, - -	"	–	15	
Solomon Butler, - -	"	–	15	
William Brewer, - -	"	–	15	
Jeremiah Bradshaw, - -	"	–	15	
Augustus Ballard, - -	"	–	15	
William Bradshaw, - -	"	–	15	
David Carr, - -	"	–	15	
Jessee Carr, - -	"	–	15	
Benjamin Council, - -	"	–	15	
Lot. W. Corbit, - -	"	–	15	
Nathan Carr, - -	"	–	15	
John Council, - -	"	–	15	
Henry W. Corbit, - -	"	–	15	
Jessee Council, - -	"	–	15	
Shadrack Cutchins, - -	"	–	15	
Hardy Council, - -	"	–	15	
Joseph Cutchins, - -	"	–	15	
Samuel Corbill, - -	"	–	15	
Absalom Daughtry, - -	"	–	15	
Richard Daughtry, - -	"	–	15	
Joseph Fowler, - -	"	–	15	
Edmund Fowler, - -	"	–	15	
Silas Fowler, - -	"	–	15	
Jobe C. Fowler, - -	"	–	15	
Abraham Fowler, - -	"	–	15	
Miles Fowler, - -	"	–	15	
John Fowler, - -	"	–	15	
John Holland, - -	"	–	15	
Meredith Holland, - -	"	–	15	
Neverson Holland, - -	"	–	15	
Jobe Holland, - -	"	–	15	

NAMES.	RANK.	TIME OF SERVICE.		REMARKS.
		Months.	Days.	
Robert Johnson, - -	Private,	1	15	
Obland Luter, - -	"	—	15	
Andrew Lester, - -	"	—	15	
Eley Owens, - -	"	—	15	
Hardy Parker, - -	"	—	15	
John Rose, - -	"	—	15	
Samuel Vaughan, - -	"	—	15	
Beverly R. Vaughan, -	"	—	15	
Thomas West, - -	"	—	15	
William Webb, - -	"	—	15	

Captain William M. Holman's Company—Seventh Regiment.

NAMES.			RANK.	TIME OF SERVICE.		REMARKS.
				Months.	Days.	
John Crouch,	-	-	Private,	–	–	Transferred to surgical staff.
Woodson Cluff,	-	-	"	–	14	
Caleb Ellis,	-	-	"	–	7	
Thomas Gray,	-	-	"	–	–	Promoted to regimental staff.
Obadiah Jordan,	-	-	"	–	–	Robt. J. Robertson his substitute.
Josiah Leake,	-	-	"	–	–	Wm. Page his sub.
John Marstin,	-	-	"	–	14	
John McKeand,	-	-	"	–	14	
James Pace,	-	-	"			
Thomas Watkins,	-	-	"	–	12	

(For rest of this company, see publication of Pay Rolls.)

PAY ROLL

Of a Detachment of Virginia Militia, commanded by Sergeant James Holt, ordered into Service by Lieutenant Colonel William Allen, from the 24th March to 5th April, 1813.

NAMES.			RANK.	TIME OF SERVICE.		REMARKS.
				Months.	Days.	
James Holt,	-	-	Sergeant,	–	8	
Thomas Adams,	-	-	Private,	–	8	
Gray Briggs,	-	-	"	–	8	
Nathl. H. Williams,	-	-	"	–	8	
Gray E. Adams,	-	-	"	–	7	
Randolph H. Price,	-	-	"	–	3	
Mark Warren,	-	-	"	–	1	

MUSTER ROLL

Of Captain William Holt's Company, from the Twentieth Regiment, Virginia Militia. commanded by Lieutenant Colonel James Robinson, in the Service of the United States, from the 8th to 13th February, from 10th to 15th March, and from 14th to 21st September, 1813.

NAMES.			RANK.	TIME OF SERVICE.		REMARKS.
				Months.	Days.	
William Holt,	-	-	Captain,	–	19	
Horatio Woodward,	-	-	Lieutenant,	–	10	
Nathaniel Larey,	-	-	Ensign,	–	14	
Benjamin Casson,	-	-	"	–	14	
Samuel Brown,	-	-	Sergeant,	–	14	
Bartlet Jeres,	-	-	"	–	14	
Jessee Jeres,	-	-	"	–	12	
Josiah Woodward,	-	-	"	–	19	
James Williams,	-	-	"	–	7	
Joel Gisborne,	-	-	"	–	19	
Jeremiah Plummer,	-	-	Corporal,	–	12	
Philip Larey,	-	-	"	–	15	
Samuel Doughty,	-	-	"	–	5	
Samuel Hill,	-	-	"	–	7	
John W. Hays,	-	-	"	–	7	
Ferebee Stanley,	-	-	Musician,	–	12	
Josiah Bell,	-	-	Private,	–	12	
John Boult,	-	-	"	–	18	
Maxey Boult,	-	-	"	–	12	
Jonathan Bonney,	-	-	"	–	12	
Willoughby Boult,	-	-	"	–	14	
William Berry,	-	-	"	–	7	
Timothy Collins,	-	-	"	–	19	
Leek Creekmere,	-	-	"	–	15	
Fenton Cummings,	-	-	"	–	19	
Hillery Caton.	-	-	"	–	12	
James Coy,	-	-	"	–	5	
John Cummings,	-	-	"	–	12	
Southall Corbit,	-	-	"	–	7	
William Davis,	-	-	"	–	9	
Thomas Etheridge,	-	-	"	–	7	
Eden Fulford,	-	-	"	–	19	
Matthias Fisher,	-	-	"	–	12	
James Gisborne,	-	-	"	–	12	
Thomas Hanners,	-	-	"	–	19	
Samuel Hill,	-	-	"	–	12	
Jessee Hanners,	-	-	"	–	12	
Geo. Suggs,	-	-	"	–	12	
William Sarey,	-	-	"	–	12	Or Larey.
Thomas Lawrence,	-	-	"	–	3	
Ivy Larey,	-	-	"	–	14	
John Larey,	-	-	"	–	7	
Matthias Mansfield,	-	-	"	–	19	
Malachi Murden,	-	-	"	–	12	
Joel Miller,	-	-	"	–	7	
David Nelson,	-	-	"	–	12	
Thomas Nelson,	-	-	"	–	3	
Kedar Old,	-	-	"	–	19	

NAMES.	RANK.	TIME OF SERVICE.		REMARKS.
		Months.	Days.	
William Parsons, - -	Private,	–	12	
Tulley Phillips, - -	"	–	19	
Uriah Simmons, - -	"	–	12	
John Simmons, - -	"	–	15	
James Sinaca, - -	"	–	14	
John Severn, - -	"	–	7	
James Wickings, - -	"	–	19	
William Wickings, - -	"	–	19	
Solomon Wallace, - -	"	–	19	
Henry Woodward, - -	"	–	12	
Arthur Willoughby, - -	"	–	12	
Nathaniel West, - -	"	–	19	
Malachi Willis, - -	"	–	14	
John Wilhorn, - -	"	–	4	
Bartlett Jones, - -	"	–	7	
Jessee Jones, - -	"	–	7	

Captain William H. Hooe's Company—Twenty-fifth Regiment.

NAMES.	RANK.	TIME OF SERVICE.		REMARKS.
		Months.	Days.	
William H. Hooe,	Captain,	2	12	
Hezekiah Potts,	Lieutenant,	2	12	
Thomas Martin,	Ensign,	–	21	
Gabriel Peed,	Sergeant,	–	21	
John C. Short,	"	–	21	
Bennet Price,	"	2	11	
Cossem Bennett,	"	2	12	
Geo. Bennett,	"	2	12	
William Bryan,	"	–	12	
Reubin Owens,	"	–	12	
Spencer Miller,	"	–	12	
Samuel Rollins, jr.	"	–	12	
Newton Jett,	Corporal,	–	12	
John A. Hodge,	"	2	12	
James D. Bryan,	"	1	23	
William J. Helm,	"	1	26	
Austin Suttle,	"	1	10	
Thos. Taylor,	"	–	12	
Robert Minnis,	Musician,	1	26	
Ire Fletcher,	"	1	20	
Robert Alsop,	Private,	2	12	
Henry Allensworth,	"	–	28	
William Armstrong,	"	–	12	
John Alsop,	"	–	12	
John Bachus,	"	2	12	
Jeremiah Bailey,	"	–	12	
Geo. Bennet,	"	–	12	
John Boyd,	"	–	8	
William Coakley,	"	1	5	
Geo. Chiveral,	"	2	2	
Geo. Chrismond,	"	2	12	
Robert Chesley,	"	2	12	
Geo. Coakley,	"	–	29	
Townshend Caver,	"	2	12	
Miles Clift,	"	2	12	
Reuben Caul,	"	2	12	
Reuben Dye,	"	1	7	
Cadwalider S. Dade,	"	1	13	Deserted.
Townshend Dade,	"	–	29	Robt. Minnis his sub. from 1st August.
James Dodd, jr.	"	1	10	
Philip Dishman,	"	–	12	
James Deatley,	"	–	12	
Nathaniel Fox,	"	–	11	
Geo. N. Grymes,	"	2	12	
Nehemiah Holland,	"	–	7	
William Humphreys,	"	2	12	
John Humphreys,	"	2	12	
Charles A. Harrow,	"	2	12	Commandant of a boat guard.
Thomas Humphries,	"	2	12	Qr. Mas. Sergeant.
Jessee Humphreys,	"	–	12	
John Hilton,	"	–	12	
Samuel Humphreys,	"	–	8	

NAMES.	RANK.	TIME OF SERVICE.		REMARKS.
		Months.	Days.	
John Jones, sr. - -	Private,	1	14	Boat Guard.
Geo. Jones, - -	"	1	8	
Thos. Jackson, - -	"	2	12	
Newton Jett, - -	"	1	2	Boat Guard.
William M. King, - -	"	–	1	
Dangerfield Lewis, - -	"	2	12	
William H. Levi, - -	"	1	10	Boat Guard.
Henry Musten, - -	"	2	11	
William N. Massey, - -	"	1	10	
William McDaniel, - -	"	1	2	Boat Guard.
Robert Massey, - -	"	–	12	
William Owens, - -	"	2	10	
William Purchase, - -	"	2	12	
John Purchase, - -	"	2	12	
John H. Peyton, - -	"	–	7	
Richard Potts, jr. - -	"	1	2	
William Quesenberry, -	"	–	12	
Cornelius Reynolds, - -	"	1	2	Boat Guard.
Henry Rollings, - -	"	2	11	
Samuel Rollings, - -	"	1	2	
William Rose, sr. - -	"	–	12	
Geo. Rogers, - -	"	–	12	
William M. Rollings, - -	"	–	12	
Samuel Reynolds, - -	"	–	12	
Henry Rose, - -	"	–	12	
James Rollings, jr. - -	"	–	12	
Benjamin Sedwrick, - -	"	2	12	
William Scrivner, - -	"	2	11	
Richard Stuart, - -	"	2	11	Jerem'h. Butler his sub.
Jacob W. Stuart, - -	"	2	12	Boat Guard.
John Stith, - -	"	1	22	Deserted.
Thomas Ship, - -	"	–	27	
Henry Stuart, - -	"	–	27	
Robert Scott, - -	"	–	12	
William B. Stuart, - -	"	–	12	
John Trunnels, - -	"	–	27	
William Trunnels, - -	"	–	27	
Henry Turner, - -	"	–	27	
Asa Truslow, - -	"	–	27	
Langhorn Taylor, - -	"	–	12	
William Vaughan, - -	"	–	6	
Marshall Wilkerson, - -	"	1	24	
Needham L. Washington, -	"	–	27	
Henry Williams, - -	"	–	11	

(For rest of this company, see publication of Pay Rolls.)

Captain Armistead Hoomes' Company.

NAMES.	RANK.	TIME OF SERVICE.		REMARKS.
		Months.	Days.	
William Hoomes, - -	Private,	1		

(For rest of this company, see publication of Pay Rolls.)

Captain William Harrison's Company—First Regiment.

NAMES.			RANK.	TIME OF SERVICE.		REMARKS.
				Months.	Days.	
Lunsford Broaddus,	-	-	Ensign,	–	9	
Henry Philips,	-	-	Sergeant,	–	9	
Henry Dunn,	-	-	"	–	9	
Elias Taylor,	-	-	"	–	9	
John Cole,	-	-	"	–	9	
Robert Smithers,	-	-	Corporal,	–	9	
John Page,	-	-	"	–	9	
Willis Kidd,	-	-	"	–	9	
Reuben Sorrel,	-	-	"	–	9	
James Bell,	-	-	Private,	–	9	
Edmund Cecil,	-	-	"	–	9	
Larkin Duling,	-	-	"	–	9	
Edmond Goleman,	-	-	"	–	9	
Mefrom Garnet,	-	-	"	–	9	
William Harrison,	-	-	"	–	9	
John Houston,	-	-	"	–	9	
William Jones,	-	-	"	–	9	
John Key,	-	-	"	–	9	
Barnett Moore,	-	-	"	–	9	
Coleman Pitts,	-	-	"	–	9	
Robert Pitts,	-	-	"	–	9	
James Sthreshley,	-	-	"	–	9	
Thomas Sthreshley,	-	-	"	–	9	
William Sthreshley,	-	-	"	–	9	
Benjamin Seal,	-	-	"	–	9	
Hiram Sorrel,	-	-	"	–	9	
Geo. Trout,	-	-	"	2	20	

(For rest of this company, see publication of Pay Rolls.)

MUSTER ROLL

Of Captain Thomas C. Hoome's Company of Artillery, attached to the Ninth Regiment, Virginia Militia, commanded by Lieut. Col. William Boyd, in the Service from the 3d to 10th December, 1814.

NAMES.	RANK.	TIME OF SERVICE.		REMARKS.
		Months.	Days.	
Thomas C. Hoomes, - -	Captain,	–	8	
Arch'd R. Harwood, - -	1st Lieutenant,	–	8	
James Gresham, - -	2d "	–	8	
Francis Row, - -	1st Sergeant,	–	8	
Dudley Diggs, - -	2d "	–	8	
Jacob D. Warker, - -	3d "	–	8	
William Walden, - -	4th "	–	8	
Geo. C. Jeffries, - -	1st Corporal,	–	8	
William Eubank, - -	2d "	–	8	
Adelard Barrot, - -	3d "	–	8	
E. G. Brushwood, - -	4th "	–	8	
William Pines, -	Fifer,	–	8	
Peter Albright, - -	Private,	–	8	
Henry Barton, - -	"	–	8	
Arch'd R. Burton, - -	"	–	8	
Thos. Bulman, - -	"	–	8	
Campbell Burton, - -	"	–	8	
Sterling Carr, - -	"	–	7	
Charles Collier, - -	"	–	8	
Thos. G. Crittenden, - -	"	–	8	
Leonard Carlton, - -	"	–	8	
Thomas Carlton, - -	"	–	8	
Geo. Crane, - -	"	–	8	
Thomas S. Carlton, - -	"	–	8	
Geo. Carlton, - -	"	–	8	
John Carlton, - -	"	–	8	
William Carlton, - -	"	–	8	
Christoph Eubank, - -	"	–	8	
John Eubank, - -	"	–	8	
Thomas Fleming, - -	"	–	8	
Robt. Griffith, - -	"	–	8	
Thos. Hugget, - -	"	–	8	
Thos. Heningway, - -	"	–	8	
Arch'd C. Hoskins, - -	"	–	7	
Ambrose Jackson, - -	"	–	8	
John Leigh, - -	"	–	8	
James Mitchell, - -	"	–	8	
William Morris, - -	"	–	8	
Thomas Milby, - -	"	–	8	
Alexander P. Muse, - -	"	–	7	
John Milby, - -	"	–	8	
James Muire, - -	"	–	8	
John Orrill, - -	"	–	8	
Philip B. Pendleton, - -	"	–	8	
Thomas Pemberton, - -	"	–	8	
John Roane, - -	"	–	8	
Leonard Richeson, - -	"	–	8	
Spencer Roane, - -	"	–	8	

NAMES.	RANK.	TIME OF SERVICE.		REMARKS.
		Months.	Days.	
Leonard Richerson, - -	Private,	–	8	
Larkin Smith, - -	"	–	8	
Robert Trice, - -	"	–	8	
Benj. Thruston, - -	"	–	8	
Richard Walden, - -	"	–	8	
John J. Willis, - -	"	–	8	

MUSTER ROLL

Of Captain Thomas Hoskins' Company, from the Ninth Regiment, Virginia Militia, commanded by Lieutenant Colonel William Boyd, in the Service from the 7th to 17th April, 1813, and from 2d to 10th December, 1814.

NAMES.	RANK.	TIME OF SERVICE.		REMARKS.
		Months.	Days.	
Thomas Hoskins, - -	Captain,	–	20	
Geo. Wyatt, - -	Lieutenant,	–	10	
Geo. Hoskins, - -	Ensign,	–	10	
Hugh Campell, - -	"	–	20	
Geo. Buckner, - -	Sergeant,	–	10	
Leonard Wortham, - -	"	–	10	
Edmond Smithey, - -	"	–	10	
Richard Perryman, - -	"	–	10	
William H. Roane, - -	"	–	10	
John Smith, - -	"	–	10	
Lewis Bucker, - -	Corporal,	–	20	
Anderson Scott, - -	"	–	10	
James Steward, - -	"	–	10	
Charles Southall, - -	"	–	10	
William K. Stuart, - -	"	–	10	
Henry Cooke, - -	"	–	10	
Thomas Atkins, - -	Private,	–	19	
Gabriel Alexander, - -	"	–	10	
William Allen, - -	"	–	9	
Joseph Allen, - -	"	–	9	
Clayton Atkins, - -	"	–	9	
William Broach, - -	"	–	10	
James Barstul, - -	"	–	10	
Richard Brown, - -	"	–	10	
Andrew Broach, - -	"	–	10	
Benjamin Coftin, - -	"	–	10	
Ludy Cauthorn, - -	"	–	20	
Giles Cooke, - -	"	–	9	
Isaac Duling, - -	"	–	9	
John Edwards, - -	"	–	10	
Pitman Fodler, - -	"	–	10	
John Gatewood, - -	"	–	10	
William Gatewood, - -	"	–	10	
John Griffith, - -	"	–	10	
Thomas Street Green, -	"	–	9	
William A. Garnett, - -	"	–	9	
Thomas Howell, - -	"	–	18	
Thomas Hill, - -	"	–	18	
Joseph Hiskew, - -	"	–	10	
William T. Jones, - -	"	–	10	
Daniel Longest, - -	"	–	10	
Lindsey Longest, - -	"	–	8	
Robert Lumpkin, - -	"	–	10	
Geo. Marshall, - -	"	–	6	
Laban Martin, - -	"	–	2	
Leroy Martin, - -	"	–	2	
Archibald Norris, - -	"	–	8	
Edmund Perryman, - -	"	–	8	

NAMES.			RANK.	TIME OF SERVICE.		REMARKS.
				Months.	Days.	
Lewis Phillip,	-	-	Private,	—	20	
Layton Prince,	-	-	"	—	8	
Phillip Prince,	-	-	"	—	10	
James Prince,	-	-	"	—	10	
James H. Prince,	-	-	"	—	10	
Henry Robertson,	-	-	"	—	10	
George Saunders,	-	-	"	—	10	
Gouldman Smithey,	-	-	"	—	10	
Phillip Sorrell,	-	-	"	—	8	
Edmund Taylor,	-	-	"	—	8	
Henry Taylor,	-	-	"	—	10	
William Tinsbloom,	-	-	"	—	5	
Robert Wilson,	-	-	"	—	18	
Phillip Watkins,	-	-	"	—	8	
William A. Wright,	-	-	"	—	10	
Richard Whiting,	-	-	"	—	10	
Anderson Wilson,	-	-	"	—	10	
Leroy Wilson,	-	-	"	—	10	
Samuel Wilson,	-	-	"	—	10	
Reuben Wilson,	-	-	"	—	10	
Charles Wray,	-	-	"	—	10	
James Owens,	-	-	"	—	10	

Captain Henry Howard's Company—One Hundred and Fifteenth Regiment.

NAMES.	RANK.	TIME OF SERVICE.		REMARKS.
		Months.	Days.	
Henry Howard, - -	Captain,	–	16	
William Langhorne, -	Lieutenant,	–	4	
Robert Shield, - -	"	–	12	
Robert Shield, jr. -	Ensign,	–	12	
John Moreland, - -	Sergeant,	–	16	
Edm'd Curtis, - -	"	–	12	
Edw'd Wright, - -	"	–	12	
Lewis Charles, - -	"	–	12	
James Smith, - -	Corporal,	–	12	
Henry Smith, - -	"	–	12	
William Moss, - -	"	–	12	
John Moss, - -	"	–	4	Joined Capt. Cooper's
		–		troop July 1st, 1813.
Robert Lee, - -	"	–	4	
Charles Philips, - -	"	–	4	
Charles Paul, - -	Drummer,	–	4	
John Gay, - -	Fifer,	–	4	
William Powell, - -	Drummer,	–	12	
William Wood, - -	Fifer,	–	12	
Smith Aymes, - -	Private,	–	4	
William Blackburn, -	"	–	4	
Jacob Bailey, - -	"	–	12	
Leroy Beacham, - -	"	–	4	
Quarles Bohanon, -	"	–	12	
James Bohannan, -	"	–	19	Belongs to Capt. Pres-
		–		sey's company.
Thomas Belvin, - -	"	–	12	
Robert Belvin, - -	"	–	12	
John Bennett, - -	"	–	12	
Thomas Chisman, -	"	–	10	
Joshua Cox, - -	"	–	9	
Joel Cox, - -	"	–	12	
Geo. Cooper, - -	"	–	12	
William Cook, - -	"	–	12	
Kemp Charles, - -	"	–	12	
Absalom Cox, - -	"	–	4	
Henry Drewry, - -	"	–	4	
Robert Dunn, · -	"	–	4	
Dolphin Drewry, -	"	–	4	
Seaton Elliott, - -	"	–	12	
Jonathan Frazer, -	"	–	4	
William Fox, - -	"	–	12	
Edward Gisburn, -	"	–	4	
Joseph Hopkins, -	"	–	16	
James Hogg, - -	"	–	16	
James Hopkins, - -	"	–	4	
Thomas Harwood, -	"	–	4	
Humphrey Harwood,	"	–	4	
John Hogg, sen. -	"	–	12	
John Hogg, jr. - -	"	–	12	
William Howard, -	"	–	12	
Matthias Insby, - -	"	–	4	
Willo'y Jordan, - -	"	–	12	
Nath'l Insley, - -	"	–	4	

NAMES.	RANK.	TIME OF SERVICE.		REMARKS.
		Months.	Days.	
William Jinkins, - -	Private,	—	12	
Miles Lebbee, - -	"	—	12	
Solomon Marshall, - -	"	—	12	
George Middleton, - -	"	—	19	Substitute for Joseph
	"	—		Bushel.
Samuel McIntosh, - -	"	—	4	
Robert Melson, - -	"	—	4	
John Moore, - -	"	—	4	
William Morris, - -	"	—	4	
Joseph Nottingham, - -	"	—	4	
William Notts, - -	"	—	12	
Edm'd C. Patrick, - -	"	—	12	
James Prasson, - -	"	—	12	
John Perrin, - -	"	—	4	
Walter Patrick, - -	"	—	4	
William Philips, - -	"	—	4	
Davidson Provoo, - -	"	—	4	
John A. Rogers, - -	"	—	12	
Thomas Rowe, - -	"	—	12	
James Stroad, - -	"	—	12	
Thomas Stroad, - -	"	—	12	
William Stacy, - -	"	—	12	
John Stacy, - -	"	—	12	
Levin Smith, - -	"	—	12	
William Stakes, - -	"	—	4	
Geo. W. R. Sneed, - -	"	—	12	
William Tabb. - -	"	—	12	
William Wood, - -	"	—	12	
Nelson Wright, - -	"	—	13	
John Wright, - -	"	—	12	
Edw'd Wright, jr. - -	"	—	12	
Matt. Wood, - -	"	—	4	
John Wronton, - -	"	—	4	

(For rest of this company, see publication of Pay Rolls.)

MUSTER ROLL

Of Captain Alexander Howison's Company, from the Thirty-Sixth Regiment, Virginia Militia, commanded by Colonel Enoch Renoe, in the Service from the 21st to 26th July, 1813, from 31st July to 7th August, and from 24th to 30th August, 1814.

NAMES.	RANK.	TIME OF SERVICE.		REMARKS.
		Months.	Days.	
Alexander Howison,	Captain,	–	20	
William Brundige,	Lieutenant,	–	6	
Travers Davis,	"	–	6	
Benjamin Cannon,	Ensign,	–	6	
Phillip Langfit,	"	–	6	
Daniel Grant,	Sergeant,	–	8	
Joseph B. Lunebough,	"	–	8	
Charles Rennoe,	"	–	4	
James D. Boughanan,	"	–	8	
John Webster,	"	–	6	
William Allen,	"	–	6	
John Bland,	"	–	6	
Thomas Burroughs,	"	–	6	
John Lynn,	"	–	6	
James Arnold,	"	–	6	
Vincent Calvent,	"	–	6	
William Phillips,	Corporal,	–	8	
John Bridwill,	"	–	8	
John S. Harrison,	"	–	8	
James Jourdan,	"	–	8	
Geo. Boswell,	"	–	6	
William Dowell,	"	–	6	
Allison Johnston,	"	–	6	
Thomas Molair,	"	–	6	
Thomas Able,	Private,	–	14	
James Able,	"	–	14	
Richard Allen,	"	–	14	
Thomas Addams,	"	–	14	
John Arnold,	"	–	14	
Larkin Arrington,	"	–	6	Joined the cavalry.
Moses Arnold,	"	–	6	
Leroy Athy,	"	–	6	
Geo. Appleby,	"	–	12	
Washburn Arrington,	"	–	6	
Sandford Anderson,	"	–	6	
James Allen,	"	–	6	
Horatio Athey,	"	–	6	
John Athey,	"	–	6	
Rowland Bates,	"	–	8	
Henry Brawner,	"	–	8	Sub. for W. F. Moore
Fantly Ball,	"	–	14	Sub. for Aug. Ball.
Doctor John Bronaugh,	"	–	8	
William S. Parker,	"	–	6	
John Brammel,	"	–	6	
Thomas Burroughs,	"	–	6	
Seth Brawner,	"	–	6	
Joseph Brawner,	"	–	6	
William Carter,	"	–	8	

NAMES.	RANK.	TIME OF SERVICE.		REMARKS.
		Months.	Days.	
Geo. Cornwell, - -	Private,	–	14	
William Cornwell, - -	"	–	20	
James Carter, - -	"	–	8	
William Calvert, - -	"	–	8	
Peter Cockrell, - -	"	–	14	
Alexander Chick, - -	"	–	8	
Nimrod Carr, - -	"	–	14	Substitut'd himself previous to this call.
David Carter, - -	"	–	8	Sub. for Jas. Smith.
John Cornwell, - -	"	–	6	
Peyton Calvert, - -	"	–	6	
Bland Currie, - -	"	–	6	
Harrison Cornwell, - -	"	–	6	
Richard Calvert, - -	"	–	6	
Geo. Crosby, - -	"	–	6	
Willis Chicks, - -	"	–	6	
James Chicks. - -	"	–	6	
Jessee Dowell, - -	"	–	8	
John Disney, - -	"	–	8	
Jessee Davis. - -	"	–	8	
Walter Dodson, - -	"	–	14	
Presley Davis, - -	"	–	8	Sub. for Seth Brown.
Walter Davis, - -	"	–	8	
William Davis, - -	"	–	8	
John P. Duvall, - -	"	–	6	
William H. Duvall, - -	"	–	6	
Geo. Duvall. - -	"	–	6	
John B. Davis, - -	"	–	6	
Nathaniel Ellicot, - -	"	–	8	
John English. - -	"	–	6	
Alfred Ewell, - -	"	–	6	Joined the cavalry.
James Epps, - -	"	–	6	
William Foxworthy, - -	"	–	8	
Edmond Fair, - -	"	–	8	
Harrison Fox, - -	"	–	6	
Michael Floudy, - -	"	–	6	Or Floridy.
John Goslin, - -	"	–	8	Substitute for William Selickman.
Townley Guy, - -	"	–	8	
Charles Guy, - -	"	–	8	
Culthbert Harrison, - -	"	–	8	
Corbin Hall, - -	"	–	8	
John Hancock, - -	"	–	14	
Thomas Homes, - -	"	–	8	
John Harrison, - -	'	–	6	
William Harris, - -	"	–	6	
James Hopwood, - -	"	–	6	
Stephen Harrison, - -	"	–	6	
Rhodam Henry, - -	"	–	6	
Richard Johnston, - -	"	–	6	
Fielding Jewill, - -	"	–	8	
Jacob Janny, - -	"	–	8	
James Keys, - -	"	–	8	
Michael Koon, - -	"	–	8	
Geo. Kees, - -	"	–	8	
Thomas Keys, - -	"	–	6	
William King, - -	"	–	6	
Elias King, - -	"	–	6	
Richard Lee, - -	"	–	8	
Michael Lennox, - -	"	–	8	Substitute for Stephen Howison.
William Martin, - -	"	–	8	
Ignatious Milsted, - -	"	–	8	
Geo. Maddox, - -	"	–	8	Sub. for D. Davis.

NAMES.	RANK.	TIME OF SERVICE.		REMARKS.
		Months.	Days.	
Walter Maddox,	Private,	–	6	
Elias McCuin,	"	–	6	
Thomas McQueen,	"	–	6	
Thomas Nelson,	"	–	14	
Geo. Norman,	"	–	8	
Thomas Pearson,	"	–	6	
William Patterson, jr.	"	–	14	
Richard Pell,	"	–	6	
Jessee Pilcher,	"	–	6	
William Patterson, sr.	"	–	6	
William Pierson,	"	–	6	
Hugh Petty,	"	–	14	
William Purnel,	"	–	8	
John Patterson,	"	–	8	
John Pinson,	"	–	8	
Alexander Pattison,	"	–	8	
Travis Payne,	"	–	8	
Cumberland Pinson,	"	–	8	Sub. for Wm. Pinson.
Madden Rennoe,	"	–	14	
Arthur S. Robinson,	"	–	8	
William Robey,	"	–	8	
Jacob Rolls,	"	–	6	
Geo. Renoe,	"	–	6	
James Rison,	"	–	6	
John Smith,	"	–	8	
Townley Smith,	"	–	14	
William Smith,	"	–	8	
James Smith,	"	–	14	
Larkin Strawther,	"	–	8	
James Scott,	"	–	6	
Raleigh Spinks,	"	–	6	
Charles Shaw,	"	–	6	
Jessee Sincoks,	"	–	6	
Peter Trone,	"	–	6	Joined the cavalry.
Henry Tasker,	"	–	8	
Thomas Tebbs,	"	–	8	Appointed surgeon's mate, transferred to the staff.
Joseph Tyler,	"	–	8	
David Willet,	"	–	8	Sub. for John Willet.
Geo. Woodward,	"	–	8	
Phillip Wurchoof,	"	–	8	
Randolph Welch,	"	–	8	
Thomas West,	"	–	6	
Henry West,	"	–	6	
Zachariah Winne,	"	–	8	Sub. for John Britain.
Geo. Britain,	"	–	8	
Uriah Bell,	"	–	8	Sub. for D. Larkin.
Thomas Bouroughs,	"	–	8	
Elijah Campell,	"	–	8	Substitute for Moses Cockrell.
Jonathan Campbell,	"	–	8	
Josiah Copen,	"	–	8	Substitute for John F. Jackson.
John Franklin,	"	–	8	
Elijah Fryer,	"	–	8	
William Graham,	"	–	8	
William Gardiner,	"	–	8	Sub. for D. Cannon.
James Hope,	"	–	8	
John Hill,	"	–	8	
William Hope,	"	–	8	Sub for Joshua Huff.
Thomas Huff,	"	–	8	
James Keach,	"	–	8	
John King,	"	–	8	

NAMES.			RANK.	TIME OF SERVICE.		REMARKS.
				Months.	Days.	
Henry Langfit,	-	-	Private,	–	8	
James Mason,	-	-	"	–	8	
Thomas Mason,	-	-	"	–	8	
Charles Ogden,	-	-	"	–	8	
Richard Payne,	-	-	"	–	8	
Martin Robertson,	-	-	"	–	8	
William Riley,	-	-	"	–	8	
David Ramie,	-	-	"	–	8	
James Roach,	-	-	"	–	8	
William Larkin,	-	-	"		8	

MUSTER ROLL

Of Captain James Hubbard's Company, of Sixty-eighth Regiment.

NAMES.			RANK.	TIME OF SERVICE.		REMARKS.
				Months.	Days.	
James Hubbard,	-	-	Captain,	–	19	
Philmer Clarke,	-	-	Lieutenant,	–	19	
Will. Whitaker,	-	-	"	–	19	
William Williams,	-	-	Sergeant,	–	19	
Robert Hawkins,	-	-	"	–	19	
Thos. Thomas,	-	-	"	–	19	
Bennett Kirby,	-	-	"	–	19	
John Patterson,	-	-	Corporal,	–	19	
Thomas Jones,	-	-	"	–	19	
James Hayes,	-	-	"		19	
R. Hubberd,	-	-	"	–	19	
John Anderson,	-	-	Drummer,	1	7	
Dick,	-	-	-	"	–	22	
Robert Baptist,	-	-	Private,	1	10	
William Bryan,	-	-	"	–	19	
George Boothe,	-	-	"	–	19	
William Buffin,	-	-	"	–	19	
John Boothe,	-	-	"	–	19	
Aaron Brown,	-	-	"	–	19	
Lewis Brown,	-	-	"	–	19	
Gabriel Boothe,	-	-	"	–	19	
George Bristol,	-	-	"			
Hays Burcher,	-	-	"	–	18	
John Cowan,	-	-	"	–	19	
A. Chapman,	-	-	"	–	19	
Thomas Chisman,	-	-	"	–	21	
Will. Dixon,	-	-	"	–	19	
James Fenton,	-	-	"	–	19	
Leroy Fernoeth,	-	-	"			
Reuben Graves,	-	-	"	–	19	
John Gatley,	-	-	"	–	19	
James Gray,	-	-	"	–	19	
Thomas Gayle,	-	-	"			
Charles Hubbard,	-	-	"	–	19	
H. Hubbard,	-	-	"	–	19	
Thomas Hughs,	-	-	"	–	19	
Ben. Hansford,	-	-	"	–	19	
Wm. Hubbard,	-	-	"	–	19	
Charles Hansford,	-	-	"	–	19	
J. W. Hubbard,	-	-	"	–	19	
James Hay,	-	-	"	–	21	
John Hansford,	-	-	"	–	21	
Robert Jackson,	-	-	"	–	19	
John D. Johnson,	-	-	"	1	7	
Row. Jones,	-	-	"	–	19	
James Kerr,	-	-	"	–	19	
Joshua Lester,	-	-	"	–	19	
William Lewis,	-	-	"	1	10	
Robert Larke,	-	-	"	–	19	
James Lebby,	-	-	"	–	21	

NAMES.			RANK.	TIME OF SERVICE.		REMARKS.
				Months.	Days.	
John Moore,	-	-	Private,			
Charles Moore,	-	-	"		19	
H. S. Nance,	-	-	"	–	19	
Thos. Orill,	-	-	"	–	19	
James Proove, jr.	-	-	"	–	19	
James Proove, sen.	-	-	"	–	19	
Daniel Pointer,	-	-	"	1	7	
Thomas Pointer,	-	-	"	1	7	
Francis Peters,	-	-	"	–	19	
Thomas Fresson,	-	-	"	–	19	
John Roe,	-	-	"	–	19	
Jacob Roe,	-	-	"	–	19	
Gid'n Ratchliffe,	-	-	"	–	19	
Geo. Roper,	-	-	"	–	19	
James Roane,	-	-	"	–	19	
Jas. Sullivan,	-	-	"	–	19	
John Stokes,	-	-	"	–	18	
John D. Smith,	-	-	"	1	9	
James Selby,	-	-	"	–	19	
James Taylor,	-	-	"	–	19	
William D. Taylor,	-	-	"			
Thomas Valentine,	-	-	"			
John Vale,	-	-	"	–	19	
James Wair,	-	-	"	–	19	
Thomas Wade,	-	-	"	–	19	
				–	19	

(For rest of this company, see publication of Pay Rolls.)

Captain William Hudnall's Company—Thirty-seventh Regiment.

NAMES.			RANK.	TIME OF SERVICE.		REMARKS.
				Months.	Days.	
James Brown,	-	-	Private,	–	3	
John Bryan,			"	–	10	
Thos. Dozier,	-	-	"	–	6	
John Davis,	-	-	"	1	13	
William Edwards,	-	-	"	–	6	
William France,	-	-	"	–	6	
Warner Hudnall,	-	-	"	–	4	
Charles Haydon,	-	-	"	–	1	
William Hill,	-	-	"	–	12	
Willis Ingram,	-	-	"	–	6	
George Jones,	-	-	"	–	8	
Andrew J. Khrom,	-	-	"	–	1	
Henry Low,	-	-	"	–	6	
Royston Marsh,	-	-	"	–	16	
Collin Nutt,	-	-	"	–	28	
Cyrus Pitman,	-	-	"	–	1	
George Rains,	-	-	"	–	7	
Thos. Rains,	-	-	"	–	1	
Wm. Revere,	-	-	"	–	18	
Thomas L. Sydnor,	-	-	"	–	5	
George Swanson,	-	-	"	–	20	
Vincent Thomas,	-	-	"	–	8	
George Thomas,	-	-	"	–	8	
Richard Waide,	-	-	"	–	3	

(For rest of this company, see publication of Pay Rolls.)

Captain Gabriel Hughes' Company—Sixty-first Regiment.

NAMES.	RANK.	TIME OF SERVICE.		REMARKS.
		Months.	Days.	
Josiah Foster, - -	Sergeant,	–	3	
Cyrus B. James, - -	"	–	11	On detachment from Capt. Jarvis' co.
Thomas Eddins, sen'r, -	"	–	11	On detach't from Capt. L. B. Eddins' co.
William March, - -	"	–	11	On detachment from Capt. B. Digges' co.
Gabriel Miller, -	"	–	10	On detachment from Capt. B. Digges' co.
William Foster, - -	"	–	10	On detach'; from Capt. H. W. Sales's co.
George Culley, - -	"	–	10	On detachment from Capt. T. James' co.
James Jarvis, - -	"	–	10	On detachment from Capt. P. Foster's co.
John Knight, - -	"	–	10	On detachment from Capt. J. Billups' co.
William Powell, - -	Corporal,	–	10	On detachment from Capt. C. Lewis' co.
Beverley H. Yates, - -	"	–	10	On detach't from Capt. H. W. Sales' co.
George Brooks, - -	"	–	10	On detachment from Capt. B. Digges' co.
Spencer Brown, - -	"	–	10	On detachment from Capt. T. James' co.
James Davis, - -	"	–	8	On detachment from Capt. F. Jarvis' co.
Thomas Eddins, - -	"	–	10	On detachment from Capt. J. Billups' co.
James Parrish, - -	"	–	10	On detachment from Capt. F. Foster's co.
Cary James, - -	Drummer,	–	16	
James Armistead, - -	Private,	–	2	
Francis Armistead, - -	"	–	9	
Isaac Armistead, - -	"	–	8	On detachment from Capt. F. Jarvis' co.
Isaac Ayres, - -	"	–	6	
Robert Armistead, sen'r. -	"	–	8	On detachment from Capt. F. Jarvis' co.
John Brownly, - -	"	–	11	
George K. Brooks, - -	"	–	11	
John Bassett, - -	"	–	16	
John Brownley, - -	"	–	10	On detachment from Capt. F. Foster's co.
Joseph Brownley, - -	"	–	8	On detachment from Capt. F. Jarvis' co.
William Brownley, - -	"	–	10	On detachment from Capt. B. Digges' co.
John Brownley, - -	"	–	10	On detachment from Capt. J. Billups' co.

NAMES.	RANK.	TIME OF SERVICE.		REMARKS.
		Months.	Days.	
William Brooks, - -	Private,	–	10	On detachment from Capt. B. Digges' co.
Jacob Blake, - -	"	–	1	
Joshua Banks, - -	"	1	18	
John Callis, - -	"	–	10	
Ambrose Callis, - -	"	–	10	On detachment from Capt. B. Digges' co.
Richard Cray, - -	"	–	10	On detachment from Capt. P. Foster's co.
Anthony Digges, - -	"	–	11	
William Davis, - -	"	–	10	On detachment from Capt. T. James' co.
Samuel Digges, - -	"	–	10	On detachment from Capt. T. James' co.
Thomas Dawson, - -	"	–	10	On detachment from Capt. F. Foster's co.
Tinly Dixon, - -	"	–	10	On detachment from Capt. F. Foster's co.
Humphrey Davis, - -	"	–	8	On detachment from Capt. F. Jarvis' co.
Christopher Davis, -	"	–	8	On detachment from Capt. F. Jarvis' co.
Joel Digges, - -	"	–	10	On detachment from Capt. B. Digges' co.
Job Digges, - -	"	–	10	On detachment from Capt. B. Digges' co.
Augustine Digges, -	"	–	10	On detachment from Capt. B. Digges' co.
William Dance, - -	"	–	10	On detachment from Capt. Sales' co.
William Dunbar, -	"	–	11	On detachment from Capt. Sales' co.
Michael Drisgale, -	"	–	10	On detachment from Capt. Sales' co.
Thomas Eaton, - -	"	–	10	On detachment from Capt. Sales' co.
Josiah Foster, - -	"	–	12	
John D. Fitchett, - -	"	–	7	
George Forrest, - -	"	–	4	
Matt. Forrest, - -	"	–	10	On detachment from Capt. T. James' co.
Philip Forrest, - -	"	–	10	On detachment from Capt. T. James' co.
Edm'd Forrest, - -	"	–	10	On detachment from Capt. B. Digges' co.
Thos. Fitchett, - -	"	–	10	On detachment from Capt. J. Billups' co.
Bailey Foster, - -	"	–	10	On detachment from Capt. J. Billups' co.
George Forrest, - -	"	–	10	On detachment from Capt. J. Billups' co.
George Forrest, sr. -	"	–	10	On detachment from Capt. J. Billups' co.
Jesse Forrest, - -	"	–	10	On detachment from Capt. J. Billups' co.
Salathiel Fitchett, -	"	–	10	On detachment from Capt. Sales' co.
Robert Gibson, - -	"	–	10	On detachment from Capt. Sales' co.
William Hudgin, - -	"	–	11	
Gabriel Hudgin, - -	"	–	11	
William Hobday, - -	"	–	10	

NAMES.	RANK.	TIME OF SERVICE.		REMARKS.
		Months.	Days.	
William Hundley, - -	Private,	—	16	
Bailey Hudgin, - -	"	—	10	On detachment from Capt. James' co.
John W. Hudgin, - -	"	—	10	On detachment from Capt. B. Digges' co.
Daniel Hickman, -	"	—	10	On detachment from Capt. J. Billups' co.
Edward Hurst, -	"	—	10	
Isaac Hudgin, - -	"	—	11	
Matthew Hanley, - -	"	—	22	
James Hudgin, - -	"	—	11	
Thomas Hughett, -	"	—	10	
John Jarvis, - -	"	—	4	
Richard James, - -	"	—	3	
Robert Lewis, - -	"	—	4	
Elijah Linton, - -	"	—	10	On detachment from Capt. B. Digges' co.
Richard Morgan, -	"	—	10	On detachment from Capt. P. Foster's co.
William Minter. - -	"	—	10	On detachment from Capt. B. Digges' co.
Thomas Newbern, -	"	—	3	
William Owen, - -	"	—	11	
Thomas Owen. - -	"	—	8	
William Oven. - -	"	—	10	On detachment from Capt. B. Digges' co.
Thomas Oven. - -	"	—	10	On detachment from Capt. B. Digges' co.
Levy Oven. -	"	—	10	On detachment from Capt. B. Digges' co.
George Oven, -	"	—	10	On detachment from Capt. J. Billups' co.
Elias Pugh. - -	"	—	11	
Caleb Peed, - -	"	—	10	
Ransome Parrott, -	"	—	20	
John Plummer, -	"	—	9	
William Ripley, -	"	—	11	
William Ripley, -	"	—	8	On detachment from Capt. F. Jarvis' co.
John Ripley, -	"	—	11	
Armistead Smith, -	"	—	2	
Robert Sampson. -	"	—	11	
Anthony Smith. -	"	—	10	
William Simmons, -	"	1	8	
John Singleton. -	"	—	8	On detachment from Capt. F. Jarvis' co.
John Scott, -	"	—	8	On detachment from Capt. F. Jarvis' co.
Isaac Sadler, -	"	—	10	On detachment from Capt. J. Billups' co.
Joshua Smith. -	"	—	10	On detachment from Capt. J. Billups' co.
Seymour Shackleford, -	"	—	10	On detachment from Capt. Sales' co.
Robert Sampson, -	"	—	10	On detachment from Capt. Sales' co.
Edward Sadler, -	"	—	8	On detachment from Capt. Sales' co.
Armistead Thomas, -	"	—	8	On detachment from Capt. Jarvis' co.
Simon B. Terrier, -	"	—	10	On detachment from Capt. Sales' co.

NAMES.			RANK.	TIME OF SERVICE.		REMARKS.
				Months.	Days.	
Thomas Tabour,	-	-	Private,	–	10	On detachment from Capt. Billups' co.
Francis Williams,	-	-	"	–	10	On detachment from Capt. James' co.
Dudley White,	-	-	"	–	10	On detachment from Capt. Digges' co.
James Wood,	-	-	"	–	10	On detachment from Capt. Sales' co.
William Wise,	-	-	"	–	10	On detachment from Capt. Sales' co.

(For rest of this company, see publication of Pay Rolls.)

MUSTER ROLL

Of Captain Nelson Humphries' Company of Virginia Militia, of the One Hundred and Ninth Regiment, commanded by Lieutenant Colonel Elliott Muse, in the Service from the 6th to 11th August, and from 30th November to 4th December, 1813, from 18th to 19th April, from 22d to 30th April, and from 9th to 15th August, 1814.

NAMES.	RANK.	TIME OF SERVICE.		REMARKS.
		Months.	Days.	
Nelson Humphries, - -	Captain,	–	26	
Robert Wake, - -	Lieutenant,	–	26	
Edmund Healy, - -	Ensign,	–	26	
Opie Palmer, - -	Sergeant,	–	26	
Thomas Palmer, - -	"	–	26	
Nelson Humphries, jr. - -	"	–	21	
James Bray, - -	"	–	15	
John Bray, - -	Corporal,	–	26	
John Brizendine, - -	"	–	10	
Andrew South, - -	"	–	26	Or Louth.
John Wehmore, - -	"	–	26	
Loddy South, - -	"	–	24	Or Louth.
Henry Palmer, - -	"	–	16	
Moses Walker, - -	"	–	15	
John Andrews, - -	Private,	–	8	
William Bristew, - -	"	–	26	
Samuel Blake, - -	"	–	14	
James Blake, - -	"	–	8	
Edmund Bristow, - -	"	–	14	
James Barker, - -	"	–	14	
William Barke, - -	"	–	5	
Spencer Coleman, - -	"	–	19	
Thomas Davis, - -	"	–	11	
Richard Garrett, - -	"	–	8	
Absalom Griffin, - -	"	–	8	
William Hackney, - -	"	–	10	
Benjamin Hackney, - -	"	–	10	
John Hall, - -	"	–	7	
James Johnson, - -	"	–	10	
Phillip Orrel, - -	"	–	16	
Philip Patterson, - -	"	–	8	
William Robertson, - -	"	–	13	
Peter Robertson, - -	"	–	8	
Peter B. Robertson, - -	"	–	8	
Benjamin F. Robertson, - -	"	–	8	
Bushard Rivere, - -	"	–	6	
Daniel B. Sibley, - -	"	–	26	
William N. Still, - -	"	–	26	
Thomas H. Still, - -	"	–	13	
John South, - -	"	–	29	
John Sibley, - -	"	–	8	
Daniel S. Ward, - -	"	–	20	
Robert Wilkins, - -	"	–	26	
William Ward, - -	"	–	8	
John Webb, - -	"	–	6	
James Yarington, - -	"	–	14	

MUSTER ROLL

Of Captain William Hundley's Company, from the Seventy-fourth Regiment, Virginia Militia, commanded by Lieut. Col. Wm. Trueheart, in the Service of the United States, from the 20th to 29th March, from 27th to 29th June, and from 1st to 2d July, 1813.

NAMES.	RANK.	TIME OF SERVICE.		REMARKS.
		Months.	Days.	
William Hundley,	Captain,	–	22½	
John D. Hendrick,	Lieutenant,	–	14	
Nathaniel Cross,	Ensign,	–	22½	
John King,	Sergeant,	–	22½	
John England,	"	–	22½	
John Frazer,	"	–	20	
John L. England,	"	–	22½	
Robert B. Bowles,	Drummer,	–	22½	
Bowler Whipple,	Fifer,	–	13	
William Andrew,	Private,	–	22½	
Geo. W. Adams,	"	–	19	
Thomas Adams,	"	–	18	
Thomas Bowles, (P.)	"	–	19	
Thomas Bowles, (F.)	"	–	19	
William Bowles,	"	–	20½	
John Bampass,	"	–	22½	
John Bowles,	"	–	21	
Thomas Bowles, (son of Ben,)	"	–	22½	
John Brock,	"	–	22½	
Joseph Bowles,	"	–	4	
Henry Cross, (son of John,)	"	–	22½	
William Cameron,	"	–	22½	
John Cross, jr.	"	–	20½	
James Christian,	"	–	20½	
James Donnally,	"	–	19½	
Wyatt Davis,	"	–	22½	
John Donnally,	"	–	22½	
Thomas Davis,	"	–	21	
James Davis, jr.	"	–	22½	
David Edwards,	"	–	22½	
John Glazebrook,	"	–	22½	
Andrew Grubbs,	"	–	22½	
Richard Glazebrook,	"	–	22½	
Richard P. Green,	"	–	22½	
Joel Hanes,	"	–	22½	
James Hooper,	"	–	13	
Moses Harris,	"	–	22½	
Fleming Harris,	"	–	18	
Garland Harris,	"	–	22½	
Benjamin Jenkins,	"	–	18½	
William Jenkins,	"	–	22½	
Thomas King,	"	–	21	
William King,	"	–	22½	
Benjamin Langford,	"	–	22½	
James Lynn,	"	–	14	
Sterling Langford,	"	–	17	
William Norvell,	"	–	19	

NAMES.	RANK.	TIME OF SERVICE.		REMARKS.
		Months.	Days.	
James Parseley, - -	Private,	–	22½	
John Perkins, - -	"	–	22½	
Samuel Priddy, - -	"	–	22½	
John Priddy, - -	"	–	22½	
Samuel Patterson, - -	"	–	22½	
Fendall Ragland, - -	"	–	20	
John Starke, - -	"	–	17	
John Sims. - -	"	–	22½	
Phillip Sheppard, - -	"	–	20½	
John A. Smith, - -	"	–	6	
John Stone, - -	"	–	6	
Benjamin Snead, - -	"	–	22½	
Wyatt Tinsley, - -	"	–	22½	
William Toler, - -	"	–	22½	
Parke Tinsley, - -	"	–	8	
Walter Tucker, - -	"	–	8	
Henry R. Winston, - -	"	–	22½	
Jessee Winn, - -	"	–	22½	
John S. West. - -	"	–	20½	
Christopher Winfield, -	"	–	22½	
Palmer Whipple, - -	"	–	2	

Captain Henry Hungerford's Company—One Hundred and Eleventh Regiment.

NAMES.	RANK.	TIME OF SERVICE.		REMARKS.
		Months.	Days.	
Henry Hungerford, - -	Captain,	2	8	
James Jett, - -	Lieutenant,	2	6	
William L. Mothershead, -	Ensign,	1	11	
William R. Smith, - -	Sergeant,	2	8	
Richard Neale, - -	"	2	8	
Westley Butler, - -	"	2	8	
Thomas Muse, - -	"	1	12	Detailed as assistant to
William H. Brown, - -	Drummer,	2	7	Q. M.
Ray Massey, - -	Fifer,	2	8	
James Anthony, - -	Private,	2	8	
Reuben Briscoe, - -	"	2	7	
Daniel Briscoe. - -	"	2		
Henry W. Butler, - -	"	2	2	
James Coats, - -	"	2	8	
James Cooke, - -	"	2	8	
Peter Callison, - -	"	2	7	
James Dickens, - -	"	2	8	
John Dickens, - -	"	2	8	
William Drake, - -	"	1	7	
Jeremiah Edmonds, - -	"	1	12	
Thomas Good, - -	"	2	8	Deserted.
James Harris, - -	"	2	8	
Spencer Lucas, - -	"	2	8	
Meredith Lucas, - -	"	2	8	
John Lawrence, - -	"	2	8	
Philip Matthews, - -	"	2	4	
William Mark. - -	"	1	13	
Reubin D. Oliff, - -	"	–	13	
John D. Redman, - -	"	2	6	
J. P. Robinson, - -	"	1	8	
Richard H. Simms, - -	"	1	3	Enlisted in troop of ca-
Bathel Tallant, - -	"	1	12	valry.
William Tate, - -	"	2	8	
Caleb S. Weaver, - -	"	2	8	
James Wingfield, - -	"	1	12	Deserted.
Samuel Weaver, - -	"	2	7	
James Yardley, - -	"	2	8	
William Yardley, - -	"	2	8	

(For rest of this company, see publication of Pay Rolls.)

Captain James Hurst's Company—Thirty-seventh Regiment.

NAMES.			RANK.	TIME OF SERVICE.		REMARKS.
				Months.	Days.	
Thomas Crowder,	-	-	Private,	1	15	
James Champion,	-	-	"	–	9	
Thomas Gaskins,	-	-	"	–	27	Appointed Qr. Master 11th April.
Isaac Hurst,	-	-	"	–	5	
Abnor Haydon,	-	-	"	–	5	
Francis Potts,	-	-	"	–	5	
James Spiller,	-	-	"	–	25	Enlisted in the regular service.
Beauman Darius,	-	-	Servant,	2	24	

(For rest of this company, see publication of Pay Rolls.)

MUSTER ROLL

Of Captain William Hutcherson's Company, from the Ninth Regiment, Virginia Militia, commanded by Lieutenant Colonel William Boyd, in the Service from the 7th to 17th April, 1813, and from 2d to 10th December, 1814.

NAMES.	RANK.	TIME OF SERVICE.		REMARKS.
		Months.	Days.	
William H. Hutcherson, -	Captain,	—	19	
Philip Gatwood, - -	Lieutenant,	—	9	
Thomas Kidd, - -	Ensign,	—	19	
Benjamin Gresham, - -	"	—	10	
William Dix, - -	Sergeant,	—	9	
Philip Noel, - -	"	—	19	
Larkin Cason, - -	"	—	9	
Robert Pitman, - -	"	—	9	
John Faulconer, - -	"	—	10	
John Dix. - -	"	—	10	
William Hill, - -	Corporal,	—	9	
Gabriel Dix, - -	"	—	9	
John Prewitt, - -	"	—	9	
Thomas Fogg, - -	"	—	19	
Philip Gatewood, - -	"	—	10	
Reuben M. Garratt, - -	"	—	10	
Larkin Cozen, - -	"	—	10	
Robert Tate, - -	Drummer,	—	10	
Thomas Allen, - -	Private,	—	19	
William Allen, - -	"	—	10	
William Acre, - -	"	—	10	
Joseph Allen, - -	"	—	10	
Henry Alexander, - -	"	—	19	
Richard Alexander, - -	"	—	9	
William Broach, - -	"	—	10	
James Berry, - -	"	—	10	
Ambrose Bland, - -	"	—	9	
Elliott Blake, - -	"	—	9	
Silas Cook, - -	"	—	10	
Henry Cook, - -	"	—	10	
John Cramprey, - -	"	—	10	
John Cook, - -	"	—	10	
John Clark, - -	"	—	9	
John Cole, - -	"	—	9	
Thomas Cooke, - -	"	—	9	
William Dix, - -	"	—	10	
William Dew, - -	"	—	9	
Joseph Fogg, - -	"	—	10	
Thomas Graves, - -	"	—	10	
Robert Graves, - -	"	—	10	
Gabriel Gatewood, - -	"	—	10	
Thomas Greenstead, - -	"	—	10	
Walker Hutcherson, - -	"	—	10	
Taliaferro Hutcherson, -	"	—	10	
Leroy Hutcherson, -	"	—	10	
Henry Hutcherson, - -	"	—	10	
John Harper, - -	"	—	19	
Benjamin Haskins, - -	"	—	10	

NAMES.	RANK.	TIME OF SERVICE.		REMARKS.
		Months.	Days.	
James Harper, - -	Private,	—	19	
Henry Lumpkins, - -	"	—	19	
John Kidd, - -	"	—	10	
Robert Kay, - -	"	—	10	
Owen Minor, - -	"	—	19	
Ephraim Minor, - -	"	—	10	
Richard Minor, - -	"	—	10	
Andrew Mahon, - -	"	—	19	
John Martin, - -	"	—	10	
Richard Marshall, - -	"	—	19	
Jessee Mayfield, - -	"	—	10	
Coleman Minor, - -	"	—	9	
William Minor, - -	"	—	9	
John Noel, - -	"	—	10	
Charles Philips, - -	"	—	10	
John Pewett, - -	"	—	10	
Solomon Pallen, - -	"	—	10	
Robert Pitman, - -	"	—	10	
Gabriel Philips, - -	"	—	19	
Spencer Riddle, - -	"	—	10	
Edmund Smither, - -	"	—	10	
William Shelton, - -	"	—	19	
Robert Sherwood, - -	"	—	10	
William Taylor, - -	"	—	10	
John Watkins, - -	"	—	19	
Leroy Wilson, - -	"	—	10	
Richard Wilkins, - -	"	—	10	
Philip Watkins, - -	"	—	9	
William Finsbloom, - -	"	—	10	

Captain *William Jackson's* Company—*Seventh Regiment.*

NAMES.	RANK.	TIME OF SERVICE.		REMARKS.
		Months.	Days.	
Joseph Perkins, - -	Corporal,	–	13	Transferred to general staff as assistant wagon master Sept. 16, 1814.
David Anderson, - -	Private.	–	16	
William Anthony, - -	"			
Thomas Arnett, - -	"	–	17	
Robert Brodas, - -	"			
Thomas Baker, - -	"			
John H. Coleman, - -	"	–	4	Transferred to general staff as assistant wagon master.
Archibald Christmas, -	"			
Walter Chisholme, -	"	–	27	
Armistead Cole, - -	"	–	6	Transferred to wagon yard as wagoner.
Thomas Davis, -	"			
Leonard Dunnavant, -	"	–	26	
Dudley A. Gibson, - -	"	–	3	Enlisted in U. States service.
Wm. B. Harris, - -	"	–	3	Enlisted in U. States service.
Charles C. Jennings, -	"			
William Minor, - -	"	–	25	
Joseph Morton, - -	"	–	25	
John F. Wash, - -	"			

(For the rest of this company, see publication of Pay Rolls.)

MUSTER ROLL

Of Captain David Jacobs' Troop of Cavalry, of the Twenty-eighth Regiment, Virginia Militia, in the County of Nelson, called into actual Service under the general orders of the 26th August, 1814, from the 2d to the 12th of September, 1814.

NAMES.	RANK.	TIME OF SERVICE.		REMARKS.
		Months.	Days.	
David Jacobs,	Captain,	–	12	
Richard Phillips,	Lieutenant,	–	12	
Peter C. Jacobs,	"	–	12	
Alexander Roberts,	Cornet.	–	12	
Nathaniel Harlow, jr.	Sergeant,	–	12	
John P. Scruggs,	"	–	12	
Nath'l H. Ragland,	"	–	12	
William Miggison,	"	–	12	
Chapel Devcanport,	Corporal,	–	12	
Nicholas Fortune,	"	–	12	
William Crisp,	"	–	12	
Patterson Scruggs,	"	–	12	
Kendol Brent,	Private,	–	12	
James Bibb,	"	–	12	
Benjamin Bradshaw,	"	–	12	
Peter Clarkeson,	"	–	12	
James Campbell,	"	–	12	
John Carr.	"	–	12	
William Campbell,	"	–	12	
Samuel Denny,	"	–	12	
William Davis,	"	–	12	
John Demastus,	"	–	12	
James Demastus,	"	–	12	
Jordan Edmunds,	"	–	12	
Thomas Fortune,	"	–	12	
John W. Green,	"	–	12	
Henry M. Green,	"	–	12	
Elias Hamlet,	"	–	12	
John Hamlet,	"	–	12	
Nathaniel Hill,	"	–	12	
Wyatt Hare,	"	–	12	
Robert Hunter,	"	–	12	
John Hensley,	"	–	12	
Augustin Henlow,	"	–	12	
Robert Johnson,	"	–	12	
Holeman Jopling,	"	–	12	
William C. Kidd,	"	–	12	
William J. Kidd,	"	–	12	
Lavender London,	"	–	12	
Richard Ligon,	"	–	12	
Samuel P. Lane.	"	–	12	
Charles Langford,	"	–	12	
Edmund T. Lively,	"	–	12	
James B. Lane,	"	–	12	
John Lavender,	"	–	12	
Reuben T. Mitchell,	"	–	12	
Aaron H. Morrison,	"	–	12	

NAMES.	RANK.	TIME OF SERVICE.		REMARKS.
		Months.	Days.	
James McAlexander, -	Private,	–	12	
Vincent Marks, - -	"	–	12	
Davis R. Patterson, - -	"	–	12	
Charles Philips, - -	"	–	12	
James Panock, - -	"	–	12	
Lucas Powell, - -	"	–	12	
Nelson Philips, - -	"	–	12	
Richard C. Pollard, - -	"	–	12	
Lymore Powell, - -	"	–	12	
Conyers Philips, - -	"	–	12	
Nathaniel Powell, - -	"	–	12	
William Reppetoe, - -	"	–	12	
Giles Richardson, - -	"	–	12	
Joseph Seay, - -	"	–	12	
John Scruggs, - -	"	–	12	
Richard Saunders, - -	"	–	12	
David Shields, - -	"	–	12	
John Statham, - -	"	–	12	
James Smith, - -	"	–	12	
George Shields, - -	"	–	12	
Lemuel Turner, - -	"	–	12	
James S. Thomas, - -	"	–	12	
James Thomas, - -	"	–	12	
Henry Turner, - -	"	–	12	
Lewis White, - -	"	–	12	
William Watkins, - -	"	–	12	
John Willoughby, - -	"	–	12	
Nelson Wanick, - -	"	–	12	
Hudson Watkins, - -	"	–	12	
Milliner Wilkinson, - -	"	–	12	
Augustin Wright, - -	"	–	12	
Robert Woody, - -	"	–	12	
Nelson Wright, - -	"	–	12	
James Wright, - -	"	–	12	

Captain Edward James' Company—at Cape Henry.

NAMES.			RANK.	TIME OF SERVICE.		REMARKS.
				Months.	Days.	
Edward James,	-	-	Captain,	–	16	
Henry Styron,	-	-	Lieutenant,	–	8	
John Barnes,	-	-	Ensign,	–	8	
James Senaca,	-	-	Sergeant,	–	16	
Francis Williamson,	-	-	"	–	16	
Reuben Doudge,	-	-	"	–	8	
Kedar Whitehurst,	-	-	"	–	8	
Willoughby Doudge,	-	-	"	–	8	
Henry Capps,	-	-	"	–	8	
Simon Whitehurst,	-	-	Corporal.	–	8	
Malachi Williamson,	-	-	"	–	8	
Francis Batten,	-	-	"	–	8	
Hillary Styron,	-	-	"	–	8	
John Bonney,	-	-	"	–	8	
William Ward,	-	-	"	–	8	
William Dawley,	-	-	"	–	8	
Benjamin Capps,	-	-	"	–	8	
Jonathan J. Lindsay,	-	-	Drummer,	–	8	
William White,	-	-	"	–	8	
Jonathan Ackiss,	-	-	Fifer,	–	16	
Benjamin Barnes,	-	-	Private,	–	16	
William Batten,	-	-	"	–	16	
Jonathan Bonney,	-	-	"	–	8	
Francis Batten,	-	-	"	–	8	
Tully Barnes,	-	-	"	–	8	
Ancil Cox,	-	-	"	–	16	
Benjamin Cox,	-	-	"	–	8	
Thomas Craft,	-	-	"	–	8	
Enoch Capps,	-	-	"	–	16	
Henry Capps,	-	-	"	–	8	
John Craft,	-	-	"	–	8	
Elijah Capps,	-	-	"	–	8	
Charles Dyer,	-	-	"	–	8	
William Dawley,	-	-	"	–	8	
Joshua Frizle,	-	-	"	–	16	
Luke Hill,	-	-	"	–	8	
David Idlet,	-	-	"	–	8	
Henry James,	-	-	"	–	8	
Willoughby Kemp,	-	-	"	–	8	
David Kincey,	-	-	"	–	16	
Henry Kincey,	-	-	"	–	16	
Solomon Kincey,	-	-	"	–	16	
Solomon Lane,	-	-	"	–	8	
Jesse Lane,	-	-	"	–	16	
Nathaniel Land,	-	-	"	–	8	
Charles Land,	-	-	"	–	8	
Tully McClanen,	-	-	"	–	16	
Caleb Malbane,	-	-	"	–	8	
Perrin Smith,	-	-	"	–	16	
Hillary Styron,	-	-	"	–	8	
Jesse Smith,	-	-	"	–	8	
Stephen Sherwood,	-	-	"	–	8	
William Smith,	-	-	"	–	8	

NAMES.			RANK.	TIME OF SERVICE.		REMARKS.
				Months.	Days.	
Henry Sherwood,	-	-	Private,	–	8	
James Salmons,	-	-	"	–	8	
John Whitehead,	-	-	"	–	8	
Simon Whitehurst,	-	-	"	–	8	
William White,	-	-	"	–	8	
Caleb Whitehurst,	-	-	"	–	8	
Malachi Williamson,	-	-	"	–	8	
James Williamson,	-	-	"	–	8	
William Woodland,	-	-	"	–	8	
William Whitehurst,	-	-	"	–	8	
Henry Williams,	-	-	"	–	8	
Hillary Whitehurst,	-	-	"	–	8	
James Whitehurst,	-	-	"	–	8	
Francis Whitehurst,	-	-	"	–	16	
John Whitehurst,	-	-	"	–	16	
David Whitehurst,	-	-	"	–	8	
James Williams,	-	-	"	–	8	
George Whitehurst,	-	-	"	–	8	
William Ward,	-	-	"	–	8	
Charles Waterman,	-	-	"	–	8	

(For rest of this company, see publication of Pay Rolls.)

MUSTER ROLL

Of Lieutenant John James' Company, of the Ninety-second Regiment, Virginia Militia, in the County of Lancaster, called into actual Service under regimental orders of the 7th August, 1813.

NAMES.			RANK.	TIME OF SERVICE.		REMARKS.
				Months.	Days.	
John James,	-	-	Lieutenant,	–	6	
John Kirk.	-	-	Sergeant,	–	3	
Coleman Doggett,	-	-	"	–	2	
Charles Kelly,	-	-	"	–	1	
James Brent,	-	-	"	1		
Thomas Miller.	-	-	Corporal,	–	4	
John Yerby,	-	-	"	–	4	
Armstead Haydon,	-	-	"	–	4	
Elias Fendley,	-	-	"	–	4	
James Ashburn.	-	-	Private,	–	4	
William Driver,	-	-	"	–	4	
James Doggett,	-	-	"	–	3	
Joseph Dasher.	-	-	"	–	1	
John Flowers,	-	-	"	1		
James Gains,	-	-	"	1		
John W. Hunton,	-	-	"	–	4	
Oswell Haydon,	-	-	"	–	4	
Lewis Hammond,	-	-	"	–	4	
Bedy Hughlett,	-	-	"	–	4	
Abner Haydon,	-	-	"	–	4	
Griffin Haydon,	-	-	"	–	3	
William Keeling,	-	-	"	–	4	
Eppa Lunce,	-	-	"	–	4	
Rodolph Miller,	-	-	"	–	1	
Robert Miller,	-	-	"	–	1	
Thomas B. Oliver,	-	-	"	–	1	
John Richardson,	-	-	"	–	2	
Daniel Shelton,	-	-	"	–	4	
Thomas Schofield.	-	-	"	–	3	
James R. Tankersley,	-	-	"	–	4	
Thornton B. Tankersley,	-	-	"	1		
Joseph Talman,	-	-	"	1		
George Wale,	-	-	"	–	2	

Captain Thomas James' Company—Sixty-first Regiment.

NAMES.	RANK.	TIME OF SERVICE.		REMARKS.
		Months.	Days.	
Joshua G. Brown, - -	Lieutenant,	–	3	
Matthias James, - -	"	–	15	
John Billups, - -	"	–	4	
A. G. Cushman, - -	Sergeant,	–	4	
John Hudgin, - -	"	–	3	
Nicholas Terrill, - -	"	–	4	
William Minter, - -	"	–	3	
Humphrey Hunley,	Drummer,	1	19	
John Adams, - -	Private,	–	2	
Richard Ayres, - -	"	–	3	
John Anderton, - -	"	–	3	
Ralph Armistead, - -	"	–	2	
Joseph Bohannon, - -	"	–	2	
George Brooks, - -	"	–	3	
Thomas Bassett, - -	"	–	2	
Samuel W. Brown, - -	"	–	23	
Joseph Bohannon, - -	"	–	2	
Joseph Brown, - -	"	–	16	
William Butler, - -	"	–	2	
Joseph Brownley, - -	"	–	13	
Robert Billups, - -	"	–	2	
James Brownley, - -	"	–	6	
Thomas Billups, - -	"	–	4	
George Brownley, - -	"	–	4	
James Brooks, - -	"	–	3	
Alden G. Cushman, - -	"	–	2	
John Callis, jr. - -	"	–	4	
Robert Dixon, - -	"	–	20	
Augustin Digges, - -	"	–	8	
Jarvis Deale, - -	"	–	7	
John Digges, - -	"	–	3	
Edward Davis, - -	"	–	2	
William Dunlavy, - -	"	–	2	
Samuel Eddins, - -	"	–	3	
Thomas Eddins, - -	"	–	4	
Jesse Foster, - -	"	–	4	
Joshua Foster, - -	"	–	4	
John Forrest, - -	"	–	3	
Edm'd Forrest, - -	"	–	2	
Joseph Foster, - -	"	–	3	
John Gayle, - -	"	–	3	
Thomas Gayle, (of Josh.) -	"	–	26	
Thomas Gayle, (of Matt.) -	"	–	5	
William Green, - -	"	–	4	
Hugh Hudgin, - -	"	–	13	
Warner Hudgin, - -	"	–	4	
Lewis Hudgin, - -	"	–	2	
Humphrey Hudgin,	"	–	5	
Anthony Hudgin, - -	"	–	17	
Richard Hunley, - -	"	–	4	
Beverley Hudgin, - -	"	–	6	
Matthew Hunley, - -	"	–	7	
Josiah Huggett, - -	"	–	8	
John Hughes, - -	"	–	5	

NAMES.	RANK.	TIME OF SERVICE.		REMARKS.
		Months.	Days.	
Jesse Hurst, - -	Private,	–	4	
Matthias James, - -	"	–	29	
Francis Jarvis, - -	"	–	15	
Cary James, - -	"	1		
George W. Litchfield, -	"	–	2	
James McBride, - -	"	–	6	
William Minter, - -	"	–	11	
Robert Minor, - -	"	–	3	
John Morgan, - -	"	–	3	
Zachary Owen, - -	"	–	4	
Josiah Pugh, - -	"	–	4	
James Peed, - -	"	–	3	
Lewis Peed, - -	"	–	3	
Thomas Robbins, -	"	–	3	
William Richardson, -	"	–	4	
William Robbins, - -	"	–	3	
Thomas Sampson, -	"	–	3	
James G. Simmons, - -	"	–	2	
Robert Sadler, - -	"	–	3	
James Saunders, - -	"	–	4	
Absalom Sadler, - -	"	–	4	
Isaac Sadler, - -	"	–	3	
John Sadler, - -	"	–	4	
William Treackle, -	"	–	3	
Christopher Weston, -	"	–	3	
Samuel D. White, -	"	–	13	
Matthew Weston, - -	"	–	28	
John Weston, - -	"	–	14	
Thos. White, - -	"	–	9	
Jno. White, sen. - -	"	–	2	

(For rest of this company, see publication of Pay Rolls.)

MUSTER ROLL

Of Captain Joseph Janey's Company, of the Sixth and One Hundred and Eleventh Regiments, Virginia Militia, commanded by Colonel Archibald Ritchie, and Lieutenant Colonel Richard E. Parker, respectively, in the Service of the United States, from 28th July to 25th September, and from 5th to 9th December, in the year 1814.

NAMES.	RANK.	TIME OF SERVICE.		REMARKS.
		Months.	Days.	
Joseph Janey, - -	Captain,	2	7	
Winter Bray, - -	Lieutenant,	–	28	
Francis W. Quarles, - -	"	1		
John Saddler, - -	Ensign,	2	7	
Alexander S. Boughton, -	Sergeant,	2	7	
William S. Young, - -	"	2	7	
Leroy D. Beale, - -	"	2	7	
Samuel May, - -	"	2	7	
Leroy Cauthorn, - -	Corporal,	2	7	
Walker Street, - -	"	1	28	
Kemp Evans, - -	"	1	28	
Baylor Carlton, - -	"	1	28	
Thomas Collins, jr. - -	"	–	9	
Larkin Hunley, - -	"	–	9	
Thomas Hunley, jr. - -	"	–	9	
Sylvanus Allen, - -	Private,	–	25	Transferred from Capt. Thomas' company,
Ambrose Armstrong, - -	"	–	25	" " "
Matta Ball, - -	"	–	25	" " "
Reubin Boughton, - -	"	1	4	" " "
Anderson Brizendine, -	"	2	3	
Travis Brizendine, - -	"	1	28	
Richard Brooks, - -	"	2	7	
Lewis Boughton, - -	"	2	7	
John Brooks, - -	"	2	5	
James Boughton, - -	"	2	7	
William Blake, - -	"	1	27	Godfrey Davis his sub.
Philip Brooks, - -	"	1	23	
Peter Brooks, - -	"	2	7	
Baylor Carlton, - -	"	–	5	
Curtis Chamberlaine, -	"	–	9	
Beverley Carroll, - -	"	2	6	
William Clarke, - -	"	1	2	Transferred from Capt. Thomas' company.
Green Coleman, - -	"	–	25	" " "
Benjamin Coghill, - -	"	–	25	" " "
William Cauthorn, - -	"	–	25	" " "
John Chamberlain, - -	"	–	25	" " "
John Cauthorn, - -	"	–	25	" " "
John Carter, - -	"	1	28	
William Coleman, - -	"	1	28	
Thomas Clarke, - -	"	1	28	
Godfrey Cauthorn, - -	"	–	25	
Absalom Cloudas, - -	"	1	16	
William Dyke, - -	"	2	7	
William Dyke, - -	"	1	28	

NAMES.	RANK.	TIME OF SERVICE.		REMARKS.
		Months.	Days.	
James Dyke, - -	Private,	—	9	
Thomas Dunn, - -	"	—	8	
Caleb Elliott, - -	"	2	7	
Thomas Elliott, - -	"	1	28	
Beverly Elliott, - -	"	—	25	
Samuel Fenton, - -	"	2	3	
William Fogg. - -	"	—	25	
Thomas Gordon, - -	"	1	28	
Stephen H. Garrett, - -	"	2	7	
Travis Gatewood, - -	"	2	6	
George Gordon, - -	"	—	25	
Richard Golman, - -	"	—	25	
James Gatewood, - -	"	—	25	
John Harmon, - -	"	1	28	
Anthony Haynes, - -	"	2	7	
James Howerton, - -	"	1	28	
Thomas Hunley, - -	"	2	7	
Larkin Hunley, - -	"	1	28	
John Hunley, - -	"	2	7	
Philip Howerton, - -	"	1	28	
Henry Haile, - -	"	—	25	
Benjamin Hunley, - -	"	—	7	
James Howard, - -	"	—	9	
George M. Hunley, - -	"	—	9	
William James, - -	"	—	25	
Martin Lipscomb, - -	"	2	6	
Henry Latham, - -	"	—	25	
Richard Mann, - -	"	2	7	
John Marshall, - -	"	2	7	
Latane Montigne, - -	"	—	9	
Peter Newbill, - -	"	2	6	
Major Oakes, - -	"	—	9	
Austin Oliver, - -	"	—	25	Transferred from Capt. Thomas' company.
Richard Phillips, - -	"	2	7	
William Perry, - -	"	—	25	
Richard Richards, - -	"	2	7	
Mourning Smith, - -	"	2	7	
Henry Saunders, - -	"	—	25	.. .. ..
John Steward, - -	"	—	20	
Francis Smith, - -	"	—	9	
Henry Samuels, - -	"	—	9	
Rolley Taff, - -	"	1	28	
Lewis Thomas, - -	"	—	25	" " "
Robert Thomas, - -	"	—	25	.. .. ..
Samuel Williamson, - -	"	2	1	

MUSTER ROLL

Of Captain William N. Jarrett's Troop of Cavalry, of the Third Regiment, in the County of Monongalia, called into actual Service under the order of the Governor, from the 22d to the 26th January, in the year 1813.

NAMES.	RANK.	TIME OF SERVICE.		REMARKS.
		Months.	Days.	
William N. Jarrett, - -	Captain,	–	5	
Robert Hawthorn, - -	Lieutenant,	–	5	
Ralph Barkhire, - -	"	–	5	
Marmaduke Evans, - -	Cornet,	–	5	
Daniel Balzet, - -	Private,	–	5	
Cornelius Barkshire,	"	–	5	
Francis Billingly, - -	"	–	5	
Benjamin Dowey, - -	"	–	5	
Henry Darby, - -	"	–	5	
James Doran. - -	"	–	5	
John Davis, - -	"	–	5	
John Evans, - -	"	–	5	
Matthew Gay, - -	"	–	5	
Archibald Hamilton, - -	"	–	5	
Reason Holland, - -	"	–	5	
Brice Holland, - -	"	–	5	
John Jolliff, - -	"	–	5	
Fielding Kizer, - -	"	–	5	
William B. Linsey, - -	"	–	5	
Nehemiah Power, - -	"	–	5	
Henry Runner, - -	"	–	5	
James Runner, - -	"	–	5	
George Reed, - -	"	–	5	
Thomas S. Swaringer, -	"	–	5	
Jonathan Salyards, - -	"	–	5	
Frederick Snisher, - -	"	–	5	
Alpheus P. Wilson, - -	"	–	5	
Augustus Werminger, -	"	–	5	

Captain Francis Jarvis' Company—Sixty-first Regiment.

NAMES.			RANK.	TIME OF SERVICE.		REMARKS.
				Months.	Days.	
Jesse Hudgin,	-	-	Ensign,	–	7	
Cary James,	-	-	Drummer,	–	7	
Francis Hudgin,	-	-	Fifer,	–	7	
Foster Brownley,	-	-	Private,	–	7	
Spencer Brown,	-	-	"	–	7	
George Culley,	-	-	"	–	7	
Langley Culley,	-	-	"	–	7	
Joseph Gayle,	-	-	"	–	7	
Sam'l Hudgin,	-	-	"	–	20	
John Hudgin, jr.	-	-	"	–	2	
Francis Hudgin,	-	-	"	–	7	
Thomas Jarvis, sen'r,	-	-	"	–	15	
Cary James,	-	-	"	–	18	
Robert Lewis,	-	-	"	–	1	
James Pleasy,	-	-	"	–	5	
John D. Pleasy,	-	-	"	–	8	
John Ripley,	-	-	"	–	7	
Edw'd Smith,	-	-	"	–	7	
William Turner,	-	-	"	–	11	
James Thomas,	-	-	"	–	5	
Robert Weston,	-	-	"	–	25	

(For rest of this company, see publication of Pay Rolls.)

Captain William Jarvis' Company—Twenty-seventh Regiment.

NAMES.	RANK.	TIME OF SERVICE.		REMARKS.
		Months.	Days.	
John Nelson, - -	Sergeant,	–	22	
Nathaniel Nottingham, -	"	–	22	
William Jarvis, jr. - -	"	–	15	
Severn Wingate, - -	Drummer,	–	22	
John Anderson, - -	Private,	–	22	
John Adams, - -	"	–	22	
Rich'd Bell, - -	"	–	22	
John Bell, - -	"	–	2ᴊ	
William Clay, - -	"	–	22	
Nat. Costin, - -	"	–	2	
James Clay, - -	"	–	22	
John Causley, - -	"	–	15	
Thomas Dixon, - -	"	–	15	
William S. Evans, - -	"	–	15	
Thomas Fitchett, - -	"	–	24	
John Floyd, - -	"	–	22	
Littleton Griffith, - -	"	–	22	
John Griffith, - -	"	–	22	
William Goffigon, - -	"	–	15	
Andrew Humpleton, - -	"	–	22	
George Hichins, - -	"	–	15	
Thomas Hickman, - -	"	–	22	
George Hickman, - -	"	–	22	
William Jarvis, jr. - -	"	–	22	
John Jacob, - -	"	–	15	
James Jones, - -	"	–	15	
Nathaniel Jones, - -	"	–	15	
Matthew Moore, - -	"	–	22	
John Moore, - -	"	–	22	
Thomas Powell, - -	"	–	22	
Charles Roe, - -	"	–	22	
Thos. B. Snead, - -	"	–	22	
Thos. Speakman, - -	"	–	22	
Southey Spady, - -	"	–	15	
William Travis, - -	"	–	15	
James Taylor, - -	"	–	15	
Abner Thuston, - -	"	–	9	
John Wilson, - -	"	–	22	
Josias Willis, - -	"	–	22	
William Wilson, - -	"	–	22	
Thomas Wheeler, - -	"	–	22	
Thomas Wingate, - -	"	–	15	
Nat. Williams, - -	"	–	15	
William Wilkins, - -	"	–	15	

(For rest of this company, see publication of Pay Rolls.)

Captain Tilmon E. Jeter's Troop of Cavalry—First Regiment.

NAMES.	RANK.	TIME OF SERVICE.		REMARKS.
		Months.	Days.	
Anderson Jeter, - -	Private,	–	27	
Thomas Wilson, - -	"	–	27	

(For rest of this company, see publication of Pay Rolls.)

Captain Edward Johnson's Company—Second Regiment.

NAMES.			RANK.	TIME OF SERVICE.		REMARKS.
				Months.	Days.	
John Booton,	-	-	Private	–	15	
Ro. R. Miller,	-	-	"	–	5	

(For rest of this company, see publication of Pay Rolls.)

Captain Samuel B. Jeter's Company—Seventh Regiment.

NAMES.	RANK.	TIME OF SERVICE.		REMARKS.
		Months.	Days.	
George Brooks, - -	Sergeant,	3	25	
Thomas Bentley, - -	Private,	–	14	
John M. Clark, - -	"	4	5	Deserted.
Henry R. James, - -	"			
John Rudd, - -	"	–	–	Deserted.

(For rest of this company, see publication of Pay Rolls.)

Captain William Jett's Company—Thirty-seventh Regiment.

NAMES.	RANK.	TIME OF SERVICE.		REMARKS.
		Months.	Days.	
Edward Oldham, - -	Corporal,	–	7	
John Dawson, - -	Drummer,	–	5	
Royston Betts, sen. -	Private,	–	25	
William Hudnall, jr. -	"			
John L. Kirk, - -	"	–	8	
John Kirk, - -	"			
David H. Pitts, - -	"	–	6	

(For rest of this company, see publication of Pay Rolls.)

MUSTER ROLL

Of Captain Isaiah Johnson's Company of Infantry of the Thirty-third Regiment, Virginia Militia, commanded by Lieutenant Colonel Charles Bagwell, in the Service of the United States, from the 28th to the 30th May, 1813.

NAMES.	RANK.	TIME OF SERVICE.		REMARKS.
		Months.	Days.	
Isaiah Johnson, - -	Captain,	–	3	
Thorogood Taylor, - -	Lieutenant,	–	3	
John S. Johnson, - -	Ensign,	–	3	
David Mears, - -	Qr. M. Serg't,	–	3	
John Bird, - -	Sergeant,	–	3	
Geo. Russell, - -	"	–	3	
Southey Northam, - -	"	–	3	
John F. Fisher, - -	Corporal,	–	3	
Joseph Gladding, - -	"	–	3	
Thomas Hinmond, - -	"	–	3	
Gilbert M. Leatherbury, -	"	–	3	
Isaac Marshall, - -	Drummer,	–	3	
James Stant, - -	Fifer,	–	3	
Jacob Andrews, - -	Private,	–	2	
Henry Ayres, - -	"	–	3	
James Bayly, - -	"	–	3	
William Bell, - -	"	–	3	
Johannas Bird, - -	"	–	3	
Selby Bloxom, - -	"	–	3	
Elisha Bayley, - -	"	–	3	
James Bloxom, - -	"	–	3	
Major Bird, - -	"	–	3	
Eli Bloxom, - -	"	–	3	
Upshur Bailey, - -	"	–	3	
John Bailey, (of Robert.) -	"	–	3	
William Bloxom, - -	"	–	3	
Robert P. Brodwater, - -	"	–	2	
John Bayly, (of Southy,) -	"	–	2	
Richard Bloxom, - -	"	–	2	
Daniel T. Bird, - -	"	–	1	
William Christopher, - -	"	–	3	
John Christopher, - -	"	–	3	
Ephraim Chessee, - -	"	–	1	
Eli Chesson, - -	"	–	1	
Jesse Dickerson, - -	"	–	3	
Edmund Duncan, - -	"	–	3	
Zadock Davis, - -	"	–	3	
William Davis, - -	"	–	2	
Henry Fletcher, - -	"	–	3	
William Hutson, - -	"	–	3	
John Harmon, - -	"	–	3	
Galen Hindmand, - -	"	–	3	
Levin Harmon, - -	"	–	1	
James Hoffman, - -	"	–	1	
Richard Hart, - -	"	–	1	
John Jester, - -	"	–	3	
Isaiah Johnson, jr. - -	"	–	3	
Major Kelly, - -	"	–	3	
Thomas Kelley, - -	"	–	3	

NAMES.	RANK.	TIME OF SERVICE.		REMARKS.
		Months.	Days.	
James Kelley, - -	Private,	—	3	
Elijah Lucas, - -	"	—	2	
Selby Lankford, - -	"	—	3	
Sampson Marshall, - -	"	—	3	
John Marshall, - -	"	—	3	
George Mears, - -	"	—	3	
William Mears, - -	"	—	3	
Henry Marshall, - -	"	—	3	
John Russell, - -	"	—	3	
James Russell, - -	"	—	3	
Noah Riggin, - -	"	—	3	
John Rew, - -	"	—	2	
William Riley, - -	"	—	2	
William Silvertherer, - -	"	—	3	
William Tatham, - -	"	—	3	
Abbott Trader, - -	"	—	3	
William Trader, - -	"	—	3	
Nathaniel Taylor, - -	"	—	3	
Nathaniel Taylor, jr. - -	"	—	1	
Levi Trader, - -	"	—	3	
Southey Walker, - -	"	—	3	
George Wilson, - -	"	—	2	
Henry Young, - -	"	—	3	

MUSTER ROLL

Of Captain Jeptha Johnson's Company, of the Twenty-seventh Regiment, Virginia Militia, in the County of Northampton, called into actual Service under the general orders of the 8th March, 1813, from 8th to 14th April, 1813.

NAMES.			RANK.	TIME OF SERVICE.		REMARKS.
				Months.	Days.	
Jeptha Johnson,	-	-	Captain,	—	7	
James D. Turpine,	-	-	Lieutenant,	—	7	
Johannes Johuston,	-	-	Ensign,	—	7	
James Bilcout,	-	-	Sergeant,	—	7	
Edm'd Bele,	-	-	"	—	7	
Jonathan Boole,	-	-	"	—	7	
William Cary,	-	-	"	—	7	
James Tatham,	-	-	Drummer,	—	7	
Thomas Wyatt,	-	-	Fifer,	—	7	
Bowden Aleilill,	-	-	Private,	—	7	
Patrick Benson,	-	-	"	—	7	
James Barcraft,	-	-	"	—	7	
Cas. Bradford,	-	-	"	—	7	
Robertson Custis,	-	-	"	—	7	
Benj. Dunton,	-	-	"	—	7	
Thos. Dorety,	-	-	"	—	7	
Edm'd Fitcher,	-	-	"	—	7	
Richard Garrito,	-	-	"	—	7	
Thomas Metcalf,	-	-	"	—	7	
Jno. Mapp,	-	-	"	—	7	
Samuel Warrington,	-	-	"	—	7	
Beasey Watson,	-	-	"	—	7	

Captain Richard Johnson's Company—Twenty-seventh Regiment.

NAMES.			RANK.	TIME OF SERVICE		REMARKS.
				Months.	Days.	
Richard Johnson,	-	-	Captain,	—	10	
William G. Pitts,	-	-	Lieutenant,	—	10	
Thomas Amos,	-	-	Ensign,	—	10	
July S. Ward,	-	-	Sergeant,	—	10	
Thos. Widgion,	-	-	"	—	10	
William Clark,	-	-	"	—	10	
Jno. Hansley,	-	-	"	—	10	
James Twiford,	-	-	Corporal,	—	10	
Jno. Andrews,	-	-	"	—	10	
Jno. Joynes,	-	-	"	—	10	
Jno. Pritlove,	-	-	"	—	10	
Newton Harrison,	-	-	Drummer,	—	10	
Jno. Dunton,	-	-	Fifer,	—	10	
Jno. G. Ames,	-	-	Private,	—	10	
Thomas Addison,	-	-	"	—	10	
Joseph Berrier,	-	-	"	—	10	
James Belote,	-	-	"	—	10	
James Beach,	-	-	"	—	10	
Caleb Core,	-	-	"	—	10	
William Cary,	-	-	"	—	10	
Thomas Clark,	-	-	"	—	10	
Charles Carpenter,	-	-	"	—	10	
Samuel Dalby,	-	-	"	—	10	
Major Dennis,	-	-	"	—	10	
Rowland Dowty,	-	-	"	—	10	
Samuel Dennis,	-	-	"	—	10	
Richard Garriatt,	-	-	"	—	10	
William Harrison,	-	-	"	—	10	
Joseph Hickman,	-	-	"	—	10	
Thomas Hosin,	-	-	"	—	10	
Smith Joynes,	-	-	"	—	10	
William Matthews,	-	-	"	—	10	
William Richardson,	-	-	"	—	10	
Jno. Ross,	-	-	"	—	10	
Jno. Seaton,	-	-	"	—	10	
James Turner,	-	-	"	—	10	
James Tatum,	-	-	"	—	10	
Zachariah Wise,	-	-	"	—	10	
Meshack Waterfield,	-	-	"	—	10	
Stephen Wiscot,	-	-	"	—	10	
Samuel Warrington,	-	-	"	—	10	

(For rest of this company, see publication of Pay Rolls.)

MUSTER ROLL

Of a Guard stationed at Nomony Ferry, by order of Colonel R. E. Barker, of the One Hundred and Eleventh Regiment, from the 21st August to the 14th September, in the year 1813.

NAMES.			RANK.	TIME OF SERVICE.		REMARKS.
				Months.	Days.	
Willam Johnston,	-	-	Sergeant,	–	21	
James H. Bailey,	-	-	Private,	–	21	
Owen Brimmore,	-	-	"	–	21	
James Kirk,	-	-	"	–	21	
Thos. Palmer,	-	-	"	–	18	

MUSTER ROLL

Of Captain Catesby Jones' Company—Twenty-first Regiment.

NAMES.			RANK.	TIME OF SERVICE.		REMARKS.
				Months.	Days.	
Catesby Jones,	-	-	Captain,	–	27	
Horatio G. Harwood,		-	Lieutenant,	–	28	
Philip W. Lewis.	-	-	"	–	17	
Thomas C. Amory,	-	-	Ensign,	–	26	
Isaac Broocke,	-	-	Sergeant,	–	18	
Henry Sears,	-	-	"	–	7	
James Dillard,	-	-	"	–	26	
James W. Howard,	-	-	"	–	8	
William Newcomb,	-	-	"	–	26	Promoted from corporal January 30, 1814; served 4 days as a corporal.
Bowden Newcomb,		-	Corporal,	–	26	
George Hibbe,	-	-	"	–	18	Promoted corporal January 30th, 1814; served four days as private.
Francis S. Wyatt,	-	-	"	–	26	Promoted corporal January 30th, 1814; served four days as private.
John Walker,	-	-	"	–	22	Promoted corporal January 30th, 1814; served four days as private.
William Johnson,	-	-	"	–	16	
Vincent Hudson,	-	-	Drummer,	–	8	
Joseph R. Powell,	-	-	"	–	11	
Peter Camp,	-	-	Fifer,	–	5	
Jacob Acra,	-	-	Private,	–	18	
William Acra,	-	-	"	–	26	
Jno. H. Brister,	-	-	"	–	4	
Daniel Bayne,	-	-	"	–	24	
Meckings Browning,	-	-	"	–	7	
George Bonsh,	-	-	"	–	24	
Robertson Bridges,	-	-	"	–	22	
Richard Coleman,	-	-	"	2	5	
Thomas Collier,	-	-	"	–	16	
James Carney,	-	-	"	–	5	
James Dutton,	-	-	"	–	12	
Henry Dutton,	-	-	"	–	26	
James Dutton, jr.	-	-	"	–	26	
Richard Dutton,	-	-	"	–	18	
Paul Drummond,	-	-	"	–	26	
Lewis Dutton,	-	-	"	–	21	
Thomas Davis,	-	-	"	–	16	
Samuel Daniel,	-	-	"	–	16	
John Drisgale,	-	-	"	–	17	
John Edwards,	-	-	"	–	18	
Samuel Enos,	-	-	"	2	17	
George B. Field,	-	-	"	–	16	

NAMES.	RANK.	TIME OF SERVICE.		REMARKS.
		Months.	Days.	
John Figg, - -	Private,	–	8	
Tunstall German, - -	"	–	24	
Matt. Hall, - -	"	–	18	
William Hall, - -	"	–	25	
Thomas Hall, - -	"	–	17	
James Hall. - -	"	–	8	
Francis Hall. - -	"	–	22	
James Hibble, - -	"	–	18	
William Hardy, - -	"	–	27	
Matthew Harmanson, -	"	–	29	
Matt. Hopkins. - -	"	–	16	
George Jackman, - -	"	–	16	
Charles King. - -	"	–	16	
Hiram Lankford. - -	"	–	18	
Willlam Lettwyche, - -	"	–	16	
Thomas Mason, - -	"	–	8	
John Minor, - -	"			
John Mason, - -	"	–	3	Served as corporal till Jan. 29, 1814—Joined Capt. Rogers.
George Norton. - -	"	–	7	
Joseph Newcomb. - -	"	–	26	
William O'Dean, - -	"	–	18	
William Padgett, - -	"	–	18	
John Philpotts, - -	"	–	24	
Julian Palester, - -	"	–	4	
William Roane, - -	"	–	25	
John Rowe, - -	"	–	5	
Thomas Roane, - -	"	–	25	
William A. Rogers, - -	"	–	9	
James B. Sheppard, -	"	–	8	
Henry Stalker, - -	"	–	26	
John Sheppard, - -	"	–	4	
James South. - -	"	–	24	
Robert J. Sadler, - -	"	–	17	
Robert Sadler, - -	"	–	12	
Edm'd N. Sale, - -	"	–	8	
Jacob S. Saunders, - -	"	–	16	
Thomas Travillian, - -	"	–	8	
Isaac Walton, - -	"	–	8	
James Ware, - -	"	–	8	
John Wood, - -	"	–	3	
Edward Waller. - -	"	–	8	
James Wiatt, - -	"	–	25	
John Wilkins, - -	"	–	8	
William Walden, - -	"	–	8	
William Wiatt, - -	"	–	16	
Overton Wiatt, - -	"	–		
John R. Wiatt, - -	"	–		
Isaac Wilcox. - -	"	–		
James C. West, - -	"	–		
William Young, - -	"	–		

(For rest of this company, see publication of Pay Rolls.)

MUSTER ROLL

Of Captain Irby Jones' Company, of the Seventy-first Regiment, Virginia Militia, commanded by Lieutenant Colonel William Allen, in the Service of the United States, from 30th June to 10th of July, 1813, and from 31st August to 11th September, 1814.

NAMES.	RANK.	TIME OF SERVICE.		REMARKS.
		Months.	Days.	
Irby Jones, - -	Captain,	–	23	
John Watkins, - -	Lieutenant,	–	12	
Isham Inman, - -	"	–	12	
Richard Cock, - -	"	–	11	
Alexander Davis, - -	Ensign,	–	11	
William Maynard, - -	"	–	12	
Cilas Marks, - -	Sergeant,	–	11	
William Milby, - -	"	–	12	
Thomas Richardson, - -	"	–	11	
John Bishop, - -	"	–	11	
Carter Marks, - -	"	–	11	
Richard Carsley, - -	Corporal,	–	11	
Herman Bishop, - -	"	–	11	
Pleasant Bishop, - -	"	–	11	
Thomas Lunsford, - -	"	–	11	
Melville Newell, - -	Musician,	–	12	
William Arriss, - -	Private,	–	23	
Bartholomew Andrews, -	"	–	12	
John Bishop, - -	"	–	12	
Pleasant Bishop, - -	"	–	12	
James P. Bell, - -	"	–	12	Jesse Little his sub.
David Booth, - -	"	–	11	
Mason Bishop, - -	"	–	11	
Hamblin Bishop, - -	"	–	11	
Mark Booth, - -	"	–	7	
Littleberry Chappell, - -	"	–	23	
David Cocke, jr. - -	"	–	12	
Samuel Cocke, - -	"	–	12	
Champion Carter, - -	"	–	12	
William Cockes, jr. - -	"	–	12	
James Clinch, - -	"	–	12	
Foster Cook, - -	"	–	11	
Bird C. Dewell, - -	"	–	12	
Bailey Davis, - -	"	–	11	
John Emery, - -	"	–	12	
Drewry Emery, - -	"	–	12	
Ezekiah Emery, - -	"	–	11	
Stephen Ellis, - -	"	–	11	
Claiborne Emery, - -	"	–	11	
Bell Goodrich, - -	"	–	12	
John S. Gwaltney, - -	"	–	12	
Charnel Hite, - -	"	–	23	
Herman S. Hite, - -	"	–	12	
John N. Hunnicutt, - -	"	–	12	
William Holloway, - -	"	–	12	
Robinson M. Hargrave, -	"	–	12	
Henry Holt, - -	"	–	12	

NAMES.			RANK.	TIME OF SERVICE.		REMARKS.
				Months.	Days.	
Miles Johnson,	-	-	Private,	—	12	
Levy Johnson,	-	-	"	—	12	
David Johnson,	-	-	"	—	12	
Joseph P. Judkins,	-	-	"	—	12	
Joseph Judkins,	-	-	"	—	12	
William Judkins, jr.	-	-	"	—	12	
John C. Judkins,	-	-	"	—	12	
Ranolph Johnston,	-	-	"	—	11	
Alexander Johnston,	-	-	"	—	11	
John Johnston,	-	-	"	—	11	
John Justice,	-	-	"	—	11	
David Johnston,	-	-	"	—	11	
Thaddeus Lunsford,	-	-	"	—	11	
Stephen Lucas,	-	-	"	—	11	
Thomas Lashly,	-	-	"	—	11	
Blanks Moody,	-	-	"	—	12	
Daniel Marks,	-	-	"	—	11	
Archibald Mderey,	-	-	"	—	11	
Ishaw Newell,	-	-	"	—	23	
Edward Newell,	-	-	"	—	12	
Matthew Pond,	-	-	"	—	12	
Samuel Price,	-	-	"	—	12	Henry Price his sub.
John Stiles,	-	-	"	—	12	
Pleasant Sheffield,	-	-	"	—	12	
Henry Sheffield,	-	-	"	—	11	
John L. Smith,	-	-	"	—	12	
James Sheffield,	-	-	"	—	11	
John E. Thomson,	-	-	"	—	12	
James Thompson,	-	-	"	—	12	
Willis D. Warren,	-	-	"	—	12	
Joel Wall,	-	-	"	—	12	
John Wilson,	-	-	"	—	12	
Samuel Warren,	-	-	"	—	12	
John Westmore,	-	-	"	—	11	
William Wrenn,	-	-	"	—	11	

Captain John Jones' Company—Twelfth Regiment.

NAMES.	RANK.	TIME OF SERVICE.		REMARKS
		Months.	Days.	
John Jones, - -	Captain,			
Valentine Mayo, - -	Lieutenant,			
James G. Mayo, - -	Ensign,			
Richard Holland, - -	Sergeant,			
David Wildy, - -	"			
Robert Kent, - -	"			
Callom Jones, - -	"			
Alfred Wren, - -	"			
John Bailey, - -	Corporal,			
Reubin Martin, - -	"			
Wilson Parrish, - -	"			
Allen R. Bomard, - -	"			
David Ross, - -	"			
John Lovins, - -	Drummer,			
Bartholomew K. Johnston, -	Fifer,			
James Aston, - -	Private,			
William R. Allen, - -	"			
Mark Blumcoe, - -	"			
James Bartlett, - -	"			
David Brown, - -	"			
Obadiah Bransam, - -	"			
Stephen Fitzgerald, - -	"			
Dudley Gilman, - -	"			
Joseph Holland, - -	"			
Samuel Hardesty, - -	"			
William B. Howard, - -	"			
Joshua Harlow, - -	"			
James Jones, - -	"			
Armager Lilly, - -	"			
Elijah Lowry, - -	"	–	–	Sub for David Wildy.
Thomas Mayo, - -	"			
James Ross, - -	"			
Thomas Snead, - -	"			
William Saunders, - -	"			
William D. Statham, - -	"			
Thomas Sadler, - -	"			
Benj. Smith, - -	"	–	12	
William Tencer, - -	"			
John Thomas, - -	"			
William Thomas, - -	"			
Henry Taylor, - -	"			
John Venable, - -	"			
Garland White, - -	"			
Dabney White, - -	"			

(For rest of this company, see publication of Pay Rolls.)

MUSTER ROLL

Of Captain John R. Jones' Company, of the Nineteenth Regiment, Virginia Militia, in the County of Henrico, commanded by Lieutenant Colonel John Ambler, in the Service of the United States, from 18th to the 27th March, 1813, and from 26th August to 8th September, 1814.

NAMES.			RANK.	TIME OF SERVICE.		REMARKS.
				Months.	Days.	
John R. Jones,	-	-	Captain,	—	24	
Patrick Coutts,	-	-	Lieutenant,	—	23	
David Haynes,	-	-	Ensign,	—	17	
Francis Wood,	-	-	"	—	23	
Joshua Lomax,	-	-	Sergeant,	—	13	
John Parkhill,	-	-	"	—	13	
Ebenezer Jones,	-	-	"	—	13	
John Wood,	-	-	"	—	13	
Sublett Magruder,	-	-	"	—	10	
James Williams,	-	-	"	—	10	
Charles Keesee,	-	-	"	—	10	
Francis Wood,	-	-	"	—	10	
Henry Robinson,	-	-	Corporal,	—	23	
John Parkhill,	-	-	"	—	10	
John Wood,	-	-	"	—	10	
Samuel T. Chandler,	-	-	"	—	10	
William Crane,	-	-	"	—	13	
Charles J. Payne,	-	-	"	—	13	
John Southall,	-	-	"	—	13	
Samuel Andrews,	-	-	Private,	—	13	
S. Alaquin,	-	-	"	—	10	
Edward Adams,	-	-	"	—	10	
Samuel Adams,	-	-	"	—	10	
Andrew Bryson,	-	-	"	—	10	
Richard Bohannan,	-	-	"	—	10	
Campbell Blades,	-	-	"	—	10	
Arch'd Blair,	-	-	"	—	10	
John G. Beck,	-	-	"	—	13	
Benj. W. Coleman,	-	-	"	—	10	
Marcus Cochran,	-	-	"	—	10	
William Crane,	-	-	"	—	10	
Frs. W. Coleman,	-	-	"	—	10	
Joseph B. Colton,	-	-	"	—	10	
Henry Clarke,	-	-	"	—	10	
Geo. W. Clarke,	-	-	"	—	10	
Frederick Clarke,	-	-	"	—	13	
Josephus B. Colton,	-	-	"	—	13	
Elisha Copland,	-	-	"	—	13	
Milton Clarke,	-	-	"	—	13	
William Dixon,	-	-	"	—	10	
Thos. S. Dicken,	-	-	"	—	10	
William Dabney,	-	-	"	—	23	
Edw'd Eubank,	-	-	"	—	23	
Saml. C. Faulkner,	-	-	"	—	10	

NAMES.	RANK.	TIME OF SERVICE.		REMARKS.
		Months.	Days.	
Richard Fitzgerald, - -	Private,	–	10	
William Finch, - -	"	–	15	
Macon Ford, - -	"	–	23	
John B. Finley, - -	"	–	10	
Thomas Foster, - -	"	–	10	
Simon Frayser, - -	"	–	10	
James Gray, - -	"	–	13	
A. T. Gordon, - -	"	–	10	
James Gentry, - -	"	–	10	
Robert H. Goldthwaite, -	"	–	13	
Th. P. Hutchinson, - -	"	–	10	
And. Hetherton, - -	"	–	10	
John C. Hobson, - -	"	–	10	
C. Hubbard, - -	"	–	10	
John S. Hughes, - -	"	–	13	
Wyatt Hynes, - -	"	–	11	
George Irwin, - -	"	–	10	
John Johnson, - -	"	–	10	
L. Jones, - -	"	–	10	
Moses Jackson, - -	"	–	10	
John Jenks, - -	"	–	10	
Ellis Juan, - -	"	–	10	
Philip Jackson, - -	"	–	10	
Moses H. Judah, - -	"	–	13	
Jacob King, - -	"	–	15	Transferred to flying artillery.
John Kelso, - -	"	–	10	
Henry King, - -	"	–	13	
Caleb Lownes, - -	"	–	10	Transferred to cavalry.
Geo. B. Lafong, - -	"	–	10	
Joshua Lomax, - -	"	–	10	
Joseph Lovell, - -	"	–	10	
John Ludden, - -	"	–	5	Transferred to flying artillery.
William Lenieve, - -	"	–	13	
James Lownes, jr. - -	"	–	13	
Caleb Lownes, - -	"	–	5	
John Miller, - -	"	–	23	
Thomas Massie, - -	"	–	10	
Hector M. Organ, - -	"	–	23	
Asa Otis, - -	"	–	10	
Geo. B. Poe, - -	"	–	10	
Benjamin Poe, - -	"	–	10	
Thomas A. Ponsonby, -	"	–	13	
Bernard Phillips, - -	"	–	8	
Reuben Ragland, - -	"	–	10	
L. Read, - -	"	–	10	
Nath. Ragland, - -	"	–	10	
Theod'k Robinson, - -	"	–	10	
Nicholas Rind. - -	"	–	13	
William Richard, - -	"	–	13	
Henry Rogers, - -	"	–	5	
John Rynax, - -	"	–	13	
Elias Reed, - -	"	–	13	
Richard Reddy, - -	"	–	6	
F. Sydnor, - -	"	–	10	
Wm. Sanderson, - -	"	–	10	
Burnett Scott, - -	"	–	10	
Robert Shapard, - -	"	–	10	
William Shapard, - -	"	–	10	
Edward Staples, - -	"	–	10	
William Shepherd, - -	"	–	10	
C. Vail, - -	"	–	10	
Otway Wilkinson, - -	"	–	10	

NAMES.	RANK.	TIME OF SERVICE.		REMARKS.
		Months.	Days.	
Isaac White, - -	Private,	–	10	
Edward Walford, - -	"	–	10	
Edward Williams, - -	"	–	10	
David Wilson, - -	"	–	10	
William Wild, - -	"	–	10	
Austin Williams, - -	"	–	10	

(For rest of this company, see publication of Pay Rolls.)

Captain Richard Jones' Company—Twenty-first Regiment.

NAMES.	RANK.	TIME OF SERVICE.		REMARKS
		Months.	Days.	
Richard Jones, - -	Captain,	–	18	
Smith Hall, - -	Lieutenant,	1	9	
John Thruston, - -	"	1	5	
Richard G. Morriss, -	Sergeant,	–	25	
Daniel Fletcher, - -	"	–	27	
John Leigh, - -	"	–	18	
William Andrews, - -	"	–	22	
Laurence Stubbs, - -	"	–	22	
John Davis, - -	"	–	4	
Samuel Enos, - -	"	–	4	
John Thomas, - -	"	–	21	
William Andrews, - -	Corporal,	–	27	
Robert Kemp, - -	"	1	3	
Abraham Insley, - -	"	–	23	
John Kercheval, - -	"	–	24	
Joseph Robinson, - -	"	1	5	
John B. Clayton, - -	"	–	29	
Thomas Hall, - -	"	–	24	
Thomas Baytop, - -	"	–	8	
William Beverage, - -	Private,	–	17	
Bevion Brooking, - -	"	–	11	
Benj. R. Brooking, - -	"	–	11	
Austin Brown, - -	"	1	1	
Iverson Boswell, - -	"	1	3	
James Booker, - -	"	–	18	
Lewis C. Booker, - -	"	–	10	
Cary Booker, - -	"	–	4	
Benjamin Booker, - -	"	5		
George Booker, - -	"			
Samuel Brooking, - -	"			
Thomas Bassett, - -	"	–	11	
Leroy Bridgett, - -	"	–	29	
John Coats, - -	"	–	3	
William Croswell, - -	"	1	1	
Mordecai Cooke, - -	"	–	8	
William Carney, - -	"	–	12	
John Cullis, - -	"	–	21	
Thomas Carney, - -	"	–	21	
William Dudley, - -	"	–	23	
John Davis, - -	"	–	27	
Theo'k Dame, - -	"	–	18	
Warner Dunston, - -	"			
Lewis Dunston, - -	"			
John Dame, - -	"	–	2	
Samuel Enos, - -	"	–	25	
Colton Eubank, - -	"	–	4	
George Enos, - -	"	–	26	
Henry Fletcher, - -	"	1	10	
Lewis Fletcher, - -	"	1	3	
John Gressitt, - -	"	–	21	
John Guthrie, - -	"	–	8	
George Hains, - -	"	–	3	
Matt. Harminson, - -	"	–	8	
James Hart, - -	"	–	15	

NAMES.	RANK.	TIME OF SERVICE.		REMARKS.
		Months.	Days.	
Holder Hudgin, - -	Private,	–	9	
Thomas Hall, - -	"	1	9	
Warner Hall, - -	"	–	3	
John B. Hall, - -	"			
Hugh Hudgin, - -	"	1	12	
William Hunt, - -	"	–	21	
Jesse Hunt, - -	"	–	21	
Griffin Henry, - -	"	–	26	
Reuben Ison, - -	"	–	14	
Richard Kercheval, -	"	1	5	
John Kemp, sen'r, -	"	–	8	
John Kemp, jr. -	"	–	26	
William Lambeth, -	"	–	4	
William Lutwyche, -	"	–	2	
William Lawson, -	"	–	12	
John Lewis, - -	"	–	26	
John Martin, - -	"	1	1	
Thomas Muire, - -	"	–	27	
James Miller, - -	"	–	4	
Dunford Moore, - -	"	–	8	
Lewis Oliver, - -	"	–	10	
James Oliver, - -	"	–	26	
William Philpotts, -	"	–	19	
Joseph Puller, - -	"	1	1	
Henry Priddy, - -	"	1	5	
James P. Purcell, -	"	1	5	
Thos. Purcell. - -	"	–	15	
Christopher Proctor, -	"	1	3	
John Philpotts, - -	"	–	2	
Paul Philpotts, - -	"	1	3	
William Padgett, -	"	–	7	
William Powell, - -	"	–	3	
Thomas Rilee, - -	"	1	1	
James Roy, - -	"	–	7	
James Robins, - -	"	1	3	
James Ransone, - -	"	–	10	
Ab'm Satterwhite, -	"	–	25	
Thomas Sears, - -	"	–	8	
Laurence Stubbs, -	"	–	2	
Robert Sampson, -	"	–	21	
Joshua Smith, - -	"	–	21	
Thomas Trevillian, -	"	–	16	
William Treakle, -	"	–	21	
Thomas Wright, - -	"	–	25	
James West, - -	"	1	5	
Nathan Wilkins, - -	"	1	2	
John Wilson, - -	"			
Solomon Woodland, -	"	–	4	
Lewis Wright, - -	"	–	4	
James Williams, - -	"	–	21	
Matthew Winston, -	"	–	21	

(For rest of this company, see publication of Pay Rolls.)

MUSTER ROLL

Of Captain Samuel Jones' Company, of the Nineteenth Regiment, Virginia Militia, commanded by Lieutenant Colonel John Ambler, in the Service of the United States, from the 18th to the 27th March, and from the 28th June to the 3rd day of July, 1813.

NAMES.	RANK.	TIME OF SERVICE.		REMARKS.
		Months.	Days.	
Samuel Jones,	Captain,	–	16	
John B. Ogg,	Lieutenant,	–	10	
John H. Royster,	Ensign,	–	16	
John W. Wood,	Sergeant,	–	13	
N. K. Thomas,	"	–	13	
Thomas Oliver,	"	–	16	
Trebourne Crenshaw,	"	–	10	
F. J. Crenhard,	"	–	6	Or Crenshaw.
G. H. Bacchus,	"	–	6	
James Armstrong,	"	–	3	
A. Wiley,	Corporal,	–	3	
George Davis,	"			
James Laughline,	"	–	6	
D. Ball,	"	–	4	
Charles Anthony,	Private,	–	10	
Richard Anderson,	"	–	16	
Myer Alden,	"	–	10	
James Armstrong,	"	–	3	
Samuel J. Blair,	"	–	14	
Simon Block,	"	–	16	
Gurdon H. Bacchus,	"	–	13	
James Burley,	"	–	10	
George W. Bristow,	"	–	10	
James Bennett,	"	–	10	
Albert Booker,	"	–	10	
Hillary Baker,	"	–	13	
Wm. Bradley,	"	–	16	
Robert Bullington,	"	–	10	
William Barksdale,	"	–	6	
Samuel Brooks,	"	–	4	
James Bailey,	"	–	4	
Leo. Bowers,	"	–	3	
Lewis Brawner,	"	–	3	
William Crawford,	"	–	16	
William Caulfield,	"	–	16	
Joseph R. Crouch,	"	–	10	
Andrew Crew,	"	–	16	
William Colquhoun,	"	–	16	
William H. Carroll,	"	–	16	
Seaman Charlton,	"	–	10	
Jonathan Carlile,	"	–	13	
William H. Carlile,	"	–	16	
James A. Campbell,	"	–	16	
Peter Cotton,	"	–	6	
Robert Craig,	"	–	6	
Nathan. Dunlop,	"	–	16	
William Dunn,	"	–	16	

NAMES.	RANK.	TIME OF SERVICE.		REMARKS.
		Months.	Days.	
Charles Doyle, - -	Private,	—	16	
George Dabney, - -	"	—	10	
William Davenport, -	"	—	16	
George Davis, -	"	—	10	
Jos. W. Dickenson, - -	"	—	16	
Saml. C. Dickenson, -	"	—	16	
Thos. T. Dickenson, -	"	—	16	
Russell Dutton, - -	"	—	6	
William Dandridge, - -	"	—	6	
Geo. W. Fuzzell, - -	"	—	16	
William Foushee, jr. -	"	—	16	
James Fellows, - -	"	—	16	
Francis Graves, - -	"	—	16	
James Gray, - -	"	—	16	
William Gentry, - -	"	—	16	
John B. Green, - -	"	—	16	
John Gray, - -	"	—	6	
Edward Gay, - -	"	—	6	
Edward Hallam, - -	"	—	16	
Ellis Hudnall, - -	"	—	16	
John Henry, - -	"	—	16	
George W. Hill, - -	"	—	16	
Gideon Hatcher, - -	"	—	16	
John Holderfield, - -	"	—	16	
James Howard, - -	"	—	16	
Charles Hubbard, - -	"	—	16	
Axiom Hubbard, - -	"	—	16	
Richard Hines, - -	"	—	10	
James Henderson, - -	"	—	16	
Robert Hughes, - -	"	—	10	
Robert Henderson, - -	"	—	16	
Richard Henderson, - -	"	—	16	
D. Higginbotham, - -	"	—	3	
John Ireson, - -	"	—	12	
Solomon Jacobs, - -	"	—	13	
Richard Jordan, - -	"	—	11	
John James, - -	"	—	16	
Harrison James, - -	"	—	13	
John Jones, - -	"	—	10	
Abraham Kimball, - -	"	—	16	
Bennett Kirby, - -	"	—	16	
Frederick Kuhn, - -	"	—	16	
John King, - -	"	—	16	
Henry King, - -	"	—	10	
John Leslie, - -	"	—	16	
James Lughlam, - -	"	—	10	
Isaac Leabetts, - -	"	—	10	
Conrad Lotz, - -	"	—	4	
Isaac Leadbetter, - -	"	—	6	
Gamaliel Monroe, - -	"	—	16	
John McMarra, - -	"	—	16	
James McKildoe, - -	"	—	16	
James McNally, - -	"	—	16	
Andrew Moore, - -	"	—	16	
William S. Murphy, -	"	—	13	
Thomas Montague, -	"	—	13	
Adam Maury, - -	"	—	10	
Charles M. Mitchell, -	"	—	13	
Garland Mitchell, - -	"	—	10	
And. Murray, - -	"	—	3	
Elijah May, - -	"	—	3	
B. Morrison, - -	"	—	6	
J. G. Mosby, - -	"	—	6	
Littleberry Mosby, - -	"	—	6	

NAMES.	RANK.	TIME OF SERVICE.		REMARKS.
		Months.	Days.	
Matthew Mosby, - -	Private,	–	6	
Andrew Moorland, - -	"	–	6	
Opie Norris, - -	"	–	16	
William Neckervis, - -	"	–	16	
D. P. Organ, - -	"	–	6	
Samuel Pointed, - -	"	–	10	
Allen Pollock, - -	"	–	16	
Jonathan Palmer, - -	"	–	16	
Sherloch Palmer, - -	"	–	16	
Munford Perks, - -	"	–	13	
Fleming Park, - -	"	–	13	
James Pakes, - -	"	–	10	
John Parker, - -	"	–	13	
F. D. Peters, - -	"	–	1	
John Perkins, - -	"	–	3	
John Rowland, - -	"	–	13	
Leonard Rowlett, - -	"	–	10	
Edward W. Rootes, - -	"	–	16	
Alexander Reed, - -	"	–	13	
Samuel Read, - -	"	–	13	
Pascal Robinson, - -	"	–	10	
G. H. Stanback, - -	"	–	16	
Nathaniel Smith, - -	"	–	10	
George W. Smith, - -	"	–	10	
John M. Smith, - -	"	–	16	
Jacob Stally, - -	"	–	10	
Wm. M. Samuel, - -	"	–	10	
Jos. Smith, - -	"	–	6	
William Scott, - -	"	–	6	
Alexander Sharp, - -	"	–	6	
John Southall, - -	"	–	6	
Edward W. Trent, - -	"	–	13	
James Talley, - -	"	–	10	
Robert Tucker, - -	"	–	13	
Exra Talmadge, - -	"	–	10	
John L. Thomas, - -	"	–	10	
John Vaughan, - -	"	–	16	
Hez. Veach, - - -	"	–	16	
Geo. W. Valentine, - -	"	–	16	
Joseph A. Weed, - -	"	–	13	
Edward Wanton, - -	"	–	16	
William W. Walker, - -	"	–	16	
David Woodward, - -	"	–	16	
Ro. Wilson, - -	"	–	6	
Sylvester Walkley, - -	"	–	6	
Alex. Wiley, - -	"	–	3	

MUSTER ROLL

Of Captain Thomas Jones' Company, of the Seventy-fourth Regiment, Virginia Militia, commanded by Colonel William Truehart, in the Service of the United States, from 20th to 29th March, from 28th to 30th June, and from 1st to 2d July, in the year 1813.

NAMES.	RANK.	TIME OF SERVICE.		REMARKS.
		Months.	Days.	
Thomas Jones, - -	Captain,	—	15	
David R. Jones, - -	Lieutenant,	—	15	
Charles K. Bowles, -	Ensign,	—	15	
James Colley, - -	Sergeant,	—	15	
John G. Childres, -	"	—	15	
Thomas Carter, -	"	—	15	
Harman A. Pulliam, - -	"	—	15	
Joseph Anderson, -	Private,	—	15	
Archibald Atkinson, - -	"	—	15	
Anderson Bowles, - -	"	—	9	
Robert Blunkall, -	"	—	12	
Elkanah A. Brooks, - -	"	—	15	
Joseph Burnard, -	"	—	15	
Thomas Carver, - -	"	—	15	
William Childress, -	"	—	15	
Charles Colley, jr. -	"	—	15	
Alex'r Chisholm, -	"	—	15	
Pendleton R. Childress,	"	—	15	
John S. Crutchfield, -	"	—	15	
Richard Childress, -	"	—	15	
Richard Childress, jr.	"	—	15	
Daniel Couch, -	"	—	15	
Spotswood Childress,	"	—	9	
Theophilus Chewning,	"	—	15	
John R. Chisholm, -	"	—	15	
Nathaniel W. Dandridge, -	"	—	15	
Archibald B. Dandridge,	"	—	15	
Robert A. Dandridge,	"	—	15	
Allen Denton, -	"	—	15	
Thomas Denton, -	"	—	10	
James Denton, -	"	—	12	
Richard S. Duke, -	"	—	12	
Elisha Ellis, -	"	—	12	
James Glenn, -	"	—	15	
John Glenn, jr. -	"	—	15	
William Glenn, -	"	—	15	
John Gentry, -	"	—	12	
Archibald Glenn, -	"	—	15	
Chapman Gordon, -	"	—	15	
Thomas Hunnicutt, -	"	—	15	
Edward Hatton, -	"	—	15	
Richard Johnson, -	"	—	15	
John B. Jones, -	"	—	15	
Miles B. Locknane, -	"	—	15	
Overton Mallory, -	"	—	15	
Thilman Mallory, -	"	—	15	
William Moseley, -	"	—	15	
David Mallory, -	"	—	15	

NAMES.	RANK.	TIME OF SERVICE.		REMARKS.
		Months.	Days.	
Richard Morris, - -	Private,	–	15	
Daniel Mitchell, - -	"	–	15	
John Nuchols, - -	"	–	15	
William Nuchols, - -	"	–	15	
Nathaniel Nuchols, - -	"	–	15	
Reuben Nuchols, - -	"	–	15	
Robert Pulliam, sr. - -		–	15	
Richard Philips, - -	"	–	15	
Robert J. Pulliam, - -	"	–	15	
Samuel Pulliam, - -	"	–	15	
George S. Pulliam, - -	"	–	15	
Joseph Perkins, - -	"	–	15	
Thomas Pope, - -	"	–	15	
Thomas Richardson, - -	"	–	6	
Tolevar Ragland, - -	"	–	6	
William Royster, - -	"	–	15	
George Shields, - -	"	–	15	
William Shoemaker, - -	"	–	15	
Miles Taylor, - -	"	–	15	
Edward Taylor, - -	"	–	15	
John Taylor, - -	"	–	15	
James Underwood, - -	"	–	12	
John Underwood, - -	"	–	12	
Shadrack Vaughan, - -	"	–	15	
Benjamin Vaughan, - -	"	–		
William Williams, - -	"	–	15	
Isham R. Woodson, - -	"	–	15	
William Winston, - -	"	–	2	

Captain William Jones' Company—Twenty-first Regiment.

NAMES.	RANK.	TIME OF SERVICE.		REMARKS.
		Months.	Days.	
William Jones,	Captain,	1	2	
James Wright,	Lieutenant,	1	2	
Matthew Gibbs,	Ensign,	—	5	
Thomas Ransone,	"	—	25	
Thomas Rilee,	Sergeant,	1	1	
Jeremiah Thrift,	"	1	2	
William Fields,	"	1	18	
Benjamin Thrift,	"	1	14	
Jesse Thrift,	Corporal,	1	18	
John Wright,	"	—	24	
Baylor Kenningham,	"	1	2	
Wm. G. Padgett,	"	1	2	
Joseph P. Powell,	Drummer,	1	18	
Peter Kemp,	Fifer,	1		
Wm. Almond,	Private,	1	2	
William Ambrose,	"	1	2	
John Blassingham,	"	1	18	
Wm. Blassingham,	"	—	16	
James Baytop,	"	—	16	
William Brown,	"	1	2	
Thomas Blake,	"	1		
Lewis Blake,	"	—	29	
John Coates, sen'r,	"	—	8	
William Coleman,	"	1	2	
James Coleman,	"	1	2	
Richard Douglass,	"	1	18	
Thomas C. Dillard,	"	1	2	
Lewis Dunston,	"	—	29	
Benjamin Didlake,	"	—	29	
Thomas Dunston,	"	—	10	
John Fenly,	"	1	2	
John Garrett,	"	—	16	
John Grassett,	"	1		
John M. Harwood,	"	1	2	
John W. Hilliard,	"	1	18	
Francis Hall,	"	1	18	
John Howlett,	"	1	12	
Holder Hudgin,	"	—	18	
Thomas Horsley,	"	1	2	
Isaac Hilyard,	"	1	2	
Matthias Insley,	"	1	18	
William Jones,	"	1	8	
Peter Kemp,	"	1	2	
Lewis D. Kemp,	"	1	2	
Charles Lawson,	"	—	29	
John Lawson,	"	—	8	
Thomas Minor,	"	1	11	
Dunford Moore,	"	1	10	
John Mitchell,	"	—	3	
Wm. D. Mitchell,	"	1	2	
Edw'd M. Purcell,	"	1	18	
Morgan Powell,	"	—	5	
Morgan Purcell,	'	—	9	
William R. Purcell,	"	1	2	
James Prosser,	"	—	28	

NAMES.			RANK.	TIME OF SERVICE.		REMARKS.
				Months.	Days.	
John Rilie,	-	-	Private,	1	11	
Wm. Rilie,	-	-	"	–	29	
Lewis Rilie,	-	-	"	1	2	
Francis Robins,	-	-	"	–	17	
A. Simmons,	-	-	"	1	9	
Wm. Soles,	-	-	"	1	13	
Anthony Sanders,	-	-	"	–	9	
Edward Trevillian,	-	-	"	1	18	
Christ. Trevillian,	-	-	"	1	2	
James Trevillian,	-	-	"	1	2	
James Wilson,	-	-	"	1	18	
Henry West,	-	-	"	1	17	
Christ. Whiting,	-	-	"	–	11	
Kemp Wiatt,	-	-	"	1		
Jno. Wilson,	-	-	"	1	2	

(For rest of this company, see publication of Pay Rolls.)

MUSTER ROLL

Of Captain Robert Jordan's Company, in the Twenty-seventh Regiment, Virginia Militia, commanded by Major Joseph M. Ballard, in the Service of the United States, from the 25th day of June, 1813, to the 10th day of July, 1813, inclusive.

NAMES.	RANK.	TIME OF SERVICE.		REMARKS.
		Months.	Days.	
Robert Jordan, - -	Captain,	–	16	
Willis Morriss, - -	Lieutenant,	–	16	
Jesse Roberts, - -	Ensign.	–	13	
Willis Fulgham, - -	Sergeant,	–	16	
Lewis Chapman, - -	"	–	16	
William Chapman, - -	"	–	16	
Henry Gaskins, - -	"	–	16	
Benj. Westray, - -	Corporal,	–	16	
John Joyner, - -	"	–	16	
Willis Westray, - -	"	–	16	
Robert Chapman, - -	"	–	16	
Champion Brasey, - -	Private,	–	16	
William Battin, - -	"	–	16	
Money Battin, - -	"	–	16	
Wiley Battin, - -	"	–	16	
Thomas Darden, - -	"	–	16	
John S. Dinson, - -	"	–	16	
Jonas Edwards, - -	"	–	16	
Alexander Gale, - -	"	–	16	
Andrew Gale, - -	"	–	16	
Meredith Holland, - -	"	–	16	
Thomas McLenny, - -	"	–	16	
Jesse Murphrey, - -	"	–	16	
Micajah Powell, - -	"	–	16	
Thomas Powell, - -	"	–	16	
John Parnal, - -	"	–	16	
Richard Pope, - -	"	–	16	
William Pierce, - -	"	–	16	
Jno. Smelly, - -	"	–	16	
Jordan Stepherson, - -	"	–	16	
Wiley Turner, - -	"	–	16	
Joseph Tomblin, - -	"	–	16	
Joshua Turner, - -	"	–	16	
Samuel Westray, - -	"	–	16	

Captain John G. Joynes' Company—Second Regiment.

NAMES.	RANK.	TIME OF SERVICE.		REMARKS.
		Months.	Days.	
Laban Phillips, - -	Drummer,	–	21	
Nathaniel Badger, - -	Private,	1	29	
William Bird, - -	"	–	27	
Clement Bonwell, - -	"	–	22	
John J. Bagby, - -	"	–	15	
William Carmine, - -	"	–	8	
Arthur Dunton, - -	"	–	8	
Charles East, - -	"	–	21	
Thomas H. Guy, - -	"	–	8	
Littleton Grant, - -	"	–	10	
Robert Kellam, - -	"	–	15	
Ed. Phillips, - -	"	–	14	
Gabriel Purse, - -	"	–	8	
Aaron Parker, - -	"	–	8	
John R. Revell, - -	"	–	8	
Southey W. Satchell, - -	"	–	14	
E. Smith, - -	"	–		
James Stewart, - -	"	–	4	
Joseph Turlington, - -	"	–	4	
James Taylor, - -	"	–	3	
Tully R. Wise, - -	"	1	2	

(For rest of this company, see publication of Pay Rolls.)

Captain Levin S. Joynes' Company—Second Regiment.

NAMES.	RANK.	TIME OF SERVICE.		REMARKS.
		Months.	Days.	
Aaron Parker, - -	Corporal,	1	11	
William D. Chandler, -	"			
James Badger, - -	Private,	1	2	
Henry Beasley, - -	"	—	9	
William Blackstone, - -	"	—	12	
Elijah Bull, - -	"			
Jesse Bonwell, - -	"	—	6	
Wm. Cornwell, - -	"	—	20	
Wm. D. Chandler, - -	"	—	22	
Thos. C. Gibb, - -	"	—	1	
John W. Hannaford, - -	"	—	8	
William Lingo, - -	"	—	20	
Thomas Leatherby, - -	"	—	4	
Robert Melson, - -	"	1	22	
Samuel Marshall, - -	"			
Isaac B. Moore, - -	"	—	8	
Major Parker, - -	"	—	4	
George Parker, - -	"	—	24	
Thomas Paul, - -	"	—	26	
J. Roberts, - -	"	—	8	
George C. Revell, - -	"	—	21	
James Ross, - -	"	—	21	
Thomas Scott, - -	"	—	5	
George Scott, - -	"	—	11	
Jesse Savage, - -	"	—	29	
Southey Taylor, - -	"	—	8	
Elijah A. White, - -	"	—	2	
William E. Wise, - -	"			

(For rest of this company, see publication of Pay Rolls.)

Captain Thomas R. Joynes' Company—Second Regiment.

NAMES.			RANK.	TIME OF SERVICE.		REMARKS.
				Months.	Days.	
John Finney,	-	-	Sergeant,	–	20	
John J. Wise,	-	-	Corporal,	–	10	
Robinson Waples,	-	-	"	–	28	
Jesse Bonwell,	-	-	Private,	–	16	
William Bird,	-	-	"	–	18	
John Bonwell,	-	-	"	–	28	
Charles B. Bradford,	-	-	"	–	9	
James Carruthers,	-	-	"	–	6	
Thomas Chandler,	-	-	"	–	8	
Thomas Gray,	-	-	"	–	6	
John Holeston,	-	-	"	–	22	
Robert Hall,	-	-	"	–	14	
John Hannaford,	-	-	"	–	23	
Henry Hannaford,	-	-	"	–	18	
Peter Holland,	-	-	"	–	5	
Joshua Holland,	-	-	"	–	5	
William Lewis,	-	-	"	–	16	
Levin Laylor,	-	-	"	–	8	
John Parker,	-	-	"	–	28	
Thomas Russell,	-	-	"	–	14	
James Roberts,	-	-	"	–	2	
Elijah Scott,	-	-	"	–	4	
Ezekiel Smith,	-	-	"	–	24	
George D. Wise,	-	-	"	–	12	
Robinson West,	-	-	"	–	15	
John J. Wise,	-	-	"	–	8	

(For rest of this company, see publication of Pay Rolls.)

MUSTER ROLL

Of Captain George Judkins' Company, in the Seventy-first Regiment, Virginia Militia, commanded by Lieutenant Colonel William Allen, from the 30th June to the 10th July, in the year 1813.

NAMES.	RANK.	TIME OF SERVICE.		REMARKS.
		Months.	Days.	
George Judkins,	Captain,	–	11	
Nathaniel Cocks,	Lieutenant,	–	11	
Benjamin Bailey,	Ensign,	–	11	
William Maynard,	Sergeant,	–	11	
James Douglass,	"	–	11	
David Bishop,	"	–	11	
Bartholomew Andrews,	"	–	11	
William Bailey,	Corporal,	–	11	
Miles Burgess,	"	–	11	
William Rae,	"	–	11	
Archibald Milby,	"	–	11	
Celeb Dewell,	Fifer,	–	11	
Nicholas Dewell,	Drummer,	–	11	
Henry Andrews,	Private,	–	7	
William H. Browne,	"	–	2	
Samuel Bains,	"	–	10	
John Burgess,	"	–	7	
Richard Bishop,	"	–	7	
John Bishop,	"	–	7	
James Brockwell,	"	–	7	
John Chetham,	"	–	7	
William Cauley,	"	–	7	
George C. Collier,	"	–	10	
Stephen Collier,	"	–	10	
Edward Charles,	"	–	10	
John Collier,	"	–	10	
Burd Dewell,	"	–	7	
Zachariah Dewell,	"	–	7	
David Dewell,	"	–	10	
Herbert Dewell,	"	–	2	
William B. Ellis,	"	–	10	
Wm. M. Gurriman,	"	–	7	
John Hollandsworth,	"	–	10	
Carter Harrison,	"	–	10	
Drewry Hobbs,	"	–	10	
Richard Johnson,	"	–	10	
Alexander Jeinm,	"	–	10	
Thomas D. Lucas,	"	–	7	
Willis Lane,	"	–	3	
Bernard Major,	"	–	7	
Dudley D. Maynard,	"	–	7	
Richard McColester,	"	–	10	
Edward Marks,	"	–	10	
Robert C. Maynard,	"	–	10	
Thomas Murry,	"	–	2	
Edward Newell,	"	–	6	
Gilliam Newsom,	"	–	10	
Francis Ruffin,	"	–	7	
Nathaniel Spratley,	"	–	7	

NAMES.			RANK.	TIME OF SERVICE.		REMARKS.
				Months.	Days.	
Pleasant Sheffield,	-	-	Private,	–	7	
Thomas Slade,	-	-	"	–	10	
David Sheffield,	-	-	"	–	2	
Amos Sledge,	-	-	"	–	3	
William Singleton,	-	-	"	–	3	
Stephen Stewart,	-	-	"	–	2	
Jno. M. St. George,	-	-	"	–	2	
John A. Warren,	-	-	"	–	10	

Ensign Thomas Keeling's Company—Twentieth Regiment.

NAMES.	RANK.	TIME OF SERVICE.		REMARKS.
		Months.	Days.	
James Burgess,	Sergeant,	–	17	
Jonathan Ackiss,	Private,	–	14	
Henry Airs,	"	–	14	
Stephen Bonney,	"	–	14	
John Brumley,	"	1	12	
James Bryant,	"	–	14	
Moses Bonney,	"	–	14	
Jonathan Buskey,	"	–	14	
Edward Bonney,	"	–	14	
Charles Berry,	"	–	14	
Francis Batton,	"	–	14	
Robert Burley.	"	–	14	
John Butt,	"	–	28	
William Butt,	"	–	28	
Maximilian Bolt,	"	–	14	
John Bolt,	"	–	14	
Benjamin Barnes,	"	–	28	
Joseph Benthall,	"	–	14	
Nathan Bonney,	"	–	14	
Griffin Bonney,	"	–	14	
Jonathan Bonney,	"	–	14	
Edward Bonney,	"	–	14	
Benjamin Barnes,	"	–	14	
James Brown,	"	–	14	
John Bonney, jr.	"	–	14	
John Bonney, sr.	"	–	28	
Batson Cayson,	"	–	14	
Caleb Carrell,	"	–	14	
Thomas Campbell,	"	–	14	
James Corbell,	"	–	14	
Fenton Cummings,	"	–	28	
Batson Capps.	"	–	14	
John Cox,	"	–	28	
Seth Capps,	"	1	14	
Hilery Capps,	"	–	14	
Henry Cornick,	"	–	14	
Kader Capps,	"	–	14	
Joel Carbell,	"	–	14	
John Cummings,	"	–	14	
David Capps, (of Obed.)	"	–	14	
Benjamin Cox, (of John,)	"	–	14	
Benjamin Cox,	"	–	14	
Dennis Capps,	"	–	14	
Lemuel Collins,	"	–	14	
Timothy Collins,	"	–	14	
James Capps,	"	–	14	
George Cox,	"	–	14	
Ansell Cox,	"	–	14	
William Capps,	"	–	14	
John Cuthrell,	"	–	14	
John Carr,	"	–	14	
Willoughby Cooper,	"	–	14	
Willis Cooper,	"	–	14	
Maximilian Cherry,	"	–	14	

NAMES.	RANK.	TIME OF SERVICE.		REMARKS.
		Months.	Days.	
William Capps, - -	Private,	—	14	
Jacob Chappell, - -	"	—	14	
Thomas Caton, - -	"	—	14	
Joseph Chappell, - -	"	—	14	
John Dudley, - -	"	—	14	
James Davis, sr. - -	"	—	14	
James Dyer, - -	"	—	14	
Samuel Doughty, -	"	—	14	
Jesse Dawley, - -	"	—	14	
Joshua Davis, - -	"	—	14	
Jesse Doudge, - -	"	—	14	
Henry Davis, - -	"	—	14	
James Davis, jr. - -	"	—	14	
Horatio Davis, - -	"	—	14	
John Edwards, - -	"	—	28	
Henry Edwards, -	"	—	14	
Simon M. Etheridge, -	"	—	14	
Robert Etheredge, - -	"	—	14	
Henry Edmunds, -	"	—	14	
David Edmunds, - -	"	—	14	
Thomas Ewell, - -	"	—	14	
John Edmunds, - -	"	—	14	
Alexander W. Edmunds, -	"	—	14	
William Eaton, - -	"	—	14	
Alexander W. Edmunds, -	"	—	14	
John Fentress, - -	"	—	14	
William Fentress, - -	"	—	14	
Jeremiah Fentress, -	"	—	14	
Edward Flannagan, -	"	—	14	
Joshua Frizzell, - -	"	—	14	
John Franklin, - -	"	—	28	
John Fisher, - -	"	—	14	
Zachariah Frizzell, -	"	—	14	
Arthur Frizzell, - -	"	—	14	
David Fentress, - -	"	—	18	
James Gisbon, - -	"	—	28	
Charles Griggs, - -	"	—	14	
Lemuel Godfrey, - -	"	—	14	
David Grimstead, - -	"	—	28	
Joshua Grimstead, - -	"	—	14	
William Griggs, - -	"	—	14	
George S. Gaskings, -	"	—	14	
Greshom Galusha, -	"	—	14	
James Harrison, - -	"	—	14	
Daniel Hargrove, -	"	—	14	
William Hebdon, - -	"	—	14	
Hillery Hunter, - -	"	—	14	
George T. Hall, - -	"	—	14	
John Haynes, - -	"	—	14	
John Holmes, - -	"	—	14	
Benjamin Holmes, -	"	—	14	
Samuel Hill, - -	"	—	14	
Jesse Hanners, -	"	—	14	
Moses Heath, - -	"	—	14	
Robin Holmes, - -	"	—	14	
Jesse Ives, - -	"	—	14	
Horatio James, - -	"	—	14	
Jonathan James, - -	"	—	14	
Smith Kilby, - -	"	—	14	
Smith Kelley, - -	"	—	14	
James Kellem, - -	"	—	14	
John K. Kays, - -	"	—	14	
Henry Land, - -	"	—	14	
William Land, - -	"	—	14	

NAMES.	RANK.	TIME OF SERVICE.		REMARKS.
		Months.	Days.	
Dennis Land, - -	Private,	–	14	
James Lovett, - -	"	–	14	
Jesse Lane, - -	"	–	14	
Simon Land, - -	"	–	14	
Willis Langley, - -	"	–	14	
Thomas Lovett, - -	"	–	14	
William McCoy, - -	"	–	14	
Willis McCoy, - -	"	–	14	
Adam Murden, - -	"	–	14	
Lemuel Malbone, - -	"	–	14	
Thomas J. Merchant, -	"	–	14	
William Moore, - -	"	–	28	
John McDonald, - -	"	–	14	
James Mullen, - -	"	–	14	
Equillar Monday, - -	"	–	28	
Zachariah Murden, - -	"	–	14	
Thomas McClannan, sr. -	"	–	28	
William Malbone, - -	"	–	14	
Edward Murden, - -	"	–	14	
William Mathias, -	"	–	14	
Dempsey McClannon, -	"	–	14	
George McClannon, - -	"	–	14	
William Moore, jr. - -	"	–	14	
John Malbone, - -	"	–	14	
Malachi Murden, - -	"	–	14	
John Morse, - -	"	–	14	
Thomas McClannon, jr. -	"	–	14	
Kader McClannon, - -	"	–	14	
Caleb Malbone, - -	"	–	14	
David Nelson, - -	"	–	28	
William Otley, - -	"	–	28	
Joseph Ottison, - -	"	–	14	
Coventon Otley, - -	"	–	14	
Jacob Petree, - -	"	1	12	
Tully Phillips, - -	"	–	28	
Robert Parsons, - -	"	–	14	
Laban Pallett, - -	"	–	14	
Luke Paden, - -	"	–	14	
Richard Pebworth, - -	"	–	14	
William Parsons, - -	"	–	14	
Enoch Rancy, - -	"	–	14	
William Reade, - -	"	–	14	
James Robinson, - -	"	–	14	
John W. Smith, - -	"	–	28	
Reuben Stone, - -	"	–	14	
John Shipp, - -	"	–	14	
Jesse Smith, - -	"	–	28	
John Shepherd, - -	"	–	28	
Malachi Stiron, - -	"	–	14	
Simeon Smith, - -	"	–	14	
Tully Smith, - -	"	–	14	
Thomas Strawhorn, - -	"	–	28	
Ebenezer Span, - -	"	–	28	
Smith Stiron, - -	"	–	14	
Joseph Sylvester, - -	"	–	14	
James Sinaker, - -	"	–	14	
Edward Suggs, - -	"	–	14	
George Throp, - -	"	–	14	
Collins Timmons, - -	"	–	14	
David Williamson, - -	"	–	14	
Jesse Wiles, - -	"	–	14	
Joel Waterman, - -	"	–	14	
John West, - -	"	–	14	
Thomas Wiles, - -	"	–	14	

NAMES.	RANK.	TIME OF SERVICE.		REMARKS.
		Months.	Days.	
Henry Williams,	Private,	—	14	
Thomas Whichard,	"	—	14	
Caleb Whitehurst,	"	—	14	
John Whitehurst, (of Jas.)	"	—	14	
George Whitehurst,	"	—	14	
Thomas Woodhouse,	"	—	14	
William H. Williams,	"	—	14	
Solomon Wallace,	"	—	14	
Malachi Williams,	"	—	14	
James Williams,	"	—	14	
Josiah Williamson,	"	—	14	
Robert Williams,	"	—	18	
Robert Williams, (of Tully,)	"	—	14	
Henry Woodhouse,	"	—	14	
Obed Whitehurst,	"	—	14	
James Woodhouse,	"	—	14	
Batson Whitehurst,	"	—	14	
William Woodland,	"	—	14	
John Whitehurst, sr.	"	—	14	
John Woodhouse,	"	—	14	
David Whitehurst,	"	—	14	
John Ward,	"	—	14	
John Whitehurst,	"	—	14	
Nathaniel West,	"	—	14	
Absalom Whitehurst,	"	—	14	
John Whichard,	"	—	14	
Noah Whitehurst,	"	—	28	
John Wilburn,	"	—	14	
Horatio Woodward,	"	—	14	
Nehemiah Whitehurst,	"	—	28	
David Williamson,	"	—	14	
Enoch Whitehurst,	"	—	14	
Patrick Whitehurst,	"	—	14	
Joshua Whitehurst, (of Jas.)	"	—	14	

(For the rest of this company, see publication of Pay Rolls.)

MUSTER ROLL

Of Captain Richard B. Kello's Company, of the Sixty-fifth Regiment, Virginia Militia, in the County of Southampton, called into the Service of the United States under the general orders of the 26th of August, from 29th August to 13th September, in the year 1814.

NAMES.	RANK.	TIME OF SERVICE.		REMARKS.
		Months.	Days.	
Richard B. Kello, - -	Captain,	—	16	
Benjamin Wilson, - -	Lieutenant,	—	16	
George B. Cobb, - -	"	—	16	
Samuel Summerell, - -	Ensign,	—	16	
Jesse Bailey, - -	Ord'ly serg't,	—	16	
Lewis N. Branch, - -	Sergeant,	—	16	
John Nicholson, - -	"	—	16	
Joseph Joiner, - -	"	—	16	
William Love, - -	Corporal,	—	16	
John Newsum, - -	"	—	16	
William Bowden, - -	"	—	16	
Nathaniel Barham, - -	"	—	16	
Robert Wellons, - -	Drummer,	—	16	
Joseph Fowler, - -	Fifer,	—	16	
Lenard Atkins, - -	Private,	—	16	
Green Adams, - -	"	—	16	
John Bristen, - -	"	—	16	
Jesse Branch, - -	"	—	16	
Orson Branch, - -	"	—	16	
George Branch, jr. - -	"	—	16	
Lemuel Beale, - -	"	—	16	
Dixon B. Bass, - -	"	—	16	
Bailey Bryant, - -	"	—	16	
Joshua Bryant, - -	"	—	16	
Elijah Beale, - -	"	—	16	
Elias Bracy, - -	"	—	16	
Willis Brown, - -	"	—	16	
Burwell Branch, - -	"	—	16	
James Calthorpe, - -	"	—	16	
John Cooper, - -	"	—	16	
Cooper Cawling, - -	"	—	16	
John Davis, - -	"	—	16	
Elisha Darden, - -	"	—	16	
Humphrey Drewry, - -	"	—	16	
Jeremiah E. Edwards, - -	"	—	16	
Tyler Edwards, - -	"	—	16	
Jesse Gardner, - -	"	—	16	
Robert Hart, - -	"	—	16	
William Hancock, - -	"	—	16	
Joseph Harriss, - -	"	—	16	
Jordan Jones, - -	"	—	16	
Irajah Johnson, - -	"	—	16	
Ichabod Johnson, - -	"	—	16	
John Linter, - -	"	—	16	
John Norsworthy, - -	"	—	16	
William Pierce, - -	"	—	16	
Benj. C. Hancock, - -	"	—	16	
Talton Scott, - -	"	—	16	

NAMES.	RANK.	TIME OF SERVICE.		REMARKS.
		Months.	Days.	
Martin P. Stephens, - -	Private,	—	16	
Brittain Travis, - -	"	—	16	
Benj. Travis, - -	"	—	16	
Dawson Vaughan, - -	"	—	16	
Henry Vaughan, - -	"	—	16	
Bartimeus Wellons, - -	"	—	16	
James Willis, - -	"	—	16	

MUSTER ROLL

Of Captain William Kendall's Company, of the Twenty-fifth Regiment, Virginia Militia, in the County of King George, called into actual Service under the general orders of the 14th of July, from the 15th to the 26th July, in the year 1813.

NAMES.		RANK.	TIME OF SERVICE.		REMARKS.
			Months.	Days.	
William Kendall,	- -	Captain,	—	8	
Samuel Davis,	- -	Lieutenant,	—	8	
Joseph Suttle,	- -	Ensign,	—	8	
James Baker,	- -	Sergeant,	—	8	
Lemuel Davis,	- -	"	—	12	
William Spilman,	- -	"	—	12	
Thomas McKenney,	- -	"	—	12	
James Rollins,	- -	Corporal,	—	12	
James Frank,	- -	"	—	8	
Massey Thomas,	- -	"	—	3	
John Frank,	- -	Drummer,	—	8	
Robert Rollins,	- -	Fifer,	—	8	
Thornton Atwell,	- -	Private,	—	8	
George D. Ashton,	- -	"	—	3	
James Bailey,	- -	"	—	8	
John Baily,	- -	"	—	10	
Thomas Bernard,	- -	"	—	8	
Bennett Chrismond,	- -	"	—	12	
Henry Chrismond,	- -	"	—	12	
John Cox,	- -	"	—	8	
John Curley,	- -	"	—	5	
John Dishman,	- -	"	—	12	
Hiram Davis,	- -	"	—	8	
James Dishman,	- -	"	—	8	
James Fricker,	- -	"	—	3	
Willis Ferrell,	- -	"	—	8	
Wm. D. Greer,	- -	"	—	12	
William Hailes,	- -	"	—	8	
John Hutt,	- -	"	—	8	
Joseph Harrison,	- -	"	—	12	
John Jones, jr.	- -	"	—	12	
Philip H. Jones,	- -	"	—	8	
William J. Jett,	- -	"	—	8	
Joel Jones,	- -	"	—	8	
Jacob Levy,	- -	"	—	8	
Thomas Lyons,	- -	"	—	8	
William P. Massey,	- -	"	—	9	
Powell Massey,	- -	"	—	8	
Reuben Massey,	- -	"	—	12	
William Massey,	- -	"	—	6	
John Massey,	- -	"	—	8	
Nathaniel Owens,	- -	"	—	12	
Joel Reynolds,	- -	"	—	12	
Cornelius Reynolds,	- -	"	—	12	
William Rollins,	- -	"	—	8	
Gust. G. Rogers,	- -	"	—	8	
Benjamin Reynolds,	- -	"	—	12	

NAMES.	RANK.	TIME OF SERVICE.		REMARKS.
		Months.	Days.	
John Sebastian, - -	Private,	–	12	
James Staples, - -	"	–	7	
John Spilman, jr. - -	"	–	8	
Richard Steel, - -	"	–	8	
Austin Suttle, - -	"	–	8	
George White, - -	"	–	8	
William S. Wilkinson, - -	"	–	5	
Augustin Weidon, - -	"	–	8	

MUSTER ROLL

Of Captain Charles Kent's Company, of the Thirty-ninth Regiment, Virginia Militia, in the County of Dinwiddie, called into actual Service under the general orders of the 30th June, from the 30th June to the 12th July, in the year 1813.

NAMES.	RANK.	TIME OF SERVICE.		REMARKS.
		Months.	Days.	
Charles Kent, - -	Captain,	–	13	
Thomas Wallace, - -	Lieutenant,	–	13	
George W. Stainback, -	Ensign,	–	13	
Seth Heath, - -	Sergeant,	–	13	
Stephen Paer, - -	"	–	13	
Abial Camp, - -	"	–	13	
Charles Hunt, - -	"	–	13	
Thomas Wilson, - -	Corporal,	–	13	
Wauglin W. Biggers, -	"	–	13	
Major L. Drinkard, - -	Private,	–	13	
Samuel Woodfolk, - -	"	–	13	
Alexander Crosland, - -	"	–	13	
Daniel C. Townes, - -	"	–	13	
Nelson Alley, - -	"	–	13	
Richard J. Andrews, - -	"	–	13	
John C. Armistead, - -	"	–	13	
Robert Adams, - -		–	13	
Edward Atkinson, - -	"	–	13	
Charles W. Brewer, - -	"	–	13	
Daniel Brown, - -	"	–	13	
Robert Burge, - -	"	–	13	
Thomas Braner, - -	"	–	13	
Benjamin Barnes, - -	"	–	13	
Benjamin E. Cook, - -	"	–	13	
Sampson Clements, - -	"	–	13	
William Dosh, - -	"	–	13	
Nathaniel Denby, - -	"	–	13	
Augustine Ellis, - -	"	–	13	
Ephraim Eckles, - -	"	–	13	
Martin Eanes, - -	"	–	13	
William Edwards, - -	"	–	13	
Nathaniel Friend, - -	"	–	13	
Robert Firn, - -	"	–	13	
William Fennell, - -		–	13	
William P. Graham, - -	"	–	13	
Walthal Hatcher, - -	"	–	13	
Jared Hotchkiss, - -	"	–	13	
Parham Hobbs, - -	"	–	13	
Joseph Heath, - -	"	–	13	
George Irvine, - -	"	–	13	
James B. Kendall, - -	"	–	13	
Thomas Lee, - -	"	–	13	
James P. Lownes, - -	"	–	13	
M. P. Mays, - -	"	–	13	
Jeremiah McIntosh, - -	"	–	13	
William McCay, - -	"	–	13	

NAMES.	RANK.	TIME OF SERVICE.		REMARKS.
		Months.	Days.	
Peter McCulloch, - -	Private,	–	13	
John McLarren, - -	"	–	13	
Nathaniel McTaimon, - -	"	–	13	
William Matthews, - -	"	–	13	
Thomas Neilson, - -	"	–	13	
Charles O'Harra, - -	"	–	13	
Timothy R. Ryan, - -	"	–	13	
William C. Rawlings, - -	"	–	13	
Burwell Rosser, - -	"	–	13	
Thornby Schoolar, - -	"	–	13	
Thomas Stewart, - -	"	–	13	
John Stewart, - -	"	–	13	
Charles Stewart, - -	"	–	13	
Robert Stewart, - -	"	–	13	
James Smith, - -	"	–	13	
Daniel Thompson, - -	"	–	13	
Nathan Vincent, - -	"	–	13	
Nathaniel H. Whitlow, - -	"	–	13	
William Wallace, - -	"	–	13	
Silas Webb, - -	"	–	13	
William Weeks, - -	"	–	13	
Leighton Wood, - -	"	–	13	
Jonas Wood, jr. - -	"	–	13	

Captain James Kirk's Company—Ninety-second Regiment.

NAMES.	RANK.	TIME OF SERVICE.		REMARKS.
		Months.	Days.	
Richard Towell, - -	Lieutenant,	—	17	
John James, - -	"	—	6	
Timothy McNamara, -	Ensign,	—	23	
Ellis L. B. Tapscott, - -	Sergeant,	—	11	
Thomas Mason, - -	"	—	17	
Coleman Doggett, - -	"	—	9	
Charles Hilleey, - -	"	—	2	
John Kirk, - -	"	—	3	
John Thrall, - -	"	—	9	
Thomas Mason, jr. - -	"	—	6	
Bailey George, - -	Corporal,	—	17	
Thomas N. Ford, - -	"	—	17	
Hiram Locke, - -	"	—	17	
Benj. George, - -	"	—	17	
James Doggett, - -	"	—	7	
John Yerby, - -	"	—	5	
Armstead Haydon, - -	"	—	5	
James Thrall, - -	Drummer,	—	17	
George Pullen, - -	"	—	10	
James Ashburn, - -	Private,	—	17	
Abel Alford, - -	"	—	20	
John Alford, - -	"	—	20	
Robert Bean, - -	"	—	17	
Thomas Bottoms, - -	"	—	17	
Nicholas P. Buchan, - -	"	—	11	
Arthur Brent, - -	"	—	6	
Isaac Brent, - -	"	—	6	
George L. Corbin, - -	"	—	11	
Nicholas Carter, - -	"	—	17	
Thomas Cottrell, - -	"	—	11	
George Carter, - -	"	—	17	
Thomas Carter, - -	"	—	17	
Thomas Cornelius, - -	"	—	11	
Isaac Currell, - -	"	—	17	
Isaac Currell, jr. - -	"	—	6	
Gawin Corbin, - -	"	—	11	
George L. Corbin, - -	"	—	6	
Daniel Chilton, - -	"	—	7	
Charles Carter, - -	"	—	2	
Hiram Chilton, - -	"	—	4	
Newman Chilton, - -	"	—	6	
William Driver, - -	"	—	5	
James Doggett, - -	"	—	2	
Joseph Dosher, - -	"	—	2	
Richard Edwards, - -	"	—	10	
Zamoth George, - -	"	—	17	
John Gains, - -	"	—	17	
Griffin Gains, - -	"	—	17	
Martin George, - -	"	—	11	
William Gibson, - -	"	—	11	
Lewis Gains, - -	"	—	10	
John George, - -	"	—	6	
Osbourn Haydon, - -	"	—	7	
Thomas Haydon, - -	"	—	6	

NAMES.	RANK.	TIME OF SERVICE.		REMARKS.
		Months.	Days.	
Griffin Haydon, - -	Private,	—	5	
Abner Haydon, - -	"	—	12	
Addison Hall, - -	"	—	22	
William Hammonds, -	"	—	17	
Richard Hinton, - -	"	—	11	
Thomas Hughes, - -	"	—	11	
Augustin Hughlett, -	"	—	22	
George H. Hutchings, -	"	—	8	
Lewis Hammonds, - -	"	—	12	
Royston Hughlett, - -	"	—	23	
John W. Hunton, - -	"	—	5	
Oswall Haydon, - -	"	—	5	
Bedy Hughlett, - -	"	—	5	
Lewis Hammon, - -	"	—	5	
Armstead Haydon, - -	"	—	7	
Richard Ingram, - -	"	—	11	
Charles James, - -	"	—	11	
William James, - -	"	—	17	
James Jefferson, - -	"	—	17	
Ludwell Locke, - -	"	—	17	
Eppa Lawson, - -	"	—	22	
Eppa Lunce, - -	"	—	5	
John Mason, - -	"	—	17	
William Martin, - -	"	—	11	
John McNamara, - -	"	—	17	
James Mott, - -	"	—	6	
Alexander Noel, - -	"	—	3	
Thomas L. Norris, - -	"	—	10	
James Plunket, - -	"	—	12	
Cyrus Pitman, - -	"	—	20	
John Roberts, - -	"	—	17	
John Richardson, - -	"	—	2	
Henry Schofield, - -	"	—	11	
Spencer C. Smith, - -	"	—	17	
Moses Short, - -	"	—	20	
Charles Simmonds, - -	"	—	20	
Daniel Shelton, - -	"	—	5	
George Spilman, - -	"	—	10	
William Thrall, - -	"	—	13	
Dempsey Treacle, - -	"	—	11	
Thomas Towell, - -	"	—	17	
John Toleman, - -	"	—	17	
John Wilder, - -	"	—	17	
Thomas Yerby, - -	"	—	17	
John Yerby, - -	"	—	7	

(For rest of this company, see publication of Pay Rolls.)

MUSTER ROLL

Of Captain Archer Lacy's Company, from the Fifty-second Regiment, Virginia Militia, New Kent County, commanded by Lieutenant Colonel John H. Christian, in the Service from 28th June to 13th July, 1813.

NAMES.			RANK.	TIME OF SERVICE.		REMARKS.
				Months.	Days.	
Archer Lacy,	-	-	Captain,	–	16	
Parker Ball,	-	-	Lieutenant,	–	16	
Rich'd Crump,	-	-	Ensign,	–	16	
John Curle,	-	-	Sergeant,	–	16	
John W. Langley,	-	-	"	–	16	
Henry Vaughan,	-	-	"	–	16	
Samuel Trower,	-	-	"	–	16	
Gideon Trower,	-	-	Corporal,	–	16	
Florance H. Walker,	-	-	"	–	16	
John Austin,	-	-	Private,	–	16	
William Walker,	-	-	"	–	16	
William Boswell,	-	-	"	–	16	
John Wilks,	-	-	"	–	16	
John Stuart,	-	-	"	–	16	
Henry Woodward,	-	-	"	–	16	
Phil'n Lacy,	-	-	"	–	16	
Robert E. Jones,	-	-	"	–	16	
John H. Walker,	-	-	"	–	16	
Joshua Martin,	-	-	"	–	16	
Thomas Watts,	-	-	"	–	16	
John Tandy,	-	-	"	–	16	
Thomas Vaiding,	•	-	"	–	16	

Captain Griffin Lamkin's Company—One Hundred and Twenty-first Regiment.

NAMES.			RANK.	TIME OF SERVICE.		REMARKS.
				Months.	Days.	
Robert Beard,	-	-	Sergeant,	–	20	
Jacob Good,	-	-	Fifer,	1	8	
William Linton,	-	-	Private,	–	17	
David Morton,	-	-	"	–	9	
Carter Meen,	-	-	"	–	23	
John Window,	-	-	"	–	23	
Reuben Zenherty,	-	-	"	–	23	

(For rest of this company, see publication of Pay Rolls.)

Captain Lunsford Loving's Company—at Camp Holly.

NAMES.	RANK.	TIME OF SERVICE.		REMARKS.
		Months.	Days.	
Robert Hunter, - -	Corporal,	1	27	

(For rest of this company, see publication of Pay Rolls.)

(This captain is Lunsford instead of Loving in the index of the Pay Rolls.)

MUSTER ROLL

Of Captain James Land's Company, from the Twentieth Regiment, Virginia Militia, commanded by Lieutenant Colonel James Robinson, in the Service from 6th to 18th February, from 10th to 15th March, and from 24th to 30th September, 1813.

NAMES.			RANK.	TIME OF SERVICE.		REMARKS.
				Months.	Days.	
James Land,	-	-	Captain,	—	23	
Peter Land,	-	-	Lieutenant,	—	23	
Enoch Land,	-	-	Ensign,	—	23	
William Morriss,	-	-	Sergeant,	—	17	
John P. Biddle,	-	-	"	—	17	
John Burgess,	-	-	"	—	17	
William Whitehurst,	-	-	"	—	6	
Amos Brown,	-	-	"	—	6	
Whitington Cox,	-	-	"	—	6	
Amos Brown,	-	-	Private,	—	17	
Thomas L. Brown,	-	-	"	—	17	
John Butt,	-	-	"	—	12	
William S. Brown,	-	-	"	—	23	
William Bishop,	-	-	"	—	17	
William Butt,	-	-	"	—	17	
John Brown,	-	-	"	—	12	
Enoch Cannon,	-	-	"	—	15	
Whitington Cox,	-	-	"	—	12	
Geo. Cox,	-	-	"	—	17	
John Cannon,	-	-	"	—	17	
Joshua Cannon,	-	-	"	—	12	
John Cox,	-	-	"	—	17	
Henry Cannon,	-	-	"	—	12	
Tully Doudge,	-	-	"	—	12	
William Etheridge,	-	-	"	—	12	
John Ewell,	-	-	"	—	23	
Geo. S. Gaskings,	-	-	"	—	23	
Joshua Holmes,	-	-	"	—	23	
Isaac Johnson,	-	-	"	—	23	
Henry Land,	-	-	"	—	5	
Joshua Lovitt,	-	-	"	—	6	
Moses Moore,	-	-	"	—	12	
Kedar Moore,	-	-	"	—	17	
William McCoy,	-	-	"	—	17	
James McClaten,	-	-	"	—	17	
William Morriss,	-	-	"	—	6	
Henry Pattet,	-	-	"	—	23	
Matthew Pattet,	-	-	"	—	17	
John L. Pebworth,	-	-	"	—	17	
James Pebworth,	-	-	"	—	11	
Reuben Shipp,	-	-	"	—	18	
William Shipp,	-	-	"	—	23	
John W. Smith,	-	-	"	—	23	
Geo. Scott,	-	-	"	—	23	

NAMES.	RANK.	TIME OF SERVICE.		REMARKS.
		Months.	Days.	
Josiah Styron, - -	Private,	–	18	
William Whitehurst, -	"	–	12	
Nehemiah Whitehurst, -	"	–	23	
Charles M. Woodhouse, -	"	–	17	
James Woodhouse, - -	"	–	11	

MUSTER ROLL

Of Captain Peter Land's Company, from the Twentieth Regiment, Virginia Militia, commanded by Lieutenant Colonel James Robinson, in the Service of the United States from the 5th to the 14th February, from 9th to 15th Marcl., and from 7th to 15th September, 1813.

NAMES.	RANK.	TIME OF SERVICE.		REMARKS.
		Months.	Days.	
Peter Land, - -	Captain,	—	21	
William Whitehurst, - -	Lieutenant,	—	15	
Daniel Lovitt, - -	Ensign,	—	15	
Thomas L. Brown, - -	Sergeant,	—	19	
Robert Murden, - -	"	—	21	
Moses Murden, - -	"	—	6	
Henry Murden, - -	"	—	14	
Reubin Brown, - -	"	—	15	
James Murden, - -	"	—	21	
Zachariah Fentress, - -	"	—	6	
John Fentress, - -	"	—	21	
William Murden, - -	Corporal,	—	15	
James Whitehurst, - -	"	—	15	
William Ward, - -	"	—	15	
William Simmons, - -	Fifer,	—	21	
John West, - -	Drummer,	—	21	
Batson Brown, - -	Private,	—	21	
Kedar Brown, - -	"	—	14	
Thomas Corprew, - -	"	—	21	
Joshua Corprew, - -	"	—	6	
Benjamin Capps, - -	"	—	6	
Benjamin Copes, - -	"	—	6	
John Campbell, - -	"	—	6	
William Fentress, - -	"	—	21	
Thomas Fentress, - -	"	—	12	
Rich'd Frentress, - -	"	—	9	
William Fentress, jr. - -	"	—	15	
Nathan Fentress, - -	"	—	9	
William Godfrey, - -	"	—	11	
William C. Henly, - -	"	—	15	
Erasmus Haynes, - -	"	—	15	
Daniel Hugrow, - -	"	—	15	
James Huddleston, - -	"	—	6	
John Huddleston, - -	"	—	9	
William Jobson, - -	"	—	15	
John Jobson, - -	"	—	9	
William Land, sr. - -	"	—	21	
Thomas Lovitt, - -	"	—	10	
William Land, jr. - -	"	—	21	
Simon Land, - -	"	—	12	
Lancaster Lovett, - -	"	—	17	
John Land, - -	"	—	6	
Willoughby Land, - -	"	—	11	
James Lovitt, - -	"	—	15	
Langley Lovett, - -	"	—	6	
Francis Lovett, - -	"	—	15	
Major Land, - -	"	—	6	

NAMES.			RANK.	TIME OF SERVICE.		REMARKS.
				Months.	Days.	
Dennis Land,	-	-	Private,	—	15	
David Land,	-	-	"	—	9	
Adam Lovett,	-	-	"	—	9	
William Malbone,	-	-	"	—	21	
Lemuel Malbone,	-	-	"	—	21	
Malachi Murden,	-	-	"	—	12	
Edward Murden,	-	-	"	—	15	
James Murden, jr.	-	-	"	—	6	
Thomas Stokes,	-	-	"	—	19	
Hilary Shipp,	-	-	"	—	9	
Balson Shipp,	-	-	"	—	14	
Malachi Styron,	-	-	"	—	20	
William Stone,	-	-	"	—	15	
James Stokes,	-	-	"	—	15	
Lemuel Stokes,	-	-	"	—	10	
Reubin Shipp,	-	-	"	—	6	
John Stone,	-	-	"	—	10	
Peter Stone,	-	-	"	—	4	
Henry Simmons,	-	-	"	—	4	
Batsen Whitehurst,	-	-	"	—	11	
Thomas Wright,	-	-	"	—	20	
John Woodhouse,	-	-	"	—	15	
Thos. Woodhouse,	-	-	"	—	6	
William West,	-	-	"	—	15	
Willoughby West,	-	-	"	—	15	
John Williamson,	-	-	"	—	9	

MUSTER ROLL

Of Captain Littleton Lanier's Company, from the Second Regiment, Virginia Militia, commanded by Lt. Col. William Allen, in the Service of the United States, from the 1st to 11th September, 1814.

NAMES.	RANK.	TIME OF SERVICE.		REMARKS.
		Months.	Days.	
Littleton Lanier, - -	Captain,	–	11	
Robert Rochelle, - -	Lieutenant,	–	11	
Walter Blunt, - -	Ensign,	–	11	
Joseph Jarrad, - -	Sergeant,	–	11	
John Jarrad, - -	"	–	11	
Thomas Peete, - -	"	–	11	
John C. Owen, - -	"	–	11	
Augustine Shands, - -	Corporal,	–	11	
Gilliam Fletcher, - -	"	–	11	
Geo. Birdsong, - -	"	–	11	
Jessee Hurgrave, - -	"	–	11	
Micajah H. Adkins, - -	Private,	–	11	
Johnson Atkinson, - -	"	–	11	
Thomas Birdsong, - -	"	–	11	
James Birdsong, - -	"	–	11	
Benjamin Birdsong, - -	"	–	11	
Nelson Bryant, - -	"	–	11	
Frederick Bryant, - -	"	–	11	
Burnwell B. Bryant, - -	"	–	11	
Benjamin Bains, - -	"	–	11	
Zachariah Bains, - -	"	–	11	
Geo. Blow, - -	"	–	11	
Richard Booth, - -	"	–	11	
Edmond Barrett, - -	"	–	11	
Littleberry Clarke, - -	"	–	11	
Frederick H. Clarke, - -	"	–	11	
John Clarke, - -	"	–	11	
Robert B. Cooper, - -	"	–	11	
Charles Christian, - -	"	–	11	
Zenos. Chappell, - -	"	–	11	
Cary Cotton, - -	"	–	11	
Pleasant Cotton, - -	"	–	11	
Charles Davis, - -	"	–	11	
Samuel Davis, - -	"	–	11	
William Davis, - -	"	–	11	
William B. Ellis, - -	"	–	11	
Richard Ellis, - -	"	–	11	
Micajah Ellis, - -	"	–	11	
James Fason, - -	"	–	11	
Thomas Graves, - -	"	–	11	
Geo. Hargrave, - -	"	–	11	
Robert Hargrave, - -	"	–	11	
John Hargrave, - -	"	–	11	
Joseph Hargrave, - -	"	–	11	
David Hargrave, - -	"	–	11	
Geo. Hallcome, - -	"	–	11	
Geo. Helvin, - -	"	–	11	
Gilliam Harrup, - -	"	–	11	

NAMES.	RANK.	TIME OF SERVICE.		REMARKS.
		Months.	Days.	
Henry Hobbs, - -	Private,	—	11	
Willie Hines, - -	"	—	11	
Robert Hite, - -	"	—	11	
Geo. Judkins, - -	"	—	11	
Samuel W. Judkins, - -	"	—	11	
Thomas B. Jarrad, - -	"	—	11	
Caleb Jones, - -	"	—	11	
Jessee Little, - -	"	—	11	
Warren Murphy, - -	"	—	11	
James Scoggin, - -	"	—	11	
Henry Underhill, - -	"	—	11	

MUSTER ROLL

Of Ensign John Lare's Company of Infantry, from the Twenty-third Regiment, Virginia Militia, Chesterfield County, commanded by Lieutenant Colonel William Brown, in the Service from the 18th to 21st March, 1813.

NAMES.	RANK.	TIME OF SERVICE.		REMARKS.
		Months.	Days.	
John Lare, - - -	Ensign,	–	3	Lara or Lore.
Thomas Ball, - -	Sergeant,	–	3	
Geo. N. Brichan, - -	"	–	3	
Thomas Drake, - -	"	–	3	
Bennet Goode, - -	"	–	3	
Robert H. Adkins, - -	Private,	–	3	
Joseph C. Adams, - -	"	–	3	
Andrew Adkins, - -	"	–	3	
Andrew Adkinson, - -	"	–	3	
John Brooks, - -	"	–	3	
William Brightwell, - -	"	–	3	
Geo. W. Branch, - -	"	–	3	
Thomas A. Brookin, -	"	–	3	
Thomas A. Bookin, - -	"	–	3	
Charles Cuntiff, - -	"	–	3	Or Cunliff.
John W. Dandridge, -	"	–	3	
Bal'a Furnia, - -	"	–	3	
James Fore, - -	"	–	3	
William Goff, - -	"	–	3	
Wilson Lain, - -	"	–	3	
Lewis Jeffers - -	"	–	3	
Drewry L. Lockadoe, -	"	–	3	
Jacob Lora, - -	"	–	3	
John McColum, - -	"	–	3	
Riley Moore, - -	"	–	3	
John Norman, - -	"	–	3	
Samuel Nelson, - -	"	–	3	
Samuel Nelson, - -	"	–	3	
Josiah Olds, - -	"	–	3	
William Paul, - -	"	–	3	
John L. Pleasants, - -	"	–	3	
John Rozell, - -	"	–	3	
Henry Sumpler, - -	"	–	3	
Samuel Short, - -	"	–	3	
John Simpson, - -	"	–	3	
James Short, - -	"	–	3	
John L. Vaughan, - -	"	–	3	
Waller T. Winfree, - -	"	–	3	

MUSTER ROLL

Of Captain John Lawrence's Company, attached to the Twenty-ninth Regiment, Virginia Militia, commanded by Major Joseph W. Ballard, in the Service from the 29th June to the 10th July, 1813.

NAMES.			RANK.	TIME OF SERVICE.		REMARKS.
				Months.	Days.	
John Lawrence,	-	-	Captain,	—	12	
Exum Eley,	-	-	Lieutenant,	—	12	
John Whitfield,	-	-	Ensign,	—	12	
Nathaniel Moody,	-	-	Sergeant,	—	12	
Benjamin Coggin,	-	-	"	—	12	
Thomas Norsworthy,	-	-	"	—	12	
Henry Wright,	-	-	"	—	12	
Jesse Saunders,	-	-	Corporal,	—	12	
Amos Powell,	-	-	"	—	12	
Robert Hancock,	-	-	"	—	12	
Joel W. Baugh.	-	-	"	—	12	
Elisha Bradshaw,	-	-	Private,	—	12	
Robert Bateman,	-	-	"	—	12	
Jessee Britt,	-	-	"	—	12	
Nathaniel Barrett,	-	-	"	—	12	
Samuel Batton,	-	-	"	—	12	
James Bridger,	-	-	"	—	12	
James Bowden,	-	-	"	—	12	
Thomas Bowden,	-	-	"	—	12	
John G. Bracy,	-	-	"	—	12	
John Bullock,	-	-	"	—	12	
Samuel Bridger,	-	-	"	—	12	
Joshua Coggin,	-	-	"	—	12	
Seth Copeland,	-	-	"	—	12	
John Clark,	-	-	"	—	12	
Lewis Coggin,	-	-	"	—	12	
Jacob Darden,	-	-	"	—	12	
John Davis,	-	-	"	—	12	
John B. Eley,	-	-	"	—	12	
Horatio Eley,	-	-	"	—	12	
Levy Edwards,	-	-	"	—	12	
Cary Eley.	-	-	"	—	12	
Matthew Edwards,	-	-	"	—	12	
Allen Fulgham,	-	-	"	—	12	
Miles Gay,	-	-	"	—	12	
Edwin Gray,	-	-	"	—	12	
Jessee Gay,	-	-	"	—	12	
Samuel Gay,	-	-	"	—	12	
John Hall.	-	-	"	—	12	
Joseph Holland,	-	-	"	—	12	
Matthew Johnson,	-	-	"	—	12	
Robert Lawrence,	-	-	"	—	12	
Thomas Pierce,	-	-	"	—	12	
Mitchman Pierce,	-	-	"	—	12	
Joshua Powell,	-	-	"	—	12	
Arthur Pierce,	-	-	"	—	12	
Willis Pope,	-	-	"	—	12	
William Powell,	-	-	"	—	12	
Hartwell Powell,	-	-	"	—	12	

NAMES.	RANK.	TIME OF SERVICE.		REMARKS.
		Months.	Days.	
William Roberts, - -	Private,	–	12	
John W. Roberts, - -	"	–	12	
James Roberts, - -	"	–	12	
Barden Roberts, - -	"	–	12	
Willis Roberts, - -	"	–	12	
John Saunders, jr. - -	"	–	12	
Thomas Stevens, - -	"	–	12	
Johnson Stevens, - -	"	–	12	
Mathew Turner, - -	"	–	12	
Thomas Underwood, - -	"	–	12	
Randolph Whitley, - -	"	–	12	
Henry Whitley, - -	"	–	12	

Captain Richard H. L. Lawson's Company—Twentieth Regiment.

NAMES.	RANK.	TIME OF SERVICE.		REMARKS.
		Months.	Days.	
Richard H. L. Lawson, -	Captain,	–	28	
Simon Hancock, - -	Lieutenant,	1	2	
William T. Nimmo, -	Ensign,	1	3	
James Scarfe, - -	Sergeant,	1	12	
Charles Moseley, - -	"	1	12	
Henry A. Dalbey, - -	"	1	12	
William Corbell, - -	"	1	12	
Henry K. Manning, - -	"	–	26	
Thomas Barkwell, - -	"	–	28	
James Johnston, - -	"	–	13	
James Hunter, - -	"	–	21	
James Throwgood, - -	Corporal,	1	12	
Hillary M. Hunter, - -	"	–	15	
Geo. T. Hall, - -	"	1	22	
Hillary Snale, - -	"	–	13	
James Walmsley, - -	"	–	25	
Thomas Fountain, - -	"	–	11	
Stephen Bonney, - -	Private,	1	16	
James Bryant, - -	"	1	2	
Amos Benson, - -	"	–	28	
Thaddeus Bowman, - -	"	–	29	
John Bevin, - -	"	1	2	
Geo. Bashaw, - -	"	1	2	
Joseph Benthall, - -	"	–	18	
John Care, - -	"	1	3	
Joel Cuterell, - -	"	1	2	
James Collins, - -	"	1	2	
Lemuel Collins, - -	"	2		
Jessee Cartwright, - -	"	1	12	
William Core, - -	"	–	26	
Jeremiah Cain, - -	"	–	13	
Benjamin Dixon, - -	"	1	16	
Samuel Drayton, - -	"	1	2	
Geo. Dudley, - -	"	–	25	
Ralph Dixon, - -	"	–	27	
William Ellegood, - -	"	1	2	
Thomas Ewell, - -	"	1	2	
John Edmonds, - -	"	1	2	
James Ewell, - -	"	1	2	
Thomas Fountain, - -	"	1	12	
Geo Fentress, - -	"	–	13	
John Gains, - -	"	1	2	
James Haynes, - -	"	1	19	
William Harrison, - -	"	1	2	
John Holmes, - -	"	1	12	
John Haynes, - -	"	–	13	
John Henderson, - -	"	–	13	
James Jarrell, - -	"	1	2	
James Johnston, - -	"	–	28	
Edmond Johnston, - -	"	–	28	
James Kellum, - -	"	–	28	
Major Kellum, - -	"	1	2	
John Kellum, - -	"	–	11	
William Lockwood, - -	"	1	12	

NAMES.	RANK.	TIME OF SERVICE.		REMARKS.
		Months.	Days.	
Henry Lemount, - -	Private,	1	12	
John Lester, - -	"	1	12	
John McDonald, - -	"	1	2	
John Mills, - - -	"	1	19	
Nathaniel Mears, - -	"	1	14	
John Moore, - - -	"	1	8	
Bagwell Moore, - -	"	—	24	
Leven Pettet, - -	"	1	16	
Richard Pebworth, - -	"	1	12	
Henry Pebworth, - -	"	1	16	
Erasmus Smith, - -	"	1	12	
Wesley Smith, - -	"	1	12	
Enoch Smith, - -	"	1	12	
Hillary Snale, - -	"	—	20	
David Scott, - -	"	—	27	
Geo. Throp, - -	"	1	12	
John B. Vaughan, - -	"	—	25	
Moses Williams, jr. - -	"	—	28	
James Walmsley, - -	"	—	3	
Jacob Hunter, - -	"	—	13	

(For rest of this company, see publication of Pay Rolls.)

MUSTER ROLL

Of Lieutenant Haynes Lee's Company, from the Sixty-eighth Regiment, Virginia Militia, in the Service of the United States, from the 3d to 19th January, 1815.

NAMES.			RANK.	TIME OF SERVICE.		REMARKS.
				Months.	Days.	
Haynes Lee,	-	-	Lieutenant,	–	16	
Anthony King.	-	-	Ensign,	–	16	
William Gibbs.	-	-	Sergeant,	–	14	
Thomas Thomas,	-	-	"			
Thomas D. Harris.	-	-	"			
Lewis Pangan,	-	-	"			
Thomas Newman,	-	-	Corporal,	–	16	
Richard Hubbard,	-	-	"			
James V. Shields,	-	-	"			
John Lucas,	-	-	"			
Wm. E. Barrett,	-	-	Private,			
Ro. H. Boalton,	-	-	"	–	8	
John A. Chandler,	-	-	"	–	9	
William Calivan,	-	-	"			
Christopher Dixon,	-	-	"			
Leroy Feroneth,	-	-	"			
Leven Gordon,	-	-	"	–	10	
Matthew Holt,	-	-	"			
Henley Hazelwood,	-	-	"			
William Lively,	-	-	"			
James Lawson,	-	-	"			
James Leppy,	-	-	"			
James Lively,	-	-	"			
Henry S. Nace,	-	-	"			
John Pumphry,	-	-	"	–	9	
Francis Peters,	-	-	"			
Geo. Roper.	-	-	"			
Otway B. Shields,	-	-	"			
James V. Shields,	-	-	"			
Bailey Smith,	-	-	"			
William Soles,	-	-	"			
Richard T. Vaughan,	-	-	"			
Samuel Williford,	-	-	"			
Joseph Wade,	-	-	"			
Benjamin Walls,	-	-	"			
Roberson Wade,	-	-	"	–	5	
Nathaniel Wilson,	-	-	"	–	16	
Edward Jenkins,	-	-	"	–	16	
James Judkins,	-	-	"	–	16	

Captain Lewis Lee's Company—One Hundred and Ninth Regiment.

NAMES.			RANK.	TIME OF SERVICE.		REMARKS.
				Months.	Days.	
William Jesse,	-	-	Lieutenant,	–	3	
Matthew Major,	-	-	Saddler,	–	3	
Parmenus Bird,	-	-	Private,	–	12	
Geo. Dudley,	-	-	"	–	3	
Richard Jackson,	-	-	"	–	15	
John B. Roane,	-	-	"	–	3	
Jessee Thomas,	-	-	"	–	12	
Thomas Trice, jr.	-	-	"	–	3	
Thomas Walker,	-	-	"	–	3	

(For the rest of this company, see publication of Pay Rolls.)

MUSTER ROLL

Of Lt. William Lee's Company, attached to the Sixty-eighth Regiment, Virginia Militia, commanded by Lt. Col. Crutchfield, in the Service from 26th June to 14th July, 1813.

NAMES.	RANK.	TIME OF SERVICE.		REMARKS.
		Months.	Days.	
William Lee.	Lieutenant,	—	19	
William Gilliam,	Ensign,	—	19	
John Steadmen,	Sergeant,	—	19	
William Hubbard.	"	—	19	
Arch'd B. Campbell,	"	—	19	
William M. Walter,	"	—	19	
Zack. Shackleford,	Corporal,	—	19	
Lewis Hogg,	"	—	19	
Thomas Austin,	"	—	19	
Banister Kerby,	"	—	19	
Charles Harris,	Private,	—	19	
Ransom Austin,	"	—	19	
Edmund Bacon,	"	—	12	
Simon Block,	"	—	19	
William Charles,	"	—	19	
Samuel J. Dycher,	"	—	19	
William Ernest,	"	—	19	
John Garrett,	"	—	19	
Louis Germain,	"			
John Heath,	"	—	19	
Thomas Harwood,	"	—	19	
William Holland,	"	—	19	
John Lee,	"	—	19	
John Mounett,	"	—	19	
Jos. Nottingham,	"	—	19	
James Newman,	"	—	19	
William Proby,	"	—	19	
William Patrick,	"	—	19	
William M. Patrick,	"	—	19	
Robert Provoo,	"	—	19	
Abram Rider,	"	—	19	
Elijah Rider,	"	—	19	
Geo. Southall,	"	—	4	
John Seeborne,	"	—	19	
Aaron Walker,	"	—	19	
William H. Wynne,	"			
Matt. Wills,	"	—	19	
William Wright,	"	—	4	
Nathaniel Young,	"	—	19	

Captain James Leftwich's Company.

NAMES.	RANK.	TIME OF SERVICE.		REMARKS.
		Months.	Days.	
John Everett,	Private,	2	27	

(For rest of this company, see publication of Pay Rolls.)

Captain Andrew Lewis' Company.

NAMES.			RANK.	TIME OF SERVICE.		REMARKS.
				Months	Days.	
James Hopkins,	-	-	Private,			
James Plunkett,	-	-	"			
Joseph Ritenger,	-	-	"	1	14	
George Stagg,	-	-	"	–	25	

(For rest of this company, see publication of Pay Rolls.)

Captain Christopher T. Lewis' Company—Sixty-first Regiment.

NAMES.			RANK.	TIME OF SERVICE.		REMARKS.
				Months.	Days.	
Moses Atherton,	-	-	Private,	–	4	
Richard Ayres,	-	-	"	–	7	
Ben. Adams,	-	-	"	–	4	
Jacob Blake,	-	-	"	–	2	
Iverson Carney,	-	-	"	–	8	
Richard Cray,	-	-	"	–	3	
John Callis,	-	-	"	–	2	
Tinley Dixon,	-	-	"	–	5	
Robert Sadler,	-	-	"	–	7	
John Sadler,	-	-	"	–	7	

(For rest of this company, see publication of Pay Rolls.)

Captain William Leigh's Company—Second Elite Corps.

NAMES.			RANK.	TIME OF SERVICE.		REMARKS.
				Months.	Days.	
Thomas Pate,	-	-	Sergeant,	–	18	
Stephen E. Wood,	-	-	Corporal,	–	–	Dead.
Alexander Asher,	-	-	Private,	–	12	
Vincent Birch,	-	-	"	–	20	Sub. for Vin. Carlton.
Edward Carlton,	-	-	"	–	21	" " Ambrose Hart.
William Dickey,	-	-	"	–	14	" " John Dickey.
Samuel Harwood,	-	-	"	–	20	Sub. for John Crenshaw.
Elijah Rives,	-	-	"	–	14	
Charles Read,	-	-	"	–	14	
John Simmons,	-	-	"			
Thomas Simmons,	-	-	"	–	13	Sub. for John Simmons.
Chesley Taylor,	-	-	"	–	13	
James Walton,	-	-	"	–	11	

(For rest of this company, see publication of Pay Rolls.)

MUSTER ROLL

Of Captain John Linton's Troop of Cavalry, from the Thirty-sixth Regiment, Virginia Militia, commanded by Lieutenant Colonel Enoch Rennoe, in the Service from 21st to 27th August, and from 30th August to 7th September, 1814.

NAMES.			RANK.	TIME OF SERVICE.		REMARKS.
				Months.	Days.	
John Linton,	-	-	Captain,	—	12	
John Gibson,	-	-	Lieutenant,	—	12	
James E. Heath,	-	-	"	—	12	
Burr Harrison,	-	-	Cornet,	—	12	
William C. Williams,		-	Sergeant,	—	12	
Lemuel Stone,	-	-	"	—	12	
Geo. Norman,	-	-	"	—	12	
Jonathan C. Gibson,	-	-	"	—	8	
Hugh Adie,	-	-	Corporal,	—	8	
Thomas Dowell,	-	-	"	—	18	
Larkin Arrington,	-	-	Private,	—	12	
Geo. Bell,	-	-	"	—	7	
Thomas Charlton,	-	-	"	—	12	
David Carter,	-	-	"	—	12	
John Carney,	-	-	"	—	12	
Alexander Chick,	-	-	"	—	12	
Richard Davis, jr.	-	-	"	—	12	
Alfred Ewell,	-	-	"	—	12	
Henley Groves,	-	-	"	—	12	
Matthew Guy,	-	-	"	—	7	
Harrison Graham,	-	-	"	—	7	
James Harrison,	-	-	"	—	12	
James Hawley,	-	-	"	—	12	
Colin Hays,	-	-	"	—	12	
Thos. W. Hewit,	-	-	"	—	9	
Lemuel Hedge,	-	-	"	—	11	
Philip Harrison,	-	-	"	—	7	
Robert Hamilton,	-	-	"	—	7	
Allison Johnston,	-	-	"	—	5	
Elias King,	-	-	"	—	5	
James McAboy,	-	-	"	—	12	
Thos. J. Newman,	-	-	"	—	5	
William Patterson,	-	-	"	—	5	
John C. Stone,	-	-	"	—	12	
John Stoke,	-	-	"	—	12	
William H. Tebbs,	-	-	"	—	12	
Peter Tone,	-	-	"	—	12	
Thomas Turner,	-	-	"	—	12	
Warden Walter,	-	-	"	—	7	

MUSTER ROLL

Of Captain John T. Lomax's Company, from the Forty-first Regiment, Virginia Militia, commanded by Lieutenant Colonel Vincent Bramhan, in the Service from the 20th to the 31st of July, 1813.

NAMES.	RANK.	TIME OF SERVICE.		REMARKS.
		Months.	Days.	
John T. Lomax,	Captain,	—	10	
William K. Bragg,	Lieutenant,	—	11	
T. M. Bragg,	Ensign,	—	11	
James Renolds,	Sergeant,	—	11	
Geo. Newman,	"	—	11	
James Saunders,	"	—	11	
William Burgess,	"	—	11	
Thomas Mosingo,	"	—	11	
James Balderson,	Private,	—	11	
Shelton Brinnon,	"	—	4	
Josiah Brown,	"	—	11	
John Bowen,	"	—	11	
Gilbert H. Balderson,	"	—	11	
John Brown,	"	—	11	
William Brown,	"	—	11	
Hudson Brown,	"	—	11	
Jessee Brown,	"	—	11	
William Balderson,	"	—	11	
Robert Connille,	"	—	11	
Meredith Carpenter,	"	—	11	
William Carpenter,	"	—	11	
James Fones,	"	—	11	
Robert P. Headley,	"	—	11	
Meredith Hammond,	"	—	11	
William Hall,	"	—	11	
Newman Hall,	"	—	11	
James Henson, jr.	"	—	11	
Augustin Henson,	"	—	11	
William Henson,	"	—	11	
Presley Henson,	"	—	11	
James Henson,	"	—	11	
James Henson, jr.	"	—	11	
John Jenkins,	"	—	11	
Thos. Jones,	"	—	11	
Robert Jenkins,	"	—	11	
William Kendal,	"	—	11	
Reub. McKenny,	"	—	11	
James Mothersaid,	"	—	11	
William Marx,	"	—	11	
James Mothersaid, jr.	"	—	11	
James McKenny,	"	—	6	
Reuben Marx,	"	—	11	
Pierce Mosingo,	"	—	11	
Samuel McGinnis,	"	—	11	
John Marx,	"	—	11	
James Newman,	"	—	11	
Tapley Nash,	"	—	11	
James Quesenberry,	"	—	11	

NAMES.	RANK.	TIME OF SERVICE.		REMARKS.
		Months.	Days.	
William Quesenberry, -	Private,	–	11	
Richard Renolds, - -	"	–	11	
Vincent Renolds, - -	"	–	11	
John Rayals, - -	"	–	11	
Geo T. Spilman, - -	"	–	11	
Reuben Sanford, - -	"	–	11	
John Sandy, - -	"	–	11	
William Sanders, - -	"	–	11	
Benjamin White, - -	"	–	11	
Thomas Weldon, - -	"	–	11	
Matthew V. Yeatman, -	"	–	11	
John H. Yeatman, - -	"	–	11	

Captain Gabriel Long's Company—Sixteenth Regiment.

NAMES.	RANK.	TIME OF SERVICE.		REMARKS.
		Months.	Days.	
Gabriel Long, - -	Captain,	–	27	
Charles McCalley, - -	Ensign,	–	27	
George B. Hopkins, -	Sergeaut,	–	27	
Gerrald Bland, - -	"	1	5	
Lewis Stevenson, - -	Corporal,	–	27	
William Kirby, - -	"	–	27	
Edmund Hogans, - -	"	–	27	
William Acres, - -	Private,	–	27	
Barnett Andrews, - -	"	–	27	Substitute for Robt. S. Coleman, jr.
Charles Beazley, - -	"	–	27	
William Bradford, - -	"	–	2	
John Cox, - -	"	–	4	
Joseph Carnahan, - -	"	–	27	
Lewis Coats, - -	"	–	22	
Henry Carpenter, - -	"	–	27	
Whitefield Cash, - -	"	–	27	
William Cash, - -	"	–	27	
Elijah Carnal, - -	"	–	8	
Robert Cammack, - -	"	–	8	
John Duerson, jun'r, -	"	–	5	Joined artillery.
Jonathan Gibson, - -	"	–	27	
John Heslop, - -	"	–	23	
Horace Heslop, - -	"	–	8	Substitute for Chas. Beazley.
Benj. Hicks, - -	"	–	27	Substitute for Wm. Spindle.
George K. Holland, - -	"	–	27	Substitute for Robt. Cammack.
James McCalley, - -	"	–	27	
Robert Y. Pendleton, -	"	1	2	Substitute for Thos. D. Herndon.
Thos. G. Peyton, - -	"	–	8	Substitute for Robt. S. Coleman.
Robert Pendleton, - -	"	–	27	
James Stewart, - -	"	–	27	
Edmund Turnley, - -	"	–	27	
William True, - -	"	–	29	
Thos. G. Tupman, - -	"	–	8	Substitute for Geo. P. Hopkins.
George Yates, - -	"	–	27	Sub. for Jno. Johnson.

(For rest of this company, see publication of Pay Rolls.)

MUSTER ROLL

Of Lieutenant Peter Lucas' Company, from the Sixteenth Regiment, Virginia Militia, commanded by Lieutenant Colonel Waller, in the Service from the 22nd July to the 17th day of August, 1814.

NAMES.	RANK.	TIME OF SERVICE.		REMARKS.
		Months.	Days.	
Peter Lucas, - -	Lieutenant,	—	25	
William P. Goodman, -	Ensign,	—	25	
James Williams, - -	Sergeant,	—	25	
John Harrison, - -	"	—	25	
John Sedwidge, - -	"	—	25	Or Ledwidge.
Lawrence Slaughter, - -	"	—	25	
Nicholas Thornton, - -	Corporal,	—	25	
Richard B. Thornton, -	"	—	25	
Baylor Banks, - -	"	—	25	
George P. Shepherd, -	"	—	25	
Moses, - -	Drummer,	—	22	
Henry W. Ashton, - -	Private,	—	25	
Fontaine Bell, -	"	—	25	
Thomas Ball, - -	"	—	25	
George Brent, -	"	—	25	
Thomas B. Bloxton, -	"	—	25	
Richard T. Banks, -	"	—	25	
John Brown, - -	"	—	25	
Henry Berry, - -	"	—	25	
John Banks, - -	"	—	17	
Edward Carmichael, -	"	—	25	
Henry Connody, -	"	—	13	
William Cox, - -	"	—	25	
Thomas C. Camp, -	"	—	25	
George Cox, - -	"	—	25	
Jeremiah Covert, -	"	—	25	
James Cooke, - -	"	—	25	
Thomas J. Dennison, -	"	—	25	
William Fletcher, -	"	—	25	
German Goodloe, -	"	—	25	
Alexander Gallop, -	"	—	25	
John Green, - -	"	—	25	
Charles Goodwyn, -	"	—	25	
John Garner, - -	"	—	25	
Henry Green, - -	"	—	25	
Turner Hudson, -	"	—	25	
James Harrison, -	"	—	25	
Peter Horde, - -	"	—	25	
William Hewlett, -	"	—	25	
Archibald Heart, -	"	—	25	
Joseph Henry, - -	"	—	6	
Thomas Johnson, -	"	—	25	
Richard L. Johnson, -	"	—	25	
Dunett Lons, -	"	—	25	
Butler Maury, -	"	—	25	
William Martin, -	"	—	25	
Thompson Murrian, -	"	—	25	
Joseph Mitchell, -	"	—	25	

NAMES.			RANK.	TIME OF SERVICE.		REMARKS.
				Months.	Days.	
Henry McGeeham,	-	-	Private,	—	25	
John Noble,	-	-	''	—	25	
Hugh Nelson,	-	-	''	—	25	
Henry Nicholson,	-	-	''	—	25	
Charles F. Pope,	-	-	''	—	25	
William F. Philips,	-	-	''	—	25	
George Pollett,	-	-	''	—	25	
John Patterson,	-	-	''	—	25	
Reuben T. Thom,	-	-	''	—	25	
Joseph B. Redd,	-	-	''	—	25	
Gernard Simpson,	-	-	''	—	25	
John Sexsmith,	-	-	''	—	25	
John Shutt,	-	-	''	—	25	
William Strut,	-	-	''	—	25	
John Scott,	-	-	''	—	25	
Joseph D. Thompson,	-	-	''	—	25	
Philip Tutt,	-	-	''	—	25	
Presley Thornton,	-	-	''	—	25	
Archibald R. Taylor,	-	-	''	—	25	
John Teasley,	-	-	''	—	25	
James Waddle,	-	-	''	—	25	
Nathaniel Webb,	-	-	''	—	25	
William T. Williams,	-	-	''	—	25	
Harris Walker,	-	-	''	—	25	
Joseph Clark,	-	-	Wagoner,	—	25	
Harrison,	-	-	Waiter,		25	

Lieutenant Moore Lurtey's Company—Twenty-fifth Regiment.

NAMES.	RANK.	TIME OF SERVICE.		REMARKS.
		Months.	Days.	
John W. Taliaferro, - -	Ensign,	–	8	
James Anderson, - -	Private,	–	8	
Charnock Cox, - -	"	–	8	
Duff Chadwell, - -	"	–	8	
Thornton Clift, - -	"	–	9	
James Jones, - -	"	–	6	
Fantley Kennedy, - -	"	–	8	
Stewart Marks, - -	"	–	19	
John Murphy, - -	"	–	8	
Thomas Sullivan, - -	"	–	8	
William Tallant, - -	"	–	8	
William F. Taliaferro, -	"	–	8	

(For rest of this company, see publication of Pay Rolls.)

Captain Thomas R. Magee's Company—Sixteenth Regiment.

NAMES.	RANK.	TIME OF SERVICE.		REMARKS.
		Months.	Days.	
John T. Parke, - -	Lieutenant,	–	12	
John Minor, - -	Ensign,	–	12	
Thomas M. Horn, - -	"	–	26	
William Jackson, - -	"	–	12	
William Johnson, - -	Sergeant,	–	12	
David McWhirt, - -	"	–	12	
William Stewart, - -	"	–	12	
Charles Martin, - -	"	–	12	
William Beazley, - -	"	–	26	
Waller L. Brightwell, -	Corporal,	–	26	
Benjamin Carter, - -	"	–	12	
John McWhirt, - -	"	–	12	
Whitehead Coleman, -	"	–	12	
Benjamin P. Waller, -	"	–	12	
Hezekiah Reeder, - -	"	–	12	
Darling Anderson, - -	Private,	–	12	
Samuel Almond, - -	"	–	26	Substitute for Henry Almond.
Absalom Brightwell, -	"	–	26	
William Bronough, -	"	–	12	
Edward Brown, - -	"	–	12	
James Beazley, - -	"	–	12	
Lewis Bowling, - -	"	–	12	
John Burnett, - -	"	–	12	
Joseph Chewning, - -	"	–	26	
Thomas Curtis, - -	"	–	26	
John Carnall, - -	"	–	12	
Durrett Cammack, -	"	–	12	
James Coleman, - -	"	–	12	
Lewis Coats, - -	"	–	12	
Charles Cosby, - -	"	–	12	
Adcock Carter, - -	"	–	12	
Levi Catlin, - -	"	–	12	
James Daniel, - -	"	–	12	
William Doggett, - -	"	–	12	
James Duerson, - -	"	–	12	
James Driver, - -	"	–	12	
John Donathan, - -	"	–	12	
Thos. Furneyhough, -	"	–	12	
Nicholas Fisher, - -	"	–	21	
George Farish, - -	"	–	12	
William Fletcher, - -	"	–	12	
William Fisher, - -	"	–	26	Substitute for Claiborne Duval.
James T. Falconer, -	"	–	26	
Thomas M. Falconer, -	"	–	21	
Walter Gimbo, - -	"	–	12	
James L. Goodwin, -	"	–	12	
Charles Gyer, - -	"	–	12	
Thomas Hicks, - -	"	–	12	
John Haydon, - -	"	–	12	
Alexander Hawkins, -	"	–	26	
William L. Hill, - -	"	–	12	
Elisha Hazel, - -	"	–	12	
Martin Hicks, - -	"	–	12	

NAMES.	RANK.	TIME OF SERVICE.		REMARKS.
		Months.	Days.	
Horace Heslop, - -	Private,	—	12	
Edmond Hogan, - -	"	—	12	
Robert Hart, - -	"	—	12	
George B. Hopkins, - -	"	—	12	
John Jones, - -	"	—	26	
Richard Johnson, - -	"	—	26	
Gibson Jenkins, - -	"	—	12	
Archibald Johnson, - -	"	—	12	
James Jenkins, - -	"	—	12	
John S. Jenkins, - -	"	—	12	
Bland Jerrald, - -	"	—	12	
Thomas Lewis, - -	"	—	12	
Willis Landrum, - -	"	—	12	
Robert Lancaster, - -	"	—	12	
William Lipscomb, - -	"	—	12	
Azeriah Lanceley, - -	"	—	26	
Harris Murphy, - -	"	—	12	
Aden C. Morris, - -	"	—	12	
Thornton Mattox, - -	"	—	12	
Edward D. Meredith,	"	—	12	
Wiley Magee, - -	"	—	12	
Charles Mullin, - -	"	—	12	
John Mannan, - -	"	—	12	
John B. Martin, - -	"	—	12	
Thornton Mead, - -	"	—	12	
James H. Martin, - -	"	—	26	
James O. Massey, - -	"	—	26	
Thomas Martin, - -	"	—	26	
Peter McDormant, - -	"	—	26	
Robert Oliver, - -	"	—	21	
William Proctor, - -	"	—	26	
John Puller, - -	"	—	12	
John Pulliam, - -	"	—	12	
Benjamin Pendleton, -	"	—	12	
James Puller, - -	"	—	12	
John Penn, - -	"	—	12	
Henry Pendleton, - -	"	—	12	
Alden Pusey, - -	"	—	12	
George Robinson, - -	"	—	12	
William Red, - -	"	—	12	
Presley Stone, - -	"	—	12	
James Scott, - -	"	—	12	
John M. Stevens, - -	"	—	12	
Day Scott, - -	"	—	12	
John Stine, - -	"	—	12	
George Stubblefield, - -	"	—	21	
Newton Sullivan, - -	"	—	8	
James Scofield, - -	"	—	12	
Benj. Stivers, - -	"	—	26	
Edward Stivers, - -	"	—	26	
Wiley Sullivan, - -	"	—	26	
Francis B. Sullivan, - -	"	—	26	
George Taylor, - -	"	—	12	
William True, - -	"	—	12	
John True, - -	"	—	12	
Fielding True, - -	"	—	12	
John Thomas, - -	"	—	21	
William Tamplain, - -	"	1	6	
Thomas Towles, - -	"	—	5	
James True, - -	"	—	15	
Thornel Twyman, - -	"	—	12	
Ambrose Underwood, - -	"	—	12	
James Wallace, - -	"	—	26	
Stephen Williams, - -	"	—	26	

NAMES.			RANK.	TIME OF SERVICE.		REMARKS.
				Months.	Days.	
John Whiting,	-	-	Private,	–	12	
Nathaniel Wheeler,	-	-	"	–	12	
William McWhirt,	-	-	"	–	12	
Josiah·White,	-	-	"	–	12	
Leonard Wharton,	-	-	"	–	12	
Benjamin Wharton,	-	-	"	–	12	
John Watts,	-	-	"	–	12	
Nimrod Young,	-	-	"	–	12	

(For rest of this company, see publication of Pay Rolls.)

Captain James Mallory's Company—At Camp Holly.

NAMES.			RANK.	TIME OF SERVICE.		REMARKS.
				Months.	Days.	
James Mallory,	-	-	Captain,	1		
William Boyan,	-	-	Lieutenant,	1		
Jessee Katspon,	-	-	Ensign,	1		Or Katsfon.
Jeremiah Sullivan,	-	-	Sergeant,	1		
Martin Tutwiler,	-	-	"	1		
John Holliday,	-	-	"	1		
Philip Holt,	-	-	"	1		
Solomon Ritchie,	-	-	Corporal,	1		
Florence Mahoney,	-	-	"	1		
Philip Parrott,	-	-	"	1		
John S. Herring,	-	-	"	1		
Jonas Hinchie,	-	-	Drummer,	1		
Burgess Grady,	-	-	Fifer,	1		
Geo. Armenstreet,	-	-	Private,	1		
Christopher Armentrout,	-		"	1		
John Baker,	-	-	"	1		
John Bryan,	-	-	"	1		
Jacob Bargahiser,	-	-	"	1		
John Brown,	-	-	"	1		
John Barrick,	-	-	"	1		
Philip Baker,	-	-	"	1		
James Brown,	-	-	"	1		
Daniel Bazzil,	-	-	"	1		
William Brackney,	-	-	"	1		
James Bryan,	-	-	"	1		
Michael Clinefelter,	-	-	"	1		
John Clabough,	-	-	"	1		
Valentine Dotherby,	-	-	"	1		
Michael Dever,	-	-	"	1		
Geo. Done,	-	-	"	1		
John Hin,	-	-	"	1		
John Hortinger,	-	-	"	1		
David Hughes,	-	-	"	1		
Geo. Jenkins,	-	-	"	1		
William Jenkins,	-	-	"	1		
John Kenny,	-	-	"	1		
Jacob Lawson,	-	-	"	1		
James McCulley,	-	-	"	1		
Edward Moonley,	-	-	"	1		
Timothy Mahoney,	-	-	"	1		
John Miller,	-	-	"	1		
John Ott,	-	-	"	1		
Adam Pierce,	-	-	"	1		
Massie Rush,	-	-	"	1		
Phillip Ritchie,	-	-	"	1		
Phillip Rudy,	-	-	"	1		
Henry Ritchie,	-	-	"	1		
William Spangler,	-	-	"	1		
Henry Shoemaker,	-	-	"	1		
Christian Shoemaker,	-	-	"	1		
Andrew Stoneburner,	-	-	"	1		
David Summers,	-	-	"	1		
Jacob Spraher,	-	-	"	1		
Balsor Shaver,	-	-	"	1		

NAMES.			RANK.	TIME OF SERVICE.		REMARKS.
				Months.	Days.	
Joseph Spangler,	-	-	Private,	1		
Sampson Tinsley,	-	-	"	1		
Andrew Tencke,	-	-	"	1		
Abraham Tishlor,	-	-	"	1		
David Turner,	-	-	"	1		
Jacob Vance,	-	-	"	1		
Jacob Varner,	-	-	"	1		
Isaac Witsell,	-	-	"	1		
John Weller,	-	-	"	1		
James Wilson,	-	-	"	1		

(For rest of this company, see publication of Pay Rolls.)

MUSTER ROLL

Of Captain Geo. Markham's Company, from the Twenty-third Regiment, Virginia Militia, commanded by Lieutenant Colonel William Brown, in the Service from the 13th to 30th March, from 27th to 28th June, and from 1st to 2d July, 1813.

NAMES.			RANK.	TIME OF SERVICE.		REMARKS.
				Months.	Days.	
Geo. Markham,	-	-	Captain,	—	21	
John L. Morgan,	-	-	Lieutenant,	—	21	
James Martin,	-	-	Ensign,	—	21	
Lewis Neal,	-	-	Sergeant,	—	21	
Reuben Cross,	-	-	"	—	21	
James Burrute,	-	-	"	—	21	
Leroy Branch,	-	-	"	—	21	
Willey Andrews,	-	-	Private,	—	21	
William Adkins,	-	-	"	—	21	
Ambrose Alexander,	-	-	"	—	21	
John Andrews,	-	-	"	—	2	
James Adkins,	-	-	"	—	2	
Woodford Alvis,	-	-	"	—	2	
John Anderson,	-	-	"	—	17	
Zephaniah Alvis,	-	-	"	—	1	
Eleuzer Bennet,	-	-	"	—	21	
William Burton,	-	-	"	—	21	
Samuel Bridgewater,	-	-	"	—	21	
John Burton,	-	-	"	—	21	
Thomas Branch,	-	-	"	—	21	
Caleb Bradley,	-	-	"	—	21	
John Branch,	-	-	"	—	5	
Matthew Branch,	-	-	"	—	3	
Samuel B. Collin,	-	-	"	—	19	
John W. Cardwell,	-	-	"	—	21	
William Cary,	-	-	"	—	2	
Francis Cheatham,	-	-	"	—	17	
Darius H. Furgison,	-	-	"	—	21	
Nathaniel Foster,	-	-	"	—	21	
Owen Franklin,	-	-	"	—	17	
Edmond George,	-	-	"		19	
Radford C. Gooding,	-	-	"	—	21	
William Good,	-	-	"	—	2	
Jeremiah Huccoe,	-	-	"	—	19	
Benjamin Horace,	-	-	"	—	21	
Samuel Horace,	-	-	"	—	21	
Caleb Hartgrove,	-	-	"	—	21	
James Holman,	-	-	"	—	21	
Benjamin Hatcher,	-	-	"	—	19	
Edward Henry,	-	-	"	—	2	
John Johnson,	-	-	"	—	21	
Leonard Jones,	-	-	"	—	21	
Watson Johnson,	-	-	"	—	21	
John Murrinder,	-	-	"	—	21	
James Miles,	-	-	"	—	21	
Nathaniel Mason,	-	-	"	—	21	
Overton Mason,	-	-	"	—	19	

NAMES.			RANK.	TIME OF SERVICE.		REMARKS.
				Months.	Days.	
John Moore,	-	-	Private,	—	3	
Peter Mason,	-	-	"	—	17	
William Nash,	.	-	"	—	17	
Claiborne Nash,	-	-	"	—	21	
Francis Patram,	-	-	"	—	20	
Stephen Russell,	-	-	"	—	17	
John Sorrell,	-	-	"	—	19	
William Shell,	-	-	"	—	2	
Richard Sassue,	-	-	"	—	21	
Moses Stanley,	-	-	"	—	19	
Thomas Winfrey,	-	-	"	—	21	
Samuel Winfrey,	-	-	"	—	21	
Abner Winfrey,	-	-	"	—	21	
Green Wood,	-	-	"	—	21	
Francis O. Watkins,	-	-	"	—	17	
Christopher Thomas,	-	-	"	—	21	
Matthew Winfrey,	-	-	"	—	17	
Joseph Smith,	-	-	"	—	17	
John Vickers,	-	-	"	—	21	
Philip H. Vest,	-	-	"	—	21	
Charles Zebmme,	-	-	"	—	4	Or Zebmure.

Captain Edward Marks' Company—Sixty-second Regiment.

NAMES.			RANK.	TIME OF SERVICE.		REMARKS.
				Months.	Days.	
Edward Marks,	-	-	Captain,	–	9	
John B. Williams,	-	-	Lieutenant,	1	13	
Charles H. Marks,	-	-	"	1	11	
Joel Marks,	-	-	Cornet,	–	9	
Elisha Newcomb,	-	-	Sergeant,	1		
Peyton A. Waymack,	-	-	"	1	2	
Grief Grammer,	-	-	"	1		
William H. Baugh,	-	-	"	1	17	
R. Wilkins,	-	-	Corporal,	–	23	
Richard Bland,	-	-	"	1	26	
Edmond H. Harrison,	-		"	–	17	
Henry G. Heath,	-		"	–	17	
Gabriel Grantham,	-	-	"	1		
Edward H. Niblett,	-		"	–	17	
Herbert Harrison,	-		"	–	9	
Edward Davenport,	-		"	–	9	
E. T. Harrison,	-		"	–	15	
William H. Harrison,	-		Commissary,	–	27	
William Baxter,	-		Trumpeter,	–	9	
Anthony Allen,	-		Private,	–	9	
Pat. Andrew,			"	2	6	
George D. Adams,	-	-	"	–	9	
William Allen,	-	-	"	–	9	
Thomas Adams,	-	-	"	–	9	
Lawrence G. Acres,	-	-	"	–	26	
William Baxter,	-	-	"	1	9	
William Brown,	-	-	"	1	2	
Lewis Batte,			"	1	2	
Ro. Batte,	-	-	"	–	13	
Alford Butts,	-	-	"	–	9	
John Brichett,	-	-	"	–	9	
Robert Bonner,	-	-	"	–	9	
Thomas Comer,	-	-	"	1	5	
Colin R. Cooke,	-	-	"	–	9	
Colin Cocke,	-	-	"	1		
James Comer,	-	-	"	–	9	
Drury Dunn,	-	-	"	1	2	
William Eppes, jr.	-	-	"	–	21	
Peter Friend,	-	-	"	–	24	
Josias Gilbert,	-	-	"	1		
James W. Harrison,	-		"	–	9	
James Harrison,	-	-	"	1	11	
Colin Harrison,	-	-	"	1	7	
H. Harrison,	-	-	"	–	24	
James Hite,	-	-	"	1	3	
H. Heath,	-	-	"	–	24	
H. G. Heath,	-	-	"	–	24	
David Heath,	-	-	"	–	9	
Robert Harrison,	-	-	"	–	9	
B. Harrison,	-	-	"	–	20	
David Jamison,	-	-	"	–	9	
William Kirkland,	-	-	"	–	9	
Benjamin Marks,	-	-	"	1		
William Marks,	-	-	"	1	3	

NAMES.	RANK.	TIME OF SERVICE.		REMARKS.
		Months.	Days.	
Harrison Marks, - -	Private,	—	10	
John Moody, - - -	"	—	24	
Joseph Mason, - -	"	—	9	
Thomas B. Mitchell, - -	"	—	9	
E. H. Niblett, - - -	"	—	15	
Travis Perkinson, - -	"	—	15	
T. Perkins, - - -	"	—	15	
William Peebles, - -	"	1	3	
S. Perkins, - - -	"	—	24	
Nathaniel B. Sturdivant, -	"	—	9	
Lodowick Traylor, - -	"	—	29	
P. B. Thweatt, - -	"	1	15	
Peter Tatum, - -	"	—	29	
David Todd, - - -	"	—	9	
James Tatum, - - -	"	—	9	
Jeremiah Vaughan, - -	"	—	9	
Thomas Vaughan, - -	"	—	9	
Alford Wilkins, - -	"	—	29	

(For rest of this company, see publication of Pay Rolls.)

MUSTER ROLL

Of Captain M. M. Marmaduke's Company, from the One Hundred and Eleventh Regiment, Virginia Militia, Westmoreland County, commanded by Major William Nelson, in the Service from 5th to 11th November, 1813.

NAMES.	RANK.	TIME OF SERVICE.		REMARKS.
		Months.	Days.	
M. M. Marmaduke, - -	Captain,	–	6	
Wm. M. Walker, - -	Lieutenant,	–	6	
Edward Spence, - -	"	–	5	
Alexander Spence, - -	Sergeant,	–	6	
Thomas Huchings, - -	"	–	6	
Samuel Templeman, - -	"	–	6	
Jeremiah Lanford, - -	Private,	–	6	Or Sanford.
Vincent Marmaduke, - -	"	–	6	
James Weaver, - -	"	–	2	
James Roles, - -	"	–	3	
John Hunter, - -	"	–	3	
Joseph Dozier, - -	"	–	6	
Tutt Lampkin, - -	"	–	6	
Joseph Robertson, - -	"	–	5	
William Roles, - -	"	–	5	
Samuel S. Davis, - -	"	–	4	
Gerard Garner, - -	"	–	2	
John Norwood, jr. - -	"	–	3	
Randsal Pegg, - -	"	–	2	
Henry Brawner, - -	"	–	6	
Bowen Bashaw, - -	"	–	6	
William Sanford, jr. - -	"	–	6	
Christopher Moxley, - -	"	–	5	
James Hinson, - -	"	–	6	
Austin Hinson, - -	"	–	6	
Meroditt Carpenter, - -	"	–	6	
William Noah, - -	"	–	6	

Captain Samuel Marshall's Company.

NAMES.	RANK.	TIME OF SERVICE.		REMARKS.
		Months.	Days.	
Samuel Marshall, - -	Captain,	1	8	
Samuel Davis, - -	"	–	23	
Richard Moseley, - -	Ensign,	1	8	
Nelson Cary, - -	Sergeant,	1	8	
Benjamin T. Davis, - -	"	1	8	
Lendrey J. Mann, - -	"	–	15	
Thomas Cheatham, - -	"	–	23	
Woodson Winfree, - -	"	–	23	
Jonathan Powell, - -	"	–	23	
Joseph Sublett, - -	Corporal,	1	8	
Mark Taylor, - - -	"	1	8	
William Gill, - - -	"	–	23	
Thomas Maxey, - -	"	–	23	
Jessee Taylor, - -	Drummer,	–	23	
William Gates, - -	Fifer,	–	23	
Creed Aminette, - -	Private,	–	23	
Henry Bowles, - -	"	–	23	
William Bowles, - -	"	–	23	
William Bransford, - -	"	–	23	
Pleasant S. Bowler, - -	"	–	23	
Henry Bowman, - -	"	–	23	
James Blankenship, - -	"	–	23	
Litty Boatwright, - -	"	–	15	
David Battray, - -	"	–	15	
Matt. Baker, - -	"	–	15	
James Criddle, - -	"	–	23	
Walthall Davis, - -	"	–	23	
Chesley Davis, - -	"	–	23	
Berkley Farley, - -	"	–	23	
Daniel Farley, - -	"	1	8	
Soammi Frost, - -	"	–	23	
Alexander Farley, - -	"	–	15	
Fielding Gardner, - -	"	–	15	
Joel Gathwright, - -	"	–	15	
David Hall, - - -	"	–	23	
Willey Jackson, - -	"	1	8	
Benjamin Jennings, - -	"	–	23	
Elias Jackson, - -	"	–	15	
John Jessee, - - -	"	–	15	
Jacob Ingram, - -	"	–	23	
Rolling M. Langden, - -	"	–	15	
David Lacy, - - -	"	–	23	
Elijah Maxey, - - -	"	1	8	
Eli Moore, - - -	"	1	8	
James Moore, - - -	"	–	15	
John Mosby - - -	"	–	23	
Linsey J. Mann, - -	"	–	23	
John Miller, - - -	"	–	23	
George Mosby, - -	"	–	15	
Robert McLaurin, - -	"	–	15	
Elijah Nunnally, - -	"	–	15	
William B. Pemberton, - -	"	–	23	
William Smith, - -	"	–	23	
Thomas Stratton, - -	"	–	23	

NAMES.	RANK.	TIME OF SERVICE.		REMARKS.
		Months.	Days.	
Michal Squiggins, - -	Private,	—	15	
James Syms, - -	"	—	15	
John A. Smith, - -	"	—	15	
Jeff. Swann, - -	"	—	15	
Richard A. Swann, - -	"	—	15	
John H. Steger, - -	"	—	15	
Jessee Tillottson, - -	"	—	23	
Major Tinsley, - -	"	—	23	
Lapole Tencer, - -	"	—	23	
James Taylor, - -	"	—	23	
Anderson Traylor, - -	"	—	15	
Satterwhite Tyre, - -	"	—	15	
James R. Vaughan, - -	"	—	23	
Woodson Winfrey, - -	"	—	15	

(For rest of this company, see publication of Pay Rolls.)

Captain Daniel Mason's Company—Forty-fifth Regiment.

NAMES.	RANK.	TIME OF SERVICE.		REMARKS.
		Months.	Days.	
Edw'd Shelton, - -	Sergeant,	—	27	
Burton Johnson, - -	"	—	27	
James Armstrong, - -	"	—	11	
Obadiah Cox, - -	"	—	11	
Jeremiah Knight, - -	Corporal,	1	3	
Daniel Grigsby, - -	"	—	8	
John Knox, - -	"	—	8	
William Guy, - -	"	1	3	
James Boling, - -	Private,	—	8	
William Chisam, - -	"	—	27	
John Gragg, - -	"	—	27	
Henry Calender, - -	"	—	27	
William Ensor, - -	"	—	27	
Joseph Ensor, - -	"	—	8	
Bartlett Fritter, - -	"	—	27	
Barnett Fritter, - -	"	—	27	
John Gollahorn, jr. - -	"	—	27	
John Guy, - -	"	—	27	
John Knox, - -	"	—	27	
John King, - -	"	—	27	
William Limbrick, - -	"	—	27	
John Philips, - -	"	—	27	
William Payne, - -	"	—	27	
James Presley, - -	"	—	8	
Gustavus Raye, - -	"	—	8	
Peter Rankins, - -	"	—	8	
Arch'd Rye, - -	"	—	27	
Geo. Rankins, - -	"	—	27	
John Richerson, - -	"	—	27	
Geo. G. Shelton, - -	"	—	27	
William Sullivant, - -	"	—	8	
James Smith, - -	"	—	8	
John Skinmore, - -	"	—	8	
John Tongate, - -	"	—	27	
William Thompson, - -	"	—	27	
William West, - -	"	—	8	

(For rest of this company, see publication of Pay Rolls.)

MUSTER ROLL

Of Captain Nicholas Massenburg's Company, from the Fifteenth Regiment, Virginia Militia, commanded by Lieutenant Colonel William Allen, in the Service of the State of Virginia from the 1st to 11th September, 1814.

NAMES.	RANK.	TIME OF SERVICE.		REMARKS.
		Months.	Days.	
Nicholas Massenburg, -	Captain,	–	11	
Smith Parham, -	Lieutenant,	–	11	
William C. Goodrich, -	Ensign,	–	11	
Richard B. Grigg, -	Sergeant,	–	11	
Jones Wilburne, -	"	–	11	
James Thomas, -	"	–	11	
William O. Chambliss, -	"	–	11	
Isaac Robertson, -	Corporal,	–	11	
James May, -	"	–	11	
Pinkey B. Tyns, -	"	–	11	
Samuel Owen, -	"	–	11	
William Thorn, -	Drummer,	–	11	
Thomas Sledge, -	Fifer,	–	11	
John Adams, -	Private,	–	11	
Robert Anderson, -	"	–	11	
Jessee Andrews, -	"	–	11	
Laborn Bailey, -	"	–	11	
Hermen Bailey, -	"	–	11	
Washington Bailey, -	"	–	11	
David Bailey, -	"	–	11	
Edmund Bailey, -	"	–	11	
Patrick Culhoun, -	"	–	11	
David Congo, -	"	–	11	
William Clairy, -	"	–	11	
Geo. Dowden, -	"	–	11	
Robert Ellis, -	"	–	11	
Nicholas Gilliman, -	"	–	11	
James Gilliman, -	"	–	11	
John Green, -	"	–	11	
Ambrose Griggard, -	"	–	11	
Edwin Hayse, -	"	–	10	Deserted 10th September, 1814.
Jessee Horn, -	"	–	11	
John Hogwood, -	"	–	11	
David Horn, -	"	–	11	
William Hogwood, -	"	–	11	
Thomas Harwood, -	"	–	11	
Archibald Holdsworth, -	"	–	11	
Frederick Jackson, -	"	–	11	
John Johnston, -	"	–	11	
Josiah Johnston, -	"	–	11	
William Jarratt, -	"	–	11	
David Jones. -	"	–	11	
Hinchey Knight, -	"	–	11	
Robert Key, -	"	–	11	
Benjamin Lamb, -	"	–	11	
Robert Lessenburg, -	"	–	11	
Ethelred Massenburg, -	"	–	11	
William Malone, -	"	–	11	

NAMES.	RANK.	TIME OF SERVICE.		REMARKS.
		Months.	Days.	
William Manary, - -	Private,	—	11	
William Myrick, - -	"	—	11	
Matthew Moore, - -	"	—	11	
Matthew Muge, - -	"	—	11	
Allen Owen, - -	"	—	11	
Asa Oliver, - -	"	—	11	
Frederick Parrish, - -	"	—	11	
Jones Parish, - -	"	—	11	
Littleberry Robertson, -	"	—	11	
Howell Robertson, - -	"	—	11	
Edward Relse, - -	"	—	11	
Joseph Rowland, - -	"	—	11	
William Spiers, - -	"	—	11	
Thomas Spain, - -	"	—	11	
John Spain, - -	"	—	11	
Joseph Tyns, - -	"	—	11	
Reuben Underwood, -	"	—	11	
John Underhill, - -	"	—	11	
Thomas Vaughan, - -	"	—	11	
John Wilbourn, - -		—	11	
John T. Weathers, - -	"	—	11	
Carrel Whittington, - -	"	—	11	
William Whitehorn, - -	"	—	11	
James White, - -	"	—	11	

Captain Gideon Massie's Company—Eigth Regiment.

NAMES.			RANK.	TIME OF SERVICE.		REMARKS.
				Months.	Days.	
Robert Ware,	-	-	Ensign,	–	11	Promoted to adjutant.
Frederick Johnson,	-	-	Private,	1	25	
Noel Lowry,	-	-	"	–	17	
Arch'd Lingo,	-	-	"	–	20	
William Tompkins,	-	-	"	1	26	

(For rest of this company, see publication of Pay Rolls.)

Captain Daniel Matthews' Company—One Hundred and Sixteenth Regiment.

NAMES.			RANK.	TIME OF SERVICE.		REMARKS.
				Months.	Days.	
John T. Salouge,	-	-	Sergeant,	1	14	
Jesse Harrison,	-	-	"	1	14	
M. Markwood,	-	-	Drummer,	–	6	
Tandy Carnel,	-	-	Private,	–	22	
John Jack, -	-	-	"	1	14	
Abraham Orebough,	-	-	"	–	22	
Jacob Rust,	-	-	"	–	25	

(For rest of this company, see publication of Pay Rolls.)

Captain John Miller's Company—Seventeenth Regiment.

NAMES.	RANK.	TIME OF SERVICE.		REMARKS.
		Months.	Days.	
Edmund Lee, - -	Private,	1	4	
James Wilkinson, - -	"	1	6	Sub. for Carter Wilkinson,
John Woodson, - -	"	1	4	

(For rest of this company, see publication of Pay Rolls.)

MUSTER ROLL

Of Captain William McCabe's Company, from the Nineteenth Regiment, Virginia Militia, commanded by Lieutenant Colonel John Ambler, in the Service of the United States, from the 18th to the 27th March, 1813.

NAMES.	RANK.	TIME OF SERVICE.		REMARKS.
		Months.	Days.	
William McCabe,	Captain,	–	10	
Archelaus Hughes,	Lieutenant,	–	10	
John McPherson,	Ensign,	–	10	
Richard Crouch,	Sergeant,	–	10	
David Hanna,	"	–	10	
Robert Triplett,	"	–	10	
Joshua Crump,	"	–	10	
Christian Bohn,	Private,	–	10	
James Wallace,	"	–	10	
Charles J. Shelton,	"	–	10	
John Southall,	"	–	10	
James Lucadoe,	"	–	10	
David Mason,	"	–	10	
James Roberts,	"	–	10	
Matthew Moody,	"	–	10	
William Franklin,	"	–	10	
Leroy Hipkins,	"	–	10	
James McBride,	"	–	10	
Beverly Gale,	"	–	10	
Jos. W. Vaughan,	"	–	10	
Richard Archer,	"	–	10	
Charles Ellis,	"	–	10	
Joseph Todd,	"	–	10	
Walker Y. Meriwether,	"	–	10	
Robert Poore,	"	–	10	
David Poore,	"	–	10	
John Cooley,	"	–	10	
Edmund Leneve,	"	–	10	
James Atkinson,	"	–	10	
Thomas W. Walker,	"	–	10	
David Merry,	"	–	10	
Robert Walker,	"	–	10	
Westwood James,	"	–	10	
John Anderson,	"	–	10	
Benjamin Read,	"	–	10	
Thomas Hatcher,	"	–	10	
William Matthew,	"	–	10	
James Barnes,	"	–	10	
Graves Matthews,	"	–	10	
William T. Archer,	"	–	10	
Geo. W. Spooner,	"	–	10	
William Price.	"	–	10	
Edward Cunningham,	"	–	10	
Geo. Atkinson,	"	–	10	
Benj. James Harris,	"	–	10	
James Bridges,	"	–	10	
Michael Gretter,	"	–	10	

NAMES.	RANK.	TIME OF SERVICE.		REMARKS.
		Months.	Days.	
Leonard Wheeler, - -	"		10	
Samuel Hawkins, - -	"		10	
Alexander Brander, - -	"		10	
Gustavus Lucke, - -	"		10	
William H. Hubbard, -	"		10	
Horatio H. Chittenden, -	"		10	
David Timberlake, - -	"		10	
Jessee Higginbottom, -	"		10	
George Winston, - -	"		10	
Caleb Terrell,	"		10	
Samuel Winston, - -	"		10	
Cyrus Christian, - -	"		10	
Walter Childers, - -	"		10	
John Winston, - -	"		10	
Valerius Campbell, - -	"		10	
Lewis Webb, - -	"		10	
George Stillman, - -	"		10	
Hugh McNamare, - -	"		10	
James S. Smithers, - -	"		10	
John Hill, - -	"		10	
John D. Miller, - -	"		10	
Samuel D. Daniel, - -	"		10	
Thomas E. Brown, - -	"		10	
Osmond Bowler, - -	"		10	
John H. Sublett, - -	Private,		10	
James Scott, - -	"		10	
James Reat, - -	"		10	
Thomas Hubbard, - -	"		10	
William Rhodes, - -	"		10	
Jacob Cheadle, - -	"		10	
John L. Buckner, - -	"		10	
John Hockiday, - -	"		10	
Joseph S. James, - -	"		10	

Lieutenant Robert McCandlish's Company—Sixty-Eighth Regiment.

NAMES.			RANK.	TIME OF SERVICE.		REMARKS.
				Months.	Days.	
Wilson Matthews,	-	-	Drummer,	—	20	
Hayes Burcher,	-	-	Private,	—	23	
Lewis Browne,	-	-	"	—	25	
George Earnest,	-	-	"	—	20	
Reuben Graves,	-	-	"	—	29	
James Gray,	-	-	"	—	26	
John Hogg,	-	-	"	—	27	
John Hansford,	-	-	"	—	22	
Thomas Pressley,	-	-	"	—	25	
Jacob Roe,	-	-	"	—	22	
Zack. Shackleford,	-	-	"	—	10	

(For rest of this company, see publication of Pay Rolls.)

Captain Robert McCulloch's Company—Seventh Regiment.

NAMES.			RANK.	TIME OF SERVICE.		REMARKS.
				Months.	Days.	
Wilson Ballard,	-	-	Ensign,	–	15	
Thomas Clark,	-	-	Corporal,	–	23	
John Dickinson,	-	-	"	1	15	
Andrew Broach,	-	-	Private,	–	27	Sub. for David Huckstep.
John Dickerson,	-	-	"	1	28	Sub. for Mich'l Ansel.
John Dickinson,	-	-	"	–	12	Promoted to corporal.
John B. Ellis,	-	-	"	–	21	
William Gillarsby,	-	-	"	–	14	

(For rest of this company, see publication of Pay Rolls.)

Captain William L. Montague's Company—One Hundred and Ninth Regiment.

NAMES.			RANK.	TIME OF SERVICE.		REMARKS.
				Months.	Days.	
Major Oaks,	-	-	Private,	–	8	
John Owen,	-	-	"	–	5	
Thomas Palmer,	-	-	"	–	2	
John Rousee,	-	-	"	–	7	
Ben. Sale,	-	-	"	–	7	
John Saunders,	-	-	"	–	7	
James Trice, sr.	-	-	"	–	5	
Henry Thuston,	-	-	"	–	7	
Henry Woodward,	-	-	"	–	9	
Henley Woodward,	-	-	"	–	7	
Philemon Woodward,	-	-	"	–	9	
Ben. Williams,	-	-	"	–	7	
Carter Williams,	-	-	"	–	11	

(For rest of this company, see publication of Pay Rolls.)

MUSTER ROLL

Of Captain John McPherson's Company, from the Nineteenth Regiment, Virginia Militia, commanded by Lieutenant Colonel John Ambler, in the Service of the United States, from 26th August to the 7th day of September, 1814.

NAMES.			RANK.	TIME OF SERVICE.		REMARKS.
				Months.	Days.	
John McPherson,	-	-	Captain,	—	14	
John Bootwright,	-	-	Lieutenant,	—	14	
John Perry,	-	-	Ensign,	—	14	
Jos. S. James,	-	-	Sergeant,	—	14	
James Reat,			"	—	14	
Joshua Crump,	-	-	"	—	14	
Thos. Cushing,	-	-	"	—	14	
Westwood W. James,	-		Corporal,	—	14	
Josiah Poore,	-	-	"	—	6	Joined Aug. 28, 1814.
David Reat,	-	-	"	—	4	" 31, "
William Poe,	-	-	"	—	4	" 31, "
Richard Archer,	-	-	Private,	—	9	Joined the blues Sep. 3.
Richard Alltin,	-	-	"	—	8	
Christian Bohn,	-	-	"	—	9	Flying artillery Sept. 3.
William Boulware,	-	-	"	—	19	" " "
Water Childress,	-	-	"	—	19	" " "
Wilson B. Clark,	-	-	"	—	8	" " "
Edwin Clark,	-	-	"	—	19	" " "
Michael Gretter,	-	-	"	—	19	" " "
Parke Glenn,	-	-	"	—	14	
Thos. Gillian,	-	-	"	—	9	" " "
Jessee Higginbotham,	-	-	"	—	9	Appointed secretary Sept. 3.
David Hanna, -	-	-	"	—	9	Appointed serg't major Sept. 3.
James Hubbard,	-	-	"	—	9	Flying artillery.
Isaac Harper,	-	-	"	—	9	" "
Thomas Hill,	-	-	"	—	3	" "
John Hill.	-	-	"	—	4	" "
William Jones,	-	-	"	—	14	
Nath'l Ireson,	-	-	"	—	4	Transferred.
David Kenney,	-	-	"	—	14	
Read Kire.			"	—	14	
Gustavus Luke,	-	-	"	—	14	
Adam Murray,	-	-	"	—	14	
David Mason.	-	-	"	—	14	
William McEnery,	-	-	"	—	14	
James Madison,	-	-	"	—	9	Joined the blues Sep. 3.
Charles Melna,	-	-	"	—	3	
Robert Neilson,	-	-	"	—	14	
Robert Poore,	-	-	"	—	14	
Nath'l Perkins,	-	-	"	—	9	
James Roper.			"	—	10	
Geo. H. Stanback,	-	-	"	—	9	Flying artillery.
James S. Smithers,	-	-	"	—	14	
John H. Sublett,	-	-	"	—	9	
Joseph Todd,	-	-	"	—	14	

NAMES.			RANK.	TIME OF SERVICE.		REMARKS.
				Months.	Days.	
Lewis Webb,	-	-	Private,	–	14	
John Walden,	-	-	"	–	9	Flying artillery 3.
John Winston,	-	-	"	–	14	
James Winston,	-	-	"	–	14	
Thos. N. Walker,	-	-	"	–	9	Joined the blues Sep. 3.

MUSTER ROLL

*Of Captain Isaac Medley's Company, from the Sixty-ninth Regiment, Virginia
Militia, Halifax County, in the Service, from the 5th to 20th July, 1813.*

NAMES.	RANK.	TIME OF SERVICE.		REMARKS.
		Months.	Days.	
Isaac Medley, - -	Captain,	–	15	
William Edmundson, - -	Lieutenant,	–	15	
William Kirby, -	Ensign,	–	15	
William Howerton, /. -	Sergeant,	–	15	
Thomas Howerton, - -	"	–	15	
Thornton Puryear, - -	"	–	15	
Jeremiah Morgan, - -	"	–	15	
William Hughes, - -	"	–	15	
Hopkins G. Jones, - -	"	–	15	
Austin Brigg, - -	"	–	15	
Samuel Edmundson, -	"	–	15	
Elias Smith, - -	"	–	15	Or Elas.
Coleman Burton, - -	"	–	15	
Lewis Siah, - -	"	–	15	
Martin Blalock, - -	"	–	15	
Frederick Briggs, - -	"	–	15	
William Drummond, - -	"	–	15	
Joseph Clardy, - -	"	–	15	
Daniel Clark, - -	"	–	15	
Thomas Chambers, - -	"	–	15	
John Hart, - -	"	–	15	
Joel Henderson, - -	"	–	15	
Elias Washer, - -	"	–	15	Or Walker.
Quiller Carlton, - -	"	–	15	
Larbome Cooper, - -	"	–	15	
Joseph G. Griesham, - -	"	–	15	
John L. Whitland, - -	"	–	15	
John Goode, - -	"	–	15	
Powell Tuck, - -	"	–	15	
Isby Wall, - -	"	–	15	
Seth P. Pool, - -	"	–	15	
Irby Duberry, - -	"	–	15	
Alexander Cumbo, - -	"	–	15	
Thomas Watkins, - -	"	–	15	
Richard Arrington, - -	"	–	15	
John Warren, - -	"	–	15	
Samuel Hailey, - -	"	–	15	
Joseph Drumman, - -	"	–	15	
Henry Elliott, - -	"	–	15	
Joseph Lizmore, - -	"	–	15	
Thomas Duncan, - -	"	–	15	
John Turpin, - -	"	–	15	
Claiborne Rice, - -	"	–	15	
Thomas Taylor, - -	"	–	15	
John Davis, - -	"	–	15	
Edward Murphy, - -	"	–	15	
William L. Boyd, - -	"	–	15	
Thomas Poinor, - -	"	–	15	
John Bennett, - -	"	–	15	
William Stainley, - -	"	–	15	

NAMES.	RANK.	TIME OF SERVICE.		REMARKS.
		Months.	Days.	
John Anderson, - -	Private,		15	
Francis State, - -	"		15	
Vines Browder, - -	"		15	
Brooking C. Griffin, - -	"		15	
William Lofter, - -	"		15	
William Guthrie, - -	"		15	
William Saunders, - -	"		15	
Robert Harris, - -	"		15	
Henry McCarter, - -	"		15	
Pool White, - -	"		15	

582

MUSTER ROLL

Of Captain John Merchant's Company, from the Eighty-ninth Regiment, Virginia Militia, commanded by Lieutenant Colonel Gerrard Alexander, in the Service of the United States from the 24th to 30th August, and from 31st August to September 7th, 1814.

NAMES.		RANK.	TIME OF SERVICE.		REMARKS.
			Months.	Days.	
John Merchant,	- -	Captain,	–	14	
William French,	- -	Lieutenant,	–	8	
Barnaby Cannon,	- -	Ensign,	–	8	
Thomas Burrough,	- -	Sergeant,	–	8	
Cuthbart Harrison,	- -	2d "	–	8	
Daniel Cole,	- -	3d "	–	14	
William Martin,	- -	Corporal,	–	8	
James Merchant,	- -	2d "	–	8	
Otley Crosby,	- -	3d "	–	8	
Matthias Cole,	- -	"	–	6	
Lewis Athey,	- -	Private,	–	8	
James Abel,	- -	"	–	8	
Samuel Anderson,	- -	"	–	6	
John Arnold,	- -	"	–	8	
James Arnold,	- -	"	–	8	
Thomas Abel,	- -	"	–	8	
Thomas Adams,	- -	"	–	8	
Richard Allen,	- -	"			
Zephaniah Brawner,	- -	"	–	8	
Fantley Ball,	- -	"	–	8	
Benjamin Carney,	- -	"			
Vincent Calvert,	- -	"	–	8	
Thomas Cock,	- -	"			
Alexander Crosby,	- -	"	–	6	
William Cornwell,	- -	"	–	8	
Harrison Cornwell,	- -	"	–	8	
Jessee Dowell,	- -	"	–	14	
Walter Davis,	- -	"	–	14	
John B. Davis,	- -	"	–	8	
Walter Dodson,	- -	"	–	8	
Jessee Davis,	- -	"	–	6	
Thomas Davis,	- -	"	–	6	
Edward Fair,	- -	"	–	8	
Cathbert Harrison,	- -	"	–	8	
Zachins Holloday,	- -	"	–	14	Or Zacheus.
Stephen Harrison,	- -	"	–	8	
James Jordan,	- -	"	–	8	
William King,	- -	"	–	8	
Geo. Keys,	- -	"	–	14	
James Keys,	- -	"	–	14	
Archibald Lawson,	- -	"	–	8	
William Moore,	- -	"	–	8	
Ignatius Milstead,	- -	"	–	8	
Thomas Nelson,	- -	"	–	14	
William Murphy,	- -	"	–	6	
William Martin,	- -	"	–	6	
William Muck,	- -	"			

NAMES.	RANK.	TIME OF SERVICE.		REMARKS.
		Days.	Months.	
Alexander Patterson, -	Private,	—	14	
John Payne, - -	"	—	14	
William Phillips, - -	"	—	8	
Geo. Pierson, - -	"	—	8	
Hugh Petty, - -	"	—	8	
Ashford Posey, - -	"	—	6	
Ace Pierson, - -	"	—	6	
John Patterson, - -	"	—	6	
Travis Payne, - -	"	—	6	
John Roles, - -	"	—	14	
Arthur S. Robertson, -	"	—	8	
Madden Rennoe, - -	"	—	8	
George Rennoe, - -	"	—	8	
William Rymes, - -	"	—	6	
John Smith, - -	"	—	14	
James Smith, - -	"	—	8	
Smallwood Truman, -	"	—	6	
Henry Tasker, - -	"	—	8	
Eliphalet Umberfield, -	"	—	8	

MUSTER ROLL

Of Captain John Merry's Company, from the Fifty-second Regiment, Virginia Militia, New Kent County, commanded by Lieutenant Colonel John H. Christian, in the Service from the 28th June to the 13th July, 1813, and from 4th to 18th of September, 1814.

NAMES.		RANK.	TIME OF SERVICE.		REMARKS.
			Months.	Days.	
John Merry,	- -	Captain,	1		
Edward V. Graves,	- -	Lieutenant,	–	14	
William H. Vaiden,	- -	Ensign,	–	14	
William New,	- -	"	–	16	
William Cook,	- -	Sergeant,	–	14	
Sims Vaiden,	- -	"	1		
John Edloe,	- -	"	1		
Samuel Trower,	- -	"	–	14	
Jones French,	- -	"	–	16	
Henry H. Wilcox,	- -	"	–	16	
Turner Southall,	- -	Corporal,	–	16	
John W. Rodgers,	- -	"	–	16	
Henry Southall,	- -	"	–	16	
Henry H. Southall,	- -	"	–	16	
Gideon Trower,	- -	"	–	14	
William P. Wyatt,	- -	"	–	14	
Croshor Graves,	- -	"	–	14	
Florence H. Walker,	- -	"	–	14	
John T. Brown,	- -	Private,	–	14	
John Brewer,	- -	"	1		
William Brown,	- -	"	–	14	
Edmond Bullifant,	- -	"	–	16	
William Chandler,	- -	"	–	14	
James Charles,	- -	"	–	14	
Thomas Clarke,	- -	"	–	16	
William Collier,	- -	"	–	16	
John Davis,	- -	"	–	14	
John Dillard,	- -	"	–	14	
James Evans,	- -	"	–	14	
Bartholo. Graves,	- -	"	–	14	Sub. for Edw'd. Major.
Carter Harmon,	- -	"	–	7	
William Holdcropt,	- -	"	–	14	Or Holdcroft.
John Hughes,	- -	"	–	14	
John G. Hillard,	- -	"	–	14	
Patrick Hendren,	- -	"	–	–	Acting as secretary to the commandant.
Robert Holdcroft,	- -	"	–	14	
Edward E. Harwood,	- -	"	–	8	
Robert Hillard,	- -	"	–	16	
William Holdworth,	- -	"	–	16	
Edward Isham,	- -	"	–	14	
William Jane,	- -	"	1		
Robert E. Jones,	- -	"	–	14	
Richard H. Meaux,	- -	"	–	14	
Thomas Morriss,	- -	"	–	14	
Joshua Martin,	- -	"	–	14	
Thomas Moss,	- -	"	–	14	

NAMES.	RANK.	TIME OF SERVICE.		REMARKS.
		Months.	Days.	
Christian Mountcastle, -	Private,	—	16	
William Pointer, - -	"	—	16	
Philip Perry, - -	"	—	16	
Daniel Roberts, - -	"	—	16	
Marston Shell, - -	"	—	14	
Richard L. Smith, - -	"	—	14	
William Smith, - -	"	—	14	
Clement Taylor, - -	"	—	14	
Henry D. Timberlake, -	"	—	14	
John Tandy, - -	"	—	14	
George Temple, - -	"	—	16	
Major Wilcox, - -	"	—	14	
Geo. Sweaney, - -	"	—	14	
William Wells, - -	"	—	14	
Thomas Walls, - -	"	—	14	
John H. Walker, - -	"	—	14	
Henry Woodward, - -	"	—	14	
Thomas W. Walker, -	"	—	14	
Harmon Walker, - -	"	—	7	
Jacob Vaiden, - -	"	—	14	
Isaac H. Vaiden, - -	"	—	14	
John Wilson, - -	"	—	14	

MUSTER ROLL

Of Captain John Middleton's Company, from the Thirty-seventh Regiment, Virginia Militia, Northumberland County, in the Service from the 4th to 7th April, and from 15th to 29th July, 1813.

NAMES.	RANK.	TIME OF SERVICE.		REMARKS.
		Months.	Days.	
John Middleton, - -	Captain,	—	12	
John C. Straughan, - -	Lieutenant,	—	6	
Geo. Downing, - -	Ensign,	—	9	
William Smithers, - -	Sergeant,	—	17	
Benjamin Landsdell, - -	"	—	4	
Joseph Boothe, - -	"	—	12	
James Headley, jr. - -	"	—	11	
John Dawson, - -	Drummer,	—	4	
Thomas T. Brown, - -	Fifer,	—	16	
Alexander Newsom, - -	"	—	11	
Samuel Ashburn, - -	Private,	—	12	
John Anderson, jr. - -	"	—	9	
Ewell Alexander, - -	"	—	6	
Rodham H. Booth, - -	"	—	12	
William Burris, - -	"	—	12	
Hezekiah Baker, - -	"	—	3	
Isaac Bray, - -	"	—	12	
Alpheus Barnes, - -	"	—	11	
William R. Booth, - -	"	—	12	
John Beacham, - -	"	—	10	
Vincent Barnes, - -	"	—	11	
Tarlton Barnes, - -	"	—	3	
Geo. Coles, - -	"	—	6	
John Conolley, - -	"	—	9	
Stephen Crowther, - -	"	—	12	
Geo. Conolley, - -	"	—	12	
Williamson Conolley, - -	"	—	3	
Jeremiah Dawson, - -	"	—	8	
Eppa Dawson, - -	"	—	8	
John Dawson, jr. - -	"	—	7	
Samuel Dawson, - -	"	—	9	
Thomas Davis, - -	"	—	12	
Richard Denny, - -	"	—	12	
Daniel Edwards, - -	"	—	12	
William France, - -	"	—	12	
John Hunt, - -	"	—	11	
Chichester Haynie, - -	"	—	11	
William Hughlett, - -	"	—	11	
John Littrell, - -	"	—	12	
Thomas Littrell, - -	"	—	12	
Richard C. Littrell, - -	"	—	11	
James Littrell, - -	"	—	12	
Charles Lumpkin, - -	"	—	12	
Holland Marsh, - -	"	—	4	
Thomas Neale, - -	"	—	12	
Richard Nelms, - -	"	—	3	
Elijah Pitman, - -	"	—	3	
Thomas Pope, - -	"	—	7	
Enoch H. Potts, - -	"	—	3	

NAMES.			RANK.	TIME OF SERVICE.		REMARKS.
				Months.	Days.	
John Sullivan,	-	-	Private,	–	9	
William Ticer,	-	-	"	–	12	
Lewis Ticer,	-	-	"	–	8	
Champion Talley,	-	-	"	–	12	
Moses Talley,	-	-	"	–	12	
Daniel Welch,	-	-	"	–	6	
James L. Straughan,	-	-	"	–	3	

MUSTER ROLL

Of Captain William Middleton's Company of Artillery, from the One Hundred and Eleventh Regiment, Virginia Militia, Westmoreland County, commanded by Lieutenant Colonel Richard E. Parker, in Service from 15th to 26th July, from 3d to 5th August, from October 30th to 17th November, in the year 1813, and from 18th July to 25th September, 1814.

NAMES.			RANK.	TIME OF SERVICE.		REMARKS.
				Months.	Days.	
William Middleton,	-	-	Captain,	3	2	
William Wright,	-	-	Lieutenant,	1	16	
Richard Wright,	-	-	"	2	13	
Thomas Pinckard,	-	-	Ensign,	–	15	
Walter Self,	-	-	Sergeant,	2	13	
William King,	-	-	"	2	12	
William M. Crabb,	-	-	"	2	7	
Elliot S. Minor,	-	-	"	–	2	
Henry Parker,	-	-	"	–	4	
Jeremiah Middleton,	-	-	"	–	20	
Richard Batten,	-	-	"	–	2	
William Johnson,	-	-	"	–	16	
Austin Dozier,	-	-	"	–	16	
John Brown,	-	-	"	–	16	
John Beale,	-	-	"	–	16	
Vincent Moore,	-	-	Drummer,	2	3	
George V. C. Hudson,	-	-	Fifer,	2	7	
Orville Austin.	-	-	Private,	–	15	
John Anthony,	-	-	"	–	15	
John Allen,	-	-	"	–	16	
Samuel Booth,	-	-	"	1	9	
John Beale,	-	-	"	2	14	
Beckwith Butler,	-	-	"	–	17	
John Brinn,	-	-	"	1	20	
William Brown,	-	-	"	–	3	
Richard Batten,	-	-	"	–	17	
Samuel Brann,	-	-	"	2	24	
Vincent Brann,	-	-	"	2	24	
Joseph Brown,	-	-	"	–	16	
Corbin Brown,	-	-	"	–	16	
Sheldon Brinnon,	-	-	"	–	16	
John Barber,	-	-	"	–	2	
William Butler,	-	-	"	–	9	
William Brann,	-	-	"	–	7	
John Bennett,	-	-	"	1	20	
William Brickey,	-	-	"	2	7	
John T. Courtney,	-	-	"	–	22	
Thomas McFarlane Cox,	-	-	"	2	13	
William M. Crabb,	-	-	"	–	14	
George B. Carey,	-	-	"	1	13	
Bend't M. Crabbe,	-	-	"	–	15	
Vincent Douglass,	-	-	"	2	23	
James Donnaubow,	-	-	"	–	16	
James Davis,	-	-	"	1	23	
John Davis,	-	-	"	1	2	
John Davis,	-	-	"	–	2	

NAMES.	RANK.	TIME OF SERVICE.		REMARKS.
		Months.	Days.	
George Davis, - -	Private,	2	7	
John C. Dawson, - -	"	2	19	
William Enniss, - -	"	2	9	
William Hazzard, - -	"	2	23	
Daniel Hardwick, - -	"	—	16	
William Harper, - -	"	—	16	
Thomas O. Harrow, -	"	—	15	
Tressel Hall, - -	"	—	4	
Parker Hall, - -	"	—	4	
John Harrison, - -	"	2	20	
James Johnson, - -	"	1	16	
John Jewell, - -	"	3	1	
Griffin T. King, - -	"	2	23	
James Kertley, - -	"	—	16	
James King, - -	"	—	12	
John Kirk, - -	"	1	9	
William B. Lewis, - -	"	2	20	
Jeremiah Middleton, - -	"	—	12	
William McKildoe, - -	"	1	23	
William Moore, - -	"	2	23	
Allen McKenny, - -	"	1	17	
Alexander McGrier, -	"	—	13	
Newman McKenny, - -	"	—	16	
Elliott S. Minor, - -	"	2	12	
Ro. Middleton, - -	"	—	4	
Wm. G. Morris, - -	"	1	2	
James Morse, - -	"	2	8	
Travis McGrew, - -	"	—	7	
William Newman, - -	"	—	16	
Bena't M. Oldham, -	"	1	4	
William A. M. Parker, -	"	2	19	
Fleet B. Plummer, -	"	2	17	
Thomas Pillion, -	"	—	19	
Henry Pritchell, -	"	—	15	
Henry Parker, -	"	2	12	
Nimrod Rockluster, -	"	—	16	
William Reynolds, -	"	—	13	
Peter N. Rust, -	"	2	6	
Thomas Scutt, - -	"	2	14	
Francis Self, - -	"	2	23	
James Smith, - -	"	2	22	
John Shackleford, -	"	2	21	
Patrick S. Sandford, -	"	—	15	
William H. Sandford, -	"	2	24	
Samuel Smith, -	"	—	15	
Owen Sullivan, -	"	—	9	
Peyton Sesson, -	"	—	12	
William Sutton, sr. -	"	—	16	
James T. Scott, -	"	—	16	
William Stone, -	"	—	16	
William Sutton, jr. -	"	—	10	
James Sutton, -	"	—	10	
John Seycock, -	"	—	16	
James Sorrell, -	"	2	16	
James Thomas, -	"	—	16	
William Thomas, -	"	—	10	
William Williams, -	"	1	28	
Presley C. Wright, -	"	2	23	
John Weathers, - -	"	—	2	

MUSTER ROLL

Of Captain Anderson Miller's Company, from the Nineteenth Regiment, Virginia Militia, commanded by Lieutenant Colonel John Ambler, in the Service of the United States, from the 18th to 27th March, and from 28th June to 3d July, 1813, and from 26th August to 7th September, 1814.

NAMES.	RANK.	TIME OF SERVICE.		REMARKS.
		Months.	Days.	
Anderson Miller, - -	Captain,	–	28	
Michael B. Portiaux, - -	Brevet Lieut.	–	28	Promoted from corp'l.
Geo. E. Tiffin, - -	Lieutenant,	–	16	
William H. Hughes, - -	Ensign,	–	16	
Fred. M. McCraw, - -	"	–	12	
Geo Fisher, - -	Sergeant,	–	16	
Edward Bailey, - -	"	–	16	
Thomas Cushing, - -	"	–	16	
Dabney Eubank, - -	"	–	6	
Charles Carter, ⌣ -	"	–	10	
Gordon H. Backus, - -	"	–	12	
James Herron, - -	"	–	8	
Thomas Hatcher, - -	"	–	12	
John H. Norman, - -	"	–	12	
William R. Butler, - -	"	–	9	
William H. Prince, - -	Corporal,	–	16	
John Dryman, - -	"	–	6	
John Roberts, - -	"	–	28	
Edmund Banks, - -	"	–	10	
James Armstrong, - -	"	–	10	
John Crouch, - -	"	–	10	
William Burke, - -	"	–	12	
Geo. Bosher, - -	"	–	12	
Elias Carlton, - -	"	–	8	
Richard Davis, - -	"	–	8	
Robert Moreland, - -	"	–	8	
Robert Andrews, - -	Private,	–	18	
Thos. M. Ambler, - -	"	–	22	
Geo. Allen, - -	"	–	10	
Philip Aylett, - -	"	–	10	
Robert Atkinson, - -	"	–	10	
Thomas Baish, - -	"	–	12	
Daniel Baugh, - -	"	–	12	
Wilson Brackett, - -	"	–	12	
James Brook, - -	"	–	12	
Geo. Bosher, - -	"	–	12	
William Banks, - -	"	–	12	
Edmund Banks, - -	"	–	12	
Samuel D. Brame, - -	"	–	12	
William R. Butler, - -	"	–	12	
William Burke, - -	"	–	2	
John Brakenbrough, - -	"	–	16	
John H. Blair, - -	"	–	13	
William V. Butler, - -	"	–	16	
James Blair, - -	"	–	3	
Hickman Bachelor, - -	"	–	16	
Robert Bradford, - -	"	–	16	

NAMES.	RANK.	TIME OF SERVICE.		REMARKS.
		Months.	Days.	
John Banks, - -	Private,	–	6	
Lewin Blake, - -	"	–	10	Or Levin,
Washington Berry, - -	"	–	10	
Geo. R. Cocke, - -	"	–	3	
Lemuel Churchill, - -	"	–	12	
William Cook, - -	"	–	12	
John Campbell, - -	"	–	22	
Elias Carlton, - -	"	–	12	
Samuel N. Cardozo, - -	"	–	8	
Thomas Cook, - -	"	–	6	
Micajah Clarke, - -	"	–	10	
Josiah Cushing, - -	"	–	10	
John W. Dance, - -	"	–	12	
Richard Davis, - -	"	–	12	
John Day, - -	"	–	16	
Francis Dunington, - -	"	–	16	
Philip Duval, - -	"	–	6	
John Drinan, - -	"	–	6	
Johnson Eubank, - -	"	–	16	
Miles Egleston, - -	"	–	6	
John H. Eustace, - -	"	–	16	
Joseph Ellis, - -	"	–	6	
Theoderick Furguson, - -	"	–	12	
Alexander Fulcher, - -	"	–	7	
James Fisher, - -	"	–	6	
Henry Frobus, - -	"	–	6	
Robert Fuller, - -	"	–	10	
Jesse Franklin, - -	"	–	10	
John Grantland, - -	"	–	12	
Gideon B. Green, - -	"	–	12	
Robert Gordon, - -	"	–	16	
Thomas Gibbs, - -	"	–	16	
Matthew Gentry, - -	"	–	6	
James Gunn, - -	"	–	6	
John P. Grantland, - -	"	–	6	
Wiltshur Golden, - -	"	–	6	
Martin Gentry, - -	"	–	10	
Geo. Greenhow, - -	"	–	10	
Richard Graves, - -	"	–	10	
Martin Holloway, - -	"	–	28	
Henry Hucksford, - -	"	–	12	
John Hays, - -	"	–	12	
John Holman, - -	"	–	12	
James Herron, - -	"	–	22	
Thomas G. Hull, - -	"	–	16	
John Hocady, - -	"	–	6	
John Holman, - -	"	–	6	
John Herrick, - -	"	–	10	
Daniel Higginbotham, - -	"	–	10	
Christopher Hudson, - -	"	–	10	
Joseph Hill, - -	"	–	10	
Sterling R. Hood, - -	"	–	10	
Charles A. Jacobs, - -	"	–	22	
Joseph Jenkins, - -	"	–	16	
Thomas Jefferys, - -	"	–	6	
James Jefferys, - -	"	–	10	
William Johnston, - -	"	–	10	
John M. Key, - -	"	–	12	
Matthew Lacy, - -	"	–	12	
Alexander Lithgow, - -	"	–	16	
Fleming Lacy, - -	"	–	10	
Charles J. McMurdo, - -	"	–	28	
William McCabe, - -	"	–	12	
William Minor, - -	"	–	12	

NAMES.	RANK.	TIME OF SERVICE.		REMARKS.
		Months.	Days.	
Robert Moreland, - -	Private,	–	12	
William McCaw, - -	"	–	3	
William Mann, - -	"	–	6	
Robert McCullough, - -	"	–	6	
William McKenny, - -	"	–	10	
Edmund Mosby, - -	"	–	6	
Thomas Muir, - -	"	–	10	
William Neale, - -	"	–	10	
Norborne Norton, - -	"	–	16	
Lewell Osgood, - -	"	–	16	
Walter Porter, - -	"	•	12	
Henry Pettus, - -	"	–	10	
Kincheon Parker, - -	"	–	10	
William B. Price, - -	"	–	6	
William Perry, - -	"	–	16	
Edward Petticola, - -	"	–	12	
John Quarles, - -	"	–	12	
Richard Ross, - -	"	–	16	
Alexander Strother, - -	"	–	16	
Jacob Smith, - -	"	–	10	
Philip Sturdivant, - -	"	–	10	
Fendal J. Sebree, - -	"	–	16	
Philip Southall, - -	"	–	10	
Walter J. Steptoe, - -	"	–	10	
George Smith, - -	"	–	16	
William C. Shields, - -	"	–	12	
William Sadler, - -	"	–	12	
Isaac Sturdivant, - -	"	–	12	
Chiles Terrell, - -	"	–	16	
Thomas Terrell, - -	"	–	10	
Benjamin Thomas, - -	"	–	22	
James Taylor, - -	"	–	16	
Richard D. Taylor, - -	"	–	6	
Wilson Thomas, - -	"	–	12	
James Taylor, - -	"	–	12	
Rodney Walters, - -	"	–	16	
William Wickham, - -	"	–	16	
Charles Wade, - -	"	–	10	
Edmund Wade, - -	"	–	10	
John Wills, - -	"	–	10	
William C. Williams, - -	"	–	10	

MUSTER ROLL

Of Captain Morris L. Miller's Company of Riflemen, from the Thirty-third Regiment, Virginia Militia, Henrico County, in the Service from the 19th to 29th March, 1813.

NAMES.	RANK	TIME OF SERVICE.		REMARKS.
		Months.	Days.	
Morris L. Miller,	Captain,	–	5	
Samuel Gathright,	Lieutenant,	–	5	
Richard H. Frazer,	Ensign,	–	5	
Robert Redford,	Sergeant,	–	5	
David W. Robinson,	"	–	5	
Anthony Matthews,	"	–	5	
William Tussle,	Corporal,	–	5	
Geo. Whitten,	"	–	5	
Thomas Epperson,	"	–	5	
Reuben George,	"	–	5	
George V. Angle,	Private,	–	5	
Thomas Barbour,	"	–	5	
Charles Breeding,	"	–	5	
James Bridgwater,	"	–	5	
James Brightwell,	"	–	5	
Benjamin Cotten,	"	–	5	
Thomas Childrey,	"	–	5	
Rolling Childress,	"	–	5	
Reuben Childress,	"	–	5	
Charles G. Carter,	"	–	4	
Theodrick Carter,	"	–	5	
Charles Childress,	"	–	5	
Joseph G. Carter,	"	–	5	
William H. Childress,	"	–	5	
Nathaniel Enroughty,	"	–	5	
Richard Enroughty,	"	–	5	
Peter Francis,	"	–	4	
Charles Fussle,	"	–	5	
John Fussle,	"	–	5	
Martin Farrell,	"	–	5	
Anderson Gathwright,	"	–	5	
Thomas Goode,	"	–	5	
Jackson Hampton,	"	–	5	
Henry Johnson,	"	–	5	
William M. Laster,	"	–	5	
Hartwell M. Manners,	"	–	5	
Benjamin Morriss,	"	–	5	
Robert Sharp,	"	–	5	
Price Sharpe,	"	–	4	
Thomas Salmon,	"	–	5	
Eaton Tyler,	"	–	4	
Isaac Truman,	"	–	5	
Matthew Vaughan,	"	–	5	
Wyatt Wade,	"	–	5	
John Wade,	"	–	5	
Elisha Williams,	"	–	5	
Samuel Warriner,	"	–	5	

MUSTER ROLL

Of Captain Isaac Mitchell's Company, from the Fifteenth Regiment, Virginia Militia, commanded by Lieutenant Colonel William Allen, in the Service of the United States, from the 1st to 11th of September, 1814.

NAMES.			RANK.	TIME OF SERVICE.		REMARKS.
				Months.	Days.	
Isaac Mitchell,	-	-	Captain,	–	11	
Richard Eppes,	-	-	Lieutenant,	–	11	
Jacob Mitchell,	-	-	Ensign,	–	11	
John Mitchell,	-	-	Sergeant,	–	11	
John Brown,	-	-	"	–	11	
Henry W. Epps,	-	-	"	–	11	
Joel Jones,	-	-	"	–	11	
Nicholas Jarratt,	-	-	Corporal,	–	11	
Thomas Malone,	-	-	"	–	11	
Henry W. Adams,	-	-	"	–	11	
Harrison Randolph,	-	-	"	–	11	
David Rainey,	-	-	Drummer,	–	11	
Geo. Bailey,	-	-	Fifer,	–	11	
William Bailey,	-	-	Private,	–	11	
Joshua Bass,	-	-	"	–	11	
Green H. Booth,	-	-	"	–	11	
Wiley Brill,	-	-	"	–	11	
William Brister,	-	-	"	–	11	
Robert Curtis,	-	-	"	–	11	
Joel Davis,	-	-	"	–	11	
Thomas P. Davis,	-	-	"	–	11	
Francis Eppes,	-	-	"	–	11	
John Edwards,	-	-	"	–	11	
Jessee Grigg,	-	-	"	–	11	
Geo. Graves,	-	-	"	–	11	
Carter Hogwood,	-	-	"	–	11	
Frederick J. Judkins,	-	-	"	–	11	
Enos Kitchen,	-	-	"	–	11	
Bowling M. King,	-	-	"	–	11	
Augustin Loftin,	-	-	"	–	11	
James Mosley,	-	-	"	–	11	
Thomas Malvre, jr.	-	-	"	–	11	
Jessee Murtland,	-	-	"	–	11	
Charles Newsome,	-	-	"	–	11	
Leonard Parham,	-	-	"	–	11	
Chadrick P. Pool,	-	-	"	–	11	
David Parrish,	-	-	"	–	11	
Thomas C. Peebles,	-	-	"	–	11	
Robert Rainey,	-	-	"	–	11	
Adam Spires,	-	-	"	–	11	
James Spires,	-	-	"	–	11	
Henry Spires,	-	-	"	–	11	
Charles Stewart,	-	-	"	–	11	
Burwell Whitehorne,	-	-	"	–	11	
John Whitehorne,	-	-	"	–	11	
John Winfield,	-	-	"	–	11	
John Woodford,	-	-	"	–	11	
James Washer,	-	-	"	–	11	

NAMES.			RANK.	TIME OF SERVICE.		REMARKS.
				Months.	Days.	
James Winfield,	-	-	Private,	–	11	
Jessee Williams,	-	-	"	–	11	
Joel T. Wingfield,	-	-	"	–	11	
William Wingfield,	-	-	"	–	11	
Morress Zells,	-	-	"	–	11	

MUSTER ROLL

Of a Company of Artillery, detached from the Thirty-sixth Regiment of Virginia Militia, commanded by Major Thomas Chapman, in Service of the State of Virginia, from 31st August to 7th September, in the year 1814.

NAMES.	RANK.	TIME OF SERVICE.		REMARKS.
		Months.	Days.	
Thomas Montgomerie, -	Sergeant,	–	8	
James D. Boughanan, -	Private,	–	8	
William Cannon, - -	"	–	8	
David Davis, - -	"	–	3	
John Dickinson, - -	"	–	8	
Moses Duffey, - -	"	–	8	
Robert Forgie, - -	"	–	8	
Robert Forsythe, - -	"	–	8	
John Hall, - -	"	–	8	
John S. Harrison, - -	"	–	8	
John Hammill, - -	"	–	8	
George F. Huber, - -	"	–	8	
John Lansdown, - -	"	–	8	
Judah Lord, - -	"	–	8	
Frederick Muschett, - -	"	–	8	
Francis Purnell, - -	"	–	8	
William Smith, - -	"	–	8	
James Watson, - -	"	–	8	

MUSTER ROLL

Of Captain Richard Monroe's Company, from the One Hundred and Eleventh Regiment, Virginia Militia, Westmoreland, commanded by Major William Nelson, in the Service from the 15th to 25th July, 1813.

NAMES.	RANK.	TIME OF SERVICE.		REMARKS.
		Months.	Days.	
Richard Monroe, - -	Captain,	—	10	
William Hungerford, -	Lieutenant,	—	8	
Alexander Tindley, -	Ensign,	—	6	
Meredith Marmaduke, -	"	—	4	
Newton Berryman, - -	"	—	3	
James McDaniel, -	Sergeant,	—	10	
William White, -	"	—	10	
William Reymy, -	"	—	10	
Robert P. Marshall, -	"	—	2	
Abner James, - -	"	—	4	
William Frank, -	"	—	2	
Taliaferro Jett, - -	"	—	4	
William Anthony, -	Private,	—	2	
John Barrott, -	"	—	2	
William Barrott, -	"	—	2	
Thomas Bulger, -	"	—	5	
Lewis Bell, -	"	—	5	
Joseph Barker, -	"	—	5	
Robert Brewer, -	"	—	4	
John Barker, -	"	—	8	
Daniel Barker, -	"	—	2	
Bowen Boshaw, -	"	—	2	
James Boshaw, -	"	—	2	
Daniel Briscoe, -	"	—	3	
Thomas Brann, -	"	—	5	
William Berkley, -	"	—	2	
Abner Carter, -	"	—	3	
James Crosk, -	"	—	2	
David Curley, -	"	—	2	
John Crosk, -	"	—	10	
Nelson Craidling, -	"	—	10	
Lovel Carpenter, -	"	—	6	
William Coats, -	"	—	10	
William Coghill, -	"	—	10	
John Deatley, jr. -	"	—	1	
James Dosier, -	"	—	2	
Henry Deatley, -	"	—	3	
James Gurtridge, -	"	—	10	
John Gurtridge, -	"	—	10	
Spencer Head, -	"	—	6	
Warner Hudson, -	"	—	2	
Weadson Jett, -	"	—	2	
George Johnston, -	"	—	2	
Thomas Jenkins, -	"	—	2	
James H. Jenkins, -	"	—	2	
Bennet Knight, -	"	—	10	
Fenies Lefever, -	"	—	1	
Fleet Lampkin, -	"	—	2	

NAMES.	RANK.	TIME OF SERVICE.		REMARKS.
		Months.	Days.	
Bald'n M. Lee, - -	Private,	—	2	
James Lampkin, - -	"	—	2	
William Lampkin, - -	"	—	2	
William Mitchell, - -	"	—	1	
John Mitchell, - -	"	—	4	
William McClanihan, -	"	—	4	
Washington Mariner, -	"	—	5	
William McKenny, - -	"	—	2	
Geo. McKenny, - -	"	—	2	
Jo. H. Mothershead, -	"	—	2	
William Marmaduke, -	"	—	5	
Vincent Marmaduke, -	"	—	2	
James Nash, - -	"	—	2	
William Nash, - -	"	—	2	
Lofty Olliff, - -	"	—	2	
William Olliff, - -	"	—	10	
James Pead, - -	"	—	10	
John Pead, - -	"	—	10	
John Purseley, - -	"	—	2	
John Purseley, jr. - -	"	—	2	
Thos. Pegg, - -	"	—	2	
John Pierce, - -	"	—	5	
Geo. Picket, - -	"	—	5	
Edward Porter, - -	"	—	2	
William Ralls, - -	"	—	2	
James Ralls, - -	"	—	2	
Major Roly, - -	"	—	10	
Jonathan P. Robinson, -	"	—	5	
Josh'a Raymy, - -	"	—	10	
Thomas Sampson, - -	"	—	6	
Benjamin Sims, - -	"	—	2	
Abram Selvy, - -	"	—	4	
Benj. P. Smith, - -	"	—	2	
Francis C. Triplett, - -	"	—	5	
Richard Wilkins, - -	"	—	10	

MUSTER ROLL

Of Captain William B. Moody's Company, attached to the Twenty-Ninth Regiment, Virginia Militia, commanded by Major Joseph W. Ballard, in the Service from the 24th June to the 10th July, 1813.

NAMES.	RANK.	TIME OF SERVICE.		REMARKS.
		Months.	Days.	
William B. Moody, - -	Captain,	–	16	
David Dick, - -	Lieutenant,	–	16	
Isaac Moody, - -	Ensign,	–	16	
Pleasant Stagg, - -	Sergeant,	–	16	
Nelson Harriss, - -	"	–	16	
William Turner, - -	"	–	16	
Benjamin Philips, - -	"	–	16	
Robert Marshall, - -	Corporal,	–	16	
Joseph Villines, - -	"	–	16	
William Stephens, - -	"	–	16	
Peter Turner, - -	"	–	16	
Pleasant Casey, - -	Drummer,	–	16	
Francis Whiteley, - -	Fifer,	–	16	
Zachariah Atkins, - -	Private,	–	16	
Jeremiah Atkins, - -	"	–	16	
Francis Chapman, - -	"	–	16	
Armstrong Edwards, - -	"	–	16	
Josiah Edwards, - -	"	–	16	
Philip Edwards, - -	"	–	16	
Hezekiah Edwards, - -	"	–	16	
James Edwards, - -	"	–	16	
John Fulgham, - -	"	–	16	
William Gaskins, - -	"	–	16	
Gillum Hatchell, - -	"	–	16	
Nelson Hatchell, - -	"	–	16	
John Herring, - -	"	–	16	
Harman Hatchell, - -	"	–	16	
Willis Johnson, - -	"	–	16	
Harrison Kimbell, - -	"	–	16	
Zachariah Matthew, - -	"	–	16	
Drewry Mints, - -	"	–	16	
Joseph Parkerson, - -	"	–	16	
William Parr, - -	"	–	16	
John Sikes, - -	"	–	16	
Thomas Smith, - -	"	–	16	
John Turner, (of Wm.) - -	"	–	16	
Joseph Turner, - -	"	–	16	
Wilsa Turner, - -	"	–	16	
John Turner, (of John,) - -	"	–	16	
George Turner, - -	"	–	16	
Benjamin Turner, - -	"	–	16	
Jordan Turner, - -	"	–	16	
Joseph Turner, (of E.) - -	"	–	16	
Henry Turner, - -	"	–	16	
John Villines, - -	"	–	16	
Elisha Whitley, - -	"	–	16	
Isaac Whitley, - -	"	–	16	
Robert Whitley, - -	"	–	16	

Captain George Morris' Company—Fortieth Regiment.

NAMES.	RANK.	TIME OF SERVICE.		REMARKS.
		Months.	Days.	
Francis Anderson, - -	Private,	–	25	
Benj. Chapman, - -	"	–	26	
Joseph Coats, - -	"	–	26	
Obadiah Gordon, - -	"	–	21	Transferred to Capt. Jackson's company.
Fontaine McGehee, - -	"	3	26	Substitute for Jno. R. Cheek.
Richard Robertson, - -	"	–	21	
Nathaniel Talley, - -	"	–	16	
Nathaniel Thompson, -	"	–	27	

(For rest of this company, see publication of Pay Rolls.)

Captain Robert Magill's Company—Fifty-eighth Regiment.

NAMES.			RANK.	TIME OF SERVICE.		REMARKS.
				Months.	Days.	
Abraham Koots,	-	-	Private,	1	23	
Early Taylor,	-	-	"	–	28	

(For rest of this company, see publication of Pay Rolls.)

MUSTER ROLL

Of Captain William Moseley's Company of Cavalry, attached to the First Regiment, Virginia Militia, in the Service of the United States, from the 29th August to 13th of Sept, 1814.

NAMES.	RANK.	TIME OF SERVICE.		REMARKS.
		Months.	Days.	
William Moseley, - -	Captain,	–	16	
Charles Moseley, - -	Lieutenant,	–	16	
Thomas Jurticum, - -	"	–	16	
Bernard Booker, - -	Cornet,	–	16	
Thomas Cobbs, -	1 Sergeant,	–	12	
Samuel Gordon, - -	2 "	–	16	
Robert Bonderant, -	3 "	–	16	
Nathan Spencer, - -	4 "	–	16	
Pleasant Abbott, - -	Private,	–	16	
Felix Brown, -	"	–	16	
John Chadsin, - -	"	–	–	On wagon guard.
James Coleman, -	"	–	16	
Richard W. Chick, -	"	–	16	
Matthew W. Cason, -	"	–	16	
William J. Dunn, -	"	–	16	
George W. Eldridge, -	"	–	16	
Thomas Eldridge, -	"	–	16	
Stephen Fossee, - -	"	–	16	
William B. Gray, -	"	–	16	
William Gordon, -	"	–	16	
John Gibson, - -	"	–	16	
Obediah Gordon, - -	"	–	16	
William Harris, -	"	–	–	On wagon guard.
Peter Hales, - -	"	–	16	
James Holbeman, -	"	–	16	
Henry Hall, - -	"	–	16	
William H. Jones, -	"	–	16	
William B. Jones, -	"	–	16	
William D. Jones, -	"	–	–	On vidette.
Thomas Jeffries, -	"	–	16	Sub. for Thos. Rush.
Josas Jones, - -	"	–	–	Sub. for Wm. Moore.
Robert B. Jones, -	"	–	16	
James W. Jones, -	"	–	16	
David Johnson, -	"	–	16	
John Linticum, -	"	–	16	
Thomas Lewis, -	"	–	16	
David Marriner, -	"	–	16	
Merit Milton, -	"	–	16	
Charles May, - -	"	–	16	
Matthew Moseley, -	"	–	16	
John Moore, - -	"	–	16	
Thomas Nowlin, -	"	–	16	Sub. for R. Patterson.
Miller Copton, -	"	–	16	
Edward Perkins, -	"	–	16	
Turner H. Patterson, -	"	–	–	On vidette.
Stephen Pankey, -	"	–	16	
Thomas Saunders, -	"	–	16	

NAMES.	RANK.	TIME OF SERVICE.		REMARKS.
		Months.	Days.	
Francis Saunders, - -	Private,	–	16	
Samuel Saunders, - -	"	–	16	
Absalom Stephens, - -	"	–	16	
Thomas Stephens, - -	"	–	16	
Arthur Woodmore, - -	"	–	16	
Geo. W. Word, - -	"	–	16	
Geo. Wooldridge, - -	"	–	16	
Robert Walker, - -	"	–	16	
Geo. Webb, - -	"	–	16	
Joseph Walker, - -	"	–	16	
Robert Walton, - -	"	–	16	
Thomas Walton, - -	"	–	16	
Walter C. Wilkerson, -	"	–	16	

PAY ROLL

Of a Boat Guard, detached and continued in the Service, by Major William N°-son, commanding One Hundred and Eleventh Regiment, Virginia Militia, by an order bearing date 1st November 1813.

NAMES.			RANK.	TIME OF SERVICE.		REMARKS.
				Months.	Days.	
Samuel Mothershead, -			–	–	17	
William Nash,	-	-	–	–	16	
Whiting Green,	-	-	–	–	17	
Warner Hudson,	-	-	–	–	17	
Spencer B. Worth,	-	-	–	–	8	
Spencer B. Worth,	-	-	–	–	6	

PAY ROLL.

Of a Boat Guard, called into Service by order of Lieutenant Colonel Richard E. Parker, by an order dated 23d August, 1813.

NAMES.			RANK.	TIME OF SERVICE.		REMARKS.
				Months.	Days.	
Stephen S. Motherheed,	-	-	–	–	21	
John Lucass,	-	-	–	–	21	
Elijah M. Oliff,	-	-	–	–	21	
William Oliff,	-	-	–	–	21	
Silas Short,	-	-	–	–	21	
John B. Deatley,	-	-	–	–	21	

Captain William McMahon's Company, One Hundred and Sixteenth Regiment.

NAMES.			RANK.	TIME OF SERVICE.		REMARKS.
				Months.	Days.	
Enoch Wortham,	-	-	Sword Master,	–	24	
John Cusman,	-	-	Private,	–	12	
Daniel Ettinger,	-	-	"	–	12	

(For rest of this company, see publication of Pay Rolls.)

Captain William Murphy's Company—Nineteenth Regiment.

NAMES.	RANK.	TIME OF SERVICE.		REMARKS.
		Months.	Days.	
William Murphy, - -	Captain,	–	5	
David J. Burr, - -	Lieutenant,	–	5	
Thomas Diddep, - -	Ensign,	–	5	
John G. Blair, - -	Sergeant,	–	5	
William Finney, - -	"	–	5	
Edw. C. Cook, - -	"	–	5	
Philip Duval, - -	"	–	5	
James Rawlings, - -	Corporal,	–	5	
William J. Cole, - -	"	–	5	
Robert Lyman, - -	"	–	4	
John W. Cheadle, - -	"	–	5	
Henry J. Arnhold, - -	Private,	–		
Bentley Anderson, - -	"	–	3	
John M. Armistead, - -	"	–	3	
Charles Beck, - -	"	–	5	
Albert Booker, - -	"	–	3	
William Barrett, - -	"	–	5	
James Brown, jr. - -	"	–	5	
Thomas Bendle, - -	"	–	5	
Alexander Brown, - -	"	–	3	
Beverly Blair, - -	"	–	5	
John Bootright, - -	"	–	5	
John H. Blair, - -	"	–	10	
Peter Copland, - -	"	–	5	
Benj. Cheigneau, - -	"	–	5	
William Cowan, - -	"	–	5	
Samuel Carey, - -	"	–	2	
Edward V. Crandall, - -	"	–	5	
Sterling I. Crump, - -	"	–	5	
Thomas Cheadle, - -	"	–	5	
William Craig, - -	"	–	5	
Flem. B. Cross, - -	"	–	4	
Thomas Cowles, - -	"	–	5	
Nat. Dick, - -	"	–	10	
Thos. S. Dickerson, - -	"	–	2	
Geo. Dabney, - -	"	–	2	
Rivers Drake, - -	"	–	5	
John Darrac. - -	"	–	5	
Simon Frazer, - -	"	–	3	
Charles J. Fox, - -	"	–	5	
John Fore, - -	"	–	5	
John G. Gamble, - -	"	–	2	
William R. Geddy, - -	"	–	5	
Robert Hughes, - -	"	–	3	
William Hooper, - -	"	–	4	
Peter Hohn, - -	"	–	5	
Manuel Judah, - -	"	–	5	
John Jones, - -	"	–	2	
Flem'g James, - -	"	–	3	
James Liggon, - -	"	–	5	
E. V. Lachaize, - -	"	–	5	
Thomas Morgan, - -	"	–	2	
William Minton, - -	"		5	

NAMES.	RANK.	TIME OF SERVICE.		REMARKS.
		Months.	Days.	
Fred. McCraw, - -	Private,	—	5	
Theo. Nash, - -	"	—	5	
Jacob Philips, - -	"	—	5	
Arch'd Pleasants, - -	"	—	5	
Thos. S. Pope, - -	"	—	5	
Walter Potter, - -	"	—	5	
Ro. M. Pulliam, - -	"	—	5	
Fred. Pleasants, - -	"	—	5	
Geo. Robertson, - -	"	—	3	
Joseph Robbins, - -	"	—	5	
Youell Rust, - -	"	—	5	
Henry Rodgers, - -	"	—	5	
T. Y. Roddy, - -	"	—	5	
Theo. Robertson, - -	"	—	4	
John H. Strobia, - -	"	—	5	
Isaac B. Seixas, - -	"	—	5	
John G. Smith, - -	"	—	5	
James Sizer, - -	"	—	1	
Philip T. Shelton, - -	"	—	5	
Frs. Strobia, - -	"	—	5	
E. Sandford, - -	"	—	5	
William H. Shields, - -	"	—	5	
Sam'l Scott, - -	"	—	5	
Elisha Turpin, - -	"	—	5	
Harry Tompkins, - -	"	—	5	
John L. Thomas, - -	"	—	3	
John Wilson, - -	"	—	5	
Charles Watson, - -	"	—	2	
Geo. Wells, - -	"	—	5	
Abel Webster, - -	"	—	5	
Robert Wilkins, - -	"	—	5	
Corbin Warwick, - -	"	—	5	
William Warwick, - -	"	—	5	

(For rest of this company, see publication of Pay Rolls.)

MUSTER ROLL

Of Lieutenant David Murray's Company, from the Twentieth Regiment, Virginia Militia, commanded by Lieutenant Colonel James Robertson, in the Service of the United States, from the 10th to 15th March, 1813.

NAMES.	RANK.	TIME OF SERVICE.		REMARKS.
		Months.	Days.	
David S. Murray,	Lieutenant,	–	5	
Henry Sparrow,	Ensign,	–	5	
William C. Burrough,	Sergeant,	–	5	
Caleb Whitehurst,	"	–	5	
Edward Moseley,	"	–	5	
Isaac Land,	"	–	5	
Malicha Wiles,	Corporal,	–	5	
Gresham Gulasha,	"	–	5	
Patrick Whitehurst,	"	–	5	
Jonathan Williamson,	"	–	5	
John T. Calvert,	Private,	–	5	
Horatio Davis,	"	–	5	
Hillary Davis,	"	–	5	
Ralph Dickson,	"	–	5	
Henry Edwards,	"	–	5	
David Edwards,	"	–	5	
Jeremiah Fentress,	"	–	5	
Caleb Godfrey,	"	–	5	
William Godfrey,	"	–	5	
Lemuel Godfrey,	"	–	5	
Charles Griggs,	"	–	5	
Joshua Hopkins,	"	–	3	
John Lee,	"	–	5	
William Lyen,	"	–	5	
William Mooring,	"	–	5	
William Matthias,	"	–	5	
John Mosley,	"	–	5	
Richard Murray,	"	–	5	
Hyram Nellams,	"	–	5	
William Otley,	"	–	5	
John Paynter,	"	–	5	
Nathaniel Paynter,	"	–	5	
Robert Parsons,	"	–	5	
Josiah W. Slack,	"	–	5	
Joseph Stafford,	"	–	5	
John Shipps,	"	–	5	
Bartlett Shipps,	"	–	5	
William Truss,	"	–	4	
Henry Williamson,	"	–	5	
James Williamson,	"	.—	5	
David Whitehurst,	"	–	5	
Peter Williamson,	"	–	5	
William Williamson,	"	–	5	
Josiah Williamson,	"	–	5	
John Wood,	"	–	5	
John Ward,	"	–	5	
David Whitehurst,	"	–	5	
Tulley Whitehurst,	"	–	4	

MUSTER ROLL

*Of Captain Samuel Muse's Company, from the Sixth Regiment, Virginia Militia,
in the Service from the 5th to 16th April, 1813.*

NAMES.	RANK.	TIME OF SERVICE.		REMARKS.
		Months.	Days.	
Samuel Muse, - -	Captain,	–	11	
Alexander L. Bonathon, -	Lieutenant,	–	11	
Robert Dobbins, - -	Ensign,	–	11	
Vincent Ramsey, - -	Sergeant,	–	11	
Chaney Brizendine, - -	"	–	11	
Reuben Cauthon, - -	"	–	11	
John St. John, - -	"	–	11	
James Durhame, - -	Corporal,	–	11	
William Davis, - -	"	–	11	
John Townley, - -	"	–	11	
James Trible, - -	"	–	11	
Mourning Armstrong, -	Private,	–	11	
Lindy Brizendine, - -	"	–	11	
Ervin Brizendine, - -	"	–	11	
Vincent Brizendine, - -	"	–	11	
James Brizendine, - -	"	–	11	
Leonard Burnett, - -	"	–	11	
James Brooks, - -	"	–	11	
Godfrey Brizendine, - -	"	–	11	
Lewis D. Brooks, - -	"	–	11	
Dabney Brooks, - -	"	–	11	
William Brizendine, - -	"	–	11	
Lewis Coleman, - -	"	–	11	
Reuben Cox, - -	"	–	11	
John Cauthorn, - -	"	–	11	
Richard Coats, - -	"	–	11	
Henry Crutchfield, - -	"	–	11	
Nathaniel S. Crow, ↓ -	"	–	11	
Gabriel Dix, - -	"	–	11	
Thomas Durhone, - -	"	–	11	
Joshua Davis, - -	"	–	11	
Jackson Dunn, - -	"			
Samuel Fenton, - -	"	–	11	
John Greenwood, - -	"	–	11	
Geo. Gordon, - -	"	–	11	
Jessee Griggs, - -	"	–	11	
Geo. Greenwood, - -	"	–	11	
Ewin Goode, - -	"	–	11	
Philip Howerton, - -	"	–	11	
John Heath, - -	"	–	11	
Joseph Jones, - -	"	–	11	
Thomas Marlow, - -	"	–	11	
James McFarling, - -	"	–	11	
Elijah McCann, - -	"	–	11	
Edward Rose, - -	"	–	11	
Ludy Taylor, - -	"	–	11	
James Taylor, - -	"	–	11	
Major Taylor, - -	"	–	11	
William Taylor, - -	"	–	11	

NAMES.	RANK.	TIME OF SERVICE.		REMARKS.
		Months.	Days.	
Warner Shackelford, - -	Private,	–	11	
William Williamson, - -	"	–	11	
Upton Williamson, - -	"	–	11	Or Upshur.
John Webb, - -	"	–	11	

MUSTER ROLL

Of Lieutenant William Newsum's Company, of the Ninth Regiment, Virginia Militia, commanded by Lieutenant Colonel William Boyd, called into Service by Lieutenant Colonel Elliott Muse, from the 2d to the 10th December, 1814.

NAMES.	RANK.	TIME OF SERVICE.		REMARKS.
		Months.	Days.	
William Newsum, - -	Lieutenant,	–	9	
Richard Taliaferro, - -	Ensign,	–	9	
Wm. S. Willis, - -	Sergeant,	–	9	
Richard Crittenden, - -	"	–	9	
John Atkins, - -	"	–	9	
Leonard Smither, - -	"	–	9	
Benjamin Pitts, - -	Corporal,	–	7	
Pascal Cooke, - -	"	–	9	
Benjamin Williams, - -	"	–	9	
William Taylor, - -	"	–	9	
Lewis J. Atkins, - -	Private,	–	7	
Robert S. Anderson, -	"	–	6	
Robert Busby, - -	"	–	9	
Elijah Brookes, - -	"	–	9	
Anderson Broach, - -	"	–	9	
Wm. D. Brookes, - -	"	–	6	
William Bland, - -	"	–	9	
Joyeux Collins, - -	"	–	9	
Joseph Collier, - -	"	–	9	
John Collier, - -	"	–	9	
John Corr, - -	"	–	8	
Thomas Crittenden, -	"	–	9	
Henry P. Crittenden, -	"	–	9	
Wm. Currie, - -	"	–	9	
Jeremy Darling, - -	"	–	9	
Richard Dudley, - -	"	–	9	
Thomas Dudley, - -	"	–	9	
Paulin Dudley, - -	"	–	8	
James Didlake, - -	"	–	6	
John Douglass, - -	"	–	7	
Obadiah Fogg, - -	"	–	8	
John Gardiner, - -	"	–	8	
William Ison, - -	"	–	9	
James Lemon, - -	"	–	8	
William Muire, - -	"	–	9	
Richard Muire, - -	"	–	6	
Spencer Major, - -	"	–	9	
Peyton Massey, - -	"	–	9	
Taylor Pitts, - -	"	–	9	
Major Roane, - -	"	–	9	
Leonard Stevens, - -	"	–	9	
Samuel Smither, - -	"	–	9	
William Sears, - -	"	–	2	
Gregory Taylor, - -	"	–	9	
John Williams, - -	"	–	9	
John Willis, - -	"	–	7	
John A. Ware, - -	"	–	9	

NAMES.			RANK.	TIME OF SERVICE.		REMARKS.
				Months.	Days.	
Lewis Williams,	-	-	Private,	–	9	
John Walden,	-	-	"	–	5	
Richard Ware,	-	-	"	–	9	
James Wright,	-	-	"	–	9	

Captain Edward J. Northen's Company—Forty-first Regiment.

NAMES.	RANK.	TIME OF SERVICE.		REMARKS.
		Months.	Days.	
John Literal, - -	Ensign,	–	3	
John English, - -	"	–	4	
Samuel M. Dameron, -	Corporal,	–	12	
Robert Scott, - -	"	–	3	
John Hardwick, - -	"	–	12	
Charles Dodson, - -	Fifer,	–	19	
Elijah Ambrose, - -	Private,	–	3	
William Beale, - -	"			
Ludwell Bell, - -	"			
Wm. T. Clarke, - -	"	–	12	
Edward Douglass, - -	"	–	11	
John Douglass, jr. - -	"	–	8	
Austin Dodson, - -	"			
Conway Dozier, - -	"	1	6	
Griffin G. Dudley, - -	"	–	19	
William Efford, jr. - -	"	–	12	
John English, - -	"	–	9	
Eppa Headley, - -	"	–	10	
Griffin Headley, - -	"	–	8	
Henry W. Headley, - -	"			
John Hardwick, - -	"			
George Jones, - -	"			
Eppa Jones, - -	"	–	5	
Edm'd R. Jeffries, - -	"	–	21	
Richard Jones, - -	"			
James Jennings, - -	"	–	28	
John Jenkins, - -	"	–	28	
Matthew Jenkins, - -	"	–	28	
John Literal, - -	"	–	9	
James Lewis, - -	"	–	9	
Ro. B. Mitchell, - -	"	–	5	
John Spelman, - -	"	–	6	
John Scott, - -	"	–	12	
Robert Scott, - -	"	–	9	
Reuben Sandford, - -	"	–	28	
John Sanders, - -	"	–	27	
John Stott, - -	"			
John Thrift, jr. - -	"	–	3	
John Wise, - -	"	–	4	
John Wilcox, - -	"			
James Wilcox, - -	"			

(For rest of this company, see publication of Pay Rolls.)

MUSTER ROLL

*Of Lieutenant William Oliver's Company, of the Ninth Regiment, Virginia Mi-
litia, commanded by Lieutenant Colonel William Boyd, called into Service by
Lieutenant Colonel Elliott Muse, of the One Hundred and Ninth Regiment,
from 2d to 10th December, 1814.*

NAMES.	RANK.	TIME OF SERVICE.		REMARKS.
		Months.	Days.	
William Oliver,	Lieutenant.	–	9	
William B. Hoskins,	Ensign,	–	9	
John Motley,	Sergeant,	–	9	
Thomas Williams,	"	–	9	
James Phillips,	"	–	9	
Ambrose Durham,	"	–	9	
Daniel Watts,	Corporal,	–	9	
Thomas Redd,	"	–	9	
William Broockes,	"	–	9	
William T. Ware,	"	–	9	
William C. Bynes,	Private,	–	9	
Christopher Carlton,	"	–	9	
John Cauthorn,	"	–	9	
Edward Garrett,	"	–	1	
William Hillyard,	".	–	9	
Ralph Mitchell,	"	–	9	
Henry Mactyre,	"	–	9	
John Newcomb,	"	–	9	
John Newbill,	"	–	9	
Benjamin Newcomb,	"	–	4	
Fleming Oglesby,	"	–	9	
Robert Orrill,	"	–	9	
Phillip Sears,	"	–	9	
Robert Smith,	"	–	1	
William Sears,	"	–	9	
Thomas Sears,	"	–	9	
Richerson Stone,	"	–	9	
Richard Stone,	"	–	9	
John Turner,	"	–	9	
Henry Williams,	"	–	9	

MUSTER ROLL

Of Captain Richard Omohundro's Company, of the One Hundred and Eleventh Regiment, Virginia Militia, in the County of Westmoreland, called into actual Service under the battalion orders of Major William Nelson, from the 15th to the 16th July, 1813.

NAMES.	RANK.	TIME OF SERVICE.	
		Months.	Days.
Richard Omohundro, -	Captain,	—	2
John H. Doleman, - -	Lieutenant,	—	2
John R. McNeale, - -	Ensign,	—	2
Tarpley Bryant, - -	Sergeant,	—	2
Reuben Marks, - -	"	—	2
Levin Jones, - -	"	—	2
Richard Crask, - -	"	—	2
Thos. Jenkins, - -	Corporal,	—	2
William Dodd - -	"	—	2
Sam'l Mothershead, -	"	—	2
James Airs, - -	Private,	—	2
Jno. Briant, - -	"		
Richard T. Brown, -	"	—	2
John Barrett, - -	"	—	2
Richard Croxton, - -	"	—	2
William Doleman, - -	Wagoner,		
Vincent Dozier, - -	Private,	—	2
Jno. Davis, - -	"	—	2
Jeremiah Edmonds, -	"	—	2
Gerard Garner, - -	"	—	2
Thos. W. Jones, - -	"	—	2
Henry Mothershead, -	"	—	2
Thomas S. Muse, - -	"	—	2
Daniel Mothershead, -	"	—	2
Thomas Mothershead, -	"	—	2
James R. Nash, - -	"	—	2
Joseph Read, - -	"	—	2
James Raimy, - -	"	—	2
Sam'l M. Rust, - -	"	—	2
Alex'r Spence, - -	"	—	2
Wm. Scates, - -	"	—	2
Henry Sisson, - -	"	—	2
Augustine Sanford, -	"	—	2
William True, - -	"	—	2
Christopher Tallant, -	"	—	2
George R. Weldon, -	"	—	2
Elfred Weaver, - -	"	—	2
Jennins Yeatman, - -	"	—	2

Captain Walter Otey's Company—Tenth Regiment.

NAMES.	RANK.	TIME OF SERVICE.		REMARKS.
		Months.	Days.	
William Woodford, - -	Serg't Major,	1	14	
Thomas Moorman, - -	Private,	6		
Benj. H. Mansfield, - -	"	6		
William McGeorge, - -	"	6		
Edward Perkins, - -	"	3	17	Substitute for James Calland.
William Smith, - -	"	–	–	Substitute for Thomas Pegram.

(For rest of this company, see publication of Pay Rolls.)

Captain William D. Outten's Company—Second Regiment.

NAMES.	RANK.	TIME OF SERVICE.		REMARKS.
		Months.	Days.	
George Drummond, - -	Lieutenant,	–	7	
Samuel Walston, - -	Ensign,	–	14	
Henry Finney, - -	"	–	24	
Leonard Gurney, - -	Sergeant,	–	6	
John A. Bundick, - -	Q. M. Serg't,	–	8	
William Thomas, - -	Corporal,	–	25	
Elijah Bloxom, - -	Private,	–	8	
William Budd, - -	"	–	7	
John P. Berry, - -	"	–	6	
George Bull, - -	"	–	5	
Tully Beysley, - -	"	–	5	
Isaac Benston, - -	"	–	14	
Sebastian Cropper, - -	"			
Laban Chandler, - -	"	–	8	
Thomas Custis, - -	"	–	7	
Geo. Dunton, - -	"			
Severn Dakes, - -	"	–	6	
Peter Duberly, - -	"	–	6	
William Dunton, - -	"	1		
Revel Dix, - -	"	–	8	
John Edwards, - -	"	–	8	
George H. Ewell, -	"			
William East, (of S.) -	"			
John Groten, - -	"	–	11	
Arthur Hickman, - -	"	–	12	
Richard Kelley, - -	"	–	5	
Edmund Lilliston, - -	"	–	14	
Zadoc Lewis, - -	"	–	4	
William Lewis, - -	"			
Isaac B. Moore, - -	"	–	6	
William Metcalf, - -	"	–	25	
John Mason, - -	"	–	6	
George Middleton, - -	"	–	5	
Ephraim Outten, - -	"	–	5	
John Phillips, - -	"	–	8	
James Ross, - -	"	–	13	
Samuel Russell, - -	"	–	6	
Nat. Russell, - -	"	–	6	
John Tignal, - -	"	–	14	
Samuel Taylor, - -	"	–	8	
Major Turnal, - -	"	–	8	
Wiley J. Twiford, - -	"	–	8	
Levin Taylor, - -	"	–	3	
James Twiford, - -	"	–	10	
James White, - -	"	1	8	
Isaac Wright, - -	"	–	8	
George Willis, - -	"	–	8	
William White, - -	"	–	18	
Dennis Wright, - -	"	–	7	
John Waters, - -	"	–	5	
John B. Walker, - -	"	–	20	

(For rest of this company, see publication of Pay Rolls.

Captain Meacham Owen's Company—One Hundred and Ninth Regiment.

NAMES.	RANK.	TIME OF SERVICE.		REMARKS.
		Months.	Days.	
Ben. H. Williams,	Sergeant,	–	13	
John Seward,	Corporal,	–	12	
Elijah Bird,	"	–	11	
Ben. Leonard,	"	–	2	
Richard Montague,	Drummer,	–	13	
Lewis Montague,	Fifer,	–	12	
John Alcock,	Private,	–	12	
Lewis Beaman,	"	1		
Alex'r Bristow,	"	–	11	
Ben. Clowdas,	"	–	2	
Joseph Cullendon,	"	–	8	
Samuel Cropfield,	"	–	7	
Branton Clarke,	"	–	6	
Lewis Daniel,	"	–	13	
Bev. Daniel,	"	–	10	
James Didlake,	"	–	11	
Lewis George,	"	–	13	
James George,	"	–	13	
John Good, jr.	"	–	2	
James Hackney,	"	–	11	
John Hardy,	"	–	3	
James Howard,	"	–	9	
John Hare,	"	–	13	
Allen Howard, jr.	"	–	12	
John Hardy,	"	–	12	
William Hudgin,	"	1		
Thomas L. Haley,	"	1		
Isaac Kidd, jr.	"	–	8	
William Mullins,	"	–	13	
John B. Roane,	"	1		
Edmund Reade,	"	–	12	
Henry Sears,	"	3	8	
Elliott Seward,	"	1	18	
Thos. St. John,	"	–	12	
Thos. H. Stiff,	"	1		
John R. Smith,	"	1		
William Sibly,	"	1		
John Shackleford,	"	–	3	
Carter Trice,	"	1		
William Watts,	"	–	26	
Major Wiatt,	"	–	13	

(For rest of this company, see publication of Pay Rolls.)

Captain George S. Pace's Company—One Hundred and Ninth Regiment.

NAMES.			RANK.	TIME OF SERVICE.		REMARKS.
				Months.	Days.	
John C. Montague,	-	-	Sergeant,	1		
Edward Trice,	-	-	Corporal,	–	29	
John Robinson,	-	-	Fifer,	–	9	
Robert Brooken,	-	-	Private,	–	29	
Ben. Boughton,	-	-	"	1		
John Calice,	-	-	"	–	5	
Thomas Clare,	-	-	"	1		
John A. Mills,	-	-	"	–	11	
Isham Miller,	-	-	"	–	16	
Thomas Mountjoy,	-	-	"	–	8	
John Robinson,	-	-	"	1	3	
Robert Reade,	-	-	"	–	2	
Levy Smith,	-	-	"	–	12	
William Sibly,	-	-	"	1		
James Trice,	-	-	"	1		
James Wilkins,	-	-	"	2		
William Wilkins,	-	-	"	1		
Moses Walker,	-	-	"	1		

(For rest of this company, see publication of Pay Rolls.)

MUSTER ROLL

Of Ensign William Pace's Company, of the Ninth Regiment, Virginia Militia, commanded by Colonel William Boyd, called into Service by Colonel Elliott Muse, of the One Hundred and Ninth Regiment, from the 2d to the 10th December, in the year 1814.

NAMES.	RANK.	TIME OF SERVICE.		REMARKS.
		Months.	Days.	
William Pace, - -	Ensign,	—	8	
John B. Jefferey, - -	Sergeant,	—	8	
Carlton Isaac, - -	Private,	—	8	
Richard Carlton, sr. - -	"	—	8	
Richard Carlton, jr. - -	"	—	8	
Quiller Carlton, - -	"	—	8	
Robert Carlton, - -	"	—	8	
William Dillard, - -	"	—	8	
William Gibson, - -	"	—	8	
John Hart, - -	"	—	8	
Mitcham Spencer, - -	"	—	8	
Benamy Stone, - -	"	—	8	
George Walton, - -	"	—	8	

MUSTER ROLL

Of Sergeant Opie Palmer's detachment of Infantry and Cavalry, from the One
Hundred and Ninth Regiment, Virginia Militia, in the County of Middlesex,
called into actual Service at Stingray Point, by order of the Executive Council,
from 26th August to 20th September, in the year 1813.

NAMES.	RANK.	TIME OF SERVICE.		REMARKS.
		Months.	Days.	
Opie Palmer,	Sergeant,	–	26	
James Rice,	Corporal,	–	26	Of Cavalry.
John Bray,	Private,	–	26	
John Brown,	"	–	26	"
Thomas Edwards,	"	–	26	"
William Jefferson,	"	–	26	
William D. Robertson,	"	–	26	"
Andrew Toath,	"	–	26	
William Ward,	"	–	26	
Robert Wilkins,	"	–	26	
John Welmore,	"	–	26	
Daniel S. Ward,	"	–	26	See Captain Blakey's pay roll.

Sergeant Thomas S. Palmer's Company—One Hundred and Ninth Regiment.

NAMES.	RANK.	TIME OF SERVICE.		REMARKS.
		Months.	Days.	
Nelson Humphries, - -	Sergeant,	–	3	
Henry C. Palmer, - -	Corporal,	–	3	
John Wedmore, - -	"	–	3	
Thomas L. Healey, - -	"	–	3	
John Andrew, - -	Private,			
William Bristow, - -	"	–	3	
James Baker, - -	"			
Samuel Blake, - -	"			
Thomas Davis, - -	"			
James Hardy, - -	"			
Philip Orrell, - -	"			
Wm. Robinson, sr. - -	"			
John South, - -	"			
Thomas H. Stiff, - -	"			
Andrew South, - -	"	–	3	
Daniel R. Sibly, - -	"	–	3	
Robert Wilkins, - -	"	–	3	
James Yarrington, - -	"			

(For rest of this company, see publication of Pay Rolls.)

MUSTER ROLL

Of Lieutenant James Parker's Company, of the Thirtieth Regiment, Virginia Mi-
litia, commanded by Major Reuben Tankersley, in the Service of the State of
Virginia, from the 3rd to the 9th December, in the year 1814.

NAMES.	RANK.	TIME OF SERVICE.		REMARKS.
		Months.	Days.	
James Parker, - -	Lieutenant,	—	7	
John Summerson, - -	Sergeant,	—	7	
John Parker, - -	"	—	7	
Richard Ship, - -	"	—	7	
Richard Summerson, -	"	—	7	
Samuel T. Vaughan, -	Corporal,	—	5	
Dudley Johnson, - -	Wagoner,	—	7	
John C. Bowie, - -	Private,	—	4	
Lawson Barber, - -	"	—	7	
John Claytor, - -	"	—	7	
James Dunn, - -	"	—	7	
Francis Evans, - -	"	—	7	
Henry Hill, - -	"	—	7	
Robert Lumpkin, - -	"	—	5	
John P. Miller, - -	"	—	7	
William Mason, - -	"	—	7	
Thomas L. Oneale, -	"	—	7	
Robert Pace, - -	"	—	7	
William Powers, - -	"	—	6	
William Phillips, - -	"	—	3	
James Reamy, - -	"	—	7	
Lewis Reynolds, - -	"	—	7	
Mordecai Shaddock, -	"	—	7	
John Saunders, - -	"	—	7	
Robert Toombs, - -	"	—	7	

MUSTER ROLL

Of Captain Severn E. Parker's Company of Riflemen, of the Twenty-seventh Regiment, Virginia Militia, commanded by Lieutenant Colonel Major S. Pitt, in the Service of the United States, from 3rd to 10th December, in the year 1814.

NAMES.	RANK.	TIME OF SERVICE.		REMARKS.
		Months.	Days.	
Severn E. Parker,	Captain,	–	8	
Abel Powell,	Lieutenant,	–	8	
Harold L. Wilson,	Ensign,	–	8	
Nathaniel Collins,	Sergeant,	–	8	
John Evans,	"	–	8	
Silas Jefferson,	"	–	8	
John Adams,	"	–	8	Wm. Scott his sub.
Rickets Dunton,	Drummer,	–	8	
Matthew Floyd,	Fifer,	–	8	
Peter S. Bodoin,	Private,	–	8	Geo. Luke his sub.
John N. Brickhouse,	"	–	8	
Thomas S. Brickhouse,	"	–	8	Allen Brown his sub.
Smith Brickhouse,	"	–	8	
Benjamin F. Dunton,	"	–	8	
William Dalby,	"	–	8	
George Eshon, sr.	"	–	8	Southey Simpson his sub.
Thomas Evans,	"	–	8	
Sheppard Floyd,	"	–	8	Christ. Freshwater his sub.
Kendall Groten,	"	–	8	
Littleton Griffith,	"	–	8	
Edward Hickman,	"	–	8	
William Harmon,	"	–	8	
Teackle Jacob,	"	–	8	
Smith Milliner,	"	–	8	
Thomas Nottingham,	"	–	8	
Richard Nottingham,	"	–	8	
Richard Prescott,	"	–	8	
Stewart Pettit,	"	–	8	
Patrick Rooks,	"	–	8	
John Simpson,	"	–	8	
Hillary Scott,	"	–	8	
Charles Scarborough,	"	–	8	
William S. Speakman,	"	–	8	
Thomas W. Scott,	"	–	8	
Samuel Taylor,	"	–	8	
James Taylor,	"	–	8	John Prane his sub.
William Teackle,	"	–	8	
Nathaniel West,	"	–	8	
James West,	"	–	8	Wm. H. Williams his sub.
John S. Williams,	"	–	8	James Scott his sub.
Thomas Wilkins,	"	–	8	
John Wilkins, (of Ben.)	"	–	8	
James Wilkins,	"	–	8	

Captain James Paxton's Company—Second Elite Corps.

NAMES.	RANK.	TIME OF SERVICE.		REMARKS.
		Months.	Days.	
Adam Zolman, - -	Private,	–	20	Transferred to Capt. Campbell.

(For rest of this company, see publication of Pay Rolls.)

Captain John Pollock's Company—Seventh Regiment.

NAMES.	RANK.	TIME OF SERVICE.		REMARKS.
		Months.	Days.	
Nicholas Ware, - -	Sergeant,	–	18	Promoted ensign and transferred.
Bolling Britt, - -	"	–	18	
Rich'd Leake, - -	Corporal,	–	5	
Harrod Anderson, - -	Private,	–	–	Jno. Bernard his sub.
Philip Bevins, - -	"	–	20	
Daniel Boyce, - -	"	–	22	
John Crutchfield, - -	"			
Price Frazer, - -	"			
Joseph Grady, - -	"			
Benj'n B. Harris, -	"			
Elijah Hawkins, - -	"			
John Hoggard, - -	"	–	27	
Jeremiah Harris, - -	"	–	27	
Thomas Hall, - -	"			
Samuel Jones, - -	"			
Richard Leake, - -	"	–	7	
Anderson Lowry, - -	"	–	3	
John F. Mallory, - -	"			
Benj. Nuckolds, - -	"	–	–	R. Childress his sub.
Henry F. Pleasants, - -	"	–	19	
Peter M. Puryear, - -	"			
Ro. S. Smith, - -	"			

(For rest of this company, see publication of Pay Rolls.)

Captain Josiah Penick's Company—Seventh Regiment.

NAMES.	RANK.	TIME OF SERVICE.		REMARKS.
		Months.	Days.	
Peter Berry, - -	Private,	4	16	
Jesse Brightwell, - -	"	3	16	
George Cardwell, - -	"	–		
Thomas Holt, - -	"	–	23	
John Maddox, - -	"	–		
Nathaniel Wilson, - -	"	–		

(For rest of this company, see publication of Pay Rolls.)

Captain Baker Pegram's Company—First Regiment.

NAMES.				RANK.	TIME OF SERVICE.		REMARKS.
					Months.	Days.	
Billy,	-	-	-	Driver,	2	16	
Chavers,	-	-	-	"	3	4	

(For rest of this company, see publication of Pay Rolls.)

MUSTER ROLL

Of Captain Nat. Perkins' Company of Artillery, attached to the Fourth Brigade of Virginia Militia, in the Service from the 1st to the 13h September, 1814.

NAMES.	RANK.	TIME OF SERVICE.		REMARKS.
		Months.	Days.	
Nathaniel Perkins, - -	Captain,	–	13	
Robert French, - -	Lieutenant,	–	13	
John Stevens, - -	"	–	7	
Joseph Hopkins, - -	Ensign,	–	7	
Edward H. Poor, - -	Sergeant,	–	13	
David Cardin, - -	"	–	13	
David Lemay, - -	"	–	13	
Robert Meriwether, - -	"	–	13	
John M. Williams, - -	"	–	13	
Robert Thompson, - -	Corporal,	–	13	
Robert Singleton, - -	"	–	13	
John H. Pryor, - -	"	–	13	
Thomas H. Scruggs, - -	"	–	13	
William Pryor, jr. - -	"	–	13	
Thomas Eades, - -	Drummer,	–	13	
James Thruston, - -	Fifer,	–	13	
William Armistead, - -	Private,	–	7	
James Armistead, - -	"	–	7	
John Bradway, - -	"	–	7	
John Boatwright, - -	"	–	7	
Benjamin Bradshaw, -	"	–	8	
Alexander Burnley, -	"	–	13	
Archibald M. Bagwell, -	"	–	13	
Merideth Belloway, -	"	–	13	
John Bradshaw, jr. -	"	–	13	
Seth F. Bowler, - -	"	–	13	
Robert Chumley, - -	"	–	7	
John Conner, - -	"	–	7	
Robert Carden, jr. -	"	–	13	
Stephen G. Cheatham, -	"	–	13	
John A. Cheatham, -	"	–	13	
Benjamin Crutchfield, -	"	–	13	
James Carden, - -	"	–	13	
David M. Carden, - -	"	–	13	
Richard H. Crutchfield, -	"	–	13	
William W. Crank, -	"	–	13	
Joshua Davidson, - -	"	–	7	
Griffith Dickerson, -	"	–	7	
John F. Duke, - -	"	–	7	
Richard Davis, - -	"	–	13	
George Davis, - -	"	–	13	
Tarlton Davenport, -	"	–	13	
Jacob Deals, - -	"	–	13	
William A. Ford, - -	"	–	10	
Jennings Fowlks, - -	"	–	7	
Daniel French, - -	"	–	13	
Pleasant Gaulding, - -	"	–	7	

NAMES.	RANK.	TIME OF SERVICE.		REMARKS.
		Months.	Days.	
James Goulden, - -	Private,	–	13	
Martin Glass, - -	"	–	13	
James Halsey, - -	"	–	13	
John Halsey, - -	"	–	13	
James Herndon, - -	"	–	13	
Thomas Herndon, - -	"	–	13	
John Hudson, - -	"	–	7	
John B. Hurt, - -	"	–	7	
Godfrey Isbell, - -	"	–	13	
Mason Johns, - -	"	–	13	
William Jackson, - -	"	–	7	
William Leneive, - -	"	–	7	
William Lowry, - -	"	–	13	
Anderson Lowry, - -	"			
Charles Lacy, - -	"	–	13	
John H. Long, - -	"	–	13	
Pryor Layne, - -	"	–	13	
David Layne, jr. - -	"	–	13	
Archer Layne, - -	"	–	13	
James B. Medley, - -	"	–	7	
Howell McBride, - -	"	–	13	
Philip Murrer, - -	"	–	13	
Thomas Matthews, jr. -	"	–	13	
James Matthews, - -	"	–	13	
Isaac Murrer, - -	"	–	13	
John F. Morrison, - -	"	–	13	
William A. Massie, - -	"	–	13	
Presley Nash, - -	"	–	7	
William Nash, - -	"	–	7	
Thomas P. O'Brien, - -	"	–	7	
David M. Parrish, - -	"	–	13	
John Perkins, jr. - -	"	–	13	
Henry Pace, - -	"	–	13	
Samuel Pryor, jr. - -	"	–	13	
Jonathan S. Payne, - -	"	–	13	
William O. Payne, - -	"	–	13	
John W. Payne, - -	"	–	13	
David Richards, - -	"	–	13	
William Rutherford, - -	"	–	13	
Sharp Spencer, - -	"	–	7	
John Smith, - -	"	–	13	
Elkanah Talley, - -	"	–	13	
George Tiller, - -	"	–	13	
William Thruston, jr. - -	"	–	13	
Thomas C. Turner, - -	"	–	13	
George Turner, - -	"	–	13	
Samuel Whitlock, - -	"	–	13	
William H. Whitlock, - -	"	–	13	
Uriah Willard, - -	"	–	7	

Captain Robert Perkins' Company—Fifty-second Regiment.

NAMES.	RANK.	TIME OF SERVICE.		REMARKS.
		Months.	Days.	
Anselm Bailey, - -	Ensign,	–	16	
James Roper, - -	Sergeant,	–	16	
Francis Marshall, - -	"	–	16	
John A. Smith, - -	"	–	15	
John Walker, - -	"	–	15	
Isaiah Austin, - -	Corporal,	–	15	
Anderson Meanley, - -	"	–	16	
Thomas Crum, - -	"	–	16	
William Morris, - -	Drummer,	–	15	
Major R. Apperson, - -	"	–	16	
Josiah Austin, - -	Private,	–	16	
Richard Atkinson, - -	"	–	15	
Edward Bradley, - -	"	–	16	
John Boswell, - -	"	–	16	
William G. Bowers, - -	"	–	14	
Parkes Bailey, - -	"	–	15	
Robert W. Crump, - -	"	–	15	
Nelson Clarke, - -	"	–	15	
George Crump, - -	"	–	16	
Robert Chandler, - -	"	–	16	
Hannon Crump, - -	"	–	16	
Charles Crump, - -	"	–	16	
John W. Crump, - -	"	–	16	
John Dixon, - -	"	–	16	
James Dennett, - -	"	–	16	
Robert Dennett, - -	"	–	20	
Dandridge Dixon, - -	"	–	16	
Richard Eanes, - -	"	–	15	
Richard Y. Eanes, - -	"	–	15	
William Freeman, - -	"	–	15	
Jeduthan Gibson, - -	"	–	15	
William Green, - -	"	–	16	
Isaac Howle, - -	"	–	16	
Thomas Hilliard, - -	"	–	15	
John Ironmonger, - -	"	–	15	
George S. Johnson, - -	"	–	16	
Carver Mercer, - -	"	–	15	
B. D. McKenzie, - -	"	–	15	
William R. Meanley, - -	"	–	16	
Armistead Pumphrey, - -	"	–	15	
Wm. M. Ross, - -	"	–	16	
William Smith, - -	"	–	16	
James Thompson, - -	"	–	15	
James Tandy, - -	"	–	15	
Colin Turner, - -	"	–	16	
Gideon Wade, - -	"	–	15	
Henry Whitt, - -	"	–	16	
William Word, - -	"	–	16	
John Woodrum, - -	"	–	16	

(For rest of this company, see publication of Pay Rolls.)

Captain William K. Perrin's Company—Fourth Regiment.

NAMES.	RANK.	TIME OF SERVICE.		REMARKS.
		Months.	Days.	
William K. Perrin, - -	Captain,	1	25	
William S. Thornton, -	Lieutenant,	1	25	
Mann Page, - -	"	1	25	
Thomas Dobson, - -	Sergeant,	1	25	
Charles Chilton, - -	"	1	25	
Thomas G. Cluverius, -	"	1	25	
Wm. F. Thomas, - -	"	1	25	
William West, - -	Corporal,	1	25	
Augus'n Brown, - -	"	1	25	
John Hogg, - -	"	1	25	
Wm. Brown, - -	"	1	25	
Vincent Hudson, - -	Fifer,	1	25	
Wm. Hudson, - -	Drummer,	1	25	
George Brown, - -	Private,	1	25	
Charles Brown, - -	"	1	25	
Ralph Belvin, - -	"	1	25	
John Belvin, - -	"	1	25	
Thomas Bland, - -	"	1	25	
Iverson Boswell, - -	"	1	25	
Holt Cluverius, - -	"	1	14	
James Deal, - -	"	1	25	
James Davis, - -	"	1	25	
Lewis Green, - -	"	1	25	
William Graves, - -	"	1	25	
Geo. Green, - -	"	1	25	
Thomas Howard, - .	"	1	25	
Edmund Heywood, - -	"	1	25	
James Hogg, - -	"	1	25	
Rich'd Hogg, - -	"	1	25	
Lewis Hogg, - -	"	1	25	
William Hogg, - -	"	1	25	
John Hall. - -	"	1	25	
Charles Heywoood, - -	"	1	25	
Rich'd Heywood, - -	"	1	25	
Edward Heywood, - -	"	1	25	
John Hogg, jr. -	"	1	25	
William Heywood, - -	"	1	25	
Armistead Jenkins, - -	"	1	25	
Samuel Jenkins, - -	"	1	25	
Edmond Jenkins, - -	"	1	25	
James Jenkins, jr. -	"	1	25	
Harwood Jenkins, - -	"	1	25	
James Jenkins, sen'r, -	"	1	25	
Lewis Jenkins, - -	"	1	25	
Robert Keeble, - -	"	1	25	
Hiram Lankford, - -	"	–	7	
Read Owens, - -	"	2	28	
William Pate, - -	"	1	25	
James Powell, - -	"	–	7	
John Ransome, - -	"	4	16	
Thomas Robins, - -	"	1	25	
Abraham Rider, - -	"	1	25	
William Spencer, - -	"	–	3	
Thomas Smith, - -	"	1	25	

NAMES.	RANK.	TIME OF SERVICE.		REMARKS.
		Months.	Days.	
William Smith, - -	Private,	1	25	
Stephen Smith, - -	"	1	25	
Michael Smith, - -	"	1	25	
Robert Stokes, - -	"	1	25	
John Thomas, - -	"	1	25	
Ambrose West, - -	"	1	25	
James West, - -	"	1	25	

(For rest of this company, see publication of Pay Rolls.)

MUSTER ROLL

Of Captain Edward Pescud's Company, of the Thirty-ninth Regiment, Virginia Militia, called into the Service under the general orders of the 30th June, 1813, from the 30th June to the 12th July, in the year 1813.

NAMES.			RANK.	TIME OF SERVICE.		REMARKS.
				Months.	Days.	
Edward Pescud,	-	-	Captain,	–	13	
Richard B. Batte,	-	-	Lieutenant,	–	13	
John Pollard,	-	-	Ensign,	–	13	
William Moore,	-	-	Sergeant,	–	13	
Stephen Townes,	-	-	"	–	13	
James Gibbon,	-	-	"	–	13	
Gideon Johnson,	-	-	"	–	13	
Collin Alfriend,	-	-	Private,	–	13	
William Allison,	-	-	"	–	13	
James Andrews,	-	-	"	–	13	
John L. Andrews,	-	-	"	–	13	
Samuel Boothe,	-	-	"	–	13	
Daniel Bass,	-	-	"	–	13	
Hector Brander,	-	-	"	–	13	
John H. Banister,	-	-	"	–	13	
John W. Bell,	-	-	"	–	13	
Stephen Barnes,	-	-	"	–	13	
Ezra Beal,	-	-	"	–	13	
James Bagley,	-	-	"	–	13	
George Brown,	-	-	"	–	13	
John Bragg,	-	-	"	–	13	
William Bradley,	-	-	"	–	13	
John Bennett,	-	-	"	–	13	
William Clarke,	-	-	"	–	13	
Samuel Christian,	-	-	"	–	13	
George Cooper,	-	-	"	–	13	
Joseph Cooper,	-	-	"	–	13	
Robert Cohen,	-	-	"	–	13	
William Cumming,	-	-	"	–	13	
Moses Cohen,	-	-	"	–	13	
George Dunn,	-	-	"	–	13	
John Dunlop,	-	-	"	–	13	
Thomas Dunn,	-	-	"	–	13	
Samuel Dilworth,	-	-	"	–	13	
Daniel Dugger,	-	-	"	–	13	
Henry Fernando,	-	-	"	–	13	
Francis Fraser,	-	-	"	–	13	
George Fein,	-	-	"	–	13	
Lawson B. Flack,	-	-	"	–	13	
Peter D. Gibbs,	-	-	"	–	13	
J. L. George,	-	-	"	–	13	
William B. Harwood,	-	-	"	–	13	
Travis Harwood,	-	-	"	–	13	
Daniel Hanson,	-	-	"	–	13	
John Hardy,	-	-	"	–	13	
Arthur Johnson,	-	-	"	–	13	
William Johnson,	-	-	"	–	13	
James Lockhead,	-	-	"	–	13	
John Lemosuirer,	-	-	"	–	13	

NAMES.	RANK.	TIME OF SERVICE.		REMARKS.
		Months.	Days.	
Thomas Lownes, - -	Private,	–	13	
A. S. Lockhead, - -	"	–	13	
Dabney Lipscomb, - -	"	–	13	
William Laird, - -	"	–	13	
Jacob Melliman, - -	"	–	13	
Nathaniel Massenburg, -	"	–	13	
Peter McLean, - -	"	–	13	
Henry Mountcastle, - -	"	–	13	
Thomas T. Miller, - -	"	–	13	
John McDowell, - -	"	–	13	
Samuel Nargen, - -	"	–	13	
William Neal, - -	"	–	13	
Griffin Orgain, - -	"	–	13	
John Patterson, - -	"	–	12	
Samuel Pearce, - -	"	–	13	
George Read, - -	"	–	13	
Justus Smith, - -	"	–	13	
Henry Shroyer, - -	"	–	13	
Robert Simmons, - -	"	–	13	
J. M. Shaul, - -	"	–	13	
Jeremiah Sadler, - -	"	–	13	
Samuel Snow, - -	"	–	13	
Nathaniel Snelson, - -	"	–	13	
Thomas Smith, - -	"	–	13	
Lewis Timmer, - -	"	–	13	
John D. Townes, - -	"	–	13	
William Thweatt, - -	"	–	13	
William Thompson, - -	"	–	13	
Peter Tatum, - -	"	–	13	
John Taliaferro, - -	"	–	13	
John Thompson, - -	"	–	13	
Charles Wise, - -	"	–	13	
Thomas G. Warthine, -	"	–	13	
Pleasant Womack, - -	"	–	13	
John U. Wilcox, - -	"	–	13	
John Withers, - -	"	–	13	
Paskal Wells, - -	"	–	13	
Francis G. Yancey, - -	"	–	13	

MUSTER ROLL

Of Captain Rice B. Pierce's Company, of the Sixty-fifth Regiment, Virginia Militia, in the County of Southampton, called into the Service of the United States, under the general orders of the 28th of August, 1814, from the 29th August to the 13th September, in the year 1814.

NAMES.			RANK.	TIME OF SERVICE.		REMARKS.
				Months.	Days.	
Rice B. Pierce,	-	-	Captain,	–	16	
Samuel Pond,	-	-	Lieutenant,	–	16	
Henry Gurley,	-	-	"	–	16	
John Williams,	-	-	Ensign,	–	16	
Wiley Wellons,	-	-	Sergeant,	–	16	
John Vaiser,	-	-	"	–	16	
Henry Applewhite,	-	-	"	–	16	
Jesse Davis,	-	-	"	–	16	
Wm. Kitchen,	-	-	Corporal,	–	16	
Daniel Vick,	-	-	"	–	16	
Wilson Wellons,	-	-	"	–	16	
Benjamin Hines,	-	-	"	–	16	
Edwin Council,	-	-	Drummer,	–	16	
James Council,	-	-	Fifer,	–	16	
Matthew Adams,	-	-	Private,	–	16	
Claiborne Booth,	-	-	"	–	16	
Alex'r Briggs,	-	-	"	–	16	
Rawley Barrot,	-	-	"	–	16	
James Bell,	-	-	'	–	16	
Elias Barrot,	-	-	"	–	16	
John Briggs,	-	-	"	–	16	
James Barham,	-	-	"	–	16	
Wm. Boykin,	-	-	"	–	16	
James Brasswell,	-	-	"	–	16	
Geo. Blow,	-	-	"	–	16	
Richard Beal,	-	-	"	–	16	
James Bradshaw,	-	-	"	–	16	
Elias Bradshaw,	-	-	"	–	16	
Edwin Beale,	-	-	"	–	16	
Benjamin Bradshaw,	-		"	–	16	
Mark Clanton,	-	-	"	–	16	
John Cobb,	-	-	"	–	16	
Stephen Carter,	-	-	"	–	16	
Henry Council,	-	-	"	–	16	
William Davis,	-	-	"	–	16	
Mark Drake,	-	-	"	–	16	
John Daughety,	-	-	"	–	16	
Edmund Doyle,	-	-	"	–	16	
Etheldred Daughtry,	-		"	–	16	
David Doyl,	-	-	"	–	16	
Alfred Denson,	-	-	"	–	16	
Jeremiah Doyl,	-	-	"	–	16	
Samuel Denson,	-	-	"	–	16	
Philip Doyl,	-	-	"	–	16	
Robert Exum,	-	-	"	–	16	
Wm. English,	-	-	"	–	16	
Jno. Foster,	-	-	"	–	16	

NAMES.	RANK.	TIME OF SERVICE.		REMARKS.
		Months.	Days.	
Wm. Felts, - -	Private,	—	16	
Robert Fort, - -	"	—	16	
Jeremiah Gay, - -	"	—	16	
Henry Gardner, - -	"	—	16	
Harrison Griffin, - -	"	—	16	
Ro. Gillum, - -	"	—	16	
Ely Griffin, - -	"	—	16	
Armstead Grizzard, - -	"	—	16	
John Hargrave, - -	"	—	16	
Etheldred Hart, - -	"	—	16	
John Harris, - -	"	—	16	
Mills Hobbs, - -	"	—	16	
James Harris, - -	"	—	16	
Wm. Joyner, - -	"	—	16	
Kinchin Iray, - -	"	—	16	
Gillum Jones, - -	"	—	16	
Aaron Johnson, - -	"	—	16	
Jonas W. Johnson, - -	"	—	16	
Wm. Joyner, - -	"	—	16	
Sinclair Joyner, - -	"	—	16	
Hardy Johnson, - -	"	—	16	
Ro. Johnson, - -	"	—	16	
Lawrence Joyner, - -	"	—	16	
Lemuel Jones, - -	"	—	16	
John Lewis, - -	"	—	16	
Zach. Lankfort, - -	"	—	16	
Alex'r Myrick, - -	"	—	16	
James Mumfort, - -	"	—	16	
Nath. Mumfort, - -	"	—	16	
Wm. Norsworthy, - -	"	—	16	
Nathan Oberry, - -	"	—	16	
Richard Owen, - -	"	—	16	
Lem'l Pond, - -	"	—	16	
Samuel Powers, - -	"	—	16	
Joseph Pope, - -	"	—	16	
Nathan Pope, - -	"	—	16	
Ely Pope, - -	"	—	16	
Thos. Pond, - -	"	—	16	
Mike Stephenson, - -	"	—	16	
John P. Slade, - -	"	—	16	
Jordan Spivey, -	"	—	16	
Gideon Scarborough, -	"	—	16	
Harrison Summerell, -	"	—	16	
Thomas Stephenson, -	"	—	16	
Edmund Spencer, - -	"	—	16	
Miles Slade, - -	"	—	16	
Herod Summerell, - -	"	—	16	
John Travis, - -	"	—	16	
Jordan Vaiser, - -	"	—	16	
Jesse Vick, - -	"	—	16	
Levi Wellons, - -	"	—	16	
Benja. Wood, - -	"	—	16	
Dan'l Wood, - -	"	—	16	
Geo. Williams, - -	"	—	16	
Elisha Wade, - -	"	—	16	
Wm. Worrel, - -	"	—	16	
Machlin Whitehead, - -	"	—	16	

MUSTER ROLL

Of Captain John Pinckard's Company of Riflemen, of the One Hundred and Tenth Regiment, Virginia Militia, commanded by Lieutenant Colonel Robert Innes, in the Service of the United States, from the 11th to the 23rd of September, in the year 1814.

NAMES.	RANK.	TIME OF SERVICE.		REMARKS.
		Months.	Days.	
John Pinchard,	Captain,	–	12	
John Clay,	Lieutenant,	–	12	
Hezekiah Gill,	Ensign,	–	12	
James Pinckard,	Sergeant,	–	12	
Samuel Young,	"	–	12	
John Patton,	"	–	12	
John Kidd,	"	–	12	
David Moore,	Corporal,	–	12	
Lewis Potter,	"	–	12	
Martin McGeehee,	"	–	12	
Thomas Dunn,	"	–	12	
Francis Belcher,	Fifer,	–	12	
Tubal Brock,	Drummer,	–	12	
Elijah Bird,	Private,	–	12	
Isham Belcher,	"	–	12	
Phillip Carter,	"	–	12	
Elijah Cooley,	"	–	12	
Robert Cooley,	"	–	12	
Chapman Cooley,	"	–	12	
Zachariah Cooley,	"	–	12	
Ezekiel Clay,	"	–	12	
Thomas Dawson,	"	–	12	
Robert N. Dickenson,	"	–	12	
George Dickenson,	"	–	12	
Alexander Fortune,	"	–	12	
Tandy Foster,	"	–	12	
Britton Fuller,	"	–	12	
Richard Haizlip,	"	–	12	
Billy Hutchinson,	"	–	12	
John Hood,	"	–	12	
Henry Haizlip,	"	–	12	
Joab Hodges,	"	–	12	
Chamell Hix,	"	–	12	
Ashford Hodges,	"	–	12	
Dibdell Hix,	"	–	12	
Elijah Hodges,	"	–	12	
Elijah Hodges,	"	–	12	
Peyton Hodges,	"	–	12	
Howard Hix,	"	–	12	
William Jefferson,	"	–	12	
Ashford Keen,	"	–	12	
Peyton Law,	"	–	12	
William Merriman,	"	–	12	
James Murrell,	"	–	12	
Nelson McGeehee,	"	–	12	
Angers McGeehee,	"	–	12	

NAMES.	RANK.	TIME OF SERVICE.		REMARKS.
		Months.	Days.	
Charles McBride, - -	Private,	—	12	
Thomas Marcom, - -	"	—	12	
James Marcom, - -	"	—	12	
Doctor Pierson, - -	"	—	12	
Robert Pinkard, -	"	—	12	
Theodorick Ramsey, - -	"	—	12	
Edmund Richards, - -	"	—	12	
Waterman Richards, -	"	—	12	
Joel Richards, - -	"	—	12	
William Stagall, - -	"	—	12	
Hamilton Steward, - -	"	—	12	
Brice Steward, -	"	—	12	
Benjamin Sermonds, -	"	—	12	
William Steward, - -	"	—	12	
Littleberry Thornton, -	"	—	12	
Josiah Warren, - -	"	—	12	
William Zrigler, - -	"	—	12	
John Zrigler, - -	"	—	12	
Jacob Zrigler, - -	"	—	12	

MUSTER ROLL

Of Captain Thomas D. Pitts' Company of the Sixth Regiment, Virginia Militia, in the County of Essex, called into actual Service under the orders of Colonel John Dangerfield, of the 21st July, from the 6th to 7th April, from 21st to 23rd July, 1813, and from 21st to 25th September, 1814.

NAMES.			RANK.	TIME OF SERVICE.		REMARKS.
				Months.	Days.	
Thomas D. Pitts,	-	-	Captain,	2	10	
William Gray,	-	-	Lieutenant,	2	7	
Thos. W. Hill,	-	-	"	–	3	
Lewis Hord,	-	-	Ensign.	2	5	
Lewis Ward,	-	-	"	–	3	
Edward Parker,	-	-	Sergeant,	2	5	
Richard Coghill,	-	-	"	2	5	
Reuben L. Pitts,	-	-	"	–	25	Appointed Serg't Sep. 1, 1814.
James Fields,	-	-	"	2	8	
Henry Wering,	-	-	"	–	3	
Thomas Clarkson,	-	-	"	–	3	
William Blackburn,	-	-	"	–	2	
Benjamin Coghill,	-	-	"	–	2	
Bowler Vawter,	-	-	"	–	2	
Robert Samuel,	-	-	"	–	3	
John Thomas,	-	-	"	–	2	
Asee Gouldman,	-	-	Corporal,	2	5	
Lindsay Reynolds,	-	-	"	2	5	
William Parker,	-	-	"	–	25	App'd Corp'l 1 Sept'r, 1814, transfer'd Sep. 1, 1814.
Leonard Sale,	-	-	"	–	25	App'd Corp'l Sept. 1, 1814.
James Parker,	-	-	"	–	2	
John Bell,	-	-	"	–	2	
Alex'r Parker,	-	-	"	–	3	
Rich'd Beazley,	-	-	"	–	3	
Math. Ball,	-	-	"	–	3	
John Mahon,	-	-	"	–	3	
John Atkinson,	-	-	Private,	–	5	
Livin Ayres,	-	-	"	2	5	
Thomas P. Andrews,	-	-	"	2	5	
John Blackburn,	-	-	"	–	2	
Richard Beazley,	-	-	"	–	2	
Wm. T. Brooke,	-	-	"	–	2	
Philip Bastin,	-	-	"	–	3	
James Bartin,	-	-	"	–	3	
John Bastin,	-	-	"	2	5	
Thomas Boulware,	-	-	"	–	3	
Richard Coghill,	-	-	"	–	2	
Gouldman Carter,	-	-	"	2	8	
Thomas Coghill,	-	-	"	–	3	
Brooking Clark,	-	-	"	2	8	
Burkett Clarke,	-	-	"	2	8	
Benjamin Coghill,	-	-	"	–	3	
Lewis Clark,	-	-	"	2	5	

NAMES.	RANK.	TIME OF SERVICE.		REMARKS.
		Months.	Days.	
Larkin Clark, - -	Private,	2	5	
David Dishman, - -	"	2	7	
William Dickinson, - -	"	–	2	
Samuel Dishman, - -	"	2	5	
James Fields, - -	"	–	2	
Lewis Fisher, - -	"	–	5	
Lewis Farmer, - -	"	–	2	
William Fisher, - -	"	2	10	
John Fisher, - -	"	–	5	
William W. Fogg, - -	"	–	3	
Major Fogg, - -	"	–	3	
John Gray, - -	"	2	7	
Muscoe Garnett, - -	"	–	2	
Ozwald Goldman, - -	"	–	5	
Reuben Garrett, - -	"	2	10	
Robert G. Garnett, - -	"	–	2	
Philip Gatewood, - -	"	–	2	
Asa Gouldman, - -	"	–	5	
Jesse Gouldman, - -	"	–	3	
John S. Garrett, - -	"	2	5	
Obed Gray, - -	"	2	5	
William Gale, - -	"	2	5	
Philip Gatewood, - -	"	–	25	Transf'd from Captain Thomas' company, Sept. 1, 1814.
Lewis Hord, - -	"	–	2	
William Halbert, - -	"	–	27	" " " "
William Hill, - -	"	–	3	
James Halbert, - -	"	–	28	Detached from this regiment as wagoner to the 9th reg't, and transf'd to my company Sept. 1, 1814.
Larkin Haddock, - -	"	–	3	
Thomas Halbert, - -	"	2	5	
Richard T. Haile, - -	"	–	25	Transf'd from Captain Thomas' company, Sept. 1, 1814.
John Howard, - -	"	–	25	" " " "
Spencer Ingram, - -	"	2	8	
Orison Ingram, - -	"	–	28	" " " "
Moore Ingram, - -	"	2	5	
Thomas Kay, - -	"	–	13	
John Loyal, - -	"	–	2	
James Loyal, - -	"	–	5	
Philip Lee, - -	"	2	8	
Davis Longest, - -	"	2	5	
Brookin Lee, - -	"	2	5	
Francis Monday, - -	"	–	2	
Hickman Mitchell, - -	"	–	3	
Coleman Minor, - -	"	–	3	
Nathaniel J. Mothershead, -	"	–	28	Transf'd Sept. 1, 1814.
Mereday Munday, - -	"	–	3	
Thomas Munday, - -	"	–	3	
Robert Mercy, - -	"	1	20	
Thomas Mariner, - -	"	2	27	
Johnston Munday, - -	"	–	25	Transf'd from Captain Thomas' company, Sept. 1, 1814.
John B. Micou, - -	"	2	25	
Pan C. Micou, jr. - -	"	1	5	Appointed ensign in Essex county.
Achilles Noel, sr. -	"	–	28	Transf'd from Captain Thomas' company, Sept. 1, 1814.

NAMES.			RANK.	TIME OF SERVICE.		REMARKS.
				Months.	Days.	
Muscoe Noel,	-	-	Private,	2	28	
Achilles Noel, jr.	-	-	"	–	25	Transferred from Capt. Thomas' company, Sept. 1, 1814.
Edmond Noel,	-	-	"	–	25	" " "
Andrew Noel,	-	-	"	–	25	" " "
Oswald Noel,	-	-	"	2	25	
Lewis Noel,	-	-	"	2	25	
Austin Oliver,	-	-	"	–	5	
Larkin Pitts,	-	-	"	2	7	
Samuel Parker,	-	-	"	–	2	
Warren Parker,	-	-	"	–	2	
Younger Pitts,	-	-	"	–	3	
Edward Pilkerton,	-	-	"	–	3	
Robert Parker,	-	-	"	2	8	
James Parker,	-	-	"	–	3	
Mann Page,	-	-	"	2	5	
Thomas Parker,	-	-	"	2	5	
Ely Pitts,	-	-	"	2	5	
Thos. H. Pitts,	-	-	"	2	5	
Thomas Pitts,	-	-	"	2	5	
Andrew Rennolds,	-	-	"	1	–	" " "
Daniel Rennolds,	-	-	"	–	2	
John Rousee,	-	-	"	–	2	
Lindsey Rennolds,	-	-	"	–	3	
Richard Rennolds,	-	-	"	2	8	
Henry Rouse,	-	-	"	2	5	
Larkin Shaddock,	-	-	"	–	2	
Robert Samuel,	-	-	"	–	2	
William Sullivan,	-	-	"	2	7	
John Smither,	-	-	"	–	28	" " "
William Smither,	-	-	"	–	3	
Sthreshley Stokes,	-	-	"	–	28	" " "
Thomas Schools,	-	-	"	2	5	
Brookin Stokes,	-	-	"	2	5	
Anthony Samuel,	-	-	"	2	5	
Wm. D. Thomas,	-	-	"	–	3	
Robert Thomas,	-	-	"	–	3	
John Thomas,	-	-	"	2	5	
Humphrey B. Thomas,	-	-	"	–	25	" " "
Bowler Varler,	-	-	"	–	8	
Henry Waring,	-	-	"	–	2	
Richard Waters,	-	-	"	–	3	
Leonard Walthim,	-	-	"	–	25	" " "

Captain Thomas Pollard's Company—Twenty-fifth Regiment.

NAMES.	RANK.	TIME OF SERVICE.		REMARKS.
		Months.	Days.	
John Arnold, - -	Lieutenant,	–	9	
Ellis Gravatt, - -	Sergeant,	–	9	
John Johnson, - -	"	–	12	
John Massey, - -	Corporal,	–	8	
Gabriel Peed, - -	"	–	12	
James Baker, - -	Private,			
Gideon Bradley, - -	"	–	4	
S. J. S. Brown, - -	"	–	8	
Nathan Burchel, - -	"	–	8	
Harris Betty, - -	"	–	8	
William Carver, - -	"	–	8	
Charles Chrismond, - -	"	–	16	
William Humphries, jr. -	"	–	6	
Charles Jones, - -	"	–	2	
David Jones, - -	"	–	2	
William H. Levi, - -	"	–	8	
Gabriel Levi, - -	"	–	8	
George Mahoney, - -	"	–	8	
George Miffleton, - -	"	–	8	
Charles Massey, - -	"	–	–	Deserted.
Henry Staples, - -	"	–	2	
Archibald Tacket, - -	"	1	6	Deserted.
Richard Turner, - -	"	–	29	
George White, jr. - -	"	–	9	Robt. Rollings his sub.
Robert C. Wade, - -	"	–	8	
Reuben Wilkerson, - -	"	–	13	

(For rest of this company, see publication of Pay Rolls.)

MUSTER ROLL

Of Captain Erastus Poulson's Company, of the Ninety-ninth Regiment, Virginia Militia, commanded by Lieutenant Colonel Charles Bagwell, in the Service of the United States, from the 28th day of May to the 4th day of June, in the year 1814.

NAMES.	RANK.	TIME OF SERVICE.		REMARKS.
		Months.	Days.	
Erastus Poulson,	Captain,	–	7	
Martin Lewis,	Lieutenant,	–	7	
George Marshall,	Ensign,	–	7	
George Hope,	Sergeant,	–	7	
Elijah Hope,	"	–	7	
Parker Lucas,	"	–	7	
William Gillespie,	"	–	7	
Wm. H. Beavans,	Q. M. Serg't,	–	7	
William Archbold,	Private,	–	7	
John Cowley,	"	–	7	
George Christopher,	"	–	7	
John Core,	"	–	7	
Levy Core,	"	–	7	
Zadock Davis,	"	–	7	
James Fisher,	"	–	7	
Riley Fisher,	"	–	7	
Henry Fisher,	"	–	7	
Tully Fisher,	"	–	7	
William Garrett,	"	–	7	
Jas. Hope,	"	–	7	
Elijah Hutson,	"	–	7	
Thomas Hope,	"	–	7	
William Justice,	"	–	7	
Luke Lucas,	"	–	7	
Samuel Mapps,	"	–	7	
Charles Matthews,	"	–	7	
Thomas Nock,	"	–	7	
Charles Nock,	"	–	7	
Southey Northen,	"	–	7	
William Nock, (of T.)	"	–	7	
Custis Nathan,	"	–	7	
Daniel Price,	"	–	7	
Whitington B. Pool,	"	–	7	
Dan'l Shay,	"	–	7	
John Savage,	"	–	7	
Robert Townsend,	"	–	7	
John Taylor,	"	–	7	
John Thornton,	"	–	7	
Staton Taylor,	"	–	7	
Savage Taylor,	"	–	7	
Purnell Taylor,	"	–	7	
Zadock Taylor,	"	–	7	
Archibold Traydon,	"	–	7	
William Walker,	"	–	7	

NAMES.			RANK.	TIME OF SERVICE.		REMARKS.
				Months.	Days.	
John Walker,	-	-	Private,	–	7	
Robt. Williams,	-	-	"	–	7	
Gillet Watson,	-	-	"	–	7	
Samuel Walston,	-	-	"	–	7	
John Wright,	-	-	"	–	7	
Isaac Young,	-	-	"	–	7	

MUSTER ROLL

Of Cornet George Powell's Troop of Cavalry, of the Twenty-seventh Regiment, commanded by Lieutenant Colonel Major S. Pitts, in the Service of the United States, from 10th to 18th May, and from 2nd October to 2nd November, in the year 1814.

NAMES.	RANK.	TIME OF SERVICE.		REMARKS.
		Months.	Days.	
George Powell, - -	Cornet,	1	9	
John Widgeon, - -	Sergeant,	–	15	
William Dalby, - -	"	–	10	
Thomas Spady, - -	"	–	22	
Thomas S. Brickhouse, -	Private,	–	17	
Smith Brickhouse, - -	"	–	16	
George Brickhouse, - -	"	1		
Thomas Brickhouse, - -	"	–	9	
Nathaniel Collins, - -	"	–	9	
William Dalby, - -	"	–	9	
George Eshum, - -	"	–	17	
John T. Elliott, - -	"	–	19	
Thomas Henderson, - -	"	–	19	
John H. Harmanson, - -	"	–	20	
Seth D. Heth, - -	"	–	19	
Silas Jefferson, - -	"	–	19	
William D. James, - -	"	–	19	
Richard Nottingham, - -	"	–	19	
William E. Nottingham, -	"	1	1	
Abel Powell, - -	"	–	19	
William Ridley, - -	"	–	19	
Thomas S. Satchell, - -	"	–	21	
John G. Stratton, - -	"	–	19	
Edmund Scarborough, -	"	–	19	
Thomas Spady, - -	"	–	9	
George Savage, - -	"	–	29	
John Simpson, - -	"	–	9	
Levin J. Thomas, - -	"	–	19	
Bart. Taylor, - -	"	–	9	
Amos Underhill, - -	"	–	19	
William White, - -	"	–	19	
John B. Waddy, - -	"	–	7	
John S. Williams, - -	"	–	9	
John Widgeon, - -	"	–	9	
Nathaniel West, - -	"	–	9	

MUSTER ROLL

Of Lieutenant William B. Power's Company, of the Sixty-eighth Regiment, Virginia Militia, stationed at York Town, from the 4th October to the 2nd November, in the year 1814.

NAMES.	RANK.	TIME OF SERVICE.		REMARKS.
		Months.	Days.	
William B. Power,	Lieutenant,	–	29	
Dabney Brown,	Ensign,	–	29	
William B. Chaplin,	Sergeant,	–	29	
Robert Deneufville,	"	–	29	
Augustus Deneufville,	"	–	29	
John Lucas,	Corporal,	–	29	
William Powell,	"	–	29	
Frederick Bryan,	"	–	29	
Charles Lindsey,	"	–	29	
Richard Preston,	Musician,	–	29	
Miles Austin,	Private,	–	29	
Thomas Brooks,	"	–	29	
Henry Charles,	"	–	29	
William K. Charles,	"	–	29	
Henry Finch,	"	–	29	
Charles Hansford,	"	–	29	
John Hansford,	"	–	29	
Benjamin Hazlewood,	"	–	29	
Jordan Harrison,	"	–	29	
William Inge,	"	–	29	
Rowland Jones,	"	–	29	
Allen Jones,	"	–	29	
William Lee,	"	–	29	
Thomas Lucas,	"	–	29	
Francis Moody,	"	–	29	
Joseph Monett,	"	–	29	
Thomas Newman,	"	–	29	
William Norris,	"	–	29	
Hezekiah Rider,	"	–	29	
Thomas Stroud,	"	–	29	
William Tinney,	"	–	15	
Aaron Walker,	"	–	29	
John Wilson,	"	–	29	
William Williamson,	"	–	29	
William N. Walker,	"	–	29	
William Washer,	"	–	29	

MUSTER ROLL

Of Captain Joseph F. Price's Company, of the Seventy-fourth Regiment, Virginia Militia, commanded by Colonel William Trueheart, called into the Service of the United States, from 28th to 29th June, and from 1st to 2nd July, in the year 1813.

NAMES.	RANK.	TIME OF SERVICE.		REMARKS.
		Months.	Days.	
Joseph F. Price, - -	Captain,	–	14	
William Day, - -	Lieutenant,	–	14	
Francis Blunt, - -	Ensign,	–	14	
John Goodwin, - -	Sergeant,	–	14	
John Chesterman, -	"	–	14	
Edward Valentine, - -	"	–	14	
William D. Winston, -	"	–	10	
Walker Taylor, - -	"	–	4	
Henry Arnall, sr. - -	Private,	–	14	
Henry Arnall, jr. - -	"	–	10	
Charles D. Alvis, - -	"	–	14	
Len. P. Anderson, -	"	–	14	
Edmund M. Anderson, -	"	–	14	
Richard Arnall, - -	"	–	14	
Lemuel Alvis, - -	"	–	14	
Thomas Austin, - -	"	–	10	
Joseph Arnall, - -	"	–	14	
Davis Arnall, - -	"	–	14	
Robert Alvis, - -	"	–	14	
John Blunt, - -	"	–	14	
Lewis Berkley, - -	"	–	14	
Thomas Bowles, - -	"	–	14	
Samuel Busick, - -	"	–	14	
William Byars, - -	"	–	14	
Michael B. Blankenbiker, -	"	–	14	
Isaac Butler, - -	"	–	14	
James Baber, - -	"	–	14	
Joseph Blunt, - -	"	–	10	
Nelson Brooks, - -	"	–	10	
Thomas B. Cosby, - -	"	–	14	
William Dabney, - -	"	–	14	
John Darracott, - -	"	–	14	
Thomas Doswell, - -	"	–	14	
Abram W. Davis, -	"	–	14	
Walter C. Day, - -	"	–	14	
Miles C. Eggleston, -	"	–	14	
George Eggleston, -	"	–	10	
James Fortson, - -	"	–	14	
John Grubbs, - -	"	–	14	
Samuel Grantland, -	"	–	14	
Richard Hope, - -	"	–	14	
William O. Harris, -	"	–	14	
William Harris, - -	"	–	10	
Epaphroditus Howle, -	"	–	14	
Winfield Harris, -	"	–	14	
Richard B. Hendrick, -	"	–	14	
William Hope, - -	"	–	14	

NAMES.	RANK.	TIME OF SERVICE.		REMARKS.
		Months.	Days.	
William Haines, - -	Private,	—	10	
David Hackney, - -	"	—	10	
John Haley, - -	"	—	10	
Winston M. Hicks, - -	"	—	10	
Johnson Jones, - -	"	—	14	
Richard C. B. Jones, - -	"	—	14	
John Jones, jr. - -	"	—	14	
Edward W. Kimbrough, -	"	—	14	
James Lowry, - -	"	—	14	
Jasper Lane, - -	"	—	11	
Solomon Lowry, - -	"	—	14	
Samuel Lowry, - -	"	—	14	
Claiborne Lowry, - -	"	—	14	
William Lumay, - -	"	—	14	
Timothy P. R. Lester, -	"	—	14	
William Long, - -	"	—	10	
William Lambert, - -	"	—	4	
Claiborne Mallory, - -	"	—	10	
William Mallory, - -	"	—	14	
William Mallory, jr. - -	"	—	14	
Turner Mallory, - -	"	—	14	
Fleming Mallory, - -	"	—	14	
Stephen Mallory, - -	"	—	14	
James May, - -	"	—	14	
James M. Morriss, - -	"	—	10	
Pleasant Mathiss, - -	"	—	14	
William Norvell, - -	"	—	14	
Thomas W. Norvell, - -	"	—	14	
Mordecai Page, - -	"	—	14	
John Patterson, - -	"	—	14	
Samuel Patterson, - -	"	—	14	
Joseph Patterson, - -	"	—	14	
Edmund Patterson, - -	"	—	10	
William Pearson, - -	"	—	14	
Plummer Potter, - -	"	—	14	
Thomas R. Rootes, - -	"	—	14	
Archibald Richardson, - -	"	—	14	
Landon Richardson, - -	"	—	14	
Nathaniel Stephens, - -	"	—	14	
Julius Stephens, - -	"	—	4	
John Seddons, - -	"	—	14	
Thomas Southward, - -	"	—	14	
Simeon Souther, - -	"	—	14	
William Sheppard, - -	"	—	14	
John Southward, - -	"	—	14	
William Shirley, - -	"	—	14	
Pleasant Terrell, - -	"	—	14	
Anthony Thornton, - -	"	—	14	
William D. Taylor, - -	"	—	10	
Armistead Thornton, - -	"	—	14	
John D. Thilman, - -	"	—	14	
Thomas Trevilian, - -	"	—	14	
Walker Taylor, - -	"	—	10	
William Terrell, - -	"	—	14	
Meredith Thacker, - -	"	—	10	
George Valentine, - -	"			
William C. Williams, - -	"	—	14	
Samuel Williams, - -	"	—	14	
James Winston, - -	"	—	14	
Phil. B. Winston, - -	"	—	14	
John Williams, jr. - -	"	—	14	
Thomas Yarbrough, - -	"	—	10	
Jesse Yarbrough, - -	"	—	14	
Elisha Yarbrough, - -	"	—	14	

MUSTER ROLL

Of Captain Thomas H. Prosser's Troop of Cavalry, in the Thirty-third Regiment, Virginia Militia, in the County of Henrico, called into the Service of the United States, under the general order of the 26th August, from 27th August to 10th September, 1814.

NAMES.	RANK.	TIME OF SERVICE.		REMARKS.
		Months.	Days.	
Thomas H. Prosser, - -	Captain,	–	15	
John M. Radford, - -	Lieutenant,	–	15	
Richard C. Gilliam, - -	"	–	15	
Reuben Burton, - -	Cornet,	–	15	
Spotswood Austin, - -	Private,	–	15	
Lyddell Bowles, - -	"	–	15	
Thomas O. Burton. - -	"	–	15	
Samuel Burton, - -	"	–	11	
John Burton, - -	"	–	11	
Josiah Blackburn, - -	"	–	11	
Wm. M. Burton, - -	"	–	11	
Samuel Carlisle, - -	"	–	11	
Samuel Conway, - -	"	–	11	
Reuben Cottrell, - -	"	–	11	
Wm. Jas. Cawthorn, - -	"	–	11	
Wm. Cottrell, - -	"	–	11	
Jos. Cottrell, - -	"	–	11	
Peter Coutts, - -	"	–	11	
Frank R. Ellis, - -	"	–	11	
Bartholomew Ellis, - -	"	–	11	
John Goode, - -	"	–	11	
William Gentry, - -	"	–	11	
Matthew Jordan, - -	"	–	11	
William Hooker, - -	"	–	11	
David Hughes, - -	"	–	11	
Nathaniel Holman, - -	"	–	11	
William Layne, - -	"	–	11	
Benj. Mann, - -	"	–	11	
John Mann, - -	"	–	11	
Thomas Mallory, - -	"	–	11	
Reuben Meredith, - -	"	–	11	
James Nuckolds, - -	"	–	11	
Robert Priddy, - -	"	–	11	
Overton Pettit, - -	"	–	11	
John C. Pleasants, - -	"	–	11	
Smith Puryear, - -	"	–	11	
Jacob Smith, - -	"	–	11	
David Sheet, - -	"	–	11	
Andrew Todd, - -	"	–	11	
James Todd, - -	"	–	11	
Malachi Tinsley, - -	"	–	11	
Christopher Taliaferro, -	"	–	11	
Jacob Woodrum, - -	"	–	11	
Frederick Woodson, - -	"	–	11	
Joseph Webber, - -	"	–	11	

Captain John C. Pryor's Troop of Cavalry—Twenty-first Regiment.

NAMES.	RANK	TIME OF SERVICE.		REMARKS.
		Months.	Days.	
John C. Pryor, - -	Captain,	1	2	
William Minor, - -	Lieutenant,	–	25	
Thomas Kemp, - -	"	–	12	
John Kemp, - -	"	–	19	
John Bracken, - -	Cornet,	–	15	
John D. Gressett, - -	Sergeant,	1	6	
Thomas T. Tabb, - -	"	–	15	
Edward B. S. Cary, -	"	–	22	
Jno. M. Gayle, - -	"	–	6	
Jno. Stubblefield, - -	"	–	6	
Warner Whiting, - -	"	–	17	
Warner Whiting, - -	Corporal,	–	6	
William S. Camp, - -	"	4	17	
William E. Gressett, -	"	2	20	
Henry Sincore, - -	"	1	5	
Thomas Throckmorton, -	"	–	27	
Peter Kemp, - -	"	–	9	
William E. Gressett, -	Quar. Master,	–	9	
Thomas Acra, - -	Private,	–	6	
John Buckner, - -	"	–	23	
James Baine, - -	"	2	3	
Matt. M. Brooke, - -	"			
William Crittenden, -	"	1	8	
Simon Cook, - -	"	1	8	
William Cook, - -	"	1	1	
Thomas G. Cluverius, -	"	1	3	
Benj. Cluverius, - -	"	1	9	
Miles Camp, - -	"	–	27	
John Dunston, - -	"	1	17	
William Dennis, - -	"	1	2	
John Douglass, - -	"	–	9	
William Edwards, - -	"	2	21	
Henry Enos, - -	"	1	6	
John Fleming, - -	"	1	24	
E. L. Ferrill, - -	"	–	23	
William Farinholtz, -	"	–	23	
John T. Gayle, - -	"	–	18	
Nath. Gressett. - -	"	2	27	
Thomas Goulden, - -	"	–	17	
John Goulden, - -	"	–	23	
John Glass, - -	"			
William Hughs, - -	"	2	7	
John Hughs, - -	"	1	11	
John Hall, - -	"	1	8	
John Hobday, - -	"	1	2	
Sowersby Hughs, - -	"	2		
William Harwood, - -	"			
John Howlett, jun'r, -	"	–	18	
John Howlett, sen'r, -	"	–	4	
Thomas M. Johnson, -	"	–	20	
Gabriel Jones, - -	"	–	14	
John Johnson, - -	"	–	20	
William Johnson, - -	"	–	2	
James Johnson, - -	"	3	12	

NAMES.	RANK.	TIME OF SERVICE.		REMARKS.
		Months.	Days.	
Peter Kemp, sen'r, - -	Private,	–	20	
Robert Kemp, - -	"	–	10	
Cary Kemp, - -	"	–	17	
Matt. Kemp, - -	"	–	6	
Peter Kemp, jr. - -	"	–	25	
M. Kemp, (son of Robt.) -	"	1	4	
M. Kemp, (son of Matt.) -	"	–	12	
Thomas R. Leigh, - -	"	1	13	
Christopher Lewellin, -	"	–	6	
William Lear, - -	"	–	6	
William Leavitt, - -	"	–	9	
Jacob Moore, - -	"	1	6	
John Major, - -	"	–	17	
Hazolem Nuttall, - -	"	2	2	
Bowden Newcomb, - -	"	–	22	
Thomas Pointer, -	"	2	3	
Willis Perrin, -	"	–	12	
Thomas M. Ryland, - -	"	–	6	
Robert Ransone, - -	"	–	9	
Jasper C. Rowe, - -	"	1	6	
John Ransone, - -	"	–	6	
William Shields, - -	"	1	10	
Richard Singleton, - -	"	2	25	
William Stevens, - -	"	–	6	
William Stubblefield, -	"	1	7	
Fielding Shields, - -	"	1	1	
Baylor Stubblefield, - -	"	1	7	
Seth Stubblefield, - -	"	1	20	
Robert Stubblefield, - -	"	1	17	
Waid Stubblefield, - -	"	1	8	
Francis Stubbs, - -	"	1	16	
Robert Sadler, - -	"	–	17	
William Sears, - -	"	–	15	
Dawson Soles, - -	"	–	8	
John Stubblefield, - -	"	–	25	
Richard Thornton, - -	"	–	18	
Warner Throckmorton, -	"	–	21	
Robert Waddle, - -	"	–	20	
Nath'l Watlington, - -	"	–	20	
Matt. Wood, - -	"	1		
Paul Watlington, - -	"	1	14	
John West, - -	"	1	26	
Edward Williams, - -	"	3	5	
Armstead Watlington, -	"	–	18	
James Williams, - -	"	1	19	
John B. Whiting, - -	"	1	8	
Robert Wilkins, - -	"	–	9	

(For rest of this company, see publication of Pay Rolls.)

PAY ROLL

Of Captain B. Wms. Pryor's Company of Artillery, of Virginia Militia, called into actual Service under the general orders of the 6th February, from the 8th February to the 3d March, 1813.

NAMES.			RANK.	TIME OF SERVICE.		REMARKS.
				Months.	Days.	
B. Wms. Pryor,	-	-	Captain,	—	24	
Robert Lively,	-	-	Lieutenant,	—	24	
John W. Jones,	-	-	"	—	24	
Elijah Smith,	-	-	Sergeant,	—	24	
Samuel Lively,	-	-	"	—	24	
James V. Moore,	-	-	"	—	24	
John H. Outten,	-	-	"	—	24	
John S. Parker,	-	-	Corporal,	—	24	
William Hawkins,	-	-	"	—	24	
William Wood,	-	-	"	—	24	
William Gooch,	-	-	"	—	24	
John Whitfield,	-	-	Drummer,	—	24	
Andrew Bully,	-	-	Private,	—	24	
John Bully,	-	-	"	—	24	
Caleb Bonwell,	-	-	"	—	24	
Baldwin Bushell,	-	-	"	—	24	
James Benthall,	-	-	"	—	24	
William Bailey,	-	-	"	—	24	
William Backhouse,	-	-	"	—	24	
William Burke,	-	-	"	—	24	
William Clarke,	-	-	"	—	4	
John Daws,	-	-	"	—	24	
Holmes Dewbre,	-	-	"	—	24	
Ezekiel Drummond,	-	-	"	—	24	
Joseph Evans,	-	-	"	—	20	
Levy Guy,	-	-	"	—	14	
Nathaniel Giddens,	-	-	"	—	24	
Henry Guy,	-	-	"	—	24	
William Guy,	-	-	"	—	24	
Thomas Holland,	-	-	"	—	24	
Samuel Hickman,	-	-	"	—	24	
Robert Hatton,	-	-	"	—	24	
William Langley,	-	-	"	—	17	
Thomas Lewis,	-	-	"	—	24	
Samuel Lewis,	-	-	"	—	24	
Moses Lawrence,	-	-	"	—	23	
John Lewis,	-	-	"	—	24	
John Laurence,	-	-	"	—	18	
Thomas Melson,	-	-	"	—	24	
George Melson,	-	-	"	—	24	
William Melson,	-	-	"	—	24	
Allen McHolland,	-	-	"	—	24	
George Middleton,	-	-	"	—	24	
Thomas Mowring,	-	-	"	—	18	
William Minson,	-	-	"	—	21	
Samuel Metcalf,	-	-	"	—	19	
Walter Mayland,	-	-	"	—	4	
John Pool,	-	-	"	—	24	

NAMES.	RANK.	TIME OF SERVICE.		REMARKS.
		Months.	Days.	
Eppy Pierce, - -	Private,	–	17	
Robert Russell, - -	"	–	24	
George Routen, - -	"	–	24	
Zorobabel Roberts, - -	"	–	24	
William Russell, - -	"	–	24	
Thomas Skinner, - -	"	–	13	
John S. Simpson, - -	"	–	24	
John Shield, - -	"	–	24	
Joseph Tennis, - -	"	–	7	
Robert Terlington, - -	"	–	24	
Branson Turner, -	"	–	24	
Patrick Walker, - -	"	–	17	
John Wayland, - -	"	–	24	
Robert Wilson, - -	"	–	24	
Richard Wilson, - -	"	–	24	
William Whitfield, - -	"	–	24	
John Wilson, - -	"	–	24	
Richard Vaughan, - -	"	–	21	

Captain John Quarles' Company—Sixteenth Regiment.

NAMES.	RANK.	TIME OF SERVICE.		REMARKS.
		Months.	Days.	
John Arnold, - -	Lieutenant,	–	19	
William H. Fulcher, -	Ensign,	–	27	
James R. Holladay, -	"	–	27	
Oswald N. Pemberton, -	Sergeant,	–	19	
Stephen Pratt, - -	"	–	19	
Thomas Tutt, - -	"	–	14	
Edmond Hoomes, -	"	–	19	
George T. Riding, -	"	–	19	
John P. Corthron, -	"	–	26	
Thomas Boxley, -	"	–	26	
Bailey Dawson, -	Corporal,	–	19	
William Alexander, -	"	–	19	
Alexander Donaphon, -	"	–	14	
John B. Taylor, -	"	–	19	
Wm. G. A. Jones, -	"	–	9	
Richard D. Taylor, -	"	–	26	
Benj. Jenkins, -	"	–	26	
Ralph Dickinson, -	"	–	26	
Jesse Humphries, -	Fifer,	–	19	
Ritchie Alsop, -	Private,	–	14	
James Allen, -	"	–	9	
James M. Bell, -	"	–	26	
George H. Bullard, -	"	–	–	Deserted.
John B. Burchell, -	"	–	14	
James Bevard, -	"	–	14	
Thomas Berry, -	"	–	–	Deserted.
David Bradley, -	"	–	19	
Charles Brimmer, -	"	–	19	
Samuel Burruss, -	"	–	19	
Reuben D. Bullard, -	"	–	15	
James Bruce, -	"	–	–	Deserted.
James Bailey, -	"	–	9	
William Boxley, -	"	–	29	
Fielding Curtis, -	"	–	19	
John Combs, -	"	–	14	
Benjamin Combs, -	"	–	14	
Berryman Cox, -	"	–	19	
Joseph Crim, -	"	–	19	
Robert Clift, -	"	–	10	
Henry Chrismal, -	"	–	10	
William Cox, -	"			
John Cox, -	"	–	8	
Obadiah Cox, -	"	–	19	
Lewis Cross, -	"	–	12	
John Child, -	"	–	11	
William Curtis, -	"	–	5	
John Curtis, -	"	–	5	
George Davis, -	"	–	29	
John Dodd, -	"	–	19	
John Davis, -	"	1	15	
Henry Deatley, -	"	–	19	
Daniel B. Doggett, -	"	–	14	
James Dodd, -	"	–	15	
Nathaniel Dismukes, -	"	–	26	

NAMES.	RANK.	TIME OF SERVICE.		REMARKS.
		Months.	Days.	
John England, - -	Private,	–	19	
Jeremiah Elkins, - -	"	–	9	
John Elkins, - -	"	–	9	
John A. Edwards, - -	"	–	18	
William Faulkner, - -	"	–	26	Substitute for Elijah Quesenberry.
Joel Fant. - -	"	–	19	
William Frank, - -	"	–	16	
Willis Fewell, - -	"	–	13	
John Fisher, - -	"	–	5	
William Gibson, - -		–	–	Deserted.
James Garrison, - -	"	–	19	
John Gaulph, - -	"	–	19	
Bartlett Guthrie, - -	"	–	–	Deserted.
Rhody S. Green, - -	"	–	15	
John Goldsmith, - -	"	–	15	
John Garner, - -	"	–	9	
Thornton Garner, - -	"	–	9	
Daniel Grinnan, - -	"	–	13	
James Gardner, - -	"	–	26	
Reuben Grady, - -	"	–	26	
Richard Howard, - -	"	–	26	Sub. for John White.
Waller Holloday, - -	"	–	2	Aden C. Morris his substitute.
Robert Henderson, - -	"	–	14	
Robert Hildrup, - -	"	–	14	
John Horton, - -	"	–	19	
Nathan Hallaway, - -	"	–	19	
Joel Harding, - -	"	–	14	
Joseph Homes, - -	"	–	19	
Samuel Humphreys, - -	"	–	19	
James Holladay, - -	"	–	14	
Charles Henderson, - -	"	–	14	
William Hay, - -	"	–	19	
Burdett Hefferlin, - -	"	–	19	
William Hilton, - -	"	–	13	
Charles Humphreys, - -	"	–	18	
Edward Inscoe, - -	"	–	9	
Elijah Inscoe, - -	"	–	9	
Colbert Jones, - -	"	–	19	
Sidney Jones, - -	"	–	9	
Gibson Jenkins, - -	"	–	26	
Benjamin Jenkins. - -		–	–	Presley Stone his substitute.
Joel Jones, - -	"	–	8	
Joseph Jones, - -	"	–	19	
Lewis W. Johnson, - -	"	–	26	Substitute for Waller Holladay.
Lewis Jenkins, - -	"	–	26	
John C. Johnson, - -	"	–	26	
John S. Jenkins, - -	"	–	26	
Absalom King, - -	"	–	19	
Branson Knight, - -	"	–	19	
William Kindall, - -	"	–	14	
James Lee, - -	"	–	19	
Barnes Lawson, - -	"	–	19	
Lewis Lawless, - -	"	–	19	
William Latham, - -	"	–	5	
Fontaine Laine, - -	"	–	26	
Jacob Levi, - -	"	–	14	
Thomas Lyons, - -	"	–	8	
John McCarty, - -	"	–	19	
Thomas Minton, - -	"	–	19	
Elijah Million, - -	"	–	14	

NAMES.	RANK.	TIME OF SERVICE.		REMARKS.
		Months.	Days.	
Benjamin Murphy, - -	Private,	—	14	
William Murry, - -	"	—	19	
John Murry, - -	"	—	19	
Robert McO. Boy, - -	"	—	19	
John Moore, - -	"	—	19	
Rodman Mires, - -	"	—	14	
Fenner Marks, - -	"	—	19	
John Mardis, - -	"	—	19	
John H. Micoe, - -	"	—	15	
Thomas H. Micoe, - -	"	—	15	
George Miffleton, - -	"	—	9	
William Mardis, - -	"	—	14	
Henry Martin, - -	"	—	14	
Robert P. Marshall, - -	"	—	11	
Aden C. Morris, - -	"	—	6	Substitute for Waller Holladay.
Benjamin Massey, - -	"	—	26	
Fielding Owens, - -	"	—	8	
Nathaniel Owens, - -	"	—	8	
Elias Owens, - -	"	—	5	
Nathan G. Parker, - -	"	—	26	
Daniel Pilcher, - -	"	—	19	
John Potts, - -	"	—	14	
John Payne, - -	"	—	19	
Bailey Pottes, - -	"	—	19	
James Prim, - -	"	—	13	
George Payne, - -	"	—	6	
George Pickett, - -	"	—	9	
John Payne. - -	"	—	5	
Valentine Rolls, - -	"	—	14	
Jesse Rowe, - -	"	—	19	
William Rose, - -	"	—	9	
William M. Rawlings, - -	"	—	14	
Joel Reynolds, - -	"	—	6	
Garrett Schooler, - -	"	—	26	
Presley Stone, - -	"	—	8	Substitute for Benj. Jenkins.
Dawson Swillivan, - -	"	—	19	
Thornton Shilton, - -	"			
William B. Stuart, - -	"	—	10	
Thomas Short, - -	"	—	14	
Philip J. Spilman, - -	"	—	11	
Martin Swillivan, - -	"	—	13	
Benj. Tolson, - -	"	—	19	
Joseph D. Thompson, - -	"	—	16	
Thornel Twyman, - -	"	—	8	
Edward Thomas, - -	"	—	26	
Samuel Taylor, - -	"	—	14	
James Tricker, - -	"	—	8	
Abraham Tricker, - -	"	—	4	
Washington Taylor, - -	"	—	13	
Keeling Terrell, - -	"	—	27	
Archibald Tackett, - -	"	—	2	
Nathaniel Wheeler, - -	"	—	26	
George White, - -	"	—	19	
Henry Williams, - -	"	—	14	
William Williams, - -	"	—	14	
Bailey Watson, - -	"	—	19	
James Williams, - -	"	—	8	
Isaac Wilkerson, - -	"	—	8	
Nathaniel Webb, - -	"	—	16	

(For rest of this company, see publication of Pay Rolls.)

MUSTER ROLL

Of a Detachment, Volunteer Militia, commanded by Sergeant Frederick Ragsdale, of the Sixty-second Regiment, in the Service of the State of Virginia, from the 21st February to 28th May, 1814.

NAMES.	RANK.	TIME OF SERVICE.		REMARKS.
		Months.	Days.	
Frederick Ragsdale, - -	Sergeant,	3	6	
Jeremiah Aldridge, - -	Private,	3	6	
John Crider, - -	"	3	6	
William Epis, - -	"	3	6	
Hampton Epis, - -	"	3	6	
Carter Harrison, - -	"	3	6	
Hartwell Hackney, - -	"	3	6	
Hartwell Heath, - -	"	3	6	
Littleberry Murry, - -	"	3	6	
Jessee Mustlewhite, - -	"	3	6	
Joseph Phillips, - -	"	3	6	
David Simmons, - -	"	3	6	
Nathaniel Wamack, - -	"	3	6	

MUSTER ROLL

Of Captain Ephraim Raines' Company of Infantry, from the Sixty-second Regiment, Virginia Militia, commanded by Lieutenant Colonel Miles Selden, in the Service from the 28th June to the 10th July, 1813.

NAMES.	RANK.	TIME OF SERVICE.		REMARKS.
		Months.	Days.	
Ephraim Raines, - -	Captain,	—	13	
Henry Williams, - -	Lieutenant,	—	13	
Jeremiah Clements, - -	Ensign,	—	13	
John Woodlief, - -	Sergeant,	—	13	
Hudson Tucker, - -	"	—	13	
William W. Rives, - -	"	—	13	
Robert Tench, - -	"	—	13	
Richard Raines, - -	Corporal,	—	13	
William Rives, jr., - -	"	—	13	
William Parham, - -	"	—	13	
Hardiman Webb, - -	"	—	13	
Joel Butler, - -	Drummer,	—	13	
Geo. Abomb, - -	Private,	—	13	
James Brockwell, - -	"	—	10	
John Brockwell, - -	"	—	13	
Elisha Brockwell, - -	"	—	13	
Daniel Brockwell, - -	"	—	13	
John Butler, jr., - -	"	—	7	
Kennon Burge, - -	"	—	13	
Henry M. Cate, - -	"	—	13	
James Cotton, - -	"	—	13	
Francis Fern, - -	"	—	13	
Benjamin Figg, - -	"	—	12	
John Figg, - -	"	—	8	
Wm'son Grammer, - -	"	—	13	
Travis Grammar, - -	"	—	13	
Thomas Hadden, - -	"	—	13	
Elisha Herrins, - -	"	—	13	
James Hare, - -	"	—	3	
Thomas Hare, - -	"	—	10	
Armstead Heath, - -	"	—	13	
Jones Heath, - -	"	—	12	
Edmund Ledbetter, - -	"	—	12	
Bartholomew Kirtland, -	"	—	—	Or Kirkland
Charles Livesay, - -	"	—	13	
Frederick Livesay, - -	"	—	12	
John Livesay, - -	"	—	12	
Peterson Livesay, - -	"	—	12	
Geo. Mitchell, - -	"	—	12	
William Parr, - -	"	—	12	
Moses Rollings, - -	"	—	12	
Henry Tatum, - -	"	—	12	
John Tatum, - -	"	—	12	
Richard Tatum, - -	"	—	13	
William L. Wills, - -	"	—	13	
John Wood, - -	"	—	13	
Josiah Wood, - -	"	—	13	

MUSTER ROLL

Of Cornet Richard Randolph's Troop of Cavalry, from the Nineteenth Regiment, Virginia Militia, commanded by Lieutenant Colonel J. Ambler, in the Service from the 17th of April to 2nd May, 1813.

NAMES.			RANK.	TIME OF SERVICE.		REMARKS.
				Months.	Days.	
Richard Randolph,	-	-	Cornet,	–	15	
William Randolph,	-	-	Sergeant,	–	15	
James Whitlocke,	-	-	Private,	–	15	
Jed'h Allen,	-	-	"	–	15	
Richard Brooke,	-	-	"	–	15	
T. Burton,	-	-	"	–	15	
William Bootwright,	-	-	"	–	15	
B. F. Cocke,	-	-	"	–	15	
Charles Childrey,	-	-	"	–	15	
Thos. Gay,	-	-	"	–	15	
Charles Hay,	-	-	"	–	15	
Lightfoot Janney,	-	-	"	–	15	
James Lynch,	-	-	"	–	15	
Nath'l Nelson,	-	-	"	–	15	
T. Redmond,	-	-	"	–	15	
William Richardson,	-	-	"	–	15	
—— Miller,	-	-	"	–	15	
John Stagg,	-	-	"	–	15	
James Gawthmey,	-	-	"	–	15	
William Preston,	-	-	"	–	15	
H. Tompkins,	-	-	"	–	15	
John Watson,	-	-	"	–	15	
J. Webster,	-	-	"	–	15	
John Woodfin,	-		"	–	15	

Captain Jeremiah Rawls' Company—Fifty-ninth Regiment.

NAMES.			RANK.	TIME OF SERVICE.		REMARKS.
				Months.	Days.	
Jeremiah Rawls,	-	-	Captain,	—	12	
Simons Pierce,	-	-	Sergeant,	—	18	
Tho's Saunders,	-	-	"	—	18	
Jethro Butler,	-	-	Corporal,	—	18	
Riddick Pierce,	-	-	"	—	18	
Stephen Abdel,	-	-	Private,	—	18	
Edw'd Ashborne,	-	-	"	—	18	
Amos Banes,	-	-	"	—	18	
David Baker,	-	-	"	—	18	
Henry Evans,	-	-	"	—	15	
Wilson Ellis,	-	-	"	—	18	
John Grant,	-	-	"	—	18	
John Graham,	-	-	"	—	18	
Joseph J. Holland,	-	-	"	—	18	
Andrew Holland,	-	-	"	—	18	
Elarkin F. Holland,	-	-	"	—	18	
Miles Heffiton,	-	-		—	18	
Benj. King,	-	-	"	—	18	
Bembridge Laster,	-	-		—	18	
Jesse Lamb,	-	-	"	—	13	
Hannon Mintz,	-	-	"	—	18	
David Nelms,	-	-	"	—	13	
John Norfleet,	-	-	"	—	18	
Samuel Parker,	-	-	"	—	8	
William Parker,	-	-	"	—	18	
John Redmon,	-	-	"	—	18	
Matthew Right,	-	-	"	—	18	
Griffin Ross,	-	-	"	—	18	
James Riddick,	-	-		—	18	
Acy Smith,	-	-	"	—	18	
Jethro Taylor,	-	-	"	—	13	
James Vaughan,	-	-	"	—	18	

(For rest of this company, see publication of Pay Rolls.)

Captain John Reade's Company—Twentieth Regiment.

NAMES.	RANK.	TIME OF SERVICE.		REMARKS.
		Months.	Days.	
John Reade, - -	Captain,	1	3	
David S. Murray, - -	Lieutenant,	1	9	
Henry Sparrow, - -	Ensign,	1	22	
Edward Moseley, - -	Sergeant,	1	9	
Caleb Whitehurst, - -	"	–	19	
William C. Boroughs, -	"	–	19	
John Keeling, - -	"	–	15	
Isaac Land, - -	"	–	21	
Henry Williamson, - -	"	–	6	
Malachi Miles, - -	Corporal,	1	1	
Gerham Galusha, - -	"	–	23	
Patrick Whitehurst, - -	"	1	16	
Jonathan Williamson, -	"	–	22	
David Edmonds, - -	"	–	7	
Jonathan Berry, - -	Private,	–	21	
John T. Calvert, - -	"	–	11	
Horatio Davis, - -	"	–	17	
Hillery Davis, sr. - -	"	1	13	
Hillery Davis, jr. - -	"	–	17	
Ellison A. Doughty, - -	"	–	15	
Ralph Dickenson, - -	"	–	27	
Alexander W. Edmonds, -	"	–	21	
Henry Edmonds, - -	"	–	17	
David Edmonds, - -	"	–	10	
John Etheridge, - -	"	–	19	
Jeremiah Fentress, - -	"	1	10	
Hillery Fentress, - -	"	–	15	
Caleb Godfrey, - -	"	–	21	
William Godfrey, - -	"	–	25	
Samuel Godfrey, - -	"	–	17	
Charles Griggs, - -	"	–	15	
Joshua Hopkins, - -	"	–	23	
Samuel Hosier, - -	"	–	13	
Batson Land, - -	"	–	20	
Caleb Land, - -	"	–	11	
John Lee, - -	"	1	10	
William Lyon, - -	"	–	6	
David Matthias. - -	"	–	15	
Geo. McClanahan, - -	"	–	15	
William Matthias, - -	"	–	13	
John Moseley, - -	"	1	1	
William Mooring, - -	"	–	6	
Richard Murray, - -	"	–	6	
Hiram Nellam, - -	"	–	27	
John Otley, - -	"	–	21	
William Otley, - -	"	–	16	
John Payntor, - -	"	–	24	
Nat. Payntor, - -	"	–	25	
Robert Parsons, - -	"	–	16	
John Quick, - -	"	1	2	
Joseph Stafford, - -	"	1	10	
Simeon Smith, - -	"	–	19	
Josiah W. Slack, - -	"	–	15	
Bartlett Shipps, - -	"	–	27	

NAMES.			RANK.	TIME OF SERVICE.		REMARKS.
				Months.	Days.	
John Shipps,	-	-	Private,	–	16	
David Shirley,	-	-	"	–	21	
Aaron Timberlake,	-	-	"	–	26	
William Truss,	-	-	"	–	17	
Henry Williamson,	-	-	"	1	4	
Tully Whitehurst,	-	-	"	–	24	
David Whitehurst, jr.		-	"	–	23	
James Williamson,	-	-	"	1	7	
Anthony Walk,	-	-	"	–	7	
Edwin Walk,	-	-	"	–	7	
John Ward,	-	-	"	1	12	
David Whitehurst, sen'r,		-	"	–	15	
William Williamson,		-	"	1	12	
Josiah Williamson,	-	-	"	–	28	
Charles Williamson,	-	-	"	–	26	
Peter Williamson,	-	-	"	1	2	
John Wood,	-	-	"	–	6	
Miles Wood,	-	-	"	–	6	

(For rest of this company, see publication of Pay Rolls.)

MUSTER ROLL

Of a detachment from Captain Thos. Redd's Company, of Virginia Militia, from the Sixty-third Regiment, in the Service from the 30th August to 6th September, 1814.

NAMES.			RANK.	TIME OF SERVICE.		REMARKS.
				Months.	Days.	
John Stevens,	-	-	2d Lieutenant,	–	8	
John B. Hunt,	-	-	Drummer,	–	8	
William Armistead,	-	-	Private,	–	8	
James Armistead,	-	-	"	–	8	
John Conner,	-	-	"	–	8	
Robert Chumleigh,	-	-	"	–	8	
John Broadway,	-	-	"	–	8	
John Boatright,	-	-	"	–	8	
Griffin Dickerson,	-	-	"	–	8	
John T. Dicke,	-	-	"	–	8	
Joshua Davidson,	-	-	"	–	8	
Jennings Fowlkes,	-	-	"	–	8	
Pleasant Gauldin,	-	-	"	–	8	
John Hudson,	-	-	"	–	8	
William Jackson,	-	-	"	–	8	
William Leneve,	-	-	"	–	8	
James B. Medley,	-	-	"	–	8	
William D. Nash,	-	-	"	–	8	
Presley Nash,	-	-	"	–	8	
Thomas P. O'Brien,	-	-	"	–	8	
Sharp Spencer,	-	-	"	–	8	
Willard Uriah,	-	-	"	–	8	

MUSTER ROLL

Of Captain Joseph Reddish's Company, from the Forty-fifth Regiment, Virginia Militia, commanded by Lieutenant Colonel Samuel H. Peyton, in the Service of the United States from the 22nd July to 18th August, 1814.

NAMES.	RANK.	TIME OF SERVICE.		REMARKS.
		Months.	Days.	
Joseph Reddish,	Captain,	–	12	
Geo. Billingsley,	Lieutenant,	–	12	
Edward Templeman,	Ensign,	–	12	
Thomas Paine,	Sergeant,	–	12	
Samuel Geter,	"	–	12	
Jessee Curtice,	"	–	12	
William Lunceford,	"	–	12	
Ephraim Fritter,	Corporal,	–	12	
James Final,	"	–	12	
Abner Leitch,	"	–	12	
William Alexander,	Private,	–	12	
William Bryant,	"	–	12	
William Brown,	"	–	12	
John Boling,	"	–	12	
James Brummet,	"	–	12	
James Boling,	"	–	12	
William Brittice,	"	–	12	
Moseley Battalley,	"	–	12	
Richard Crop,	"	–	12	
James Conner,	"	–	12	
John Cristy,	"	–	12	
Lemuel Cox,	"	–	12	
Thomas Custice,	"	–	12	
Geo. Davill,	"	–	12	
Thomas Davice,	"	–	12	
Cad. J. Dade,	"	–	12	
Geo. Fergerson,	"	–	12	
Robert Final,	"	–	12	
John Fines,	"	–	12	
Geo. B. Fant,	"	–	12	
Richard Fant,	"	–	12	
Elijah Garrison,	"	–	12	
William Henry,	"	–	12	
William Harding,	"	–	12	
Geo. Holloway,	"	–	12	
G. M. Jamison,	"	–	12	
Peter Jett,	"	–	12	
William Jones,	"	–	12	
Jos. Jones,	"	–	12	
Silas Leich,	"	–	12	
William Limbrick,	"	–	12	
James Limbrick, sr.	"	–	12	
James Limbrick, jr.	"	–	12	
Thornton Lathram,	"	–	12	
John More,	"	–	12	
John McCarty,	"	–	12	
John McFee,	"	–	12	

NAMES.			RANK.	TIME OF SERVICE.		REMARKS.
				Months.	Days.	
John Maquis,	-	-	Private,	–	12	
Daniel Monson,	-	-	"	–	12	Or Monroe.
Fielding Monroe,	-	-	"	–	12	
John McColley,	-	-	"	–	12	
Lewis Pearman,	-	-	"	–	12	
Yelverton Perch,	-	-	"	–	12	
James Quisenberry,	-	-	"	–	12	
James Robertson,	-	-	"	–	12	
Jones Sullivant,	-	-	"	–	12	
James Smith,	-	-	"	–	12	
Morning Smith,	-	-	"	–	12	
James Spillman,	-	-	"	–	12	
William Tilley,	-	-	"	–	12	
Alexander Turner,	-	-	"	–	12	
William Templeman,	-	-	"	–	12	
Henry Turner,	-	-	"	–	12	
Ephram Templeman,	-	-	"	–	12	
Sidney Weshand,	-	-	"	–	12	
Jessee Williams,	-	-	"	–	12	
James Watson,	-	-	"	–	12	
Sincefield Young,	-	-	"	–	12	

Ensign Isaac Revere's Company—One Hundred and Ninth Regiment.

NAMES.	RANK.	TIME OF SERVICE.		REMARKS.
		Months.	Days.	
Nelson Humphreys, - -	Sergeant,	–	14	

(For rest of this company, see publication of Pay Rolls.)

Captain John Rothwell's Company—Seventh Regiment.

NAMES.	RANK.	TIME OF SERVICE.		REMARKS.
		Months.	Days.	
Samuel Johnson, - -	Fifer,	–	29	
Thomas Aude, - -	Private,			
Peter Belew, - -	"	3	20	Deserted.
Smedley Garnett, - -	"	–	–	Deserted.
David Higginbotham, -	"	–	8	Geo. Mills his sub.
Langsdon Henley, - -	"			
Benjamin Knight, - -	"			
Howell Lewis, - -	"	–	19	J. B. Linehaugh his sub.
Jos. B. Linehaugh, - -	"	–	–	Deserted.
Alexander McClure, - -	"	2	7	Sub. for Andrew Alexander.
John Mansfield, - -	"			
Pleasant Martin, - -	"	3	12	Sub. for Daniel Scott.
Fortunatus Nappier, - -	"	1	19	Deserted.
Philip Phillips, - -	"	1	15	
Amos Thacker, - -	"			
Rowland B. Wood, - -	"	2	29	Sub. for Chap .Maupin.

(For rest of this company, see publication of Pay Rolls.)

MUSTER ROLL

Of Captain Mills Riddick's Company—Fifty-ninth Regiment.

NAMES.	RANK.	TIME OF SERVICE.		REMARKS.
		Months.	Days.	
Mills Riddick, - -	Captain,	–	15	
Harrison Minton, - -	2d Lieutenant,	–	15	
Robert Riddick, - -	Cornet,	–	16	
Thomas P. Smith, - -	Sergeant,	–	21	
Charles Driver, - -	"	–	15	
Willis Cowling, - -	"	–	14	
Christopher Vandaman, -	Corporal,	–	29	
George Kelley, - -	"	–	22	
Thomas Green, - -	"	–	6	
David Godwin, - -	"	–	15	
Moses Ash, - -	Trumpeter,	–	6	
Jennings Bidgood, - -	Private,	–	21	
David Butler, - -	"	–	15	
Stephen Butler, - -	"	–	14	
Blake Campbell, - -	"	–	21	
William Dashall, - -	"	–	21	
Joseph Denson, - -	"	–	19	
William Denby, - -	"	–	29	
James Denby, - -	"	–	21	
William Gwinn, - -	"	–	22	
George Godwin, - -	"	–	6	
Thomas Holladay, - -	"	–	6	
John Johnson, - -	"	–	15	
Landawich Matthews, -	"	–	16	
Nathaniel Norfleet, -	"	–	15	
Wm. Oldham, - -	"	–	21	
Lebin Pitt, - -	"	–	14	
Thomas Rodgers, - -	"	–	15	
James Stallings, - -	"	–	16	
Robert Smith, - -	"	–	22	
Edward Wright, - -	"	–	16	
Seth Williams, - -	"	–	16	

(For rest of this company, see publication of Pay Rolls.)

MUSTER ROLL

Of Captain Thomas Ridley's Company, from the Sixty-fifth Regiment, Virginia Militia, commanded by Major Henry W. Wills, in the Service of the State of Virginia, from the 29th August to the 8th September, 1814.

NAMES.	RANK.	TIME OF SERVICE.		REMARKS.
		Months.	Days.	
Thomas Ridley,	Captain,	–	10	
Henry J. N. Westbrook,	Lieutenant,	–	10	
Archibald Washington	"	–	10	
Howell Nicholson,	Cornet,	–	10	
Richard Nick,	Sergeant,	–	10	
Alfred Simmons,	"	–	10	
Washington Clements,	"	–	10	
John Carr,	Corporal,	–	10	
Mike Harris,	"	–	10	
Jerry Gardner,	"	–	10	
James Miller,	"	–	10	
Bolling Barnes, (of John,)	Private,	–	10	
Bolling Barnes,	"	–	10	
Nathaniel Boush,	"	–	10	
John Barham,	"	–	10	
Alfred Baley,	"	–	10	
John Boykin,	"	–	10	
Joseph Cland,	"	–	10	
Joshua Cland,	"	–	10	
Jessee Clanton,	"	–	10	
Leonard Cobb,	"	–	10	
Joseph Drury,	"	–	10	
Richard Day,	"	–	10	
Josiah Eley,	"	–	10	
John Gardner,	"	–	10	
John Holleman,	"	–	10	
Hardy Harriss,	"	–	10	
Isaac O. Hollan,	"	–	10	
John Harriss,	"	–	10	
Charles Jennings,	"	–	10	
Nathan Jones,	"	–	10	
Joshua Joiner,	"	–	10	
James Newsom,	"	–	10	
John Norvel,	"	–	10	
Matthew Parker,	"	–	10	
Thomas Porter,	"	–	10	
Johnson Pope,	"	–	10	
Geo. Reaves,	"	–	10	
Amos Stephenson,	"	–	10	
Cyer Simmons,	"	–	10	
Bennett Stephenson,	"	–	10	
Jessee H. Summurel,	"	–	10	
John Tiller.	"	–	10	
Elisha Williams,	"	–	10	
Nicholas Williams,	"	–	10	
Geo. Whitfield,	"	–	10	
Ethelored Warren,	"	–	10	

NAMES.			RANK.	TIME OF SERVICE.		REMARKS.
				Months.	Days.	
James Wright,	-	-	Private,	–	10	
Henry Wiggins,	-	-	"	–	10	
James Wist,	-	-	"	–	10	
Willis Williamson,	-	-	"	–	10	

MUSTER ROLL

Of Captain Edward Robertson's Troop of Cavalry, from the Eleventh Regiment, Virginia Militia, in the Service of the State of Virginia, from the 28th August to 3d September, 1814.

NAMES.	RANK.	TIME OF SERVICE.		REMARKS.
		Months.	Days.	
Edward Robertson,	Captain,	—	7	
Charles J. Evans,	Lieutenant,	—	7	
Francis Nash,	"	—	7	
Isaac Morrice,	Cornet,	—	7	
Peyton Dosivell,	Sergeant,	—	7	Or Doswell.
Asa Cabaniss,	"	—	7	
Joseph S. Clarke,	"	—	7	
Richard Garrett,	Corporal,	—	7	
Anthony Cabiness,	"	—	7	
Moses Overton,	"	—	7	
John B. Oliver,	"	—	7	
James Burton,	Private,	—	7	
Peyton Baughn,	"	—	7	
Jessee Butler,	"	—	7	
Edward Bruce,	"	—	7	
John R. Bell,	"	—	7	
James Baram,	"	—	7	
Kenner Cralle,	"	—	7	
Moses Collier,	"	—	7	
Francis Carter,	"	—	7	
Pleasant Clarke,	"	—	7	
William Crittenden,	"	—	7	
John Dunevant,	"	—	7	
John Dickerson,	"	—	7	
Gabriel Folkes,	"	—	7	
Gideon Foster,	"	—	7	
Pascal Foster,	"	—	7	
John Foster,	"	—	7	
Cradock Foulks,	"	—	7	
James N. Fletcher,	"	—	7	
James Fletcher,	"	—	7	
James Goodwin,	"	—	7	
Daniel Hardaway,	"	—	7	
Joshua Hames,	"	—	7	
Thomas L. Hanley,	"	—	7	
John B. Holmes,	"	—	7	
William Hardaway,	"	—	7	
Freeman Jordon,	"	—	7	
John C. Jackson,	"	—	7	
Edmund Jefferies,	"	—	7	
Joseph B. Jregham,	"	—	7	
John W. Jennings,	"	—	7	
Sewelen Jones,	"	—	7	Or Lewelin.
Benj'n Jenkins,	"	—	7	
Simon C. Jackson,	"	—	7	
Tiscamer Knight,	"	—	7	
Sygnal Moore,	"	—	7	
Temple Lipscomb,	"	—	7	

NAMES.	RANK.	TIME OF SERVICE.		REMARKS.
		Months.	Days.	
Francis Nash, - -	Private,	–	7	
Rice Numan, - -	"	–	7	
Thomas Nelson, - -	"	–	7	
Robert Oliver, - -	"	–	7	
Thomas Pinch, - -	"	–	7	
Charles Rideant, - -	"	–	7	
Thomas Richardson, - -	"	–	7	
Shadwick Saidsburg, - -	"	–	7	
William Smith, (son of Hall,)	"	–	7	
Cumon Smith, - -	"	–	7	
Ezekiel Saidsbury, - -	"	–	7	
Thomas Salmons, - -	"	–	7	
William Smith, - -	"	–	7	
Daniel Verser, - -	"	–	7	
Bassett Watson, - -	"	–	7	
Anderson Jackson, - -	"	–	7	
Samuel Thomas, - -	"	–	7	
Anderson Gills, - -	"	–	7	
Green Holloway, - -	"	–	7	
John Stanley, - -	"	–	7	

MUSTER ROLL

Of Captain Michael Robins' Company, from the Ninety-ninth Regimen Virginia Militia, commanded by Lieutenant Colonel Charles Bagwell, in the Service of the United States, from the 28th May to 1st June, 1814.

NAMES.	RANK.	TIME OF SERVICE.		REMARKS.
		Months.	Days.	
Michael Robins, - -	Captain,	–	3	
James Duncan, -	Lieutenant,	–	1	
William S. Matthews, -	Ensign,	–	1	
James Milbourn, - -	Sergeant.	–	3	
James Missick, - -	"	–	3	
Crippin Delastatius, - -	"	–	3	
Geo. Bunting, - -	"	–	3	
Elijah Bunting, - -	Corporal,	–	3	
Elijah Hinman, - -	"	–	3	
Luther Hall, - -	"	–	3	
James Jenkins, - -	"	–	3	
Asa Matthews, - -	Drummer,	–	3	
John Porter, - -	Fifer,		3	
John Silverthorn, - -	Private,	–	3	
Noah Smith, - -	"	–	3	
Geo. Smith. - -	"	–	3	
Severn Wilson, - -	"		3	

Captain William A. Rogers' Company—Fourth Regiment.

NAMES.			RANK.	TIME OF SERVICE.		REMARKS.
				Months.	Days.	
William A. Rogers,	-	-	Captain,	1	29	
John B. Seawell,	-	-	Lieutenant,	1	29	
Hugh B. Gwyn,	-	-	"	1	29	
James Baytop,	-	-	Sergeant,	1	29	
Cornelius Livingston,		-	"	2	18	
Overton Sewell,	-	-	"	–	11	
John H. Saunders,	-	-	"	2	22	
Holt Claverius,	-	-	"	1	29	
James Leigh,	•	-	Corporal,	1	29	
Meakins Browning,	-	-	"	2	27	
Charles Burton,	-	•	"	1	29	
Henry L. Guthrie,	-	-	"	2	14	
Geo. D. Brister,	-	-	Private,	1	29	
John Bohannon,	-	-	"	1	29	
Robert Brown,	-	-	"	1	29	
Reuben B. Buckley,	-	-	"	1	29	
John Brown,	-	-	"	1	29	
James Bentley,	-	-	"	2	16	
Thomas Baytop,	-	-	"	3	19	
Leroy Brister,	-	-	"	2	8	
Thomas Coleman,	-	-	"	1	29	
James Crewdson,	-	-	"	2	17	
Thomas Douglas,	-	-	"	1	29	
Geo. W. Dare,	-	-	"	1	29	
John Dunston,	-	-	"	1	29	
Carter B. Dunlary,	-	-	"	1	29	
John Dawson,	-	-	"	1	29	
Henry Eaton,	-	-	"	–	3	
John Figg,	-	-	"	2	14	
William Flemming,	-	-	"	1	29	
Thos. Flemming,	-	-	"	1	29	
William Gibbs,	-	-	"	2	18	
Thomas Gayle,	-	-	"	2	4	
Edward Griffin,	-	-	"	1	29	
Robert Gwyn,	-	-	"	1	29	
Thomas Green,	-	-	"	–	19	
Ptolemy Graves,	-	-	"	–	11	
Thomas R. Hobday,	-	-	"	1	29	
Aderson Hall,	-	•	"	1	29	
James Hardy,	-	-	"	2	8	
James Jarvis,	-	-	"	1	29	
James H. Jones,	-	-	"	1	29	
William Jackmon,	-	-	"	1	29	
Samuel Jackmon,	-	•	"	1	29	
Edward Jarvis,	-	-	"	1	29	
Geo. Jackmon,	-	-	"	1	29	
Thomas Jarvis,	-	-	"	3	1	
William Kemp,	-	-	"	1	29	
William Leigh,	-	-	"	3	15	
William Lawson,	-	-	"	1	29	
Henry Mourning,	-	-	"	1	29	
Benjamin Minor,	-	-	"	1	29	
Joseph Minor,	-	-	"	1	29	
Joel Mitchim,	•	-	"	1	29	
John Minor,	-	-	"	1	29	

NAMES.	RANK.	TIME OF SERVICE.		REMARKS.
		Months.	Days.	
Richard Minor, - -	Private,	1	29	
James Philpotts, - -	"	1	29	
James Powers, - -	"	3		
Samuel Puller, - -	"	1	29	
Stephen Puller, - -	"	1	29	
John A. Pointer, - -	"	1	29	
Wm. Ransone, - -	"	—	17	
Thomas Robius, - -	"	1	29	
John Rowe, - -	"	—	15	
Edward Shurlds, - -	"	1	29	
Robert Saunders, - -	"	1	29	
Jacob Saunders, - -	"	2	11	
John Singleton, - -	"	2	15	
John H. Saunders, - -	"	—	16	
Charles E. Tompkins, -	"	2	3	
Francis West, - -	"	1	29	
Geo. West,, - -	"	1	29	
Richard West, - -	"	1	29	
William Wood, - -	"	1	29	
William Ransou, - -	"	1	29	
John Right, - -	"	1	29	

(For rest of this company, see publication of Pay Rolls.)

MUSTER ROLL

Of Captain William Ross' Company, from the Eighty-third Regiment, Virginia Militia, commanded by Lieutenant Colonel James Scott, in the Service of the United States, from the 1st to the 5th July, 1813, and from 28th August to 13th September 1814.

NAMES.	RANK.	TIME OF SERVICE.		REMARKS.
		Months.	Days.	
William Ross, - -	Captain,	–	22	
Edward Scott, - -	Lieutenant,	–	22	
Francis Scott, - -	"	–	22	
Thomas Rogers, - -	Cornet,	–	22	
Hamlin Hargrave, - -	Sergeant,	–	5	
Alex'r E. Bolling, -	"	–	5	
Thomas A. Oliver, -	"	–	22	
John C. Hambleton,	"	–	22	
Benjamin Pegram, - -	"	–	15	Transferred to Captain Pryor's troop 10th September.
Joel Manlove, - -	"	–	15	Transferred to Captain Pryor's troop 10th September.
William B. Clemans, -	Corporal,	–	5	
Andrew Waugh, - -	"	–	5	
William E. Booth, -	"	–	5	
Hartwell H. Hobbs, -	"	–	17	
Hardaway T. Rives, -	"	–	17	
Thomas Rose, -	"	–	17	
David Westmoreland, -	"	–	15	Transferred to Captain Pryor's comp'y 10th September.
John Abernathy, - -	Private,	–	20	Transferred to Captain Pryor's comp'y 10th September.
John Atkerson, - -	"	–	17	
Robert Bolling, - -	"	–	22	
John Bolling, - -	"	–	17	
Peterson Burge, - -	"	–	17	
Samuel P. Bolling, - -	"	–	17	
Alex'r E. Bolling, - -	"	–	15	Transferred to Captain Pryor's comp'y 10th September.
William E. Boothe, - -	"	–	15	Transferred to Captain Pryor's comp'y 10th September.
James Boothe, - -	"	–	5	
Robert Chappell, jr. - -	"	–	17	Substitute for John Chappell.
Benjamin H. Copeland, -	"	–	6	App'ted surgeon's mate 2d September.
John Chappell, - -	"	–	5	
John Dabney, - -	"	–	22	
Griffin Demovill, - -	"	–	5	
Lucas Elder, - -	"	–	5	
John Field, - -	"	–	1	Appointed hospital surgeon's mate 23d August.

NAMES.	RANK.	TIME OF SERVICE.		REMARKS.
		Months.	Days.	
John Grubbs, - -	Private,	—	15	Substitute for Sterling Woodward, and transferred to Captain Pryor's troop.
Merewether S. Gilliam, - -	"	—	22	
Benjamin Harris, - -	"	—	22	
Hartwell Hitchcock, - -	"	—	20	Transferred to Captain Pryor's troop on 10th Sept.
Burwell Hitchcock, - -	"	—	20	" " "
Alexander G. Hall, - -	"	—	15	" " "
Hartwell H. Hobbs, - -	"	—	5	
Benjamin Jackson, - -	"	—	—	Never joined.
Littleberry Jackson, - -	"	—	5	
John Lantroop, - -	"	—	15	Transferred to Captain Pryor's troop.
Peter M. Leadbetter, - -	"	—	17	" " "
Gustavus A. Muir, - -	"	—	17	
Isaac Oliver, - -	"	—	22	
William Pryor, - -	"	—	15	Transferred to Pryor's troop, 10th Sept.
Peter Pryde, - -	"	—	15	" " "
Nicholas Roney, - -	"	—	5	
Cincinatus Stith, - -	"	—	6	Appointed wagon master.
Peter Scott, - -	"	—	17	
William Stepperdson, -	"	—	20	Transferred to Captain Pryor's troop.
Anthony W. Smith, - -	"	—	15	" " "
Cary Wilkerson, - -	"	—	22	
Isaac Williamson, - -	"	—	22	
Charles Williamson, - -	"	—	17	
Vines C. Williamson, -	"	—	17	
Alexander Wells, - -	"	—	17	Substitute for Thomas Firth.
Sterling Woodward, - -	"	—	5	
John Watkins, - -	"	—	5	

MUSTER ROLL

Of Captain Richard Rouzee's Company from the Fourth Regiment, Virginia Militia, commanded by Lieutenant Colonel Archibald Ritchie, in the Service of the State of Virginia, from the 5th to 8th April, 1813, from 5th to 20th September, and from 1st to 9th of December, 1814.

NAMES.	RANK.	TIME OF SERVICE.		REMARKS.
		Months.	Days.	
Richard Rouzee,	Captain,	–	27	
Thos. Perkins,	Lieutenant,	–	3	
Lewis Crittenden,	"	–	3	
Edwin Upshaw,	"	–	24	
Archibald Gibson,	"	–	24	
Thomas Harper,	Sergeant,	–	27	
Edmund Munday,	"	–	3	
Meriday Munday,	"	–	3	
Robert Harper,	"	–	27	
Robert Coxton,	"	–	24	
James Wood,	"	–	23	
Edwin Davis,	Corporal,	–	24	
Josiah Stokes,	"	–	24	
Hugh Cox,	"	–	15	
Lewis Halbert,	"	–	15	
Stephen H. Garrett,	"	–	3	
Thos. M. Jones,	"	–	3	
Pitman Johnson,	Drummer,	–	14	
William Saunders,	Fifer,	–	15	
John Armstrong,	Private,	–	24	
Lawrence Andrews,	"	–	10	
William B. Banks,	"	–	26	
Austin Brooks,	"	–	24	
Henry H. Baughan,	"	–	15	
John Bragg,	"	–	25	
William Ball,	"	–	24	
John S. Revan,	"	–	26	
Meriday Brown,	"	–	24	
Thompson Beazley,	"	–	11	
William Beazley,	"	–	3	
Robert Clarke,	"	–	27	
Anthony D. Crow,	"	–	27	
Thomas Clark,	"	–	22	
John Collin,	"	–	24	
John Croxton,	"	–	24	
Zacha. Carter,	"	–	21	
Martin Coleman,	"	–	21	
William Coleman,	"	–	15	
Robert Crow,	"	–	8	
Robert Croxton,	"	–	2	
Hugh Cox,	"	–	2	
William Collin,	"	–	9	
Tanday Davis,	"	–	15	
James Davidson,	"	–	24	
Geo. Davis,	"	–	24	
Josiah Davis,	"	–	15	
Othnill Davis,	"	–	27	

NAMES.	RANK.	TIME OF SERVICE.		REMARKS.
		Months.	Days.	
Dunstead Davis, - -	Private,	—	24	
John Doggins, - -	"	—	25	
Edward Davis, - -	"	—	3	
Thomas Davis, - -	"	—	2	
John B. Elliott, - -	"	—	2	
Robert T. Evans, - -	"	—	2	
James Ferrill, - -	"	—	14	
Thomas Ferrill, - -	"	—	15	
William Ferrill, - -	"	—	17	
Daniel Gouldman, - -	"	—	23	
Whitefield Gatewood, -	"	—	23	
Edmond Goudy, - -	"	—	27	
Samuel Greenwood, - -	"	—	26	
Gabriel Gatewood, - -	"	—	15	
Waller L. Garrett, - -	"	—	4	
James Gatewood, - -	"	—	2	
Ranstell Hill, - -	"	—	17	
Robert Howerton, - -	"	—	25	
Major Harper, - -	"	—	3	
William Jefferis, - -	"	—	24	
Pitman Johnson, - -	"	—	2	
Richard Jones, - -	"	—	24	
Edmond Munday, - -	"	—	24	
William Munday, - -	"	—	26	
Harrison Munday, - -	"	—	18	
Thomas Minter, - -	"	—	24	
Baldwin S. Matthews, -	"	—	3	
Latane Montague, - -	"	—	3	
Reuben Noel, - -	"	—	15	
Thomas Pilcher, - -	"	—	27	
William Saunders, - -	"	—	2	
John Saunders, - -	"	—	25	
Thomas Stokes, - -	"	—	25	
Edmond P. Smith, - -	"	—	20	
Edmond Stokes, - -	"	—	3	
Stephen Smith, - -	"	—	14	
Edmund C. Smither, -	"	—	3	Or Smitcher.
Major J. B. Turner, - -	"	—	27	
John Tounger, - -	"	—	17	
William Taylor, - -	"	—	15	
Thomas Turner, - -	"	—	24	
Lemuel L. Woolard, - -	"	—	3	
James Wood, - -	"	—	3	
Samuel Harriss, - -	Servant,	—	15	

MUSTER ROLL

Of Captain John B. Royall's Troop of Cavalry, from the First Regiment, Virginia Militia, Halifax County, in the Service of the United States, from the 30th of August to 21st September, 1814, commanded by Lieutenant Colonel P. Halcomb.

NAMES.			RANK.	TIME OF SERVICE.		REMARKS.
				Months.	Days.	
John B. Royall,	-	-	Captain,	–	22	
R. D. Palmer,	-	-	Lieutenant,	–	22	
William Collins,	-	-	Cornet,	–	22	
John Abbott,	-	-	Sergeant,	–	22	
J. D. Spragins,	-	-	"	–	22	
D. P. Snead,	-	-	"	–	22	
Elisha Collins,	-	-	"	–	22	
William P. Carr,	-	-	Corporal,	–	22	
Lorenzo Thomas,	-	-	"	–	22	
John Wilbourne,	-	-	"	–	22	
James M. Cooper,	-	-	Musician,	–	22	
Fleming Mayard,	-	-	"	–	22	
Charles Bardette,	-	-	Private,	–	22	
James Bomar,	-	-	"	–	22	
Joseph Bass,	-	-	"	–	22	
James Bower,	-	-	"	–	22	
Samuel Barley,	-	-	"	–	22	
John Beadle,	-	-	"	–	22	
John Barley,	-	-	"	–	22	
William Bunting,	-	-	"	–	22	
Edward Baptist,	-	-	"	–	22	
Thomas Clarke,	-	-	"	–	22	
Allen Claybrooke,	-	-	"	–	22	
Robert Claybrooke,	-	-	"	–	22	
John Carr,	-	-	"	–	22	
Thomas T. Carr,	-	-	"	–	22	
Thomas Carr, sr.	-	-	"	–	22	
Philip Clay,	-	-	"	–	22	
Joseph M. Crews,	-	-	"	–	22	
George M. Crews,	-	-	"	–	22	
John B. Callahan,	-	-	"	–	22	
Drury Dunaway,	-	-	"	–	22	
James Elam,	-	-	"	–	22	
Mark L. Elam,	-	-	"	–	22	
Henry Fisher,	-	-	"	–	22	
James Y. Franklin,	-	-	"	–	22	
John Faris,	-	-	"	–	22	
William Fletcher,	-	-	"	–	22	
John Glascock,	-	-	"	–	22	
Elisha Hodges,	-	-	"	–	22	
Nathan Hensley,	-	-	"	–	22	
James Hankley,	-	-	"	–	22	
John Hubbard,	-	-	"	–	22	
Frederick Hodges,	-	-	"	–	22	
Joel Hubbard,	-	-	"	–	22	
Isaac Kirk,	-	-	"	–	22	

NAMES.	RANK.	TIME OF SERVICE.		REMARKS.
		Months.	Days.	
Curtis D. Kates, - -	Private,	–	22	
William Lee,	"	–	22	
William Moore, - -	"	–	22	
Edmund Martin, - -	"	–	22	
Zachariah Martin, - -	"	–	22	
William Martin, - -	"	–	22	
Philip McKenny, - -	"	–	22	
Thomas Meret, - -	"	–	22	
James Pettey, - -	"	–	22	
Banister Pridie, - -	"	–	22	
William Prindle, - -	"	–	22	
John Prindle, - -	"	–	22	
Banister J. Pindle, - -	"	–	22	
Hardaway Pindle, - -	"	–	22	
Lewis D. Poindexter, -	"	–	22	
Samuel Price, - -	"	–	22	
William Royall, - -	"	–	22	
James Rudder, - -	"	–	22	
William Ridgeway, - -	"	–	22	
Geo. Reaves, - -	"	–	22	
Francis Smith, - -	"	–	22	
Parhan Seamore, - -	"	–	22	
Paul Street, - -	"	–	22	
John Shuffield, - -	"	–	22	
William Tins, - -	"	–	22	
Elijah Vasser, - -	"	–	22	
Joseph Wilker, - -	"	–	22	
John Walker, - -	"	–	22	
Henry Wade, - -	"	–	22	
John Walne, - -	"	–	22	
Ambrose Walker, - -	"	–	22	
Robert L. Wilbourn, - -	"	–	22	
John Yates, - -	"		22	
Joel Younger, - -	"		22	
Thomas Younger, - -	"	–	22	
Wm'son Younger, - -	"		22	

MUSTER ROLL

Of Captain Thomas Royston's Company, from the Thirtieth Regiment, Virginia Militia, commanded by Major Reuben Tankersley, in the Service of the State of Virginia, from the 3d to 9th December, 1814.

NAMES.	RANK.	TIME OF SERVICE.		REMARKS.
		Months.	Days.	
Thomas Royston, - -	Captain,	–	6	
Richard Buckner, -	Lieutenant,	–	6	
Michael W. Yates, - -	Ensign,	–	6	
Austin Robinson, - -	Sergeant,	–	6	
Robert G. Holloway, - -	"	–	6	
Reuben Long, - -	"	–	6	
James C. Wiatt, - -	"	–	6	
Corbet Royston, - -	Corporal,	–	4	
Reuben Long, - -	"	–	6	
Eastus Woodford, - -	"	–	6	
John T. Bullock, - -	"	–	6	
Henry Baxter, - -	Private,	–	6	
Thornton Baxter, - -	"	–	6	
Charles Catlett, - -	"	–	6	
James Carter, - -	"	–	6	
Robert Catlett, - -	"	–	6	
William Callawn, - -	"	–	2	
Benjamin Catlett, - -	"	–	3	
Geo. Doggett, - -	"	–	6	
William Edwards, - -	"	–	6	
William Emberson, - -	"	–	6	
Thomas Farmer, - -	"	–	6	
William Graves, - -	"	–	6	
John Holloway, - -	"	–	6	
William Jones, - -	"	–	6	
James Long, - -	"	–	6	
Benjamin Long, - -	"	–	6	
John Lefoe, - -	"	–	6	
Abner Lefoe, - -	"	–	6	
Catlett Lawson, - -	"	–	6	
John Lawson, - -	"	–	6	
John Leland, - -	"	–	6	
Presley Merryman, - -	"	–	6	
Prewit Charles, - -	"	–	6	
William Peak, - -	"	–	6	
John Rose, - -	"	–	6	
Richard W. Royston, - -	"	–	6	
Anthony Rawlins, - -	"	–	6	
Abner Saunders, - -	"	–	6	
Leonard Samuels, - -	"	–	6	
Leonard S. Samuel, - -	"	–	3	
Thompson Samuel, - -	"	–	3	
Richard Satterwhite, - -	"	–	4	
Catlett Thomas, - -	"	–	6	
Philip W. Thornton, - -	"	–	6	
James Whitice, ● - -	"	–	3	

Captain Cornelius Sales' Company—Eighth Regiment.

NAMES.	RANK.	TIME OF SERVICE.		REMARKS.
		Months.	Days.	
Jacob Bogert, - -	Private,			
Nelson C. Dawson, - -	"	2		
John Hatton, - -	"	–	5	Sub. for J. Hatton.
Alexander N. Jones, - -	"	1	20	
Ambrose R. Marr, - -	"	1	11	Sub. for A. D. Marr.
Thomas Terry, - -	"			
Lawson G. Tyler, - -	"	–	6	Detached to Captain Johnson's company.

(For rest of this company, see publication of Pay Rolls.)

Captain George Shrum's Company—Thirteenth Regiment.

NAMES.	RANK.	TIME OF SERVICE.		REMARKS.
		Months.	Days.	
Jacob Sprecker, - -	Lieutenant,	–	14	
Daniel Hisey, - -	Private,	–	5	

(For rest of this company, see publication of Pay Rolls.)

Captain Henry W. Sales' Company—Sixty-first Regiment.

NAMES.	RANK.	TIME OF SERVICE.		REMARKS.
		Months.	Days.	
Robert Brooks, - -	Sergeant,	–	6	
Samuel Lewis, - -	"	–	9	
John Hughes, - -	"	–	9	
John Brownley, - -	"	–	6	On detach't from Capt. Jarvis' company.
Wm. Borum, - -	"	–	6	" "
John Thomas, - -	"	–	5	" "
John Billups, - -	"	–	6	On detach't from Capt. Billups' company.
John Foster, - -	"	–	6	" "
George Cully, - -	"	–	5	On detach't from Capt. James' company.
William Digges, - -	"	–	6	" "
Robert Hunley, - -	"	–	5	" "
Samuel D. White, - -	"	–	5	" "
John G. Culveres, - -	"	–	6	On detach't from Capt. Foster's company.
John Digges, - -	"	–	6	On detach't from Capt. B. Digges' compa'y.
Edward White, - -	"	–	6	On detach't from Capt. Hughes' company.
Joseph Brownley, -	Corporal,	–	5	On detach't from Capt. Jarvis' company.
James Davis (of Wm.) -	"	–	5	" "
Daniel Davis, - -	"	–	6	" "
Armistead Miller, - -	"	–	10	" "
Spencer Brown, - -	"	–	5	On detach't from Capt. James' company.
Elias Pugh, - -	"	–	6	" "
William Turner, - -	"	–	6	" "
Joseph White, - -	"	–	5	" "
Robert Dibnam, - -	"	–	6	On detach't from Capt. Hughes' company.
Robert Parrott, - -	"	–	6	On detach't from Capt. Foster's company.
Leonard D. Thompson, -	"	–	4	
John Hughes, - -	"	–	8	
Jesse White, - -	"	–	9	
George Digges, - -	"	–	9	
Humphrey Hunley, . -	Drummer,	–	16	On detach't from Capt. Hughes' company.
Carey James, - -	"	–	5	On detach't from Capt. James' company.
Richard Blake, - -	Fifer,	–	9	
John Plummer, - -	"	–	16	" "
Robert Armistead, - -	Private,	–	5	" "
Ben. Adams, - -	"			
Isaac Armistead, - -	"	–	5	On detach't from Capt. James' company.
Richard Ayres, - -	"	–	4	
John Ayres, - -	"	–	6	On detach't from Capt. Billups' company.
Ralph Armistead, - -	"	–	10	On detach't from Capt. Jarvis' company.

NAMES.	RANK.	TIME OF SERVICE.		REMARKS.
		Months.	Days.	
Moses Atherton,	Private,	–	2	
Robert Armistead,	"	–	5	On detachment from Capt. Jarvis' co.
James Adams,	"	–	10	On detachment from Capt. Foster's co.
Thomas Anderton,	"	–	7	
Robert Anderson,	"			
John D. Anderson,	"			
George Brownley,	"	–	6	On detachment from Capt. Hughes' co.
Foster Brownley,	"	–	6	On detachment from Capt. James' co.
John Borum,	"	–	6	" " "
John Basset,	"			
George Borum,	"	–	15	On detachment from Capt. Jarvis' co.
James Brown,	"	–	1	
Conrad A. Booze,	"	–	1	On detachment from Capt. Billups' co.
Thomas Billups,	"	–	6	" " "
Thomas Basset,	"	–	4	
Thomas Brownley,	"	–	11	On detachment from Capt. James' co.
William Blake, sr.	"	–	3	
Arch'd Brownley,	"	–	5	On detachment from Capt. Jarvis' co.
John Brownley,	"	–	4	
Edm'd Borum,	"	–	5	" " "
William D. Butler,	"	–	4	
William Brooks,	"	–	9	
Joseph Brownley,	"	–	9	
Wm. Brownley,	"	–	8	
Wm. F. Blake, sr.	"	–	4	
William Brown,	"	–	5	
William Carter,	"	–	3	
Arthur Clayton,	"	–	2	
James Callis,	"	–	11	On detachment from Capt. Foster's co.
John S. Clayton,	"	–	3	
Robert Callis,	"	–	1	" " "
John Callis,	"			
Iverson Carney,	"	–	9	
Richard Cray,	"	–	4	
John Dudley,	"	1	7	
George E. Dudley,	"	–	4	
John Davis,	"	–	15	On detachment from Capt. Jarvis' co.
William Davis,	"	–	13	On detachment from Capt. James' co.
Miles H. Dawson,	"			
Humphrey Davis,	"	–	5	On detachment from Capt. Jarvis' co.
Christopher Davis,	"	–	5	" " "
William Dance,	"	–	4	
James Davis, (of James,)	"	–	10	" " "
Job Digges,	"	–	9	
Augustin Digges,	"	–	9	
Tinley Dixon,	"	–	9	
Robert Dixon,	"	–	8	
Armistead Davis,	"			
Wm. D. Drisdale,	"	–	24	
Henry F. Everidge,	"	–	9	
Jesse Forrest,	"	–	6	On detachment from Capt. James' co.
Henry Fleet,	"	–	19	
James Fleetwood,	"	–	6	On detachment from Capt. Foster's co.

NAMES.	RANK.	TIME OF SERVICE.		REMARKS.
		Months.	Days.	
Thomas Forrest, - -	Private,	–	4	
Armistead Flipping, - -	"	–	6	On detachment from Capt. Billups' co.
Matthew Forrest, - -	"	–	5	On detachment from Capt. James' co.
Phillip Forrest, - -	"	–	5	" "
George Finch, - -	"	–	13	
Rowland W. Finch, - -	"	–	6	
Thomas Fitchett, - -	"	–	9	
Horace Fitchett, - -	"	–	2	
Henry Griffin, - -	"	–	17	
Robert Gwyn, - -	"	–	8	
Armistead Griffin, - -	"	–	26	
Bartlett Gayle, - -	"			
Ebenezer Gray, - -	"	–	3	
Thomas Hugett, - -	"	–	6	On detachment from Capt. B. Digges' co.
Hugh Hudgin, - -	"	–	6	" "
Matthew Hunley, - -	"	–	3	On detachment from Capt. Hughes' co.
Isaac Hudgin, - -	"	–	6	On detachment from Capt. James' co.
Peter Hudgin, - -	"	–	6	" "
Bailey Hudgin, - -	"	–	6	" "
Patrick Horan, - -	"			
Warner Hudgin, - -	"	–	6	" "
William Hudgin, - -	"	–	6	On detachment from Capt. Jarvis' co.
Houlder Hudgin, - -	"	–	6	" "
Matthew Hunley, - -	"	–	6	On detachment from Capt. Foster's co.
Leroy Hudgins, - -	"	–	4	
Lewis Hudgins, - -	"	–	19	" "
Bartlett Hurst, - -	"	–	5	On detachment from Capt. James' co.
William Hobday, - -	"	–	6	
Edward Hughes, - -	"	–	9	
Thos. Hurst, - -	"	–	9	
William Hurst, - -	"	–	5	
Josiah Hugel, - -	"	–	9	
Philip Hughes, - -	"	–	4	
William Hudgins, - -	"	–	9	
Richard L. Hilling, - -	"	–	2	
Anthony Hudgins, - -	"	–	9	
John Jarvis, - -	"	–	10	On detachment from Capt. Jarvis' co.
John Jarvis, (of Francis,) -	"	–	4	" "
Thomas James, - -	"	–	10	Substitute for R. Lightburn.
James Jarvis, - -	"	–	4	
Robert Lightburn, - -	"	–	3	On detachment from Capt. Jarvis' co.
James Litchfield, - -	"	–	3	
James Minter, (of Jno.) -	"	–	6	On detachment from Capt. James' co.
Josiah Minter, - -	"	–	6	" "
Thomas Minter, - -	"	–	6	" "
Robert Matthews, - -	"	–	5	" "
James Minter, - -	"	–	9	
Mark Morgan, - -	"	–	4	
Rich'd Morgan, - -	"			
Edward Owen, - -	"	–	6	On detachment from Capt. Jarvis' co.
Zacheus Owen, - -	"	–	6	On detachment from Capt. Billups' co.

NAMES.	RANK.	TIME OF SERVICE.		REMARKS.
		Months.	Days.	
Ransone Párrott, - -	Private,	–	10	On detachment from Capt. Foster's co.
Robert Pead, - -	"	–	14	On detachment from Capt. James' co.
Jerry Parish, -	"	–	6	Sub. for J. Anderson, Capt. Foster's co.
John Parrott, - -	"	–	9	
Henry Powell, - -	"	–	8	
Absalom Parsons, - -	"	–	4	
John Parsons, - -	"	–	5	
John Ripley, - -	"	–	6	On detachment from Capt. James' co.
William Richardson, -	"	–	9	
William Ripley, -	"	–	5	On detachment from Capt. Jarvis' co.
William Simmons, -	"	–	6	On detachment from Capt. Hughes' co.
George Simmonds, -	"	–	4	
John Scott, -	"	–	15	On detachment from Capt. Jarvis' co.
Edward Smith, - -	"	–	5	" " "
John Sadler, - -	"	–	10	On detachment from Capt. Foster's co.
Robert Sadler, - -	"	–	3	
Armistead Smith, - -	"	–	6	" " "
Philip W. Spark, - -	"	–	3	
William Simmons, -	"	–	6	On detachment from Capt. Billups' co.
Richard Sadler, - -	"	–	6	
James Saunders, - -	"			
James Spratt, - -	"	–	8	
Joshua Smith, - -	"	–	14	
John Thomas, - -	"	–	6	On detachment from Capt. James' co.
Leonard D. Thompson, -	"	–	6	On detachment from Capt. Foster's co.
Armistead Thomas, -	"	–	5	On detachment from Capt. James' co.
Hunley Thomas, - -	"	–	9	
Moses Terrier, - -	"	1	3	
James M. Vaughan, -	"	–	13	
Daniel Wise, - -	"	–	1	
John White, - -	"	–	6	Sub. for Jno. Davis, on detachment from Capt. Hughes' co.
William White, - -	"	–	6	Sub. for Ed. Smith.
Christ. Weston, - -	"	–	6	On detachment from Capt. Digges' co.
Robert Weston, - -	"	–	6	On detachment from Capt. James' co.
Thomas Willis, -	"	–	6	On detachment from Capt. Foster's co.
John Watson, - -	"	–	6	" " "
Lewis B. Wyatt, - -	"	–	6	" " "
Abram Williams, -	"	–	6	On detachment from Capt. Billups' co.
Francis Williams, -	"	–	5	On detachment from Capt. Jarvis' co.
James White, -	"	–	6	On detachment from Capt. Hughes' co.
Isaac White, - -	"	–	8	
Absulom White, - -	"	–	8	
James Wood, - -	"	–	15	
Thomas Willis, - -	"			

(For rest of this company, see publication of Pay Rolls.)

MUSTER ROLL

Of Captain Joseph Sandford's Company of Cavalry, from the Sixty-ninth Regiment, Virginia Militia, in the County of Halifax, called into Service under general orders of the 27th June, 1813, from 27th June to 19th August, in the year 1813.

NAMES.			RANK.	TIME OF SERVICE.		REMARKS.
				Months.	Days.	
Joseph Sandford,	-	-	Captain,	1	23	
Benjamin Marable,	-	-	Lieutenant,	1	23	
Stephen Davenport,	-	-	"	1	23	
William Martin,	-	-	Cornet,	1	23	
Clement Ragland,	-	-	Sergeant,	1	23	
Jeremiah Moore,	-	-	"	1	23	
Beverley Sydnor,	-	-	"	1	23	
William Chambers,	-	-	"	1	23	
Richard Oliver,	-	-	Corporal,	1	23	
Pleasant Farmer,	-	-	"	1	23	
Edward Stubblefield,	-	-	"	1	23	
Samuel H. McCraw,	-	-	"	1	23	
Elisha Bell,	-	-	Private,	1	23	
Charles Brice,	-	-	"	1	23	
William Brance,	-	-	"	1	22	
Harrison Bowen,	-	-	"	1	23	
John Britton,	-	-	'	1	23	
John Claiborne,	-	-	"	1	23	
Paul Carrington,	-	-	"	1	23	
Aansy Carrington,	-	-	"	1	23	
George Claughton,	-	-	"	1	23	
William S. Craddock,	-	-	"	1	23	
Theo. Carter,	-	-	"	1	23	
John B. Dodson,	-	-	"	1	23	
Elisha Dodson,	-	-	"	1	23	
Caleb Dodson,	-	-	"	1	23	
Thomas Dodson,	-	-	"	1	23	
Richard Edmonson,	-	-	"	1	23	
Edmund Edmundson,	-	-	"	1	23	
Martin Ferrill,	.	-	"	1	23	
Richard Fling,	-	-	"	1	23	
James Gann,	-	-	"	1	23	
Thomas Gresham,	-	-	"	1	23	
Thomas Glascock,	-	-	"	1	23	
John Hobson,	-	-	"	1	23	
Thomas C. Hoskins,	-	-	"	1	23	
Edward P. Hughs,	-	-	"	1	23	
Daniel Irvine,	-	-	"	1	23	
Richard Jordan,	-	-	"	1	23	
Bird Janner,	-	-	"	1	23	
Isham Lane,	-	-	"	1	23	
Edward Morriss,	-	-	"	1	23	
Samuel Major,	-	-	"	1	23	
John Oliver,	-	-	"	1	23	
Samuel Pate,	-	-	"	1	23	
Roper Ribis,	-	-	"	1	23	
Joseph Royall,	-	-	"	1	23	

NAMES.	RANK.	TIME OF SERVICE.		REMARKS.
		Months.	Days.	
Dabner Ragland, - -	Private,	1	23	
Josiah Robertson, - -	"	1	23	
John W. Scott, - -	"	1	23	
Joel Tynes, - -	"	1	23	
John Talknor, - -	"	1	23	
James P. Vass, - -	"	1	23	
Philip Vass, - -	"	1	23	
Robert Williams, - -	"	1	23	
Christopher Wooding, -	"	1	23	

Captain Robert Saunders' Troop of Cavalry—Sixty-eighth Regiment.

NAMES.	RANK.	TIME OF SERVICE.		REMARKS.
		Months.	Days.	
Ro. Saunders, - -	Captain,			
Geo. R. Avery, - -	Sergeant,	—	24	
Edward Teagle, - -	Corporal,	—	24	
Edward Turner, - -	"	—	29	
John E. Allen, - -	Private,	—	29	
William S. Bacon, - -	"	—	28	
Carter Burwell, - -	"			
Ancelm Bailey, - -	"	—	19	
Henry Bolton, - -	"	—	11	
Roscoe Cole, - -	"	—	11	
John Coggin, - -	"	—	26	
Will. Hankins, - -	"	—	29	
Parke Jones, - -	"	—	13	
William A. Lucy, - -	"			
Wm. C. Mountcastle, -	"	1	2	
John Powell, - -	"	—	16	
Baker Perkins, - -	"			
Philip Smith, - -	"	—	29	

(For rest of this company, see publication of Pay Rolls.)

·MUSTER ROLL

Of Captain George Scarborough's Company, of the Second Regiment, Virginia Militia, in the County of Accomack, called into the Service under the general orders of the 22nd of May, 1813, from the 22nd to the 29th May, in the same year.

NAMES.	RANK.	TIME OF SERVICE.		REMARKS.
		Months.	Days.	
George Scarborough, -	Captain,	—	8	
William Custis, - -	Lieutenant,	—	8	
Henry Finney, - -	Ensign,	—	8	
James R. Ashmead, - -	Q. Sergeant,	—	8	Joined artillery.
Wm. Dix, - -	Sergeant,	—	8	
Thomas Sturgis, - -	"	—	8	
Thomas C. Gibb, - -	"	—	8	" "
Edward S. Snead, - -	"	—	8	" "
McKeel Bonwell, - -	Drummer,	—	4	" "
Charles Bradford, - -	Private,	—	4	
George Bloxsom, - -	"	—	8	
Elijah Bloxsom, - -	"	—	8	
Jesse Belote, - -	"	—	8	
Walter Belote, - -	"	—	8	
Charles Belote, - -	"	—	8	
Jesse Bonwell, - -	"	—	8	
William Charrock, - -	"	—	8	
Henry Custis, - -	"	—	8	
George Carmine, - -	"	—	8	" "
Edward Charnock, - -	"	—	8	
George Chandler, - -	"	—	8	
Edmund Cow, - -	"	—	4	
Carvey Dunton, - -	"	—	8	
Lemuel Dalby, - -	"	—	4	
John Finney, jr. - -	"	—	8	
Walter Finney, - -	"	—	8	
John Grant, - -	"	—	4	
John Hallet, - -	"	—	8	
William Hannaford, - -	"	—	8	" "
Revel Kellam, - -	"	—	4	
James Kellam, - -	"	—	4	
Edmund Leatherburg, -	"	—	8	
Thomas Leatherburg, -	"	—	8	" "
George. P. Leatherburg, -	"	—	8	" "
Jedediah Lester, - -	"	—	8	
James Lester, - -	"	—	8	
William Lawrence, - -	"	—	8	
Kendull Lawrence, - -	"	—	8	
William Moddleston, - -	"	—	8	
Jacob Mayron, - -	"	—	8	
Thomas F. Matthews, - -	"	—	8	
Jesse Minter, - -	"	—	4	
Francis Ounley, - -	"	—	8	
Jacob Phillips, - -	"	—	8	
John Phillips, - -	"	—	8	
William Rodgers, - -	"	—	8	" "
John Savage, - -	"	—	4	

NAMES.			RANK.	TIME OF SERVICE.		REMARKS.
				Months.	Days.	
Edmund Savage,	-	-	Private,	—	8	
John Satchell,			"	—	8	Joined artillery.
James Savage,	-	-	"	—	8	
Levin Savage,	-	-	"	—	8	
Jacob Savage,	-	-	"	—	8	" "
Aaron Shores,	-	-	"	—	8	
James Smith,	-	-	"	—	4	
Ezekiel Smith,	-	-	"	—	4	
George Turner,	-	-	"	—	8	" "
Samuel Winder,	-	-	"	—	4	
Zoro. E. Wise,	-	-	"	—	8	" "
John B. Warrington,	-	-	"	—	8	
John K. Warrington,	-	-	"	—	8	

Captain Henry Scarborough's Company of Artillery—Twenty-seventh Regiment.

NAMES.	RANK.	TIME OF SERVICE.		REMARKS.
		Months.	Days.	
Henry Scarborough, - -	Captain,	—	11	
William Simkins, - -	Lieutenant,	—	11	
Henry Kendall, - -	"	—	11	
Thomas Williams, - -	Sergeant,	—	11	
Jas. Fisher, - -	"	—	11	
Wm. Floyd, - -	"	—	11	
Thos. Willis, - -	"	—	11	
Allen Brown, - -	Corporal,	—	11	
Reavel Savage, - -	"	—	11	
Litt'n Hyslop, - -	"	—	11	
Jacob Nottingham, - -	"	—	11	
Jno. Ewing, - -	Drummer,	—	11	
James Williams, - -	Fifer,	—	11	
Rich'd Bell, - -	Private,	—	11	
Jno. Bishop, - -	"	—	11	
Thomas Capes, - -	"	—	11	
Isaac Caple, - -	"	—	11	
Charles Dilliard, - -	"	—	11	
Ely Dowtry, - -	"	—	11	
Thos. Downs, - -	"	—	11	
George Esham, - -	"	—	11	
Luke Griffit, - -	"	—	11	
George Halt, - -	"	—	11	
Shaddarick Hall, - -	"	—	11	
Nathaniel Jones, - -	"	—	11	
George Luke, - -	"	—	11	
Wm. Nottingham, - -	"	—	11	
Thomas L. Nolin, - -	"	—	11	
Joseph Nottingham, - -	"	—	11	
Jarret Palker, - -	"	—	11	
James Privot. - -	"	—	11	
Zoro. Pratt, - -	"	—	11	
Temple N. Rabers, - -	"	—	11	
Calvin H. Read, - -	"	—	11	
George Scott, - -	"	—	11	
John Smaw, - -	"	—	11	
Harry Smaw, - -	"	—	11	
Michael Savage, - -	"	—	11	
William Teakle, - -	"	—	11	
Nath. Triosh, - -	"	—	11	
John Taylor, - -	"	—	11	
Robert F. Williams, - -	"	—	11	
Wm. Wilson, sen'r, - -	"	—	11	
Josiah Willis, - -	"	—	11	
Jno. Wilson, - -	"	—	11	
Levin G. Winder, - -	"	—	11	
John Warrington, - -	"	—	11	
Jno. Welch, - -	"	—	11	
Jno. Yateman, - -	"	—	11	

(For rest of this company, see publication of Pay Rolls.)

Captain William M. Scarbrough's Company—Second Regiment.

NAMES.	RANK.	TIME OF SERVICE.		REMARKS.
		Months.	Days.	
Shadrack Ames,	Cornet,	–	10	
Smith Stringer,	Sergeant,	–	10	
John Robins,	"	–	10	
Thomas H. Bradford,	Musician,	–	4	
William Addison,	Private,	1	5	
Thomas H. Ames,	"	–	16	
James Ames,	"	–	22	
James Bunting,	"	–	18	
Thomas H. Bradford,	"	–	21	
George Babe,	"	–	8	
James Benson,	"	–	6	
William Colony,	"	–	17	
Shadrack Darley,	"	–	19	
Isaac Duncan,	"	–	5	
Shadrack Darby,	"	–	8	
Isaac Dunton,	"	–	15	
Richard W. East,	"	–	23	
Benj. Floyd,	"	–	25	
John Funio,	"	–	5	
Henry Folio,	"	–	28	
Edmund Garretson,	"	–	24	
Edw'd Gandun,	"	–		
Tho's U. Hack,	"	–		
Tho's Holmes,	"	–	2	
Benj. Holmes,	"	1	2	
Abel B. Johnston,	"	–	1	
John Jacobs,	"	–	5	
Johnson Kellam,	"	–	27	
John Lilliston,	"	–		
Richard Mears,	"	–	20	
William Mason,	"	–	8	
William Major,	"	–	8	
James W. Parker,	"	–	11	
William A. Parker,	"	–	10	
Richard Rodgers,	"	–	9	
William H. Rodgers,	"	–		
Richard H. Rodgers,	"	–	8	
John Robins,	"	–	6	
Bowden Robins,	"	–	6	
James Savage,	"	–		
S. Stringer,	"	–	13	
James Savage,	"	–	6	
Hillery B. Skinner,	"	–	3	
Hillery Stringer,	"	–	8	
Shadrack Starling,	"	–	21	
William Stockley,	"	–	28	
John Smith, jr.	"	–	20	
Mitchell Scarborough,	"	–	10	
George Scott,	"	–	5	
Edwin Teackle,	"	–	5	

NAMES.			RANK.	TIME OF SERVICE.		REMARKS.
				Months.	Days.	
Samuel Trader,	-	-	Private,	–	15	
Shepherd Wilkins,	-	-	"	–	13	
John Wilkins,	-	-	"	1	28	
John R. West,	-	-	"	–		
Mitchell S. West,	-	-	"	–	25	

(For rest of this company, see publication of Pay Rolls.)

Captain Richard B. Scervant's Company—One Hundred and Fifteenth Regiment.

NAMES.	RANK.	TIME OF SERVICE.		REMARKS.
		Months.	Days.	
Richard B. Scervant,	Captain,	–	3	
James Banks,	Ensign,	–	3	
William Face,	Sergeant,	–	3	
Wilson W. Jones,	"	–	3	
Thomas L. Nicholson,	"	–	3	
James Face,	"	–	3	
Thomas French,	Corporal,	–	3	
Michel King,	"	–	3	
William Patrick,	"	–	3	
William Budd,	"	–	3	
Michel Burkman,	Musician,	–	3	
William B. Armistead,	Private,	–	3	
John C. Brown,	"	1	4	
James Briggs,	"	–	3	
William Beird,	"	–	3	
Edward Barris,	"	–	3	
Edward Baines,	"	–	23	
John Crandal,	"	–	3	
Charles Cooper,	"	–	3	
Alex'r J. Calvert,	"	–	3	
Levy Core,	"	–	3	
Thomas Dixon,	"	–	3	
Gilbert Davis,	"	–	3	
John Field,	"	–	3	
Nathaniel Hawthorn,	"	–	3	
Thomas Hope,	"	–	3	
Wilton Hope,	"	–	3	
William Hope,	"	–	3	
Cornelius Hicks,	"	–	3	
Stephen Hopkins,	"	–	3	
John Hope,	"	–	3	
William C. Hicks,	"	–	24	
Henry Jenkins,	"	–	3	
Henry King,	"	–	3	
George Latimer,	"	–	3	
Joseph S. Latimer,	"	–	3	
Thomas A. Marion,	"	–	3	
William Massenburg,	"	–	3	
Edward Moss,	"	–	3	
William V. Nettles,	"	–	3	
John Prisson,	"	–	3	
John Page,	"	–	3	
Richard Poll,	"	–	3	
William Parrish,	"	–	3	
John Poole,	"	–	24	
Thomas Roberts,	"	–	3	
Butts Roberts,	"	–	3	
Henry Robinson,	"	–	3	
George Randolph,	"	–	24	
William Sealey,	"	–	3	
Bowman Siliston,	"	–	3	
William Smalt,	"	–	3	
James Saunders,	"	–	3	

NAMES.			RANK.	TIME OF SERVICE.		REMARKS.
				Months.	Days.	
Johnson Smith,	-	-	"	—	3	
Samuel Thomas,	-	-	"	—	3	
Charles Thompson,	-	-	"	—	3	
William Tompkins,	-	-	"	—	3	
Henry Thompson,		-	"	—	24	
Edward Whitaker,	-	-	"	—	4	
John Willings,	-	-	"	—	3	
William Westwood,	-	-	"	—	3	

(For rest of this company, see publication of Pay Rolls.)

MUSTER ROLL

Of Captain Wm. S. Sclater's Company, of the One Hundred and Fifteenth Regiment, Virginia Militia, in the County of York, called into actual Service under the orders of the Lieutenant Colonel, from 26th June to 7th July, 1813.

NAMES.			RANK.	TIME OF SERVICE.		REMARKS.
				Months.	Days.	
William S. Sclater,	-	-	Captain,	–	12	
Miles C. Chesman,	-	-	Lieutenant,	–	12	
Robert Pescud,	-	-	Ensign,	–	12	
William Wilson,	-	-	Sergeant,	–	12	
John Hunt,	-	-	"	–	12	
Wm. S. Wills,	-	-	"	–	12	
John Powell,	-	-	"	–	12	
Thos. Phillips,	-	-	Corporal,	–	12	
Wm. M. Dixon,	-	-	"	–	12	
Ro. Howard,	-	-	"	–	12	Joined Capt. Cooper's troop July 4, 1813.
Edward Baptist,	-	-	"	–	12	
Absalom Cox,	-	-	Private,	–	12	
Henry Drewry,	-	-	"	–	12	
Henry Freeman,	-	-	"	–	12	
James Hopkins,	-	-	"	–	12	
Wm. Hopkins,	-	-	"	–	12	
Mathias Jusley,	-	-	"	–	12	
John Jusley,	-	-	"	–	12	
Naboth Jusley,	-	-	"	–	12	
Henry Martin,	-	-	"	–	12	
George Martin,	-	-	"	–	12	
Anthony Morris,	-	-	"	–	12	
Middleton Melson,	-	-	"	–	12	
Ambrose Morris,	-	-	"	–	12	
Wm. Morris,	-	-	"	–	12	
Wm. Moore,	-	-	"	–	12	
Custis Myrick,	-	-	"	–	12	
Merill Moore,	-	-	"	–	12	
Wm. Phillips,	-	-	"	–	12	
Rooksberry Roberts,	-	-	"	–	12	
Joseph Rollins,	-	-	"	–	12	
John R. Topping,	-	-	"	–	12	
James Wilson,	-	-	"	–	12	
Peter Wright,	-	-	"	–	12	
Dudley Wright,	-	-	"	–	12	
Nelson Wright,	-	-	"	–	12	
Wm. Wright,	-	-	"	–	12	

Captain William C. Scott's Company—Twenty-eighth Regiment.

NAMES.	RANK.	TIME OF SERVICE.		REMARKS.
		Months.	Days.	
Mathew Lanford, - -	Lieutenant,	–	15	
James Edmonds, - -	Sergeant,	–	9	
Jesse Becknal, - -	Private,			
Woodson Fitzgerald, - -	"			
Alexander Fitzpatrick, -	"	–	29	
John Harris, jr. - -	"			
John Henderson, - -	"	–	16	
William Hudson, - -	"	–	26	
Larkin Miller, - -	"			
Walker Nicholas, - -	"			
Abram Polack, - -	"	–	20	
Alexander B. Rose, - -	"			
William Settles, - -	"			

(For rest of this company, see publication of Pay Rolls.)

Captain Samuel Steele's Company—At Camp Holly.

NAMES.	RANK.	TIME OF SERVICE.		REMARKS.
		Months.	Days.	
James Blair, - -	Private,	–	–	No time given.
William Howman, - -	"			
Amos Pharp, - -	"			

(For the rest of this company, see publication of Pay Rolls.)

MUSTER ROLL

Of Captain Clement Shackleford's Company, from the Forty-first Regiment, Virginia Militia, commanded by Lieutenant Colonel Vincent Branham, in the Service of the United States, from the 21st to 29th September, from 5th to 8th October, and from 30th November to 8th December, in the year 1814.

NAMES.	RANK.	TIME OF SERVICE.		REMARKS.
		Months.	Days.	
Clement Shackleford, -	Captain,	—	13	
Daniel Garland, - -	Lieutenant,	—	13	Adjutant to the regiment.
Edmond Northen, - -	"	—	9	
Jeremiah Garland, - -	Ensign,	—	13	
Samuel B. Kilsick, - -	Sergeant,	—	12	
Thomas P. Ball, - -	"	—	12	
Thomas T. Reynolds, -	"	—	4	
William Burgess, - -	"	—	8	
Thomas Bryant, - -	"	—	8	
Charles Damron, - -	"	—	8	
Samuel Bryant, - -	Corporal,	—	8	
Samuel L. Damron, - -	"	—	8	
Ewel Hanks, - -	"	—	8	
John Bryant, - -	"	—	8	
Eidson Matthew, - -	Fifer,	—	8	
Mozingo Thomas, - -	Drummer,	—	7	
James Adams, - -	Private,	—	8	
Elijah Ambrose, - -	"	—	7	
Thomas Brown, - -	"	—	7	
Edward Brown, - -	"	—	8	
Samuel Bearcraft, - -	"	—	8	
John Brown, - -	"	—	7	
Thomas Berrick, - -	"	—	9	
Hudson Brown, - -	"	—	7	
Isaac Bishop, - -	"	—	12	
John Billings, - -	"	—	5	
Jesse Bowen, - -	"	—	8	
Thaddeus Bryant, - -	"	—	6	
William Brown, - -	"	—	8	
Christopher Brown, -	"	—	8	
Jonathan W. Bowen, -	"	—	7	
John Bowing, - -	"	—	9	
James Crain, - -	"	—	12	
John Cash, - -	"	—	12	
William T. Clark, - -	"	—	8	
Austin Dodson, - -	"	—	8	
William Duff, - -	"	—	8	
Edward Douglass, - -	"	—	5	
Samuel Donoway, - -	"	—	8	
Achilles Dale, - -	"	—	8	
Lindsey Davenport, - -	"	—	8	
Rawleigh Dodson, - -	"	—	5	
Thomas Dodson, - -	"	—	2	
John English, - -	"	—	8	
William Forister, - -	"	—	8	
Samuel Fones, - -	"	—	5	
James M. Fones, - -	"	—	8	

NAMES.	RANK.	TIME OF SERVICE.		REMARKS.
		Months.	Days.	
Thomas Glascock, - -	Private,	–	3	
Reuben Gutridge, - -	"	–	13	
James Hansberry, - -	"	–	8	
Thornton Hinson, - -	"	–	7	
Griffin Headley, - -	"	–	8	
Eppa J. Hinson, - -	"	–	7	
James Hazard, - -	"	–	9	
Newman Hall, - -	"	–	9	
William Henson, - -	"	–	4	
John Jones, - -	"	–	8	
Sandford Jones, - -	"	–	5	
Matthew Jenkins, - -	"	–	8	
Benjamin Jenkins, - -	"	–	8	
James Jennings, - -	"	–	7	
John Jenkins, - -	"	–	8	
Richard H. Jones, - -	"	–	4	
Reuben Jenkins, - -	"	–	7	
Eppa Jones, - -	"	–	8	
Samuel Lyell, - -	"	–	7	
Thomas Moss, - -	"	–	7	
Samuel Muly, - -	"	–	8	
James McKinny, - -	"	–	4	
Reuben McKinny, - -	"	–	12	
Reuben Marks, - -	"	–	8	
John Marks, - -	"	–	8	
James Newman, - -	"	–	8	
George Newman, - -	"	–	9	
Samuel Prichard, - -	"	–	8	
Samuel Pursell, - -	"	–	8	
Henry Packett, - -	"	–	12	
William A. Packett, -	"	–	12	
William Quesenberry,	"	–	9	
James Quesenberry, -	"	–	9	
Benjamin Reynolds, -	"	–	8	
James Reynolds, - -	"	–	7	
William Richards, - -	"	–	12	
Peyton Sisson, - -	"	–	8	
Robert Scott, - -	"	–	8	
John Thrift, - -	"	–	6	
John Wroe, - -	"	–	8	
William J. Win, - -	"	–	8	
William Webb, - -	"	–	14	
John H. Yeatman, - -	"	–	7	

MUSTER ROLL

Of Captain Vincent Shackleford's Company of Artillery, from the Fourth Regiment of Virginia Militia, commanded by Lieutenant Colonel Vincent Branham, in the Service of the United States, from 6th to 10th April, from 20th to 26th July, 1813, from 5th to 9th October, and from 1st to 8th December, in the year 1814.

NAMES.	RANK.	TIME OF SERVICE.		REMARKS.
		Months.	Days.	
Vincent Shackleford,	Captain,	—	20	
Benjamin Boughton,	Lieutenant,	—	23	
Vincent Garland,	"	—	25	
John Garland,	Sergeant,	—	25	
James E. Jones,	"	—	20	
Newby Barrick,	"	—	15	
Cyrus Chilton,	"	—	17	
Wm. D. McCarthy,	"	—	3	
James Greenlaw,	"	—	3	
William Garland,	Corporal,	—	13	
Eppa Weathers,	"	—	10	
Daniel Flinn,	"	—	9	
Chichester Dobyns,	"	—	9	
John Alderson,	Private,	—	20	
Samuel Baker,	"	—	23	
George Beale,	"	—	24	
Reuben Beale,	"	—	20	
William S. Bulger,	"	—	23	
Charles Beale,	"	—	7	
Thomas M. Bellfield,	"	—	6	
William Baker,	"	—	11	
William Beckwith,	"	—	11	
John Billings,	"	—	5	
Thomas P. Ball,	"	—	1	
Hudson Brown,	"	—	1	
John Bulger,	"	—	1	
Christopher Brown,	"	—	1	
William Brown,	"	—	1	
Samuel Bryant,	"	—	1	
Henry Crewdson,	"	—	21	
Thornton Connellee,	"	—	11	
Robert W. Carter,	"	—	12	
David Clarke,	"	—	12	
Thomas Clarke,	"	—	12	
Richard Clarke,	"	—	8	
John Cash,	"	—	1	
James Crane,	"	—	1	
Washington Clarke,	"	—	15	
John Donahau,	"	—	25	
John Davis, sen'r,	"	—	7	
Chichester Dobyns,	"	—	11	
Jesse Dobyns,	"	—	9	
John Davis, jr.,	"	—	1	
Charles Dameron,	"	—	1	
Joseph Dozier,	"	—	1	
Thomas Douglass,	"	—	1	

NAMES.	RANK.	TIME OF SERVICE.		REMARKS.
		Months.	Days.	
William Duff, - -	Private,	–	1	
William Elmore, - -	"	–	3	
John English, - -	"	–	1	
Daniel Flinn, - -	"	–	12	
John Ferguson, - -	"	–	18	
Charles Fulks, - -	"	–	1	
William Ferguson, - -	"	–	7	
William Garland, - -	"	–	12	
Thomas How, - -	"	–	17	
William Henson, - -	"	–	1	
Griffin Hedley, - -	"	–	1	
Griffin Jones, - -	"	–	25	
Samuel B. Jasper, - -	"	–	19	
Samuel B. Kelsick, - -	"	–	13	
Armistead Kelly, - -	"	–	25	
Vincent Landman, - -	"	–	18	
Richard Lewis, - -	"	–	18	
John P. Laycock, - -	"	–	7	
John Literal, - -	"	–	1	
Richard W. Minter, - -	"	–	20	
Thomas Miles, - -	"	–	7	
Thomas Mitchell, - -	"	–	15	
James McKenney, - -	"	–	1	
Reuben McKenney, - -	"	–	1	
Samuel Meadley, - -	"	–	1	
James B. Newman, - -	"	–	7	
Samuel W. Neasom, - -	"	–	12	
Augustine Neale, - -	"	–	3	
George Pursell, - -	"	–	19	
Richard Packet, - -	"	–	12	
William Packet, - -	"	–	1	
Henry Packet, - -	"	–	1	
Samuel Pursell, - -	"	–	1	
Vincent Reynolds, - -	"	–	18	
Jesse D. Reynolds, - -	"	–	14	
James Rose, - -	"	–	8	
Richard Reynolds, - -	"	–	13	
Thomas T. Reynolds, - -	"	–	1	
James Reynolds, - -	"	–	1	
William Richards, - -	"	–	1	
Foxhall Sturman, - -	"	–	25	
Edward Spence, - -	"	–	12	
William Smith, - -	"	–	19	
James Smith, - -	"	–	24	
William Stanley, - -	"	–	7	
John P. Sacock, - -	"	–	7	
Elijah Seates, - -	"	–	9	
Miskell Saunders, - -	"	–	6	
John Sisson, - -	"	–	18	
John B. Sisson, - -	"	–	13	
James Scrimger, - -	"	–	13	
William Settle, - -	"	–	5	
Thomas Smith, - -	"	–	5	
Isaac Smith, - -	"	–	3	
Thaddeus Shurley, - -	"	–	1	
Samuel A. Self, - -	"	–	1	
John Scott, - -	"	–	1	
Williamson B. Tomlin, - -	"	–	7	
Thomas G. Tarpley, - -	"	–	10	
John Thrift, jr, - -	"	–	1	
John Webb, - -	"	–	12	
Eppa Weathers, - -	"	–	12	
William Webb, - -	"	–	1	

NAMES.	RANK.	TIME OF SERVICE.		REMARKS.
		Months.	Days.	
John Wroe, - -	Private,	–	1	
Anthony Wilcox, - -	"	–		
Thomas Yeatman, - -	"	–	5	
Thomas Yerby, - -	"	–	3	

Captain Samuel M. Shearman's Company—Ninety-second Regiment.

NAMES.	RANK.	TIME OF SERVICE.		REMARKS.
		Months.	Days.	
John James,	Lieutenant,	–	6	
William George,	Ensign,	–	24	
Robert Clarke,	Corporal,	–	6	
Isaac Tilman,	"	–	6	
John M. S. Tapscott,	"	–	5	
Isaac Pitman,	"	–	7	
George Gundry,	Drummer,	–	13	
Ben. Doggett,	"	–	10	
Eppa Hill,	Fifer,	–	10	
Griffin Ashburn,	Private,	2	5	
Archibald Anderson,	"	–	4	
Arthur Brent,	"	–	5	
Spencer Brown,	"	–	24	
Theodore Bland,	"	–	10	
Theodorick Bland,	"	1	1	
William Boatman,	"	–	24	
Middleton Brent,	"	–	24	
Robert Biscoe,	"	–	19	
James G. Cottrell,	"	2	29	
Isaac Currell, jr.	"	–	5	
Gawin Corbin,	"	–	17	
Armistead Currie,	"	1	10	
Robert Clarke,	"	–	19	
Edward Currell,	"	2	8	
Jacob Currell,	"	–	5	
James Currell,	"	2	2	
Wm. H. Chowning,	"	–	24	
John Carrell,	"	–	10	Sub. for Henry Scho-field.
John Carter,	"	–	10	
William Danson,	"	–	11	
Isaac Danson,	"	–	12	
William George,	"	–	24	
Eppa George,	"	–	13	
William Gibson,	"	–	10	Sub. for Wm. Spilman.
Calvin George,	"	–	24	
Thomas D. George,	"	–	24	
James Gains,	"	–	24	
Jesse George,	"	–	10	Sub. for William H. George.
James Hammond,	"	–	7	
William Hughlett,	"	–	6	
William Hinton,	"	–	7	
Addison Hall,	"	–	10	
Martin Hughlett,	"	–	29	
Rawleigh Hazzard,	"	–	24	
Augustin Hughlett,	"	–	11	
Raustin Hughlett,	"	1	4	
Charles Ingram,	"	–	12	
John Kemp,	"	–	12	
Richard Kemm,	"	–	24	
James Mott,	"	–	11	
Joseph Merryman,	"	–	24	
Thomas Mason, jr.	"	–	6	

NAMES.	RANK.	TIME OF SERVICE.		REMARKS.
		Months.	Days.	
John Mason, - -	Private,	–	24	
Thos. B. Oliver, - -	"	–	24	
William Pullen, - -	"	–	24	
John Schofield, - -	"	–	24	
William Spillman, - -	"	–	9	
Portues Towles, - -	"	–	23	
Thomas Towill, - -	"	–	19	
Charles Yerby, - -	"	–	10	Sub. for Thos. Yerby.

(For rest of this company, see publication of Pay Rolls.)

MUSTER ROLL

Of Captain Thomas Shelly's Company, from the Seventy-first Regiment of Virginia Militia, commanded by Colonel William Allen, in Surry County, in Service from 30th June to 10th July, 1813.

NAMES.	RANK.	TIME OF SERVICE.		REMARKS.
		Months.	Days.	
Thomas Shelly, - -	Captain,	–	11	
Robert Hunnicutt, - -	Lieutenant,	–	11	
Meshack Goodrich, - -	Ensign,	–	11	
John Hunnicutt, - -	Sergeant,	–	11	
Joseph Barham, - -	"	–	11	
James Goodrich, - -	"	–	11	
James Gray, - -	"	–	11	
Alexander Moore, - -	Corporal,	–	11	
Edwin Hasty, - -	"	–	11	
Thomas Judkins, - -	"	–	11	
William Carter, - -	"	–	11	
Edwin Eppes, - -	Drummer,	–	11	
Thomas B. Adams, -	Private,	–	11	
James Bell, - -	"	–	11	
John H. Bell, - -	"	–	11	
Joseph Berryman, - -	"	–	11	
William Binns, - -	"	–	11	
Nathaniel Berryman,	"	–	11	
John Bell, - -	"	–	11	
Joseph Carey, - -	"	–	11	
John Carroll, - -	"	–	11	
David Davis, - -	"	–	11	
John Davis, - -	"	–	11	
John Druce, - -	"	–	11	
James Davis, - -	"	–	11	
Samuel Edwards, -	"	–	11	
Thomas C. Edwards, -	"	–	11	
Rich'd H. Edwards, -	"	–	11	
Benjamin Edwards, -	"	–	11	
Shadrick Goodrich, -	"	–	11	
Fred. Gray, - -	"	–	11	
Abednego Goodrich,	"	–	11	
Francis Holt, - -	"	–	11	
William Hunnicutt, -	"	–	11	
Henry Harrison, - -	"	–	11	
Caufield Hunnicutt, -	"	–	11	
John N. Hunnicutt, -	"	–	11	
John W. Judkins, - -	"	–	11	
William Judkins, - -	"	–	11	
Blanks Moody, - -	"	–	11	
Willis Moore, - -	"	–	11	
John Norris, - -	"	–	11	
Thomas Pitman, - -	"	–	11	
Burwell Persons, - -	"	–	11	
Samuel Price, - -	"	–	11	
Thomas M. Price, - -	"	–	11	
Jeremiah Proctor, - -	"	–	11	
William Pettit, - -	"	–	11	
Philip Phones, - -	"	–	11	

NAMES.			RANK.	TIME OF SERVICE.		REMARKS.
				Months.	Days.	
James Price,	-	-	Private,	–	11	
Nathaniel Phillips,	-	-	"	–	11	
Thomas Rowell,	-	-	"	–	11	
Richard Rowell,	-	-	"	–	11	
Cary Seward,	-	-	"	–	11	
Charles Taylor,	-	-	"	–	11	
Nicholas Taylor,	-	-	"	–	11	
Patrick Warren,	-	-	"	–	11	
Samuel Wilkinson,	-	-	"	–	11	
Archibald Wright,	-	-	"	–	11	
John M. Williams,	-	-	"	–	11	
Abraham Williams,	-	-	"	–	11	
Samuel Wilson,	-	-	"	–	11	

Captain Tunstall Shelton's Company—Second Elite Corps.

NAMES.			RANK.	TIME OF SERVICE.		REMARKS.
				Months.	Days.	
Beverley Shelton,	-	-	Ensign,	–	12	
Charles L. Adams,	-	-	Private,	–	14	Transferred to wagon department.
James Roper,	-	-	"	–	22	Sub. for John Black.
Reuben Brown,	-	-	Servant,	–	21	

(For rest of this company, see publication of Pay Rolls.)

Sergeant William D. Shackleford's Company—One Hundred and Ninth Regiment.

NAMES.	RANK.	TIME OF SERVICE.		REMARKS.
		Months.	Days.	
William Boughton, - -	Private,	—	3	
Bartlett Blake, - -	"	—	3	
Fred'k Meynadier, - -	"	—	3	
Ben. Pierce, - -	"	—	3	
Major Turner, - -	"	—	3	
Thomas Trice, jr. - -	"	—	3	
Carter Williams, - -	"	—	3	

(For rest of this company, see publication of Pay Rolls.)

MUSTER ROLL

Of Captain Arthur Simkins' Company, from the Twenty-seventh Regiment, Virginia Militia, in the County of Northampton, called into Service under the general orders of the 8th March, 1813, from the 10th of March to the 23rd of the same month, inclusive, in the year 1813.

NAMES.	RANK.	TIME OF SERVICE.		REMARKS.
		Months.	Days.	
Arthur Simkins, - -	Captain,	–	13	Or Sinkins.
William Jarvis, - -	Lieutenant,	–	13	
John Trower, - -	Ensign,	–	13	
Abram Castin, - -	Sergeant,	–	13	
Charles Fitchell, - -	"	–	13	
Moses Griffith, - -	"	–	13	
Thomas Graves, - -	"	–	13	
John Adams, - -	Private,	–	13	
John T. Belook, - -	"	–	13	
John Costin, - -	"	–	13	
Charles S. Capes, - -	"	–	13	
James Clay, - -	"	–	13	
Nathaniel Costin. - -	"	–	13	
Thomas Dixon, - -	"	–	13	
Wm. S. Evans, - -	"	–	13	
Thomas Elliott, - -	"	–	13	
John Evans, - -	"	–	13	
Thos. Fitchew, - -	"	–	13	
John Griffith, - -	"	–	13	
Michael Habett, - -	"	–	13	
Jno. Hyslop, sen'r, - -	"	–	13	
Laban Kelly, - -	"	–	13	
Sam'l Kellam, - -	"	–	13	
Wm. Nottingham, - -	"	–	13	
John Parsons, - -	"	–	13	
Robert Peake, - -	"	–	13	
Marriatt Parsons, - -	"	–	13	
Thomas Scott, - -	"	–	13	
John Shads, - -	"	–	13	
Wm. Smith, - -	"	–	13	
Elliott Travis, - -	"	–	13	
Jno. Whitehead, jr., - -	"	–	13	
Peter Williams, - -	"	–	13	
William Watkins, - -	"	–	13	
Thos. Williams, - -	"	–	13	
Thomas Wilson, - -	"	–	13	
Ezekiel Younger, - -	"	–	13	

Captain John Simpkins' Company—Twenty-seventh Regiment.

NAMES.	RANK.	TIME OF SERVICE.		REMARKS.
		Months.	Days.	
John Simpkins, - -	Captain,	–	21	
Littleton Kendall, - -	Lieutenant,	–	21	
Thomas Graves, - -	Sergeant,	–	10	
James Goffigon, - -	"	–	10	
William Jarvis, - -	"	–	10	
John Spady, - -	"	–	10	
Nat. Collins, - -	"	–	12	
William Dalby, - .	"	–	17	
Severn Wingate, - -	Drummer,	–	10	
John Adams, - -	Private,	–	10	
Nathaniel Bishop, - -	"	–	10	
Christopher Biggs, - -	"	–	10	
Thomas S. Brickhouse, -	"	–	24	
Smith Brickhouse, - -	"	–	22	
William Clay, - -	"	–	10	
John Costin, jr. - -	"	–	10	
Isaac Costin, - -	"	–	10	
Francis Costin, - -	"	–	10	
John Costin, jr. - -	"	–	10	
Thomas Dawson, - -	"	–	10	
William Dulby, - -	"	–	8	
George Eshum, - -	"	–	20	
John T. Elliott, - -	"	–	22	
John Floyd, - -	"	–	10	
James Fisher, - -	"	–	10	
John Griffith, - -	"	–	10	
John Hyslop, - -	"	–	10	
Thomas Henderson, - -	"	–	25	
John H. Harmanson, - -	"	–	29	
S. D. Heath, - -	"	–	28	
Silas Jefferson, - -	"	–	25	
William D. James, - -	"	–	25	
Samuel Kellam, - -	"	–	10	
John McKown, - -	"	–	10	
William Nottingham, - -	"	–	10	
Richard Nottingham, - -	"	1	5	
Severn E. Nottingham, -	"	–	10	
Nat. Nottingham, - -	"	–	10	
Robert Pake, - -	"	–	10	
Abel Powell, - -	"	–	25	
William Ridley, - -	"	–	26	
John G. Stratton, - -	"	–	15	
Edmund Scarborough, -	"	–	25	
John Simpson, - -	"	–	15	
James Spady, - -	"	–	10	
Thomas W. Scott, - -	"	–	10	
Levin T. Thomas, - -	"	–	25	
Bart Taylor, - -	"	–	16	
John S. Williams, - -	"	–	18	
John Whitehead, - -	"	–	10	
James Wingate, - -	"	–	10	
William White, - -	"	–	25	
Southy Wingate, - -	"	–	10	

NAMES.	RANK.	TIME OF SERVICE.		REMARKS.
		Months.	Days.	
John R. Waddy, - -	Private,	-	14	
William Warren, - -	"	—	10	
Nat. West, - -	"	—	15	
Amos Underhill, - -	"	—	25	
	"	—		

(For rest of this company, see publication of Pay Rolls.)

MUSTER ROLL

Of Captain Daniel Slater's Company, from the Fifty-second Regiment, Virginia Militia, in the County of New Kent, called into actual Service under the general orders of the 2d September, 1814, from the 4th to the 18th of September, in the same year.

NAMES.	RANK.	TIME OF SERVICE.		REMARKS.
		Months.	Days.	
Daniel Slater,	Captain,	–	15	
Robert Irby,	Lieutenant,	–	15	
Richard Crump,	Ensign.	–	15	
Edward Philbates,	Sergeant,	–	15	
James Richardson,	"	–	15	
Benjamin Hix,	"	–	15	
Thomas Stagg,	"	–	15	
John Ratcliffe,	Corporal,	–	15	
Dudley Williams,	"	–	15	
Robert Cassaday,	"	–	15	
Edward Wadal,	"	–	15	
Gillam Adams,	Private,	–	15	
John Adams,	"	–	15	
Jesse Barnes,	"	–	15	
Edward Craddock,	"	–	15	
Robert Drake,	"	–	15	
William Edwards,	"	–	15	
William Fowler,	"	–	15	
John Folks,	"	–	15	
Edward Farthing,	"	–	15	
Walker Gregory,	"	–	15	
William Gill,	"	–	15	
James Gregory,	"	–	15	
Henry Gill,	"	–	15	
Arthur Hamlet,	"	–	15	
John Hamlet,	"	–	15	
Randolph Hardiman,	"	–	15	
John T. Harwood,	"	–	15	
James Jordan,	"	–	15	
Ezekiel Lawson,	"	–	15	
Henry Ladd,	"	–	15	
Thomas S. Morriss,	"	–	15	
Jonathan Mountcastle,	"	–	15	
Zachariah Nance,	"	–	15	
Joseph Pond,	"	–	15	
John Philbates,	"	–	15	
John Phillips,	"	–	15	
John Ratcliffe,	"	–	15	
William Slater,	"	–	15	
George Taylor,	"	–	15	

MUSTER ROLL

Of Captain William Slater's Company, of the Fifty-second Regiment of Virginia Militia, called into actual Service under general orders of the 26th June 1813, from 28th June to 13th July, in the same year.

NAMES.			RANK.	TIME OF SERVICE.		REMARKS.
				Months.	Days.	
William Slater,	-	-	Captain,	–	16	
Daniel Slater,	-	-	Lieutenant,	–	16	
Rich'd Hilliard,	-	-	Ensign,	–	16	
Chesley Jones,	-	-	Sergeant,	–	16	
Edward Tilbates,	-	-	"	–	16	
James Hilliard,	-	-	"	–	16	
Jno. Ball,	-	-	"	–	16	
Jon'n Williams,	-	-	Corporal,	–	16	
John Parrish,	-	-	"	–	16	
Jas. Saunders,	-	-	"	–	16	
Jno. Ratcliffe,	-	-	"	–	11	
William Day,	-	-	Private,	–	16	
Edward Farthing,	-	-	"	–	16	
James Glaisbrook,	-	-	"	–	16	
Rich'd B. Hix,	-	-	"	–	16	
James Hughes,	-	-	"	–	16	
Wm. R. Hix,	-	-	"	–	16	
David Jones,	-	-	"	–	16	
Edward Knewstep,	-	-	"	–	16	
Thos. S. Morris,	-	-	"	–	16	
Jno. A. Moore,	-	-	"	–	16	
Jno. Phillips,	-	-	"	–	16	
Thomas Ratcliffe,	-	-	"	–	16	
Turner Richardson,	-	-	"	–	16	
William Slater,	-	-	"	–	16	
Benj. Tyree,	-	-	"	–	16	
Bolling Vaughan,	-	-	"	–	16	
Archer Williams,	-	-	"	–	16	
Bart. D. Williams,	-	-	"	–	16	
Dudley Williams,	-	-	"	–	16	
David Williams,	-	-	"	–	16	
Meredith Williams,	-	-	"	–	16	

Captain Arthur Smith's Company—Twenty-seventh Regiment.

NAMES.	RANK.	TIME OF SERVICE.		REMARKS.
		Months.	Days.	
Henry Joyner, - -	Ensign,	–	22	
Mallory G. Todd, - -	"	–	18	
Pleasant Casey, - -	Drummer,	–	22	
Francis Whitley, - -	Fifer,	–	22	
John Barradal, - -	Private,	–	22	
William Bransby, - -	"	–	17	
Henry Deford, - -	"	–	22	
Davis Gray, - -	"	–	27	
Kinchin Godwin, - -	"	–	18	
Beeph. Gibbs, - -	"	–	22	
Joseph Goodwin, , -	"	–	18	
Teucle Heath, - -	"	–	28	
Major Heath, - -	"	–	18	
Robert Jordan, - -	"	–	16	
Peter Knight, - -	"	–	22	
James Moody, - -	"	–	22	
John Pope, - -	"	–	22	
Willis Pitman, - -	"	–	24	
Jacob Person, - -	"	–	22	
Richard Reynolds, - -	"	–	9	
Mallory Todd, - -	"	–	3	
Thomas Wrenn, - -	"	–	22	
Thomas Wail, - -	"	–	7	
Charles Wail, -	"	–	16	
Willauby Williamson, -	"	–	16	

(For rest of this company, see publication of Pay Rolls.)

MUSTER ROLL

Of Lieutenant Arthur Smith's Company, of the Fifty-ninth Regiment of Virginia Militia, commanded by Lieutenant Colonel Josiah Riddick, jr., called into Service from the 16th April to 1st May, in the year 1813.

NAMES.			RANK.	TIME OF SERVICE.		REMARKS.
				Months.	Days.	
Arthur Smith,	-	-	Captain,	–	16	
Benjamin Riddick,	-	-	Ensign,	–	16	
William M. Jones,	-	-	Sergeant,	–	16	
Joseph B. Baker,	-	-	"	–	16	
John W. Dardan,	-	-	"	–	16	
Christopher Lawrence,	-	-	Corporal,	–	16	
Joseph Vaughan,	-	-	"	–	16	
William Archer,	-	-	Private,	–	16	
Anthony Birdsong,	-	-	"	–	16	
Lewis Cogstal,	-	-	"	–	16	
Pewis Dildey,	-	-	"	–	16	
William B. Godwin,	-	-	"	–	16	
William Howell,	-	-	"	–	16	
George W. Holland,	-	-	"	–	16	
Thomas Holland,	-	-	"	–	16	
Ely Harrell,	-	-	"	–	16	
Nathaniel Jones,	-	-	"	–	16	
Abraham Jones,	-	-	"	–	16	
Kader Lassiter,	-	-	"	–	16	
Thomas Lassiter,	-	-	"	–	16	
Isaac Luke,	-	-	"	–	16	
James Northcut,	-	-	"	–	16	
Joseph Orom,	-	-	"	–	16	
Jeremiah Parker,	-	-	"	–	16	
Francis Sketer,	-	-	"	–	16	
James Shepherd,	-	-	"	–	16	
James Wright,	-	-	"	–	16	

MUSTER ROLL

Of Captain Gulielmus Smith's Company, of the Sixteenth Regiment, Virginia Militia, commanded by Lieutenant Colonel Aylette Waller, in the Service of the United States, from 22d July to 17th August, in the year 1814.

NAMES.	RANK.	TIME OF SERVICE.		REMARKS.
		Months.	Days.	
Gulielmus Smith,	Captain,	—	26	
Joseph Duerson,	Lieutenant,	—	26	
John Robins,	Ensign,	—	26	
Joseph Ledwidge,	Sergeant,	—	26	Sub. for Elijah D. Robins.
Walker B. Luck,	"	—	26	
Thompson Schooler,	"	—	26	
Abraham Ryan,	"	—	26	
Walker Wilson,	Corporal,	—	26	
William Clark,	"	—	26	
Lewis Olive,	"	—	26	
John Payne,	"	—	26	
Henry Etherton,	Drummer,	—	26	
John Devenport,	Fifer,	—	26	
Matthew B. Duff,	Wagoner,	—	26	
William Alsop,	Private,	—	26	
William Buckhanan,	"	—	26	
Thomas Buckhanan,	"	—	26	
Thomas Beazley,	"	—	26	
John Beazley,	"	—	26	
Edward Burk,	"	—	26	
William Chewning,	"	—	26	
William Crutchfield,	"	—	26	
William Darnaby,	"	—	26	
John Duerson,	"	—	26	
Gideon Duerson,	"	—	26	
John Duerson, jr.	"	—	26	
Alsop Y. Daniel,	"	—	26	
William Ellis,	"	—	26	
Robert D. Foster,	"	—	26	
William D. Goodler,	"	—	26	
Edward Holladay,	"	—	26	
Alexander Humphreys,	"	—	26	
Thomas Hart,	"	—	26	
William Hart,	"	—	26	
Linsfield Jones,	"	—	26	
Daniel Landrum,	"	—	26	
Fountain Landrum,	"	—	26	
David Lewis,	"	—	26	
William Ledwidge,	"	—	26	
Andrew Mitchell,	"	—	26	
John Martin,	"	—	25	
William Martin,	"	—	25	
William McKenny,	"	—	25	
John McDormant,	"	—	25	
Charles Oliver,	"	—	26	
James K. Olive,	"	—	26	
John Penny,	"	—	26	
Nathaniel Pulliam,	"	—	26	

NAMES.	RANK.	TIME OF SERVICE.		REMARKS.
		Months.	Days.	
Benjamin Pilcher, - -	Private,	—	26	
John Perry, - -	"	—	26	
William Perry, - -	"	—	26	
John Patton, - -	"	—	26	
John Puller, - -	"	—	26	
William Pierce, - -	"	—	26	
James Payne, - -	"	—	26	
James M. Richardson, -	"	—	26	
William B. Stubblefield, -	"	—	26	
James Smallwood, - -	"	—	26	
James Stewart, - -	"	—	26	
George Stewart, - -	"	—	26	
Walker Vass, - -	"	—	26	
Daniel B. White, - -	"	—	26	
John Wilson, - -	"	—	26	
James Willaby, - -	"	—	26	
Trueman Willaby, - -	"	—	26	

Captain Isaac Smith's Company—Second Regiment.

NAMES.	RANK.	TIME OF SERVICE.		REMARKS.
		Months.	Days.	
William D. Outen, - -	Lieutenant,	–	12	
William Henderson, - -	"	–	12	
Jno. H. Husley, - -	Ensign,	–	12	
Peter Martin, - -	Sergeant,	–	12	
William Bloxham, - -	"	–	12	
Zoro. Hutchinson, - -	"	–	8	
Ezekiel Ashby, - -	Private,	–	21	
Abel Abdell, - -	"	–	10	
John N. Ames, - -	"	–	12	
Major Abdell, - -	"	–	5	
William C. Adams, - -	"	–	12	
George Ardis, - -	"	–	12	
William Ashby, - -	"	–	12	
Theo. W. Adair, - -	"	–	8	
Caleb Belote, - -	"	–	10	
James Badger, - -	"	–	22	
William Bloxom, - -	"	–	14	
Abbot Bloxom, - -	"	–	3	
Nat. Badger, - -	"	–	5	
Ezekiel Badger, - -	"	–	12	
Anderson Bloxom, - -	"	–	12	
Edw'd Boisnard, - -	"	–	12	
Henry Bagwell, - -	"	–	12	
William Bell, - -	"	–	12	
Wilson Boughton, - -	"	–	7	
Michael Casey, - -	"	–	4	
John Chandler, - -	"	–	2	
Isaac Coleburn, - -	"	–	3	
Thomas Chandler, - -	"	–	10	
James Creathers, - -	"	–	1	
James Chandler, - -	"	–	5	
Nat. Copes, - -	"	–	8	
William Colonna, - -	"	–	6	
Samuel Colonna, - -	"	–	19	
John C. Copes, - -	"	–	12	
Thomas Custis, (of Only,) -	"	–	12	
Shadrack Darby, - -	"	–	10	
James Doughty, - -	"	–	5	
Isma Doughty, - -	"	–	23	
William Davis, - -	"	–	12	
Isaac Edwards, - -	"	–	8	
Jesse Edwards, - -	"	–	6	
Severn East, - -	"	–	5	
Bay. Edwards, - -	"	–	6	
Sellery Edwards, - -	"	–	6	
John Fleaherty, - -	"	–	12	
Elijah Floid, - -	"	–	12	
William Grinalds, - -	"	–	12	
Edward Hickman, - -	"	–	12	
Edmund Hutchinson, -	"	–	12	
Stephen Hopkins, - -	"	–	12	
Ben. Harrison, - -	"	–	12	
Stephen Hannason, - -	"	–	5	
Littleton Hyslop, - -	"	–	12	

NAMES.	RANK.	TIME OF SERVICE.		REMARKS.
		Months.	Days.	
Henry Hannaford, - -	Private,	–	12	
James Harrison, - -	"	–	12	
Richard Hickman, - -	"	–	12	
Jno. Ironmonger, - -	"	–	12	
Levin James, - -	"	–	12	
James Jester, - -	"	–	12	
William P. Johnson, - -	"	–	4	
William Jones, - -	"	–	12	
Esau Kellam, - -	"	1	8	
Evans Kellam, - -	"	–	12	
Ezekiel Killman, - -	"	–	12	
Timothy Kelly, - -	"	–	12	
Robert Kellam, - -	"			
Revelle Kellam, - -	"	–	12	
John Leatherby, jr. - -	"	–	8	
William Long, - -	"	–	3	
John Leatherberry, - -	"	–	5	
Thomas Lewis, - -	"	–	12	
Jesse Lewis, - -	"	–	12	
Nathaniel Long, - -	"	–	12	
Richard Lewis, (of Rich'd) -	"	–	7	
James Marting, - -	"	–	9	
James Mears, (of Sev.) -	"	–	14	
Jno. Mears, (of Jno.) -	"	1	5	
Littleton Mears, -	"	–	4	
James Mears, (of Sol.) -	"	–	5	
William Mears, (of Jno.) -	"	–	4	
John Mason, - -	"	–	12	
Abel Mason, - -	"	–	12	
Jesse Martin, - -	"	–	12	
Isaac Mister, - -	"	–	12	
F. S. Noel, - -	"	–	20	
Z'l Noel, - -	"	–	8	
Jno. Nock, (of Jno.) - -	"	–	12	
Jno. Nock, (of Sol.) - -	"	–	12	
William O. Parker, - -	"	–	10	
Jno. Phillips, (of Jno.) -	"	–	12	
Jas. Parker, (of Ro.) -	"	–	5	
Jas. Parker, - -	"	–	5	
Major Pickett, (of Sam'l) -	"	–	5	
Gabriel Purse, - -	"	–	12	
William Person, - -	"	–	12	
Major Pickett, - -	"	–	5	
Jas. W. Parker, - -	"	–	5	
Zoro. Richardson, - -	"	–	10	
Asa J. Rodgers, - -	"	–	10	
William Rue, - -	"	–	12	
Dennis Rue, - -	"	–	12	
John Savage, (of Wm.) -	"	1	1	
Thos. B. Snead, - -	"	–	7	
Jesse Savage, - -	"	–	8	
Major Savage, - -	"	–	21	
Bay. Savage, - -	"	–	6	
Revell Sherrod, - -	"	–	12	
William Snead, (of Pres.) -	"	–	12	
Ezekiel Smith, - -	"	–	12	
Hillery B. Stringer, - -	"	–	12	
Jno. Scott, (of Wat.) -	"	–	12	
Robert Twiford, - -	"	1	21	
Ricketts Tatham, - -	"	–	26	
Robert Twiford, (of Geo.) -	"	–	17	
James Twiford, - -	"	–	13	
James Taylor, - -	"	–	6	
Nath. Twiford, - -	"	–	12	

NAMES.	RANK.	TIME OF SERVICE.		REMARKS.
		Months.	Days.	
Nath. Turner, - -	Private,	–	12	
Aug. Waterfield, - -	"	–	28	
Aug. Waterford, - -	"	–	5	
Peter Wise, - -	"	–	22	
Littleton Wyatt, - -	"	–	10	
Jno. Wilburn, jr. - -	"	–	12	
Jno. B. Walker, - -	"	–	6	
Jno. D. Wallon, - -	"	–	6	
George West, (of Jno.) -	"	–	12	
Waitman Willet, - -	"	–	12	

(For rest of this company, see publication of Pay Rolls.)

MUSTER ROLL

Of Captain James W. Smith's Company, (commanded by Lieut. Pryor C. Shepperson,) from the Eighty-third Regiment, in the County of Dinwiddie, called into actual Service under the general orders of the 30th June, 1813, from 1st to 6th July, in the same year.

NAMES.	RANK.	TIME OF SERVICE.		REMARKS.
		Months.	Days.	
James W. Smith,	Captain,	–	6	
Pryor C. Shepperson,	Lieutenant,	–	6	
Jesse Abernathy,	Ensign,	–	6	
John H. Davis,	Sergeant,	–	6	
Manson Harwell,	"	–	6	
Abner Adams,	"	–	6	
John B. Brodnax,	"	–	6	
Jesse Pearce,	Corporal,	–	6	
John Bolling,	"	–	6	
Miles King,	"	–	6	
David Westmoreland,	"	–	6	
Frederica Adams,	Private,	–	6	
John Adams,	"	–	6	
William Barrow,	"	–	6	
Freeman W. Brodnax,	"	–	6	
William H. Brodnax,	"	–	6	
Burwell Cross,	"	–	6	
Richard C. Claiborne,	"	–	6	
Joseph E. Davis,	"	–	6	
David Draper,	"	–	6	
Richard Evans,	"	–	6	
John Goode,	"	–	6	
William Holloway,	"	–	6	
Robert Harwell,	"	–	6	
William Jackson,	"	–	6	
Carey Jones,	"	–	6	
Hamlin Lewis,	"	–	6	
James Lunceford,	"	–	6	
Joseph Lunceford,	"	–	6	
Christopher Manlove,	"	–	6	
Thomas B. Manlove,	"	–	6	
William Mason,	"	–	6	
Robert Manlove,	"	–	6	
Thomas Parsons,	"	–	6	
Anderson Parrish,	"	–	6	
Christopher Shepperson,	"	–	6	
John F. Sherman,	"	–	6	
John M. Vaughan,	"	–	6	
William Wells,	"	–	6	
Daniel Wall,	"	–	6	
Burwell Williams,	"	–	6	
David W. Withers,	"	–	6	
Thomas Wells,	"	–	6	
Joseph Wells,	"	–	6	
James Wilson,	"	–	6	
Hartwell Westmoreland,	"	–	6	
Thomas Wilson,	"	–	6	

MUSTER ROLL

Of Captain Joseph Smith's Company, of the Thirty-sixth Regiment, Virginia Militia, in the County of Prince William, called into actual Service under the regimental orders of the 24th August, 1814, from the 24th to the 30th August, 1813.

NAMES.	RANK.	TIME OF SERVICE.		REMARKS.
		Months.	Days.	
Joseph Smith,	Captain,	–	7	
William French,	Lieutenant,	–	7	
George Lansdowne,	Ensign,	–	7	
John Webster,	Sergeant,	–	7	
John Lansdowne,	"	–	7	
Edward Austin,	"	–	7	
John Athy,	Private,	–	7	
Willis Bridwell,	"	–	7	
Chapman Copen,	"	–	7	
James Cooper,	"	–	7	
Harrison Cornwell,	"	–	7	
Alexander Chick,	"	–	7	
Peter Cockrell,	"	–	7	
Elijah Dawson,	"	–	7	
Harrison Fox,	"	–	7	
Edward Fair,	"	–	7	
Samuel Florence,	"	–	7	
Michael Floriday,	"	–	7	
Daniel Grant,	"	–	7	
George Godfrey,	"	–	7	
Cathbert V. Harrison,	"	–	7	
Thomas Homes,	"	–	7	
Benson Jewel,	"	–	7	
Sandy Keys,	"	–	7	
William F. Moore,	"	–	7	
Isaac Murphy,	"	–	7	
William Norman,	"	–	7	
Edward Norman,	"	–	7	
Watson Person,	"	–	7	
John Person,	"	–	7	
Whittenton Person,	"	–	7	
George Person,	"	–	7	
Cumberlain Person,	"	–	7	
George Rennoe, sr.	"	–	7	
George Rennoe, jr.	"	–	7	
Madden Rennoe,	"	–	7	
Matthew H. Smoote,	"	–	7	
Willis Turner,	"	–	7	
Henry Webster,	"	–	7	

MUSTER ROLL

Of Captain Martin Smith's Company, of the Thirty-third Regiment, in the County of Henrico, called into actual Service under the general orders of the 13th March, 1813, from 19th to 29th March, in the same year.

NAMES.			RANK.	TIME OF SERVICE.		REMARKS.
				Months.	Days.	
Martin Smith,	-	-	Captain,	–	5	
Wm. Shepperson,	-	-	Lieutenant,	–	5	
James Whitelaw,	-	-	Ensign,	–	5	
Wm. S. Blackburn,	-	-	Sergeant,	–	5	
Matt. H. Owen,	-	-	"	–	5	
John Burton,	-	-	"	–	5	
Lyddall Cornet,	-	-	"	–	5	
Joseph V. Owen,	-	-	Corporal,	–	5	
Granvill Ford,	-	-	"	–	5	
Isham Lucas,	-	-	"	–	5	
Samuel Blackbron,	-	-	"	–	5	
William Alley,	-	-	Private,	–	5	
Edmund Bowles,	-	-	"	–	5	
Royall Blackburn,	-	-	"	–	5	
Thomas Blackburn,	-	-	"	–	5	
William Blackburn,	-	-	"	–	5	
Claiborne Boone,	-	-	"	–	5	
Lyddall Bowles,	-	-	"	–	5	
Wm. B. Chamberlain,	-	-	"	–	5	
Thomas Courtney,	-	-	"	–	5	
Allen Cornet,	-	-	"	–	5	
Thomas Cawthorn,	-	-	"	–	5	
Ephraim Clark,	-	-	"	–	5	
Patrick Daniel,	-	-	"	–	5	
Lewis S. Edwards,	-	-	"	–	5	
David Elmore,	-	-	"	–	5	
Robert England,	-	-	"	–	5	
Dabney Eubank,	-	-	"	–	5	
Dabney Ford,	-	-	"	–	5	
Daniel Ford;	-	-	"	–	5	
Martin Ford,	-	-	"	–	5	
Gilley Ford,	-	-	"	–	5	
Zachariah Francis,	-	-	"	–	5	
James Griffin,	-	-	"	–	5	
Charles Griffin,	-	-	"	–	5	
Benj. Gromes,	-	-	"	–	5	
Daniel Horner,	-	-	"	–	5	
Austin Hill,	-	-	"	–	5	
Samuel Jennings,	-	-	"	–	5	
Allen Jennings,	-	-	"	–	5	
Jesse Jennings,	-	-	"	–	5	
David Jennings,	-	-	"	–	5	
William Jennings,	-	-	"	–	5	
Hezekiah Jennings,	-	-	"	–	5	
George King,	-	-	"	–	5	
Benjamin Lay,	-	-	"	–	5	
George Miller,	-	-	"	–	5	
Thomas Mallory,	-	-	"	–	5	

NAMES.	RANK.	TIME OF SERVICE.		REMARKS.
		Months.	Days.	
John Melton, - -	Private,	–	5	
David Melton, - -	"	–	5	
John G. Nelson, - -	"	–	5	
Henry Owen, - -	"	–	5	
Thomas Owen, - -	"	–	5	
Samuel Owen, - -	"	–	5	
William Owen, - -	"	–	5	
Thomas Phillips, - -	"	–	5	
Isaac Phillips, - -	"	–	5	
Smith Puryear, - -	"	–	5	
Mosby Sheppard, - -	"	–	5	
Benj. Sheppard, - -	"	–	5	
Thomas Smith, - -	"	–	5	
Wilson Staples, - -	"	–	5	
Charles A. Stanley, - -	"	–	5	
Walter Thacker, - -	"	–	5	
John Toler, - -	"	–	5	
Eleazer Vest, - -	"	–	5	
Isaac Winston, - -	"	–	5	
Wm. Warbleton, - -	"	–	5	
Wm. Winston, - -	"	–	5	
John Walton, - -	"	–	5	
Edmund West, - -	"	–	5	

Captain Peter Smith's Company—Eighty-first Regiment.

NAMES.			RANK.	TIME OF SERVICE.		REMARKS.
				Months.	Days.	
Abel Jackson,	-	-	Private,	–	20	
David Johnson,	-	-	"	–	20	
Edwin Irvine,	-	-	"	1	8	

(For rest of this company, see publication of Pay Rolls.)

Captain Hugh Stewart's Company—Eighth Regiment.

NAMES.	RANK.	TIME OF SERVICE.		REMARKS.
		Months.	Days.	
James W. Colton, - -	Private,	–	18	
William Santer, - -	"	1	13	

(For rest of this company, see publication of Pay Rolls.)

MUSTER ROLL

Of Captain Washington Smith's Company, in the Fifty-ninth Regiment, Virginia Militia, Nansemond County, commanded by Lieutenant Colonel J. Riddick, jr., called into actual Service by Colonel Commandant, from March 20 to April 17, in the year 1813.

NAMES.	RANK.	TIME OF SERVICE.		REMARKS.
		Months.	Days.	
Washington Smith,	Captain,	–	28	
Benjamin Goodman,	Lieutenant,	–	10	
Abram Parker,	Ensign,	–	10	
John Harrell,	Sergeant,	–	28	
Wm. Bubb,	"	–	15	
John March,	"	–	28	
Samuel Smith,	"	–	10	
William Jones,	Corporal,	–	28	
William Barnes,	"	–	28	
Williams Adkins,	Private,	–	15	
Kedar Byrd,	"	–	28	
Aaron Byrd,	"	–	15	
David Baker,	"	–	15	
Wm. E. Copeland,	"	–	28	
Thomas Cornelius,	"	–	28	
Samuel Citizen,	"	–	28	
Jessee Griffin,	"	–	28	
David Harrell,	"	–	15	
Isaac Horton,	"	–	28	
Wilkerson Jones,	"	–	15	
Harrison Jones,	"	–	28	
Dempsey Langston,	"	–	15	
Abram Philps,	"	–	15	
Abram Parker,	"	–	15	
Wm. Pierce,	"	–	28	
John Parker,	"	–	15	
James Parker,	"	–	15	
Riddick Peal,	"	–	15	
Willis Parker,	"	–	15	
John Russell,	"	–	15	
Adam Raby,	"	–	28	
Isaac Smith,	"	–	15	
John Smith,	"	–	28	
Joseph Stallings,	"	–	12	
John Staples,	"	–	28	
William Shelton,	"	–	15	
Levin Turlington,	"	–	15	
James Wiatt,	"	–	28	
Willis Wiggins,	"	–	28	
Conrad Woolfrey,	"	–	15	
Jesse Wiggins,	"	–	28	

MUSTER ROLL

Of Captain William Smith's Company, of the Second Regiment, Virginia Militia, in the County of Orange, called into actual Service, under the general orders of the 28th of June, 1813, from the 5th July to the 10th August, in the same year.

NAMES.	RANK.	TIME OF SERVICE.		REMARKS.
		Months.	Days.	
William Smith, - -	Captain,	1	12	
Hay Taliaferro, - -	Lieutenant,	1	12	
George W. Spotswood, -	"	1	12	
Patrick Pitty, - -	Cornet,	1	12	
John T. Mann, - -	Sergeant,	1	12	
Henry Conway, - -	"	1	12	
James Yager, - -	"	1	12	
Charles S. Stone, - -	"	1	12	
William S. Jinkins, - -	Corporal,	1	12	
Thomas Tombs, - -	"	1	12	
Henry Clark, - -	"	1	12	
George H. Inskeep, - -	"	1	12	
Daniel Anderson, - -	Private,	1	12	
Roland Bradley, - -	"	1	12	
Peter Bogarder, - -	"	1	12	
John Bradley, - -	"	1	12	
James Brown, - -	"	1	12	
Thomas Brown, - -	"	1	12	
William Clarke, - -	"	1	12	
Jonathan Cathin, - -	"	1	12	
John Clarke, - -	"	1	12	
Edward Colling, - -	"	1	12	
Jacob Davis, - -	"	1	12	
Horatio Dade, - -	"	1	12	
John Dickson, - -	"	1	12	
William Foard, - -	"	1	12	
Francis Ford, - -	"	1	12	
William Fanbooner, - -	"	1	12	
Thomas Getting, - -	"	1	12	
John C. Harris, - -	"	1	12	
Monroe Hancock, - -	"	1	12	
Linsfield Jones, - -	"	1	12	
William Jones, - -	"	1	12	
John J. Lewis, - -	"	1	12	
John Lewis, - -	"	1	12	
Conway Mower, (or Mawr,) -	"	1	12	
Moses McKenny, - -	"	1	14	
Braxton Osborn, (or Oborn,)	"	1	12	
Abner Pitts, - -	"	1	12	
Isaac Right, - -	"	1	12	
Thomas Stubblefield, -	"	1	12	
Lawrence Sandford, - -	"	1	12	
William Talken, - -	"	1	12	
Lawrence Taliaferro, -	"	1	12	
William Taylor, - -	"	1	12	
Hay Taliaferro, - -	"	1	12	
James Webb, - -	"	1	12	
James Waller, - -	"	1	12	
John H. Weeks, - -	"	1	12	

MUSTER ROLL

Of Videttes, of the Second Battalion, One Hundred and Eleventh Regiment, Westmoreland County, ordered into Service by Major John Turberville, in July 1813.

NAMES.			RANK.	TIME OF SERVICE.		REMARKS.
				Months.	Days.	
James Sorrel,	-	-	Commander,	–	7	
James H. Bailey,	-	-	Private,	–	5	
Stephen Bailey,	-	-	"	–	3	
Presley Cox,	-	-	"	–	5	
John Crenshaw,	-	-	"	–	7	
George Glascock,	-	-	"	–	6	
James Lett,	-	-	"	–	6	
Samuel Lewis,	-	-	"	–	5	
Henry Parker,	-	-	"	–	5	
Thomas Pinckard,	-	-	"	–	2	
James Robinson,	-	-	"	–	5	

Captain James H. Sowers' Company—Fifty-first Regiment.

NAMES.			RANK.	TIME OF SERVICE.		REMARKS.
				Months.	Days.	
Maholon Colman,	-	-	Drummer,	2	25	
Abner Hughes,	-	-	Fifer,	2	25	
Alexander Gordon,	-	-	Private,	–	22	
Jeremiah Lahud,	-	-	"	–	15	
Wm. T. Rowsee,	-	-	"	–	22	

(For rest of this company, see publication of Pay Rolls.)

Captain Archibald Stuart's Company—Ninety-third Regiment.

NAMES.			RANK.	TIME OF SERVICE.		REMARKS.
				Months.	Days.	
James Black,	-	-	Private.	–	14	
Hyram Byas,	-	-	"	–	22	
William Cason,	-	-	"	1	16	
Richard Freeman,	-	-	"	–	20	
W. Lilley,	-	-	"	–	22	
Ralph A. Eoftus,	-	-	"	–	12	
Henry Miller,	-	-	"	–	22	
Thomas Rowsey,	-	-	"	–	5	
T. H. Shanklin,	-	-	"	–	22	
Conrad Sciders,	-	-	"	–	14	
William Spence,	-	-	"	–	18	
Nat. Tarbet,	-	-	"	–	12	
Abner Whitsel.	-	-	"	1	14	

(For rest of this company, see publication of Pay Rolls.)

MUSTER ROLL

Of Captain John |Staton's Company, of the Ninety-ninth Regiment, Virginia Militia, called into actual Service of the United States, under the general orders of Lieutenant Colonel Charles Bagwell, from the 28th May to 2d June, 1814.

NAMES.	RANK.	TIME OF SERVICE.		REMARKS.
		Months.	Days.	
John Staton,	Captain,	–	3	
Jacob Warner,	Lieutenant,	–	3	
William Matthews,	Ensign,	–	2	
James Staton,	Sergeant,	–	2	
Kendal Silverthorn,	"	–	5	
Walter Wessels,	"	–	5	Or Wepels.
Levin Matthews,	"	–	5	
John Cutler,	Corporal,	–	5	
Noah Johns,	"	–	5	
William Trotter,	Musician,	–	5	
Stephen Lumber,	"	–	5	
Archibald Annis,	Private,	–	5	
John Adams,	"		5	
Kendal Bloxom,	"	–	5	
Jacob Bloxom,	"	–	5	
James Conquest,	"	–	5	
William Conquest,	"		5	
Joseph Conquest,	"		5	
Richard Coke,	"	–	5	
John C. Drummond,	"	–	5	
John Drummond, (of David,)	"	–	5	
Samuel Delartatsions,	"	–	5	
Thomas Fletcher,	"	–	5	
John Fletcher,	"	–	5	
Thomas Hall,	"	–	5	
Henry Hall,	"	–	5	
John Henderson, (of Butt,)	"	–	5	
John Jackson,	"	–	5	
William Justice, (of Robert,)	"	–	5	
Thomas Johns,	"	–	5	
Raymond Lewis,	"	–	5	
Revil Lewis,	"	–	5	
Elijah Linton,	"	–	5	
William Linton,	"	–	5	
Samuel W. Milhowm,	"	–	5	
John Mears,	"	–	5	
William Marshall,	"	–	5	
John Mudut,	"	–	5	
William McReady,	"	–	5	
Aaron Marshall,	"	–	5	
William Northan,	"	–	5	
Henry Northan,	"	–	5	
William Only,	"	–	5	
Josiah Starling,	"	–	5	
Geo. Smith,	"	–	5	
Thomas Smith,	"	–	5	
Ishmael Trader,	"	–	5	

NAMES.			RANK.	TIME OF SERVICE.		REMARKS.
				Months.	Days.	
Staton Trader,	-	-	Private,	–	5	
John White,	-	-	"	–	5	
Geo. Winder,	-	-	"	–	5	
Isaac Whaley,	-	-	"	–	5	

MUSTER ROLL

Of Captain Andrew Stevenson's Company, of the Nineteenth Regiment, Virginia Militia, commanded by Lieutenant Colonel John Ambler, called into the Service of the United States, from 18th to 27th of March, in the year 1814.

NAMES.	RANK.	TIME OF SERVICE.		REMARKS.
		Months.	Days.	
Andrew Stevenson, -	Captain,	–	10	
Charles Bosher, - -	Lieutenant,	–	10	
Ralph Allen, -. -	"	–	10	
Chs. Z. Abrahams, - -	Sergeant,	–	10	
John P. Prentis, - -	"	–	10	
Nath. Charter, - -	"	–	10	
James Golding, - -	"	–	10	
Abner Allen, - -	Private,	–	10	
John Bath, - -	"	–	10	
Elias Bennett, - -	"	–	10	
James Bosher, - -	"	–	10	
John Bosher, - -	"	–	10	
Jonas Crane, - -	"	–	10	
Zach. Clarke, - -	"	–	10	
Joseph Danforth, - -	"	–	10	
James Edwards, - -	"	–	10	
Richard Finch, - -	"	–	10	
Jas. A. Grant, - -	"	–	10	
William Gardner, - -	"	–	10	
Felix Grant, - -	"	–	10	
Wm. Henderson, - -	"	–	10	
Alex'r Hare, - -	"	–	10	
Mitchum Hudgins, -	"	–	10	
Bathford Irvine, - -	"	–	10	
G. F. Kohler, - -	"	–	10	
William Keesee, - -	"	–	10	
William Lee, - -	"	–	10	
Thomas Lane, - -	"	–	10	
Samuel Liggon, - -	"	–	10	
Peter Lemons, - -	"	–	10	
Barrett Moss, - -	"	–	10	
H. Mettert, - -	"	–	10	
Joseph Murdock, - -	"	–	10	
—— Miller, - -	"	–	10	
Richard Norris, - -	"	–	10	
William O. Nash, - -	"	–	10	
James Ogden, - -	"	–	10	
John Patton, - - -	"	–	10	
H. Pickrill, - - -	"	–	10	
Solomon Robins, - -	"	–	10	
William Talman, - -	"	–	10	
James Thompson, - -	"	–	10	
James Tounley, - -	"	–	10	
Charles Wills, - -	"	–	10	
Amiel Williams, - -	"	–	10	
John Walker, - -	"	–	10	

MUSTER ROLL

Of Captain William Stone's Company, of the Twentieth Regiment, Virginia Militia, commanded by Lieutenant Colonel James Robinson, called into the Service of the United States from 5th to 18th February, from 10th to 15th March, and from 10th to 17th September, in the year 1813.

NAMES.			RANK.	TIME OF SERVICE.		REMARKS.
				Months.	Days.	
William Stone,	-	-	Captain,	—	20	
Samuel Veale,	-	-	Lieutenant,	—	28	
Charles Burgess,	-	-	Ensign,	—	28	
John Smith,	-	-	Sergeant,	—	28	
John Keeling,	-	-	"	—	20	
David Butt,	-	-	"	—	8	
John Burgess,	-	-	"	—	8	
Moses Murden,	-	-	"	—	14	
Robert Hays,	-	-	"	—	20	
George Whitehurst,	-	-	"	—	6	
Willis Whitehurst,	-	-	Corporal,	—	27	
Henry Davis,	-	-	"	—	27	
William Griggs,	-	-	"	—	14	
Robert Williamson,	-	-	"	—	8	
George Whitehurst,	-	-	"	—	14	
William Hibden,	-	-	"	—	6	
Amos Benson,	-	-	Private,	—	6	
David Butt.	-	-	"	—	20	
Hillary Berry,	-	-	"	—	20	
Anthony Butt,	-	-	"	—	20	
John Brumley,	-	-	"	—	20	
Henry Batton,	-	-	"	—	17	
John Brinson,	-	-	"	—	14	
Jonathan Berry,	-	-	"	—	20	
William Banks,	-	-	"	—	3	
Robert Burby,	-	-	"	—	6	
William Cason,	-	-	"	—	27	
John Dennett,	-	-	"	—	28	
Charles Dennett,	-	-	"	—	20	
James Etheridge,	-	-	"	—	14	
William Etheridge,	-	-	"	—	13	
Edward Etheridge,	-	-	"	—	20	
David Fentress,	-	-	"	—	20	
Charles Griggs,	-	-	"	—	8	
William Griggs,	-	-	"	—	14	
John Griffin,	-	-	"	—	20	
William Godfrey,	-	-	"	—	20	
William Hudgins,	-	-	"	—	14	
Jonathan James,	-	-	"	—	14	
John Johnson,	-	-	"	—	14	
Henry Keeling,	-	-	"	—	26	
Nath. Keeling,	-	-	"	—	20	
Isaac Keeling,	-	-	"	—	28	
William Luffman,	-	-	"	—	20	
Isaac Matthias,	-	-	"	—	14	
Willis B. McCoy,	-	-	"	—	28	
David Matthias,	-	-	"	—	18	

NAMES.	RANK.	TIME OF SERVICE.		REMARKS.
		Months.	Days.	
Christopher Moseley, -	Private,	–	19	
George McClanahan, -	"	–	14	
Coventon Otley, - -	"	–	20	
Henry Petty, - -	"	–	25	
James Stone, - -	"	–	27	
David Shirley, - -	"	–	6	
Thomas Ward, - -	"	–	20	
John Ward, - -	"	–	26	
Thomas Wiles, - -	"	–	26	
Enoch Whitehurst, - -	"	–	20	
Joshua Williamson, - -	"	–	26	
John Whitehurst, sr. - -	"	–	20	
John Whitehurst, jr. - -	"	–	19	
Oden Whitehurst, - -	"	–	20	
Robert Williamson, - -	"	–	20	
Botson Whitehurst, - -	"	–	14	

MUSTER ROLL

Of Captain Barton S. Stone's Company, of the Forty-fifth Regiment, Virginia Militia, commanded by Lieutenant Colonel Samuel H. Peyton, called into the Service of the United States, from 22d July to the 18th August, in the year 1814.

NAMES.	RANK.	TIME OF SERVICE.		REMARKS.
		Months.	Days.	
Barton S. Stone,	Captain,	–	28	
Archibald Rowley,	Ensign,	–	28	
Thomas Graves,	Sergeant,	–	28	
John Latham,	"	–	28	
Willis Brown,	Corporal,	–	28	
William Horton,	"	–	28	
Alexander Obryhim,	"	–	28	
George Coakley,	Musician,	–	28	
Henry Bradley,	Private,	–	28	
David Bradley,	"	–	28	
William Black,	"	–	28	
John Berry,	"	–	28	
Samuel Bloxton,	"	–	28	
Richard M. Beckwith,	"	–	28	
Thomas W. Cowne,	"	–	28	
John Fant,	"	–	28	
John Foushee,	"	–	28	
William Gregory,	"	–	28	
Joseph Graves,	"	–	28	
John Horton,	"	–	28	
George Honey,	"	–	28	
James Hewitt,	"	–	28	
Daniel Hall,	"	–	28	
Cossum Horton,	"	–	28	
Zachariah Jones,	"	–	28	
Perry Patterson,	"	–	28	
Lewis Payne,	"	–	28	
Thomas Schooler,	"	–	28	
John Sudduth,	"	–	28	
Benjamin Snelling,	"	–	28	
Bradford Smith,	"	–	28	
George Wine,	"	–	28	

Captain John G. Stuart's Company—Twenty-fifth Regiment.

NAMES.	RANK.	TIME OF SERVICE.		REMARKS.
		Months.	Days.	
West Ashton, - -	Corporal,	—	13	
George N. Grymes, - -	"	—	13	
John S. Burnbury, - -	Private,	—	13	
Thomas Bryan, - -	"	—	13	
James Cox, - -	"	—	13	
Walter Clark, - -	"	—	12	
Miles Clift, - -	"	—	5	
Cadw'r J. Dade, - -	"	—	6	
Henry Fitzhugh, - -	"	—	13	
A. B. Hooe, - -	"	—	13	
John Hooe, - -	"	—	13	
Dangerfield Lewis, - -	"	—	8	
Herbert Mason, - -	"	—	13	
John H. Peyton, - -	"	—	7	
Edward Reynolds, - -	"	—	8	
Gustavus G. Rogers, - -	"	—	13	
James Williams, - -	"	—	13	
Jacob W. Stewart, - -	"	—	13	
John Shropshire, - -	"	—	4	

(For rest of this company, see publication of Pay Rolls.)

Captain John Sizer's Company—Thirtieth Regiment.

NAMES.	RANK.	TIME OF SERVICE.		REMARKS.
		Months.	Days.	
John Pearson, - -	Private,	6	7	
William Peatross, - -	"	6	7	
Hugh N. Thompson, -	"	6	7	

(For rest of this company, see publication of Pay Rolls.)

MUSTER ROLL

Of Lieutenant John S. Stubbs' Company, in the Nineteenth Regiment, Virginia Militia, commanded by Lieutenant Colonel John Ambler, called into the Service of the United States, from the 26th August to the 7th September, 1814.

NAMES.			RANK.	TIME OF SERVICE.		REMARKS.
				Months.	Days.	
John S. Stubbs,	-	-	Lieutenant,	—	13	Appointed adjutant.
Jacob Weisiger,	-	-	Ensign,	—	13	
Francis J Lewis,	-	-	Sergeant,	—	13	Appointed assistant F. master.
Edmund Redford,	-	-	"	—	13	Appointed assistant Q. master.
George Watt,	-	-	"	—	10	Appointed Qr. master.
Edmund S. Norvell,	-	-	"	—	13	
John Ormond,	-	-	Corporal,	—	13	
Reuben Nash,	-	-	"	—	13	
Jabez Parker,	-	-	"	—	13	
John A. Lancaster,	-	-	"	—	13	
Wiliam Armistead,	-	-	Private,	—	7	F. artillery.
James Asby,	-	-	"	—	13	
Wm. Archer,	-	-	"	—	7	" "
Alexander Auter,	-	-	"	—	7	" "
Charles Bennett,	-	-	'	—	13	
William Brasie,	-	-	"	—	13	
Royal Brown,	-	-	"	—	13	
Joshua Brotherhood,	-	-	"	—	13	
Leonard Bowers,	-	-	"	—	7	Union artillery.
Benj. W. Coleman,	-	-	"	—	13	
George Charter,	-	-	"	—	13	
Andrew Crew,	-	-	"	—	13	
John Drinkard,	-	-	"	—	13	
Christ. Drummond,	-	-	"	—	7	F. artillery.
Andrew Dunn,	-	-	"	—	13	
Charles Elliott,	-	-	"	—	7	" "
John Enders,	-	-	"	—	13	
Wm. Fleming,	-	-	"	—	7	" "
Robert Fagg,	-	-	"	—	7	" "
John Goode,	-	-	"	—	13	
William Garrow,	-	-	"	—	13	
Isaac Hamard,	-	-	"	—	13	
George P. Hadin,	-	-	"	—	7	" "
Daniel Jones,	-	-	"	—	13	
John Johnson,	-	-	"	—	13	
Uriah Johnson,	-	-	"	—	13	
William Loyall,	-	-	"	—	13	
Nathaniel Long,	-	-	"	—	13	
Thomas Lee,	-	-	"	—	13	
Isaac Leonard,	-	-	"	—	13	
Carter Mallory,	-	-	"	—	7	" "
George Mettert,	-	-	"	—	7	" . "
James McAllister,	-	-	"	—	13	
William Masonberg,	-	-	"	—	13	
Richard Minor,	-		"	—	7	" "

NAMES.	RANK.	TIME OF SERVICE.		REMARKS.
		Months.	Days.	
Alexander Morris, - -	Private,	–	7	F. artillery.
G. W. Pam, - -	"	–	7	" "
Thomas Pickerell, - -	"	–	13	
Samuel Quay, - -	"	–	13	
James H. Royster, - -	"	–	6	
Richard Redford, - -	"	–	13	
James Rudd, - -	"	–	7	" "
Jacob Smith, - -	"	–	13	
George Smith, - -	"	–	13	
William Sheran, - -	"	–	13	
James Shell, - -	"	–	13	
Reuben M. Sizer, - -	"	–	13	
George F. Shifter, - -	"	–	10	
Simon Solomon, - -	"	–	13	
Samuel Smith, - -	"	–	8	
Michael Tucker, - -	"	–	13	
Watson Tyler, - -	"	–	7	
Roddy Towers, - -	"	–	7	" "
Charles Word, -	"	–	13	Appointed F. master.
Thomas Whitlow -	"	–	7	F. artillery.
Edmund Warner -	"	–	7	
John Warwick, -	"	–	13	
Matthew Watts, -	"	–	7	" "
Benjamin Waller, - -	"	–	13	
Samuel Winston, - -	"	–	13	
Hugh Warden, - -	"	–	13	
George Woodfin, - -	"	–	6	Sutler.

MUSTER ROLL

Of Lieutenant Henry Styron's Company, in the Twentieth Regiment, Virginia Militia, commanded by Lieutenant Colonel James Robinson, called into the Service of the United States, from the 10th to the 15th March, 1813.

NAMES.			RANK.	TIME OF SERVICE.		REMARKS.
				Months.	Days.	
Henry Styron,	-	-	Lieutenant,	–	6	
John Barnes,	-	-	Ensign,	–	6	
James Seneca,	-	-	Sergeant,	–	6	
Francis Williamson,	-	-	"	–	6	
Kader Whitehurst,	-	-	"	–	6	
William Ward,	-	-	Corporal,	–	6	
Francis Batten,	-	-	"	–	6	
Hillary Styron,	"	-	"	–	6	
Jonathan Ackiss,	-	-	Fifer,	–	6	
Caleb Whitehurst,	-	-	Drummer,	–	6	
Benjamin Cox,	-	-	Private,	–	6	
Ancil Cox,	-	-	"	–	6	
Elijah Capps,	-	-	"	–	6	
John Craft,	-	-	"	–	3	
William Dawley,	-	-	"	–	6	
Joshua Frizzle,	-	-	"	–	6	
Reuben Flanagan,	-	-	"	–	3	
Henry Kinsey,	-	-	"	–	6	
Solomon Lane,	-	-	"	–	6	
Tully McClanen,	-	-	"	–	6	
James Robinson,	-	-	"	–	6	
Perin Smith,	-	-	"	–	6	
Jesse Smith,	-	-	"	–	6	
Stephen Sharwood,	-	-	"	–	6	
James Whitehurst,	-	-	"	–	3	
Charles Waterman,	-	-	"	–	6	
James Williamson,	-	-	"	–	6	
Simon Whitehurst,	-	-	"	–	6	
John Whitehurst,	-	-	"	–	6	
William Woodland,	-	-	"	–	6	
Malachi Williamson,	-	-	"	–	6	
Henry Williams,	-	-	"	–	6	

Captain James Sutton's Company—Thirty-seventh Regiment.

NAMES.	RANK.	TIME OF SERVICE.		REMARKS.
		Months.	Days.	
Cal. Harcum, - -	Sergeant,	–	6	
John Robinson, - -	Drummer,	–	5	
Ralph Beatley, - -	Private,	–	29	
William Blackwell, - -	"	–	19	
Samuel Church, - -	"	–	13	
Peter P. Cockarill, - -	"	–	5	
Richard P. Coles, - -	"	–	9	
Jos. Coles, - - -	"	–	7	
Joseph Dudley, - -	"	–	4	
Robert Edwards, - -	"	–	6	
Griffin Edwards, - -	"	–	12	
Elisha Fallin, - -	"	–	5	
William H. Juques, - -	"	–	19	
William Kirkham, - -	"	–	7	
John McAdam, - -	"	1	21	Appointed surgeon's mate.
Rhodam Neal, - -	"	–	10	
Reves Owens, - -	"	–	17	
John Tary, - - -	"	1	11	
John Throp, - -	"	–	3	
James Throp, - -	"	–	18	
Catesby Toulson, - -	"	–	5	
Thomas Tignor, - -	"	–	6	
Collins Willey, - -	"	–	24	
James Williams, - -	"	–	8	
Joseph Wood, - -	"	–	11	

(For rest of this company, see publication of Pay Rolls.)

MUSTER ROLL

Of Captain Levi Swelnam's Company of Virginia Militia, commanded by Lieutenant Colonel Samuel H. Peyton, in the Service of the United States, from 22d July to 16th August, 1814.

NAMES.	RANK.	TIME OF SERVICE.		REMARKS.
		Months.	Days.	
Levi Swelnam, - -	Captain,	—	26	
Jer'h B. Templeman, - -	Lieutenant,	—	28	
George T. Shelkeet, - -	Ensign,	—	28	
John R. Bohannan, - -	Sergeant,	—	28	
George Curtis, - -	"	—	28	
Andrew Ross, - -	"	—	28	
William Burton, - -	"	—	28	
Rodham Graves, - -	Corporal,	—	28	
Oswell Pemberton, - -	"	—	28	
Wm. Marquiss, - -	"	—	28	
John H. Cochran, - -	"	—	28	
Isaac Barton, - -	Private,	—	28	
Fielding Batty, - -	"	—	28	
Wm. Bryant, - -	"	—	28	
Wm. Bowling, - -	"	—	28	
Charles Bowling, - -	"	—	28	
James Bowling, - -	"	—	28	
John Burton, - -	"	—	28	
Abija Bowling, - -	"	—	28	
George Bowling, - -	"	—	28	
Joshua Beach, - -	"	—	28	
Joseph Burnham, - -	"	—	28	
James Briggs, - -	"	—	.28	
Thornton Cropp, - -	"	—	28	
Richard Curtis, - -	"	—	28	
Robert Child, - -	"	—	28	
Fielding Curtis, - -	"	—	28	
Presley Cropp, - -	"	—	28	
Thomas Cropp, - -	"	—	28	
Lewis Courtney, - -	"	—	28	
Lovel Fant, - -	"	—	28	
James Foreakers, - -	"	—	28	
Thomas Graves, - -	"	—	28	
Joseph Graves, - -	"	—	28	
Fielding Humphrey, - -	"	—	28	
Early Humphrey, - -	"	—	28	
John Jackson, jr. - -	"	—	28	
Wm. Jackson, - -	"	—	28	
James Jackson, - -	"	—	28	
James Knight, - -	"	—	28	
Rolly Latham, - -	"	—	28	
Thornton Martin, - -	"	—	28	
Jesse Mussleman, - -	"	—	28	
John Martin, - -	"	—	28	
John Mussleman, - -	"	—	28	
Elliott Patton, - -	"	—	28	
Perry Patterson, - -	"	—	28	
Samuel Pater, - -	"	—	28	

NAMES.	RANK.	TIME OF SERVICE.		REMARKS.
		Months.	Days.	
William Pemberton, - -	Private,	–	28	
William Richerson, - -	"	–	28	
John Ryan, - -	"	–	28	
Benjamin Simms, - -	"	–	28	
Joseph Tyson, - -	"	–	28	
James Tyson, - -	"	–	28	
Creed True, - -	"	–	28	
Thornton Taylor, - -	"	–	28	
John Trussel, - -	"	–	28	
William Trussel, - -	"	–	28	
James Williams, - -	"	–	28	
Thomas Watts, - -	"	–	28	
Thomas Young, - -	"	–	28	

MUSTER ROLL

Of Captain John T. Sydnor's Company of the Eighty-third Regiment, Virginia Militia, in the County of Dinwiddie, called into actual Service under the general orders of the 30th June, 1813, from 1st to 6th July in the year 1813.

NAMES.	RANK.	TIME OF SERVICE.		REMARKS.
		Months.	Days.	
John T. Sydnor,	Captain,	–	6	
Isaac Daney,	Lieutenant,	–	6	
Edward H. Jones,	Ensign,	–	6	
Joel Stowe,	Sergeant,	–	6	
Enoch Rather,	"	–	6	
John Candle, sen.	"	–	6	
Arch'd Candle,	"	–	6	
William Parham,	Corporal,	–	6	
Daniel Wells,	"	–	6	
Daniel Browder,	"	–	6	
Joshua Young,	"	–	6	
Epes Allen,	Private,	–	6	
Rich'd Browder,	"	–	6	
Tilman Butler,	"	–	6	
Geo. Browder,	"	–	6	
Thos. Browder,	"	–	6	
Henry Barnes,	"	–	6	
Edward Birchett,	"	–	6	
John Coleman,	"	–	6	
Charner Crowder,	"	–	6	
Jacob Crowder,	"	–	6	
John G. Dyson,	"	–	6	
Isham Eppes,	"	–	6	
Elisha Eanes,	"	–	6	
Wm. Elder,	"	–	6	
Rice Eanes,	"	–	6	
Wm. French,	"	–	6	
John Grant,	"	–	6	
Rich'd Goode,	"	–	6	
Everard Green,	"	–	6	
Wm. Hambleton,	"	–	6	
John Hughes,	"	–	6	
Green Moss,	"	–	6	
Abel T. Puckett,	"	–	6	
John Pandle, jr.	"	–	6	
Branch Perkinson,	"	–	6	
Jesse Reames,	"	–	6	
Wm. Slaughter,	"	–	6	
Fendal T. Sutherland,	"	–	6	
Wm. Sandiford,	"	–	6	
Joshua Spain,	"	–	6	
Wm. Spain,	"	–	6	
Jno. B. Spain,	"	–	6	
Thompson Stewart,	"	–	6	
Joel Wells,	"	–	6	
James Williams,	"	–	6	
Herbert Williams,	"	–	6	

NAMES.			RANK.	TIME OF SERVICE.		REMARKS.
				Months.	Days.	
John A. Waugh,	-	-	Private,	–	6	
James Young,	-	-	"	–	6	
Elliott Young,	-	-	"	–	6	
John Young, jr.	-	-	"	–	6	

Lieutenant Thomas T. T. Tabb's Company—Sixty-first Regiment.

NAMES.	RANK.	TIME OF SERVICE.		REMARKS.
		Months.	Days.	
Thomas T. T. Tabb, - -	Lieutenant,	–	10	
Thomas B. Yeatman, -	Ensign,	–	9	
Jos. C. Mayne, (or Marigne,)	Sergeant,	–	14	
Jesse Degges, - -	"	–	10	
William L. Smith, - -	"	–	9	
John Foster, - -	"	–	9	
Felix T. Sharples, - -	Corporal,	–	10	
Bailey Hudgin, - -	"	–	10	
Josiah Evans, - -	"	–	9	
John Degges, - -	"	–	9	
Richard Ayres, - -	Private,	–	8	
John Adams, - -	"	–	10	
John Ayres, - -	"	–	2	
Josiah Brooks, - -	"	–	10	
Thomas Basset, - -	"	–	14	
George Brown, - -	"	–	9	
Barber Degges, - -	"			
Jarvis Deale, - -	"	–	12	
Cole Degges, - -	"	–	10	
Anthony Deggs, - -	"	–	10	
John Deggs, - -	"	–	10	
Samuel Eddins, - -	"			
John Forrest, - -	"	–	9	
Isaac Foster, - -	"	–	10	
Joseph Foster, - -	"			
Abraham Forrest, - -	"	–	10	
James Foster, - -	"			
Joshua Foster, - -	"	–	8	
Josiah Foster, - -	"			
Elijah Gayle, - -	"	2	18	
Thomas Gayle, - -	"	–	22	
Thomas Gayle, - -	"	–	22	
Bartlett Hudgin, - -	"	–	9	
Meredith Hurst, - -	"	–	10	
John Hurst, - -	"	–	14	
William Hurst, - -	"	1	14	
Jesse Hurst, - -	"	–	10	
Holder Hudgin, - -	"	–	10	
William Hunley, - -	"	–	9	
Peter S. Hunley, - -	"	–	3	
John Hunley, jr. - -	"			
John Hughes, - -	"	–	9	
Philip Hughes, - -	"	–	8	
Lewis Hudgin, - -	"	–	9	
Richard L. Hilling, - -	"			
William Hudgin, - -	"	–	9	
John Morris, - -	"	–	9	
Thomas Morton, - -	"			
John Morgan, - -	"	–	9	
Thomas Owen, - -	"	–	8	
Edward Owen, - -	"	–	1	
Matthew Pickett, - -	"	–	14	
John Parsons, - -	"	–	9	
Absalom Parsons, - -	"			

NAMES.		RANK.	TIME OF SERVICE.		REMARKS.
			Months.	Days.	
George Parrott,	- -	Private,	–		
Thomas Palmer,	- -	"	–	10	
William Parrott,	- -	"	–	1	
James Ripley,	- -	"	–	2	
Thomas Sampson,	- -	"	–	9	
Isaac Smith,	- -	"	–		
Robert Sadler,	- -	"	–	9	
John Sadler,	- -	"	–	8	
Philip W. Spark,	- -	"	–		
William Treakle,	- -	"	–	16	
John Turner,	- -	"	–	9	
James Willis,	- -	"	–	-1	
Abram Williams,	- -	"	–	11	
William D. White,	- -	,,	–	8	

(For rest of this company, see Captain Thomas T. T. Tabb's company in publication of Pay Rolls.)

MUSTER ROLL

Of Captain Joseph Tarney's Company, from the Sixth Regiment, Virginia Militia, in the County of Essex, called into actual Service from the 5th to 8th April, in the year 1813.

NAMES.			RANK.	TIME OF SERVICE.		REMARKS.
				Months.	Days.	
Joseph Tarney,	-	-	Captain,	—	4	Or Tarey.
Philip Brooks,	-	-	Sergeant,	—	4	
Richard Cronton,	-	-	"	—	4	Or Croxton.
Perkins Armstrong,	-	-	Private,	—	4	
Wm. Blake,	-	-	"	—	4	
Leroy D. Beal,	-	-	"	—	4	
John Brooks,	-	-	"	—	4	
Reuben Boughton,	-	-	"	—	4	
Richard Boughton,	-	-	"	—	4	
John Cronton,	-	-	"	—	4	Or Croxton.
Leroy Cauthorn,	-	-	"	—	4	
Absalom Candas,	-	-	"	—	4	
Baylor Carlton,	-	-	"	—	4	
Wm. Dyke,	-	-	"	—	4	
Moses Dyke,	-	-	"	—	4	
James Dyke,	-	-	"	—	4	
James Dix,	-	-	"	—	4	
Kemp Evans,	-	-	"	—	4	
Archibald Gibson,	-	-	"	—	4	
Benj. Hundley,	-	-	"	—	4	
Thos. Hartey,	-	-	"	—	4	
Anthony Haynes,	-	-	"	—	4	
James R. Micou,	-	-	"	—	4	
Richard Mann,	-	-	"	—	4	
John Marshall,	-	-	"	—	4	
Wm. McLyre,	-	-	"	—	4	
Wm. Perry,	-	-	"	—	4	
Richard Richards,	-	-	"	—	4	
John Stuart,	-	-	"	—	4	
Joseph Tompkins,	-	-	"	—	4	
Godfrey Young,	-	-	"	—	4	

Captain Alexander Taylor's Company.

NAMES.			RANK.	TIME OF SERVICE.		REMARKS.
				Months.	Days.	
Reuben Moss,	-	-	Ensign,	–	23	
Daniel Pegram,	-	-	Corporal,	–	23	
John Anderson,	-	-	Private,	–	23	
Wylie Burge,	-	-	"	–	23	
William Cameron,	-	-	"	–	23	
Patrick Durkin,	-	-	"	–	23	
Samuel Davis,	-	-	"	–	23	
David Fowler,	-	-	"	–	23	
Joseph Gray,	-	-	"	–	23	
Theodore Hart,	-	-	"	–	23	
Benjamin Johnson,	-	-	"	–	23	
John Joiner,	-	-	"	–	23	
Thomas Lockhead,	-	-	"	–	23	
Francis Pace,	-	-	"	–	23	
John B. Ponsonby,	-	-	"	–	23	
Ro. G. Simmons,	-	-	"	–	23	
Thomas Taylor,	-	-	"	–	23	
William Worsham,	-	-	"	–	23	
Davis Wills,	-	-	"	–	23	
William B. Wills,	-	-	"	–	6	

(For rest of this company, see publication of Pay Rolls.)

Cnptain Robert P. Taylor's Company—Sixty-eighth Regiment.

NAMES.	RANK.	TIME OF SERVICE.		REMARKS.
		Months.	Days.	
Anthony King, - -	Ensign,	–	17	
Armistead Lightfoot, - -	Sergeant,	–	26	
William Gibbs, - -	"	–	15	
Whitaker Lee, - -	"	–	11	
George Thomas, - -	"	1	2	
Thomas Newman, - -	Corporal,	–	17	
Bennett K. Barhern, - -	"	–	11	
Joseph C. Valentine, - -	"	1	9	
James V. Shields, - -	"	–	11	
Jno. W. Judkins, - -	"	–	11	
George James, - -	"	1	2	
John Tyree, - -	"	–	29	
William E. Barnett, - -	Private,			
Elisha Bates, - -	"			
Robert Boalton, - -	"	–	9	
William Calivan, - -	"	–	9	
George Cooper, - -	"	–	20	
Johnson Coggin, - -	"	–	11	
John Crawley, - -	"	1	1	
Miles Crowdus, - -	"	–	16	
William S. Ellis, - -	"	–	25	
John T. Earnest, - -	"	–	11	
Thomas Goode, - -	"	–	10	
Leaven Gordon, - -	"	–	11	
John Hockaday, - -	"			
Benj. Hockaday, - -	"			
Benj. Hazelwood, - -	"			
Gordon Harrison, - -	"			
Matthew Holt, - -	"	–	10	
Thomas Hazelwood, - -	"			
Jourdan Harrison, - -	"			
Benj. Hansford, - -	"	–	23	Sub. for Henry Finch.
James Jenkins, - -	"	–	15	
Park Jones, - -	"	1	1	Joined cavalry.
Benj. Jolley, - -	"	–	29	
John A. James, - -	"	–	11	
Chesley Jones, - -	"	–	29	
William Lively, - -	"			
James McKendall, - -	"	–	11	
Daniel M. Mills, - -	"	–	11	
William Mure, - -	"			
John Pearman, - -	"			
Thomas Pointer, - -	"	–	29	
John Pumphrey, - -	"	–	21	
Abner Piggott, - -	"			
Reuben Ratcliff, - -	"	–	25	
Wade Robinson, - -	"	–	6	
Bailey Smith, - -	"	1	1	Sub for Allen Jones.
William W. Taylor, - -	"	–	7	
—— Thornton, - -	Wagoner,			
Wm. D. Williamson, - -	Private,	–	16	
Benjamin Walls, - -	"	–	16	
William A. Walker, - -	"	–	9	

NAMES.	RANK.	TIME OF SERVICE.		REMARKS.
		Months.	Days.	
Samuel Willeford, - -	Private,	–	24	
Edmund Waller, - -	"	–	4	
Dennis Williamson, - -	"	–	26	
John Wilson, - -	"	1	12	

(For rest of this company, see publication of Pay Rolls.)

MUSTER ROLL

Of Captain Thomas T. Taylor's Company, from the Ninty-ninth Regiment, Virginia Militia, called into actual Service of the United States, under general orders of Lieutenant Colonel Charles Bagwell, from 2d to 9th June, and from 7th to 8th September, in the year 1814.

NAMES.			RANK.	TIME OF SERVICE.		REMARKS.
				Months.	Days.	
Thomas T. Taylor,	-	-	Captain,	—	10	
James White,	-	-	Lieutenant,	—	10	
Skinner Wallop,	-	-	Ensign,	—	10	
David Davis,	-	-	Sergeant,	—	10	
William Wallop,	-	-	"	—	9	
George Showard,	-	-	"	—	10	
William Hickman,	-	-	"	—	10	
William Hancock,	-	-	Corporal,	—	10	
Henry Tunnall,	-	-	"	—	9	
William Ewell,	-	-	"	—	9	
John D. Cropper,	-	-	"	—	10	
John Taylor,	-	-	Drummer,	—	10	
John Dunton,	-	-	Fifer,	—	10	
George Addison,	-	-	Private,	—	10	
Richard Addison,	-	-	"	—	10	
George Arbuckle,	-	-	"	—	10	
Arthur Adderson,	-	-	"	—	8	
Reuben Adams,	-	-	"	—	2	
James Bowles,	-	-	"	—	8	
Woodman Bloxom,	-	-	"	—	9	
Samuel Bowles,	-	-	"	—	8	
Thomas Bloxom,	-	-	"	—	10	
John Buttingham,	-	-	"	—	2	
William Buckler,	-	-	"	—	2	
Arthur Coard,	-	-	"	—	8	
Joseph Covington,	-	-	"	—	8	
John T. Collins,	-	-	"	—	10	
William Collins,	-	-	"	—	10	
Parker Coard,	-	-	"	—	2	
William Coard,	-	-	"	—	2	
George Ewell,	-	-	"	—	10	
Edward Ewell,	-	-	"	—	10	
Thomas Fletcher,	-	-	"	—	8	
Richard Hastings,	-	-	"	—	9	
John Jacobs,	-	-	"	—	10	
Caleb Massey,	-	-	"	—	10	
John Marshall,	-	-	"	—	10	
Thomas Matthews,	-	-	"	1	10	
Luther Massey,	-	-	"	—	10	
John Parramore,	-	-	"	—	4	
Thomas Russell,	-	-	"	—	10	
Wm. Ross,	-	-	"	—	2	
Robert Russell,	-	-	"	—	10	
Wm. Rowley,	-	-	"	—	2	
Elisha Smith,	-	-	"	—	10	
William M. Taylor,	-	-	"	—	10	
Evans Taylor,	-	-	"	—	10	

NAMES.	RANK.	TIME OF SERVICE.		REMARKS.
		Months.	Days.	
William Taylor, - -	Private,	–	10	
Tully Taylor, - -	"	–	10	
Southey Townsend, - -	"	–	10	
Samuel Taylor, - -	"	–	10	
Richard Taylor, - -	"	–	9	
John Tatham, - -	"	–	10	
Teackle Taylor, - -	"	–	7	
James Wishart, - -	"	–	10	
John Wheatley, - -	"	–	10	
George Whealton, - -	"	–	10	
Daniel Watkins, (or David,)	"	–	10	
Elisha Whealton, -	"	–	10	
William Walters, - -	"	–	10	
Charles Whealton, - -	"	–	10	
John H. Watts, - -	"	–	10	
John Wallop, - -	"	–	10	

Captain William Taylor's Company—Fifty-second Regiment.

NAMES.	RANK.	TIME OF SERVICE.		REMARKS.
		Months.	Days.	
Nathaniel Hix, - -	Sergeant,	–	16	
John Harmon, - -	Corporal,	1	1	
John F. Richardson, -	"	–	15	
Francis Ratcliff, - -	"	–	16	
Wm. P. Wyatt, - -	"	–	16	
George Ball, - -	Private,	–	16	
Dennis Binns, - -	"	–	15	
William Curle, - -	"	–	15	
Nelson Cumbo, - -	"	–	16	
William R. Crawley, -	"	–	16	
J. V. Dilliard, - -	"	–	15	
William Day, - -	"	–	15	
Thomas Furbush, -	"	–	15	
John Franks, - -	"	–	5	
Benjamin Hill, - -	"	–	16	
Richard Hall, - -	"	–	16	
Philip Hockaday, - -	"	–	15	
Samuel Hix, - -	"	–	15	
William Harman, - -	"	–	15	
John Jones, - -	"	–	16	
Charles Jones, - -	"	–	16	
Edward Jones, - -	"	–	16	
John R. Moore, - -	"	1	1	
Samuel Meredith, -	"	–	16	
Armistead R. Manning, -	"	–	23	
Arthur Mitchell (or Archer,) -	"	–	24	
James T. Morris, - -	"	–	15	
William Peay, - -	"	–	15	
Isaac Roper, - -	"	–	16	
John Sweeney, - -	"	–	16	
Meredith Slater, - -	"	–	16	
Reuben Skelton, - -	"	–	16	
William R. Taylor, - -	"	–	15	
Roscow Taylor, - -	"	–	16	
William Woodward, -	"	–	15	
Warwick Woodward, -	"	–	15	
John F. Woodward, -	"	–	16	
John Williams, jr. - -	"	–	16	
David A. Walker, - -	"	–	16	

(For rest of this company, see publication of Pay Rolls.)

Captain **James** *S. Teackle's Company—Second Regiment.*

NAMES.	RANK.	TIME OF SERVICE.		REMARKS.
		Months.	Days.	
Elijah Lilliston,	Lieutenant,	–	5	
Samuel Read,	Sergeant,	–	9	
Ezekiel Ashby,	Private,	–	24	
Abel Bradford,	"	–	3	
Jno. Bonwell, (of Jno.)	"	–	18	
William Bloxom,	"	–	22	
Jno. Bonwell, (of Jas.)	"	–	5	
Jno. Bonwell,	"	–	5	
Galen Conner,	"	–	5	
Samuel Colonna,	"	–	12	
Jehu Davis,	"	–	27	
John Ewell,	"			
George Floyd,	"	–	24	
Ben. Harrison,	"	–	5	
William Harmon.	"			
William Harmon, (of Jno.)	"	–	1	
James Jester,	"	1	13	
Levin James,	"	–	29	
John Lewis,	"	–	5	
John Mears, (of R.)	"	–	13	
James Mears, (of E.)	"	–	19	
John B. Mears,	"	–	27	
James Mears, (of G.)	"	–	8	
Samuel Mears, (of Jno.)	"	–	8	
Levin Nock, (of Jno.)	"	1	7	
William Nock,	"	–	6	
George Nock,	"			
John Nock, (of Sol.)	"	1	13	
Thomas Nock.	"	–	7	
George Nock, (of Geo.)	"	–	1	
George Nock, jr.	"	–	8	
William Phillips,	"	–	3	
Arthur Powell.	"	–	16	
James Roberts,	"	–	24	
Kendal Richardson,	"	–	5	
William Richardson,	"	–	20	
Calvin Read,	"	–	3	
Major Savage,	"			
Major R. Savage,	"	–	8	
William Tatham,	"	–	26	
Thomas Underhill,	"	–	24	
William Wallace,	"	–	21	
Jno. W. Watson,	"			
Jesse Willet,	"	–	5	
Jno. Watson,	"			
Littleton Wyatt,	"	–	11	
Littleton Watson,	"	–	18	
Isma Wyatt,	"	–	3	

(For rest of this company, see publication of Pay Rolls.)

MUSTER ROLL

Of Captain Foushee G. Tebbs' Company, of the Forty-first Regiment, Virginia Militia, commanded by Lieutenant Colonel Vincent Branham, in the Service of the United States, from 6th to 9th April, from 20th to 27th July, 1813, and from 21st July to 25th September, from 5th to 9th October, and from 30th November to 9th December, 1814.

NAMES.	RANK.	TIME OF SERVICE.		REMARKS.
		Months.	Days.	
Foushee G. Tebbs, - -	Captain,	3		
Samuel Northen, - -	Lieutenant,	3	2	
Richard L. Shackleford, -	Ensign,	3	2	
John Plummer, - -	Sergeant,	2	21	
Charles D. Smith, - -	"	2	21	
Charles Barnes, - -	"	–	17	
Henry Miskel, - -	"	2	29	
John Gordon, - -	"	–	4	
Robert Moore, - -	"	–	12	
Henry Hartford, - -	"	–	4	
Thomas S. Davis, - -	"	–	8	
John G. White, - -	"	2	6	
Geo. T. Garland, - -	Corporal,	2	29	
Joseph Palmer, - -	"	2	28	
James V. Bell, - -	"	–	8	
Wm. Shackleford, - -	"	–	9	
John Davis, sr. - -	"	2	11	
Chapman Austin, - -	"	2	11	
Charles D. Smith, - -	"	–	12	
Lewis Hammack, - -	"	–	4	
George Crutcher, - -	"	–	8	
George Lewis, jr. - -	Drummer,	–	8	
David Austin, - -	"	1	6	
Henry Hudson, - -	"	–	10	
Thomas Bryant, - -	Fifer,	2	21	
Thornton Hinton, - -	"	–	6	
David Austin, - -	Private,	–	12	
Chapman Austin, - -	"	–	12	
John Alderson, jr. - -	"	–	6	
Alexander Bryant, - -	"	2	26	
Samuel Bryant, - -	"	2	9	
Ludwell Bell, - -	"	–	8	
Thomas N. Bell, - -	"	1	10	
Gilbert H. Balderson, -	"	–	5	
Berryman Balderson, -	"	–	5	
Thomas Bryant, - -	"	–	13	
John Bryant, - -	"	–	5	
William Bryant, - -	"	–	5	
Charles Barnes, - -	"	2	9	
Travers Barnes, - -	"	–	10	
James Bradbury, - -	"	–	12	
John Courtney, - -	"	3	3	
Leonard Courtney, - -	"	2	16	
Samuel Coats, - -	"	–	5	
Robert Carnella, - -	"	–	5	
George Crutcher, - -	"	1	24	

NAMES.	RANK.	TIME OF SERVICE.		REMARKS.
		Months.	Days.	
George Curtis, - -	Private,	–	4	
Bichard Clark, - -	"	–	4	
Randall Clarke, - -	"	–	24	Enlisted in U. S. service.
Joseph Deschamps, - -	"	1	17	
Thomas S. Davis, - -	"	2	22	
Linsey Davenport, - -	"	–	5	
Archiles Dale, - -	"	–	5	
Thomas Dodson, - -	"	–	9	
Charles Dameron, - -	"	–	4	
Chichester Dobyns, - -	"	–	12	Joined artillery.
Joseph Dozier, - -	"	–	4	
John Dozier, - -	"	–	4	
John Davis, - -	"	–	8	
Thomas Everett, - -	"	3	3	
Williamson Efford, - -	"	3	2	
John Efford, - -	"	1	13	
William Everett, - -	"	–	14	
Samuel French, - -	"	2	15	
Samuel Finch, - -	"	–	2	
Famous Ficklin, - -	"	1	5	
Benjamin Foster, - -	"	1	–	Enlisted in U. S. service.
Thomas Glasscock, - -	"	–	5	
Griffin Garner, - -	"	1	16	
John Gordon, - .	"	–	7	
John Harris, - -	"	3	2	
Eppa Headley, - -	"	–	4	
John Hammack, - -	"	–	12	Joined artillery.
Henry Harford, jr. - -	"	2	27	
James Hazzard, - -	"	–	4	
Robert P. Headley, - -	"	–	12	
George Harris, - -	"	2	20	
Robert Hammack, - -	"	1	21	
Reuben Hart, - -	"	–	5	
Meredith Hammon, - -	"	–	5	
George Henson, - -	"	–	5	
Ewell Hanks, - -	"	–	5	
Henry Harford, sr. - -	"	1	16	
Lewis Hammack, - -	"	–	8	
William Harford, jr. - -	"	–	16	
John Jenkins, - -	"	3	3	
Thomas Jones, - -	"	2	27	
Thomas Jenkins, - -	"	3	3	
Thomas Jasper, - -	"	3	3	
John Jenkins, jr. - -	"	–	5	
Thomas Jenkins, jr. - -	"	–	5	
John Jackson, - -	"	1	25	
George Lewis, - -	"	2	14	
Samuel Lewis, - -	"	–	7	
Richard E. Matthews, - -	"	2	18	
Robert Mitchell, - -	"	–	7	
Hudson Morris, - -	"	–	5	
Daniel Morris, - -	"	–	5	
James Mothershead, - -	"	–	5	
Reuben Marks, - -	"	–	5	
Samuel Moore, - -	"	–	10	
James Monroe, jr. - -	"	–	4	
Peter Morgan, - -	"	–	6	Joined cavalry.
Robert Moore, - -	"	1	9	
Elias Northern, - -	"	2	20	
William Newman, - -	"	–	5	
Henry Nash, - -	"	–	5	
John Nash, - -	"	–	5	

NAMES.	RANK.	TIME OF SERVICE.		REMARKS.
		Months.	Days.	
James Nash, - -	Private,	—	5	
Eppa L. Newsom, - -	"	—	10	Joined cavalry.
Samuel W. Newsom, -	"	—	10	
Abraham Proctor, - -	"	1	23	
Hansford Purcell, - -	"	—	23	
Edward M. Purcell, - -	"	2	17	
John M. Proctor, - -	"	2	12	
James Pratt, - -	"	—	5	
Samuel Pritchett, - -	"	—	5	
William R. Packet, - -	"	—	12	
John Plumer, - -	"	—	12	
George Purcell, - -	"	—	4	
George H. Rust, - -	"	2	28	
Lemuel Rust, - -	"	2	19	
Nimrod Rochester, - -	"	2	21	
William L. Rust, - -	"	1	16	
John Rice, - -	"	—	4	
John Rust, - -	"	—	15	
Samuel Sydnor, - -	"	2	22	
Thomas P. Smith, - -	"	2	29	
George H. Smith, - -	"	2	29	
Eppa Sydnor, - -	"	2	21	
Eppa Stott, - -	"	2	22	
George N. Stonum, - -	"	—	11	
James Scrimger, - -	"	—	12	
Thomas Swan, - -	"	—	10	
Henry Stonum, - -	"	—	4	
James Scott, - -	"	—	4	
William Stonum, - -	"	—	10	
Harrison Sydnor, - -	"	—	6	
Wm. Shackleford, - -	"	2	6	
Wm. R. Shackleford, -	"	—	5	
Daniel Saunders, - -	"	—	5	
James Saunders, - -	"	—	5	
Allen Saunders, - -	"	—	5	
James Saunders, jr. - -	"	—	5	
John Sutton, - -	"	—	5	
Travers Tune, - -	"	2	28	
George D. Tune, - -	"	2	20	
Henry Tarpley, - -	"	—	9	
George Thrift, - -	"	2	20	
Peter Todd, - -	"	—	4	
Samuel Thrift, - -	"	—	4	
Thomas Thrift, - -	"	—	-6	
Benj. Vanlandingham, -	"	2	20	
Joseph Woollard, jun'r. -	"	2	22	Substitute for Joseph Woollard.
William Weathers, - -	"	2	29	
Jeremiah Webb, - -	"	2	29	
Jno. G. White, - -	"	—	11	
John Wilcocks, - -	"	—	-4	

MUSTER ROLL

Of Captain William Thomas' Company, from the Sixth Regiment, Virginia Militia, commanded by Colonel Archibald Ritchie, in the Service of the United States, from 1st to 9th December, 1814.

NAMES.	RANK.	TIME OF SERVICE.		REMARKS.
		Months.	Days.	
William Thomas, - -	Captain,	–	9	
William H. Falconer, -	Lieutenant,	–	9	
Reuben Corthon, - -	Ensign,	–	9	
Amos Corthen, - -	Sergeant,	–	9	
James Montague, - -	"	–	9	
John Shearwood, - -	"	–	9	
Castin Boughan, - -	"	–	9	
Samuel Johnson, - -	Corporal,	–	9	
Asa Goldman, - -	"	–	9	
Lewis Brown, - -	"	–	9	
Henry Latham, - -	"	–	9	
Philip Clarke, - -	Drummer,	–	9	
Lawson Johnson, - -	Fifer,	–	9	
Levin Ayres, - -	Private,	–	6	
Richard Bearfoot, - -	"	–	7	
John Bastin, - -	"	–	5	
James Brooks, - -	"	–	7	
Josiah Blan, - -	"	–	8	
Motta Ball, - - -	"	–	8	
John Brown, - -	"	–	8	
Robert Clarke, : -	"	–	8	
Larkin Clarke, - -	"	–	9	
Brooking Clarke, - -	"	–	9	
Benjamin Coghill, - -	"	–	8	
Goldman Carter, - -	"	–	5	
Jackson Dunn, - -	"	–	8	
John Dix, - - -	"	–	8	
Robert Elliott, - -	"	–	8	
James Fields, - -	"	–	5	
Thomas Gardin, - -	"	–	8	
George Gardin, - -	"	–	8	
William Gale, - -	"	–	9	
Lewis Gatewood, - -	"	–	7	
Philip Gatewood, - -	"	–	6	
Jessee Griggs, - -	"	–	8	
Samuel Gressom, - -	"	–	8	
William Gophney, - -	"	–	8	
John T. Hill, - -	"	–	8	
Orson Ingram, - -	"	–	8	
Philip Lee, - -	"	–	7	
Nathaniel J. Mothershead, -	"	–	6	
James McFarlane, - -	"	–	7	
John B. Micou, - -	"	–	3	
Mann Page, - -	"	–	3	
Andrew Rennolds, - -	"	–	9	
John Smither, - -	"	–	7	
William Sullivan, - -	"	–	6	
Anthony Samuel, - -	"	–	9	

NAMES.			RANK.	TIME OF SERVICE.		REMARKS.
				Months.	Days.	
Robert Thomas,	-	-	Private,	–	8	
Richard Thomas,	-	-	"	–	8	
Wm. D. Thomas,	-	-	"	–	4	
John H. Webb,	-	-	"	–	7	

MUSTER ROLL

Of Captain Christopher Tompkins' Company of Rifle Volunteers, from the Sixty-first Regiment of Virginia Militia, in the County of Matthews, commanded by Lieutenant Colonel Leavin Gayle, in Service from 10th to 11th March, on the 12th May, and from 27th to 31st May, in the year 1813.

NAMES.			RANK.	TIME OF SERVICE.		REMARKS.
				Months.	Days.	
Christopher Tompkins,	-		Captain,	—	6	
Thomas T. T. Tabb,	-		Lieutenant,	—	3	
Thomas R. Yeatman,	-		Ensign,	—	6	
Joseph C. Maigne,	-	-	Sergeant,	—	6	
Jesse Degges,	-	-	"	—	6	
William L. Smith,	-	-	"	—	6	
John Foster,	-	-	"	—	6	
Felix T. Sharples,	-	-	Corporal,	—	1	
Bailey Hudgin,	-	-	"	—	6	
Josiah Evans,	-	-	"			
John Degges,	-	-	"	—	6	
Humphrey Hunley,	-	-	Musician,	—	5	
John Adams,	-	-	Private,	—	5	
Richard Ayres,	-	-	"	—	6	
George Brown,	-	-	"	—	7	
Thomas Bassett,	-	-	"	—	6	
A. G. Cushman,	-	-	"	—	2	
John Degges,	-	-	"	—	8	
Anthony Degges,	-	-	"	—	6	
Cole Degges,	-	-	"	—	6	
Jesse Degges,	-	-	"	—	2	
George E. Dudley,	-	-	"	—	2	
John Degges,	-	-	"	—	2	
James Deale,	-	-	"	—	1	
Barber Degges,	-	-	"	—	5	
Samuel Eddins,	-	-	"	—	2	
Josiah Evans,	-	-	"	—	2	
John Forrest,	-	-	"	—	6	
James Foster,	-	-	"	—	6	
Isaac Foster,	-	-	"	—	7	
Joseph Foster,	-	-	"	—	2	
Abraham Forrest,	-	-	"	—	6	
Joshua Foster,	-	-	"	—	2	
Bartlett Hudgin,	-	⊢	"	—	8	
Meredith Hurst,	-	-	"	—	8	
John Hurst,	-	-	"	—	8	
William Hurst,	-	-	"	—	8	
Jesse Hurst,	-	-	"	—	8	
Holder Hudgin,	-	-	"	—	8	
William Hunley,	-	-	"	—	6	
Peter S. Hunley,	-	-	"	—	6	
John Hunley, jr.	-	-	"	—	5	
John Hughes,	-	-	"	—	6	
Philip Hughes,	-	-	"			
Lewis Hudgin,	-	-	"	—	6	
Richard L. Hilling,	-	-	"	—	5	
William Hudgin,	-	-	"	—	6	

NAMES.	RANK.	TIME OF SERVICE.		REMARKS.
		Months.	Days.	
Patrick Hovan, - -	Private,	–	2	
Hugh Hudgin, - -	"	–	2	
Peter Hudgin, - -	"	–	2	
John Morgan, - -	"	–	6	
John Morriss, - -	"	–	1	
Joseph C. Maigne, - -	"	–	2	
Thomas Norton, - -	"	–		
Thomas Owens, - -	"	–	7	
John Plummer, - -	"	–	5	
John Parsons, - -	"	–	6	
Absalom Parsons, - -	"	–	6	
George Parrott, - -	"	–	6	
Thomas Palmer, - -	"	–	6	
Matthew Pickett, - -	"	–	2	
John Sadler, - -	"	–	1	
Philip M. Spark, - -	"	–		
Robert Sadler, - -	"	–	6	
Thomas Sampson, - -	"	–	6	
Isaac Smith, - -	"	–	7	
Wm. L. Smith, - -	"	–	2	
Felix T. Sharples, - -	"	–	2	
William Treakle, - -	"	–	6	
John Turner, - -	"	–	7	
Thomas T. T. Tabb, - -	"	–	2	
James Willis, - -	"	–	7	
William Willis, - -	"	–		
Thomas R. Yeatman, -	"	–	2	

MUSTER ROLL

Of Captain Charles Thompson, jr.'s Company, from the Seventy-fourth Regiment,
Virginia Militia, commanded by Colonel William Trueheart, in the Service of
the United States, from 20th to 29th March, from 28th to 29th June, and
from 1st to 2d July, in the year 1813.

NAMES.		RANK.	TIME OF SERVICE.		REMARKS.
			Months.	Days.	
Charles Thompson, jr.	-	Captain,	—	14	
Edmund Higgason,	-	Lieutenant,	—	14	
Henry H. Jones,	-	Ensign,	—	14	
Michael R. Jones,	-	Sergeant,	—	14	
John Higgason,	-	"	—	14	
George S. Netherland,	-	"	—	14	
Frederick Shoemaker,	-	"	—	14	
William Callis,	-	Private,	—	14	
William Corker,	-	"	—	14	
Richard Callis,	-	"	—	14	
Daniel Corker,	-	"	—	2	
William S. Dandridge,	-	"	—	2	
Gideon Hanes,	-	"	—	14	
Martin Hall,	-	"	—	14	
Pleasant Hanes,	-	"	—	14	
Garland Higgison,	-	"	—	14	
Richard Higgason,	-	"	—	14	
Christopher Hanes,	-	"	—	14	
Samuel R. Jones,	-	"	—	14	
Will.. .. ills,	-	"	—	14	
W..		..	—	1.	
Jas.. .. .. ..,	-	..	..	...	
Fleming Puryear,	-	"	—	14	
David Sims, jr.	-	"	—	14	
William Stanley,	-	"	—	14	
Thomas Swift,	-	"	—	14	
Chapman Stuard,	-	"	—	14	
Richmond Terrell,	-	"	—	14	
William A. Thompson,	-	"	—	14	
Thomas W. Thacker,	-	"	—	14	
William Walton, jr.	-	"	—	14	
Joseph Watson,	-	"	—	14	

MUSTER ROLL

Of Captain William B. Thompson's Company, of the Eighty-third Regiment, Virginia Militia, in the County of Dinwiddie, called into actual Service under the general orders of the 30th June, 1813, from the 1st to the 6th July, in the same year.

NAMES.	RANK.	TIME OF SERVICE.		REMARKS.
		Months.	Days.	
William B. Thompson,	Captain,	–	6	
Stith Thompson,	Lieutenant,	–	6	
Anderson Harper,	Ensign,	–	6	
Charles W. Bristow,	Sergeant,	–	6	
John Wainwright,	"	–	6	
Daniel Connolly,	"	–	6	
Peter Davis,	"	–	6	
Benjamin Rives,	Corporal,	–	6	
Samma Clark,	"	–	6	
Samuel H. Kirkes,	"	–	6	
Charles S. Tucker,	"	–	6	
John Atkinson,	Private,	–	6	
Daniel Algood,	"			
William Baily,	"	–	6	
Robert C. Booth,	"	–	6	
Laban Beames,	"			
William Booth,	"	–	6	
John Crawford,	"	–	6	
John B. Clarke,	"	–	–	On duty at Norfolk.
William Davis,	"	–	6	
Daniel E. Elder,	"	–	6	
John Evans,	"	–	6	
Petersen Elder,	"	–	6	
Alexander Fraser,	"	–	6	
William Ferguson,	"	–	6	
Thomas Gee,	"	–	–	" "
John Grubbs,	"	–	6	
William Grigg,	"			
Bartholomew Ingram,	"			
Richard K. Jones,	"	–	6	
T. John Jott,	"	–	6	
Nelson Jones,	"	–	6	
William Locke,	"	–	6	
Thomas Locke,	"	–	6	
William Malone,	"	–	–	" "
William Mason,	"	–	6	
Gustavus A. Muir,	"	–	6	
Daniel Malone,	"	–	6	
Anthony North,	"	–	6	
Hardaway T. Rives,	"	–	6	
James Sandiford,	"	–	6	
William N. Tucker,	"	–	6	
Isaac Tucker,	"	–	6	
David Tucker,	"	–	6	Jas. Eiples his sub.
George Trotter,	"	–	6	
Littleberry West,	"	–	–	On duty at Norfolk.
Burwell Whitmore,	"	–	–	" " "
McKie Wainwright,	"	–	6	

NAMES.	RANK.	TIME OF SERVICE.		REMARKS.
		Months.	Days.	
Joseph Whitmore, - -	Private,	–	6	
Thomas Whitmore, - -	"	–	6	
Samuel Wainwright, -	"	–	6	
Freeman Wainwright, -	"	–	6	

MUSTER ROLL

Of Captain Anthony R. Thornton's Company, from the Sixteenth Regiment, commanded by Lieutenant Colonel Aylett Waller, in the Service of the State of Virginia, from 22d July to 17th August, in the year 1814.

NAMES.	RANK.	TIME OF SERVICE.		REMARKS.
		Months.	Days.	
Anthony R. Thornton, -	Captain,	–	27	
John T. Parke, - -	Lieutenant,	–	27	
Thomas N. Grymes, - -	Ensign,	–	27	
James W. Blair, - -	Sergeant,	–	27	
Richard R. Maury, - -	"	–	25	
P. B. Mayer, - -	"	–	27	
Nathaniel Brown, - -	"	–	27	
Thomas Wright, - -	Corporal,	–	27	
John S. Carter, - -	"	–	27	
Thomas N. Berkely, - -	"	–	27	
George D. Storke, - -	"	–	27	
Bevin Ashly, - -	Private,	–	27	
Charles Baggett, - -	"	–	27	
George Baggett, sr. - -	"	–	27	
Zachariah Brimmer, - -	"	–	27	
William Biscoe, - -	"	–	27	
George Baggett, jr. - -	"	–	27	
John Burnett, sr. - -	"	–	27	
John Burnett, jr. - -	"	–	27	
John B. Benson, - -	"	–	27	
James Baggett, - -	"	–	27	
John W. Carter, - -				
. . . . ,				
Aug. Conne, - -	"	–	27	
John Carter, - -	"	–	27	
James Carter, sr. - -	"	–	27	
James Carter, jr. - -	"	–	27	
Daniel Curtis, - -	"	–	27	
Isaac Donnelly, - -	"	–	27	
Thomas Daniel, - -	"	–	27	
Will. H. Drake, - -	"	–	27	
Lemuel Doggett, - -	"	–	27	
James Daniel, - -	"	–	17	
John B. Edelin, - -	"	–	27	
George Ellis, - -	"	–	27	
John Frost, - -	"	–	27	
Richard G. Fult, - -	"	–	27	
James Frazier, - -	"	–	27	
Edward Gerald, - -	"	–	27	
Charles Gregory, - -	"	–	27	
James L. Hill, - -	"	–	27	
Will. Hereford, - -	"	–	27	
Will. L. Hill, - -	"	–	27	
Daniel Hickey, - -	"	–	27	
James D. Harrow, - -	"	–	27	
Charles J. Johnson, - -	"	–	27	
Isaac M. King, - -	"	–	27	
William Morton, - -	"	–	27	

NAMES.	RANK.	TIME OF SERVICE.		REMARKS.
		Months.	Days.	
Charles Mullen, - -	Private,	—	27	
Wiley Magee, - -	"	—	27	
William Murphey, - -	"	—	27	
John Morgan, - -	"	—	27	
Joshua Myers, - -	"	—	27	
William McFarlane, - -	"	—	27	
John Murphey, - -	"	—	27	
James Mercer, - -	"	—	1	
Thornton Northwood, -	"	—	27	
William Proctor, - -	"	—	27	
George Purvis, - -	"		27	
George Rothrock, -	"	—	27	
Robert Richards, -	"	—	27	
Hez. Reeder, - -	"	—	17	
John Ross, - -	"	—	27	
William Stimpson, - -	"	—	27	
John L. Sheltuce, - -	"	—	27	
Robert Stewart, - -	"	—	27	
Hugh Stevens, - -	"	—	27	
Clai. Simpson, - -	"	—	27	
Spencer Sullivan, - -	"	—	27	
Stephen Stuart, - -	"	—	27	
R. D. Throckmorton, -	"	—	27	
John Taylor, - -	"	—	27	
Edward R. Victor, - -	"	—	27	
Robt. Wilson, -	"	—	27	
Jno. M. Wiedmeyer, - -	"	—	27	
John T. Wilson, -	"	—	27	
William Wines, - -	"	—	27	
Austin West, - -	"	—	17	
John Whiting, - -	"	—	27	
Nimrod Young, - -	"	—	27	

MUSTER ROLL

Of Captain Robert Thruston's Company, of the Twenty-first Regiment, Virginia Militia, commanded by Lieutenant Colonel William Jones, in the Service of the United States, from 16th February to 25th March, from 1st May to 3d July, from 24th to 31st July, and from 28th of August, in the year 1813, to 23d of March, in the year 1814.

NAMES.			RANK.	TIME OF SERVICE.		REMARKS.
				Months.	Days.	
Robert Thruston,	-	-	Captain,	3	22	
Sterling Seawell,	-	-	Lieutenant,	3	22	Promoted.
Thomas Cary,	-	-	"	2		
Warner Lewis,	-	-	Ensign,	1	22	
Philip W. Lewis,	-	-	"	1	21	
John Lucas,	-	-	Sergeant,	3	22	
Absolem Simcoe,	-	-	"	3	22	
Joseph Tilledge,	-	-	"	3	22	
Bartlett Yates,	-	-	"	2	8	
Ch. C. Chilton,	-	-	"	1	14	
Thomas West,	-	-	Corporal,	1	22	
Robert Barrett,	-	-	"	2	8	
Anthony Smith,	-	-	"	2	8	
Ch. Dodson,	-	-	"	1	14	
Bartlett Yates,	-	-	"	1	14	
John Hogg,	-	-	"	3	14	
Robert Heywood,	-	-	"	2		
William Hudson,	-	-	Drummer,	2	8	
Vincent Hudson,	-	-	"	1	14	
Vincent Hudson,	-	-	Fifer,	2	8	
William Hudson,	-	-	"	1	14	
Michael Ambrose,	-	-	Private,	2	22	
Richard Allard,	-	-	"	1	9	
James Acree,	-	-	"	2		
Robert Barrett,	-	-	"	1	14	
George Brown,	-	-	"	–	13	Detached from Captain Perrin's company.
Charles Brown,	-	-	"	–	13	" " "
Wm. Brown,	-	-	"	–	13	" " "
August Brown,	-	-	"	–	13	" " "
Wm. Buckner,	-	-	"	2		
Ro. Brumley,	-	-	"	2		
John Crew,	-	-	"	3	22	
Major Colonna,	-	-	"	1	14	
Charles Dodson,	-	-	"	2	8	
Wm. Dudley,	-	-	"	1	22	
Walker Dyke,	-	-	"	3	22	
Ranks Dudley,	-	-	"	1	22	
James Deal,	-	-	"	–	13	" " "
John B. Daner,	-	-	"	2		
Sam'l Dudley,	-	-	"	2		
Lewis Enus,	-	-	"	2	–	Promoted to sergeant 24th January 1814.
Geo. Enus,	-	-	"	2		
Jo. Edwards,	-	-	"	2		
Warner Enus,	-	-	"	2		

NAMES.	RANK.	TIME OF SERVICE.		REMARKS.
		Months.	Days.	
Lemuel Foxwell, - ·	Private,	3	1	
Henry Fleming, - -	"	3	22	
John Foxwell, - -	"	3	1	
John Fields, - -	"	2		
Lewis Flutcher, - -	"	2		
William Flutcher, - ·	"	2		
Wm. Graves, - -	"	1	22	
John Golden, - -	"	–	13	
Samuel S. Griffin, - -	"	2		
Jno. M. Gale, - -	"	2		
Ivison Hall, - -	"	3	22	
William Hogg, - -	"	3	22	
Daniel Hogg, - -	"	3	22	
John Heywood, - -	"	3	22	
William Heywood, - -	"	3	22	
Seymour Hudgins, - -	"	–	13	
Lewis Hogg, - -	"	–	13	Detached from Captain Perrin's company.
John Hogg, - -	"	–	13	" " "
James Hogg, - -	"	–	13	" " "
Charles Heywood, - -	"	–	13	" " "
John Hall, - -	"	–	13	" " "
Ch. Hobday, - ·	"	2		
Edm'd Hobday, - -	"	2		
Abram Insley, - -	"	2		
John Jessee, - -	"	3	21	
James Jenkins, - -	"	–	13	" " "
Lewis Jenkins, - -	"	–	13	" " "
Richard Janson, - -	"	–	13	" " "
Edw'd Jenkins, - -	"	–	13	" " "
Armist'd Jenkins, - -	"	–	13	" " "
Samuel Jenkins, - -	"	–	13	" " "
Matt. Kemp, - -	"	–	13	
Thomas Lucas, - -	"	3	22	
William Lutridge, - -	"			
Hyram Langford, - -	"	2		
Jno. Lewis, - -	"	2		
Samuel Minor, - -	"	3	22	
John March, (or Joseph,) -	"	3	22	
Ab. M. Moore, - -	"	2		
Joel Mitchell, - -	"	2		
Th. Mure, - -	"			
William Moore, - -	"			
Nath. Nelson, - -	"	2		
William Oliver, - -	"	3	22	
James Oliver, - -	"	3	14	
William Potts, - -	"	1	9	
William Powell, - -	"	–	13	" " "
Paul Philpotts, - -	"	2		
Thomas Purcell, - -	"	2		
Geo. ·Pigg, - -	"	2		
Armistead Robins, - -	"	3	17	
George Rowe, - -	"	2	6	
Jasper C. Rowe, - -	"	1	1	
Francis Robins, - -	"	1	14	
John Ransome, - -	"	1	14	
Wm. Robins, - -	"	–	13	
Thomas Robins, - -	"	–	13	" " "
Baylor Smith, - -	"	1	9	
James South, - -	"	3	19	Deserted.
Anthony Smith, - -	"	1	14	
Baily Smith, - -	"	2		
Coleman Stubbs, - -	"	2		

NAMES.	RANK.	TIME OF SERVICE.		REMARKS.
		Months.	Days.	
Thomas Smith, - -	Private,	–	13	Detached from Captain Perrins' company.
William Smith, - -	"	–	13	" " "
Mich'l Smith, - -	"	–	13	" " "
William Tilledge, - -	"	1	1	
Foster Thomas, - -	"	1	1	
William Walker, - -	"	1	6	
William Wilkins, - -	"	3	14	
Armistead Watlington, -	"	–	13	
James Williams, - -	"	-.	13	
Robert Wilkins, - -	"	2		Dead.
Thomas West, - -	"	2		
Cliver Watlington, (or Oliver,)	"	2		
Turner West, - -	"	2		

Captain Horace Timberlake's Company—Seventh Regiment.

NAMES.			RANK.	TIME OF SERVICE.		REMARKS.
				Months.	Days.	
Patrick Childers,	-	-	Private,	2	–	Detailed to work in boats.
Patrick Childress,	-	-	"	1	24	Deserted.
William Clasby,	-	-	"	3	26	Substitute for George F. Southerland, and deserted.
Thomas Davis,	-	-	"	–	1	Substitute for Temple Gentry.
Robert Fleming,	-	-	"	–	29	
George K. Holland,	-	-	"	2		
William D. Statum,	-	-	"	3	25	Sub. for W. C. Wain, and deserted.
William Wilkinson,	-	-	"	2		
William Wilkerson,	-	-	"	1	23	Deserted.

(For rest of this company, see publication of Pay Rolls.)

Captain Isaac Tinsley's Company—Eighth Regiment.

NAMES.	RANK.	TIME OF SERVICE.		REMARKS.
		Months.	Days.	
William Fuqua, - -	Lieutenant,	–	25	
Samuel Anderson, - -	Private,	–	12	
William Cohoon, - -	"			
Beverley Cox, - -	"	1	24	Sub. for H. Ellington.
John Collier, - -	"	1	18	Sub. for Jno. Bayne.
James Davidson, - -	"	1	23	Sub. for Wm. Davidson in general hospital.
William Dawson, - -	"			
Peyton Fleming, - -	"	–	3	Sub. for Jos. Woodson.
John Gee, - -	"			
James Hickman, - -	"	–	23	
John Johnson, - -	"	–	22	
Joseph Mays, - -	"	1	6	Sub. for D. Clasby.
Jesse Martin, - -	"	2	12	Sub. for Conyers.
Joshua Phillips, - -	"	2	29	
Hezekiah Stone, - -	"	–	12	Transferred to Capt'n Massey.
Stake Whittington, - -	"			
Joseph Warrener, - -	"	–	18	

(For rest of this company, see publication of Pay Rolls.)

MUSTER ROLL

Of Quarter Master Sergeant Joel Titmarsh's detachment of Volunteers, from the Sixty-second Regiment, Virginia Militia, in the County of Prince George, called into actual Service, under the general orders of the 4th of November, 1813, from the 7th November, 1813, to the 21st February, 1814.

NAMES.	RANK.	TIME OF SERVICE.		REMARKS.
		Months.	Days.	
Joel Titmarsh, - -	Qr. M. Serg't,	3	15	
Edm'd Wilkins, - -	Sergeant,	3	15	
Samuel Fuqua, - -	Corporal,	3	15	
Thomas H. Allen, - -	"	3	15	
Samuel Womack, - -	Drummer,	3	15	
Joseph Beckley, - -	Private,	3	15	
Robert Cummings, - -	"	3	15	
Josiah Fuqua, - -	"	3	15	
Jno. Hamlin, jr. - -	"	3	15	
William Lee, - -	"	3	15	
Thomas McHan, jr. - -	"	3	15	
Waller Warthen, - -	"	3	15	
Uriah Williamson, - -	"	3	15	

Lieutenant James Todd's Company—Ninety-third Regiment.

NAMES.			RANK.	TIME OF SERVICE.		REMARKS.
				Months.	Days.	
John Beard,	-	-	Private,	1	10	
John Kilby,	-	-	"	–	19	
Jacob Shaver,	-	-	"	–	22	

(For rest of this company, see publication of Pay Rolls.)

Captain Therit Towles' Troop of Cavalry—Sixteenth Regiment.

NAMES.	RANK.	TIME OF SERVICE.		REMARKS.
		Months.	Days.	
Lewis W. Dangerfield,	Lieutenant,	–	27	
James A. Spindle,	Cornet,	–	27	
Edmund Coleman,	Sergeant,	–	27	
Edward Elly.	"	–	26	
Ira Lipscomb.	Corporal,	–	26	
John Layton,	"	–	18	
William Scott,	"	–	27	
Hezekiah Ellis,	"	–	27	
Benjamin James,	"	–	27	
William Liggin,	Musician,	–	27	
John H. Buckman.	Private,	–	22	
Carter Brock,	"	–	27	
Martin Brent,	"	–	27	
Orrill Brock,	"	–	27	
John Chewning.	"	–	11	
Oscar Crutchfield,	"	–	27	
Granville Cason,	"	–	27	
Beverley Hicks,	"	–	27	
Norborne Lafong,	"	–	27	
Charles McCloud,	"	–	8	
Benjamin S. Partlow,	"	–	27	
John Pratt,	"	–	18	
William Robinson,	"	–	25	
Belford Smith,	"	–	26	
William Shadock,	"	–	26	
Thomas Trigg,	"	–	16	
George Todd,	"	–	27	
John Walden.	"	–	26	
Byrd C. Willis,	"	–	27	
William Webber,	"	–	27	
William Walden,	"	–	27	
William Woodford,	"	–	19	
George Yates,	"	–	26	

(For rest of this company, see publication of Pay Rolls.)

MUSTER ROLL

Of Captain John L. Townes' Company of Mounted Infantry, of the First Corps d'Elite, commanded by Colonel Thomas M. Randolph, in the Service of the State of Virginia, from the 30th August to 14th September, in the year 1814.

NAMES.	RANK.	TIME OF SERVICE.		REMARKS.
		Months.	Days.	
John L. Townes, - -	Captain,	–	15	
Benjamin L. Meade, -	Lieutenant,	–	15	
John Robertson, - -	Ensign,	–	15	
Peter Rison, - -	Sergeant,	–	15	
Thomas Bolt, - -	"	–	15	
John T. Leigh, - -	"	–	15	
Joseph R. Robertson, -	"	–	15	
Francis Anderson, - -	Private,	–	15	
Wm. Anderson - -	"	–	15	
Benjamin Bridgforth, ∎	"	–	15	
Richerson Booker, - -	"	–	15	
Richard Booker, - -	"	–	15	
Richard Bibb, - -	"	–	15	
John P. Bolling, - -	"	–	15	
Robert F. Branch, - -	"	–	15	
John Chaffin, · - -	"	–	15	
George Craddock, - -	"	–	15	
Armstead Coleman, - -	"	–	15	
Wm. H. Eggleston, - -	"	–	15	
Alford O. Eggleston, -	"	–	15	
Ca's H. Featherston,	"	–	15	
Edward Ford, -	"	–	15	
Marston Foster, - -	"	–	15	
Nathan Hawkins, - -	"	–	15	
Nathaniel Harrison, - -	"	–	15	
Benjamin M. Harrison, -	"	–	15	
Phil. Wm. H. Holcombe, -	"	–	15	
John W. Jones, - -	"	–	15	
Seth W. Jones, - -	"	–	10	
Benjamin Lawson, - -	"	–	15	
Wm. G. Overton, - -	"	–	15	
Leonard Puckett, - -	"	–	15	
John S. Quarles, - -	"	–	15	
John R. Robertson, - -	"	–	15	
Edward Randolph, - -	"	–	15	
Thomas Wiley, - -	"	–	15	
John Webster, - -	"	–	15	
John F. Wiley, - -	"	–	15	

Captain Henry Travers' Company—Thirty-seventh Regiment.

NAMES.			RANK.	TIME OF SERVICE.		REMARKS.
				Months.	Days.	
Lewis Lamkin,	-	-	Sergeant,	—	7	
James Winstead,	-	-	"	—	5	
Matthew Neale,	-	-	"	—	4	
Edward D. Lewis,	-	-	"	—	5	
Thomas Kirkham,	-	-	"	—	4	
Peter Moore,	-	-	"	—	12	
Edward Oldham,	-	-	"	—	12	
T. Oldham,	-	-	"	—	15	
David H. Pitts,	-	-	"	—	14	
Vincent Lewis,	-	-	"	—	12	
Samuel Anderson,	-	-	Private,	—	17	
Daniel W. Beacham,	-	-	"	—	7	
Tarlton Barnes,	-	-	"	—	27	
Samuel Brumley,	-	-	"	—	23	
Joseph Burriss,	-	-	"	—	8	
Thomas Butlar,	-	-	"	—	17	
Ewell Beale,	-	-	"	—	20	
Meredith Barnes,	-	-	"	—	15	
George Blinco,	-	,	"	—	15	
Jesse Briant,	-	-	"	—	18	
John Campbell,	-	-	"	—	17	
James R. Carter,	-	-	"	—	5	
Price Campbell,	-	-	"	—	9	
James Campbell,	-	-	"	—	16	
Henry Dawson,	-	-	"	—	12	
Christ. Dawson,	-	-	"	—	12	
Lindsay T. Dawson,	-	-	"	—	28	
Samuel Dawson,	-	-	"	—	5	
George Dawson,	-	-	"	—	17	
Charles L. Fulks,	-	-	"	—	5	
John Fulks,	-	-	"	—	5	
J. France,	-	-	"	—	5	
Presley France,	-	-	"	—	20	
Presley Garner,	-	-	"	—	20	
James C. Gill,	-	-	"	—	6	
Presley Hudson,	-	-	"	—	27	
Samuel Hudson,	-	-	"	1	4	
Thomas Headley,	-	-	"	—	16	
James Harding,	-	-	"	—	4	
Thomas Jones,	-	-	"	—	9	
Bruiston Kenner,	-	-	"	—	16	
Charles Kent,	-	-	"	—	12	
Baldwin M. Leland,	-	-	"	—	11	
John Lewis, sen.	-	-	"	—	6	
John Lewis,	-	-	"	—	17	
Joseph Lewis,	-	-	"	—	20	
William Lewis,	-	-	"	—	5	
Vincent Moore,	-	-	"	—	5	
Elijah Moore,	-	-	"	—	17	
John A. Moss,	-	-	"	—	16	
Edward Oldham,	-	-	"	—	5	
Thomas Oldham,	-	-	"	—	4	
David H. Pitts,	-	-	"	—	11	
James Pierce,	-	-	"	—	5	

NAMES.	RANK.	TIME OF SERVICE.		REMARKS.
		Months.	Days.	
John Phillips, - -	Private,	–	5	
Reuben Potter, - -	"	–	4	
John Redman, -	"	–	15	
Sam'l A. Self, - -	"	–	7	
Henry W. Travers,	"	–	14	
Henry Travers, jr. - -	"	–	14	
George B. Vanlandingham, -	"	–	14	
George Vanlandingham, -	"	–	5	
Spencer Vanlandingham, -	"	–	16	
William Winstead, - -	"	–	16	
John Weymouth, - -	"	–	7	
George Winstead, - -	"	–	17	
John Walker, - -	"	–	5	
Thomas Walker, - -	"	–	5	

(For the rest of this company, see publication of Pay Rolls.)

MUSTER ROLL

*Of Lieutenant Thomas C. Tunstall's Company, from the Fifty-second Regiment,
Virginia Militia, in the County of New Kent, called into actual Service, under
general orders of the 26th June, 1813, from 28th June to 13th July, in the
year 1813.*

NAMES.	RANK.	TIME OF SERVICE.		REMARKS.
		Months.	Days.	
Thomas C. Tunstall, - -	Lieutenant,	–	16	
Norborne Crump, - -	Ensign.	–	16	
Wm. Bailey. - -	Sergeant,	–	16	
Wm. Massie, - -	"	–	16	
John Parke. - -	"	–	16	
Thompson Turner. - -	"	–	16	
John Tomlinson. - -	Corporal,	–	16	
Carter Gaddin, - -	"	–	16	
Wm. Jontson. - -	"	–	16	Or Johnson.
John Bailey. - -	Private,	–	16	
Wm. Badkins, - -	"	–	16	
John Barker. - -	"	–	16	
Wm. Boyd, - -	"	–	12	
Charles Clarke, - -	"	–	16	
James Ellison, - -	"	–	12	
Francis Foster. - -	"	–	16	
Nath'l Fox, - -	"	–	16	
Thomas Garnet, - -	"	–	16	
Prosser Higgins, - -	"	–	16	
James Hill. - -	"	–	16	
Wm. Higgins, - -	"	–	16	
Rich'd C. Jontson, - -	"	–	16	Or Johnson.
Parker Kent, - -	"	–	16	
Thomas Kent, - -	"	–	16	
Blackwell Kent. - -	"	–	16	
Thomas Moss, - -	"	–	16	
Parke Martin, - -	"	–	16	
James Parrish, - -	"	–	16	
Pleasant Pollard, - -	"	–	16	
Wm. Smith, - -	"	–	16	
Thomas Strange, - -	"	–	16	
James Thompson, - -	"	–	16	
Richard Tyree, - -	"	–	16	
Richard C. Terrell, - -	"	–	16	
John Wright, - -	"	–	16	
John S. Webb, - -	"	–	16	
Martin Wade, - -	"	–	16	
James Wright, - -	"	–	16	
Richard A. Warren, - -	"	–	16	
Henry Webb, - -	"	–	16	

Captain Anthony Turner's Company—Nineteenth Regiment.

NAMES.	RANK.	TIME OF SERVICE.		REMARKS.
		Months.	Days.	
Anthony Turner, - -	Captain,	—	10	
William Richardson, - -	Lieutenant,	—	10	
Patrick Coutts, - -	"	—	23	
Richard Drury, jun'r, -	Ensign,	—	10	
George M. Carrington, -	"	—	23	
James M. Couling, - -	Sergeant,	—	23	
Bartholomew Graves, -	"	—	14	
Archibald Parten, - -	"	—	16	
Lewis Wray, - -	"	—	16	
Miles Turpin, - -	"	—	6	
Freeborn G. Grenshaw, -	"	—	23	
Daniel P. Organ, - -	"	—	23	
William Brown, - -	"	—	10	
James Couling, - -	Corporal,	—	13	
Josiah Poore, - -	"	—	23	
David Reat, - -	"	—	23	
Nath. M. Johnson, -	"	—	23	
Nicholas Moore, - -	"	—	6	
William Hockins, - -	"	—	10	
Henry Williams, - -	"	—	10	
William Rowlett, - -	"	—	10	
Miles Turpin, - -	"	—	10	
Thomas Cook, - -	Drummer,	—	19	
Martin Austin, - -	Private,	—	16	
Joseph Addington, - -	"	—	6	
Richard Anderson, - -	"	—	23	
John Armistead, - -	"	—	23	
Stephen Aldridge, - -	"	—	23	
Charles Blunt, - -	"	—	10	Enlisted in U. S. army.
Jonathan Brown, - -	"	—	10	
Williamson Brown, - -	"	—	10	
Simon Block, - -	"	—	17	
Alexander Brown, - -	"	—	23	
John Bluford, - -	"	—	6	
Henry H. Bowles, - -	"	—	5	
David Chalmers, - -	"	—	10	
Richard Clarke, - -	"	—	10	
John Cook, - -	"	1		
Edwin J. Clopton, - -	"	—	16	
Henry Cusor, - -	"	—	10	
Joel Callis, - -	"	—	10	
Samuel Choat, - -	"	—	6	
Francis Childers, - -	"	—	6	
John Cline, - -	"	—	23	
William M. Chick, - -	"	—	23	
Thomas Cushing, - -	"	—	23	
James Duval, - -	"	—	10	
Joseph Danforth, - -	"	—	10	
Wm. Depriest, - -	"	—	10	
Benajah Denham, - -	"	—	10	
John Dames, - -	"	1	6	
William Dunn, - -	"	—	23	
Russell Dutton, - -	"	—	23	
Nathaniel Dutton, - -	"	—	23	

NAMES.	RANK.	TIME OF SERVICE.		REMARKS.
		Months.	Days.	
Henry Ensor, - -	Private,	–	6	
Anderson K. Freeman, -	"	–	10	
Reuben Freeman, - -	"	–	16	
Jesse Franklin, sr. - -	"	–	10	
John Francis, - -	"	–	9	
John H. Foster, - -	"	–	10	
Royall Freeman, - -	"	–	4	
John Gentry, - -	"	–	10	
Benj. Grover, - -	"	–	10	
Joseph Gale, - -	"	–	10	
George W. Godwin, - -	"	–	19	
Parke Glynn, - -	"	–	23	
Archibald Gardner, - -	"	–	6	
Wm. Hewlett, jr. - -	"	–	10	
Wm. Hoskin, - -	"	–	10	
Richard Hughes, - -	"	–	10	
Nicholas Hewlett, - -	"	–	10	
William Harper, - -	"	–	16	
Samuel Haywood, - -	"	–	7	
George W. Hill, - -	"	–	23	
Eppes Hughes. - -	"	–	5	
Peter Hamel, - -	"	–	4	
Daniel Higginbotham, -	"	–	23	
John Henderson, - -	"	–	19	
Edward Hallam, - -	"	–	23	
Nathaniel Ireson, - -	"	–	23	
Moses H. Judah, - -	"	–	16	
John James. - -	"	–	10	
Solomon Jacobs, - -	"	–	23	
Westwood W. James, -	"	–	23	
William Jordan, - -	"	–	5	
Jesse G. Jones. - -	"	–	6	
Bennett Kirby, - -	"	–	23	
Read Keir, - -	"	–	–	Joined artificers.
David Kinney, - -	"	–	23	
George Lester, - -	"	–	10	
James H. Lynch, - -	"	–	23	
Gustavus Luke, - -	"	–	11	
John Morris, - -	"	–	10	
John Martin, - -	"	–	10	
Meny Maynard, - -	"	–	10	
Richard Mair, - -	"	–	10	
Nicholas Moore, - -	"	–	10	
William Maddox, - -	"	–	17	
Amzi Munson, - -	"	–	16	
William Montague, - -	"	–	10	
William Morris, - -	"	–	13	
Daniel Mitchell, - -	"	–	23	
John McMarra, - -	"	–	23	
Turner Mountcastle, - -	"	–	10	
Davis Minor, - -	"	–	23	
Elisha May. - -	"	–	23	
John Marques, - -	"	–	23	
Charles M. Mitchell, - -	"	–	15	
David Mason, - -	"	–	23	
Adam Murry, - -	"	–	11	
Leslie Mitchell, - -	"	–	6	
John D. Miller, - -	"	–	6	
Benjamin Mason, - -	"	–	2	
Reuben Nash, - -	"	–	16	
Robert Neilson, - -	"			
John B. Ogg, - -	"	–	23	
Henry O'Neal, - -	"	–	5	
William Phillips, - -	"	–	16	

NAMES.	RANK.	TIME OF SERVICE.		REMARKS.
		Months.	Days.	
Henry Porter, - -	Private,	—	15	
Robert Poore, - -	"			
Elisha Penny, - -	"	—	9	
John Perkins. - -	"	—	23	
David D. Phillips, - -	"	—	1	
Henry E. Ratford, - -	"	—	10	
Anthony Robertson, - -	"	—	10	
Armstead Russell, - -	"	—	10	
David R. Ross, - -	"	—	10	
John Royall. - -	"	—	10	
George Roper, - -	"	—	16	
Elijah Roberts, - -	"	—	10	
Reuben Ragland, - -	"	—	23	
John Rowland, - -	"	—	23	
Edward W. Rootes. - -	"	—	23	
George Reid. - -	"	—	23	
David Roper, - -	"	—	23	
Abner Robinson, - -	"	—	20	
James Reat. - -	"	—	23	
Alexander Read, - -	"	—	6	
Matthew H. Rice, - -	"	—	23	
James Roper, - -	"	—	23	
Elias Roberts, - -	"	—	4	
Henry C. Redford, - -	"	—	6	
Abner Richardson, - -	"	—	6	
John P. Schermerhorn, -	"	—	10	
Peter Stywald, -	"	—	10	
Robert Sloan, -	"	—	10	
B. Slaughter, - -	"	—	16	
Benjamin Spratley, - -	"			
John St. John, - -	"			
Robert Seayres, - -	"	—	4	
Seymour Scott, - -	"	—	23	
Larkin Smith, - -	"	—	23	
Alexander Sharp, - -	"	—	23	
Samuel Sheppard, - -	"	—	23	
James S. Smithers, - -	"	—	4	
George Smith, - -	"			
Nathan Taylor, - -	"	—	10	
Curtis Tignor, - -	"	—	16	
John E. Thurman, - -	"	—	16	
Henry Turpin, -	"	—	10	
Richardson D. Taylor, -	"	—	20	
Edward W. Trent, - -	"	—	23	
Thomas Turner, - -	"			
Martin Turner, - -	"	—	6	
John Toler, - -	"			
John Tull, - -	"	—	5	
Joseph W. Vaughan, -	"			
Hezekiah Veach, - -	"	—	23	
Wm. Williamson, - -	"	—	16	
Wm. Williams, - -	"	—	16	
Allison Winstone, - -	"	—	10	
Wm. Walker, - -	"	—	10	
John Walker, - -	"	—	10	
Caleb Walker, - -	"	—	10	
James Watson, - -	"	—	23	
Conquest Wyatt, - -	"	—	23	
Sylvester Walkley, - -	"	—	23	
John Winston, - -	"	—	8	
Lewis Webb, - -	"	—	23	
Isham Williams, - -	"	—	5	
James Young, - -	"	—	10	

(For rest of this company, see publication of **Pay Rolls.**)

MUSTER ROLL

Of Captain Benjamin Tyler's Company, of the Eighty-ninth Regiment, Virginia Militia, commanded by Lieutenant Colonel Gerard Alexander, in the Service of the United States, from 30th August to 7th September, in the year 1814.

NAMES.	RANK.	TIME OF SERVICE.		REMARKS.
		Months.	Days.	
Benjamin Tyler,	Captain,	–	9	
H. R. Payn,	Lieutenant,	–	9	
Wm. P. Dunnington,	Ensign,	–	9	
Silas Foster,	Sergeant,	–	9	
Francis T. Fitzhugh,	"	–	9	
Joseph Tyler,	"	–	9	
James Cowls,	"	–	9	
Alex'r Anderson,	Corporal,	–	9	
Joshua Hoff,	"	–	9	
Robert Therman,	"	–	9	
Reuben Franklin,	"	–	9	
Wm. Briant,	Private,	–	9	
Joseph Butler,	"	–	9	
Wm. Brawner,	"	–	9	
John Brown, jr.	"	–	9	
Thomas Bradfield,	"	–	9	
Elijah Camerl,	"	–	9	
Jonathan Camerl,	"	–	9	
William Daviss,	"	–	9	
Robt. Dunnington,	"	–	9	
Solomon Ewell, jr.	"	–	9	
David Franklin,	"	–	9	
Elijah Fryer,	"	–	9	
Presley Foley,	"	–	9	
George Garner,	"	–	9	
Wm. Garner,	"	–	9	
Wm. Graham,	"	–	9	
Thomas Hoff,	"	–	9	
James Hixon,	"	–	9	
John Hall,	"	–	9	
John Jackson, jr.	"	–	9	
Bailey Jackson,	"	–	9	
Pleasant Jeffreys,	"	–	9	
John King, sen.	"	–	9	
John King, jr.	"	–	9	
John Kinchelow,	"	–	9	
Benjamin King,	"	–	9	
John Kirkpatrick,	"	–	9	
Thos. Kirkpatrick,	"	–	9	
Wm. Learkin,	"	–	9	
Danl. Learkin,	"	–	9	
Henry Langfelt,	"	–	9	
John Milstead, jr.	"	–	9	
Thomas Mason,	"	–	9	
Martin Moredock,	"	–	9	
Burket Newman,	"	–	9	
Albert Newman,	"	–	9	
Richard Payne,	"	–	9	

NAMES.			RANK.	TIME OF SERVICE.		REMARKS.
				Months.	Days.	
Joseph Parmer,	-	-	Private,	–	9	
David Rainie,	-	-	"	–	9	
Wm. Rollins,	-	-	"	–	9	
Strother Reno,	-	-	"	–	9	
James Suttle,	-	-	"	–	9	
Westward Smithers,		-	"	–	9	
Edmond Thermon,		-	"	–	9	
Thomas Waring,	-	-	"	–	9	
Philip Winekoop,	-	-	"	–	9	
Randolph Welsh,	-	-	"	–	9	
Jesse Woodyard,	-	-	"	–	9	
John Woodyard,	-	-	"	–	9	
George Woodyard,	-	-	"	–	9	

Captain John Tyler's Company—Fifty-second Regiment.

NAMES.	RANK.	TIME OF SERVICE.		REMARKS.
		Months.	Days.	
John Tyler, - -	Captain,	–	16	
John Cole, - -	Lieutenant,	–	16	
Temple E. Demoville, -	Ensign,	–	16	
John Wilson, - -	Sergeant,	–	16	
Thomas Wilkinson, - -	"	–	16	
Colin H. Finch, - -	"	–	16	
John Hill, - -	"	–	16	
James Vaughan, - -	Corporal,	–	16	
John Knib, - -	"	–	16	
William H. Irby, - -	"	–	16	
Woodson Knib, - -	"	–	16	
Thomas T. Blackhurst, -	Private,	–	14	
William Bames, - -	"	–	16	
Thomas Butler, - -	"	–	16	
James Bradley, - -	"	–	16	
Samuel Crutchfield, - -	"	–	16	
Peter Crew, - -	"	–	16	
Lewis Crutchfield, - -	"	–	16	
Robert W. Christian, -	"	–	16	
Richard Clarke, - -	"	–	16	
John T. Eppes, - -	"	–	16	
Robert Gordon, - -	"	–	16	
William Gill, - -	"	–	16	
William Gordon, - -	"	–	16	
Thomas Gill, - -	"	–	16	
William Griffin, - -	"	–	16	
William Hardiman, - -	"	–	16	
Beverley Hardiman, - -	"	–	16	
Fra's Hardiman, jr. - -	"	–	16	
Thos. R. W. Irby, - -	"	–	16	
Anthony K. Johnston, -	"	–	16	
David Mountcastle, - -	"	–	16	
Crawley Maynard, - -	"	–	16	
Edward Scully, - -	"	–	16	
Wat. H. Tyler, - -	"	–	16	
J. Vaiden, - -	"	–	16	
Ch's Word, - -	"	–	16	
David Wilkinson, - -	"	–	16	

(For rest of this company, see publication of Pay Rolls.)

MUSTER ROLL

Of Captain Robert Tynes' Company, of the Twenty-ninth Regiment, Virginia Militia, commanded by Major Joseph W. Ballard, in Service at Smithfield, from 23d June to 10th July, 1813.

NAMES.	RANK.	TIME OF SERVICE.		REMARKS.
		Months.	Days.	
Robert Tynes, - -	Captain,	–	6	
George W. Driver, - -	Lieutenant,	–	18	
Parker Hawkins, - -	Ensign,	–	18	
John Phillips, - -	Sergeant,	–	18	
John Giles, - -	"	–	18	
Joseph Jordan, - -	"	–	18	
Joseph Holliday, - -	"	–	18	
John Parr, (of Wm.) -	Corporal,	–	17	
James Jordan, - -	"	–	18	
Hezekiah Jordan, - -	"	–	18	
Thos. Newman, - -	"	–	18	
James Beal, - -	Private,	–	6	
John Bullock, (of Jed.) -	"	–	6	
William Bullock, - -	"	–	18	
Thomas Bowles, - -	"	–	18	
James Cook, - -	"	–	6	
William Duggan, - -	"	–	18	
Henry Davis, - -	"	–	18	
Samuel Everett, - -	"	–	18	
Willis Garner, - -	"	–	18	
Jeremiah Gibbins, - -	"	–	18	
Thomas Hall, - -	"	–	18	
James Hall, - -	"	–	18	
George Hall, - -	"	–	18	
John Jolly, - -	"	–	18	
John Jordan, - -	"	–	18	
Wm. Jordan, - -	"	–	18	
Barnaba Matthews, - -	"	–	18	
Thomas Pope, - -	"	–	6	
John Parr, (of Rich'd,) -	"	–	18	
Joseph Purden, - -	"	–	18	
Lewis Powell, - -	"	–	18	
Hardy Pope, - -	"	–	7	
Thomas Pitt, - -	"	–	7	
Edward Pittman, - -	"	–	18	
John Shivers, - -	"	–	18	
Robert Shivers, - -	"	–	3	
John F. Wills, - -	"	–	18	
Stephen Whitley, - -	"	–	18	

MUSTER ROLL

Of Captain James Underwood's Troop of Cavalry, of the Fourth Regiment, in the County of Hanover, in the Service of the United States, from 31st August to 13th September, 1814.

NAMES.	RANK.	TIME OF SERVICE.		REMARKS.
		Months.	Days.	
James Underwood, - -	Captain,	–	14	
Arch'd B. Dandridge, - -	Lieutenant,	–	14	
Ro. A. Dandridge, - -	"	–	14	
John C. Underwood, - -	Cornet,	–	14	
John King, - -	Sergeant,	–	14	
John G. Childers, - -	"	–	14	
Nath. W. Dandridge, - -	"	–	14	
Joseph Woodsong, - -	"	–	14	
Fred. Shoemaker, - -	Corporal,	–	14	
Thomas Elmore, - -	"	–	14	
Nath. Anthony, jr. - -	"	–	14	
Charles Childress, - -	"	–	14	
John H. Priddy, - -	Trumpeter,		14	
Thos. S. Auil, - -	Private,	–	14	
Thos. Atkinson, - -	"	–	14	
Robt. S. Austin, - -	"		14	
Samuel J. Bulliam, - -	"		14	
Ambrose Brooks, - -	"	–	14	
Thomas Bowles, - -	"	–	14	
Nath'l Crenshaw, - -	"	–	14	
Spotswood Childers, - -	"	–	14	
Peter Copeland, - -	"	–	14	
Pendleton R. Childress, -	"	–	14	
Ed. Camron, - -	"	–	14	
James Denton, - -	"	–	14	
Nath'l Dogan, - -	"	–	14	
Allen Denton, - -	"	–	14	
John England, - -	"	–	14	
William Ford, - -	"	–	14	
Solomon Harris, - -	"	–	14	
Pleasant Hattan, - -	"	–	14	
Ed. W. Kimbrough, - -	"	–	14	
Alexander Loving, - -	"	–	14	
John Mallory, jr. - -	"	–	14	
John Mann, - -	"	–	14	
Overton W. Mallory, - -	"	–	14	
Benj. Mann, - -	"	–	14	
Nath. Mills, - -	"	–	14	
Stephen Mallory, - -	"	–	14	
John Nuckols, - -	"	–	14	
Nath. Nuckols, - -	"	–	14	
David Nuckols, - -	"	–	14	
John Nash, - -	"	–	14	
Ben. Perkins, - -	"	–	14	
William Sayre, - -	"	–	14	
Jesse Sayre, - -	"	–	14	
Christian Stone, - -	"	–	14	

NAMES.	RANK.	TIME OF SERVICE.		REMARKS.
		Months.	Days.	
John H. Taylor, - -	Private,	–	14	
Garland Thompson, - -	"	–	14	
Francis Underwood, - -	"	–	14	
Rich'd A. Woodson, - -	"	–	14	
Reuben Wood, - -	"	–	14	

Captain Littleton Upshur's Company—Twenty-seventh Regiment.

NAMES.	RANK.	TIME OF SERVICE.		REMARKS.
		Months.	Days.	
Smith Nottingham, - -	Ensign,	–	10	
Nat. Hickman, - -	Drummer,	–	10	
John Yeatman, - -	Act'g Drum'r,	–	10	
John R. Hall, - -	Fifer,	–	10	
John Nelson, jr. - -	A. Q. M. S.	–	10	
Thomas Ames, - -	Private.	–	10	
Thomas Addison, - -	"	–	10	
Hezekiah Belote, - -	"	–	1	
John Bobb, - -	"	–	10	
John Casey, - -	"	–	10	
Hill Dorsey, - -	"	–	10	
John Davis, - -	"	–	4	
John T. Elliott, - -	"	–	1	
William Floyd, - -	"	–	10	
Littleton Godwin. - -	"	–	1	
Richard Garrett, - -	"	–	10	
William Gleeson, - -	"	–	10	
Edw'd Hickman, - -	"	–	20	
Kelley Harrison, (or Riley,) -	"	1	6	
Nat. Hickman, - -	"	–	10	
Henry R. Harmanson, -	"	–	1	
James Hamilton, - -	"	–	10	
Teagle Jacob, - -	"	–	7	
Wm. Joynes, jr. - -	"	–	10	
Walter Kellam, - -	"			
Daniel Luke, - -	"	–	20	
George Luke, - -	"	–	20	
Levin Lewis, - -	"	–	10	
William Mears, - -	"	–	10	
John Ross, - -	"	–	10	
Teagle Roberts, - -	"	–	10	
John Raightield, - -	"			
Nat. Savage, - -	"	–	10	
Person Savage, - -	"	–	10	
Caleb Savage, - -	"	–	10	
John Sandford, - -	"			
John Simpson, - -	"	–	1	
Shepherd Speakman, -	"	–	20	
George Scott, jr. - -	"	–	10	
James Turner, - -	"	–	10	
Bartho. Taylor, - -	"	–	10	
Thomas H. Turpin, - -	"	–	1	
John D. Turpin, - -	"	–	1	
John Taylor, - -	"	–	1	
John Tyler, - -	"	–	20	
George Teackle, - -	"			
Arthur Upshur, - -	"			
John Upshur, - -	"	–	10	
George P. Upshur, - -	"	–	1	
Elias Waterfield, - -	"	–	10	
Samuel West, - -	"	–	10	
Charles West, - -	"	–	10	
Major Westcoat, - -	"	–	10	
John Westcoat, - -	"	–	10	

NAMES.			RANK.	TIME OF SERVICE.		REMARKS.
				Months.	Days.	
James Williams,	-	-	Private,	–	10	
Obedience White,	-	-	"	–	1	
James Wilkins,	-	-	"	–	20	
John Wilkins,	-	-	"	–	20	
Thomas Wilkins,	-	-	"	–	20	
Zorobabel Willis,	-	-	"			
William Willis,	-	-	"	–	10	
Harold L. Wilson,	-	-	"			
John Wilson,	-	-	"			
John Yeatman,	-	-	"	–	10	

(For rest of this company, see publication of Pay Rolls.)

MUSTER ROLL

Of Captain John Velvin's Company, from the Seventy-first Regiment, Virginia Militia, in Surry County, commanded by Colonel William Allen, in the Service from 30th June to 10th July, 1813.

NAMES.			RANK.	TIME OF SERVICE.		REMARKS.
				Months.	Days.	
John Velvin,	-	-	Captain,	–	11	
John Watkins,	-	-	Lieutenant,	–	11	
Robert Ellis,	-	-	Ensign,	–	11	
Jesse Warren,	-	-	Sergeant,	–	11	
James Key,	-	-	"	–	11	
Edwin Rodgers,	-	-	"	–	11	
Samuel Hargrove,	-	-	"	–	11	
Belah Williford,	-	-	Corporal,	–	11	
Lemuel Bailey,	-	-	"	–	11	
Sampson White,	-	-	"	–	11	
Nicholas Price,	-	-	"	–	11	
Jesse W. P. Bryant,	-	-	Drummer,	–	11	
Thomas Brown,	-	-	Fifer,	–	11	
Benj. B. Adkins,	-	-	Private,	–	11	
Theoderick Adkins,	-	-	"	–	11	
Robert S. Bailey,	-	-	"	–	6	
William Bryant,	-	-	"	–	11	
Richard Badget,	-	-	"	–	11	
John Brown,	-	-	"	–	11	
Benj. Brown,	-	-	"	–	11	
Richard H. S. Bailey,	-	-	"	–	11	
Benj. Clarke,	-	-	"	–	6	
John Cocks,	-	-	"	–	11	
Jesse Cocks,	-	-	"	–	11	
Henry M. Cocks,	-	-	"	–	11	
Josiah Freeman,	-	-	"	–	11	
Bell Goodrich,	-	-	"	–	11	
Cary Hargrave,	-	-	"	–	2	
Henry S. Hart,	-	-	"	–	11	
William Hargrave,	-	-	"	–	11	
Ruffin Hargrave,	-	-	"	–	11	
Henry Holt,	-	-	"	–	11	
William Holloway,	-	-	"	–	11	
James Harriss,	-	-	"	–	11	
Arthur Holleman,	-	-	"	–	11	
John Holt,	-	-	"	–	11	
James Judkins,	-	-	"	–	11	
John C. Judkins,	-	-	"	–	11	
Jacob Judkins,	-	-	"	–	11	
Moland James,	-	-	"	–	11	
Henry Johnson,	-	-	"	–	6	
Thomas Little,	-	-	"	–	11	
Jesse Lane,	-	-	"	–	11	
Jesse Little,	-	-	"	–	2	
William Matthews,	-	-	"	–	11	
Peter Oakwood,	-	-	"	–	11	
Matthew Pond,	-	-	"	–	11	
Richard Ponsonby,	-	-	"	–	11	
Richard Parr,	-	-	"	–	11	

NAMES.	RANK.	TIME OF SERVICE.		REMARKS.
		Months.	Days.	
Samuel Pretlow, - -	Private,	–	11	
Michael Rogers, - -	"	–	11	
Richard D. Riggan, - -	"	–	11	
Thomas Sharp, - -	"	–	11	
Jordan Taylor, - -	"	–	11	
Allen Warren, - -	"	–	11	
Thomas Wrenn, - -	"	–	11	
Samuel Warren, - -	"	–	6	

MUSTER ROLL

Of Lieutenant William Vesey's Company, of the Fifty-ninth Regiment, Virginia Militia, commanded by Lieutenant Colonel Josiah Riddick, jr., called into the Service of the State from 3d to 17th April, in the year 1813.

NAMES.			RANK.	TIME OF SERVICE.		REMARKS.
				Months.	Days.	
William Vesey,	-	-	Lieutenant,	–	15	
James C. Godwin,	-	-	Ensign,	–	15	
David Cutchen,	-	-	Sergeant,	–	15	
Jordan Denson,	-	-	"	–	15	
Thomas Dixon.	-	-	Corporal,	–	15	
Thos. Weatherly,	-	-	"	–	15	
John Newton,	-	-	Drummer,	–	15	
George Bartlett,	-	-	Private,	–	15	
Elijah Ball,	-	-	"	–	15	
James Brothers,	-	-	"	–	15	
James Baker,	-	-	"	–	15	
Thos. J. Coffield,	-	-	"	–	15	
William Foster,	-	-	"	–	15	
John Foster,	-	-	"	–	15	
Major Guy,	-	-	"	–	15	
James Hines,	-	-	"	–	15	
Elihu Hedgbeth,	-	-	"	–	15	
Ambrose Hill,	-	-	"	–	15	
John Minton,	-	-	"	–	15	
John Pinner,	-	-	"	–	15	
James Pitt,	-	-	"	–	15	
Matthew Powell,	-	-	"	–	15	
William Pinner,	-	-	"	–	15	
Thos. S. Stokely,	-	-	"	–	15	
Thos. Wilkins.	-	-	"	–	15	

MUSTER ROLL

Of Sergeant Ambrose Wake's Company, from the One Hundred and Ninth Regiment, in the County of Middlesex, called into actual Service at Stingray Point, by order of the Executive Council, from 26th July to 26th August, 1813.

NAMES.	RANK.	TIME OF SERVICE.		REMARKS.
		Months.	Days.	
Ambrose Wake, - -	Sergeant,	1		
Joseph K. Lipscomb, - -	Corporal,	1	–	Of cavalry.
Henry Cloudous, - -	Private,	1		
Martin Harrow, - -	"	1		
Anthony Harrow, - -	"	1		
Richard Jackson, - -	"	1		
Elliott Kidd, - -	"	1		
John Long, - -	"	1		
Isham Miller, - -	"	1		
George Revere, - -	"	1		
John Thomas, - -	"	1		
William Webmore, - -	"	1		

MUSTER ROLL

Of Captain Theodorick Walker's Company, from the Eighty-third Regiment, in the County of Dinwiddie, called into actual Service under the general orders of the 30th June, 1813, from 1st July to the 6th of the same month, in the year 1813.

NAMES.	RANK.	TIME OF SERVICE.		REMARKS.
		Months.	Days.	
Theodorick Walker, - -	Captain,	–	6	
Abraham Mitchell, - -	Lieutenant,	–	6	
Benj. Roney, - -	Ensign.	–	6	
Robert Roney, - -	Sergeant,	–	6	
Wm. G. Nunnely, - -	"	–	6	
Jno. T. Goodwin, - -	"	–	6	
Thos. Roney, - -	"	–	6	
Paschal Tucker. - -	Corporal,	–	6	
Jas. Stacy. - - -	"	–	6	
Thomas Tucker, - -	"	–	6	
Pat'k R. Smith. - -	"	–	6	
Robert Mitchell, - -	Drummer,	–	6	On duty at Norfolk.
Chas. Mitchell. - -	Fifer,	–	6	" " "
Chas. Abernathy, - -	Private,	–	6	
How'd Abernathy, - -	"	–	6	
William Alfriend, - -	"	–	6	
Martin Abernathy, - -	"	–	6	
Harm'n Abernathy, - -	"	–	6	
Freeman Abernathy, - -	"	–	6	
Geo. Abernathy. - -	"	–	6	
Jeremiah Bishop, - -	"	–	6	
Drury Bishop. - -	"	–	6	
Robt. Bolling, - -	"	–	6	Joined the cavalry.
James Bishop, jr. - -	"	–	6	
John Bailey, - -	"	–	6	
Robert Curtis, - -	"	–	6	
Henry Farlow, - -	"	–	6	
Robt. Greenway, - -	"	–	6	
Laban Harrison, - -	"	–	6	
John Hawkins. - -	"	–	6	
Green B. Hamlet, - -	"	–	6	
Robt. Harper, - -	"	–	6	
Hartwell Hartwell, - -	"	–	6	
Gardner Hankins, - -	"	–	6	
Joseph H. Jackson, - -	"	–	6	
William Jackson, - -	"	–	6	
Richard Jackson, - -	"	–	6	
Jeremiah Miles, - -	"	–	6	
Jessee Medling, - -	"	–	6	
Joseph W. Medling, - -	"	–	6	
Obadiah Nunnely, - -	"	–	6	
Charles Nunnely, - -	"	–	6	
Thomas Nunnely, - -	"	–	6	
Thos. Parch. - -	"	–	6	
Cadrick P. Poole, - -	"	–	6	
Peterson P. Poole, - -	"	–	6	In the U. S. service.
Stephen P. Poole, - -	"	–	6	

NAMES.			RANK.	TIME OF SERVICE.		REMARKS.
				Months.	Days.	
Wiley Parsons,	-	-	Private,	–	6	
James Poarch,	-	-	"	–	6	
Jeremiah Rowland,	-	-	"	–	6	
David Thrift,	-	-	"	–	6	
John Thrift.	-	-	"	–	6	
Colwell Tolley.	-	-	"	–	6	
Wm. Wilkinson,	-	-	"	–	6	
John Wells,	-	-	"	–	6	
Hubbard Wyatt,	-	-	"	–	6	Bishop Wyatt his sub.
Charles Young,	-	-	"	–	6	
Thos. Yarborough,	-	-	"	–	6	

Captain Curtis Waller's Company—Sixteenth Regiment.

NAMES.	RANK.	TIME OF SERVICE		REMARKS.
		Months.	Days.	
William H. Fulcher, -	Ensign,	–	27	
Robert E. Goodloe, - -	Sergeant,	–	27	
Belford Smith, - -	Corporal,	–	27	
William Coleman, - -	Wagoner,	–	9	
John Bohannan, - -	Private,	–	27	
Wilson M. Cary, - -	"	–	27	
John Carnohan, - -	"	–	27	
Lewis Crawford, - -	"	–	9	
Richard Coleman, - -	"	–	27	
William D. Coleman, -	"	–	27	
Stokeley Coleman, - -	"	–	27	
Herndon Carey, - -	"	–	27	Sub. for Phil. Thornton.
John Dilliard, - -	"	–	27	
Jonathan Durrett, - -	"	–	27	
William Duncan, - -	"	–	3	
Larkin F. Farish, - -	"	–	25	
Stephen Farish, - -	"	–	26	
Thomas Goodloe, - -	"	–	27	Sub. for Ed. G. Hill.
George Humphreys, -	"	–	27	
Richard Hockaday, - -	"	–	27	
Thomas Henderson, -	"	–	27	Sub. for John Cason.
Anderson Long, - -	"	–	27	Sub. for Sym B. Goodloe.
Valentine C. Long, - -	"	– ,	27	Sub. for Aquila Johnson.
Robert Lewis, - -	"	–	3	
Garland Lively, - -	"	–	1	
Garland D. Luck, - -	"	–	27	
Thomas Minor, - -	"	–	29	
Benjamin Mason, - -	"	–	27	Sub. for John Woolfolk.
Thomas McKenny, - -	"	–	27	
Larkin Morris, - -	"	–	27	
Boswell Partlow, - -	"	–	27	Sub. for John Partlow.
Thomas Payne, - -	"	–	27	
George Pearce, - -	"	–	27	
Daniel Pilcher, - -	"	–	6	
Benjamin Shackleford, -	"	–	26	
John Stanley, - -	"	–	27	
Burnley Smith, - -	"	–	9	
William Smith, - -	"	–	27	
John Thornton, - -	"	–	27	
John Truel, - -	"	–	26	
Philip Thornton, jr. - -	"	–	27	
William Thomas, - -	"	–	27	
John Woolfolk, - -	"	–		
Archer Webber, - -	"	–	27	Sub. for John Webber.
Dabney Wilkinson, - -	"	–	27	
James Wright, - -	"	–	21	
Elijah Wigglesworth, -	"	–	27	

(For rest of this company, see publication of Pay Rolls.)

MUSTER ROLL

Of Captain John Waller's Company, of the Ninth Regiment, Virginia Militia, in the County of King and Queen, called into actual Service under the general orders of the 5th of April, from 6th to 13th April, in the year 1813.

NAMES.	RANK.	TIME OF SERVICE.		REMARKS.
		Months.	Days.	
Captain John Waller, -	Major,	–	9	
Lieut. Robert Bland, -	Captain,	–	9	
Ensign Jno. Harper, -	Lieutenant,	–	9	
John Bland, - -	Sergeant,	–	9	
Edward Garrett, - -	"	–	9	
Laban Carr, - -	"	–	9	
Wm. A. Smith, - -	"	–	9	
Robt. Bowden, - -	Serg't major,	–	9	
Josiah Mactire, - -	Drum major,	–	3	
Thomas Adams, - -	Private,	–	9	
Robert Brooking, - -	"	–	9	
James Bland, - -	"	–	9	
Wm. Brown, - -	"	–	9	
Robert Brooke, - -	"	–	9	
Richard Bland, - -	"	–	9	
Samuel Brown, - -	"	–	9	
Warner Bland, - -	"	–	9	
Jno. Y. Burton, - -	"	–	9	
Charles Colley, - -	"	–	9	
Isaiah Clegg, - -	"	–	9	
George Collins, - -	"	–	9	
James Crouch, - -	"	–	9	
Laban Clegg, - -	"	–	9	
Thomas Carr, - -	"	–	9	
Henry F. Dudley, - -	"	–	9	
John Dillard, - -	"	–	9	
George G. Dame, - -	"	–	9	
Christoper Didlake, -	"	–	9	
Thornton Fleming, -	"	–	9	
Thomas Hooper, - -	"	–	9	
John Lambeth, - -	"	–	9	
Charles Lambeth, - -	"	–	9	
John Muire, - -	"	–	9	
Henry Milby, - -	"	–	9	
John Milby, - -	"	–	9	
Thos. Moore, - -	"	–	9	
Samuel Milby, - -	"	–	9	
George Moore, - -	"	–	9	
Wm. Milby, - -	"	–	9	
William Newcomb, -	"	–	9	
John Newbill, - -	"	–	9	
John Newcomb, - -	"	–	9	
John G. Rilee, - -	"	–	9	
Mourning Smith, - -	"	–	9	
Francis Smith, - -	"	–	9	
John Seward, - -	"	–	9	
James Seward, - -	"	–	9	

NAMES.	RANK.	TIME OF SERVICE.		REMARKS.
		Months.	Days.	
William Seward, - -	Private,	–	3	
Armstead Thouston, - -	"	–	9	
Wm. Thouston, - -	"	–	9	
John Tureman, - -	"	–	9	
George Tureman, - -	"	–	9	
Rob't Waldon, - -	"	–	9	

MUSTER ROLL

Of Captain Samuel Walston's Company, of the Ninety-ninth Regiment, Virginia Militia, commanded by Lieutenant Colonel Charles Burwell, called into the Service of the United States, from 8th to 9th September, 1814.

NAMES.	RANK.	TIME OF SERVICE.		REMARKS.
		Months.	Days.	
Samuel Walston, - -	Captain,	—	2	
Lewis Nock, - -	Ensign,	—	2	
Charles Nock, - -	Sergeant,	—	2	
Riley Fisher, - -	"	—	2	
Thomas Nock, - -	Corporal,	—	2	
John Cowley, - -	"	—	2	
Robert P. Brodwater, -	"	—	2	
George Prescott, - -	"	—	2	
William Abbott, - -	Private,	—	2	
William Bloxom, - -	"	—	2	
Caleb Brimore, - -	"	—	2	
Levi Core, - -	"	—	2	
William Garrett, - -	"	—	2	
John Gardner, - -	"	—	2	
Elijah Hope, - -	"	—	2	
Teackle Justice, - -	"	—	2	
Samuel Mapp, - -	"	—	2	
Southey Northum, - -	"	—	2	
Nathaniel Outten, - -	"	—	2	
Daniel Price, - -	"	—	2	
William Tatham, - -	"	—	2	
Teackle Taylor, - -	"	—	2	
Staton Taylor, - -	"	—	2	
John Taylor, - -	"	—	2	
Isaac Young, - -	"	—	2	

MUSTER ROLL

Of Captain Caleb Ward's Company, of the Twentieth Regiment, Virginia Militia, commanded by Lieutenant Colonel James Robinson, in the Service of the United States, from 21st to 29th September, 1813.

NAMES.	RANK.	TIME OF SERVICE.		REMARKS.
		Months.	Days.	
Caleb Ward,	Captain,	–	9	
David Biggs,	Ensign,	–	9	
David Morris,	Sergeant,	–	9	
Batson Dyer,	"	–	9	
David Morse,	"	–	9	
Joseph Barnes,	"	–	9	
Jonathan Grimstead,	Corporal,	–	9	
William Williams,	"	–	9	
Arthur Gornto,	"	–	9	
John Gornto,	"	–	9	
Tulley Dauge,	Fifer,	–	9	
Hillary Dyer,	Drummer,	–	9	
Cornelius Brock,	Private,	–	9	
Thomas Craft,	"	–	9	
Willoughby Capps,	"	–	9	
David Carrell,	"	–	9	
William Davis,	"	–	7	
Joshua Davis,	"	–	7	
Robert Dudley,	"	–	9	
John Fountain,	"	–	9	
Elisha Grimstead,	"	–	6	
Thomas Grimstead,	"	–	6	
Daniel Grimstead,	"	–	6	
Francis Gordon,	"	–	7	
William Gornto,	"	–	7	
Luke Hill.	"	–	9	
Joseph Lawrence,	"	–	9	
James Morris,	"	–	9	
Nathan Munden,	"	–	9	
John Spann,	"	–	9	
Francis Spann,	"	–	7	
Eustice Stripes,	"	–	5	
Ebenezer Spann,	"	–	5	
Robert Stiven,	"	–	9	
John Whitehurst,	"	–	9	
Joshua Wright,	"	–	9	
David Whitehurst,	"	–	9	
George Whitehurst,	"	–	9	
John Whitehurst,	"	–	9	
Tulley Whitehurst,	"	–	8	
Cornelius Whitehurst,	"	–	9	
Caleb Ward, jr.	"	–	9	

MUSTER ROLL

Of Captain James Warden's Company, of the Twentieth Regiment, Virginia Militia, commanded by Lieutenant Colonel James Robinson, in the Service of the United States, from 7th to 13th February, from 9th to 15th March, and from 24th to 30th September, 1813.

NAMES.	RANK.	TIME OF SERVICE.		REMARKS.
		Months.	Days.	
James Warden, - -	Captain,	–	21	
Malachi Moore, - -	Lieutenant,	–	21	
Jesse Morris, - -	Ensign,	–	21	
John Bright, - -	Sergeant,	–	9	
William Bright, - -	"	–	20	
Malachi Miller, - -	"	–	14	
Noah Brock, - -	"	–	13	
Noah Dudley, - -	"	–	6	
John Stone, - -	"	–	3	
Aaron Throp, - -	Corporal,	–	14	
Oney Brock, - -	"	–	14	
Jordan Berry, - -	"	–	21	
John Cox, - -	"	–	7	
John K. Kays, - -	"	–	14	
Thomas Dudley, - -	"	–	7	
Thomas Ackiss, - -	Private,	–	7	
Charles Berry, - -	"	–	18	
James Bonney, - -	"	–	12	
John Boughton, - -	"	–	6	
John Bonney, - -	"	–	11	
Joel Capps, - -	"	–	14	
Thomas Caton, - -	"	–	17	
John Cumberfoot, - -	"	–	13	
Joel Corbel, - -	"	–	21	
John Corbel, - -	"	–	3	
William Capps, - -	"	–	20	
Joel Cornick, - -	"	–	3	
Joseph Chappell, - -	"	–	17	
John Cox, - -	"	–	14	
Jacob Chappell, - -	"	–	17	
Caleb Carroll, - -	"	–	12	
Thomas Campbell, - -	"	–	7	
Daniel Doudge, - -	"	–	21	
Cornelius Doudge, - -	"	–	7	
John Dudley, - -	"	–	3	
Israel Fisher, - -	"	–	6	
Arthur Frizzle, - -	"	–	19	
John Fountain, - -	"	–	6	
William Gornto, - -	"	–	7	
James Gornto, - -	"	–	8	
David Grimstead, - -	"	–	6	
William King, - -	"	–	6	
James Morse, - -	"	–	3	
David Morse, - -	"	–	3	
Malachi Miller, - -	"	–	2	
Kedar McClaten, - -	"	–	14	
Thomas McClaten, - -	"	–	21	
John Matthias, - -	"	–	7	
Nathan Munden, - -	"	–	6	

NAMES.	RANK.	TIME OF SERVICE.		REMARKS.
		Months.	Days.	
William Moore, - -	Private,	–	14	
John Moore, - -	"	–	7	
William Oakham, - -	"	–	7	
Enoch Raney, - -	"	–	20	
David Riggs, - -	"	–	3	
Zephaniah Span, - -	"	–	14	
John Shepherd, - -	"	–	20	
Jesse Stone, - -	"	–	14	
Reuben Stone, - -	"	–	14	
James Salmons, - -	"	–	7	
Ebenezer Span, - -	"	–	7	
Simon Sikes, - -	"	–	7	
James Spratt, jr. - -	"	–	3	
William Timmons, - -	"	–	13	
Lodowick Williamson, -	"	–	14	
William Williams, - -	"	–	6	
Tully Whitehurst, - -	"	–	6	
Absalom Whitehurst, -	"	–	14	
John Whitehurst, - -	"	–	14	

MUSTER ROLL

Of Captain William L. Waring's Company, of the One Hundred and Eleventh Regiment, commanded by Lieutenant Colonel Richard E. Parker, in the Service of the United States, from 28th July to 25th September, in the year 1814.

NAMES.			RANK.	TIME OF SERVICE.		REMARKS.		
				Months.	Days.			
William S. Waring,	-	-	Captain,	1	29			
Richard Woodward,	-	-	Lieutenant,	1	29			
Kemp Gatewood,	-	-	Ensign,	1	29			
Joseph L. Bohannan,	-	-	Sergeant,	–	25	Transferred from Capt.		
James Booker,	-	-	"	1	29	Fisher's company.		
Thomas Sheward,	-	-	"	1	29			
James Montague,	-	-	"	1	29			
Josiah Minter,	-	-	Corporal,	1	29			
Richard Sheward,	-	-	"	1	29			
Thomas Jones,	-	-	"	1	29			
John C. Clarkson,	-	-	"	–	25	"	"	"
Philip Clarke,	-	-	Drummer,	1	29			
Obadiah Alexander,	-	-	Private,	1	29			
Morton Armstrong,	-	-	"	1	29			
Jesse Boughan,	-	-	"	1	29			
Leonard Burnett,	-	-	"	1	29			
Lewis Brooke,	-	-	"	1	29			
Lewis Brizendine,	-	-	"	1	29			
James Brooke,	-	-	"	1	29			
George Brooke,	-	-	"	1	29			
Tomson Beazley,	-	-	"	1	29			
Caston Boughan,	-	-	"	1	29			
John Bohannan,	-	-	"	–	9	"	"	"
Curtice Bawl,	-	-	"	–	25	"	"	"
John H. Brizendine,	-	-	"	–	25	"	"	"
John Brown,	-	-	"	–	25	"	"	"
Churchill Bawl,	-	-	"	–	25	"	"	"
Richard Barfoot,	-	-	"	–	25	"	"	"
Alexander S. Bohannan,	-	-	"	–	25	"	"	"
Starling Burch,	-	-	"	–	25	"	"	"
Carter Ball,	-	-	"	–	25			
Richard Ball,	-	-	"	–	25			
Reuben Brooke,	-	-	"	1	29			
Harrison Ball,	-	-	"	–	25	"	"	"
James Croxton,	-	-	"	1	29			
Thomas Coats,	-	-	"	1	29			
John Crow, sr.	-	-	"	1	29			
John Crow, jr.	-	-	"	1	29			
Peyton Crane,	-	-	"	1	29			
Philip D. Crow,	-	-	"	1	29			
Richard Coats,	-	-	"	1	29			
James Coleman,	-	-	"	–	25	Transferred from Capt.		
						Fisher's company.		
Robert Clarke,	-	-	"	–	25	"	"	"
Benjamin Clarkson,	-	-	"	–	25	"	"	"
Joseph Clarkson,	-	-	"	–	25	"	"	"
Richard Clarkson,	-	-	"	–	25	"	"	"
James Carnol,	-	-	"	–	25	"	"	"

NAMES.			RANK.	TIME OF SERVICE.		REMARKS.
				Months.	Days.	
Tolla Dunn,	-	-	Private,	1	29	
James Durham,			"	1	29	
Jackson Dunn,	-	-	"	1	29	
Samuel Duggins,	-	-	"	1	29	
Gregory Dennitt,		-	"	1	29	
Thomas Dunn,			"	1	29	
Linsey Davis,		-	"	1	29	
John Dix,	-	-	"	–	25	Transferred from Capt. Fisher's company.
Jackey Dyke,			"	–	25	" " "
Vincent Dyke,	-	-	"	–	25	" " "
William Gordon,	-	-	"	1	29	
Philip Griggs,	-	-	"	1	29	
John Howerton,	-	-	"	1	29	
Charles Hill,	-	-	"	1	29	
James McFarlane,	-	-	"	1	29	
James Owen,	-	-	"	1	29	
Warner Shackelford,	-	-	"	1	29	
Ephraim Shepard,	-	-	"	1	13	
Charles T. Southall,	-	-	"	–	9	
John Sheward,	-	-	"	–	25	" " "
Benjamin Tucker,	-	-	"	1	29	
James Wright,	-	-	"	1	13	
Philip Williamson,	-	-	"	1	29	
John H. Webb,	-	-	"	1	29	
Godfrey Young,	-	-	"	1	29	

Captain David Watson's Company.

NAMES.	RANK.	TIME OF SERVICE.		REMARKS.
		Months.	Days.	
William O. Dabney, -	Private,	1	28	

(For rest of this company, see publication of Pay Rolls.)

Captain James Watson's Company.

NAMES.			RANK.	TIME OF SERVICE.		REMARKS.
				Months.	Days.	
John H. Arnold,	-	-	Private,	–	24	
Nathan Bell,	-	-	"	–	17	
Charles Maddox,	-	-	"	1	23	
Joseph Wilson,	-	-	"	1	23	

(For rest of this company, see publication of Pay Rolls.)

Lieutenant William Waller's Company—Sixty-eighth Regiment.

NAMES.			RANK.	TIME OF SERVICE.		REMARKS.
				Months.	Days.	
William Gibbs,	-	-	Sergeant,	–	28	
Matthew Wilson,	-	-	Drummer,	–	17	
Richard Ball,	-	-	Private,	–	26	
Henry F. Charles,	-	-	"	–	28	
John Johnston,	-	-	"	–	26	
Samuel Moore,	-	-	"	–	28	

(For rest of this company, see publication of Pay Rolls.)

Captain William Way's Company—Thirty-seventh Regiment.

NAMES.	RANK.	TIME OF SERVICE.		REMARKS.
		Months.	Days.	
William Power,	Sergeant,	–	10	
Rand'l R. Kirke,	"	–	6	
William Headley,	"	3	27	
John Lewis,	Fifer,	–	9	
James Stephens,	Drummer,	–	16	
Thomas Ashburn,	Private,	–	12	
Leonard Barker,	"	–	6	
Thomas Bryant,	"	–	9	
George Brown,	"	–	12	
Frederick Booth,	"	–	12	
William Bailiss,	"	–	22	
Charles Elmore,	"	–	4	
Robert Edwards,	"	–	10	
Jeduthan Hogans,	"	–	4	
William Headley,	"	–	22	
Hancock Haynie,	"	–	5	
John Jones, jr.	"	–	16	
William Kezer,	"	–	4	
Charles Lewis,	"	–	12	
Benj. Lansdell,	"	1	16	
John Meally,	"	–	16	
James Marsh,	"	–	14	
Peter Nelms,	"	–	4	
Thomas Pullen,	"	–	16	
John Power,	"	–	12	
Joseph Rice,	"	–	8	
Richard Rice,	"	–	12	
James Rice,	"	–	16	
William Rice, jr.	"	–	4	
John Rice, jr.	"	–	10	
John Robertson,	"	–	11	
Elias Stephens,	"	–	16	
John Sebrey,	"	–	28	
William Southall,	"	–	12	
Thomas N. Smith,	"	–	5	
Griffin E. Thomas,	"	–	20	
Opie Thomas,	"	–	5	
Edwin Way,	"	–	24	

(For rest of this company, see publication of Pay Rolls.)

MUSTER ROLL

Of Captain William Watts' Company, of the Ninety-ninth Regiment, Virginia Militia, commanded by Lieutenant Colonel Charles Bagwell, in the Service of the United States, from 24th to 28th May, 1813, and from 8th to 10th June, 1814.

NAMES.	RANK.	TIME OF SERVICE.		REMARKS.
		Months.	Days.	
William Watts, - -	Captain,	–	8	
Wm. R. Drummond, - -	Lieutenant,	–	8	
Colman Bayne, - -	Ensign,	–	5	
John Gladden, - -	Sergeant,	–	8	
William Benson, - -	"	–	8	
Littleton Trader, - -	"	–	7	
Ezekiel H. James, (or Jones,)	"	–	8	
Caleb Duncan, - -	Corporal,	–	8	
John Marshall, - -	"	–	8	
Ralph White, - -	"	–	3	
Frederick Cowner, - -	"	–	5	
John Walters, - -	"	–	3	
William R. Taylor, - -	"	–	5	
James Bunting, - -	Fifer,	–	8	
Jno. Massey, - -	Drummer,	–	8	
John Allen, - -	Private,	–	6	
James Arbuckle, - -	"	–	7	
Daniel Benson, - -	"	–	8	
Ephraim Bunting, - -	"	–	6	
Nehemiah Broton, - -	"	–	8	
James Brittingham, - -	"	–	6	
Jno. F. Bayne, - -	"	–	6	
Wm. H. Brotton, - -	"	–	8	
David Banks, - -	"	–	8	
Southey Brodwater, - -	"	–	8	
Wm. Brodwater, - -	"	–	8	
Ismy Bunting, - -	"	–	8	
Isaac Bunting, - -	"	–	2	
James Bunting, - -	"	–	5	
Christopher Brodwater, - -	"	–	5	
Frederick Connell, - -	"	–	3	
William Collins, - -	"	–	7	
James Collins, - -	"	–	2	
William Delastatius, - -	"	–	8	
George Fedderman, - -	"	–	8	
John Fedderman, - -	"	–	3	
Jas. Fedderman, - -	"	–	5	
John Gladden, - -	"	–	8	
Henry Gladden, - -	"	–	7	
Jinkins Gladden, - -	"	–	5	
Jesse Gladden, - -	"	–	5	
William Hill, - -	"	–	3	
Hampton Henderson, - -	"	–	3	
George Jones, - -	"	–	8	
William Kendal, - -	"	–	2	
John S. Melvin, - -	"	–	7	
Samuel Merrell, - -	"	–	7	
George Mathews, - -	"	–	8	
Solomon Marshall, - -	"	–	7	

NAMES.	RANK.	TIME OF SERVICE.		REMARKS.
		Months.	Days.	
Stephen McCready, - -	Private,	–	5	
Robert Pitts, - -	"	–	8	
Jno. Parks, - -	"	–	5	
William Riley, - -	"	–	8	
William Ross, - -	"	–	8	
Hugh M. Stephenson, - -	"	–	8	
Geo. Satton, - -	"	–	5	
Ayres Taylor, - -	"	–	7	
James Tull, - -	"	–	8	
Nathl. Tayloe, - -	"	–	8	
Wm. S. Tunnell, - -	"	–	7	
Revel Tayloe, - -	"	–	8	
Leven Townsend, - -	"	–	5	
Jas. Taylor, - -	"	–	5	
Wm. Walters, - -	"	–	8	
John Walters, - -	"	–	5	
Jos. Walters, - -	"	–	5	
William Wilkerson, - -	"	–	8	

MUSTER ROLL

Of Captain Richard Weadon's Company, called into the Service of the United States, at Dumfries, under an order of the 24th of August, by Colonel Enoch Rennoe, Lieutenant Colonel commandant of the Thirty-sixth Regiment, from 24th to 30th August, 1814.

NAMES.			RANK.	TIME OF SERVICE.		REMARKS.
				Months.	Days.	
Richard Weadon,	-	-	Captain,	–	7	
Barnaby Cannon,	-	-	Ensign,	–	7	
Hugh Adie,	-	-	Sergeant,	–	7	
Ignatius Mitchel,	-	-	"	–	7	
Larkin Carr,	-	-	Corporal,	–	7	
Moses Duffee,	-	-	"	–	7	
William Bell,	-	-	Private,	–	7	
James Carter,	-	-	"	–	7	
William Cannon,	-	-	"	–	7	
William Calvert,	-	-	"	–	7	
Jesse Carpenter,	-	-	"	–	7	
John Dickerson,	-	-	"	–	7	
Edward Evans,	-	-	"	–	7	
Matthew Guy,	-	-	"	–	7	
Townley Guy,	-	-	"	–	7	
Corben Hales,	-	-	"	–	7	
Richard Lee,	-	-	"	–	7	
James McDaniel,	-	-	"	–	7	
Edward Mitchell,	-	-	"	–	7	
Samuel Mitchell,	-	-	"	–	7	
William Moore,	-	-	"	–	7	
Ignatius Milstead,	-	-	"	–	7	
George Mattox,	-	-	"	–	7	
William Smith,	-	-	"	–	7	

MUSTER ROLL

Of Captain John S. Webb's Company, from the Fifty-second Regiment, Virginia Militia, in the County of New Kent, called into actual Service under the general orders of the 2d day of September, 1814, from the 4th to the 18th of September, in the same year.

NAMES.	RANK.	TIME OF SERVICE.		REMARKS.
		Months.	Days.	
John S. Webb, - -	Captain,	–	15	
Alexander Walker, - -	Lieutenant,	–	15	
Tyler Hardaman, - -	Ensign,	–	15	
Waldo Clopton, - -	Sergeant,	–	15	
Samuel E. Dobson, -	"	–	15	
Thomas Clopton, - -	"	–	15	
Carrel F. Chappell, -	"	–	15	
James Parrish, - -	Corporal,	–	15	
Samuel Gaulding, - -	"	–	15	
Martin Wade, -	"	–	15	
Reuben Burch, - -	"	–	15	
Nathaniel K. Bacon, -	Private,	–	15	
William Boyd, - -	"	–	15	
John Breden, - -	"	–	15	
Beverley Crump, - -	"	–	15	
Christopher Egmon, -	"	–	15	
Francis Foster, -	"	–	15	
William K. Ferris, -	"	–	15	
Nathaniel Fox, - -	"	–	15	
Samuel Finch, -	"	–	15	
John Harper, - -	"	–	15	
Bowler Hytton, - -	"	–	15	
William Higgins, -	"	–	15	
James Hughs, -	"	–	15	
Burrel Jones, -	"	–	15	
David Jones, - -	"	–	15	
Thomas Kent, - -	"	–	15	
Blackwell Kent, - -	"	–	15	
John A. More, - -	"	–	15	
William Martin, - -	"	–	15	
Parkes Martin, - -	"	–	15	
John Richardson, - -	"	–	15	
Thomas Roberts, - -	"	–	15	
William Smith, - -	"	–	15	
Richard Tyree, - -	"	–	15	
Charles Turner, -	"	–	15	
William M. Williams, -	"	–	15	
John Williams, - -	"	–	15	
Richard A. Warren, -	"	–	15	
Samuel Webb, - -	"	–	15	
John Wright, sen. - -	"	–	15	
John Wright, jr. - -	"	–	15	

Captain Frederick Weedon's Company—Sixty-first Regiment.

NAMES.			RANK.	TIME OF SERVICE.		REMARKS.
				Months.	Days.	
James Booker,	-	-	Private,	—	2	
James Bohannan,	-	-	"	—	3	
William Blake,	-	-	"	—	2	
William Dixon,	-	-	"	—	2	
Barker Digges,	-	-	"	—	3	
John Digges,	-	-	"	—	2	
John D. Fitchett,	-	-	"	—	13	
Bartlett Gayle,	-	-	"	—	3	
Musions Spark,	-	-	"	—	5	
Moses Terrier,	-	-	"	—	10	
William Wise,	-	-	"	—	8	
James Williams,	-	-	"	—	5	

(For rest of this company, see publication of Pay Rolls.)

Captain David Weisiger's Company—Twenty-third Regiment.

NAMES.	RANK.	TIME OF SERVICE.		REMARKS.
		Months.	Days.	
David Weisiger, - -	Captain,	–	11	
James Clarke, - -	Lieutenant.	–	1	
Isaac Davis. - -	Ensign.	–	4	
Young Pankey, - -	Sergeant,	–	4	
Robert Miller, - -	"	–	4	
Thomas Winfree, - -	"	–	4	
Thomas Smith, - -	"	–	4	
Fred'k Patram. - -	"	–	7	
Jno. Fuqua, - -	"	–	7	
Jno. Emses. - -	"	–	7	
Thos. H. Bass. - -	"	–	7	
Thomas Smith, - -	Corporal,	–	4	
Wm. Bradshaw, - -	"	–	4	
Ro. Dinsworth, - -	"	–	1	
James Caskie. - -	"	–	4	
Wm. Hutchett. - -	"	–	7	
Matt. Branch. - -	"	–	7	
Edward A. May, - -	"	–	7	
Zach. Rowlett, - -	"	–	7	
Jacob Alpin, - -	Private,	–	7	
T. Brackett, - -	"	–	1	
Wm. Brackett, - -	"	–	1	
Isaac Burnard, - -	"	–	1	
John Banoff, - -	"	–	4	
Rob't F. Branch, - -	"	–	7	
Chas. Burton. - -	"	–	7	
Thomas Butts. - -	"	–	4	
James S. Bass, - -	"	–	29	
John Branch. - -	"	–	7	
E. Blankinship, - -	"	–	7	
Jno. L. Berry. - -	"	–	7	
John Bragg, - -	"	–	7	
Abel Bowman, - -	"	–	7	
Matthew H. Branch, - -	"	–	7	
William B. Clarke, - -	"	–	4	
Robert Clarke, - -	"	–	4	
Thomas Cheatham, - -	"	–	7	
John Childer. - -	"	–	1	
Miles Elam. - -	"	–	1	
Jno. Evans. - -	"	–	7	
William Elam, - -	"	–	7	
Andrew Fore. - -	"	–	4	
Mark F. Flournoy, - -	"	–	7	
Seth W. Flournoy, - -	"	–	7	
John Gilchrist, - -	"	–	4	
Nich. Garden, - -	"	–	1	
P. E. Graves, - -	"	–	4	
James Gray. - -	"	–	1	
Rand. Hatchett, - -	"	–	4	
Josiah Hobson, - -	"	–	1	
Rob't Haskins, - -	"	–	7	
J. B. Hooper, - -	"	–	4	
H. Hancock, - -	"	–	7	
Jno. Jenkins, - -	"	–	4	

NAMES.	RANK.	TIME OF SERVICE.		REMARKS.
		Months.	Days.	
Edward Johnston, - -	Private,	—	4	
Stephen Johnson, - -	"	—	4	
Wm. Long, - -	"	—	11	
James Long, - -	"	—	4	
James Lynch, - -	"	—	7	
Wastus Lockett, - -	"	—	7	
Nich. Mills, - -	"	—	4	
C. McKae, - -	"	—	1	
Henry Moody, - -	"	—	1	
B. B. Morrison, - -	"	—	4	
Philip Michaels, - -	"	—	4	
Hugh M. Miller, - -	"	—	4	
Ro. D. Murchie, - -	"	—	4	
John Moore, - -	"	—	7	
James Moyley, - -	"	—	7	
Jas. McDowell, - -	"	—	7	
Stephen Pankey, - -	"	—	4	
Wm. A. Patterson, - -	"	—	4	
Little'n Perdue, - -	"	—	7	
Peter Perkins, - -	"	—	7	
Robin Packett, - -	"	—	4	
Dennis Pastin, - -	"	—	7	
Shad. Perdue, - -	"	—	7	
Bernard Perdue, - -	"	—	7	
Cole Powell, - -	"	—	7	
Bev. Randolph. - -	"	—	4	
Edward Redford, - -	"	—	4	
William Rowlett, - -	"	—	7	
Clab. Royall, - -	"	—	7	
Bernard Roberts, - -	"	—	7	
John Rowlett, - -	"	—	7	
Richard Sizer, - -	"	—	28	
Tarlton Saunders, - -	"	—	1	
John Scott, - -	"	—	4	
Samuel Sizer, - -	"	—	4	
Joseph Spencer, - -	"	—	1	
Oba'h Short, - -	"	—	7	
Richard Tomaston, - -	"	—	7	
John Turpin, - -	"	—	7	
Thomas Turpin, - -	"	—	7	
Daniel Traylor, - -	"	—	7	
Samuel Traylor, - -	"	—	4	
T. Vaden. - -	"	—	4	
William Vaden, - -	"	—	7	
James Vast, - -	"	—	7	
Samuel Wilson, - -	"	—	7	
John Willet, - -	"	—	4	
Mans'n Watkins, - -	"	—	4	
Richard Weisiger, - -	"	—	4	
John Weisiger, - -	"	—	4	
Daniel Weisiger, - -	"	—	4	
H. Weisiger, - -	"	—	4	
Robert Warren, - -	"	—	4	
John W. Winfree, - -	"	—	1	

(For rest of this company, see publication of Pay Rolls.)

MUSTER ROLL

Of Captain Littleberry West's Company, from the Twenty-third Regiment, Virginia Militia, in the County of Chesterfield, called into actual Service under general orders, from 18th to 29th March, from 27th to 28th June, and from 1st to 2d of July, in the year 1813.

NAMES.		RANK.	TIME OF SERVICE.		REMARKS.
			Months.	Days.	
Littleberry West,	- -	Captain,	–	18	
Burwell Parkinson,	- -	Lieutenant,	–	19	
Henry P. Eanes,	- -	Ensign,	–	19	
Archer Taylor,	- -	Sergeant,	–	19	
John Rowlett,	- -	"	–	19	
Vaden Moore,	- -	"	–	19	
William Wilson,	- -	"	–	19	
Benj. Andrews,	- -	Private,	–	19	
Ledwick Andrews,	- -	"	–	19	
Daniel Andrews,	- -	"	–	19	
Erasmus Andrews,	- -	"	–	12	
Hugh Bragg,	- -	"	–	19	
Laban Blankenship,	- -	"	–	19	
John Bragg,	- -	"	–	12	
John L. Bany,	- -	"	–	12	
Andrew Costley,	- -	"	–	19	
Isaac Caulfield,	- -	"	–	19	
Jordan R. Davis,	- -	"	–	19	
Joseph Dunavant,	- -	"	–	19	
Martin Davis,	- -	"	–	15	
John Deaton,	- -	"	–	19	
Buckner Eanes,	- -	"	–	19	
Daniel Eanes,	- -	"	–	19	
Isham Eanes,	- -	"	–	19	
Thomas Eanes,	- -	"	–	12	
Arthur Fraylor,	- -	"	–	3	
Rob't Gill,	- -	"	–	7	
Will. Goodwin,	- -	"	–	12	
Will. Hatchett,	- -	"	–	12	
Alexander Moore,	- -	"	–	19	
Edward Moore,	- -	"	–	19	
Francis Mann,	- -	"	–	19	
Thomas R. Mann,	- -	"	–	19	
Charles Mann,	- -	"	–	19	
Jos. G. Mann,	- -	"	–	19	
Chastain Mann,	- -	"	–	19	
Drury Moore,	- -	"	–	19	
Cain Mann,	- -	"	–	19	
Spencer Moore,	- -	"	–	19	
Peter Moody,	- -	"	–	14	
Will. Mann, jr.	- -	"	–	19	
John Perkinson,	- -	"	–	19	
James Perdue,	- -	"	–	19	
Daniel Patram,	- -	"	–	19	
Nelson Phillips,	- -	"	–	19	
George Patram,	- -	"	–	7	

NAMES.	RANK.	TIME OF SERVICE.		REMARKS.
		Months.	Days.	
John Phillips, - -	Private,	—	16	
Peter Perdue, - -	"	—	12	
Nelson Rurtin, (or Burton,) -	"	—	12	
Daniel Rowlett, - -	"	—	19	
Joseph Ross, - -	"	—	12	
Zachariah Rowlett, - -	"	—	12	
Josiah Stringer, - -	"	—	19	
Thomas Stone, - -	"	—	19	
Michael Traylor, - -	"	—	19	
Herbert Traylor, - -	"	—	19	
John Traylor, - -	"	—	19	
Arthur Traylor, - -	"	—	19	
Matthew Traylor, - -	"	—	16	
Terray Talley, - -	"	—	16	
Daniel Traylor, - -	"	—	12	
Marshall Vaden, - -	"	—	15	
Stamander Vaden, - -	"	—	12	
Willi. Vaden, - -	"	—	12	
George Wilson, - -	"	—	19	
Ledwick Wilson, - -	"	—	19	
Willi. Wilson, - -	"	—	19	
Littleton Wilson, - -	"	—	19	
Creed Wilson, - -	"	—	19	
Henry Wilson, - -	"	—	19	
Thomas Wilson, - -	"	—	16	
John Wilkinson, - -	"	—	12	

MUSTER ROLL

Of Captain James White's Company, of the Ninety-ninth Regiment, Virginia Militia, called into actual Service of the United States, under general orders of Lieutenant Colonel Charles Bagwell, from 24th to 28th May, 1813, and from 8th to 12th September, 1814.

NAMES.	RANK.	TIME OF SERVICE.		REMARKS.
		Months.	Days.	
James White, - -	Captain,	—	10	
John Young, - -	Lieutenant,	—	10	
John Davis, - - -	Ensign,	—	10	
William White, jr. - -	Sergeant,	—	5	
William White, sen. -	"	—	5	
Isaiah E. Wise, - -	"	—	5	
Henry Bagwell, - -	"	—	5	
Dennis Bloxom, - -	"	—	5	
Edward Gunter, - -	"	—	5	
John Savage, - -	"	—	5	
Kendall Hickman, - -	"	—	5	
Elisha Ayres, - -	Corporal,	—	10	
Stephen Baker, - -	"	—	10	
William Baker, jr. - -	"	—	10	
William Baker, (of H.) -	"	—	5	
Coventon Mason, -	"	—	5	
Walter Mason, - -	Drummer,	—	5	
Alexander Ling, - -	"	—	5	
Richard Young, - -	Fifer,	—	5	
Delight James, - -	"	—	5	
Geo. Berry, - -	Private,	—	5	
Edmund Bloxom, - -	"	—	5	
Aaron Baker, - -	"	—	5	
Wm. Baker, (of Wm.) -	"	—	5	
Ezekiel Baker, - -	"	—	10	
Kendall Coloney, - -	"	—	10	
Levi Core, - -	"	—	10	
Major Fisher, - -	"	—	10	
James Gibbon, - -	"	—	5	
John Gardner, - -	"	—	5	
Edward Gunter, - -	"	—	5	
George Howard, - -	"	—	5	
Kendall Hickman, -	"	—	5	
Nathaniel Hickman, -	"	—	5	
Teackle Justice, - -	"	—	10	
John Jackson, - -	"	—	5	
James Justice, - -	"	—	5	
Geo. Lilliston, (or Littleton,) -	"	—	10	
John Laws, jr. - -	"	—	10	
Meshack Mears, - -	"	—	10	
Bennett Mason, - -	"	—	10	
Ayres Mason, - -	"	—	10	
Teackle Mason, - -	"	—	10	
William Nelson, - -	"	—	10	
George Nelson, - -	"	—	5	
William Nack, - -	"	—	5	
William Onions, sen. -	"	—	10	

NAMES.	RANK.	TIME OF SERVICE.		REMARKS.
		Months.	Days.	
William Onions, jr. - -	Private,	—	5	
John Onions, - -	"	—	5	
George Prescote, - -	"	—	5	
Richard Prescote, - -	"	—	5	
Zadock Poulson, - -	"	—	5	
Joseph Riggs, - -	"	—	5	
Joseph Savage, - -	"	—	5	
John Sparrow, - -	"	—	5	
Zorobabel Savage, - -	"	—	10	
Thomas Shreaves, - -	"	—	10	
Cuppen Silverthorn, -	"	—	10	
George White, - -	"	—	5	
William White, - -	"	—	5	
John White, - -	"	—	5	
Edward Wright, - -	"	—	10	
Henry Wright, - -	"	—	10	
Thomas Wright, - -	"	—	10	
William Wright, - -	"	—	10	
Walter Wright, - -	"	—	10	
John Wimborough, - -	"	—	10	
William Young, - -	"	—	10	

PAY ROLL

Of Captain Francis Wicker's Company of Infantry, from the Thirty-third Regiment, in the County of Henrico, called into Service from 19th to 29th March, 1813.

NAMES.	RANK.	TIME OF SERVICE.		REMARKS.
		Months.	Days.	
Francis Wicker, - -	Captain,	–	5	
John S. West, - -	Lieutenant,	–	4	
John Jourdan, - .	Sergeant,	–	5	
Nathaniel Whitelaw, -	"	–	5	
William Robinson, - -	"	–	5	
Francis Smith, - -	"	–	5	
Jacob Bowes, - -	Private,	–	5	
John Bridgewater, - -	"	–	5	
George Blakey, - -	"	–	5	
John Banks, - -	"	–	5	
Jas. M. Franklin, - -	"	–	5	
Joseph Francis, - -	"	–	5	
James Frost, - -	"	–	5	
Zachariah Franklin, - -	"	–	5	
John Gunn, - -	"	–	5	
Dandridge Garratt, - -	"	–	5	
John Hardin, - -	"	–	5	
Geo. N. Hopkins, - -	"	–	5	
Reuben Hamlett, - -	"	–	2	
William Harwood, - -	"	–	5	
Dobson Hull, - -	"	–	2	
Herbert Haynes, - -	"	–	5	
Huddleston Jourdan, - -	"	–	5	
Henry Johnson, - -	"	–	5	
Benjamin Jones, - -	"	–	5	
John Lyle, - -	"	–	5	
John Mims, - -	"	–	5	
Thomas Miller, - -	"	–	5	
William Oakley, - -	"	–	5	
Edward Roush, - -	"	–	4	
James Roush, - -	"	–	4	
Littleberry Roundtree, - -	"	–	5	
Simeon Rowland, - -	"	–	5	
James Roundtree, - -	"	–	4	
Adam Shrum, - -	"	–	5	
William Shrum, - -	"	–	5	
William Silam, - -	"	–	3	
Wm. Tenson, - -	"	–	5	
Charles Turner, - -	"	–	4	
And. Tenson, - -	"	–	5	
James Valentine, - -	"	–	5	
Josiah Via, - -	"	–	5	
Arcelm Walker, - -	"	–	5	
William Warriner, - -	"	–	5	
Brylon Waide, - -	"	–	5	
Bartlett Woodward, - -	"	–	5	

NAMES.			RANK.	TIME OF SERVICE.		REMARKS.
				Months.	Days.	
Samuel Whitelaw,	-	-	Private,	—	5	
John Whitlock,	-	-	"	—	5	
J. Whites,	-	-	"	—	4	
James Yarborough,	-	-	"	—	5	

Captain Nathaniel Widgeon's Company—Twenty-seventh Regiment.

NAMES.	RANK.	TIME OF SERVICE.		REMARKS.
		Months.	Days.	
Nathaniel Widgeon, - -	Captain,	–	10	
Keley Stott, - -	Lieutenant,	–	10	
Jno. W. Scott, ` - -	Ensign,	–	10	
Jno. Fitchett, - -	Sergeant,	–	10	
Thomas W. Scott, - -	"	–	10	
Thomas A. Wheeler, - -	"	–	10	
Jno. Wilkins, sen'r, - -	"	–	10	
Jno. Anderson, - -	Private,	–	10	
Richard Belle, - -	"	–	10	
Isaac Cuple, - -	"	–	10	
Jno. Carpenter, - -	"	–	10	
Francis Costin, • -	"	–	10	
Eli Dowty, - -	"	–	10	
Matthew Floyd, - -	"	–	10	
Matthew Fatherly, - -	"	–	10	
Shepherd Floyd, - -	"	–	15	
Wm. Godwin, - -	"	–	10	
Kendall Grotten, - -	"	–	10	
Leter Griffith, - -	"	–	10	
Richard Jones, - -	"	–	25	
W. O. Llear, - -	"	–	10	
Richard Nottingham, - -	"	–	10	
Joseph Nottingham, - -	"	–	15	
Thos. L. Nolin, - -	"	–	10	
Levi Oldham, - -	"	–	15	
Thos. Roberts, - -	"	–	10	
George Scott, - -	"	–	10	
John Smaw, - -	"	–	10	
Henry Smaw, - -	"	–	25	
Benjamin Scott, - -	"	–	10	
Jno. Tyson, - -	"	–	25	
William Taylor, - -	"	–	10	
Jno. Upshur, - -	"	–	10	
Letc'h Wilson, - -	"	–	10	
Thos. Wilkins, - -	"	–	10	
Nathaniel Wilkins, - -	"	–	10	
James Wilson, jr. - -	"	–	10	
Severn Wilkins, - -	"	–	10	
Jno. Wilson, jr. - -	"	–	10	
Sam'l Williams, - -	"	–	15	
John Yeatman, - -	"	–	15	

(For rest of this company, see publication of Pay Rolls.)

Captain Claiborne Wigglesworth's Company—Sixteenth Regiment.

NAMES.	RANK.	TIME OF SERVICE.		REMARKS.
		Months.	Days.	
Henry Washington, - -	Sergeant,	–	26	
Ezekiel Hord, - -	"	–	26	
Henry W. Rogers, - -	"	–	26	
Jesse Newton, - -	"	–	26	
John Stewart, jun'r, - -	Corporal,	–	26	
Edward Garner, - -	Drummer,	–	26	
Samuel Ames, - -	Private,	–	26	
James Alsop, - -	"	–	26	
Mark Anthon, - -	"	–	26	
Robert Bowling, - -	"	–	26	
Gray Barber, - -	"	–	26	Substitute for Yearman Smith.
Thornton Byram, - -	"	–	26	
George Bowling, - -	"	–	9	
John Byram, - -	"	–	9	
John Curtis, - -	"	–	26	
Chichester Curtis, - -	"	–	26	
Walker Chandler, - -	"	–	9	
Patrick Carnall, - -	"	–	9	
George Farish, - -	"	–	9	
William Fisher, - -	"	–	9	
Jeremiah Frank, - -	"	–	26	
Thomas Glass, - -	"	–	26	
John Garner, - -	"	–	26	
William Grady, - -	"	–	26	
Thomas S. Hicks, - -	"	–	26	Substitute for George Robinson.
William Jackson, - -	"	–	3	
Arch'd Johnson, - -	"	–	9	
Thomas Jennings, - -	"	–	26	Substitute for Wm. S. White.
Robert Lancaster, - -	"	–	12	
Willis Mills, - -	"	–	12	
Wyatte Mills, - -	"	–	9	
James Mannan, - -	"	–	9	
William Mannan, - -	"	–	26	
Alexander Magee, - -	"	–	26	
John Moore, - -	"	–	26	
James Moore, - -	"	–	26	
Henry Magee, - -	"	–	26	
Henry Oliver, - -	"	–	3	
Winslow Parker, - -	"	–	26	
George Parker, - -	"	–	29	
Thomas Peyton, - -	"	–	26	
Thomas Penn, - -	"	–	26	
William Powell, - -	"	–	26	
Thomas Powell, - -	"	–	9	
George Robinson, - -	"	–	9	
Thomas Short, - -	"	–	14	
John Sorrell, - -	"	–	26	
John Strutton, - -	"	–	26	
Benjamin Stevens, - -	"	–	7	
James Snipe, - -	"	–	26	

NAMES.			RANK.	TIME OF SERVICE.		REMARKS.
				Months.	Days.	
William Shelton,	-	-	Private,	–	26	
Richard Sidnor,	-	-	"	–	26	Sub. for J. Chewning.
John Wharton,	-	-	"	–	26	
Robert Waller,	-	-	"	–	26	
James Wren,	-	-	"	–	26	

(For rest of this company, see publication of Pay Rolls.)

Captain Henry Williams' Company—Forty-fifth Regiment.

NAMES.	RANK.	TIME OF SERVICE.		REMARKS.
		Months.	Days.	
Abner R. Alcock, - -	Ensign,	—	28	
Burdett Clifton, - -	"	—	8	
James Edward, - -	Sergeant,	—	28	
Charles Miflin, - -	"	—	8	
Edm'd Hoomes, - -	"	—	8	
William Clarke, - -	"	—	8	
Wm L. Cheeks, - -	Corporal,	—	28	
Richard Brightwell, - -	"	—	28	
Jno. H. Porter, - -	"	—	28	
Ben. Murphy, - -	"	—	28	
Lawson Wheatley, - -	"	—	8	
Thomas Curtis, - -	"	—	8	
James Carpenter, - -	"	—	8	
Jeremiah Atcheson, - -	Private,	—	8	
John Ashby, - -	"	—	28	
Peter Beach, - -	"	—	8	
Henry Bethel, - -	"	—	8	
James Butler, - -	"	—	8	
William Brent, - -	"	—	8	
James Bowling, - -	"	—	28	
Robert Benson, - -	"	—	28	
John Combs, - -	"	—	28	
Ben. Combs, - -	"	—	28	
Walter Cross, - -	"	—	8	
Thornton Cross, - -	"	—	8	
Fielding Curtis, - -	"	—	8	
William Coram, - -	"	—	8	
Jesse Carpenter, - -	"	—	8	
George Dent, - -	"	—	8	
Ben. Dawson, - -	"	—	28	
Clement Dawson, - -	"	—	28	
William Fristoe, - -	"	—	28	
Elias Fant, - -	"	—	8	
Bailey Flitter, - -	"	—	8	
Presley Gills, - -	"	—	28	
Fielding George, - -	"	—	28	
Ben. Guy, - -	"	—	28	
Josesph Guy, - -	"	—	8	
James Guy, - -	"	—	8	
Jesse Gray, - -	"	—	8	
Ben. Gray, - -	"	—	8	
Charles Humphrey, -	"	—	8	
Fielding Humphrey, -	"	—	8	
Jesse Holloway, - -	"	—	8	
Early Humphrey, - -	"	—	8	
James S. Hoomes, - -	"	—	8	
Robert Holloway, - -	"	—	8	
James Hiflin, - -	"	—	8	
John Harding, - -	"	—	28	
Jeremiah Hanes, - -	"	—	28	
Francis S. Hanes, - -	"	—	28	
Francis Jackson, - -	"	—	28	
Jeremiah Jordan, - -	"	—	28	
Henry Jones, - -	"	—	28	

NAMES.	RANK.	TIME OF SERVICE.		REMARKS.
		Months.	Days.	
Noah Jones, - -	Private,	—	8	
Charles Jones, - -	"	—	8	
Thomas Jones, - -	"	—	8	
James Latham, - -	"	—	8	
Wm. B. Mountjoy, - -	"	—	8	
Nelson Mason, - -	"	—	8	
Charles Martin, - -	"	—	8	
Horall Mitchell, - -	"	—	8	
James Mason, - -	"	—	8	
Matthew Norman, - -	"	—	28	
Jno. Payne, - -	"	—	28	
Reuben Payne, - -	"	—	28	
John Patton, - -	"	—	28	
Wm. Payne, - -	"	—	28	
Jno. Potts, - -	"	—	8	
Led. G. Payne, - -	"	—	8	
Charles Ralls, - -	"	—	8	
Alex'r G. Ratcliffe, - -	"	—	8	
Noah Reed, - -	"	—	8	
Valentine Roles, - -	"	—	28	
Jas. Sheeket, - -	"	—	28	
John Smith, - -	"	—	28	
Presley Sims, - -	"	—	28	
John Stark, - -	"	—	8	
Jas. M. Stewart, - -	"	—	8	
Joseph Starke, - -	"	—	8	
Jno. N. Tolson, - -	"	—	28	
Sanford Walters, - -	"	—	8	
Wm. Washington, - -	"	—	8	
Daniel Walmsley, - -	"	—	8	
Thomas Walters, - -	"	—	8	
Ben. Walmsley, - -	"	—	8	

(For rest of this company, see publication of Pay Rolls.)

MUSTER ROLL

Of Captain Dabney Williamson's Company, from the Thirty-third Regiment, Virginia Militia, in the County of Henrico, called into actual Service under the general orders of the 13th March, 1813, from 19th to 29th March, in the year 1813.

NAMES.	RANK.	TIME OF SERVICE.		REMARKS.
		Months.	Days.	
Dabney Williamson, - -	Captain,	–	11	
Jesse Smith, - -	Lieutenant,	–	11	
Edwin Burton, - -	Ensign,	–	11	
George Matthews, - -	Sergeant,	–	11	
George Eubank, - -	"	–	11	
George A. Kelley, - -	"	–	11	
Absalom Blackburn, - -	"	–	11	
Thomas Alley, - -	Private,	–	11	
John Alvis, - -	"	–	11	
John Brown, - -	"	–	11	
Lewis H. Brown, - -	"	–	11	
Joseph Brown, - -	"	–	11	
Robert Bigart, - -	"	–	11	
Thos. Burnett, - -	"	–	11	
Robt. Browning, - -	"	–	11	
Francis Cornett, - -	"	–	11	
James Currie, - -	"	–	11	
Henry Duke, - -	"	–	11	
Thos. Eubank, - -	"	–	11	
Daniel Edwards, - -	"	–	11	
Enoch Ford, - -	"	–	11	
Tarlton Ford, - -	"	–	11	
Reuben Ford, - -	"	–	11	
John Ford, - -	"	–	11	
Gilley Franklin, - -	"	–	11	
Abner Griffin, - -	"	–	11	
Neley Glenn, - -	"	–	11	
Joseph Green, - -	"	–	11	
James Grimstead, - -	"	–	11	
James Glenn, - -	"	–	11	
Fleming Gentry, - -	"	–	11	
Thomas W. Hill, - -	"	–	11	
Richard Harris, - -	"	–	11	
Ambrose Hutchison, - -	"	–	11	
Aaron Howard, - -	"	–	11	
Thomas Jennings, - -	"	–	11	
Woody Jennings, - -	"	–	11	
William Jentry, - -	"	–	11	
Thomas Johnson, - -	"	–	11	
William Jennings, - -	"	–	11	
Claiborn Jennings, - -	"	–	11	
Isham Jennings, - -	"	–	11	
Wilson Kelley, - -	"	–	11	
John Lawrence, - -	"	–	11	
William Lankaster, - -	"	–	11	
John McGraugh, - -	"	–	11	
James Nicholas, - -	"	–	11	

NAMES.	RANK.	TIME OF SERVICE.		REMARKS.
		Months.	Days.	
Daniel Night, - -	Private,	—	11	
David Nicholas, - -	"	—	11	
Robt. Priddy, - -	"	—	11	
Spencer Padget, - -	"	—	11	
Henry Phillips, - -	"	—	11	
Robt. Potter, - -	"	—	11	
Solomon Pursley, - -	"	—	11	
Valentine Quorrye, - -	"	—	11	
Charles Rice, - -	"	—	11	
Randolph Rice, - -	"	—	11	
William Rigdon, - -	"	—	11	
William Roach, - -	"	—	11	
Robt. Steward, - -	"	—	11	
Price Shoemaker, - -	"	—	11	
Wm. Snead, - -	"	—	11	
Jacob Smith, - -	"	—	11	
John Thorps, - -	"	—	11	
Christopher Taliaferro, -	"	—	11	
John Williamson, - -	"	—	11	
Robt. Whealey, - -	"	—	11	
James Whealey, - -	"	—	11	
Burnard Whealey, - -	"	—	11	
William Whealey, - -	"	—	11	
Saml. Whitis, - -	"	—	11	
Peter Wilkinson, - -	"	—	11	
Henry Winfree, - -	"	—	11	
John Whitis, - -	"	—	11	

Captain Henry W. Wills' Company.

NAMES.	RANK.	TIME OF SERVICE.		REMARKS.
		Months.	Days.	
Pleasant Parnell, - -	Private,	–	21	

(For rest of this company, see publication of Pay Rolls.)

Captain Allen Wilson's Company—Seventeenth Regiment.

NAMES.	RANK.	TIME OF SERVICE.		REMARKS.
		Months.	Days.	
John T. Anderson, - -	Private,	–	9	
Francis Armistead, - -	"			
Reuben Austin, - -	"	–	29	
William Armistead, - -	"	–	15	
George Bigby, - -	"	–	15	
William Bigby, - -	"	–	15	
Samuel Browning, - -	"	–	15	
William Clarke, - -	"	–	15	
George Godwin, - -	"			
Christo. Hudson, - -	"	–	15	
Samuel Hudson, - -	"	2	20	
Francis F. James, - -	"	–	15	
Carter Johnson, - -	"	–	15	
Chesley Key, - -	"	–	15	
William L. Montague, -	"	–	15	
Robert Moore, -	"			
Fleming Palmer, - -	"	–	15	
Hugh Watson, - -	"	–	15	
Maurice L. Wood, - -	"	–	15	
William H. Watkins, - -	"	–	15	

(For rest of this company, see publication of Pay Rolls.)

Captain John Wilson's Company—Twenty-sixth Regiment.

NAMES.	RANK.	TIME OF SERVICE.		REMARKS.
		Months.	Days.	
John Wilson, - -	Captain,	–	14	
Robert Wilson, - -	Lieutenant,	–	14	
Wm. C. Wilson, - -	Ensign,	–	14	
Thomas Matthews, - -	Sergeant,	–	14	
Isham Bagby, - -	"	–	14	
Dabney Jones, - -	"	–	14	
James Sisson, - -	"	–	14	
Chisholme Ellis, - -	Corporal,	–	14	
Henry Cartmill, - -	"	–	14	
Hiram Cobbs, - -	"	–	14	
John Donnally, - -	"	–	14	
John Fisher, - -	Fifer,	–	14	
Isham Bayley, - -	Private,	–	14	
Moses Brown, - -	"	–	14	
Thomas Cobbs, - -	"	–	14	
Thomas Casdrop, - -	"	–	14	
Jacob Casdrop, - -	"	–	14	
Alexander Cartwright, - -	"	–	14	
John Campbell, - -	"	–	14	
Solomon Casdrop, - -	"	–	14	
John Cooper, - -	"	–	14	
Leonard Cooper, - -	"	–	14	
Joseph Dawson, - -	"	–	14	
Gutrell Dawson, - -	"	–	14	
William Fowler, - -	"	–	14	
Asa Fowler, - -	"	–	14	
Joshua Fowler, - -	"	–	14	
Leonard Fisher, - -	"	–	14	
John Guthrie, - -	"	–	14	
Thomas Hensley, - -	"	–	14	
Thomas Lowe, - -	"	–	14	
John Medley, - -	"	–	14	
Thomas Milam, - -	"	–	14	
Moses Milam, - -	"	–	14	
Malcom McCown, - -	"	–	14	
Simeon Milam, - -	"	–	14	
Henry McLaughlin, - -	"	–	14	
James McCown, - -	"	–	14	
James Newport, - -	"	–	14	
Thomas Parrish, - -	"	–	14	
Nimrod Paul, - -	"	–	14	
Edmund Price, - -	"	–	14	
Arch'd Price, - -	"	–	14	
Samuel Presley, - -	"	–	14	
Joel Rucker, - -	"	–	14	
John Ray, - -	"	–	14	
Andrew Slaughter, - -	"	–	14	
John Smith, ; -	"	–	14	
Joseph Still, - -	"	–	14	
Elisha Smith, - -	"	–	14	
Luke Shiverdecker, - -	"	–	14	
Alexander Taylor, - -	"	–	14	
George Weldy, - -	"	–	14	
Longston Ward, - -	"	–	14	

MUSTER ROLL

Of Captain Sampson Wilson's Company, from the Seventy-first Regiment, Virginia Militia, commanded by Lieutenant Colonel William Allen, in Service from 30th June to 10th July, 1813.

NAMES.	RANK.	TIME OF SERVICE.		REMARKS.
		Months.	Days.	
Sampson Wilson, - -	Captain,	–	11	
Drewry P. Warren, - -	Lieutenant,	–	11	
Joel Lane, - -	Ensign,	–	11	
Micajah Bell, - -	Sergeant,	–	11	
Samuel Davis, - -	"	–	11	
Samuel Warren, - -	"	–	11	
Thomas Gwaltney, - -	"	–	11	
William Spratley, - -	Corporal,	–	11	
Micajah Bell, sen'r, - -	"	–	11	
William Long, - -	"	–	11	
Silas Holloway, - -	"	–	11	
Allen Savage, - -	Fifer,	–	11	
Judkins Warren, - -	Drummer,	–	11	
James P. Bell, - -	Private,	–	11	
Benj. C. Bell, - -	"	–	11	
William Cocks, - -	"	–	11	
Champion Carter, - -	"	–	11	
Sampson Clarke, - -	"	–	11	
William Delk, - -	"	–	11	
Littleberry Davis, - -	"	–	11	
William Edwards, - -	"	–	11	
Willis Gwaltney, - -	"	–	11	
James Gwaltney, - -	"	–	11	
Thomas P. Gwaltney, - -	"	–	11	
Richard Gwaltney, - -	"	–	11	
Patrick Gwaltney, - -	"	–	11	
James Holloway, - -	"	–	11	
James Hunter, - -	"	–	11	
Robert Hart, - -	"	–	11	
John Holloway, - -	"	–	11	
Elijah Hunnicutt, - -	"	–	11	
Elijah Holloway, - -	"	–	11	
Micajah Little, , -	"	–	11	
James Logan, - -	"	–	11	
Joseph Lane, - -	"	–	11	
John Lane, - -	"	–	11	
Hartwell Lane, - -	"	–	11	
Evans Moore, - -	"	–	11	
Jesse Persons, - -	"	–	7	
Thomas Presson, - -	"	–	11	
Joel Thomas, - -	"	–	11	
Josiah Turner, - -	"	–	11	
James Wright, - -	"	–	11	
Willis D. Warren, - -	"	–	11	
John Wilson, - -	"	–	11	
Austin Wright, - -	"	–	11	
James Wilson, - -	"	–	11	
James White, - -	"	–	11	
Anthony D. White, - -	"	–	7	

MUSTER ROLL

Of Captain Hudson M. Wingfield's Company, of the Seventy-fourth Regiment, Virginia Militia, in the Service of the United States, from 20th to 29th March, 1813.

NAMES.	RANK.	TIME OF SERVICE.		REMARKS.
		Months.	Days.	
Hudson M. Wingfield, -	Captain,	–	10	
William Priddy, - -	Lieutenant,	–	4	
William Cock, - -	"	–	1	
Henry A. Timberlake, -	Ensign,	–	1	
William Timberlake, - -	Sergeant,	–	10	
Francis Starke, - -	"	–	10	
Elisha Jones, - -	"	–	10	
Frederick Bowe, - -	Private,	–	10	
Absalom Browning, - -	"	–	10	
Jehu Browning, - -	"	–	10	
John C. Brocke, - -	"	–	10	
Thomas Cross, - -	"	–	10	
William Cocke, - -	"	–	10	
Hector Davis, - .	"	–	10	
William Ford, - -	"	–	10	
Robert Hicks, - -	"	–	10	
Thomas Hicks, - -	"	–	10	
Thomas Hobson, - -	"	–	10	
Thomas Kersey, - -	"	–	10	
John King, jr. - -	"	–	10	
James L. Littlepage, - -	"	–	4	
Elijah Priddy, - -	"	–	10	
James P. Ragland, - -	"	–	10	
John P. Starke, - -	"	–	10	
Henry A. Timberlake, - -	"	–	9	
Benj'n A. Timberlake, - -	"	–	9	
William Turner, - -	"	–	9	
Thomas Walker, - -	"	–	9	
Thomas Wingfield, - -	"	–	9	
Joseph Wingfield, - -	"	–	9	
John Wingfield, - -	"	–	9	
Benjamin Wingfield, - -	"	–	9	

MUSTER ROLL

Of Captain Jonathan Woodhouse's Company, of the Twentieth Regiment, Virginia Militia, commanded by Lieutenant Colonel James Robinson, in Service from 6th to 14th February, from 10th to 16th March, and from 14th to the 21st September, in the year 1813.

NAMES.	RANK.	TIME OF SERVICE.		REMARKS.
		Months.	Days.	
Jonathan Woodhouse, -	Captain,	—	23	
John Woodhouse, -	Lieutenant,	—	23	
William J. Woodhouse, -	Ensign,	—	15	
Thomas Brock, -	Sergeant,	—	14	
Edward James, -	"	—	8	
Frederick Ansell, -	"	—	15	
Edward Brown, sen. -	"	—	10	
Edward Brown, jr. -	"	—	15	
Solomon Dyer, -	"	—	9	
Charles Whitehurst, -	Corporal,	—	23	
Edward James, -	"	—	14	
Thomas Brock, -	"	—	8	
James Williamson, -	"	—	4	
Philip Malboue, -	"	—	6	
John Kelly, - -	Drummer,	—	23	
Nathan Whitehurst, -	Fifer,	—	16	
Gideon Bonny, -	Private,	—	23	
Andrew Bonny, -	"	—	17	
Nathan Bonny, -	"	—	10	
Thomas Bonny, -	"	—	19	
Edward Bonny, -	"	—	20	
Griffin Bonny, -	"	—	4	
John Cannon, -	"	—	23	
Willis Cooper, -	"	—	22	
Batson Cason, -	"	—	17	
Batson Capps, -	"	—	15	
Cornelius Dyer, -	"	—	4	
Willoughby Dyer, -	"	—	23	
James Doudge, -	"	—	23	
James Doudge, (of R.) -	"	—	4	
Enoch Doudge, -	"	—	9	
Richard Eaton, -	"	—	23	
James Eaton, -	"	—	23	
Enoch Eaton, -	"	—	18	
William Eaton, -	"	—	14	
Moses Eaton, -	"	—	13	
Moses Flanagan, -	"	—	22	
John Franklin, -	"	—	22	
Joshua Flanagan, -	"	—	8	
Edward Flanagan, -	"	—	6	
John Garrison, -	"	—	18	
Moses Heath, -	"	—	8	
Richard Heath, -	"	—	15	
Horatio James, -	"	—	8	
William James, -	"	—	14	
Smith Kelly, -	"	—	23	
David Molbane, -	"	—	18	

NAMES.	RANK.	TIME OF SERVICE.		REMARKS.
		Months.	Days.	
William Moore, - -	Private,	–	21	
Anthony Murphy, - -	"	–	6	
James Moore, - -	"	–	6	
Philip Molbane, - -	"	–	8	
Jonathan Otterson, - -	"	–	23	
Joseph Otterson, - -	"	–	15	
Jacob Petree, - -	"	–	6	
James Robinson, - -	"	–	23	
Henry Robinson, - -	"	–	23	
Richard Rainey, - -	"	–	15	
Joshua Robinson, - -	"	–	6	
Ezekiel Smith, - -	"	–	20	
George Smith, - -	"	–	11	
John Whitehurst, - -	"	–	14	
Noah Whitehurst, - -	"	–	23	
Dempsey Whitehurst, -	"	–	23	
Andrew Whitehurst, -	"	–	23	
Henry Whitehurst, - -	"	–	8	
Richard Whitehurst, -	"	–	22	
Jesse Whitehurst, - -	"	–	23	
Hillary Whitehurst, - -	"	–	15	
Philip Whichard, - -	"	–	14	
Nathan Whitehurst, -	"	–	15	
Henry Woodhouse, -	"	–	11	
Enock Whitehurst, - -	"	–	15	
John Whichard, - -	"	–	6	
Thomas Whichard, - -	"	–	4	

MUSTER ROLL

Of Captain Charles Wrenn's Company, of Twenty-ninth Regiment, Virginia Militia, commanded by Major Joseph W. Ballard, in Service at Smithfield from 23rd June to 10th July, in the year 1813.

NAMES.			RANK.	TIME OF SERVICE.		REMARKS.
				Months.	Days.	
Charles Wrenn,	-	-	Captain,	—	18	
Josh. B. Hodsden,	-	-	Ensign,	—	18	
William Jordan,	-	-	Sergeant,	—	18	
Francis Ward,	-	-	"	—	18	
Henry Casey,	-	-	"	—	18	
Samuel Stott,	-	-	"	—	18	
Benjamin Barlow,	-	-	Corporal,	—	18	
James White,	-	-	"	—	18	
Solomon Pasture,	-	-	"	—	18	
Morris Hatchell,	-	-	"	—	18	
Joseph Brantley,	-	-	Private,	—	18	
James Brantley,	-	-	"	—	18	
Eldred Brantley,	-	-	"	—	18	
Benja. Braswell,	-	-	"	—	7	
Thos. Bailey,	-	-	"	—	16	
Samuel Carroll,	-	-	"	—	18	
Solomon Dews,	-	-	"	—	18	
Henry Deford,	-	-	"	—	18	
Samuel Edwards,	-	-	"	—	18	Grey Carroll his sub.
Thomas Edwards,	-	-	"	—	18	
Herbert Edwards,	-	-	"	—	18	
Newit Edwards,	-	-	"	—	18	
Barth'l Goodrich,	-	-	"	—	18	
Samuel Glover,	-	-	"	—	18	
William Goodson,	-	-	"	—	18	
Gabriel Gibbs,	-	-	"	—	18	
Joseph Goodson,	-	-	"	—	16	
Samuel Garrison,	-	-	"	—	18	
Thomas Hardy,	-	-	"	—	18	
Hubard Hamlen,	-	-	"	—	18	
William Heath,	-	-	"	—	8	
Thomas Jones,	-	-	"	—	18	
Isaac Jones,	-	-	"	—	16	
William Mahone,	-	-	"	—	14	
Robert McMullin,	-	-	"	—	18	
Samuel Pitman,	-	-	"	—	14	
Jacob Persons,	-	-	"	—	18	Substituted Abraham Jones.
William Ripley,	-	-	"	—	18	
Womble Stringfield,	-	-	"	—	18	
Joseph Shelley,	-	-	"	—	18	
Wm. Shelley, sr.	-	-	"	—	18	
Thomas Stott,	-	-	"	—	15	
Lewis Wilson,	-	-	"	—	15	
Josiah Williams,	-	-	"	—	14	

MUSTER ROLL

Of Captain William D. Wrenn's Company, from the Nineteenth Regiment, Virginia Militia, in the City of Richmond, called into actual Service under general orders, from 18th to 27th March, and from 28th June to 3d July, in the year 1813.

NAMES.	RANK.	TIME OF SERVICE.		REMARKS.
		Months.	Days.	
William D. Wrenn, - -	Captain,	—	11	
John H. Robinson, - -	Lieutenant,	—	11	
Thomas Burling, - -	Ensign,	—	11	
Henry Fore, - -	Sergeant,	—	11	
James C. Bradley, - -	"	—	11	
Hezekiah Eubank, - -	"	—	11	
Caleb Cook, - -	"	—	11	
James Bray, - -	Corporal,	—	11	
Daniel G. Hudnall, - -	"	—	11	
Josiah Hill, - -	"	—	11	
E. Stratton, - -	"	—	5	
George Pickett, - -	Drummer,	—	5	
Prosper H. Rogers, - -	"	—	6	
Robert Atkinson, - -	Private,	—	6	
Joseph Butler, - -	"	—	11	
Henry Blacgrove, - -	"	—	11	
Robert Brooks, - -	"	—	6	
Arthur Booker, - -	"	—	4	
William Burke, - -	"	—	2	
William Cook, - -	"	—	11	
Philip Crump, - -	"	—	11	
Samuel Churchill, - -	"	—	11	
John C. Crockett, - -	"	—	11	
Charles A. Cox, - -	"	—	11	
Alexander S. Dandridge, -	"	—	11	
Richard Dunlavy, - -	"	—	11	
Wm. B. Ellis, - -	"	—	11	
Dabney Eubank, - -	"	—	3	
Herman Gentry, - -	"	—	4	
Christo. Gill, - -	"	—	6	
Jno. T. Hughes, - -	"	—	11	
Stanley F. Hudnall, - -	"	—	5	
Wm. B. Jordan, - -	"	—	11	
Jekyle Jones, - -	"	—	6	
Richard C. Johnston, - -	"	—	5	
Newin Keauns, - -	"	—	6	
Samuel M. Lewis, - -	"	—	5	
William McEnory, - -	"	—	11	
Jno. P. Morris, - -	"	—	11	
Richard C. Mills, - -	"	—	11	
Charles Norman, - -	"	—	8	
Thomas Nush, - -	"	—	5	
Benjamin Phillips, - -	"	—	11	
Richard Prince, - -	"	—	11	
Grief Price, - -		—	4	
John Quarles, - -	"	—	11	

NAMES.		RANK.	TIME OF SERVICE.		REMARKS.
			Months.	Days.	
Benoni Robins,	-	Private,	–	11	
Wm. Robins,	-	"	–	11	
Alex'r L. Robinson,	-	"	–	9	
Robert Ransom,	-	"	–	4	
Nath'l Ragland,	-	"	–	2	
Austin Talman,	-	"	–	5	
Seymour Vial,	-	"	–	4	
Claudias Vial,	-	"	–	4	
Drewry Wilkinson,	-	"	–	11	
Robert G. Williamson,	-	"	–	11	
Walker Watkins,	-	"	–	4	
John Yare,	-	"	–	2	

MUSTER ROLL

Of Captain George M. Wright's Company, of the One Hundred and Eleventh Regiment, commanded by Lieutenant Colonel E. Parker, from 18th July to 25th September, 1814.

NAMES.	RANK.	TIME OF SERVICE.		REMARKS.
		Months.	Days.	
George W. Wright, - -	Captain,	2	9	
Samuel King, - -	Lieutenant,	–	4	
Stephen Baily, - -	"	1	24	Transferred from Capt. Dozier's company.
James English, - -	Ensign.	1	17	
William Stone, - -	"	–	23	Transferred from Capt. Browns' company.
Daniel Hardwick, - -	Sergeant,	2	9	
John Crenshaw, - -	"	2	9	Transferred from Capt. Dozier's company.
Philip King. - -	"	2	5	" " " "
James Gregory, - -	"	–	25	Transferred from Capt. Brown's company.
Thomas Olive, - -	Corporal,	2	5	Transferred from Capt. Dozier's company.
William Peter, - -	"	2	9	
Charles C. Rice, - -	"	2	5	" " " "
William Stone, - -	"	–	25	Transferred from Capt. Brown's company.
Augustus Gallagher, - -	Fifer,	2	5	Transferred from Capt. Dozier's company.
Robert Anthony, - -	Private,	–	25	Transferred from Capt. Brown's company.
Richard Atwell, - -	"	2	5	
John Anthony, - -	"	–	25	
William Ambers, - -	"	–	25	
William Anthony, - -	"	–	25	
John Bryant, - -	"	–	25	" " " "
Thomas Brown, - -	"	–	25	" " " "
John Brown, - -	"	2	9	
Joseph Brown, - -	"	2	9	
William Brown, - -	"	2	7	
William Buttar, - -	"	2	5	Transferred from Capt. Dozier's company.
Thomas Bartlett, - -	"	2	5	" " " "
George Buttar, - -	"	2	9	
William Barnett, - -	"	1	25	" " " "
James H. Bailey, - -	"	2	5	
John Barrett, - -	"	–	12	
Richard Bulger, - -	"	–	25	Transferred from Capt. Brown's company.
Thomas W. Clark, - -	"	–	25	" " " "
Benedict M. Crabb, - -	"	2	5	Transferred from Capt. Dozier's company.
John Chandler, - -	"	1	19	Appointed Brigade Qr. Mast'r, Sept. 9, 1814.
William Chewning, - -	"	2	2	

NAMES.	RANK.	TIME OF SERVICE.		REMARKS.
		Months.	Days.	
Richard Crask, - -	Private,	–	25	Transferred from **Capt.** Brown's company.
Charles Callaghan, - -	"	2	9	" "
James Davis, - -	"	–	25	" "
James Dunahaw, - -	"	–	25	" "
John Elmore, - -	"	2	9	
Joseph Elmore, - -	"	2	5	Transferred from **Capt.** Dozier's company.
Edmond Elmore, - -	"	2	5	" "
John Gregory, - -	"	2	5	
Henry Gregory, - -	"	2	5	" "
Thomas Gregory, - -	"	–	25	" "
Reuben Hall, - -	"	–	25	Transferred from **Capt.** Brown's company.
John Hammond, - -	"	2	5	
William Harper, - -	"	2	9	
Robt. Hall, - -	"	–	25	" "
Jeremiah Jones, - -	"	–	17	
Leven Jones, - -	"	–	25	" "
Thomas Jenkins, - -	"	–	25	" "
Thomas King, jr. - -	"	2	5	Transferred from **Capt.** Dozier's company.
Thomas King, sen'r, - -	"	2	5	
James Kirkly, - -	"	2	4	
Samuel Lyatt, - -	"	–	25	Transferred from **Capt.** Brown's company.
Samuel Lambkin, - -	"	–	25	" "
Samuel Lewis, - -	"	–	16	
Thomas Mothershead, - -	"	–	25	" "
George G. Mothershead, - -	"	–	9	
Nathaniel Mothershead, - -	"	–	25	" "
Henry Mothershead, - -	"	–	25	" "
Jacob Millar, - -	"	–	25	" "
Newman McKenny, - -	"	–	25	" "
Presley McKenney, - -	"	2		
Jeremiah McClusky, - -	"	2	5	Transferred from **Capt.** Dozier's company.
Spencer Mullins, - -	"	–	25	Transferred from **Capt.** Brown's company.
William Marmaduke, - -	"	–	25	" "
Murdock Murphy, - -	"	2	9	
Reuben P. Marks, - -	"	–	25	" "
Charles Mothershead, - -	"	–	25	
Tarpley Nash, - -	"	–	25	" "
Thornton Nash, - -	"	2	9	
James R. Nash, - -	"	–	25	" "
William Pillion, - -	"	2	9	
Thomas Pitsburg, - -	"	2	9	
Henry Pritchett, - -	"	–	25	" "
William Robinson, - -	"	2	7	
John Reed, - -	"	–	25	" "
Reuben Rennolds, - -	"	–	7	
Samuel Ryaids, - -	"	–	25	" "
Thomas Sisson, - -	"	–	25	" "
Augustine Sandford, - -	"	–	25	" "
Owen Sullivan, - -	"	–	8	
James T. Scutt, - -	"	–	25	" "
Elisha Spurling, - -	"	2	9	
Corbin Straughn, - -	"	–	29	
James B. Stephens, - -	"	–	21	Transferred from **Capt.** Dozier's company.
William Sutton, - -	"	–	25	Transferred from **Capt.** Brown's company.
Barnett Sisson, - -	"	–	25	

NAMES.			RANK.	TIME OF SERVICE.		REMARKS.
				Months.	Days.	
Moses Shelly,	-	-	Private,	–	25	Transferred from Capt. Brown's company.
James Thomas,	-	-	"	–	25	" "
William True,	-	-	"	–	25	" "
William Thomas,	-	-	"	–	25	" "
Jennings Yeatman,	-	-	"	–	25	" "

MUSTER ROLL

Of Lieutenant George M. Wright's Company, from the One Hundred and Eleventh Regiment of Virginia Militia, in the County of Westmoreland, called into actual Service under the orders of Major John Turberville, from 15th July to the 26th of the same month, in the year 1813.

NAMES.	RANK.	TIME OF SERVICE.		REMARKS.
		Months.	Days.	
Geo. M. Wright.	Lieutenant,	–	12	
Samuel King.	Ensign,	–	12	
Samuel Gilbert.	Sergeant,	–	11	
William Johnson,	"	–	11	
James English.	"	–	12	
Charles Hazzard,	"	–	12	
Daniel Hardwick,	Corporal,	–	11	
Daniel Harrison,	"	–	11	
John Brown.	Private,	–	12	
Samuel Brann,	"	–	12	
Vincent Brann,	"	–	11	
Wm. Harper,	"	–	12	
James Harrison,	"	–	11	
Allen McHenny,	"	–	7	
Presley McHenney,	"	–	12	
Wm. Porter,	"	–	11	
Owen Sullivant,	"	–	12	
Elisha Spurlin,	"	–	12	
George Walker,	"	–	12	

MUSTER ROLL

Of Lieutenant George Wyatt's Company, of the Ninth Regiment, commanded by Lieutenant Colonel William Boyd, called into Service by Lieutenant Colonel Elliott Muse, of the 109th Regiment, from 2nd to 10th December, 1814.

NAMES.			RANK.	TIME OF SERVICE.		REMARKS.
				Months.	Days.	
George Wyatt,	-	-	Lieutenant,	—	9	
George Haskins,	-	-	Ensign,	—	9	
Robt. B. Gains,	-	-	Ord. Sergeant,	—	9	
Philip Pitts,	-	-	Sergeant,	—	9	
Franklin Scott,	-	-	"	—	9	
James Basket,	-	-	Private,	—	9	
Larkin Bromley,	-	-	"	—	7	
Beverley Boadus,	-	-	"	—	9	
Wm. Gatewood,	-	-	"	—	9	
John Gatewood,	-	-	"	—	9	
Wm. T. Jones,	-	-	"	—	9	
James H. Prince,	-	-	"	—	9	
Joseph Stewart,	-	-	"	—	9	
Reuben Wilson,	-	-	"	—	9	

MUSTER ROLL

Of Captain William P. Wyche's Troop of Cavalry, from the Fifteenth Regiment, Virginia Militia, commanded by Colonel Francis M. Boykin, called into the Service of the State of Virginia, from 1st to 8th September, in the year 1814.

NAMES.	RANK.	TIME OF SERVICE.		REMARKS.
		Months.	Days.	
William P. Wyche, - -	Captain,	—	8	
Henry P. Moss, - -	Lieutenant,	—	8	
John Key, - - -	"	—	8	
James Scammell, - -	Cornet,	—	8	
John Lanier, - -	Sergeant,	—	8	
Peyton Mason, - -	"	—	8	
James H. Jones, - -	"	—	8	
James Chappell, - -	"	—	8	
Thomas Mason, - -	Corporal,	—	8	
James L. Parham, - -	"	—	8	
Benjamin L. Harrison, -	"	—	8	
Thomas Blunt, - -	"	—	8	
Thomas Avery, - -	Private,	—	8	
Nathaniel Andrews, - -	"	—	8	
John G. Adkins, - -	"	—	8	
Edmund Chappell, - -	"	—	8	
Henry Cotton, - -	"	—	8	
Colon Cooper. - -	"	—	8	
Peter Eppes, - -	"	—	8	
Benjamin Ellis, - -	"	—	8	
Reuben Gilliam, - -	"	—	8	
John Hawthorn, - -	"	—	8	
Herbert Holt, - -	"	—	8	
William Hall, - -	"	—	8	
Williamson Howle, - -	"	—	8	
John Holloway, - -	"	—	8	
Asberry Ivy, - -	"	—	8	
Burwell Jackson, - -	"	—	8	
Thomas Jones, - -	"	—	8	
John Lanier, - -	"	—	8	
James Myrick, - -	"	—	8	
Edmund Moss, - -	"	—	8	
David E. Mason, - -	"	—	8	
John Moss, - -	"	—	8	
John Q. Moyler, - -	"	—	8	
Paul Mitchell, - -	"	—	8	
Walter Myrick, - -	"	—	8	
William B. Mason, - -	"	—	8	
Williamson G. Perkins,	"	—	8	
Archibald Parker, - -	"	—	8	
Thomas Pennington, -	"	—	8	
Edwin Petway, - -	"	—	8	
Henry Pennington, - -	"	—	8	
Robert Pennington, - -	"	—	8	
David Pennington, - -	"	—	8	
William Parham, - -	"	—	8	
John Phillips, - -	"	—	8	

NAMES.			RANK.	TIME OF SERVICE.		REMARKS.
				Months.	Days.	
Robert Petway,	-	-	Private,	–	8	
William Roe,	-	-	"	–	8	
Charles Smith,	-	-	"	–	8	
Benjamin Turner,	-	-	"	–	8	
Flowers Williams,	-	-	"	–	8	
George Williams,	-	-	"	–	8	

MUSTER ROLL

Of Captain H. H. Wynne's Company, from the One Hundred and Fifteenth Regiment, Virginia Militia, in the County of Warwick, called into actual Service under the orders of Lieutenant Colonel of the One Hundred and Fifteenth Regiment, from the 14th March to the 3rd April, in the year 1813.

NAMES.	RANK.	TIME OF SERVICE.		REMARKS.
		Months.	Days.	
H. H. Wynne, - -	Captain,	—	21	
Benj. Harwood, - -	Lieutenant,	—	21	
William Jones, - -	Ensign,	—	21	
Thomas Wynne, - -	Sergeant,	—	21	
William Charles, - -	"	—	21	
William Bendall, - -	"	—	21	
Thomas Carter, - -	"	—	21	
John Wynne, - -	Corporal,	—	21	
Robt. H. Lee, - -	"	—	21	
Bennett Wood, - -	"	—	21	
Thomas C. Carter, - -	"	—	21	
Robert Harris, - -	Fifer,	—	21	
William Blackburn, - -	Private,	—	21	
William Barnes, - -	"	—	21	
William Burcher, - -	"	—	21	
Wm. T. Crutchfield,	"	—	15	
Miles Curtis, - -	"	—	21	
Richard Davis, - -	"	—	21	
Stafford Gibbs, - -	"	—	21	
William Harris, - -	"	—	21	
Henry Howard, - -	"	—	21	
Helm Harwood, - -	"	—	21	
John Howard, - -	"	—	15	
Thomas Lee, - -	"	—	18	
John Leavy, - -	"	—	18	
Henry W. Lee, - -	"	—	18	
Wade Montfort, - -	"	—	18	
John Perrin, - -	"	—	18	
Walter Patrick, - -	"	—	18	
John Randal, - -	"	—	15	
Beverley Stubblefield, -	"	—	18	
Wm. Starey, - -	"	—	18	
James Seaburn, - -	"	—	18	
Samuel Woodey, - -	"	—	21	
Richard Wynne, - -	"	—	21	
Mathew Woods, sen. -	"	—	21	
Mathew Woods, jr. -	"	—	21	

Captain Thomas Yerby's Company—Ninety-second Regiment.

NAMES.	RANK.	TIME OF SERVICE.		REMARKS.
		Months.	Days.	
Opie Beane, - -	Lieutenant,	–	10	
William T. Yerby, - -	"	–	5	
Opie Bean, - -	Ensign,	–	5	
John Edward, - -	Sergeant,	1	1	
Hilkiah Ball, - -	"	–	5	
Thomas Y. Hunton, - -	"	–	5	
John Y. Percifull, - -	"	–	10	
John Hubbard, - -	"	–	21	
Elias Fendley, - -	"	–	5	
John Gresham, - -	"	–	10	
Wm. Stott, - -	"	–	5	
John Gresham, - -	Corporal,	–	5	
John Percifull, - -	"	–	5	
William Keeling, - -	"	–	5	
James Sutton, - -	"	–	5	
Thomas Schofield, - -	"	–	20	
Adderson Brent, - -	Private.	–	10	
Alington Brent, - -	"	–	21	
Spencer Brown, - -	"	–	10	
Thomas Barnes, - -	"	–	10	
Thomas P. Ball, - -	"	–	5	
John Boatman, - -	"	–	5	
John Cundiff, - -	"	–	15	
Isaac Cundiff, - -	"	–	5	
Thomas Cockarill, - -	"	–	10	
James Crane, - -	"	–	5	
Hiram Carpenter, -	"	–	10	
William H. Chowning, -	"	–	10	
Griffin Doggett, -	"	–	11	
Dennis Doggett, - -	"	–	5	
Daniel D. Davenport, -	"	–	10	
John Daniel, - -	"	–	10	
Daniel Edwards, - -	"	–	10	
George England, - -	"	–	6	
John Flowers, - -	"	–	20	
Eppa Fielding, - -	"	–	5	
William George, - -	"	1	15	
William Garner, - -	"	–	10	
John Gundry, - -	"	–	5	
John Gresham, - -	"	–	5	
John Hill, - -	"	–	5	
Martin Hughlett, - -	"	–	5	
John C. Hinton, - -	"	–	5	
John Hubbard, - -	"	–	5	
William O. Haydon, - -	"	–	5	
Jesse Kent, - -	"	–	5	
Epa'l Lunsford, - -	"	–	5	
Joseph Merryman, - -	"	1	6	
Rodham Miller, - -	"	–	17	
Thomas Miller, - -	"	–	5	
Robert Miller, - -	"	–	10	
John Mason, - -	"	–	5	
Cyrus Newby, - -	"	–	10	
James Nutt, - -	"	–	5	

NAMES.	RANK.	TIME OF SERVICE.		REMARKS.
		Months.	Days.	
William H. Oliver, -	Private,	–	5	
Edward Payne, - -	"	–	10	
Francis Potts, - -	"	–	5	
James Robinson, - -	"	–	5	
John Sampson, - -	"	–	5	
William Simmonds, -	"	–	5	
John Thomas, - -	"	1	10	
Thornley B. Tankersley, -	"	–	20	
Portues Towles, - -	"	–	10	
John Talley, - -	"	–	5	
Henry Tapscott, -	"	•	5	
George Talley, - -	"	–	1	
William Wilson, - -	"	–	10	
James Warwick, - -	"	–	10	
Benjamin Waddy, - -	"	–	5	

(For rest of this company, see publication of Pay Rolls.)

Captain William T. Yerby's Company—Ninety-second Regiment.

NAMES.		RANK.	TIME OF SERVICE.		REMARKS.
			Months.	Days.	
Epaphroditus Hill,	- -	Fifer,	–	10	
William Chitwood,	- -	Private,	–	4	
William George,	- -	"	–	11	
John Hill,	- -	"	–	11	
Edward Payne,	- -	"	–	11	
Benj. Waddy,	- -	"	–	24	

(For rest of this company, see publication of Pay Rolls.)

INDEX